PRAISE FOR *RESOLVING THE ISRAELI-PALESTINIAN CONFLICT*

In *Resolving the Israeli-Palestinian Conflict*, Raphael Cohen-Almagor meticulously examines the underlying causes of the numerous failures surrounding efforts to resolve this enduring conflict. Drawing upon an extensive array of interviews with key figures who were 'in or around the room' during negotiation, mediation and facilitation efforts, he offers fresh insights that inform his vision for a viable framework to achieve a just and lasting peace.

By integrating a highly diverse spectrum of perspectives, Professor Cohen-Almagor exemplifies his commitment to the Rawlsian veil of ignorance – an analytical approach he passionately advocates for in the quest for a just and sustainable resolution. This outstanding book is essential reading for anyone seeking a deep understanding of the complexities of the Israeli-Palestinian conflict and the potential pathways to peace.

More than just compelling content, *Resolving the Conflict* holds the potential to rekindle hope at a time when prospects for a negotiated settlement seem dimmer than at any point in the past three decades. Its robust analysis provides readers with not only a wealth of knowledge but also optimism grounded in a realistic sense of possibility.

—Salam Fayyad, Former Palestinian Prime Minister,
Visiting Senior Scholar and Lecturer/Distinguished Visitor in
Foreign Affairs, Princeton University

Cohen-Almagor's study of key landmarks in the ill-fated Israeli-Palestinian peace process should not be read as just one history book among many. This is a most significant contribution to the discipline of peace studies, drawing on lessons from other protracted conflicts, such as Northern Ireland. Cohen-Almagor leads us back to the forgotten fundamentals of the art of peacemaking, decodes the conditions needed for successful negotiations, strikes the right balance between the requirements of peace and the imperative of justice, addresses the philosophical question of what is a just peace, offers insights on how to deal with the ever-present spoilers, and scrutinises the indispensable role of the mediator while defending the case of small countries, such as Sweden and Norway, two moral superpowers with a keen vocation for a

Middle East peace. In an era marked by war and gloom, Cohen-Almagor's book is a reassuring call for creative peace statesmanship.

—Prof. Shlomo Ben-Ami, Israeli Minister of Foreign Affairs (2000–2001) and author of *Prophets without Honor: The 2000 Camp David Summit and the End of the Two-State Solution*

Spanning from the Oslo Accords of 1993 to the present day, this landmark volume offers the most comprehensive analysis to date of the Israel-PLO peace process. Drawing on extensive archival research and over one hundred interviews with senior officials from ten countries and the United Nations, Professor Raphael Cohen-Almagor delivers a penetrating examination of the negotiations, the role of American mediation and the enduring obstacles to peace.

With clarity and moral conviction, Cohen-Almagor unpacks the roots of the conflict and proposes a just and pragmatic framework for resolution. *Resolving the Israeli-Palestinian Conflict* is essential reading for scholars of Middle Eastern politics, conflict resolution and diplomacy – and an indispensable resource for policymakers and diplomats seeking to seize future opportunities for peace.

—Prof. Aaron Barak, President (retd) Israel Supreme Court, and Israel's senior peace negotiator, Camp David 1978

A stunning and vitally important book! Professor Cohen-Almagor deserves hearty congratulations on accomplishing an almost insuperably difficult and fraught task of making sense of the failures and near misses of Israeli-Palestinian negotiations and for synthesising decades of errors and trials into an immensely valuable and pathbreaking book.

—Robert I. Rotberg, President Emeritus, World Peace Foundation; Harvard Kennedy School

Professor Raphael Cohen-Almagor has produced a seminal and monumental work in his highly impressive book entitled *Resolving the Israeli-Palestinian Conflict*. The manuscript is a labour of years and an unrivalled commitment to contributing significantly to both the academic and political realms. It's a treasure trove for those who seek the truth, as articulated by those who were active participants in the Middle East peace process. The materials in the book are craftily analysed and presented, shedding light on the past and offering insights to future negotiators seeking to end the Israeli-Palestinian conflict and a tool for other Middle East conflict resolution experts. There are many lessons learned, offering wisdom and valuable detail. It is indispensable.

—Hiba Husseini, Attorney-at-Law and former legal advisor to the Palestinian Team to the Israeli-Palestinian Negotiations (1994–2008)

In *Resolving the Israeli-Palestinian Conflict*, Professor Raphael Cohen-Almagor offers a penetrating critical study of peace negotiations, mediation and facilitation between Israel and Palestine. Drawing on over a decade of extensive research and dozens of interviews with key participants and commentators, he presents both a rich historical analysis as well as practical recommendations for advancing peace through negotiation and mediation. This important work deserves a place in the library of every scholar and of anyone deeply interested in the history of this enduring conflict and in pursuing constructive paths toward its resolution.

—Joel Singer, Legal Adviser to the Israeli Ministry of Foreign Affairs (1993–1996) and principal negotiator of the 1993 Oslo Accord

The Abraham Accords of 2020 were indeed misrepresented as proof that Israel could circumvent the Israeli-Palestinian conflict by normalising relations with most Arab states. The events of the past two years painfully demonstrated how wrong this was. Professor Cohen-Almagor's new book is essential reading for those who wish to understand the depth of this conflict to gain fresh insights into the strategies that should be adopted for coping with it.

—Professor Itamar Rabinovich, Prime Minister Rabin's ambassador to Washington and chief negotiator with Syria

Raphael Cohen-Almagor has undertaken a critical, urgent task: to probe why the Israeli-Palestinian conflict has persisted for so long and descended into such depths of horror, despite countless attempts to resolve it. What distinguishes his work is not just the range of actors with whom he has engaged. It is that he has done so in a way few have done before, and all should emulate from now on. He listens. That is what makes his endeavour, and this book, so precious.

—Robert Malley, Senior Middle East advisor in the administrations of presidents Clinton, Obama and Biden. Co-author, with Hussein Agha, of *Tomorrow Is Yesterday: Life, Death, and the Pursuit of Peace in Israel/Palestine*

Resolving the Israeli-Palestinian Conflict brings to us the story of the conflict at one of its critical stages. With an artist's hand, Professor Cohen-Almagor outlines the course of events, brings us testimonies that have not been revealed until now, and presents a balanced, comprehensive and profound picture of the effort to achieve peace and its failure.

His personal involvement in the process and his commitment to it are important advantages of the book. Indeed, there is no doubt that the uniqueness of the effort to achieve peace between Israelis and Palestinians during those critical years lies in the intensive involvement of peace activists and the importance of Track Two (dialogue between civil society movements and organisations and peace activists), which made it possible to bridge gaps and ultimately led to direct negotiations between the Israeli and Palestinian leaderships and to historical compromises and agreements.

This book is an essential must-read for anyone seeking to understand the history of the conflict and the tumultuous trajectory of peace efforts. It leaves readers with the hope that, one day, these efforts will be renewed and a just peace will finally bring an end to this long and bloody struggle.

—Professor Eyal Zisser, Yona and Dina Ettinger Chair in Contemporary History of the Middle East, and Vice Rector, Tel Aviv University

A brilliantly written masterpiece of scholarship. Dr Cohen-Almagor combines an elegant theoretical framework, drawing from the academic literature on justice, mediation and conflict resolution, with unparalleled archival research and dozens of interviews with the key Israeli, Palestinian, American and Jordanian figures of the past four decades to deliver a gripping and clear-eyed account of why the 1993–1995 Oslo Accords, the 2000 Clinton Camp David talks and the direct Olmert-Abbas negotiations in 2008 all failed. Dr Cohen-Almagor offers his own detailed, visionary and fair proposal that – if agreed through trusted mediation and implemented in good faith by all sides – could well be the key to unlocking the elusive search for Israeli-Palestinian peaceful coexistence.

—Professor Steve Zipperstein, Director of the UCLA Y&S Nazarian Center for Israel Studies

Professor Cohen-Almagor's uniquely authoritative book, based on a wide-ranging series of interviews with many of those closely involved with attempts to resolve the tragically long-running Israeli-Palestinian conflict, provides critical insights not just into the events of the past, but also into the complexities of the issues involved and the lessons to be learnt if – and to my mind it is a big if – a serious attempt is ever again made to find a just and sustainable solution. For those, like me, who have reluctantly concluded that the window of opportunity for a two-state solution – which would have been the 'right' solution in terms of responding to two valid nationalisms – has now closed, it is a reminder that if hope should never be a strategy, despair should never be an option, and that however daunting and emotionally charged the issues involved, it is still possible to address them rationally, and to imagine the kind of leaders who would have the courage, insights and charisma to take their people down the ever-harder road to peace and security.

—Sir Tom Phillips, UK Ambassador to Israel 2006–2010 and to the Kingdom of Saudi Arabia 2010–2012

Prof. Raphael Cohen-Almagor devotes most of his academic activity to the issue of resolving the Israeli-Palestinian conflict. With his unique vision, his impressive analytical skills and his logical conclusions, he makes a very important contribution to the efforts of many of us to end the conflict that has been going on for so many years and has become the longest-running conflict in the world since the end of the Second World War. This is also reflected in his new book, which is recommended for anyone who has not lost hope that the conflict not only must end, but can end, and who understands that those who are convinced that it is insoluble simply do not want to solve it.

—Dr Yossi Beilin, former Israeli Justice Minister,
and the initiator of the Oslo Process

Raphael Cohen-Almagor makes a significant contribution to analysis of the issues surrounding Israel/Palestine, and the recent history of efforts for resolution. Suffused with insights from meticulous research, this book commands notice as deeply personal, wrapped around his own life and experiences.

But it is also a timely plea for the futures of the children of Palestine and Israel, that they may have bridges rather than the barriers which have cost the lives of countless generations.

Welcome, and thought-provoking.

—Rt Hon. Alistair Burt, UK Minister for the
Middle East 2010–2013, 2017–2019

Cohen-Almagor has woven findings of religious studies, philosophy, international relations, international law, psychology and concepts of conflict resolution into the historical narrative; combined with interviews with negotiators and decision-makers, this study offers an essential contribution for future negotiators, while sustaining the hope for peace.

—Dr Yair Hirschfeld, Israeli peace negotiator, Oslo

Resolving the Israeli-Palestinian Conflict by Raphael Cohen-Almagor is an extraordinary book about this ferocious and persistent war. Although it has been headline news for decades, most commentators take sides and are simply judgmental, with little to say about how to end the conflict. This book has a great deal to say about bringing about a peaceful settlement. Before turning to this, Cohen-Almagor gives a nuanced account of the history of the present conflict, which must be understood against a background of prior wars between Israel and the Palestinians. He evaluates the current war with a rigorous philosophical argument that makes use of one developed by John Rawls in his famous *Theory of Justice* and then moves beyond abstract ethical arguments to consider a number of political scenarios that might be considered as a way ahead. It is this focus on possible *practical* steps forward that distinguishes this book from other commentaries. These are not a set of vague bromides, but detailed policy proposals which then allow Cohen-Almagor to suggest to readers what political projects ought to be undertaken to bring about a successful resolution to this tragic conflict.

—Mervyn Frost (FKC), Professor Emeritus of
International Relations, King's College, London

Raphael Cohen-Almagor does us a great service with this book. He restores hope in the prospect of peace with justice, grounded in experience and principle, requiring hard work and compromise. He tackles three failed peace attempts forensically and draws lessons from them. Justice is the leitmotif. This book shows the way forward, marked by realism, mutual comprehension and lessons learned. Leaders should learn from it.

—Sir Vincent Fean, Trustee, Britain Palestine Project,
and British Consul-General, Jerusalem (2010–2014)

Raphael Cohen-Almagor has produced a monumental study of peace efforts between Palestinians and Israelis. In a heavily crowded field, *Resolving the Israeli-Palestinian Conflict* stands out as a veritable *chef d'oeuvre*. It is innovative both in its detailed presentation of peace initiatives and in its analysis of the benefits and drawbacks of different methods of peacemaking in the increasingly volatile context of Israeli-Palestinian relations. The addition of transcriptions of the interviews that provide the basis for the text and additional materials in the appendices makes this work especially valuable. This is a critical resource for participants in the multiple attempts to resolve the conflict, for experts in the field, for scholars studying its contours, and for anyone interested in an ongoing conflagration which will continue to generate headlines until it is equitably resolved.

—Professor Naomi Chazan, Professor (emerita) of
Political Science, Hebrew University of Jerusalem.
Member of the Knesset (1992–2003) and former
Deputy Speaker of Israel's Parliament

RESOLVING THE ISRAELI-PALESTINIAN CONFLICT

Resolving the Israeli-Palestinian Conflict is aimed at politicians, diplomats, policymakers, scholars, journalists and informed readers seeking to understand why peace efforts have repeatedly failed – and how true reconciliation remains possible. Based on over 100 interviews with Middle Eastern, European and American leaders, alongside extensive archival research, the book offers rare insight into the dynamics of diplomacy. It reveals how trust, fairness and political courage are vital for peace. By analysing pivotal moments – from Oslo to Camp David and the Abbas–Olmert talks – it identifies recurring mistakes and proposes strategies to foster mutual recognition and lasting coexistence. Both authoritative and accessible, the book blends history, law, ethics and international relations into a practical roadmap for future peace efforts. Its interdisciplinary approach and use of primary sources make it both authoritative and engaging. Readers will come away with a deeper understanding of the conflict and the tools needed to help resolve it.

RAPHAEL COHEN-ALMAGOR, DPhil Oxford, is a prolific scholar and institutional founder with 350+ publications. He held distinguished roles at Haifa, University of California, Los Angeles, Hull, Lund, University College London, Jerusalem and the Woodrow Wilson Center, and taught globally. His books span politics, law and ethics, including *The Right to Die with Dignity* (2001), *The Scope of Tolerance* (2006), *Confronting the Internet's Dark Side* (2015) and *Just, Reasonable Multiculturalism* (2021).

RESOLVING THE ISRAELI-PALESTINIAN CONFLICT

A Critical Study of Peace Negotiations, Mediation and Facilitation Between Israel and the PLO

RAPHAEL COHEN-ALMAGOR

CAMBRIDGE
UNIVERSITY PRESS

CAMBRIDGE
UNIVERSITY PRESS

Shaftesbury Road, Cambridge CB2 8EA, United Kingdom

One Liberty Plaza, 20th Floor, New York, NY 10006, USA

477 Williamstown Road, Port Melbourne, VIC 3207, Australia

314–321, 3rd Floor, Plot 3, Splendor Forum, Jasola District Centre, New Delhi – 110025, India

Cambridge University Press is part of Cambridge University Press & Assessment, a department of the University of Cambridge.

We share the University's mission to contribute to society through the pursuit of education, learning and research at the highest international levels of excellence.

www.cambridge.org
Information on this title: www.cambridge.org/9781108484398
DOI: 10.1017/9781108677059

When citing this work, please include a reference to the DOI 10.1017/9781108677059

First published 2026

Cover design: Dana Tohar Cohen-Almagor

A catalogue record for this publication is available from the British Library

Library of Congress Cataloging-in-Publication Data
Names: Cohen-Almagor, Raphael author
Title: Resolving the Israeli Palestinian conflict : a critical study of peace negotiations, mediation and facilitation between Israel and the PLO / Raphael Cohen-Almagor.
Description: 1. | New York : Cambridge University Press, 2026. |
Includes bibliographical references and index.
Identifiers: LCCN 2026006738 (print) | LCCN 2026006739 (ebook) |
ISBN 9781108484398 hardback | ISBN 9781108735827 paperback |
ISBN 9781108677059 ebook
Subjects: LCSH: Arab-Israeli conflict – Law and legislation | Arab-Israeli conflict – 1993 – Peace | Arab-Israeli conflict – Law and legislation – History – 20st century | Arab-Israeli conflict – Peace negotiations | Mediation | Israel – Foreign relations – Palestine
Classification: LCC KZ6045 .C64 2026 (print) | LCC KZ6045 (ebook)
LC record available at https://lccn.loc.gov/2026006738
LC ebook record available at https://lccn.loc.gov/2026006739

ISBN 978-1-108-48439-8 Hardback
ISBN 978-1-108-73582-7 Paperback

For Ethan
May the children of Israel and Palestine live
together in peace and tranquillity

In memory of Martin Indyk, Yitzhak Navon, Shimon
Peres, Yossi Sarid, Shabtai Shavit, Ezer Weizman
and Gad Yaacobi, visionary thinkers and doers who
inspired and enriched me with their experiences

CONTENTS

FIGURES

PREFACE

God is sitting with his loyal angels, Raphael, Michael and Gabriel, and looking down at His creation. Michael points out a tired old farmer, ploughing his land with his hands, and says, 'Dear God, this man is seventy years old. He has been working hard all his life in order to sustain his wife and six children. They live meagrely. Maybe we should lend him a hand?'

God answers laconically: 'He is not ready yet.'

The following week, God is sitting with his loyal angels, watching His creation. Michael, the stubborn angel, tries again: 'Forgive me, dear God. Look at this farmer. He has been working the field since 6 a.m. This is what he has done for more than fifty years. Maybe we can help him?'

God replies: 'He is not ready.'

The following week, Michael asks again, and God refuses again. Week after week, Michael pleads on behalf of the farmer and God declines, until one day God agrees to help. As the farmer returns home on his horse-drawn wagon, God wraps a heavy gold bar in a plain cloth and throws it on the road. The wagon hits the gold bar, and one of its wheels breaks. Cursing his bad luck, the farmer takes the wrapped gold bar and throws it away. Then he fixes the wheel and slowly makes his way back home.

God says tiredly: 'I told you, he was not ready yet.'

***

This book is much more than an academic work. I have been a peace activist since long before I was an academic. Only later in life did I merge my existential interests with my academic ones. The constructive insights I offer here are the result of research and many years of my own experience and that of many others who cooperated with me, aiming to create a new, peaceful reality in the Middle East.

I grew up in a Tel Aviv home where peace was one of our enshrined values. It was more than a lofty idea. It was a belief in its necessity for the survival of the Jewish people in Israel. My grandfather, Yoseph Chaim Cohen, who was my role model, said time and again that the key to Israel's survival is its relationships with our neighbours.

In 1967, when I was six years old, I experienced my first war. My dad left home in May, and we did not know where he was for more than a month. Struggling to cope with the pressure and the responsibility of raising my brother and me alone, my mother turned to her older sister for support and took us to live with her. We spent the month of June with my aunt's family. I remember running to the open trenches when the sirens went off. The Six-Day War left unforgettable, unpleasant scars.

Six years later, at 2 p.m. on a day in early October, the sirens went off again – the Yom Kippur War. My dad was called again for long weeks of military service and, of course, we were worried for his safety. I remember the long hours in the bomb shelter with our neighbours. The first two weeks of the war were particularly hard because the news was sombre. The war ended with the Israeli Defence Forces on the Egyptian side of the Suez Canal, and my dad finally returned home. He refused to tell us where he had been. More scars of war were added.

In 1982, I was a soldier. Although not at the front line, I was involved in the war effort. Now I had a closer taste of war, a truly ugly experience which I will never forget. Soon after completing my three-year service, I joined the peace camp in Israel.

During the 1980s, I became active in the Israeli Labour Party and got to know its leaders. At that time, the party was split into two rival camps, supporting either Yitzhak Rabin or Shimon Peres. I belonged to the Peres camp. I was active in the Tel Aviv branch and was elected to the Tel Aviv University Student Union Committee on a Labour ticket. I entered one of Peres' inner circles and watched him from close up. Peres was committed to peace but was undecided about the price that Israel needed to pay for the establishment of peace. He was willing to compromise, but only to an extent. Like all other Israeli leaders up to the time of this writing, Peres failed to reach substantive and long-lasting peace with the Palestinians.

My activity in Israeli politics, first with Labour and later with Mapam and Meretz, provided me with important insights, a foundation on which to build my academic peace research. After visiting the Occupied Palestinian Territories, I became a vocal opponent of the occupation. In the 1990s, I supported the Gaza First idea and later the two-state solution.

My commitment to peace grew over the years. I took part in meetings with peace activists from all over the world and welcomed exchanges with Palestinians. The yearning for peace became an integral part of my being. In my various capacities, both academic and non-academic, I continued to contribute to bridging gaps between Israelis and Palestinians, aiming to create cracks in the tall, overbearing walls between us.

In 2013, I decided to embark on this project: writing a book on the failed Israeli-Palestinian peace process, aiming to understand why peace has evaded us and, no less important, to decipher the formula that will help to bring about peace, if and when the right opportunity presents itself. I decided that the book will be based, in the main, on archives and comprehensive interviews with decision-makers and negotiators. My first interviewee was Shlomo Ben-Ami, whom I met in Los Angeles in 2013. I had worked for Shlomo in 1994 and had kept in touch with him over the years. This was the first of more than 100 interviews with senior people from ten countries and the United Nations.

The Israeli-Palestinian conflict is most complex. It is also most divisive. It is hard to maintain neutrality when one is discussing the conflict. We are all products of our upbringing. I am Israeli-British. I care about Israel a great deal. I am also an academic, and a peace and human rights activist. While it is difficult to maintain objectivity, I strive to offer a just solution for both parties, Israeli and Palestinian. I have always said that there are no angels in the story of the Israeli-Palestinian conflict. It is not a tale of black and white, of good people against evil people. Both sides have valid claims over the same land. Both sides have made many mistakes. Both sides need to make painful compromises if they genuinely wish to change reality and create an environment in which people can respect each other and cooperate.

At the time of writing, 2025, reality is harsh. War has been raging for two years, tensions are high and there is little appetite for peace – perceived by many as a distant dream. However, we should not fall into the fallacy of thinking that the future is bound to be similar to the present situation, and whatever situation we are in is here to stay. Time and again, history has shown that changes can be swift and dramatic. Making foes into friends is challenging, yet doable. It has happened before. It can also happen between Israelis and Palestinians.

ACKNOWLEDGEMENTS

This book is the result of many years of research and thinking. When I visited the Occupied Palestinian Territory and saw the occupation, I was startled. Since then, I have been opposed to it. Oslo 1993 gave me hope that it would be possible to create a two-state solution.

I acknowledge with gratitude Shimon Peres, who introduced me to politics; Yitzhak Navon and Ezer Weizman, who shared with me their life experiences; Gad Yaacobi, my closest friend in Israeli politics; and Yossi Sarid, whom I knew for many years from our work at the Labour and Meretz parties. May they all rest in peace. I also cherish the memory of Shabtai Shavit and Martin Indyk, who supported my research.

I thank the following interviewees who dedicated time and at times provided further help and support in the research process: Ziad Abu Zayyad, Hussein Agha, Ghaith al-Omari, Shaul Arieli, Hasan Asfour, Ami Ayalon, Gadi Baltiansky, Aharon Barak, Ehud Barak, Yossi Beilin, Shlomo Ben-Ami, Shlomo Brom, Anders Bjurner, Alistair Burt, Richard Dalton, Uzi Dayan, Udi Dekel, Jan Egeland, Stuart Eizenstat, Maher El-Kurd, Salam Fayyad, Vincent Fean, Avi Gil, Gidi Grinstein, Amos Guiora, John Hagard, Israel Hasson, Gamal Helal, Yair Hirschfeld, Ulf Hjertonsson, Hiba Husseini, John Jenkins, Ahmad Khalidi, Daniel Kurtzer, Tzipi Livni, David Makovsky, Robert Malley, Dan Meridor, Aaron David Miller, Yitzhak Mordechai, Mathias Mossberg, Francesco Motta, Marwan Muasher, Aryeh Naor, Azriel Nevo, Pär Nuder, Ehud Olmert, Tom Phillips, Jonathan Powell, William Quandt, Itamar Rabinovich, Dennis Ross, Yuval Rotem, Elyakim Rubinstein, Jonathan Schwartz, Pierre Schori, Svein Sevje, Gilead Sher, Joel Singer, Annika Söder, Sven-Eric Söder and Tor Wennesland. Some of these interviewees also kindly commented on draft chapters.

Many more people have helped me along the way. They provided advice and information, commented on chapters and kindly offered various forms of assistance. Among them, I wish to particularly note Karin

Aggestam, Fahad Albinali, Omar B. Al- Nahar, Amnon Aran, Naomi Chazan, Prince El Hassan Bin Talal, Prince Khalid bin Bandar Al Saud, Erik Berggrav, Gary Edles, Mervyn Frost, Tzippy Hauser, Mazen Kamal Homoud, James Franklin Jeffrey, Anders Lidén, Rob Litwak, Andrew J. Mainz, Matthew Palatnik, Bhikhu Parekh, Ilan Peleg, Robert I. Rotberg, Matti Steinberg, Stefan Talmon, Mike van Dusen, Roy Vilozny, Steve Zipperstein and Eyal Zisser for their support, constructive suggestions and comments.

Draft papers addressing different aspects of this research were presented at the University of Hull, the Swedish Institute of International Affairs, Lund University, Gothenburg University, Paideia Stockholm, Uppsala University, New York University, the University of Pennsylvania, the Hebrew University, the University of Haifa and the Rockefeller Foundation Center.

I am also thankful to the Israel Institute for Advanced Studies at the Hebrew University, the Woodrow Wilson International Center for Scholars, the Swedish Research Council and Lund University for providing me with invaluable resources to complete the book. Most of the book was written during my Olof Palme Visiting Professorship year at Lund Centre for Advanced Middle Eastern Studies and during my Fellowship at the Hebrew University in Jerusalem. I am indebted to these organisations for the conducive conditions provided for writing. I am also grateful to the excellent University of Hull Library for its unfailing support.

Some of the interviews were published: 'Analysis of the PLO and Hamas: Interview with Sir John Jenkins', *International Dialogue*, 14 (2024); 'Thirty Years after the Oslo Peace Accords: Interviews with Joel Singer', *Israel Studies*, 29(2) (2024): 1–29; 'Israeli-Palestinian Negotiations through the Eyes of Gamal Helal', *Israel Journal of Foreign Affairs*, 17(2) (December 2023): 159–174; 'The Role of the Arab World in the Palestinian-Israeli Conflict: Interview with Marwan Muasher', *Israel Affairs*, 29(5) (2023): 864–894; 'The Pursuit of Peace with the Palestinians: Interviews with Ehud Barak', *Israel Affairs*, 29(2) (2023): 385–450; 'Lessons from Peace Negotiations: Interview with Ehud Olmert', *Israel Affairs*, 27(6) (2021): 1160–1189; 'Stockholm and the Israeli-Palestinian Peace Process: An Interview with State Secretary for Foreign Affairs Annika Söder', *Israel Affairs*, 27(4) (2021): 732–749; 'History of Track II Peace Negotiations: Interview with Hussein Agha', *Israel Studies*, 26(1) (2021): 47–72; 'Keys for Peace in the Middle East: Interview with Ambassador Itamar Rabinovich', *Israel Affairs*, 25(4) (2019): 699–725; 'Lessons from the Israeli-Egyptian Peace Talks: An

Interview with Aharon Barak', *Israel Studies Review*, 34(2) (Autumn 2019): 1–32; 'Israel-PLO Peace Process: Interview with Ambassador Daniel Kurtzer', *Israel Studies*, 24(3) (2019): 127–156; 'Interview with Former Head of Mossad Shabtai Shavit', *Fathom* (January 2019); 'The Oslo Peace Process: Interview with Joel Singer', *Israel Affairs*, 24(5) (2018): 733–766. Other related publications are 'President Trump's Policies in the Middle East', *The Cairo Review of Global Affairs* (February 2025), www.thecairoreview.com/essays/president-trumps-policies/; 'Annapolis and the Abbas-Olmert Direct Negotiations: A Critical Analysis', *Conflict and Cooperation* (2026), https://doi.org/10.1177/00108367251397783.

Introduction

The more we sweat in peace, the less we bleed in war.

~ Vijaya Lakshmi Pandit

Israel was established in May 1948, and its boundaries have been disputed ever since. The current borders have not received official recognition from either Israel or the international community. The major controversies pertain to the West Bank, Jerusalem, the Gaza Strip and the Golan Heights – territories that Israel conquered during the Six-Day War in 1967. The Palestinian Authority (PA) seeks to end the state of occupation in the West Bank, regain control over the Gaza Strip (which has been governed by Hamas[1] since 2007) and assert claims over neighbourhoods in the eastern part of Jerusalem. The PA, like Israel, is adversely affected by the land dispute, as it lacks defined boundaries and sovereignty, essential preconditions for the declaration of an independent Palestinian state.

The history of the Israeli-Palestinian conflict is characterised by immigration, violence, expulsion, religious and national divides, and the persistent inability to replace barriers with bridges. This conflict is multidimensional and complex, directly impacting Israeli and Palestinian societies and, indirectly, their neighbours, the Middle East and the world at large. It should not be perceived merely as a political or territorial dispute; understanding it requires knowledge of ideologies, religions, politics, culture, history, security and geography. Both Israel and Palestine have legitimate claims over a small piece of land.

The complexity of the conflict arises from the dissimilarities between Israel and Palestine: a recognised state versus a non-sovereign entity. Both parties have a vested interest in the religious sites located in the West Bank but have been unable to agree on a sharing formula. Furthermore, the conflict is complicated by divisions within both societies. In Israel,

[1] Harakat al-Muqawame al-Islamiyyah, in short Hamas, is the Islamic Resistance Movement.

there is a growing divide between liberal, non-religious individuals and those who are more religious and authoritarian. In Palestine, the rift is deepening between those willing to recognise Israel and engage in dialogue, and those who advocate for eternal struggle and resistance, often characterised by more religious and authoritarian views. Additionally, Palestine faces a geographic challenge, as the West Bank and Gaza Strip are not contiguous.

The conflict is marked by inequality and asymmetry across multiple dimensions, which significantly influences relationships and negotiations. Israel, a Jewish democracy, operates within a framework of political and legal checks and balances, while the PA is in a prolonged transition from a revolutionary movement to a state-building government, characterised by authoritarian governance. Palestinians are less constrained by coalition politics than Israeli leaders are, and their governance systems differ markedly. The Palestinian populace is frustrated by their inability to elect leaders, as elections have been repeatedly postponed, compounded by systemic corruption that undermines trust in their leadership. Conversely, Israel is not immune to the democratic paradox, wherein the very foundations of democracy could lead to its own destruction. I developed the concept of the 'democratic catch' in my previous works.[2]

The 'democratic catch' aims to explain the necessity of finding a balance for the sustained functioning of democracies. A delicate equilibrium must be maintained between measures taken to protect democracy and adherence to underlying liberal values. Liberal democracy is founded on principles of liberty, tolerance, pluralism, participation and representation. However, it can be argued that these very principles may, paradoxically, undermine democracy itself. Unlimited liberty may lead to anarchy; tolerating the intolerant can result in coercion and violence; respecting all conceptions of the good may harm the most vulnerable in society, often women and children; excessive participation might overwhelm the system, rendering government functions ineffective; and no democracy can realistically ensure representation for every idea in society. Furthermore, democracy is based on majority rule while respecting the rights of

[2] Raphael Cohen-Almagor, *The Boundaries of Liberty and Tolerance* (Gainesville, FL: The University Press of Florida, 1994); *Speech, Media, and Ethics: The Limits of Free Expression* (Houndmills and New York: Palgrave Macmillan, 2001, 2005); *The Scope of Tolerance: Studies on the Costs of Free Expression and Freedom of the Press* (London and New York: Routledge, 2006); *Confronting the Internet's Dark Side: Moral and Social Responsibility on the Free Highway* (New York and Washington, DC: Cambridge University Press and Woodrow Wilson Center Press, 2015).

minorities. Respecting minority rights is no less important than majority rule. Democracy that ignores minority rights is bound to deteriorate into authoritarianism. Since 2022, Israeli democracy has been in decline. In Palestine, democracy does not exist.

Moreover, the two sides, Israel and Palestine, are unequal in terms of economic and military resources and status. Both Israeli and Palestinian leaders are acutely aware of these disparities. This asymmetry often leads the Israeli public and many populist leaders to believe that Israel can impose its will through an agreement, or at least that time will ultimately work in Israel's favour. Conversely, Palestinians believe they can garner support from the broader Arab and Muslim world, along with other international backers. This was particularly evident during the recent war between Hamas and Israel, following the Hamas onslaught on 7 October 2023, which prompted military attacks against Israel from Iran, Syria, Hezbollah in Lebanon, the Houthis in Yemen and Iraqi pro-Iranian proxies. Additionally, Russia, China and other nations openly supported the military actions against Israel. This multilateral asymmetry convinces many Palestinians and their leaders that time is on their side, leading them to believe they will either force Israel into an agreement or, ideally from their perspective, dismantle Israel and bring an end to Zionism.

More than a century of conflict has eroded trust between Israelis and Palestinians. Currently, the leaders of the two sides do not meet regularly, if at all. The involvement of a third party appears necessary, and the United States is perceived as the most suitable broker, due to its strong interests and stakes in the Middle East. As a powerful player with leverage, the US has the ability to advance the peace process; however, despite numerous attempts to mediate between the rivals, peace remains elusive.

In 1974, Secretary of State Henry Kissinger succeeded in mediating between Israel and Egypt because he was viewed as an objective and fair broker. Both sides accepted his leadership in mediating the competing interests of both nations.[3] The same can be said for President Jimmy Carter and his successful mediation at Camp David in 1978.[4] During the Camp David peace summit in 2000, however, no such perception of American neutrality was evident. The Palestinians believed that the

[3] Brian S. Mandell and Brian W. Tomlin, 'Mediation in the Development of Norms to Manage Conflict: Kissinger in the Middle East', *Journal of Peace Research*, 28(1) (1991): 43–55.

[4] Jacob Bercovitch (ed.), *Resolving International Conflicts: The Theory and Practice of Mediation* (Boulder, CO: Lynne Rienner, 1996); Tom Princen, 'Camp David; Problem-Solving or Power Politics as Usual?', *Journal of Peace Research*, 28(1) (1991): 57–69.

American negotiating team had coordinated its plans with the Israelis, a suspicion confirmed by American negotiators Daniel Kurtzer and Aaron David Miller. Miller confessed, 'not only did we consistently coordinate our positions with the Israelis, showing them our negotiating texts first – a practice I might add the Palestinians had come to expect – but we viewed the issues largely from Israel's perspective. I remember how impressed we all were when we learned that Barak was willing to concede 80 per cent of the West Bank.'[5] This lack of trust in President Bill Clinton undermined the Palestinian negotiators' confidence in his ability to relay information effectively to both parties. Currently, the Palestinians perceive President Donald Trump with suspicion, prompting them to seek involvement from other players in the process. At the same time, Palestinian leaders recognise that the American-Israeli special relationship can be advantageous for them, as only the US has the potential to compel Israel to make painful concessions.

Objectives

This book aims to analyse more than three decades of peace negotiations between Israel and the Palestine Liberation Organization (PLO), from the inception of the Oslo process in 1993 to the present day. It investigates the reasons behind the failure of the peace process, the role of third-party mediation and facilitation, and the essential elements for successful negotiations. My objective is not to provide a comprehensive historical account of all peace efforts from 1993 to the present. Instead, I focus on three critical junctures: Oslo, Camp David and the Abbas–Olmert negotiations. I seek to understand why, despite the extensive efforts of numerous individuals – including several US presidents – the peoples of Israel and Palestine remain far from achieving peace. I analyse what was accomplished, what was lacking, the mistakes made and what can be done to break the vicious cycle of violence that has inflicted profound suffering on both societies.

Furthermore, the book's objective is not solely to elucidate the reasons for these failures; it also aims to propose innovative strategies for fostering a more peaceful reality. Understanding the past may guide us towards a better future. It is imperative that we study mistakes to avoid repeating them. To ensure a brighter future for Israeli and Palestinian children, we

[5] Discussions with Aaron David Miller (October–November 2008), and Miller, 'How Not to Host a Summit', *Foreign Policy* (10 July 2012). See also Nathan Thrall, 'Israel & the US: The Delusions of Our Diplomacy', *New York Review of Books* (9 October 2014).

must devise constructive strategies to advance the peace process, develop the capacity to overcome potential obstacles, and create a practical, reasonable, innovative and achievable framework. This is a formidable undertaking. Many have attempted this task in the past, only to see their aspirations unmet and to witness a disheartening reality.

Research Questions

What role can small countries play in facilitating and mediating peace? Can small countries assist in the peace process in a way that would supplement, or even replace, American peace initiatives?
Specifically, what were/are the roles of Sweden and Norway in the context of their respective Middle East policies and bilateral relations with Israel and the Palestinians?
Was Oslo a success or a failure?
How important was the Harpsund–Stockholm process?
What role should the United States take in resolving the conflict?
Why did the 2000 Camp David Summit and the following peace summits and negotiations fail? What lessons did the parties learn?
Why, despite many efforts, is there no peace between Israel and the Palestinians?
What are the keys to successful negotiations?
What are the keys to successful mediation?
What are the keys to successful facilitation?
Is trust between the parties important?
What does ripeness mean?
How to resolve the Israeli-Palestinian conflict?

Premises and Concepts

Basic needs: All humans have the same basic needs: food, water, clothing, shelter, steady income, sleep, maintaining good health and security.
Peace: A state of peace is infinitely preferable to a state of war. As peace is a precious commodity, its achievement comes at a price. Peace is not merely a tactic. Peace needs to be the strategy of both Israel and Palestine.
Status quo: In the Israeli-Palestinian conflict, the status quo is more a theoretical concept than a real one. It is very difficult to maintain the status quo. The situation on the ground is changing all the time.
Compromise: Many of the issues that divide societies and create cleavages can be resolved via deliberations and compromises. Political conflicts

can be mitigated and tamed by compromises. While politics is bound to include a conflictual dimension, we should be engaged in a sustained quest for compromise.

Freedom vs coercion: People would like to lead their lives as free and autonomous human beings. Instinctively, coercion is foreign to us, and it might be offensive to our sensibilities and lead to an increased sense of alienation and resentment. Therefore, the occupation of the territories is abhorrent and should be removed. The occupation is bad for the Palestinians and is also bad for Israel, as it undermines its democratic foundations.

Human equality: All people should enjoy equal human and civil rights. One society is not inferior to another. Countries that endorse hierarchical order are racist.

Values: The two basic values that should guide us as humans are respect for others and not harming others. We should strive to protect and promote these values. We uphold John Stuart Mill's Harm Principle which maintains that the only purpose for which power can be rightfully exercised over any member of the community, against his or her will, is to prevent harm to others.[6] The Respect for Others Argument, derived from Kantian[7] and Rawlsian[8] philosophies, requires us to respect the dignity of people as human beings.

Balancing: Striking a balance between rights and liberties is challenging. There is no quick fix suitable for all societies. The balance must take into consideration history, politics and culture, as well as the pain and suffering of those who pay the price for belonging to a certain culture or religion and the consequences of intervention, or lack of intervention. These factors vary from one country to another, as history and politics are distinct. The challenge is becoming more difficult as a result of globalisation, immigration and the changing composition of societies.

Taking spoilers most seriously: Palestinian and Israeli spoilers have successfully undermined the peace process. They have caused an erosion of trust between the two peoples, which has led to conflict escalation. They should not merely be dealt with along the way; a concrete plan should be devised to address their challenges.

[6] J. S. Mill, *Utilitarianism, Liberty, and Representative Government* (London: J. M. Dent, 1948), Everyman's edition, at 114 or *On Liberty*, www.utilitarianism.com/ol/three.html.

[7] Immanuel Kant, *Political Writings* (Cambridge: Cambridge University Press, 1991).

[8] John Rawls, *A Theory of Justice* (Oxford: Oxford University Press, 1986).

Hypotheses

- Responsibility for the peace process failure lies with Israel, the PA and the mediating parties.
- The United States has an important role to play in the process, possibly more crucially in the advanced stages of the negotiations.
- In addition to the United States, Arab countries have an important role to play.
- Peace negotiations will only materialise when Israel and Palestine perceive peace as their strategy, not as mere tactics.

Main Arguments

The legitimacy of the Zionist and the Palestinian national movements should be recognised.

Israel's long-term survival depends not only on military strength or strategic alliances but also, fundamentally, on its acceptance within the region. The cornerstone of such regional acceptance lies in achieving a just and lasting peace with the Palestinians.

The economy of peace may be as expensive as the economy of war. However, while the economy of peace is constructive, the economy of war is destructive.

The peace pact should be fair and just for all signatories, otherwise its worth is no more than a piece of paper. The solution must be *just*. It should leave both sides satisfied. None of the sides should feel that it has been cheated. One side's satisfaction depends to a degree on making the other side sufficiently content with an agreement to want to live up to it.

Successful negotiations are not accidental; they require a convergence of several critical conditions. Key among them are:

- a ripe political moment, recognised by all parties as an urgent window of opportunity;
- thorough preparation by negotiators and stakeholders on all sides;
- open and sustained communication between negotiating parties and with their respective constituencies;
- mutual respect and good faith – not only between adversaries but also between the mediator and the parties;
- clear, reasonable goals and a willingness to make meaningful compromises;
- a fair and impartial mediation process;

- pragmatism and realism by all actors involved; and
- a coordinated strategy to identify, contain and neutralise spoilers who seek to derail the process.

Effective negotiations rest on a tripartite foundation: strategic preparation before talks begin, trust-building during the process and faithful implementation of agreements afterward. However, beyond process mechanics, substantive peace requires conducive political leadership and timing. Some essential preconditions must align: an Israeli leader who not only believes in peace but is willing to pay its political and territorial price, and who is capable of persuading his/her public that peace is in Israel's best interest; a Palestinian leader who is committed to peace, recognises its cost, and is both prepared to make concessions and capable of delivering on them; and, no less important, a ripe moment, when both sides perceive inaction as a greater threat than compromise, and when delay is seen as self-defeating, rather than strategic. Absent any of these preconditions, the prospects for peace are slim. All preconditions must be present for negotiations to move from words to transformative action.

Spoilers – whether violent extremists, political hardliners or disaffected factions – must not be underestimated. Their ability to derail peace efforts has been proven time and again. Ignoring them is not a viable strategy. Instead, any serious peace effort must include proactive, coordinated measures to manage and marginalise these actors. Peace cannot be sustained in a climate of terror and fear.

Ultimately, a sustainable solution must be both just and comprehensive. The legitimate rights and national aspirations of both Israelis and Palestinians must be reconciled. This is not a zero-sum game. Without peace, Israel faces continued cycles of violence and existential uncertainty. Its future remains perched precariously on the bayonets of occupation – an untenable position marked by insecurity, moral strain and perpetual bleeding. Without peace, the Palestinians will continue to suffer. The raging violence makes living extremely difficult for them. Peace is not a luxury; it is a strategic necessity for both nations.

Analysis

The comprehensive theoretical framework includes several layers of analysis: justice, conflict resolution, ripeness, compromise, superforecasting and dealing with spoilers.

Justice

What is a just peace process? What is a just agreement? To answer these questions, I will avail myself of John Rawls's theory of justice and fairness.[9] The protection of basic rights is instrumental in accommodating interests. Rawls viewed justice not merely as one value among many, but as the ultimate value against which conflicting values should be measured. The protection of basic rights is crucial for accommodating different interests, with Rawls's veil of ignorance serving as an analytical tool to consider various perspectives and achieve fair resolutions. Justice plays a critical role in peacebuilding, ensuring objectivity and fairness. Behind the veil of ignorance, different considerations are weighed with the aim of achieving just resolutions. Indeed, justice is the first virtue of peacebuilding. It is necessary.

Conflict Resolution, Negotiations, Mediation and Facilitation

I examine these concepts and the advantages and weaknesses of Track I (government officials), Track II (non-governmental organisations and unofficial negotiators) and mixed-track diplomacy. What were the strengths and weaknesses of the varying negotiation tracks? Official negotiations enable leaders to impact the process directly. Leaders influence the direction of negotiations and outcomes. They have the capacity to access information, intelligence and financial resources that provide high leverage and flexibility in negotiations. The art of bargaining will be explained. This line of enquiry will be informed by models for effective negotiation.[10]

Track II diplomacy brings together people who enjoy their leaders' trust to talk on an unofficial basis. Proponents believe that such a negotiation mode can help break through the barriers that official diplomacy can sometimes place on talks. This may mean entering the grey area between what governments will talk about and what they often know must be discussed if a problem is to be addressed.[11]

9 Ibid.

10 J. Bercovitch and A. Houston, 'Why Do They Do It Like This? An Analysis of the Factors Influencing Mediation Behavior in International Conflicts', *Journal of Conflict Resolution*, 44 (2000): 170–202.

11 Peter Jones, *Track Two Diplomacy in Theory and Practice* (Stanford, CA: Stanford University Press, 2015).

Ripeness

According to Zartman, there are two preconditions for ripeness: a hurtful stalemate for both sides and a mutually perceived way out.[12] Both Israeli and Palestinian leaders need to feel that the time is ripe for signing a peace deal.

Compromise

Negotiation is the art of compromise. Compromise involves finding common ground and making concessions. Negotiations require rejecting rigidity for flexibility. Communication is essential. When compromise takes place between two or more parties, the emphasis is on reciprocity, that is, mutual concessions. The parties should demonstrate mutual respect, listen actively and acknowledge what is being said. They need to speak the same language, in the sense that they share some basic norms which form the grounds for potential understanding.

I distinguish between genuine and tactical compromise, arguing that genuine negotiations require genuine compromises from both parties.

Superforecasters

A further useful model to understand the art of negotiations is Tetlock and Gardner's insights on superforecasters.[13] Superforecasters are open to diverse views; they are pragmatic and cognisant of the value of checking thinking for cognitive and emotional biases. Superforecasters are relentless, determined to continue their investigation. Reflective, they work in teams and have the ability and willingness to admit error and change the course of action when deemed necessary.

How to Deal with Spoilers?

Spoilers are those who aim to sabotage negotiations. Palestinian and Israeli terrorists and political extremists have played a critical role in the Israeli-Palestinian conflict.

[12] I. William Zartman, *Ripe for Resolution* (New York and Oxford: Oxford University Press, 1989).

[13] Philip Tetlock and Dan Gardner, *Superforecasting: The Art and Science of Prediction* (London: Random House, 2015).

Book Structure

The historical starting point of my analysis is Oslo. There is literature on Oslo with contrasting interpretations.[14] Curiously, not much has been written on the Harpsund negotiations that followed Oslo, although both Shlomo Ben-Ami (in the interview he granted me) and Ahmed Qurie, known also as Abu Ala, stressed their importance.[15] This book sheds light on how the Oslo and Harpsund talks were orchestrated and perceived by Norwegian and Swedish officials. It explains that then Prime Minister Yitzhak Rabin, who mistrusted his foreign minister, Shimon Peres, wanted to stop the Oslo talks. Peres called on attorney Joel Singer to salvage the talks, and Singer succeeded in convincing Rabin to continue them. The three chapters on Oslo analyse the first and second phases of the Oslo peace talks and evaluate the lessons that can be deduced from the Oslo negotiations.

The Oslo channel was established by Yossi Beilin, Terje Rød-Larsen and Yair Hirschfeld, who understood Yasser Arafat's need to initiate a new path for relationships with Israel.[16] The First Intifada, which erupted in 1987, constituted a threat to Arafat's leadership. He was surprised by the scale of the uprising. The rise of Hamas further threatened his leadership; Arafat felt he was losing control of the West Bank and Gaza. Moreover, his support for the Iraqi dictator Saddam Hussein during the 1991 Gulf War weakened his standing among moderate Arab nations.[17] I explain these and other factors which propelled Arafat to seek negotiations with Israel.

[14] Ron Pundak, *Secret Channel* (Tel Aviv: Aliyat Hagag, 2013) (Hebrew) and 'From Oslo to Taba: What Went Wrong?', *Survival*, 43(3) (2001): 31–45; Yair Hirschfeld, *The Israeli-Palestinian Peace Process* (Cham: Springer, 2024) and *Track-Two Diplomacy toward an Israeli-Palestinian Solution 1978–2014* (Washington, DC: Woodrow Wilson Center Press and Johns Hopkins University Press, 2014); Geoffrey R. Watson, *The Oslo Accords* (Oxford: Oxford University Press, 2000); Jane Corbin, *The Norway Channel: The Secret Talks that Led to the Middle East Peace Accord* (New York: Atlantic Monthly Press, 1994); Johan Jorgen Holst, 'Reflections on the Makings of a Tenuous Peace', *Middle East Insight*, 9(6) (September–October 1993): 30–34. See also Hilde Henriksen Waage's articles in the Bibliography.

[15] Ahmed Qurie, *Beyond Oslo* (London: I.B. Tauris, 2008). The most comprehensive source on Harpsund is Jacob Eriksson, *Swedish Mediation of the Israeli-Palestinian Conflict: A Study of the Utility of Small-State Mediation and Track II Diplomacy*, Thesis submitted for the degree of PhD (Department of Languages and Cultures of the Near and Middle East, School of Oriental and African Studies, University of London, 2011): 216–239.

[16] Interview with Yossi Beilin (13 May 2015).

[17] Interview with Shlomo Ben-Ami (26 June 2013).

The Oslo peace process was divided into two main phases. The first phase involved a mixed channel: while the PLO sent three officials, the two Israeli representatives were unofficial academics with expertise in political economy. At some point, the PLO delegation presented an ultimatum: either the Israeli government would become involved, or the Oslo channel would shut down. Peres sent Uri Savir, his loyal assistant, 'to tell the PLO that a formal official of Israel is on-board'.[18] Thus, in the second phase, an independent lawyer (Singer) and a government official (Savir) were added to the delegation alongside the two academics. Furthermore, the discussions were infused with legal jargon, and the emphasis shifted to addressing Prime Minister Rabin's major concern: security. Issues could now be developed in more depth. The endgames of the Palestinian and Israeli delegations were different: while the Palestinians aspired to end the process with an independent, sovereign state, Israel wanted them to settle for 'autonomy plus' for the Palestinians. The Israelis did not officially consider the idea of a full-fledged Palestinian state.

Many scholars wish to make a significant impact on society; very few actually do. Two of the major players in the Oslo process, Yair Hirschfeld and Ron Pundak, were Israeli academics who influenced the course of history. Adding to the very unusual story of Oslo is the fact that a third player, Joel Singer, was, at that time, a private lawyer from Washington, DC. This rare trio in the diplomatic arena, none in an official government capacity, drove the course of history.

The Oslo Accords were not a peace agreement. They established a mutual recognition agreement, intended to set the parameters for a trust-building process that would last a few years and then culminate in a signed peace agreement. The Oslo rationale was to agree on what was relatively easy to agree upon. The difficult issues would be postponed until later. As a result, major controversial and important issues were not dealt with, in the belief that as the process continued, the good faith built on both sides would create a foundation for the resolution of those tough issues. Hence, questions of borders, refugees' compensation and right of return, settlements, Jerusalem and the Temple Mount were not resolved. Rabin believed that the Oslo agreement was all about security; he was not concerned about any other aspect of the agreement. Rabin believed that if there is security, the agreement will succeed. If there is no security, even though it is otherwise perfect, the agreement will fail.[19]

[18] Interview with Joel Singer (25 March 2022), 11.
[19] Interview with Joel Singer (29 August 2014).

The Oslo Accords were meant to lead the parties to the resolution of the Israeli-Palestinian conflict and the establishment of peaceful relationships between them. The Oslo process was designed according to Rabin's cautious worldview. He wanted a slow process, so as to allow the Israelis to become accustomed to the new, emerging reality. He did not rush to make further concessions in the West Bank. As Israel's security was Rabin's first and foremost priority, he wished to test Arafat before making further concessions; he certainly did not want to see terror attacks emanating from recently evacuated territory. Rabin was also interested in pushing forward a peace initiative with Syria.[20]

Chapter 2 explains why the Israelis and the PLO representatives agreed to meet and talk. Chapter 3 analyses the talks. Chapter 4 concerns the aftermath of the Oslo talks and assesses the positive and negative aspects, lessons and implications of the peace process and the Oslo Accords.

A vicious circle hampered the success of the Oslo peace process. Internal rivalries within Israel brought about radicalisation that eroded the belief in peace, and that culminated in the assassination of Yitzhak Rabin in November 1995. Internal rivalries within Palestine spurred terrorism. That terrorism drove the Israeli electorate to elect a new leader, with a new vision contrary to the Oslo spirit. Benjamin Netanyahu came to power in 1996. Two years later, in 1998, following the signing of the Wye Plantation Accords, he lost a no-confidence vote in the Knesset. Consequently, the Knesset was dissolved and early national elections were called. When Ehud Barak came to power in 1999, he opted for resolving the Syrian conflict. A peace treaty with this large state would provide additional leverage for resolving the Palestinian issue, as the PA would be put under more pressure to yield results. Arafat, the less powerful partner in the negotiation process, needed constant assurances that he would be treated fairly and on equal terms. Only meagre assurances were provided by Netanyahu and his successor, Barak. Furthermore, Barak's tendency to dictate did not sit well with Arafat. Against this background, after failed negotiations with Syria, Barak pushed for a peace summit with Arafat under the auspices of the US.

Chapters 5, 6 and 7 are concerned with the second important peace junction: the 2000 Camp David peace summit. Camp David became part of Israeli history as the place where two peace summits were held. In 1978, President Jimmy Carter hosted the Israeli and Egyptian leaders – Menachem Begin and Anwar Sadat – and their respective delegations, in

[20] William Quandt, *Peace Process: American Diplomacy and the Arab-Israeli Conflict since 1967* (Berkeley, CA: University of California Press, 2005), 330.

an attempt to resolve the Israeli-Egyptian conflict. After intensive negotiations, the summit ended with a peace accord. In 2000, President Bill Clinton wished to follow in Carter's footsteps and resolve the Israeli-Palestinian conflict. Clinton hosted Israeli Prime Minister Ehud Barak and the Chairperson of the PA and of the PLO, Yasser Arafat, and their respective delegations for intensive talks; however, this time, the summit ended in colossal failure. It failed for many reasons, including bad timing, poor communication between the parties, differing expectations, contrasting interests, wide gaps between the Israeli and the Palestinian endgames, lack of mutual respect and courtesy, lack of transparency, lack of impartial and honest mediation, the inability of the mediator to control the agenda, unhelpful styles of negotiation of both parties and the unwillingness of the negotiating parties to pay the price for peace. I argue that the summit should not have taken place.

Some Palestinians, including Arafat, failed to understand that the use of violence corrodes the peace process and leads to a loss of faith. The early 2000s were filled with countless terror incidents.[21] Chapter 8 analyses events that took place after the peace summit. These include the al Aqsa (Second) Intifada, the Clinton Parameters, the Taba peace talks, the 2001 elections in Israel and the Arab Peace Initiative (API) of 2002. These events brought about fundamental changes in both Palestinian and Israeli societies.

Chapters 9 and 10 are concerned with the third important peace junction. I explain why the Annapolis peace process and the Abbas–Olmert direct negotiations failed, despite the considerable investment of Israel, the PA and the United States. President George W. Bush arranged an impressive international conference that supported many meetings between Olmert and Abbas, and three hundred meetings about procedures, but peace remained elusive. The chapters shed light on the proceedings and analyse the shortcomings of the process and the inability of Israel and the PA to bridge the gaps and sign a peace treaty. While Olmert presented the best peace offer to date that any Israeli prime minister was willing to sign, it still fell short of Palestinian demands. It is argued that Abbas should have signed the deal.

The second part of the book is practical. Chapter 11 outlines the keys to successful negotiations, mediation and facilitation and provides viable information on the requirements. This chapter offers insights not only for the Israeli-Palestinian context but also for conflict resolution more broadly. Building on extensive research in archives and

[21] Gilad Sharon, *Sharon – The Life of a Leader* (Tel Aviv: Matar, 2011) (Hebrew), 335–513.

in-depth interviews with senior decision-makers and negotiators who were involved in the Arab-Israeli conflict, I outline the basic qualities that negotiators, mediators and facilitators should have and things they should do. Next, I move on to what negotiators, mediators and facilitators should *not* do. The arguments are supported by examples from previous peace negotiations between Arabs and Israelis. These experiences shed important light on past events and offer yardsticks for future negotiations. I also differentiate between what negotiators are required to do *prior* to negotiations, *during* negotiations and *after* negotiations. Obviously, ideas should not merely remain on paper. They should be implemented and become reality.

This line of enquiry is informed by the work of Roger Fisher and William Ury,[22] Herbert Kelman[23] and I. William Zartman[24] on models for effective negotiation. Some elements of these models are important for good facilitation and good mediation. Other elements are specific. Mediation differs from facilitation and arbitration. Facilitation is about processes, not substance. Facilitators provide interlocutors with the conditions to negotiate. In turn, arbitration uses a judicial process and delivers a decision that the parties have previously agreed to accept.[25]

It is explained that a mediator must be perceived by the parties as credible and even-handed. The mediator must have a deep understanding of the conflict and its dynamics, as well as the ability to show flexibility, highlight progress, overcome obstacles, create opportunities and, throughout the process, speak in a language that the parties understand and appreciate. A mediator should have a degree of leverage to apply pressure when the negotiations seem to be stuck.[26] This political process of persuasion is not

22 Roger Fisher and William Ury, *Getting to Yes: Negotiating Agreement without Giving In* (London: Random House, 1991).

23 Herbert C. Kelman, *Resolving Deep-Rooted Conflicts* (London: Routledge, 2020); H. C. Kelman, 'The Political Psychology of the Israeli-Palestinian Conflict: How Can We Overcome the Barriers to a Negotiated Solution?', *Political Psychology*, 8(3) (1987): 347–363; H. C. Kelman, 'Acknowledging the Other's Nationhood: How to Create a Momentum for the Israeli-Palestinian Negotiations', *Journal of Palestine Studies*, 22(1) (Autumn 1992): 18–38; H. C. Kelman, 'Some Determinants of the Oslo Breakthrough', *International Negotiation*, 2 (1997): 183–194; H. C. Kelman, 'The Israeli–Palestinian Peace Process and Its Vicissitudes', *American Psychologist*, 62(4) (May–June 2007): 287–303.

24 I. William Zartman, *Negotiation and Conflict Management: Essays on Theory and Practice* (London: Routledge, 2007) and *Ripe for Resolution* (New York and Oxford: Oxford University Press, 1989).

25 I. William Zartman, 'Mediation Roles for Large Small Countries', *Canadian Foreign Policy Journal*, 19(1) (2013): 14.

26 Simon J. A. Mason and Damiano Angelo Sguaitamatti, *Mapping Mediators* (Zurich: Swiss Federal Institute of Technology, 2011), 10–12.

supposed to have an advance commitment from the parties to accept the mediator's ideas. It is further argued that successful mediation requires credibility, and that trust is the most basic element of mediation.[27] While the parties trust the mediator, they understand that its role is to bridge gaps, and that it may ask them to make concessions which might be too painful for them to accept. Ample time is required to exhaust the process fully and enable the parties to eliminate gaps and build bridges.

Mediators should be fair, aggressive and creative. They need to identify ways to overcome complications and reach results and know how to rise above problems and obstacles that may separate the sides. They need to have the ability to defuse tensions, erect bridges and provide a safety net for the negotiators. The book analyses the roles that the United States, Norway and Sweden played in the peace processes, and it asks whether peace can be achieved without American involvement. It explains the root causes of the failure to bring about peace and the keys for future successful negotiations.

This research is important, as the Americans continue to fail in their mediation attempts. Still, senior American diplomats continue to believe that the role of the United States is irreplaceable.[28] Studying the Oslo and the Harpsund channels is important in order to see to what extent it is possible to conduct Israeli-Palestinian peace talks without direct American involvement.

Chapter 12 is arguably the most important chapter. It surveys some of the proposed solutions that were aired as to how to resolve the Israeli-Palestinian conflict and then explicates what I perceive to be the most comprehensive solution. It argues that to resolve the Israeli-Palestinian conflict, there is a need for courageous leaders on both sides who seize the opportunities presented to them and make the most of them for their people. This book maps the main issues that must be resolved on the road to peace between Israel and the PLO. Further, it argues that of all the possible solutions presently on the table, a two-state solution, followed by a Jordanian-Palestinian confederation, is the only viable, long-term solution from which all sides can profit. While the strategy is to reach that solution, the tactics for reaching it need to address the present realities and new complexities resulting from the latest round of hostilities between Israel and Hamas.

[27] Zartman, 'Mediation Roles for Large Small Countries': 18.

[28] Discussions with Aaron David Miller (October–November 2008); interview with Daniel Kurtzer (6 April 2017).

I have dedicated a major part of my adult life to promoting peace and have been writing this book with a clear agenda. My dream is to see the children of Israel and Palestine playing and studying together. I dream that Israelis will live in tranquillity, something they have never really had, as Israel's history is saturated in blood, terror and wars. I am a proud Zionist who cares deeply about Israel and its destiny. My love for Israel is deep and strong. Because I think Israel will face severe challenges in the future, I believe that the key to its security and survival is peace. Thus, my interest in peace is not just academic. It is very practical. I want to understand why the peace process failed, and what can be done to ensure that the next attempts to bring peace will be successful. Being cognisant of my subjective feelings towards Israel, I have tried to adopt John Rawls's analytical conception of justice and his idea of the veil of ignorance.

My commitment to justice precedes my commitment to peace, as I believe Israel and the Palestinians can achieve long-lasting peace only if the terms of the agreement are just and based on liberty and human rights. I apply the Rawlsian principles to assess the policies and conduct of both sides. Behind the veil of ignorance, when one does not know one's gender, culture, nationality, religion or any other dividing factor, one would wish to ensure that justice prevails across the board, without discrimination or any form of favouritism. Justice knows no boundaries. Applying the veil of ignorance would lead to a just and reasonable peace agreement.

A note on terminology is in order. The State of Palestine has been recognised by 147 countries,[29] but it is not a full-fledged state. People refer to 'Palestine' when they speak about the West Bank and the Gaza Strip. In the West Bank, the PA governs much of day-to-day Palestinian civil life. Hamas took over Gaza in June 2007.

The term 'occupation' is contested among Israelis. A 2018 poll shows that 49 per cent of Israeli Jews perceive the West Bank as 'Liberated Territories'; 19 per cent regard the West Bank as 'held' or 'administered territory'; 11 per cent do not know. Only 21 per cent of Israeli Jews perceive the

[29] AJLabs, 'Mapping Which Countries Recognise Palestine in 2025', *Al Jazeera* (10 April 2025), https://tinyurl.com/5n98yhet; 'Which Countries Recognise Palestine in 2024?', *Al Jazeera* (29 November 2024), www.aljazeera.com/news/2024/11/29/which-countries-recognise-palestine-in-2024. See also Jason Lemon, 'Which Countries Recognize Palestine? Colombia Becomes 137th UN Member to Do So', *Newsweek* (10 August 2018), https://tinyurl.com/3986sapn; Joe Vesey-Byrne, 'Which Countries Recognise Palestine?', *Indy100* (2 November 2017), https://tinyurl.com/5n7a6pr6.

West Bank as 'Occupied Territories'.[30] Israeli governments under Prime Minister Netanyahu have been successful in legitimising the occupation. I believe we should call a spade a spade. The West Bank is under Israeli military control. Palestinians in the West Bank do not enjoy the same rights and liberties that Israeli citizens do, and they cannot have full control of their lives, as control is in the hands of Israeli authorities. At will, the latter grant rights and freedoms; at will, they take them away and deprive West Bank Palestinians of basic rights.[31] Only Jewish settlers in the West Bank enjoy rights and liberties as Israelis do. I argue that it is illogical to build new Israeli houses in a territory that is designated to be Palestinian. Gaza is devastated by the war that erupted after the 7 October 2023 Hamas terror attack on Israel. For two years, 2023–2025, the Israel Defense Forces (IDF) were fighting Hamas in Gaza. On 9 October 2025, President Donald Trump announced that Israel and Hamas had agreed to the first phase of his twenty-point peace plan in which all Israeli hostages are to be released in exchange for Palestinian prisoners, the IDF withdraw from half of the Gaza Strip and a ceasefire comes into effect.

Israeli occupation is unjust. It involves continued systematic violations of basic human rights, including ethnic and religious discrimination, denial of the right to self-determination, denial of freedom of expression and freedom of movement, subjecting Palestinians to administrative detentions, curfews, housing restrictions, roadblocks and land appropriation, as well as turning a blind eye to settler violence and aggression. Palestinians are living in constant fear and insecurity. Israel has made no indication that it intends to bring the occupation to an end. The occupation has become a constant, and there is a strong move to annexe Area C of the West Bank. Both occupation and annexation infringe upon the Rawlsian Principle of Equal Liberty, that each person should have an equal right to the most extensive liberties compatible with similar liberties for all. Basic rights secured by justice should not be subjected to political bargaining or to the calculus of social interests. Rawls argued that, being the first virtues of human activities, truth and justice are uncompromising.[32] Justice is impartial, unaffected by race, nationalism, ethnic origins, colour or religion. It should remain blind to such distinctions.

[30] Walla Editorial, 'When Did You Visit the Bank?', *Walla* (28 May 2017) (Hebrew), https://news.walla.co.il/item/3067529.

[31] Raphael Cohen-Almagor, 'Fifty Years of Israeli Occupation', *E-International Relations* (14 October 2017), www.e-ir.info/2017/10/14/fifty-years-of-israeli-occupation/.

[32] John Rawls, *A Theory of Justice* (Oxford: Oxford University Press, 1986), 3–4.

1

The Analytical Framework

Methodological and Conceptual Underpinnings

> I will not speak to you only about peace. For the precondition of peace is justice. When we have achieved justice we will have achieved peace in the Near East.
>
> ~ King Hussein bin-Talal

This is an interdisciplinary study in the fields of history, conflict resolution, diplomacy, political theory and peace mediation. It focuses on the art of negotiation, mediation and facilitation. The research deals with historical texts and events. The theoretical framework is both extensive and original, providing important tools for the analysis of the findings and for moving the peace process forward. The research provides practical advice as to what leaders should do to seize the next opportunity for peace. The other novelties of this project relate to its scope and methodology. The interviews are detailed and content analysis brings to light the array of perspectives. There is much to learn from their perspectives. Furthermore, the archival research in different countries is similarly revealing and important.

Another important aspect of the research is addressing the problem of Palestinian and Israeli spoilers who, until now, have successfully derailed the peace process time and again. Israeli right-wing extremists and Palestinian organisations such as Hamas and the Islamic Jihad do not wish to see peace between the two peoples. They are unwilling to pay the necessary price for peace. The study aims to provide guidelines for both parties on how to address spoilers, to ensure that peace can be reached and then maintained.

Methodology

This research analyses the peace process between Israel and the Palestine Liberation Organization (PLO) from Oslo 1993 up to the present. I also studied the first Camp David Summit of 1978. The research was conducted in several stages:

A) Preliminary research was conducted in libraries, where I read the relevant literature – autobiographies and monographs of peace negotiators,[1] as well as other books, journal articles and newspapers. The research project involves an extensive literature review of historic documents. These include the Oslo process (1993), the Stockholm channel (1996), the Wye River Memorandum (1998), the Sharm El Sheikh Memorandum (1999), the Harpsund negotiations (2000), the Camp David Peace Summit (2000), the Clinton Parameters (2000), the Taba peace talks (2001), the Arab Peace

[1] Many of those involved in the peace process wrote books about the negotiations from their own perspectives. These books include: Mahmoud Abbas, *Through Secret Channels* (London: Garnet Publishing, 1997); Elliott Abrams, *Tested by Zion: The Bush Administration and the Israeli-Palestinian Conflict* (New York: Cambridge University Press, 2013); Hussein Agha and Robert Malley, *Tomorrow Is Yesterday: Life, Death, and the Pursuit of Peace in Israel/Palestine* (New York: Farrar, Straus and Giroux, 2025); Hanan Ashrawi, *This Side of Peace: A Personal Account* (New York: Touchstone, 1996); Ehud Barak, *My Country, My Life: Fighting for Israel, Searching for Peace* (New York: Macmillan, 2018); Yossi Beilin, *The Path to Geneva* (New York: RDV Books, 2004) and *Touching Peace* (London: Weidenfeld and Nicolson, 1999); Shlomo Ben-Ami, *Scars of War, Wounds of Peace* (London: Phoenix, 2005) and *A Front without a Rearguard* (Tel Aviv: Yedioth Ahronoth, 2004) (Hebrew); Bill Clinton, *My Life* (New York: Knopf, 2010); Warren Christopher, *In the Stream of History: Shaping Foreign Policy for a New Era* (Stanford, CA: Stanford University Press, 1998); Avi Gil, *Shimon Peres* (London: I.B. Tauris, 2021); Yair Hirschfeld, *Track-Two Diplomacy toward an Israeli-Palestinian Solution 1978–2014* (Washington, DC: Woodrow Wilson Center Press and Johns Hopkins University Press, 2014) and *The Israeli-Palestinian Peace Process* (Cham: Springer, 2024); Martin Indyk, *Innocent Abroad* (New York: Simon and Schuster, 2009); Daniel C. Kurtzer, Scott B. Lasensky, William B. Quandt, Steven L. Spiegel, and Shibley Z. Telhami, *The Peace Puzzle: America's Quest for Arab-Israeli Peace, 1989–2011* (Ithaca, NY and Washington, DC: Cornell University Press, in Collaboration with the United States Institute of Peace, 2013); Aaron David Miller, *The Much Too Promised Land: America's Elusive Search for Arab-Israeli Peace* (New York: Bantam, 2008); Sari Nusseibeh, *Once Upon a Country: A Palestinian Life* (London: Halban, 2009); Ehud Olmert, *In First Person* (Tel Aviv: Yedioth Ahronoth, 2018) (Hebrew); Ahmed Qurie, *Peace Negotiations in Palestine* (London: I.B. Tauris, 2015), *Negotiating Palestine: From the Second Intifada to Hamas' Electoral Victory* (London: I.B. Tauris, 2013) and *Beyond Oslo* (London: I.B. Tauris, 2008); Itamar Rabinovich, *Waging Peace: Israel and the Arabs, 1948–2003* (Princeton, NJ: Princeton University Press, 2004); Shimon Peres, *For the Future of Israel* (Baltimore, MD: Johns Hopkins University Press, 1998) and *Battling for Peace: A Memoir* (London: Weidenfeld and Nicolson, 1995); Ron Pundak, *Secret Channel* (Tel Aviv: Aliyat Hagag, 2013, Hebrew); Condoleezza Rice, *No Higher Honor: A Memoir of My Years in Washington* (New York: Crown Publishers, 2012); Dennis Ross, *The Missing Peace* (New York: Farrar, Straus and Giroux, 2004); Uri Savir, *Peace First: A New Model to End War* (San Francisco, CA: Berrett-Koehler Publishers, 2008) and *The Process* (New York: Vintage, 1999); and Gilead Sher, *The Israeli-Palestinian Peace Negotiations, 1999–2001: Within Reach* (London: Routledge, 2006).

Initiative (2002), Ariel Sharon's unilateral withdrawal from Gaza (2005), Annapolis (2007), the Olmert–Abbas negotiations (2006–2008), the Kerry Initiative (2013–2014), the Trump Peace Plan and the Abraham Accords (2020).

B) I then conducted research at the National Archives in London, the Liddell Hart Centre for Military Archives at King's College, the Israel National Archives, the Israel Ministry of Foreign Affairs, the Norwegian Nobel Institute and the Library of Congress. Research in archives is fascinating, as it often reveals information not previously discussed in the literature.

C) Other important primary sources are the Palestine Papers, which shed important light on Palestinian views in real time, as negotiations were taking place. These papers are documents from the negotiation office of the Palestinian Authority (PA). They were leaked and published by *Al Jazeera* and *The Guardian*, as well as individuals including Akram Hanieh[2] and Clayton Swisher.[3]

D) Building on the literature, leading figures were contacted to request in-depth interviews. Indeed, this book is largely based on primary resources: semi-structured, in-depth elite interviews with influential decision-makers, facilitators, mediators, diplomats and negotiators from Bahrain, Egypt, Israel, Jordan, Norway, Palestine, Saudi Arabia, Sweden, the United Kingdom, the United States and the United Nations, from the highest echelons of decision-making capacity to peace implementers. I have conducted more than 100 lengthy discussions and interviews (see Appendix A), including with former prime ministers Salam Fayyad, Ehud Barak and Ehud Olmert – the latter came closest to signing a peace deal with the PA. Fifteen of the interviewees were members of the three negotiation teams at Camp David 2000 (Ghaith al-Omari, Hasan Asfour, Ehud Barak, Shlomo Ben-Ami, Gidi Grinstein, Israel Hasson, Gamal Helal, Robert Malley, Dan Meridor, Aaron David Miller, Dennis Ross, Elyakim Rubinstein, Jonathan Schwartz, Gilead Sher and the late Martin Indyk). Six were at Taba (Asfour, Yossi Beilin, Ben-Ami, Hasson, Sher and the late Yossi Sarid). I also had long conversations with five of the people who were at Camp David 1978 (Aharon Barak, Nabil Elaraby, William Quandt, Rubinstein and the late Ezer Weizman); with many people who

[2] Akram Hanieh, 'The Camp David Papers', *Journal of Palestine Studies*, 30(2) (Winter 2001): 75–97.

[3] Clayton E. Swisher, *The Palestine Papers* (London: Hesperus Press, 2011).

were involved in the Oslo and Stockholm peace process (including Hussein Agha, Asfour, Beilin, Jan Egeland, Stuart Eizenstat, Maher El-Kurd, John Hagard, Yair Hirschfeld, Ahmad Khalidi, Pär Nuder, Joel Singer and Sven-Eric Söder); with Ami Ayalon, who authored the Ayalon–Nusseibeh document; and with key figures in the Israeli-Jordanian peace accords (Hassan bin Talal, Marwan Muasher and Rubinstein). Former Deputy Prime Minister of Jordan Muasher was also one of the architects of the 2002 Arab Peace Initiative.

Most of the interviews were conducted face to face during my field trips, usually in the interviewees' offices. Some interviews were conducted at the interviewees' private homes or in 'neutral' locations, such as coffee shops, hotels and restaurants, while others were conducted at the offices kindly made available to me at the University of Hull, University College London, the Woodrow Wilson International Center for Scholars, Washington DC, Lund University and at the Israel Institute for Advanced Studies, Jerusalem. Some interviews were conducted via technology. Remote video interviews were necessary, due to the physical distance from participants. I also hosted some meetings online, in my capacity as Director of the Middle East Study Centre at the University of Hull.

Prior to the interviews, interviewees signed consent forms. I began with a general list of questions (see Appendix B), supplemented by specific questions geared to the interviewee's exact role and profession. Interviewees had the freedom to digress per their interests and concerns. During the interviews, I took notes. I also recorded the interviews. After each interview, the audiotape was transcribed, and the text was sent to the interviewee for their authorisation. Only texts authorised by the interviewees were used for analysis. Signed consent forms, interview transcripts and archival data relating to previous work are stored on secure university servers and are backed up to an off-site location. Upon completion of the book, the interviewees received an advanced draft of the manuscript to make final comments and observations if they so wished. Some of them made very useful comments that improved the quality of the arguments. The research was approved by the University of Hull Faculty of Business, Law and Politics Ethics Committee. Some of these interviews are of significant historical importance. Indeed, some have already been published as stand-alone articles.

The average length of the interviews is two hours. Some interviewees granted me more than one interview. The interviews and archival information comprise thousands of pages of text. The interviews unearth the historical processes that constituted the peace process, providing unique empirical data. Evidence provided by those who were part of the process assists in identifying the factors that move history forward. The research sheds new light on the proceedings, offering fresh insights and an in-depth explanation of the Israeli-Palestinian peace processes. It also deduces constructive lessons for effective peace negotiations, mediation and facilitation.

The interview methodology is an excellent way to elucidate issues, find new information and bring to light important evidence.[4] I found that interviews often highlight issues that are not discussed or not discussed enough in the literature. Moreover, interviews, especially face-to-face interviews, provide immediate opportunities to press and elucidate issues. Conversations with experts shed light on subjects that one can easily miss when confined to libraries. The interviews reveal that there is not one history, but many histories. People who were in the same room perceived the situation in different ways. A classic *Rashomon*.

Furthermore, evidence from people who were part of the peace process helps identify the factors that move history forward. At the same time, the interviews had some limitations. They were conducted many years after the events. Interviewees often did not remember exact details. Dates, numbers and the sequence of events might be different from what is depicted in the interviews. Interviewees might interject issues that arose after the events into the events themselves. They might resort to hindsight, consciously or unconsciously. They might paint their own roles in a positive light or magnify their own contributions. I am fully aware of the inherent problems of the interviewing methodology, including subjective memory, and the almost inevitable tendency to emphasise the interviewee's role. These are all human inclinations that need to be taken into account. In assessing the interviewees' conduct, I relied on many resources in addition to the interviewees' self-assessments. I corroborated the interviews with archival documents, media accounts, secondary sources and other interviews. I should note that I have based the writing on seven of my books[5]

[4] Nigel King, Christine Horrocks and Joanna Brooks, *Interviews in Qualitative Research* (London: Sage, 2019).

[5] Raphael Cohen-Almagor, *Speech, Media, and Ethics: The Limits of Free Expression* (Houndmills and New York: Palgrave Macmillan, 2001, 2005); *The Right to Die with Dignity: An Argument in Ethics, Medicine, and Law* (Piscataway, NJ: Rutgers University Press, 2001); *Euthanasia in the Netherlands: The Policy and Practice of Mercy Killing* (Dordrecht: Springer-Kluwer, 2004); *The Scope of Tolerance: Studies on the Costs of Free Expression and Freedom of the Press* (London and New York: Routledge, 2006, 2007); *Confronting the Internet's Dark Side: Moral and Social Responsibility on the Free Highway* (New York and Washington, DC: Cambridge University Press and Woodrow Wilson Center Press, 2015);

and many articles[6] on interviews and have vast experience in utilising interviews for research.

The second major limitation has to do with the identity of my interviewees. I have interviewed many key players in the peace process. However, I was unable to reach many of the Palestinians I wanted to interview. Some were inaccessible or refused to grant interviews, either explicitly or by ignoring my pleas (e.g., Mahmoud Abbas). Others insisted that I come to their office or to their home (e.g., Hanan Ashrawi, Ahmed Qurie). Israeli occupation and Palestinian terrorism prevented such meetings. The result is that I have less information about the Palestinian viewpoints compared with the information I garnered from other parties. Those viewpoints could have contributed to a better understanding of the Palestinian positions as the peace process evolved and encountered obstacles.

The ultimate collection of this oral history project consists of the personal accounts of leaders who played major roles in the Israeli-Palestinian peace process. They provide scholars and practitioners with the opportunity to listen to and read the personal accounts of many decision-makers, as they recall the times and events that shaped their lives and the lives of Israel and Palestine.

All the websites and web pages mentioned were accessible between 2022 and 2025.

Conceptual Underpinnings

The conceptual underpinning of this research consists of several layers: the concept of justice; the mechanisms of conflict resolution, negotiations, mediation and facilitation; the concepts of ripeness, compromise and superforecasting; and strategies for dealing with spoilers.

Just, Reasonable Multiculturalism (New York and Cambridge: Cambridge University Press, 2021); *The Republic, Secularism and Security: France versus the Burqa and the Niqab* (Cham: Springer, 2022).

6 E.g. 'The Six Day War – Interviews with Minister Ezer Weitzman and Abba Eban MK, Lessons and Insights', *Social Issues in Israel*, 6 (Summer 2008): 172–213 (Hebrew); 'The Six Day War – Interviews with General Aharon Yariv and Ambassador Shimon Shamir, Lessons and Insights', *Social Issues in Israel*, 15 (2013): 171–194 (Hebrew). Most recently, Christina Nyquist, Raphael Cohen-Almagor and Scott Kim, '"We Want to Have Our Cake and Eat It, Too": Expert Views on Medical Involvement with the Swiss Assisted Dying Practice', *AJOB Empirical Bioethics*, 15(1) (2024): 41–59; 'Thirty Years after the Oslo Peace Accords: Interviews with Joel Singer', *Israel Studies*, 29(2) (2024): 1–29; 'Analysis of the PLO and Hamas: Interview with Sir John Jenkins', *International Dialogue*, 14(3) (2024), https://digitalcommons.unomaha.edu/id-journal/vol14/iss1/3.

Justice

The concept of justice features prominently in the scriptures of Judaism and Islam. Deuteronomy 16:20 ('Judges') instructs the Israelites to appoint judges who will always deliver righteous judgments. The core principle that judges must follow is 'justice, justice shall you pursue'. The pursuit of justice must be achieved through righteous means. The Torah emphasises that judges must not distort justice in favour of one side, must not show favouritism toward the rich and powerful, and must not accept bribes. In Leviticus 19:15 it is written: 'Do not pervert justice; do not show partiality to the poor or favouritism to the great, but judge your neighbour fairly.' No one, whether rich, powerful or influential, should receive preferential treatment. Exodus 23:6 further emphasises this concern, urging, 'do not deny justice to your poor people in their lawsuits'. The prophet Isaiah envisions the Messianic age as one where the Messiah will judge the needy with righteousness: 'with justice he will give decisions for the poor of the earth' (Isaiah 11:4).

Quran 16:90 instructs: 'Indeed, Allāh orders justice and good conduct and giving [help] to relatives and forbids immorality.' Injustice is perceived as an active resistance to God's directives and wishes. There are 191 verses and more than 100 sayings in the Quran that emphasise the concept of justice. This is not the place to discuss all of them in detail, but, generally speaking, these verses uphold justice as a divine command; advocate justice as a tool for maintaining social balance; encourage standing up for what is right, even at the expense of self; and discuss fairness and the equitable distribution of wealth, and the provision of basic necessities of life for relatives, the poor and the needy.[7] The Quran instructs believers to conduct their affairs in a just manner. God loves those who uphold justice (Quran 49:9). God forbids indecency, wickedness and aggression (Quran 16:90). Believers should use fair measures in the market ('Give full measure and weigh with justice', Quran 6:152), record debts accurately ('O believers! When you contract a loan for a fixed period of time, commit it to writing. Let the scribe maintain justice between the parties. The scribe should not refuse to write as Allah has taught them to write', Quran 2:282), provide fair testimony ('If you distort the testimony or refuse to give it, then "know

[7] Mahmoud A. Al-Khatib, 'The Concept of Justice in Islam', *Journal of Ethnic and Cultural Studies*, 10(5) (2023): 53. See also Jonathan E. Brockopp, 'Justice and Injustice', *Encyclopaedia of the Qur'ān Online* (Leiden: Brill, 2018); Uri Sagie, *The Frozen Hand* (Tel Aviv: Miskal, 2011) (Hebrew), 83–84.

that" Allah is certainly All-Aware of what you do', Quran 4: 135), provide impartial judgments ('when you judge between people, judge with fairness', Quran 4:58) and treat co-wives and orphans justly (Quran 4:3, 4:10, 6: 152). There are also general instructions to act and speak in a just manner ('Whenever you speak, maintain justice – even regarding a close relative. And fulfil your covenant with Allah', Quran 6:152). The instruction is clear: 'Do not let the hatred of a people lead you to injustice. Be just! That is closer to righteousness' (Quran 5:8).

Given the centrality of justice in Judaism and in Islam, it is a fundamental aspect of this study, requiring an examination of what constitutes a just peace process and a just agreement. In the 1973 Geneva Conference, in which delegations from the United States, the Soviet Union, the United Nations, Egypt, Jordan and Israel took part, Henry Kissinger spoke of the challenge of ensuring individual justice for the common good. He stated that greater justice merges all aspirations to realise a common humanity.[8]

In *Politics*, Aristotle wrote: 'Justice is the bond of men in states, for the administration of justice, which is the determination of what is just, is the principle of order in political society.'[9] Aristotle held that the good in the sphere of politics is justice, and that justice promotes the common interest. Indeed, the idea of justice has a considerable place in our everyday life. The term 'just' is associated with positive qualities, while 'unjust' is connected to negative attributes. Justice is applicable to law and social order, as well as morality. It can be seen as a concept addressing societal order and individuals' rights, in contrast to the demands of the general social structure. The just person is often described as fair and honest, and justice is linked to spiritual elevation. People also classify things, institutions, systems, feelings, ideas and actions by using the terms just and unjust; the former is associated with 'good' notions, while the latter is always related to 'bad' notions. Our wisdom must teach us to distinguish between right and wrong, which contain concepts of 'good' and 'bad'.[10] Justice may be regarded, on the one hand, as a concept concerned with the order of society as a whole and, on the other hand, as an expression of the rights of individuals in contrast to the claims of general social order.[11]

[8] Martin Indyk, *Master of the Game: Henry Kissinger and the Art of Middle East Diplomacy* (New York: Knopf, 2022), 287.

[9] Aristotle, *Politics*, 350 BCE, http://classics.mit.edu/Aristotle/politics.1.one.html.

[10] Haim Perlman, *On Justice* (Jerusalem: The Hebrew University Law Faculty, 1962), 5.

[11] D. D. Raphael, *Problems of Political Philosophy* (London: Pall Mall Press, 1970), 165.

The moral literature regards the just man as one who is fair and honest. Justice served as an inclusive name for some forms of spiritual elevation, and many would argue that morality has no other tendency but to teach what are the things that a person is right to do, and what things a person rightly must refrain from doing. Thus, the idea of justice is used not only in the context of morality, but also in the context of law and social order. Many times in the course of history, the concept of justice was twisted and became associated with certain conspicuous qualities of human beings, where one significant attribute was preferred to all others. For instance, the distinction between different skin colours served for hundreds of years as a decisive argument against those who advocated the abolition of slavery. Black people, it was argued, are not ordinary people and are not to be considered as one of the essential species of humanity. Therefore, it was permissible to treat Black people according to inhuman principles. In much the same way, the Germans treated the Jews as inhuman creatures and employed biological and anthropological characteristics to justify discrimination – discrimination that in later stages turned into genocide.

If one finds considerable reasons for justifying discrimination between people, and if these justifications are perceived as true and right in the eyes of the public, then discrimination will take place. It can be argued that the social dimension of justice is a matter of protecting the fabric of social norms that are accepted by most members of society as advantageous to them; however, sometimes, certain people are excluded from this fabric of social norms and, in the worst cases, the advantages are achieved at the expense of some people. As there are many interpretations of what justice is, different people have different ideas about what similarities and differences among cases are morally relevant, and how various cases should be treated. Some ways of classifying cases and dealing with them are just, while others are unjust.

A plausible account of justice was suggested by John Stuart Mill, who held that moral conduct consisted in respecting moral obligations and honouring the moral rights of others. Since some moral obligations correlate with moral rights, matters of justice represent a special class of moral problems; justice consists in respecting other individuals' moral rights. 'The idea of justice supposes two things: a rule of conduct, and a sentiment which sanctions the rule. The first (rule of conduct) must be supposed to be common to all mankind, and intended for their good. The other (the sentiment) is a desire that punishment may be suffered by those who infringe the rule.'[12]

[12] John Stuart Mill, *Utilitarianism, Liberty, and Representative Government* (London: J. M. Dent & Son, 1948), 49.

What is the rule of conduct to achieve just peace? What is a just peace process? What is a just agreement? To answer these questions, I will apply Rawls's theory of justice and fairness.[13] The Rawlsian veil of ignorance is employed as an analytical tool in cases of dispute. Behind it, different considerations are weighed with the aim of achieving just resolutions. Indeed, justice is the first virtue of peacebuilding. It is necessary for maintaining objectivity.

John Rawls dedicated much of his scholarly life to articulating the idea of justice. For Rawls, justice is the single most important consideration in assessing the basic structure of society and the overall direction of social change. Justice is not just one important value among others, but rather the value by which other values are weighed, assessed and achieved. Liberals accentuated different values: liberty and truth (John Stuart Mill),[14] equality (Ronald Dworkin)[15] and tolerance (John Locke,[16] Alf Ross,[17] Alexander Meiklejohn,[18] Lee Bollinger[19]). With Rawls, I argue that justice is the value of all values, the standard by which conflicting values are reconciled and competing conceptions of the good are accommodated. If justice is achieved, all other values will be satisfied, too. The idea of justice is essential for maintaining a decent society. It is also vital for conflict resolution.

But how do we exercise justice without bias? Different philosophers have provided different answers to this question.[20] Rawls strove to ascertain principles of justice that would be accepted by liberals. To find these principles, he conceptualised an analytical exercise called the veil of ignorance. Behind this veil, people understand concepts such as

[13] John Rawls, *A Theory of Justice* (Oxford: Oxford University Press, 1986).

[14] Mill, *Utilitarianism, Liberty, and Representative Government.*

[15] Ronald M. Dworkin, 'Why Liberals Should Believe in Equality', *New York Review of Books* (3 February 1983), *A Matter of Principle* (Oxford: Clarendon Press, 1985) and *Sovereign Virtue: The Theory and Practice of Equality* (Cambridge, MA: Harvard University Press, 2002). See also Marshall Cohen, Thomas Nagel and Thomas Scanlon (eds), *Equality and Preferential Treatment* (Princeton, NJ: Princeton University Press, 1977); Paul Barker (ed.), *Living as Equals* (New York: Oxford University Press, 1999).

[16] John Locke (1689), *A Letter Concerning Toleration* (Indianapolis: Hackett, 1983).

[17] Alf Ross, *Why Democracy?* (Cambridge, MA: Harvard University Press, 1952).

[18] Alexander Meiklejohn, *Political Freedom* (New York: Oxford University Press, 1965).

[19] Lee C. Bollinger, *The Tolerant Society* (Oxford: Clarendon Press, 1986) and *Uninhibited, Robust, and Wide-Open: A Free Press for a New Century* (New York: Oxford University Press, 2010).

[20] Perlman, *On Justice*; Brian Barry, *Theories of Justice* (London: Harvester, 1989); Michael Walzer, *Spheres of Justice: A Defence of Pluralism and Equality* (New York: Basic Books, 1983).

religion, class, race, ethnicity, gender, wisdom, richness, beauty and so on, but they do not know where they fit in. They do not know their own characteristics. This abstraction would ensure that people would not choose principles of justice that are self-serving and influenced by such characteristics.[21] Justice should be blind to these considerations. Rawls then asked: behind such a veil of ignorance, what principles of justice would you choose?

Rawls argues that self-interested rational persons behind the veil of ignorance would choose two general principles of justice to structure society in the real world. The first is the egalitarian Principle of Equal Liberty: every individual has an equal right to the most extensive liberties compatible with similar liberties for all.[22] This principle relates to basic liberties, such as freedom of thought and expression, freedom of assembly and the freedom to have personal property; political liberties, such as the right to vote and to run for election; and freedom from arbitrary arrest.[23] This principle is the most important. It is supplemented by the Difference Principle, which requires that social and economic inequalities be arranged so that they are (a) to everyone's advantage, including those least advantaged in society, and (b) attached to offices and positions open to all, under conditions of equality of opportunity.[24] There is a serial order of the principles, to ensure that the lack of basic and political liberties is not compensated by economic advantages.

The concept of reasonableness is also essential in Rawlsian theory. The Oxford Dictionary defines 'reasonableness' as 'the quality of being as much as is appropriate or fair'.[25] Reasonable decision-makers are expected to weigh options for actions, try to assess short- and long-term outcomes, and gauge pros and cons. Reasonable decision-makers engage in public exchange, debate and reasoning, all of which are conducive to attaining legitimacy. Rawls's concept of reasonableness is normative, loaded with a strong moral notion, as he writes that people are reasonable when they behave fairly, seek cooperation with others and assume that others act in the same way.[26] In the Rawlsian just framework, members of society behave morally when they strive to reach an agreement. In conflict situations, they seek fair compromises that

21 Rawls, *A Theory of Justice*, 12.
22 Ibid., 60.
23 Ibid., 61.
24 Ibid., 60.
25 The Oxford Dictionary, https://en.oxforddictionaries.com/definition/reasonableness.
26 John Rawls, *Political Liberalism* (New York: Columbia University Press, 1993), 49.

balance prospects and risks. They aim to resolve tensions peacefully via deliberations. Reasonableness in conduct helps mitigate conflicts and brings about stability.

Any solution to the Israeli-Palestinian conflict should be just and reasonable, beneficial to both sides and one that will serve the interests and needs of Israelis and Palestinians. The solution should be one that both Israelis and Palestinians would choose behind a veil of ignorance, when they do not know their religion and national affiliation.

Conflict Resolution, Negotiations, Mediation and Facilitation

Conflict resolution studies integrate theoretical frameworks to address and resolve real-world disputes. These theories are interdisciplinary in nature, drawing from political science, international relations, sociology, law, economics and social psychology to inform both analysis and practice.[27] Conflict resolution requires an understanding of the other side's history, politics, constraints and goals. To be successful, negotiations must be a win–win situation. Interlocutors need to understand the constraints of the other side and, working within those constraints, try to convince the other side that what they seek to achieve is consistent with their goals and their political constraints.

Negotiators need to clarify to themselves, as well as others, what their own goals are. These goals must be realistic. Negotiators require the backing of their government. The adversary needs to be convinced that the negotiators are bargaining with the full support of the administration. Negotiators must have a certain amount of flexibility and leeway, but, at the same time, they must also have the confidence of key politicians. Successful negotiations always have an element of political risk and, therefore, negotiators must have the assurance that, at a crucial time, the decision-makers will be willing to take risks with their own political base. Politicians need to be willing to accept criticism and reach positions that may be controversial, confident that they will be able to maintain their political base and gain public approval.

[27] Kenneth Arrow, Robert H. Mnookin, Lee Ross, Amos Tversky and Robert Wilson (eds), *Barriers to Conflict Resolution* (New York: W. W. Norton, 1995); Jacob Bercovitch, Victor Kremenyuk and I. William Zartman (eds), *The Sage Handbook of Conflict Resolution* (London: Sage, 2009); Oliver Ramsbotham, *When Conflict Resolution Fails* (Cambridge: Polity, 2017); Peter Wallensteen, *Understanding Conflict Resolution: War, Peace and the Global System* (London: Sage, 2007) and *Peter Wallensteen: A Pioneer in Making Peace Researchable* (Cham: Springer, 2021).

Conflict resolution is *not* about reconciling wants or desires. It is about reconciling what each side *has to have*. When parties negotiate, it is important to distinguish between underlying interests and other considerations, often termed as 'noise'. This includes excuses, rhetoric, immaterial arguments, diversions and other tactics employed to promote their cause. Each side may always *want* certain things, having dreams and desires. The question is what they *must* have.[28] The key to resolving a conflict is ensuring that the needs of both sides are addressed, and addressed meaningfully.

Parties should not rush to the negotiation table prematurely. Slow, incremental change can be profoundly important, closing the gaps and preparing the ground for resolving the conflict. Patience is crucial, and so is leadership. History is the outcome of circumstances presented to leaders who initiate, take chances and make the most of those chances. Timing is important. Kissinger almost never put forward proposals immediately when he was engaged in a new negotiation. He first sought to fathom 'the intangibles in the position' of his interlocutor in order to 'gauge the scope as well as the limits of probable concessions.'[29] Leadership requires certain qualities and personal characteristics: courage, daring and understanding that making compromises is not a sign of weakness but a political necessity. Leaders should identify long-term and short-term goals and not confuse the two or sacrifice the former for the latter.

Resolving the Israeli-Palestinian conflict is especially difficult. It is a national, religious, ideological, political and violent conflict. It is long, protracted and one that presents unique challenges. This conflict, prima facie, involves justified claims by both parties to the conflict, as well as diverse forms of suffering, displacement, occupation and the denial of basic rights. The signing of a peace treaty intended to end more than 150 years of the Israeli-Palestinian conflict requires political capital. Writing this milestone chapter in the history of the Israeli and Palestinian people also requires considerable courage. Martin Indyk says that the key to successful negotiations is to have leaders who are committed to achieving an agreement and willing to take the risks and make the compromises necessary to reach an agreement.[30]

[28] Roger Fisher and William Ury, *Getting to Yes: Negotiating Agreement without Giving In* (London: Random House, 1991); Herbert C. Kelman, 'Contributions of an Unofficial Conflict Resolution Effort to the Israeli-Palestinian Breakthrough', *Negotiation Journal*, 11(1) (1995): 19–27.

[29] James K. Sebenius, *Kissinger the Negotiator* (New York: Harper, 2018), 222–223.

[30] Interview with Martin Indyk (9 August 2022), 6.

The interaction between leaders is important. The process of negotiations, meetings, debating, listening and persuading is beneficial to both sides. This is how they learn to appreciate each other's needs and wishes and how important they are to each side. Negotiators should study their counterparts, know their constraints, understand their weaknesses, and appreciate their needs and the points on which they might be more inclined to compromise.

Settlement may be reached through direct negotiations, without any external interference or assistance. However, sometimes parties find it difficult to negotiate directly. They need help, and then they agree to various forms of mediation, facilitation or arbitration that involve a third party who is not a disputant. It is imperative to explain the differences between mediation and facilitation, and what the keys for successful mediation and facilitation are. This is done in detail in Chapter 11. Here I briefly note that mediation is defined as a process of conflict management where disputants seek assistance or consent to accept help from a third party to prevent, manage or resolve a conflict without resorting to physical force or involving the authority of law.[31] Mediators and facilitators need to maintain equitable treatment of the adversaries and drive forward a process by which gaps are bridged and agreements replace division. The negotiating parties should have equal representation at the negotiation table. Team leaders need to be of the same or very similar ranking. Crucially, mediators and facilitators must be perceived by the parties as credible and even-handed. I explore whether the American mediators possessed a deep understanding of the conflict and its dynamics; had the ability to show flexibility, highlight progress, overcome obstacles and create opportunities; enjoyed the trust of both parties; and spoke in a language that the parties understood and appreciated. In this context, I use the scholarly writings of Bercovitch and Rubin[32] and Wallensteen,[33] and I learn from the experiences of peace practitioners such as Agha, al-Omari, Aharon Barak, Asfour, Ehud Barak, Beilin, Ben-Ami, Eizenstat, El-Kurd, Hasson, Hirschfeld, Indyk, Khalidi, Daniel Kurtzer, Tzipi Livni, Malley, Meridor,

[31] Marko Lehti (ed.), *Nordic Approaches to Peace Mediation* (Tampere: Peace Research Institute TAPRI, 2014), 19; J. Bercovitch, J. Theodore Anagnoson and Donnette L. Wille, 'Some Conceptual Issues and Empirical Trends in the Study of Successful Mediation in International Relations', *Journal of Peace Research*, 28(1) (1991): 7–17.

[32] Jacob Bercovitch and Jeffrey Z. Rubin (eds), *Mediation in International Relations: Multiple Approaches to Conflict Management* (London: Macmillan Press, 1994).

[33] Wallensteen, *Understanding Conflict Resolution* and *Peter Wallensteen: A Pioneer in Making Peace Researchable*.

Miller, Olmert, Jonathan Powell, Ross, Quandt, Itamar Rabinovich, Rubinstein, Sarid, Sher and Singer. All granted me valuable interviews.

Unlike mediation, facilitators do not actively participate in negotiations. Facilitation is a process in which the third party offers assistance in supporting negotiations, usually by providing the means for discussion and by acting as a messenger between the rival parties. While mediators are inside the negotiation room during negotiations, facilitators are outside the room. Facilitation does not focus so much on substance but on enhancing understanding among the disputants, clarifying their perceptions, interests and needs, preparing the groundwork for negotiations and fostering a conducive environment for compromise. They ensure fair representation of all parties.

Unlike mediation and facilitation, arbitration is a contract-based dispute resolution method, where an impartial third party is appointed to resolve a dispute based on pre-agreed terms. Arbitration employs judicial procedure and issues a verdict that the parties have committed themselves beforehand to accept. This third party must be acceptable to all parties and not coerced or imposed on any side. Acceptability by all parties is crucial in arbitration.

The peace negotiations between Israelis and Palestinians were extensive. They were conducted in various forms. Some were open and non-secretive, while others were secretive backchannel negotiations. Both forms may be confidential, away from the media and public knowledge. In backchannel negotiations, usually only a very small group of people is aware of the conduct. Negotiators are non-officials who are said to enjoy the confidence of the decision-makers. Because the negotiations are not official, a negotiator can fly 'test balloons' to examine the extent of receptiveness of either party.

Track I, Track II and mixed-track diplomacy have advantages and weaknesses. Track I talks concern issues that require leaders' decisions. The weaknesses of Track I diplomacy include the high stakes involved in case of failure, difficulties in maintaining secrecy, the absence of the deniability option if needed, especially when the process fails to develop as expected, and susceptibility to political and electoral pressures.

Historically, Track II has been pursued through discreet communication between leaders. It is defined as an unofficial, informal interaction between adversarial parties meant to devise strategies, develop policies, influence public opinion and organise resources in ways that might help resolve a conflict.[34] Typically, Track II involves experienced academics,

[34] Peter Jones, *Track Two Diplomacy in Theory and Practice* (Stanford, CA: Stanford University Press, 2015), 9.

religious sages and non-governmental organisation (NGO) leaders. Initially, it can serve as a monitoring group for the formal track, potentially offering suggestions. Track II can help leaders explore principles and concepts that are not discussed in public. Its informal environment may produce useful ideas to bridge gaps or package understandings. Both sides can then introduce these ideas into the formal negotiation tracks.

Unofficial Track II negotiations provide negotiators with the option of deniability, enable secrecy more easily and provide negotiators with greater flexibility. However, Track II can linger on for a long time, and some leaders lack the patience or ability to exhaust the process. Negotiators are not accountable to the public for poor decisions. A potential problem is ineffective coordination and organisation of the peace talks.

Nevertheless, Track II can become the real track to reach an overall agreement, as was the case in 1993. The Oslo peace process started with a mixed track – two Israeli academics and three PLO officials. Later, Joel Singer and Uri Savir joined. Savir was a government official and Singer was a private lawyer from Washington whom Yitzhak Rabin trusted. At this point, the negotiations changed form, shape and substance. Although the two academics were still in the room, their role became limited. Singer and Savir became the driving forces. Thus, this second phase of Oslo can be called Track I.[35]

Mahmoud Abbas was fond of Track II negotiations. He relied on his trusted advisors, Hussein Agha and Ahmad Khalidi. Unlike Abbas, Ehud Barak disliked Track II and preferred Track I. Because of these different perspectives, the Stockholm peace talks failed. While official negotiations enable leaders to impact the process directly, Track II negotiators lack executive power. Unlike leaders, Track II negotiators cannot directly decide the direction of negotiations and outcomes. They can only make recommendations to their leaders. While leaders have the capacity to access information, intelligence and financial resources that provide high leverage and flexibility in negotiations, unofficial negotiators have limited power in comparison. As negotiators lack responsibility and power, they also lack decision-making capacity. At the same time, Track II has advantages that Track I does not have. Track

[35] Rotberg writes in his comments that when he ran a six-year negotiating exercise with Turkish and Greek Cypriots, he and his colleagues started with a modified Track II gathering and then managed to convert it successfully into a Track 1.5 process that came up with an agreed-upon solution acceptable to both sides and ultimately to leaderships on both sides because the Track 1.5ers kept the bosses well informed.

II negotiators can be less formalistic and more creative, thinking outside the box. Leaders can distance themselves from the process. Formal talks can be challenging when parties fear leaks, accusations of concessions or a lack of mutual trust. In such cases, unofficial negotiations or Track II talks can be valuable. These talks allow for more freedom in discussing ideas and proposals that may not be suitable for official representatives. They also provide deniability for leaders if needed.

Formal negotiations are often constrained by political sensitivities, a lack of trust and the ever-present risk of public backlash. Parties may be hesitant to engage openly due to fears of leaks, accusations of unwarranted concessions, or concern that proposals floated prematurely may be unilaterally appropriated or 'pocketed' by the other side without reciprocal commitment. In such circumstances, informal or unofficial channels of communication – commonly referred to as Track II diplomacy – can play a critical role.

Track II negotiations, conducted by trusted emissaries or non-official actors, offer a confidential space in which parties can engage more freely, experiment with creative solutions and explore new conceptual frameworks without the burden of formal endorsement or immediate political costs. These channels enable interlocutors to test ideas and gauge the flexibility of the other side, often serving as an incubator for proposals that may later inform formal (Track I) diplomacy.

The value of Track II is particularly pronounced in contexts marked by deep-seated mistrust or political paralysis. These backchannel dialogues can address specific technical or conceptual obstacles, help build interpersonal trust and facilitate mutual understanding of each side's red lines and core interests. If the participants are perceived as accurately representing the thinking of senior leadership, Track II ideas may be taken seriously, even if unofficially.

However, the translation of Track II proposals into official policy remains a significant challenge. There is no guarantee that Track I leaders will endorse outcomes reached informally, especially if these are politically costly or not aligned with prevailing domestic narratives. Moreover, absent a formal mandate or the authority to commit, Track II participants may lack the capacity to secure implementation, and their proposals may be dismissed or rejected once brought into the official realm. Therefore, while Track II diplomacy holds promise in unlocking impasses and generating innovative approaches, its effectiveness ultimately hinges on the willingness of political leaders to engage constructively, absorb the insights it yields and incorporate them into a viable negotiation framework.

The following is a comparison between Track I and Track II negotiations.

Track I:
- Leaders and their trusted negotiators
- Tend to be in the limelight
- In democracies, leaders are democratically elected
- Full responsibility
- Full capacity to thoroughly address and agree on issues
- Formal meeting
- Formal ideas
- Issues can be developed in-depth
- Might be bogged down with linguistic differences
- Have capacity to meet or make quick progress
- Deniability is difficult
- There is a risk of leaks
- Could develop alternative plans if necessary.

Track II:
- Academics, religious authorities, NGO leaders
- Tend to be discreet
- Negotiators are not democratically elected
- Partial responsibility
- Limited capacity to thoroughly address and agree on issues. Progress is dependent on leaders' approval
- Less formal or no formal meetings
- Enable a wider exploration of options and ideas
- Limited ability to develop issues in-depth
- Flexibility in phrasing
- Limited capacity to meet or make quick progress
- Deniability is easier
- There is a risk of leaks
- Could develop alternative plans if necessary.

Ripeness

William Zartman developed the idea of ripeness in international conflict and negotiation. Ripeness is about the right timing of the initiation of peace talks.[36] Zartman argued that when parties are in a mutually

[36] Lucie Podszon, *Does Development Aid Affect Conflict Ripeness? The Theory of Ripeness and Its Applicability in the Context and Development of Aid* (Wiesbaden: VS Verlag für Sozialwissenschaften, 2011), 81.

hurting stalemate or a deadlock, they may come to the realisation that the crisis must end. To find a way out, they understand that they require a formula that takes the interests of the other party into account.[37] Both factors – a mutually hurting stalemate and having a way out – establish that peace would be beneficial to both sides, and that it is the desired goal of both parties.

Richard Haass further explains that a situation is ripe when the prerequisites for diplomatic progress exist, that is, the particular circumstances are conducive to a negotiated solution or progress.[38] Ripeness requires the existence of mutual perceptions among the parties about the need for an agreement based upon shared acceptance of the negotiation procedure, the parties' shared belief that the conflict would be exacerbated without a negotiated settlement and their understanding that a mutually satisfying settlement requires making compromises. These compromises must be mutual and adequate, so as to allow the political leadership of each party to convince their constituencies that national objectives have been preserved. Furthermore, there must be a mutually acceptable process, and there should be no diversion.[39]

An agreement is more likely when both parties think the situation might worsen; unilateral solutions are deemed inappropriate or insufficient; incentives are available to both parties; and the leaders are able and willing to take the initiative, believe that a solution is feasible, are forward looking and wish to bring their people to a better place. They may also believe that unilateral steps will not resolve the issue and that their respective horizons include a better future for their people if the damaging conflict is settled.

When parties feel the time is ripe and they come to the negotiation table, I reiterate that it is important to distinguish between underlying interests, needs, wishes and dreams. The focus should be on interests and needs. What *must* the parties achieve? Essential needs are different from desirable needs. The latter can be more easily compromised.

In the Israeli-Palestinian conflict, the 'time is ripe' means that both leaders believe that enough blood has been shed, that they need to seize

[37] William Zartman, *Ripe for Resolution* (New York: Oxford University Press, 1989). See also Oliver Ramsbotham and Amira Schiff, 'When Formal Negotiations Fail: Strategic Negotiation, Ripeness Theory, and the Kerry Initiative', *Negotiation Conflict Management Research*, 11 (2018): 321–340.

[38] Richard Haass, 'Ripeness and the Settlement of International Disputes', *Survival*, 30(3) (1988): 232.

[39] Ibid., 245–246.

the moment because things might worsen for their people, and that they have the ability to lead their respective people to accept a peace agreement and change reality for the better.

Compromise

According to the Cambridge English Dictionary, a 'compromise' is 'an agreement in an argument in which the people involved reduce their demands or change their opinion in order to agree'.[40] The act of compromise requires flexibility and letting go of rigid positions. In a compromise, two or more parties agree to an arrangement that they regard as second best.[41] Compromise happens when each side values what they can achieve more than what they have to give up. Concessions are made, acknowledging social, cultural, moral and/or political constraints. Compromises can be achieved through direct negotiations or through various forms of mediation, facilitation or arbitration.

Compromise has prerequisites. It assumes some form of cooperation between the involved parties. The parties must share basic norms forming the basis for potential understanding. Without these, compromise is impossible. In essence, compromise is about finding a balance between different demands, needs and ideas that must be satisfied, and between what is best for one party and what is best for the other. Every compromise requires a quid pro quo. After deliberation and discussion, a settlement is reached. This settlement may be achieved by mutual concessions. Agents carefully consider the nature and number of concessions required of them. They explore potential areas of agreement and strive to find shared interests. In peace negotiations, compromise involves adapting to the realities of a situation, meeting opponents halfway in equal relationships – and in a proportionate way when relationships are unequal – and sacrificing certain demands or preferences for the greater good of both parties.

Compromises tend to be motivated by self-interest, but they can also be motivated by moral reasons that might override self-interest. The act of compromise requires good faith and respect for one another. Each party has rights and can voice its claims as a free agent. When fundamental differences make compromise impossible, an appeal to common norms is

[40] *Cambridge Dictionary*, https://dictionary.cambridge.org/dictionary/english/compromise.
[41] Fabian Wendt, *Compromise, Peace and Public Justification* (London: Palgrave, 2016), 19.

necessary to reach an agreement or understanding. Parties may not agree with each other's positions, but they can still recognise the sincerity and validity of those positions. The parties need to respect each other, actively listen and acknowledge each other's viewpoints.

Compromise is not only between multiple parties. Sometimes, individuals may compromise regarding their own aims, allocating available means and determining priorities. Compromise often involves acknowledging that others are not yet ready to embrace new ideas or change their ways of life in line with these fresh ideas. *Genuine compromise* is a mutual recognition of each other's rights and interests, leading to constructive solutions. Parties must be open to reasonable concessions and participate in respectful, deliberative discussions. Conversely, *tactical compromises*, driven by constraints or deceit, lack a genuine willingness to give up interests and do not respect the rights of the opponent adversary. Such compromises are unethical and can damage trust between parties.[42] Genuine negotiations require genuine compromises, the willingness to live and abide by the consequences of the agreement.

In peace negotiations, interlocutors may make concessions in the form of acknowledging past mistakes, conceding assets, making pledges for the future, adapting to the realities of the situation at hand and sacrificing certain demands or preferences. The Israeli-Palestinian conflict is particularly complex because it is not merely a conflict over scarce resources. Fundamentally, it is an ideological conflict involving rival rights claims and the collision of opposed identities and histories. Compromises over ideological and identity issues, as is the case here, are particularly challenging and require a constructive vision to accommodate rightful claims and build bridges between competing values.

Superforecasting

Tetlock and Gardner's insights on superforecasters are instructive. Good negotiators need to be good predictors of the outcomes of their decision-making processes. Superforecasters have exceptional abilities to envisage the future. They are intellectually cautious, humble and non-deterministic.[43] They are open-minded, with a dragonfly

[42] Raphael Cohen-Almagor, 'Genuine, Principled and Tactical Compromise', *Studia Iuridica Lublinensia*, 30(2) (2021): 11–31.

[43] Philip Tetlock and Dan Gardner, *Superforecasting: The Art and Science of Prediction* (London: Random House, 2015), 191.

eye to diverse views,[44] pragmatic and cognisant of the value of checking thinking for cognitive and emotional biases. Superforecasters are relentless, determined to keep at their investigation however long it takes,[45] uncomfortable with their tentative conclusions and thus testing them with the aim to improve. Superforecasters are also reflective and comfortable with numbers.[46]

Furthermore, superforecasting involves gathering evidence from a variety of sources, learning to think probabilistically,[47] working in teams,[48] keeping score within time frameworks,[49] and having the ability and willingness to admit error and change the course of action when this is deemed necessary.[50] Tetlock and Gardner think the most important qualities for superforecasting are (a) intelligence and (b) the degree to which people are committed to belief updating and self-improvement; in their terms, these are perpetual beta people.[51] Forecasting can improve with experience and thinking that foresight is not a gift but rather a product of a particular way of thinking.[52]

Aspiring superforecasters need to learn how to strike the right balance between under- and overreacting to evidence,[53] and between under- and overconfidence, between prudence and decisiveness;[54] how to move their probability estimates fast in response to diagnostic signals;[55] and how to understand nuance, because nuance matters. The more degrees of uncertainty people can distinguish, the better superforecasters they are likely to be.[56] Furthermore, superforecasters do not try to justify or excuse their errors and failures. They try to figure out where they went wrong, the reasons for their mistakes,[57] and they bring out the best in others and let others bring out the best in them.[58]

44 Ibid., 124–127.
45 Ibid., 154–155.
46 Ibid., 128–129.
47 Ibid., 140–152.
48 Ibid., 201–204.
49 Ibid., 236.
50 Ibid., 159–166, 192.
51 Ibid., 192.
52 Ibid., 68–72.
53 Ibid., 280.
54 Ibid., 283.
55 Ibid., 281.
56 Ibid., 282.
57 Ibid., 283.
58 Ibid., 284.

Figure 1.1 Superforecasters: James Baker (speaking), Jimmy Carter (4th from right), Henry Kissinger (6th from right).
Credit: Diana Walker/Contributor/Hulton Archive/Getty Images.

I see many similarities between superforecasters and good mediators and negotiators. Examples of superforecasters are James Baker, Jimmy Carter, Henry Kissinger and possibly Moshe Dayan (see Figure 1.1).[59] All of them had good teams working for them. Baker, Kissinger and Dayan had good relationships with their respective leaders, who trusted their judgement. The best negotiator in the world cannot succeed if their leader is not fully committed and does not back their decisions. I would have included Yitzhak Rabin and Shimon Peres, but they consistently underestimated spoilers, both Jewish and Arab. Rabin paid the highest price a man can pay due to his subpar forecasting.

Dealing with Spoilers

Conflicts can be deep and bitter, making parties unwilling to negotiate. For instance, sovereign democracies often refuse to negotiate directly with terrorist organisations. They engage in counter-terrorism

[59] Joel Singer, 'Without Small Talk: Moshe Dayan Knew How to Conduct Negotiations', *Haaretz* (17 December 2024) (Hebrew).

activities that erode the possibility of constructive interaction with spoilers. In such cases, the parties opt to continue fighting each other. Sitting at the negotiation table is not a given; it is an act of willingness to compromise. For many years, Israel refused to negotiate with the PLO. In 1993, the two parties agreed to negotiate directly, and the Oslo Accords were the result. Exploring grounds for negotiations can be beneficial. This does not mean that common ground can always be found. But at the very least, exploring possibilities is important. Ideally, leaders should talk to anyone who has influence over the outcome they aspire to bring about.

'Spoilers' refers to individuals or groups that undermine or disrupt the progress of a negotiation or peace process. Some Jewish extremists believe this is a divine opportunity to fulfil God's promise to the Chosen People. Muslim fanatics believe that any territory once governed by Islamic rule must remain so forever. Since Oslo, the prime Palestinian examples are Hamas and the Islamic Jihad. Both organisations refuse to recognise the legitimacy of Israel and its right to exist. Both resort to terror and violence and reject peace negotiations.

Israel has suppressed and frustrated the Palestinians. Israel's victory in the 1947–1948 war humiliated the Palestinians. The occupation has deprived them of their basic rights. Studies in psychology show that a primordial means of attaining significance and social worth is through aggression and violence.[60] Various forms of terrorism have been employed against the Zionist enterprise, aiming to gain some recognition, esteem, dignity and honour. The jihadists' global ideology, their cell-like internal structure and access to transnational support channels constitute serious barriers to negotiation onset. Israel views Hamas as unavailable for dialogue or negotiation due to its far-ranging aims. Zartman spoke of some terrorist organisations that are 'absolute terrorists'. These are 'beyond negotiation' due to their unwillingness to compromise.[61]

Spoilers benefit from continued violence and distinguish themselves from other players by their uncompromising, violent attitude. In the Arab-Israeli conflict, religion plays a major role. Hamas is religiously and

60 Arie W. Kruglanski and Joel Singer, 'The Israeli-Palestinian Deadly Struggle for Significance', *Psychology Today* (17 June 2024), https://tinyurl.com/ye29cpfm; A. W. Kruglanski, M. Ellenberg, E. Szumowska et al., 'Frustration-Aggression Hypothesis Reconsidered: The Role of Significance Quest', *Aggressive Behavior*, 49(5) (2023): 445–468.

61 William I. Zartman, 'Negotiating with Terrorists', *International Negotiation*, 8(3) (2003): 444.

ideologically motivated, adamant about destroying Israel and the establishment of Palestine instead of Israel, built on its ruins. Palestinian as well as Israeli terrorists and political extremists (both Jewish and Palestinian) have successfully derailed the peace process.

Hamas terrorists wish to draw other parties into their fight against Israel, as is evident by their conduct on 7 October 2023, in violation of the UN Charter. They murdered 1,200 people, including some 260 mostly young men and women who were dancing at a music and peace festival.[62] In addition, thousands of people were severely wounded, and 251 Israelis and foreign nationals were kidnapped and taken to Gaza.[63] Hamas celebrated the unspeakable crimes it committed that day. Families were made to witness the torture and murder of their loved ones. There can be no doubt about Hamas's intentions: to rape, torture, mutilate, kill and kidnap as many Israelis as they could, including children and babies.[64] 7 October 2023 was a horrific day in historic terms, a day Israelis will never forget for generations to come. The terrorists were instructed to commit brutal acts that would shake the Israeli psyche – and they succeeded. Hamas's barbaric attack has traumatised the entire Israeli nation. To broaden the conflict, Hamas called upon Hezbollah and other extremists to attack Israel. Israel also suffered attacks from Lebanon, Syria, Iran, Iraq and Yemen. Notably, on 13 June 2025, Israel launched what Prime Minister Benjamin Netanyahu described as a 'pre-emptive attack' on Iran. Israel has fought many enemies, but none of them are as formidable as Iran. Netanyahu has wanted to fight Iran since 2009; but all American presidents before June 2025, including Donald Trump in his first presidency, refused to support an Israeli attack. 7 October was a sea change that convinced Israeli leaders beyond a doubt that violence should be met with more violence. Netanyahu was able to persuade Trump that attacking Iran is also in America's interest.

Israel has its own zealot spoilers. On 25 February 1994, Baruch Goldstein, an Israeli religious extremist who opposed the Oslo peace process, entered the Cave of the Patriarchs in Hebron and opened fire

[62] Roger Cohen, 'Slaughter at a Festival of Peace and Love Leaves Israel Transformed', *New York Times* (15 October 2023).

[63] *7 October Parliamentary Commission Report* (2025), https://tinyurl.com/4xyvfs42; Human Rights Watch, 'I Can't Erase All the Blood from My Mind' (17 July 2024), https://tinyurl.com/2w2antxy; Cassandra Vinograd and Isabel Kershner, 'Hamas Took More than 200 Hostages. Here's What We Know About Them', *New York Times* (19 October 2023).

[64] Ruth Halperin-Kaddari, Nava Ben-Or and Sharon Zagagi-Pinhas, *A Quest for Justice* (Jerusalem: The Dinah Project, 2025).

on Muslim worshipers, murdering twenty-nine and wounding 125 Palestinians.[65] Following the Goldstein massacre, Hamas and the Islamic Jihad carried out dozens of terror attacks against Israeli civilians. The Oslo peace process suffered a major setback, and the chances of resolving the conflict eroded considerably.

During 1994–1995, those who objected to the Oslo peace process organised a well-orchestrated campaign of incitement against the Rabin government, and the prime minister in particular. Stickers reading 'Rabin must be killed' were posted. He was branded a murderer and a traitor. Religious ceremonies called for his death. Photos were published showing him wearing a doctored SS uniform or a kaffiyeh (an Arab headdress). An atmosphere was stirred up that was conducive to promoting extremism and violence.[66] Inciting words constitute speech which is most likely to bring about harming another person or a group of people. Those words are also called speech-acts, because it is hard to ascertain where the speech ends and the action begins. The factor of time between speech and action is most vital. In cases of incitement, there is a direct and immediate link between the harmful speech and the harmful action. Israeli spoilers were delighted with their success in derailing the peace process. On 4 November 1995, an extreme zealot, Yigal Amir, murdered Prime Minister Rabin. The Oslo peace process suffered another major setback. Rabin's deputy, Shimon Peres, lost the elections. Netanyahu became prime minister and the Oslo peace process came to nearly a complete halt.

Spoilers' actions have broad implications for the Middle East, Europe and beyond. Therefore, there should be a coordinated effort to address spoilers, rather than ignoring or dismissing them. Different modes of engagement and negotiations with political extremists and terrorists have been employed.[67] Israel and Hamas have used Qatar, Egypt and the United States to mediate between them. Publicly, Israel and Hamas

[65] Ministry of Foreign Affairs, 'Suicide and Other Bombing Attacks in Israel Since the Declaration of Principles (Sept 1993)', https://tinyurl.com/2s3fbskm. See also Chronology of Terrorist Attacks in Israel Part V: 1993–1995, compiled by Wm. Robert Johnston, last updated 27 November 2016, www.johnstonsarchive.net/terrorism/terrisrael-5.html.

[66] Raphael Cohen-Almagor, 'Political Extremism and Incitement in Israel 1993–1995, 2003–2005: A Study of Dangerous Expressions', *Democracy and Security*, 3(1) (2007): 21–43, and 'Addressing Incitement in Israel', in Aharon Barak et al. (eds), *Essays in Honour of Deputy President of the Israel Supreme Court Eliyahu Mazza* (Jerusalem: Nevo, 2015), 457–488 (Hebrew).

[67] I. William Zartman and Guy Olivier Faure (eds), *Engaging Extremists* (Washington, DC: US Institute of Peace Press, 2011).

do not negotiate directly. Until 7 October 2023, Israel was willing to live next to Hamas, despite its explicit threats to destroy Israel, and enabled its funding. After 7 October, Israel can no longer afford to have Hamas in control of Gaza.

One of the things that puzzled me during my research was the attitude of decision-makers towards spoilers. I thought spoilers deserved much more consideration than was given to them by leaders. After all, they have successfully spoiled all attempts to resolve the Israeli-Palestinian conflict. To try the same methods time and time again, in the expectation of a different result, is not prudent, to say the least. 7 October 2023 proved just how wrong Israeli leaders were in underestimating threats. Granted, we must accept that spoilers will challenge the process of peacemaking, and that we must be hard-headed and keep our focus. Seriousness about getting to the goal – a peace agreement – dictates that we cannot allow any single incident to throw us off track. At the same time, peacemaking requires the continuous assessment of challenges and ways to address them, as well as the implications of spoilers' actions. Their threats must be neutralised. Leaders must remain attentive to their people and ensure that public commitment to peace remains strong and viable. This can only be done if we learn to prevent violence and terror effectively.

Thus, Israel and Palestine should not ignore zealots. Leaders should not merely say 'there will always be spoilers' and 'we will have to deal with them at the appropriate time'. A peace treaty must include an elaborate security section that recognises spoilers and sets forth a detailed plan for how to deal with them. Both countries, Israel and Palestine, should receive concrete assurances on how zealots will be mapped and what steps will be taken to deny them the possibility of upsetting the peace process. Zealots must be promptly addressed and contained. Both parties should refuse to allow zealots to dictate the agenda. It is essential that both Israel and Palestine coordinate their efforts and fight together against violence and terror.

In conclusion, the analytical framework offered in this book is inspired by theories of justice and conflict resolution, by an acute understanding of the role of negotiators and intermediaries, by drawing insights from superforecasters, and by insisting on a coordinated effort to minimise spoilers' impact. Through reasoned analysis and principled compromise, peace can be achieved.

PART I

Peace Junctions

Let me open with some personal words. In 1991, upon completing my DPhil at Oxford, I returned to Israel. Yehuda Elkana, who was then president of the Van Leer Jerusalem Institute, offered me a place at the institute in any capacity I chose, and gave me *carte blanche* to join any of the institute's activities.

I embarked on a study of the Van Leer activities and decided to join the European Project, a fascinating group that studied the connections between Europe and the Middle East. It consisted of six Israeli Jews, five Israeli Palestinians and two Germans who resided in Israel. We received a very generous grant from the Volkswagen Foundation, enabling us to meet once a month for three years. At that time in Israel, Jews and Palestinians did not have many outlets in which they could meet as equals. Van Leer provided such a forum. One of the directors of our group was Azmi Bishara, a proud Palestinian who was later elected to the Knesset, suspected of supporting terrorist activities and forced to flee the country.

In late 1993, the news of the Oslo Accords broke. The following Friday, the Jewish members of the European Project arrived at the institute elated and curious regarding the Palestinian response. We were deeply disappointed by the reaction of our Palestinian colleagues, who did not share our enthusiasm. 'This is a peace accord between occupier and occupied that would only sustain the Israeli colonialist project', they said. It was a cold shower. I understood that our joy was premature, and that peace remained elusive.

The following analysis of the extraordinary Oslo peace process is divided into three chapters. In Chapter 2, I explain why Israel and the Palestine Liberation Organization (PLO) agreed to meet in Oslo and how this channel was constructed. While the PLO sent official representatives, Yossi Beilin, Israel's deputy foreign minister, sent two academics, in an unofficial capacity, to represent Israeli interests. The meetings were conducted under the guise of an academic exercise, providing secrecy and deniability if news about the meetings was leaked. The talks were held parallel to the official Israeli-Palestinian negotiations in Washington, DC. At the second meeting, the two parties produced a paper, which the Israeli representatives gave to Beilin. Beilin showed the paper to then Foreign Minister Shimon Peres, who, in turn, immediately shared it with Prime Minister Yitzhak Rabin. Rabin was displeased by the news. While he did not stop the talks, Rabin, for some time, did not believe that anything good would result from them.[1]

Chapter 3 analyses the second phase of the peace process, when the Israeli delegation expanded and included a senior diplomat, Uri Savir, and a Washington lawyer, Joel Singer. Peres had sent Savir to Oslo because of pressure from the PLO. At some point, the PLO delegation presented an ultimatum: either the Israeli government would become involved, or the Oslo channel would shut down. Peres wanted to save Oslo by sending Savir. Chapter 4 discusses the problems in implementing the Oslo Accords, draws lessons from the Oslo precedent and explains its main achievements, short of reaching a comprehensive peace between Israel and the Palestinians.

A great deal has been written about Oslo.[2] The novelty of the present discussion is that it sheds light on the personal intricacies of the different actors, the human relationships between them, the importance of trust and mistrust in the negotiation process, the logic behind the manner and content of negotiations, the problems that arise when one party to the negotiations is comprised of official representatives while the other is

[1] Interview with Ehud Barak (25 May 2022), p. 5. In his comments on a draft of this chapter, Yair Hirschfeld wrote that Rabin wanted the Oslo channel to oblige the Palestinians to renew the Washington talks without giving in to Hamas.

[2] Jan Egeland, *A Billion Lives* (New York: Simon and Schuster, 2008); Ron Pundak, *Secret Channel* (Tel Aviv: Aliyat Hagag, 2013) (Hebrew) and 'From Oslo to Taba: What Went Wrong?', *Survival*, 43(3) (2001); Yair Hirschfeld, *Track-Two Diplomacy toward an Israeli-Palestinian Solution 1978–2014* (Washington, DC: Woodrow Wilson Center Press and Johns Hopkins University Press, 2014) and *The Israeli-Palestinian Peace Process* (Cham: Springer, 2024); Johan Jorgen Holst, 'Reflections on the Makings of a Tenuous Peace', *Middle East Insight*, 9(6) (September–October 1993): 30–34; Geoffrey R. Watson, *The Oslo Accords* (Oxford: Oxford University Press, 2000); Jane Corbin, *The Norway Channel: The Secret Talks that Led to the Middle East Peace Accord* (New York: Atlantic Monthly Press, 1994); Yossi Beilin, *Touching Peace* (London: Weidenfeld & Nicolson, 1999); Hilde Henriksen Waage, 'Explaining the Oslo Backchannel: Norway's Political Past in the Middle East', *Middle East Journal*, 56(4) (2000): 597–615, 'How Norway Became One of Israel's Best Friends', *Journal of Peace Research*, 37(2) (2000): 189–211, *Peacemaking Is a Risky Business: Norway's Role in the Peace Process in the Middle East, 1993–96* (Oslo: International Peace Research Institute PRIO, 2004) and 'Norway's Role in the Middle East Peace Talks: Between A Strong State and A Weak Belligerent', *Journal of Palestine Studies*, 34(4) (2005): 6–24.

comprised of unofficial representatives, and the problems that arise due to the specific expertise and knowledge of the negotiators. Beyond the justified criticism of Oslo, I highlight the many positives that the Oslo peace process yielded. Oslo brought both Israel and the PLO to embark on a new chapter not only in their mutual relationships, but also in the histories of Israel and the PLO, opening new markets and possibilities that previously were closed to them.

***

2

The Oslo Breakthrough

> Norway's foreign policy may be described as being pro-United States and United Kingdom to the greatest extent it dares, pro-Soviet to the extent it must, and pro-United Nations to the greatest extent it can.
>
> ~ US State Department, 1946

Introduction

Since the birth of Israel in 1948, Norway has retained a close relationship with Israel. In January 1989, Foreign Minister Thorvald Stoltenberg visited Yasser Arafat in Tunis. Arafat implored him to use his connections with Israel to arrange a public or secret meeting between the Palestine Liberation Organization (PLO) and Israel, either directly or via Norwegian research institutes. Norway widened its engagement with the Palestinians.[1] Stoltenberg conveyed Arafat's message to Prime Minister Yitzhak Shamir and Foreign Minister Moshe Arens, but they made it clear that they had no interest in meeting with the PLO. During 1991–1992, Stoltenberg had further meetings with Palestinian leaders who thought that Norway could play a positive role in the conflict. In February 1990, Jan Egeland was appointed Norwegian deputy foreign minister, and he, too, was keen to bring the two rivals together to talk.[2] All the Palestinian and Israeli meetings were handled by Egeland.[3]

In 1992, there was an opening for a peace process between Israel and the Palestinians, due to the return of Israel's Labour Party to government. This opportunity was recognised by influential people in Norway who were willing to devote resources to the pursuit of peace. They recognised that the PLO was interested in engaging with Israel and offered

1 Hilde H. Waage, *Peacemaking Is a Risky Business: Norway's Role in the Peace Process in the Middle East, 1993–96* (Oslo: International Peace Research Institute PRIO, 2004), 41.

2 Nir Levitan, *Scandinavian Diplomacy and the Israeli-Palestinian Conflict* (London: Routledge, 2023), 37.

3 Egeland's email communication (14 August 2023).

their facilitation services. While they knew that their ability to influence Israeli leaders was modest, they decided to seize the moment. Both Israel and the PLO had confidence in Norway's goodwill. Both considered Norway to be a valuable friend. Israel and the PLO perceived Norway as a responsible country with no immediate national interests in the Israeli-Palestinian conflict and, therefore, able to play the role of an impartial facilitator. The remoteness of this small Scandinavian country served them well in arranging secret negotiations away from the public eye.

The Oslo peace process was extraordinary in many respects. The three parties were Norway, Israel and the PLO. The main Norwegian player was Terje Rød-Larsen, the director of a research centre, who wanted to do good. The Israelis directly involved were a mid-level politician, Yossi Beilin, and two academics, Yair Hirschfeld and Ron Pundak (also spelled Pundik). This trio was later assisted by a private lawyer from Washington, DC, Joel Singer, and a civil servant who had never been involved in high-stakes diplomatic negotiations, Uri Savir. The Palestinian negotiators were a group of PLO officials headed by Ahmed Qurie (also known as Abu Ala). At that time, the PLO was an illegal organisation that neither the Israeli nor the American governments recognised.

While many people believed and still believe that the role of the United States is essential for any serious effort to resolve the Israeli-Palestinian conflict,[4] the Americans were not involved in the Oslo negotiations. Although the US State Department was aware of the ongoing talks in Oslo, some believed that the Norwegian track was a discussion rather than a decision-making channel,[5] whereas others took it more seriously.[6] Dennis Ross wrote that he did not fully grasp the importance of the Oslo track at the time.[7] For Martin Indyk, Oslo was a surprise. He did not know anything about the negotiating history and barely understood what exactly the Israelis and the Palestinians had agreed on.[8] For many months throughout 1993, Ross and his colleagues continued to believe that the 'real' negotiations were taking place in Washington, where Israeli officials appointed by Prime Minister Yitzhak Rabin

[4] Interviews with Ghaith al-Omari (2 September 2014); Vincent Fean (24 March 2016); Itamar Rabinovich (21 July 2017); Pär Nuder (20 August 2019); John Hagard (22 August 2019); Aaron David Miller (12 September 2019); Yuval Rotem (11 January 2021).

[5] Interview with Aaron David Miller (12 September 2019), 2.

[6] Discussion with Dan Kurtzer (7 June 2023).

[7] Dennis Ross, *The Missing Peace* (New York: Farrar, Straus and Giroux, 2004), 100.

[8] Interview with Martin Indyk (9 August 2022), 2.

negotiated with a Palestinian-Jordanian delegation that reported to the PLO but did not include Tunis officials (the PLO headquarters at that time was in Tunis).

Background

In 1987, the First Intifada erupted. On 8 December 1987, a terrible accident occurred in Gaza. A truck driver made a reckless turn and hit a Palestinian car. Four of its passengers were killed. Others were wounded. A rumour spread that the crash was intentional, planned as an act of revenge for the death of Shlomo Sekel, an Israeli who was stabbed two days earlier in a market in Gaza. It did not matter that no facts were found to establish a connection between the two incidents. Rumours have a life of their own and, in the existing atmosphere, they served as a trigger for mass rioting. On 9 December, most of those who lived in the Jabelia refugee camp did not go to work. Instead, they went to the streets to demonstrate.[9] The Intifada started with a series of public demonstrations and riots protesting against the Israeli occupation. The Intifada constituted a threat to the authority of Yasser Arafat, leader of the PLO, an organisation that was supposed to represent the Palestinian people. Arafat was surprised by the scale of the uprising, which brought thousands of protesters to the streets to fight against the Israeli occupation. He had no prior knowledge of what was coming.[10] In December 1987, the Hamas movement was established and quickly gained adherents, as the atmosphere was conducive to the group's 'resistance' and violent agenda.

The emergence of Hamas posed a significant challenge to Fatah's political dominance in the Gaza Strip and the West Bank, further weakening the position of the PLO.[11] Arafat, increasingly aware that his grip over the Palestinian territories was eroding, sought to reassert his leadership and restore his legitimacy as the central figure of the Palestinian national movement. This urgency was intensified in the wake of the 1991 Gulf War, when Arafat's decision to align with Saddam Hussein proved to be a profound strategic miscalculation. He had anticipated that such an alliance

[9] Raphael Cohen-Almagor, 'The Intifada: Causes, Consequences, and Future Trends', *Small Wars & Insurgencies*, 2(1) (1991): 12–40.

[10] Interviews with Ziad Abu Zayyad (14 May 2015), 30 and with Shlomo Ben-Ami (26 June 2013), 1.

[11] Fatah is the reverse acronym of Harakat al-Tahrir al-Filistiniya (Palestinian Liberation Movement). The name means 'conquest' in Arabic. It was founded by Arafat in the late 1950s and is now part of the PLO.

might enhance his diplomatic leverage, particularly in mediating between Iraq and Western powers; however, the outcome was the opposite. His stance alienated key actors in the Arab world – most notably Saudi Arabia, Kuwait and other Gulf states – which consequently suspended financial support to the PLO. Compounding this crisis, Iraq, one of the PLO's most dependable patrons since 1988, was rendered incapable of continuing its assistance following its military defeat.

Moreover, the Gulf War precipitated a socio-economic collapse within the Palestinian diaspora in the Gulf. Approximately 600,000 Palestinians, many of whom were economically prosperous and resided in Kuwait and the United Arab Emirates, were forcibly displaced in the aftermath of the war. This diaspora community had been a vital source of financial remittances and political support for both Fatah and the PLO. Their displacement and subsequent loss of income effectively severed a critical lifeline, exacerbating the organisation's financial crisis and diminishing its capacity to project influence and maintain its political infrastructure.[12] Arafat estimated that the PLO suffered a loss of $10 billion as a result of that war.[13]

Arafat was increasingly alarmed by the growing rapprochement between Israel and Jordan, fearing that King Hussein might follow in the footsteps of Egyptian President Anwar Sadat and become the second Arab leader to sign a peace agreement with Israel. Egypt's 1979 treaty with Israel, which notably excluded any resolution of the Palestinian question, had already set a precedent for Arab-Israeli normalisation without Palestinian input. Despite Arafat's hopes that King Hussein would either delay negotiations until Palestinian territorial claims were addressed or coordinate closely with the PLO, he recognised that such expectations were likely unfounded. The prospect of a separate Jordanian-Israeli accord threatened to further marginalise the PLO and undermine its claim to represent the Palestinian people.

In response, Arafat became increasingly focused on consolidating his political authority and securing international recognition as the legitimate leader of the Palestinian national movement. The First Intifada, however, had dramatically shifted the centre of political gravity back to the Occupied Palestinian Territory (OPT), underscoring the limitations of exile leadership. Reasserting control over the Palestinian political arena required Arafat to re-establish a presence in the West Bank and to engage in dialogue with Israel. Paradoxically, it was now Israeli cooperation that

12 Interview with Maher El-Kurd (30 January 2025), 15.

13 Sven Behrendt, *The Secret Israeli-Palestinian Negotiations in Oslo: Their Success and Why the Process Ultimately Failed* (London: Routledge, 2007), 23.

appeared essential for Arafat's political survival and the re-legitimisation of the PLO's leadership.[14]

Furthermore, the collapse of the Soviet Union during the late 1980s was a major blow to the PLO. It left the international sphere with one remaining superpower: the United States, a diplomatic actor squarely aligned with Israel.[15] Arafat could no longer count on the Soviet Union to serve as a counterbalance against American interests. He understood the need to establish ties with the Americans, who, at that time, regarded the PLO as a terrorist organisation and, by extension, Arafat as a terrorist. As he believed Israel could help him create a relationship with the United States, Arafat decided to engage with Israel. The Palestinian national movement's leaders concluded that diplomacy was the main tool for achieving their goals.[16]

In the spring of 1988, Swedish Foreign Minister Sten Andersson facilitated a series of discreet meetings between prominent American Jewish figures and representatives of the PLO. These encounters aimed to explore the possibility of establishing a framework for peace between Israel and the Palestinians. Although the Israeli government under Prime Minister Shamir remained staunchly opposed to any engagement with the PLO, the meetings nonetheless contributed to a gradual shift in US policy. US Secretary of State George Shultz articulated clear preconditions for initiating dialogue with the PLO: acceptance of United Nations Security Council Resolutions 242 and 338, formal recognition of the State of Israel and an unequivocal renunciation of terrorism. In a significant political development, the Palestine National Council (PNC) convened in November 1988 and issued a Declaration of Independence. This document affirmed the Palestinian people's right to statehood and self-determination and committed to a vision of governance rooted in democratic and pluralistic principles. 'The State of Palestine is the state of Palestinians wherever they may be. The state is for them to enjoy in it their collective national and cultural identity, theirs to pursue in it a complete equality of rights. In it will be safeguarded their political and religious convictions and their human dignity by means of a parliamentary democratic system of governance.'[17]

14 Interview with Shlomo Ben-Ami (26 June 2013), 1.

15 Vladislav Zubok, *Collapse: The Fall of the Soviet Union* (New Haven, CT: Yale University Press, 2022); Associated Press, *The Collapse of the Soviet Union: End of an Empire* (New York: AP Editions, 2015).

16 Interview with Ahmad Khalidi (5 June 2019), 2.

17 *Palestinian Declaration of Independence*, Palestine National Council, 19th Session, Algiers (15 November 1988), www.palquest.org/en/historictext/9673/palestinian-declaration-independence.

The PNC accepted UN Resolutions 242 and 338 and called for the establishment of a Palestinian state based on international legitimacy embodied in UN resolutions since 1947 and the ability of the Palestinian people to enjoy the rights of self-determination, political independence and sovereignty. Arafat declared that he condemned terrorism in all its forms, but, at the same time, he saluted those people who were sitting in the Congress Hall and who took part in battles to liberate their people from colonialism and injustice.[18]

On 6 March 1991, US President George H. W. Bush declared that 'the time has come to put an end to the Arab-Israeli conflict'.[19] He thought the time was ripe for pursuing diplomatic efforts. Bush's bold declaration was followed by eight months of intensive shuttle diplomacy by Secretary of State James Baker, culminating in the Madrid Peace Conference in October 1991. The United States and the Soviet Union declared their readiness to assist Israel and the Palestinians to achieve a just, lasting and comprehensive peace settlement, through direct negotiations between Israel and the Arab states, and between Israel and the Palestinians, based on UN Security Council Resolutions 242 and 338.[20] President Bush and Soviet President Mikhail Gorbachev co-chaired this important conference, which was attended by Israeli, Egyptian, Syrian and Lebanese delegations, as well as a joint Jordanian-Palestinian delegation. Unprecedentedly, the Palestinians were included in substantive discussions regarding their future. For the first time, all the parties to the Arab-Israeli conflict, excluding the PLO leadership, had gathered to hold direct negotiations (see Figure 2.1).[21] Substantively, however, while the Madrid Conference led to bilateral negotiations between Israel and its Arab neighbours, it did not change the political reality of the occupation. Following Madrid, Israeli, Syrian, Jordanian, Lebanese and Palestinian representatives continued to meet for bilateral talks in Washington, while multilateral talks

[18] Shafiq Al-Hout, *My Life in the PLO* (London: Pluto, 2011), 238–239.

[19] Maureen Dowd, 'After the War: The White House; Bush, Urging Wider Peace, Hints at Pressure on Israel to Yield Land for Security', *New York Times* (7 March 1991), https://tinyurl.com/38hj2j6x.

[20] 'The Madrid Peace Conference', *Journal of Palestine Studies*, 21(2) (Winter 1992): 117–149.

[21] Palestinian residents of the West Bank (excluding East Jerusalem) and Gaza Strip who had no formal links with the PLO were part of the Jordanian-Palestinian negotiating team. See Ibid.; Marvin C. Feuerwerger, Martin Indyk, Robert B. Satloff and Michael Eisenstadt, *Peacewatch Anthology: Analysis of the Arab-Israeli Peace Process from the Madrid Peace Conference to the Eve of President Clinton's Inauguration* (Washington, DC: Washington Institute for Near East Policy, 1993).

Figure 2.1 Madrid Peace Conference, October 1991.
Credit: David Ake/Staff/AFP/Getty Images.

commenced in Moscow in 1992. Yet by 1993, the Washington talks had come to a diplomatic standstill.[22]

Ahmad Khalidi, who served as an advisor to the Palestinian delegation at the Madrid/Washington and Cairo–Taba talks, regards the lack of any presence of the PLO as the key flaw of these negotiations.[23] Because the PLO was still regarded by both the US and Israel as a terrorist group and contact with its members was illegal, a PLO presence at the Washington talks was impossible. However, because the PLO was the de facto authority in Palestine, any attempt at diplomacy that excluded the PLO was rendered impotent. At the same time, the Palestinian negotiators in Washington, though not direct representatives of the PLO, received instructions from the latter.[24] These representatives, though approved by the PLO, lacked the unifying political influence that the organisation provided, causing the many rival interests within the negotiation team to further weaken the Palestinian diplomatic position. It is also possible that the PLO, offended by their lack of recognition and representation in Washington, intentionally scuttled the talks, as Elyakim Rubinstein, the chief Israeli

[22] 'The Madrid Conference, 1991', Office of the Historian, https://history.state.gov/milestones/1989-1992/madrid-conference.
[23] Interview with Ahmad Khalidi (5 June 2019), 5.
[24] Interview with Joel Singer (29 August 2014), 9.

negotiator in Washington, proposes.[25] Ziad Abu Zayyad, a member of the strategic committee that was advising the negotiating team, felt that the leadership in Tunis did not trust the local leadership in the OPT.[26] The Israeli and American insistence that the PLO could not be part of the delegation raised fears within the leadership of the PLO in Tunis that an attempt was being made to bypass them. While the Palestinian delegation in Washington assured the PLO leadership in Tunis that they would not betray their interests, Tunis remained wary of the Palestinian negotiators. They sought to establish an alternative channel, bypassing Washington. The PLO leadership in Tunis wanted to ensure that *they*, rather than the Palestinian negotiators from Jerusalem, known as the Orient House Group, would control the negotiations.[27]

Meanwhile, the Washington talks were scrutinised intensively by the press, constraining the latitude of discussion. The talks seemed to go round and round in repetitive circles, and the Americans accused Rubinstein of a policy of 'attrition'.[28] The peace talks had a built-in structural untenability; the severe power imbalance between the parties, aggravated by the United States' meddling and reluctance to put pressure on Israel, pushed the talks into a deadlock. Moreover, the Palestinians' relative inexperience and lack of expertise placed them at a significant disadvantage to Israel, whose organised army, bureaucracy and specialised diplomatic corps allowed it greater leverage on all fronts.

Only in 1997 did Ahmed Qurie and Hiba Husseini establish the Negotiations Support Unit as part of the PLO Negotiations Affairs Department, staffed with legal advisors, policy advisors and experts. It received funding from the British, Danish, Dutch, Norwegian and Swedish governments. Later, the Negotiations Support Unit was taken over by Sa'eb Erekat.[29]

Inception

It was in this environment that Terje Rød-Larsen, the director of the Fafo Research Foundation in Norway, met with Yossi Beilin, then a senior member of the Israeli Labour Party, in Tel Aviv on 29 April 1992 and offered to host meetings between the Israelis and Palestinians through

[25] Interview with Elyakim Rubinstein (28 May 2013), 4.
[26] Interview with Ziad Abu Zayyad (14 May 2015), 5.
[27] Ibid., 6.
[28] Hirschfeld's written comments on a draft of this chapter (30 June 2023).
[29] Interview with Hiba Husseini (24 December 2024), 4.

his organisation.[30] Fafo, the research institute of Norwegian trade unions, was established in 1981 and engaged in various social research projects in the OPT. Rød-Larsen, Stoltenberg and Egeland thought they could provide Israelis and Palestinians with a channel of discreet communication and creative negotiations through Fafo.[31] Rød-Larsen told Beilin that in January 1992, his wife, Mona Juul, had hosted a Palestinian delegation from Tunis headed by Qurie, Arafat's chief finance advisor. Rød-Larsen was impressed with Qurie and hoped he could find common language with the Israelis. He also thought that Faisal Husseini, a Palestinian leader from Jerusalem, would be even more appropriate for such meetings.[32] Subsequently, on 19 June 1992, Rød-Larsen, Husseini, Beilin and Hirschfeld met in Jerusalem.[33] Beilin and Hirschfeld realised that the only way to ensure a serious effort to end the conflict would be to establish a direct channel with the PLO.[34] At around the same time, Egeland, Norway's deputy foreign minister, became aware that Qurie was seeking the creation of a similar diplomatic path to circumvent the deadlocked Washington negotiations.[35] Egeland had been hoping to play a role in Israeli-Palestinian reconciliation since studying the Middle East conflict at the Hebrew University in 1984.[36] In 1988, he published a book in which he described Norway as a stable and pragmatic country whose diplomatic-bureaucratic establishment cares about and designs long-term human rights policies, and whose bilateral relationships are based on foreign assistance.[37] Because the 1992 Israeli elections had not yet taken place, and Beilin's position was uncertain, it was decided that any meeting between Israeli and PLO representatives should be postponed until after the elections, when it was hoped that the possibility of establishing a dialogue would be more assured.[38]

The elections were held on 23 June. The return of the Labour Party to power signalled a significant moment of change. Prime Minister Rabin

[30] Interview with Yossi Beilin (13 May 2015). See also Yossi Beilin, *Touching Peace* (Tel Aviv: Yedioth Ahronoth, 1997) (Hebrew), 63.

[31] Waage, *Peacemaking Is a Risky Business*, 44; Levitan, *Scandinavian Diplomacy and the Israeli–Palestinian Conflict*, 38.

[32] Beilin, *Touching Peace* (London: Weidenfeld & Nicolson, 1999), 51.

[33] Beilin, *Touching Peace* (Hebrew ed.), 67; Interview with Yossi Beilin (13 May 2015), 1.

[34] Interview with Daniel Kurtzer (6 April 2017), 14.

[35] Interview with Jan Egeland (2 September 2017), 3.

[36] Ibid. See also Jan Egeland, *A Billion Lives* (New York: Simon and Schuster, 2008), 165.

[37] Jan Egeland, *Impotent Superpower – Potent Small State* (Oslo: Norwegian University Press, 1988), 175–179.

[38] Interview with Yossi Beilin (13 May 2015), 2.

wished to move away from containment to address the core of the Israeli-Palestinian conflict: the occupation. At this point, the Labour Party's official position was that the only solution to the Palestinian issue was the establishment of internal political autonomy for the Palestinians, rather than a two-state solution, which was not considered viable by members of the Israeli government.[39] Still, there was a will to end the occupation. As Shimon Peres explained, 'we were not going to rule the Palestinians against their will. We were always looking for a way to liberate them from our occupation and to liberate ourselves as occupiers.'[40] Beilin was appointed deputy foreign minister, while Peres became foreign minister. Rabin was perpetually concerned with the integrity of his coalition and paranoid about betrayal by its members, fearing that deceit among his own might subvert his position and that of his government. Among those Rabin did not trust was Peres, his long-standing rival for leadership of the Labour Party. At that time, I was a political activist at the Labour Party and frequently witnessed the mutual distrust between the two leaders. Despite Peres's ministerial appointment in the new government, the bad blood between the two senior Labour figures meant that Peres had to be careful when engaging in bilateral peace talks. Beilin said: 'He [Peres] was not allowed to have any involvement with the bilateral talks. It was not only Palestine. It's also Jordan and Syria.'[41] However, Avi Gil said that Peres held secret meetings with Faisal Husseini and with Hanan Ashrawi. Peres also often spoke with Egyptian President Hosni Mubarak, as he was pushing the Gaza First plan and wanted Mubarak to sell the idea to Arafat. Peres thought that if he were to propose the idea to Arafat, he would immediately reject it; however, if Mubarak planted the idea in Arafat's head, he would demand it of Israel.[42]

In August 1992, the sixth round of bilateral talks commenced in Washington. They made very little progress, if any. Upon Israel's demand to bypass the PLO, a joint Palestinian-Jordanian delegation was constructed, consisting of Palestinians from the OPT. As long as the PLO was not represented, Arafat had no incentive to progress in the talks. Egeland met with Daniel Kurtzer, an expert in Middle Eastern affairs at the US State Department, who would later serve as ambassador to Israel

[39] Interview with Joel Singer (6 April 2017), 20.
[40] Shimon Peres and Robert Littell, *For the Future of Israel* (Baltimore, MD: Johns Hopkins University Press, 1998), 83.
[41] Interview with Yossi Beilin (13 May 2015), 6.
[42] Interview with Avi Gil (16 January 2025), 6–10.

and Egypt, and asked for American consent to hold peace negotiations in Oslo. Kurtzer responded that he, personally, thought this was a good idea and asked Egeland to keep the Americans informed. He also advised not conducting a dialogue behind Rabin's back.[43] On 9 September 1992, Beilin met once again with a group of Norwegian diplomats, including Egeland, Rød-Larsen and Juul, all of whom felt that the time was ripe for the creation of a direct backchannel.[44] Egeland told Beilin that his team was able and willing to discreetly connect Israelis and Palestinians on any level, anywhere.[45] Beilin brought with him his assistant, Shlomo Gur, and his close political ally and a member of the Labour Mashov circle, Yair Hirschfeld. Mashov was a group of politicians who wished to promote a social-democratic, peace-driven agenda. Hirschfeld was also a University of Haifa academic who, since 1980, arranged confidential meetings with Palestinians for Peres and Beilin.[46] In 1992, Hirschfeld completed a report to the European Union, 'Israel, the Palestinians and the Middle East: From Dependency to Interdependence'. Hirschfeld claims he had obtained supportive inputs from the Palestinians, as well as from Prime Minister Shamir's bureau, to the model, which eventually became the Oslo concept.[47] Having worked with Hirschfeld, Beilin felt that his expertise both in the development of the peace process and in dealing with Palestinian officials would prove useful.[48] At this meeting, it was left undetermined whether a dialogue could take place. Although a backchannel was possible, due to prime ministerial constraints, it would have to be undertaken, at least initially, without Rabin's direct involvement.

Such an opportunity arose on 4 December 1992. Hirschfeld met with Qurie at the recommendation of Hanan Ashrawi, the spokesperson of the Palestinian delegation in the Washington talks.[49] By doing so, Hirschfeld

[43] Discussion with Dan Kurtzer (7 June 2023).

[44] Interview with Jan Egeland (2 September 2017), 4; Yossi Beilin, *Touching Peace* (Hebrew ed.), 70–71; Hilde Henriksen Waage, 'Norwegians? Who needs Norwegians?' Explaining the Oslo Back Channel: Norway's Political Past in the Middle East, A report prepared by PRIO International Peace Research Institute, Oslo Institutt for fredsforskning (2000), 129.

[45] Egeland, *A Billion Lives*, 169.

[46] Q&A with Yair Hirschfeld (15 July 2018), 1; Hirschfeld's comments on a draft of this chapter.

[47] Q&A with Yair Hirschfeld (15 July 2018), 1.

[48] Interview with Yossi Beilin (13 May 2015), 1–2.

[49] Interview with Yossi Beilin (13 May 2015), 3; Yair Hirschfeld and Ron Pundak, 'Development of the Norwegian Channel' (1 September 1993), Israel Archives, P-6/5513: 1 (Hebrew); Hanan Ashrawi, *This Side of Peace: A Personal Account* (New York: Simon and Schuster, 1995), 267.

assumed great personal risk. He broke the law prohibiting meetings with members of the PLO to try to open a direct communication channel with them.[50] In a tense conversation, Qurie and Hirschfeld discussed the possibility of establishing a constructive dialogue and what the basis of such a backchannel dialogue might be.[51] It was at this meeting that the concept of an Israeli-Palestinian dialogue, involving direct communications with the PLO, was first proposed.

After the meeting, Hirschfeld briefed not only Beilin, but also Kurtzer, who wrote a memo to US Secretary of State Warren Christopher and the Middle East team: Dennis Ross, Martin Indyk, Aaron David Miller and Sam Lewis. The Americans were kept informed by Hirschfeld and Egeland through May 1993.[52] Although these diplomatic manoeuvres remained secretive, the Americans were kept apprised of the situation, as Kurtzer describes:

> After the initial contact with Egeland, and after this meeting and all of the subsequent meetings that I was briefed on, I would send a note 'outside the system'. In other words, it was a note with a restricted readership that would go to the Secretary of State and the peace team. The briefings I received were all memorialized ... Nothing about Oslo should have been a surprise later, as some people thought it was.[53]

Beilin proposed that the backchannel should exist under the condition of American support;[54] the Americans refused on the basis of the law prohibiting American contact with members of the PLO.[55] Beilin, who was working to repeal the law barring Israelis from contact with the PLO, told Hirschfeld to fix a date for a meeting,[56] and 20 January 1993 was selected. This was one day after the said law was repealed.[57] A few days earlier, on 8 January, Peres met with Rabin and said that as long as Arafat was in Tunis, he did not represent the Palestinians in Gaza and the West Bank and that

[50] Yair Hirschfeld, *Track-Two Diplomacy toward an Israeli-Palestinian Solution 1978–2014* (Washington, DC: Woodrow Wilson Center Press and Johns Hopkins University Press, 2014), 108.

[51] Q&A with Yair Hirschfeld (15 July 2018), 2; Yair Hirschfeld, *The Israeli-Palestinian Peace Process* (Cham: Springer, 2024), 74.

[52] Phone conversation with Dan Kurtzer (16 August 2022).

[53] Raphael Cohen-Almagor, 'Israel-PLO Peace Process: Interview with Ambassador Daniel Kurtzer', *Israel Studies*, 24(3) (2019): 129.

[54] Interview with Yossi Beilin (13 May 2015), 3.

[55] Ibid., 4.

[56] Ibid.

[57] Joel Greenberg, 'Israeli Parliament Lifts a Ban on P.L.O. Contacts', *New York Times* (20 January 1993): 3.

he would not support negotiations with Israel. Therefore, Israel should propose that Arafat return to Gaza. Peres asked Rabin to think about the idea and not respond immediately.[58]

According to Hussein Agha, a Palestinian peace negotiator, the arrangements made at Oslo were the only option available to Arafat at that point; had Arafat been asked about the contents of the Oslo agreement a mere five years before the beginning of the diplomatic process, he would have viewed it as a 'grand betrayal of the Palestinian cause'.[59] However, by the early 1990s, Arafat's position was so weak that he was left with very few options. Likewise, Egeland submits that the Palestinians were willing to meet with the Israelis, who were represented by Hirschfeld and one of his students, Ron Pundak, out of desperation. Although Hirschfeld and Pundak had no official status in the Israeli government – they were academics – the Palestinian officials were willing to engage with them. For the Norwegians, though the talks themselves offered little tangible benefit and were undertaken, as Beilin saw it, mostly out of 'goodwill',[60] the soft benefits of the peace process were significant. Through its position as a facilitator of the peace process, Norway could potentially increase its importance on the world stage as a diplomatic centre, acquiring a great deal of prestige. Additionally, Beilin states that this opportunity would also establish for Norway an important relationship with the United States, one which might prove beneficial to Norway in other, unrelated foreign policy contexts, although Beilin regards this as a result, rather than the goal of Norway's attempts to establish a dialogue.[61]

It was against this backdrop that meetings began secretly in January at a manor house in Sarpsborg, under the guise of an academic meeting. In 1990, an exercise in academic diplomacy involving Israelis and Palestinians had been conducted in Sweden but was brought to a halt a year later due to the PLO's position in the Gulf War.[62] Now, the Norwegians decided to try to facilitate further academic diplomacy.[63] They enjoyed the trust of

58 Avi Gil's comments on a draft of this chapter.

59 Interview with Hussein Agha (5 April 2019), 9.

60 Interview with Yossi Beilin (13 May 2015), 2.

61 Ibid., 3. For further discussion on the role of Norway in the Oslo negotiations, see Waage, *Peacemaking Is a Risky Business*.

62 Peter Wallensteen, *Peter Wallensteen: A Pioneer in Making Peace Researchable* (Cham: Springer, 2021), 615–624.

63 Jonathan Powell remarked: 'What I have observed around the world is, nearly always, where there are successful negotiations, whether it is South Africa, Northern Ireland, Colombia, El Salvador, ETA in Spain, all of them have started with a secret backchannel, because it is just so much easier for democratic governments to do things that way. Otherwise, they

both parties, who perceived Rød-Larsen as a credible facilitator.[64] In retrospect, Beilin said he had no idea that Oslo would lead to a breakthrough. He wanted to try it, but he knew that if he were to report it to his superiors, he might jeopardise the opportunity. The price he paid was keeping himself out of the negotiation room. By entrusting Hirschfeld and Pundak with this responsibility, he maintained deniability in case of failure, as the channel could still be portrayed as an academic seminar.[65] Hirschfeld and Pundak's expenses were covered by Fafo. They could deny any connection to the Israeli government.[66]

The initial phase of the Oslo negotiations operated as a 'mixed track', whereby Palestinian officials engaged in dialogue with unofficial Israeli interlocutors. This informal format afforded the participants greater flexibility, enabling a candid exchange of ideas and the formulation of a preliminary working document with significant conceptual depth. However, the absence of formal Israeli representation imposed clear constraints. Hirschfeld and Pundak, acting without official mandates, lacked the authority to engage substantively on certain core issues or respond swiftly to emerging proposals, as they were dependent on intermittent approval from political actors in Jerusalem. This limitation not only hampered the depth and pace of negotiations but also created a disconnect with the parallel, official track in Washington, thereby complicating coherence across diplomatic efforts.

Furthermore, the clandestine nature of the talks – conducted away from public scrutiny – risked internal political backlash and undermined transparency. A significant asymmetry between the delegations also emerged. The Palestinian negotiators were uncertain whether their Israeli counterparts were merely academic emissaries or de facto representatives of the Israeli government. This ambiguity raised concerns about the talks' legitimacy and utility, as the Palestinians were unwilling to invest in what could ultimately prove to be an academic exercise, devoid of political

face so much public pressure to stop the talks, as soon as there is an outrage.' Interview with Jonathan Powell (20 July 2022), 20.

64 Karin Aggestam, 'The Psychology of Peacemaking: Terje Rød-Larsen', in Mona Fixdal (ed.), *Ways Out of War: Peacemakers in the Middle East and the Balkans* (Houndmills: Palgrave, 2012), 77.

65 Interview with Yossi Beilin (13 May 2015); Beilin, *Touching Peace* (Hebrew ed.), 77. In his comments on a draft of this chapter (30 June 2023), Hirschfeld wrote: 'it is good to hear that Beilin needs a post-factum explanation why I led the negotiations and not he. He offered important support, without which, it would have been impossible to proceed. When Peres stopped the exercise, Beilin held his protective hand over me.'

66 Waage, 'Norwegians? Who Needs Norwegians?', 139.

consequences. The prospect of reaching a provisional agreement, only to have it dismissed by Israeli leadership, posed a serious risk and contributed to early tensions in the negotiation process.

Oslo Phase 1

Aware of the asymmetry between Israel and the PLO, Norway went out of its way to ensure that their facilitation would be symmetrical. They provided the same services, and similar logistics, used the same cars, reserved the same hotel rooms, allocated the same amount of time for presentations, and were often served the same food.[67] Equality and dignity for all.

First Meeting

On 20 January 1993, the Palestinian negotiators and their Israeli counterparts arrived at the Borregaard mansion in Sarpsborg, some 100 kilometres south of Oslo.[68] The PLO delegation to this 'academic seminar' consisted of a three-man team. It was headed by Qurie, director of multilateral negotiations and director general of the economic department of the PLO, as well as Hasan Asfour, the secretary general of the PLO Negotiations Affairs Department, which was established after the Madrid Conference in 1990. Asfour knew the details of the Washington talks; he represented Mahmoud Abbas (sometimes referred to as Abu Mazen).[69] The third member was Maher El-Kurd, an economic assistant who was Arafat's eyes and ears.[70] Hirschfeld and Pundak represented the Israeli interests.[71] Hirschfeld chose to bring Pundak with him because the two had worked together previously. Additionally, he knew Pundak's father, the prominent Danish journalist Herbert Pundik (Nahum Pundak), who wanted his son to work with Hirschfeld.[72]

67 Waage, *Peacemaking Is a Risky Business*, 8.

68 Interview with Yossi Beilin (13 May 2015), 4; David Makovsky, *Making Peace with the PLO: The Rabin Government's Road to the Oslo Accord* (Boulder, CO: Westview, 1996), 21.

69 Interviews with Joel Singer (25 March 2022), 17 and Maher El-Kurd (30 January 2025), 5.

70 Ahmed Qurie, *From Oslo to Jerusalem* (London: I.B. Tauris, 2008), 2–3; Waage, *Peacemaking Is a Risky Business*, 61.

71 I asked Hirschfeld whether Peres knew about and authorised this first meeting, and Hirschfeld replied (email 29 May 2024): 'At the time we worked closely together with Peres; before we went to Sarpsborg we discussed with him a paper we got from Hanan Ashrawi; I am not sure whether we specifically told him, but it was evident' (20 July 2018).

72 Q&A with Yair Hirschfeld (20 July 2018), 2.

The Borregaard mansion was chosen for its relative discreetness and isolation, to avoid scrutiny from the international community and the press. Shielding the talks from the media was vital for their integrity, as John Hagard, the former Swedish ambassador to Israel and one of the facilitators of later negotiations between Israel and the Palestinians, explains: 'As soon as you start to negotiate via the media, it is dead … Because then people, on either side or both, have to defend what they are doing.'[73] Secrecy was also necessary to prevent outside involvement in the talks, including that of the United States. The US State Department was aware of the talks and its members were briefed on the initial phases of negotiations by members of the Norwegian Foreign Ministry. Such briefings eventually ceased in May 1993, when an American diplomat mistakenly spoke about the process in a public place, a hotel lobby, leading the Norwegians to believe that there could be a leak.[74] Egeland explained that it was appropriate to inform the Americans only insofar as they did not break the veil of confidentiality surrounding the talks.[75] The American government, for its part, did not wish to be directly involved, as it did not want to delegitimise the Washington talks.[76]

On 21–22 January 1993, the first meetings between Hirschfeld's team and Qurie's team took place. In this meeting, the parties tried 'to feel each other'. Hirschfeld testified that it started 'a bit tough'. Qurie compared the occupation of Norway by the Nazis to the occupation of Palestine by Israel. Hirschfeld made it clear that if ever Qurie would dare to repeat such a comparison, he and Pundak would stand up, leave and never come back. Qurie never made a similar remark again.[77] Then the Israelis and Palestinians exchanged their broad concepts for discussion and their primary goals for the dialogue by passing sets of notes between them. Building on his previous work, Hirschfeld had prepared a document for his own use, charting all the Israeli and Palestinian positions, issue by issue. He therefore knew which points he could raise and which points to avoid.[78] Broadly speaking,

[73] Interview with John Hagard (22 August 2019), 12.
[74] Interview with Jan Egeland (2 September 2017), 12; Discussion with Dan Kurtzer (7 June 2023).
[75] Interview with Jan Egeland (2 September 2017), 12.
[76] Hirschfeld, *Track-Two Diplomacy*, 116. In his comments on a draft of this chapter, Singer wrote that the Americans disregarded the Oslo talks because they considered them entirely unimportant.
[77] Q&A with Yair Hirschfeld (20 July 2018), 1–2.
[78] Yair Hirschfeld, 'Learning the Lessons of the Oslo Peace Process: James Sorene Interviews Yair Hirschfeld', *Fathom* (Spring 2016), https://tinyurl.com/5n9av7ut.

the two parties discussed cooperation, the legitimacy of the Palestinian people and the PLO as their representative, and the creation of an official channel, which would form the basis of a paper they would produce.[79]

Hirschfeld laid out a roadmap for what the parties had to achieve. Qurie offered a plan in which Israel withdrew from the Gaza Strip, helped facilitate an international Marshall Plan-style development programme for the Palestinians and formed a framework for mutual Israeli-Palestinian economic and production cooperation.[80] The Palestinians also proposed a third-party (United Nations) trusteeship over Gaza to prevent instability and ensure both parties' compliance with the agreement.[81] The Palestinian negotiators brought with them several concepts for economic cooperation. These relied on resources that already existed, but which were split between the territories and Israel, and resources which remained undeveloped but could be shared.[82] The Palestinians knew that Shimon Peres was among those who supported the idea of Gaza First, having promoted the idea publicly since 1980. Qurie raised the idea of a maritime canal linking the Mediterranean Sea and the Dead Sea, and a free trade area between Ashdod and Gaza.[83]

Qurie also wanted UN Resolution 242, which called for an end to the Israeli occupation of 'territories' taken in the 1967 war,[84] and UN Resolution 338, which demanded the establishment of a durable peace in the Middle East,[85] to be inserted into the agreement as a basis for both interim and final agreements. He asked that the new Palestinian Authority (PA) govern the entire territory occupied in 1967, with agreed exceptions; that the Palestinian council controlling the transition should be allowed full legislative authority; that laws written before the transition should be reviewed; and that an international bystander/institution should oversee elections, not Israel. Qurie further wished for the implementation of the right of return for Palestinians deported in 1947–1948; for allowing PLO legitimacy in peace negotiations; and for the government of Israel to halt settlement activities.[86]

[79] Q&A with Yair Hirschfeld (20 July 2018), 2.
[80] Hirschfeld, *Track-Two Diplomacy*, 108; Waage, *Peacemaking Is a Risky Business*, 66.
[81] Hirschfeld, *Track-Two Diplomacy*, 109.
[82] Interview with Jan Egeland (2 September 2017), 5.
[83] Sarpsborg meeting 21 January 1993, Israeli Archives, https://tinyurl.com/4pcwafrw; Beilin, *Touching Peace* (English ed.), 66. See also Hirschfeld's letter to Beilin, Meeting with PLO delegation, 24 January 1993, Israel Archives (Hebrew).
[84] UN Resolution 242, http://unscr.com/en/resolutions/doc/242.
[85] UN Resolution 338, http://unscr.com/en/resolutions/doc/338.
[86] Qurie, *From Oslo to Jerusalem*, 63.

Hirschfeld was aware that these demands were unrealistic, as Rabin would not accept them. However, they did represent intriguing ground on which to attempt to build a durable agreement based on cooperation and development. After the meeting, Beilin asked Hirschfeld to produce a document that might allow the two sides to locate their points of agreement and disagreement, so as to move towards a final paper. The document Hirschfeld prepared had three main sections: a Declaration of Principles; a programme for economic, industrial and agricultural cooperation; and a section designed to act as a framework for the creation of a development plan for the territories. It became apparent that serious gaps existed. The most significant was that of territory. The Israeli clause, as written, read, 'the jurisdiction of the Palestinian Interim Council will cover control over land, as mutually agreed upon',[87] while the Palestinian version stated 'the jurisdiction of the Palestinian Interim Council will cover the Palestinian territories occupied in 1967. Any administrative exception hereto should be discussed during negotiations, stipulated these exceptions should not prejudice UN Security Council Resolutions 242 and 338 and the principles of international law'.[88] The other point of difference was over arbitration, with the Israeli stipulation that arbitration required the agreement of both sides, while the Palestinians stated that even in areas without agreement, the arbitration committee should consist of the sponsors of the Madrid Conference.[89]

Second Meeting

Throughout the initial phase of the talks, which included the second round of talks that commenced on 11 February 1993 in Borregaard, Beilin and Hirschfeld spoke often.[90] Hirschfeld also reported the meeting to Peres and Kurtzer. According to Gil, on 9 February, Peres reported the first meeting to Rabin and received his approval. Peres told Rabin that he received, through Hirschfeld and Pundak, a proposal from Qurie regarding a 'Gaza First' plan, according to which Israel would announce that it would evacuate Gaza within two to three years; a small-scale 'Marshall Plan' would be launched for Gaza; it would be stated that this would not

[87] Hirschfeld, *Track–Two Diplomacy*, 110.
[88] Ibid.
[89] Ibid.
[90] Q&A with Yair Hirschfeld (15 July 2018), 2. See also Hirschfeld's letter to Beilin, 13 February 1993, Israeli Archives, https://tinyurl.com/39p96xw9.

prejudice the continuation of negotiations regarding the West Bank; and a programme of economic cooperation between Israel and Gaza would be implemented, including the establishment of desalination plants, a port, tourism projects and a water carrier. Peres added that it was essential that the plan not become known to the local Palestinians.[91] In a visit to Washington, Rabin made clear to the American peace team that he understood the need to involve the PLO in the process. Rabin said that he 'hated Arafat' but knew that only Arafat could make decisions for the Palestinians.[92]

The informal setting enabled the negotiators to raise new ideas. Beilin encouraged Hirschfeld and Pundak to proceed with the talks, provided them with guidance, and approached Peres only if and when something concrete might arise from the dialogue. Hirschfeld explained that what Beilin offered him at this stage was not direct control, but rather indirect support through the assurance of his political backing and encouraging creative ideas:

> Beilin asked me to prepare a new concept; (he called it; 'frish-mish'); when I prepared the paper he did not change a word; he offered me all along political backing; this included political backing when Peres had thrown me out of the Knesset (early April 1993) – and he took care that I would continue to lead the dialogue in Norway afterwards.[93]

The 'frish-mish' (Yiddish: new-mix, reshuffle) included principles for negotiation and proposals for Israeli-Palestinian cooperation and for a Marshall Plan for the OPT and the region at large.[94] Hirschfeld submitted the frish-mish text in order to identify common ground. The meeting ended with 'I's' and 'P's' (Israeli vs Palestinian points). Beilin asked Hirschfeld to finalise the paper, titled Declaration of Principles (DoP). Points of agreement included a gradual process, over five years, leading to a permanent settlement. Immediately after signing the statement of principles, Israel would transfer a wide range of responsibilities to the Palestinians. A few months later, elections for the Palestinian Assembly would be held. By the end of the second year, Israel would withdraw fully

[91] Interview with Avi Gil (16 January 2025), 8 and his comments on a draft of this chapter; Hirschfeld, *The Israeli–Palestinian Peace Process*, 80. Hirschfeld wrote (email dated 29 May 2024) that Rabin did not believe Hirschfeld and Pundak would achieve anything, but he hoped they might convince the Palestinians to renew the Washington talks.

[92] Discussion with Dan Kurtzer (7 June 2023).

[93] Q&A with Yair Hirschfeld (20 July 2018), 4.

[94] Hirschfeld, *The Israeli-Palestinian Peace Process*, 76–80.

from Gaza, and talks on the permanent settlement would begin. Points of disagreement included the voting rights of the Palestinians of East Jerusalem, the powers of the Palestinian Assembly, and whether external arbitration would be welcomed in case of disagreements between Israel and the Palestinians.[95] While the Palestinians had reservations, they wanted to continue the dialogue. At that stage, it became clear to Beilin that there was something substantive in the making, and that he needed to inform Peres.[96] Beilin gave Peres the paper to read, and 'he read it, and he was quite astonished and he said, "Okay, it's a very problematic paper by the way, but I want to meet with them." Hirschfeld and Pundak came, and that was the first time in which they were exposed to him.'[97]

Peres was eager to show the document to Rabin, as the levels of mistrust and suspicion were so high between them that Peres immediately wanted to 'clear himself of conspiracy'.[98] Neither Peres, Beilin, Hirschfeld nor Pundak knew how Rabin might react to the Oslo channel, and they feared they might be stopped.[99] Indeed, Rabin did not like the informality of Oslo, the absence of experts on substantive matters or the fact that it was started by Peres's people, whom he did not trust.[100] But while Rabin was not excited by the documents presented to him by Peres, he did not halt the process.[101] He expected that the talks would pave the way for the renewal of negotiations in Washington and feed back to the ongoing

95 Beilin, *Touching Peace* (English ed.), 71.

96 Beilin, *Touching Peace* (Hebrew ed.), 87.

97 Interview with Yossi Beilin (13 May 2015), 3. Hirschfeld strongly disagreed with this statement. In his comments (30 June 2023), he wrote: 'I worked with Peres since 1981, and organised for him meetings with the pro-Jordanian Palestinian leadership; I worked closely together with Beilin and Peres during the Baker Initiative of 1989–1990; and again when Rabin became Prime Minister in 1992. I was responsible for working with Faisal and Hanan on the multilaterals; and would organise meetings between Peres, Faisal and Hanan, participate and write the protocol.'

98 Interview with Yossi Beilin (13 May 2015), 5.

99 Barak said that Rabin did not know about Oslo when it started but when Peres and Beilin came to alert him about the Norwegian track, Rabin had already heard of it from Israeli intelligence. Barak said: 'I was the chief of staff at the time, and both myself and my deputy, and the head of intelligence, we all followed it through intelligence material to the last detail. I remember, even, the nickname the Palestinians gave to Hirschfeld and Pundak. They called Pundak "The Mouse", and Hirschfeld "The Bear", because of their appearance, their physical appearance. And we knew everything. But Rabin had a kind of [dismissive] hand movement that meant "This is unimportant". He never thought that it will become the main channel to move forward.' Interview with Ehud Barak (25 May 2022), 4–5.

100 Ibid., 5.

101 Beilin, *Touching Peace* (Hebrew ed.), 89.

discussions.[102] The idea that the talks would flow back into the ongoing Washington negotiations remained Rabin's official position until nearly the end of the Oslo talks for two reasons. Firstly, Rabin, a naturally cautious person, was reluctant to offer the PLO recognition.[103] Secondly, Rabin supported Elyakim Rubinstein, his loyal representative in the official Washington channel. However, as Hirschfeld notes, the Washington negotiations had no chance of success. The Israeli position in Washington was stiff and willingness to make concessions was limited.[104] Hirschfeld explained: 'We were given the protocols of the Washington talks without dates and asked to put them into a coherent timeline; it was impossible. The Palestinian side was not able to make any concessions.'[105] Shlomo Ben-Ami further explained that Rabin was prepared to approve a track that bypassed Washington for two reasons. Firstly, in Washington, the Palestinians demanded sovereignty, Israeli withdrawal from the 1967 borders, settling the refugee problem and other basic claims of the Palestinian people. Rabin felt that he could not contend with this. Somehow, he thought Israel might get a better deal elsewhere. Secondly, Rabin wanted a subcontractor, the PLO, to suppress the Intifada.[106]

Beilin arranged for Peres to meet with Faisal Husseini on 21 and 27 February 1993. During these meetings, Husseini presented a document expressing Arafat's desire for the dialogue to continue.[107] Hirschfeld ensured that the Oslo talks were mentioned in the protocols of those meetings, as he knew they would be sent by Husseini to Tunis.[108] Hirschfeld wanted to reassure Qurie that he was connected to the Israeli leadership and not a mere academic. Meanwhile, the divisions within the Israeli leadership continued to show themselves. Although Rabin could not, at this stage, contemplate the re-admission of Arafat and the PLO to the OPT,[109] Peres ordered Hirschfeld to ask Qurie when the PLO leadership might want to return.[110] This indicates the different positions on the Oslo talks within the Israeli government.

102 Q&A with Yair Hirschfeld (20 July 2018), 2; Interview with Daniel Kurtzer (6 April 2017), 18.
103 Interview with Joel Singer (6 April 2017), 15.
104 Interview with Elyakim Rubinstein (28 May 2013), 3.
105 Q&A with Yair Hirschfeld (20 July 2018), 7.
106 Interview with Shlomo Ben-Ami (26 June 2013), 1.
107 Hirschfeld, *Track-Two Diplomacy*, 111
108 Hirschfeld, *The Israeli-Palestinian Peace Process*, 76–77.
109 Interview with Joel Singer (6 April 2017), 16.
110 Hirschfeld, *Track-Two Diplomacy*, 111

Third Meeting

The third meeting was held in Sarpsborg from 20 to 22 March 1993. Peres instructed Hirschfeld and Pundak not to reveal that he and Rabin had authorised the continuation of the talks. Rød-Larsen, however, told Qurie that the two academics had received backing from Israeli officials.[111] At this meeting, the I's and P's were eliminated and a joint paper was agreed upon. The six-page paper, 'The Principles of an Israeli-Palestinian Understanding', concerned the status of Jerusalem in Palestinian elections, Palestinian economic development and regional economic development.[112] It was agreed that the legislative powers of the Palestinian Assembly (now referred to as the Council) would be decided later and that arbitration would be confined to specific issues and invoked only as a last resort.[113] The Israelis agreed to withdraw from the Gaza Strip within two years. After a transition period, a strong Palestinian police force would take control.[114] The talks remained secret to support the ability of both parties to deny their status in the event of their failure. El-Kurd explained that open negotiations are unproductive. In open negotiations, each negotiating team is addressing its own constituency at home. They want popularity and, in order to gain popularity, they present hardline positions. They do not seek to solve problems during the negotiations.[115]

Yet deniability generated problems of trust between the Israelis and the Palestinians. It was never entirely clear to the Palestinians to whom they were speaking.[116] The ambiguous status of the Israeli participants caused anxiety on the Palestinian side. The Palestinian negotiators knew they were interacting with the Israeli government in some capacity, but to what degree was uncertain. Because of the sensitive nature of the talks, it had become increasingly important that both sides should know that their interlocutors had the backing of their authorities in Tunis and Jerusalem, to ensure a firm base on which to build further progress. Qurie emphasised this point. Still, the Palestinians, though unsure who was behind Hirschfeld and Pundak, wanted to continue the talks, hoping that they would eventually receive official recognition. The situation was extremely

111 Beilin, *Touching Peace* (Hebrew ed.), 90.
112 Summarised report of the third Sarpsborg meeting, Israel Archives, https://tinyurl.com/yfsbwys4; Makovsky, *Making Peace with the PLO*, 31.
113 Beilin, *Touching Peace* (English ed.), 76.
114 Behrendt, *The Secret Israeli-Palestinian Negotiations in Oslo*, 55.
115 Interview with Maher El-Kurd (30 January 2025), 14.
116 Interview with Ahmad Khalidi (5 June 2019), 7.

delicate, as the needs of the Israeli government had to be balanced against the necessity of trust between diplomatic parties.

At the same time, because the Americans were not directly involved, the talks had no mediator. Ghaith al-Omari, a negotiator at later talks between Israel and the Palestinians and the former director of the International Relations Department in the Office of the Palestinian President, thinks the lack of any external mediation by larger countries was a serious flaw:

> [A] superpower has the ability to mobilise all kinds of resources: the economic, diplomatic, security; has the ability to also organise various other players, that's kind of one part, that's the obvious, but another one which is maybe less obvious, it relates to the nature of United States, Israel relations. Not only in the sense that the United States can pressure Israel, because of the number of relations and the number of issues, that they have in common.[117]

Meanwhile, the Norwegian Foreign Ministry acted as a facilitator, providing the facilities in which talks could take place out of public view. They helped with logistics and communication between the parties. Terje Rød-Larsen was the key figure and the driving force behind the arrangements. His wife, Mona Juul, was the liaison between the backchannel and the Ministry of Foreign Affairs.[118] But Qurie and Hirschfeld insisted that the Norwegians were out of the room during the talks.[119]

In April 1993, a significant change took place. Foreign Minister Thorvald Stoltenberg was replaced by his brother-in-law, Johan Jørgen Holst, who was similarly committed to the peace process and who was eager to involve himself directly in the process. Beilin was relieved to hear that the Ministry would be run by a person whom he knew and liked.[120] Holst instructed Egeland and his team to do whatever they could to support the talks.[121] While Egeland, Rød-Larsen, Juul, Marianne Heiberg (an expert researcher on Middle Eastern affairs and the wife of Holst) and the

117 Interview with Ghaith al-Omari (2 September 2014), 3. Hirschfeld begs to differ. In his comments (30 June 2023) he wrote that the opposite is true. A superpower would interfere; the Norwegians were only very superficially informed about the substance of the negotiations, which made it easier to proceed.

118 Hilde Henriksen Waage, 'Proactive Peace Diplomacy: Jan Egeland', in Mona Fixdal (ed.), *Ways Out of War: Peacemakers in the Middle East and Balkans* (London: Palgrave Macmillan, 2012), 91–118.

119 Q&A with Yair Hirschfeld (20 July 2018), 3.

120 Beilin, *Touching Peace* (Hebrew ed.), 94.

121 'The Price of Oslo' (Ep. 2), *Al Jazeera World* (18 September 2013), www.youtube.com/watch?v=TgFWEVQTeHM&ab_channel=AlJazeeraEnglish.

diplomat Geir Pedersen played no role in the talks themselves,[122] Holst's contribution was in helping to clarify the positions of the parties and in intervening at crucial points, not only facilitating, but also interpreting messages from one side to the other.

At this stage, a decision was taken to renew the Washington negotiations. Rabin would oversee the negotiations while allowing Peres to manage the Oslo talks. It was unclear what the outcome of the dialogue would be. The talks were originally intended to serve primarily as 'confidence-building measures', to help facilitate progress in the Washington negotiations. It was generally believed by the Israelis, the Norwegians and the small circle of those aware of the talks within the Israeli government that the Oslo talks would not produce a stand-alone agreement, but rather a document that could feed into and help unclog the diplomatic pipeline in Washington.[123]

This belief was invoked by Rabin, who, because of his suspicious nature and rivalry with Peres, remained sceptical about the talks. Peres feared that Rabin might shut down the backchannel to safeguard the integrity of both the official Washington channel and his control over Israeli diplomacy.[124]

On 13 April 1993, Kurtzer met with Pundak and Hirschfeld. He informed them that the Americans were irritated with Elyakim Rubinstein, the chief Israeli negotiator in Washington. They regarded his negotiating tactics as counterproductive. At the same time, they remained ambivalent about the Sarpsborg negotiations and were unwilling to involve themselves, as they wished to maintain the legitimacy of the Washington talks.[125] However, following a briefing from the two Israelis, Kurtzer suggested that the Sarpsborg talks might be regarded as an alternative proposal to Washington if the gaps could not be bridged directly.[126] Although the Palestinians had already expressed a desire to merge the two talks by obtaining American approval for the document, this was the first indication that the Americans might be amenable to the idea, although they remained reluctant to abandon the Washington talks.

From the second half of April, Peres formed a working group with Beilin, Savir, Gil, Pundak, Hirschfeld and Beilin's assistant Shlomo Gur.

122 Interview with Jan Egeland (2 September 2017), 6.
123 Ibid. See also Ron Pundak, Beilin–Larsen meeting 11 April 1993, Israel Archives, P-5513–7 (Hebrew), https://tinyurl.com/bdf8yen2.
124 Avi Gil, *Shimon Peres* (London: I.B. Tauris, 2021), 80–81.
125 Interview with Daniel Kurtzer (6 April 2017), 11.
126 Hirschfeld, *Track-Two Diplomacy*, 116–117.

According to Hirschfeld, they discussed every move together.[127] Rabin provided detailed leadership from the end of April.[128]

Fourth Meeting

At the fourth round of talks, held at Holmenkollen Park Hotel in Oslo from 30 April to 1 May 1993, while Qurie agreed that the issue of Jerusalem would not be included in the interim self-rule, he demanded that, during the first phase of Israeli redeployment, the Palestinians receive, in addition to Gaza, not only Jericho, but also the King Hussein Bridge leading into Jordan. While adding Jericho to the deal was expected, the Israelis were unwilling to concede control over the King Hussein Bridge.[129] This caused friction between the parties, as such a demand required control over border security and contradicted the concept of autonomy, which only allowed Palestinians internal autonomy. Qurie raised some other interesting ideas that intrigued the Israelis. These included Israeli and Palestinian efforts to educate for peace; mobilising Saudi Arabia to finance projects in Gaza and the West Bank; transference of the PLO leadership to Gaza; and close Israeli-Palestinian security and economic cooperation. Qurie confessed that his dream was 'to establish a Jordanian-Palestinian confederation and a tripartite Israeli-Jordanian-Palestinian economic union'.[130]

The secrecy of the talks within the Israeli government and Peres's fear of being perceived as a conspirator against Rabin once again resulted in problems. Peres had raised the idea of giving the Palestinians Jericho, as well as Gaza, in a dialogue with Egyptian President Mubarak, who had in turn passed the suggestion to the Palestinians. Arafat informed Mubarak on 12 April 1993 that he would accept Peres's proposal.[131] The Palestinians therefore had assumed general Israeli support for extending authority over Jericho during the first phase of Israeli redeployment. However, Peres had failed to relay this to Rabin, Hirschfeld and Pundak. Rabin learned of this idea from the Egyptians.[132] Later, when he expressed displeasure at the demand, Peres reported falsely to Rabin that the idea had originated

[127] Hirschfeld's written comments on a draft of this chapter (30 June 2023).
[128] Hirschfeld, *The Israeli-Palestinian Peace Process*, 94.
[129] Beilin, *Touching Peace* (Hebrew ed.), 98; Behrendt, *The Secret Israeli-Palestinian Negotiations in Oslo*, 56; Qurie, *From Oslo to Jerusalem*, 120.
[130] Beilin, *Touching Peace* (English ed.), 83.
[131] Andrew S. Buchanan, *Peace with Justice* (Houndmills: Palgrave Macmillan, 2000), 102.
[132] Ibid.

with Hirschfeld and Pundak, resulting in Rabin berating the two men.[133] The Palestinians agreed to exclude East Jerusalem from interim self-rule, ambiguously stating that East Jerusalemite Palestinians could participate in elections.[134] This was an example of constructive compromise. The ambiguous statement enabled a solution. While the Palestinians wanted an explicit statement that the Palestinian residents of East Jerusalem would be able to vote in elections and stand as candidates, the Israelis refused the latter demand. The Israeli Labour position since the 1970s, as well as Menachem Begin's autonomy plan, were that East Jerusalemites could vote through absentee voting but not be candidates for elections. This meant that the Palestinians could not claim sovereignty in all places where Palestinians reside and vote. US law, for instance, allows absentee voting, although that does not mean that the United States claims sovereignty in all places where Americans reside and vote through absentee voting. The Israeli opinion prevailed. This compromise was accompanied by a Palestinian threat. In early May, Qurie told Rød-Larsen that the Oslo process would end unless the Israelis upgraded the delegation to include officials.[135] At the same time, per Israeli request, Qurie arranged that Husseini would join the talks in Washington.[136]

Fifth Meeting

The fifth round of talks, during the weekend of 8 May 1993, at the official government guest house near the Royal Palace saw a few developments. The new foreign minister, Holst, was himself involved. Qurie spoke about the need for trust-building steps and asked that Israel allow Palestinian family reunifications and release several prisoners.[137] He continued to press for bringing on board Israeli officials. Qurie told Hirschfeld and Pundak: 'You are nice gentlemen. And what I am hearing from you is very nice, but, you know, I am a representative of the PLO. Who are you guys? And Yossi Beilin is also very nice, but if we are going to progress, you need to deliver something a bit more substantial on *your* side.'[138] Hirschfeld and Pundak also felt that such an upgrade would be

133 Hirschfeld, *Track-Two Diplomacy*, 118.
134 Makovsky, *Making Peace with the PLO*, 42.
135 Ibid., 43.
136 Hirschfeld, *The Israeli-Palestinian Peace Process*, 89–90.
137 Beilin, *Touching Peace* (Hebrew ed.), 99; (English ed.), 84.
138 Interview with Ahmad Khalidi (5 June 2019), 6.

beneficial to the process.[139] Qurie made it clear to the Norwegian facilitators that the talks would cease if they did not include official Israeli representatives, knowing full well that the message would be delivered to Israelis outside the room. Indeed, Rød-Larsen delivered the message to Beilin.[140] Peres understood it was time to press Rabin to go forward. In their weekly meeting, Peres told Rabin that this was crunch time and proposed himself as the lead negotiator. Rabin preferred that a senior administrative official take the role. I assume that Rabin thought it was too early for a senior Israeli politician to be involved in the process, and he feared that his arch-rival, Peres, would become the celebrated hero if the negotiations succeeded. The last thing Rabin wanted was to see Peres getting all the credit. Peres then proposed his close confidante, Uri Savir, the newly appointed director general of the Ministry of Foreign Affairs. Peres admired Savir and trusted him to follow his instructions.[141] Rabin agreed in principle, although, at that stage, Savir was not familiar with the topics on the agenda.[142]

Peres briefed Savir and explained the positions of the Israeli government: no discussion about Jerusalem, no to arbitration and no to adding Jericho to Gaza as Rabin wanted. Insist only on Gaza.[143] Peres's further instructions to Savir were these: procure a Declaration of Principles favourable to Israeli interests, continue the talks and maintain the secrecy of the channel.[144] Savir was also made aware of Rabin's insistence on preserving Israel's security and on having complete control of its borders.[145]

The next chapters analyse Phase II of the Oslo dialogue and draw lessons and conclusions from this extraordinary milestone in diplomacy.

[139] Hirschfeld, *Track-Two Diplomacy*, 121.
[140] Levitan, *Scandinavian Diplomacy and the Israeli-Palestinian Conflict*, 46.
[141] Interview with Avi Gil (16 January 2025), 10.
[142] Beilin, *Touching Peace* (Hebrew ed.), 101.
[143] Uri Savir, *The Process* (New York: Vintage Books/Random House, 1998), 6.
[144] Beilin, *Touching Peace* (English ed.), 87.
[145] Savir, *The Process*, 6.

3

Consolidating the Oslo Accords

Blessed are the peacemakers, for they shall be called children of God.

~ Matthew 5:9

Oslo: Phase II

Sixth Meeting

The arrival of Uri Savir marked a pivotal shift in the Oslo negotiations, transforming them from an informal hybrid of Track I and Track II diplomacy into a fully-fledged Track I process. This transition had significant procedural and political ramifications. The previously flexible and exploratory nature of the talks was now constrained by requirements of official diplomacy: reduced room for improvisation, diminished plausible deniability, and an increased imperative to ensure that any proposals reflected the views and red lines of political leadership. While this elevation to official status granted the negotiators greater authority and the ability to expedite decision-making, it also placed a heavier burden of responsibility on those at the table and intensified the need for discretion. The stakes escalated markedly – any public disclosure could derail the entire process.

In parallel, internal tensions emerged within the Palestinian leadership. Yasser Arafat and Mahmoud Abbas (Abu Mazen) sought to restructure the negotiating team by appointing Yasser Abed Rabbo as its new head, relegating Ahmed Qurie (Abu Ala) to a subordinate role within the delegation. Qurie, however, resisted the move, threatening to hold a press conference to publicly reveal the existence of the secret Oslo channel. Faced with the potential collapse of the clandestine talks, Arafat and Abbas withdrew their proposal, and Qurie retained his leadership position within the Palestinian negotiating team.[1]

[1] Interview with Maher El-Kurd (30 January 2025), 6.

The sixth round of talks, and the first involving Savir, occurred from 21 to 22 May 1993.[2] The Palestine Liberation Organization (PLO) was obviously enthused when they saw Savir. However, Shimon Peres instructed Savir to travel to Oslo without Yitzhak Rabin's green light. Rabin did not know that Savir was there and had not approved his presence.[3] Peres decided to send Savir behind Rabin's back, because he feared Rabin might stall for time and then get cold feet. This was part of Peres's strategy and understanding of Rabin.[4] Peres would push Rabin and present him with facts, in order to move the prime minister to *his* way of thinking.

Savir began the session by giving a speech outlining his goals of secrecy, the continuation of talks, speed and an emphasis on the creation of an overall peace deal, without haggling over smaller details. He emphasised the need to ensure Israeli security and Israeli readiness for economic cooperation with the Palestinians. Savir said 'Israel found itself the occupying power in 1967 and our moral and political goal is to liberate ourselves from that situation'.[5] Qurie responded that he was fully in agreement while outlining his admiration for Israeli infrastructure and stating his hope that the continuing talks would yield an agreement that could allow for the mutual development of both Palestinians and Israelis.[6] Qurie said: 'We can thus open the way for your integration into the region as a nation, and you can in turn open the road to freedom for us as a people', further expressing the Palestinians' desire to create a Marshall Plan for the Middle East.[7] Israel agreed to support the Palestinian motion.[8] Savir emphasised that Palestinian autonomy could not extend to Jerusalem and expressed Israel's objection to third-party arbitration. Savir, who was new to the subjects, was surprised by the degree of Palestinian interest in establishing economic relations with Israel.[9] Recognising Israel's assurances on security, the Palestinians agreed that Gaza would be demilitarised,

[2] Yair Hirschfeld and Ron Pundak, 'Development of the Norwegian Channel' (1 September 1993), Israel Archives, P-6/5513: 3 (Hebrew), https://tinyurl.com/458kd3xw; interviews with Joel Singer (25 March 2022), 4; Uri Savir, *The Process* (New York: Vintage Books/Random House, 1998), 9–10; Yossi Beilin, *Touching Peace* (London: Weidenfeld & Nicolson, 1999), 87.

[3] Avi Gil, *Shimon Peres* (London: I.B. Tauris, 2021), 2.

[4] Interview with Avi Gil (16 January 2025), 19.

[5] Ahmed Qurie, *From Oslo to Jerusalem* (London: I.B. Tauris, 2006), 145.

[6] Mahmoud Abbas, *Through Secret Channels* (London: Garnet Publishing, 1995), 150.

[7] Qurie, *From Oslo to Jerusalem*, 146.

[8] A Guideline for Preparing a 'Marshall Plan' for the West Bank, Gaza Strip and the Region, Israel Archives, P-6/5513.

[9] Savir, *The Process*, 19.

the Palestinian police force would disarm groups that might endanger security, and the Israel Defense Forces (IDF) would redeploy outside Palestinian population centres.[10] The Palestinian police would be the only Palestinian security authority.

Savir's insertion into the talks represented an important turning point, both for the Israeli negotiating team and for the Palestinians. On the Israeli side, Yair Hirschfeld and Ron Pundak no longer took the leading role, though they would continue to be present at the talks. For the Palestinians, Savir's presence and leadership role were the sign they had been seeking, that they were negotiating with the Israeli government in an official capacity.[11] But Savir's presence also created some tensions within the talks. As mentioned, Savir outlined the Israeli conditions: no negotiations about Jerusalem or the return of refugees; no UN involvement or international arbitration; and the continuation of the Washington talks.[12] While Hirschfeld prepared Qurie for Savir's messages, upon hearing them from Savir, Qurie was unable to discern whether Savir would help or hinder the talks.[13] After initial suspicions, Qurie and Savir developed a close working relationship.[14] Terje Rød-Larsen suggested that the two negotiators have a stroll in the woods and establish a rapport between them. They spoke about their families, about Norway and about food. They joked and enjoyed each other company.[15] Qurie was impressed by Savir's statement that he wished to bring to an end the shame of the occupation and to live in peace with Israel's neighbours. Savir said: 'I wish to live in a democratic country that respects others and is respected by them.'[16]

Hirschfeld and Pundak continued to play an important role in the Oslo diplomatic process, largely due to the strong rapport they had cultivated with the Palestinian negotiators. The distinctive structure of the Oslo talks – informal, initially non-governmental and deliberately insulated

10 Uri Savir report 22–5–1993, P-5513–7S, Israel Archives (Hebrew), https://tinyurl.com/4setfwuw; Savir, *The Process*, 13–14, 29–37; David Makovsky, *Making Peace with the PLO: The Rabin Government's Road to the Oslo Accord* (Boulder, CO: Westview, 1996), 48.

11 Abbas, *Through Secret Channels*, 150; Qurie, *From Oslo to Jerusalem*, 144.

12 'The Price of Oslo' (Ep. 2), *Al Jazeera World* (18 September 2013), www.youtube.com/watch?v=TgFWEVQTeHM&ab_channel=AlJazeeraEnglish.

13 Q&A with Yair Hirschfeld (15 July 2018), 3.

14 Discussion with Yair Hirschfeld (29 October 2024); Yair Hirschfeld, *Track-Two Diplomacy toward an Israeli-Palestinian Solution 1978–2014* (Washington, DC: Woodrow Wilson Center Press and Johns Hopkins University Press, 2014), 123; Qurie, *From Oslo to Jerusalem*, 150.

15 Qurie, *From Oslo to Jerusalem*, 150.

16 Ibid.

from official oversight – proved essential to their durability. In a context defined by stark asymmetries in political and military power, these personal relationships functioned as a critical mediating force, helping to balance the inherent structural inequalities between the Israeli and Palestinian sides. The negotiations were sustained by a mutual belief that proposals were being advanced in good faith and that the process could culminate in a formal, written agreement.

Prior to the May 1993 round of negotiations, Yossi Beilin reached out to Joel Singer, a legal expert then based in the United States, summoning him urgently to Jerusalem for consultations on a matter of national significance. At first glance, Singer's selection appeared unconventional: he was a private attorney residing abroad. However, Singer had previously served as Head of the International Law Department of the IDF and had been the principal drafter of Israeli proposals during the post-Camp David autonomy talks in the late 1970s. His legal expertise, military credentials and prior experience in sensitive negotiations rendered him an ideal candidate for involvement. Moreover, Beilin was aware that Prime Minister Rabin knew and trusted Singer – a key consideration, given the delicate nature of the evolving Oslo channel. Upon reviewing the latest draft of the agreement, Singer's response was immediate and unambiguous. He said: 'What's this supposed to be … It's not the draft of an agreement! It's a blob of raw mush!'[17] The agreement was vague and unclear, and there was a discrepancy between what Hirschfeld and Pundak explained the agreement said, and what Singer read in the document. Singer was not sure what was agreed, because the terminology used in the document was so different from the normal language he was used to in international negotiations related to the West Bank and Gaza. Furthermore, important things were missing. The document spoke of economic cooperation and agricultural projects. Important as these might be, Singer felt that an agreement with an enemy should include other, more substantial issues.[18] Singer also objected to the idea of UN trusteeship over Gaza and, instead, proposed full autonomy in the Gaza Strip and partial autonomy in the West Bank.[19] Peres also objected to the trusteeship idea, because he thought this would lead to a two-state solution, something he did not support at that point in time.[20] Singer thought that these negotiations would not lead anywhere.

17 Savir, *The Process*, 27.
18 Interview with Joel Singer (29 August 2014), 3.
19 Yossi Beilin, *Touching Peace* (English ed.), 90.
20 Hirschfeld's comments on a draft of this chapter.

He was confident that he would never see Hirschfeld and Pundak again. At the same time, when he met Peres and was asked to voice his opinion, Singer diplomatically said that talking with the PLO was promising, that that was the right way to go, and that from what he heard about what the PLO representatives said, this was an interesting development. 'Nice job.'[21] When I asked Singer to explain these words, Singer replied: 'When you meet someone and you think he's ugly, you don't say that he's ugly, you say ... You look better now.'[22]

Singer returned to Washington, thinking that the Oslo document was a non-starter 'because it looked like something concocted by academics outside the government, without Rabin's blessing or guidance. And, therefore, it is not going anywhere.'[23] Singer knew Rabin's position regarding the PLO and he discounted the Oslo discussions. Savir prepared a report about his meeting with the PLO people in Oslo, which was delivered to Rabin. On 7 June 1993, Rabin sent Peres a formal, angry letter demanding that the Oslo talks be halted. Rabin might have been displeased about Savir's unauthorised trip to Oslo. He thought the Palestinian demands were too exacting.[24] Rabin wanted the Washington track to proceed and thought that Oslo was disrupting those negotiations. This was a very

[21] Interview with Joel Singer (29 August 2014), 3. See also Singer comments on Palestinian draft and suggestions, 5 June 1993, P-5513–1, Israel Archives (Hebrew), https://tinyurl.com/4cpjdb3e.

[22] Interview with Joel Singer (29 August 2014), 3. In his comments on a draft of this chapter, Hirschfeld wrote that Singer destroyed the two most important components of the agreement: the trusteeship, which would have built a functioning governmental structure and security cooperation; and the commitment to decide together, Israel and the PA, on the further use of the land, in fact freezing the settlements.

[23] Interviews with Joel Singer (25 March–5 April 2022), 8.

[24] 'Subject: Oslo Contacts Following our conversation on this matter on Sunday, 6 June 1993, I wish to reiterate the main points I raised. The so-called "Oslo contacts," in their current form, pose a serious risk to the continuation of peace negotiations based on the framework of the Madrid Conference ... The document you submitted reflects an approach that is unacceptable, both because of what it proposes and what it omits. The underlying premise of the "Declaration of Principles" appears to be: "Transfer the territories and governance authority to us first, and only then will we negotiate on the details." Sections 4 and 5 of the document articulate this position most explicitly. In this context, the other sections of the document are clear, and their proposals are entirely unacceptable and disastrous in nature ... I also regret that the "Ten Points" document was submitted on our behalf without prior consultation with me. Given that our meeting scheduled for today (7 June 1993) did not take place, I see no alternative but to request that all contacts be suspended until the negotiations resume on 15 June 1993, or until further clarification can be reached between us. Sincerely, Yitzhak Rabin.' See also Gil, *Shimon Peres*, 83–84; interview with Gil (16 January 2025), 19.

sensitive period. The Oslo track could have ended then and there. But Peres did not want to give up on Oslo, not without a fight. Although Rabin had reservations, he did not object to the entire content of the report.[25] Peres strove to continue the Oslo channel.

Singer had just returned to Washington when, to his surprise, Peres asked him to fly back to Israel. Singer thinks it was because of the angry letter Peres had received from Rabin.[26] This proved to be an astute move. Singer's involvement delighted Rabin. Rabin had worked with Singer and trusted his legal mind. The trust Rabin placed in Singer was born both from their mutual familiarity and from their similar way of thinking: unlike the other negotiators, Singer's expertise and military background meant that he and Rabin 'thought the same way'.[27]

Singer was asked to provide some written comments on the text. He wrote comments conveying criticism, but in a constructive manner. He wanted to give the process the most positive characterisation possible. As Singer explained, 'in England, teachers never tell students, "Oh, you're an idiot. Go fuck yourself." They tell the parents, "Your child is improving, and he can really do a lot more. He needs to try more but he's really showing improvement ..." So I was positive.'[28]

Subsequently, on 10 June 1993, a crucial meeting took place between Peres, Beilin, Singer and Rabin. Singer was asked for his opinion about the draft document and replied that he found some good and some bad elements in the text.[29] Even though Rabin had told Peres to stop the Oslo channel, he evidently still wanted to know whether an agreement could be reached. Hirschfeld explains that while Rabin did not believe an agreement could be reached in Oslo, he still wanted the meetings to proceed in order to convince Arafat to renew the Washington talks without returning the Hamas deportees from Lebanon.[30] In December 1992, Israel had expelled 415 activists and organisers of Hamas and the smaller terrorist group the Palestinian Islamic Jihad from the West Bank and Gaza Strip to southern Lebanon. Lebanon had refused to admit them formally, so they remained stranded in harsh winter conditions for months, which drew extensive

[25] Savir, *The Process*, 26.
[26] Interview with Joel Singer (25 March 2022), 11.
[27] Interviews with Joel Singer (29 August 2014, 25 March 2022). See also Raphael Cohen-Almagor, 'The Oslo Peace Process: Interview with Joel Singer', *Israel Affairs*, 24(5) (2018): 733–766.
[28] Interview with Joel Singer (29 August 2014), 6.
[29] Interview with Joel Singer (25 March 2022), 5.
[30] Hirschfeld's written comments on a draft of this chapter (30 June 2023).

international criticism and diplomatic pressure. Thus, Rabin asked Singer whether he could fix the document. Singer replied that he would be able to fix the agreement and then Rabin instructed him to do so. Rabin did not, however, provide Singer with any direction as to how to fix the draft. He relied on Singer's knowledge of the Labour Party's official platform, a platform that stressed Israeli security and Palestinian autonomy. Based on this platform, Singer would rework the agreement.

To fix the agreement, Singer felt that he needed to first talk with the PLO representatives directly. Hirschfeld and Pundak told him about certain things the PLO representatives had said, but Singer could not find any evidence of such remarks in the document. Singer wanted to know whether the two academics were presenting what had happened in Oslo correctly. Furthermore, Singer wanted to understand and obtain the other side's positions directly so that, should he subsequently modify the draft agreement, he could limit their objections to crucial matters.[31]

Rabin established the Oslo forum, which consisted of Rabin, Peres, Beilin and Singer. This forum met at least once and sometimes three times every week until the conclusion of the Oslo talks. No one else took part in those secret meetings. Years later, Rabin was criticised for not including senior security advisors in this forum.[32] In the 10 June meeting with Rabin, Singer raised the idea of mutual recognition between Israel and the PLO, something that no Israeli official had dared to raise and discuss until then. At this point, Rabin still did not want to openly recognise the PLO, but he told Singer that he could float the idea in a personal capacity.[33] Rabin's decision to continue the talks, despite the risks associated with meeting with the PLO, was the result of Singer's impact, together with Rabin's understanding that the Washington negotiations remained at a standstill and that time was running out. It was, as Peres acknowledged, crunch time. It is this sense of negotiations occurring under the pressure of time that Itamar Rabinovich identifies as the driving force behind both Rabin's and Arafat's decision to maintain the direct Oslo channel.[34] Additionally, as Shlomo Ben-Ami suggests, the Intifada represented a threat to both Israel and the PLO. By negotiating with the PLO directly, Rabin thought

[31] Interview with Joel Singer (25 March 2022), 11.

[32] Yossi Beilin's written remarks on a draft of this chapter (14 June 2023).

[33] Interview with Joel Singer (29 August 2014), 15. See also Joel Singer, 'The Israel–PLO Mutual Recognition Agreement', *International Negotiation*, 26 (2021): 1–25. In his comments on this chapter, Hirschfeld wrote that floating the idea in 'a personal capacity' was ridiculous. The Palestinian team knew the moment it was said, there was no way back.

[34] Interview with Itamar Rabinovich (21 July 2017), 1.

he could rely on Arafat to crack down on the Intifada in order to uphold his own authority while also supporting the goals of the Israeli security establishment.[35]

Singer's involvement represented a turning point in the talks: a shift from an emphasis on non-legalistic negotiation to one driven by legalistic thinking. As a lawyer, Singer understood how pieces of international agreements should be written. Although Hirschfeld believed that the first draft of the agreement he and Pundak had helped to produce was 'impressive',[36] Singer's view was quite different. Singer saw a document that focused too heavily on economic development while failing to address the key elements of the Labour platform: security and the scope of the Palestinian Authority (PA).[37] However, the situation presented a problem, as Beilin did not want Singer to reject all the work that Hirschfeld and Pundak had done. Singer was, therefore, asked to fix the agreement, rather than rewrite it. This proved to be exceedingly difficult, as, in Singer's own words, 'it's much easier to write a good document from scratch than to correct a bad document'.[38] Although Singer's legalistic approach heavily influenced the structure of the final document, the final version of the agreement was marred as a result of the initial negotiations having been conducted by those outside the sphere of international law, producing what Ghaith al-Omari, a critic of Oslo, calls 'partnerships based on fluff, on warm fuzzy feelings'.[39] Furthermore, the document was equally marred by the Israeli unwillingness to recognise an independent Palestinian state.

Seventh Meeting

At the next negotiating session, on 13–14 June 1993, at Heftye House, a 200-year-old building belonging to the Oslo Municipality, Singer was added to the Israeli delegation. From then on, he was in charge of the negotiations.[40] After introductions by Savir, Singer sought to understand what would be done with the document. His task was to determine whether

35 Interview with Shlomo Ben-Ami (26 June 2013), 1.

36 Hirschfeld, *Track-Two Diplomacy*, 112. In his written comments on a draft of this chapter (30 June 2023), Hirschfeld wrote that the Declaration of Principles was better than the Sarpsborg document of 21 March 1993 on the issue of elections. But the Sarpsborg document was better on the land and water development plan that would limit Israeli settlements, and also on the issue of trusteeship.

37 Interview with Joel Singer (29 August 2014), 14.

38 Ibid., 7.

39 Interview with Ghaith al-Omari (2 September 2014), 52.

40 Hirschfeld's email (29 May 2024); Savir, *The Process*, 32.

he could incorporate the PLO's reported oral commitments into the text of the draft declaration.[41] To this end, Singer asked dozens of questions about the language of the agreement, the organisation of the Palestinian administration, the status of Jerusalem, the status of the Israeli settlements, taxation, Palestinian freedom of movement, coordination between Israel and the PLO, a timeline for implementing the agreement and many other pertinent questions.[42] He couched his detailed and thoughtful questions to secure the prime minister's imperatives to ensure Israel's security and Palestinian autonomy (not sovereignty).[43] Autonomy serves Israeli interests but does little justice to the Palestinians. Still, the latter were desperate to reach some agreement. Although they were being intensely questioned, they engaged with Singer to continue the dialogue.[44] The exchange clarified the legal nature of the envisaged Palestinian institutions, including the Palestinian Assembly, the nature of both Palestinian and Israeli authority in the territories, and extensive points around how to maintain Israeli security, which had been ambiguous in the text.[45] Singer also aired the idea of mutual recognition, although, as agreed with Rabin, he made it clear this was on a personal rather than official basis.[46]

For Qurie, Singer was a mixed blessing. He represented both a further level of involvement by the Israeli leadership, serving to legitimise the previously informal talks, but also a focused interest in security issues, rather than economic cooperation.[47] At this point, it became clear, based on Singer's questioning (Qurie termed this 'interrogation'[48]) of both the

[41] Joel Singer, 'An Oral Agreement Isn't Worth the Paper It's Written On' (12 June 2019), www.joelsinger.org/an-oral-agreement-isnt-worth-the-paper-its-written-on.

[42] Archives of Israel, P-5/5514; Interviews with Joel Singer (29 August 2014, 25 March and 5 April 2022); Abbas, *Through Secret Channels*, 153; Beilin, *Touching Peace* (English ed.), 96; Savir, *The Process*, 32–33. Beilin said forty questions. Savir wrote that the list included 100 questions. Makovsky, *Making Peace with the PLO*, 53, writes that Singer asked no less than 200 questions. According to Hilde Henriksen Waage, *Peacemaking Is a Risky Business: Norway's Role in the Peace Process in the Middle East, 1993–96* (Oslo: International Peace Research Institute PRIO, 2004), 98, the Palestinians recall 300 questions. Yair Hirschfeld, *The Israeli-Palestinian Peace Process* (Cham: Springer, 2024), 90, said that Singer posed about thirty questions and argued that he did so in the May meeting. Singer himself, in my interviews with him, did not remember the exact number.

[43] Qurie, *From Oslo to Jerusalem*, 157.

[44] Interview with Joel Singer (29 August 2014), 11.

[45] Joel Singer, 'Report on the Oslo meeting' (15 June 1993), Israel Archives, P-6/5513 (Hebrew); Abbas, *Through Secret Channels*, 153.

[46] Cohen-Almagor, 'The Oslo Peace Process: Interview with Joel Singer', 751; Abbas, *Through Secret Channels*, 157.

[47] Qurie, *From Oslo to Jerusalem*, 158.

[48] Ibid., 156.

Israeli and Palestinian negotiating teams, that several fundamental points of disagreement in the negotiations remained: the references to full implementation of Security Council Resolutions 242 and 338 in the agreement, the list of subjects which would form the basis of the final status negotiations, the nature of the Israeli redeployment in Gaza and the area surrounding Jericho, the rights of displaced Palestinians and the idea of a Palestinian right of return, and the rights of Palestinians in East Jerusalem to vote and stand as candidates in Palestinian elections. With this information, Singer returned to Israel, where he reported back to Rabin and stated that he believed that agreement on both the Declaration of Principles (DoP) and a separate document, which would later become the Agreed Minutes, detailing the exact implementation of the accords, were achievable and could be aligned with the goals of Israel.[49] The DoP, in the words of Savir, described the transition from occupation to self-rule, from violence to non-violent coexistence, and from a political roadmap to reconciliation.[50] The Agreed Minutes, according to Singer, represented a legal circumvention that would allow for the retention of portions of the original text written by the Palestinians with Pundak and Hirschfeld, since Singer could not completely rewrite the agreement. Those areas of text which were problematic, but which could not be changed, would be elucidated in the Agreed Minutes. The Agreed Minutes are no less important than the main document. Singer explains:

> The Agreed Minutes are both signed by all the parties and published everywhere. It's very legalistic. Essentially, the things I wanted to really change in the agreement, I just put them in the Agreed Minutes, so as not to make too many changes in the already agreed draft Oslo agreement. Yet, I still created a lot of animosity and arguments such as, 'You can't make all of those changes at the last moment. … Because of you, all the effort that we invested will go down the drain …' And I could have attempted making even more drastic changes but I didn't want to cause the discussions to collapse. As a newcomer I had to feel what was going on, to adjust, and look for how I can find the balance between having the cake and eating it. Putting all the important things there, one way or another, and then not causing it to collapse.[51]

At this stage, Singer assessed that elections were less important to the PLO negotiators than the withdrawal of the Israelis from Gaza and Jericho, as this would allow them to establish their legitimacy and give

[49] Singer report-15–6–1993 P-5513–7, Israel Archives, https://tinyurl.com/5c2jazna; Beilin, *Touching Peace* (English ed.), 99.

[50] Savir, *The Process*, 59.

[51] Interview with Joel Singer (29 August 2014), 16.

them a better hand in elections once they were held. Based on this strategic estimation, Singer proposed that the elections be shifted to after the withdrawal.[52] His contribution was acknowledged by the Israeli leadership. Singer became an essential part of the negotiating team and was included in periodic meetings with Peres, Beilin, Savir and Avi Gil, one of Peres's close advisors. By this point, the direction of the Israeli negotiation strategy had become completely officialised, with meetings deciding the finer points of diplomatic action being held at the start of each week.

Rabin directed Singer and the negotiations.[53] He agreed to the newly drafted version of the principles written by Singer. Rabin's thinking that Oslo would feed into the Washington talks did not materialise. The latter remained stalled. Oslo became the central piece. The new draft no longer contained references to the UN trusteeship of Gaza, while withdrawal would precede the elections, with authority being transferred to the PA immediately. Following elections, discussion of the permanent settlement would begin, aligned with the framework that the interim Oslo Accords established.[54]

At this meeting, a new dynamic within the Israeli negotiation team took shape. The different delegates now represented different personalities within the Israeli government, akin to how the Palestinian delegates represented different factions within the PLO: Maher El-Kurd was Arafat's man, Hasan Asfour was a representative of Abbas, while Qurie was Qurie. He was his own person.[55] This stabilised the talks, as the members of Rabin's divided government also felt themselves represented: Peres through Savir, Rabin through Singer, and Beilin through Hirschfeld and Pundak.[56]

Meanwhile, in Washington, the Americans submitted a draft of the DoP that was very ambitious. It proposed giving the Palestinians jurisdiction over land and legislative authority, among other things. Rabin told Warren Christopher that the American draft was unacceptable and that it went too far.[57] Rabin's thinking preferred the Oslo concept, which was based on gradualism. The Oslo Accords drew on the model established by Prime Minister Menachem Begin in 1977. Begin proposed to give self-rule (autonomy) to the Palestinians in the West Bank and the Gaza Strip for a transitional period of five years. The military government would be

52 Beilin, *Touching Peace* (English ed.), 99.
53 Hirschfeld's written comments on a draft of this chapter (30 June 2023).
54 Beilin, *Touching Peace* (English ed.), 100.
55 Interview with Joel Singer (25 March 2022), 16–17.
56 Interview with Joel Singer (25 March 2022), 13.
57 Discussion with Dan Kurtzer (7 June 2023).

abolished, and the Palestinian inhabitants would elect an Administrative Council. Elected Palestinian officials would decide on finance, commerce, education, health, housing, industry, agriculture, religious affairs, social welfare, rehabilitation of refugees, administration of justice, and supervision of local police forces, tourism and transport. The seat of administration would be in Bethlehem. Security would remain under Israeli control.[58] Israelis would be entitled to acquire land and settle in the areas of Judaea, Samaria and the Gaza Strip.[59] Begin's autonomy plan relied on a defined transfer period, and Singer followed this model.[60]

Beilin, meanwhile, favoured the creation of a complete agreement, fearing that an interim agreement would collapse before a final agreement might be reached.[61] Rabin, however, refused. He told Beilin: 'You know, Yossi, you may be right, but if you go for the permanent agreement and fail, it will be very difficult to begin from the interim, but if you go to the interim and fail, you can go another time today.'[62] Singer, in line with Rabin's wishes, produced a document aligned with diplomatic precedent. As Singer understood it, the document, which had a five-year transitional period, was intended to allow time for negotiating a permanent status. Implementation of permanent status was to begin after the transitional period had been concluded. Accordingly, no settlements were to be evacuated, and no border was adjusted during the five-year transitional period.[63]

Eighth Meeting

In mid-June, El-Kurd withdrew from the PLO delegation. Prior to late May 1993, the understanding was that the interim period would be led by representatives of the West Bank and Gaza. The PLO would remain outside. The interim period, which was called the Palestine Interim Self-Governing Authority (PISGA), would consist of one council. There

[58] Interview with Bill Quandt, Washington, DC (11 September 2019); William B. Quandt, 'From Comprehensive Arab–Israeli Peace to a Separate Egyptian-Israeli Agreement: 1977–1979'. Prepared for a conference on Camp David in Oslo, Norway (28 May 2019).

[59] Seth Anziska, *Preventing Palestine: A Political History from Camp David to Oslo* (Princeton, NJ: Princeton University Press, 2018), 98–99.

[60] Interview with Aharon Barak (8 July 2018).

[61] Interviews with Yossi Beilin (13 May 2015), 8. Hiba Husseini (24 December 2024), 25, Shabtai Shavit (interview on 2 July 2018, 7) and Yossi Sarid (interview on 15 May 2015, 8) agree with this analysis.

[62] Interview with Yossi Beilin (13 May 2015), 10.

[63] Interview with Joel Singer (29 August 2014), 26; comments of Singer on a draft of this chapter.

would be no legislative council or cabinet of ministers. All these would come later. The council would consist of thirty-three people, elected from among the people in the West Bank and Gaza. They would manage and administer the transitional period for five years, and the PLO leadership would not be part of this arrangement. The latter would come back to the West Bank and Gaza only if and when a permanent status arrangement was achieved and the two-state solution was realised. Before Savir and Singer joined the negotiations, the objective was not to declare a direct Israel–PLO agreement. El-Kurd wanted to ensure deniability in case the talks failed and, therefore, he objected to the direct inclusion of the PLO in the interim management. He wanted the PLO to monitor the situation. El-Kurd thought the members of the PLO were ill-prepared and unqualified to build the institutions of a civilian government, and that the people in the territories were more qualified to do so. El-Kurd said:

> We knew nothing really on the ground about the West Bank and Gaza. So, it was preferable to let the people from the West Bank and Gaza, according to the original agreement with Uri Savir, be elected to the council, to the PISGA, in terms of the governing council, and let them manage and build the institutions in the interim period.[64]

As his grievances went unanswered, El-Kurd resigned from the PLO delegation.

Savir did not attend the meeting on 27 June 1993.[65] Singer apologised for asking so many questions in the previous meeting and expressed his appreciation of the Palestinian answers.[66] He brought with him a semi-finalised document to show Qurie. The points in the document included demands that the PLO recognise Israel's right to exist, accept UN Resolutions 242 and 338, condemn terrorism, declare all of its Charter articles that conflicted with the peace process null and void, call the Intifada to an end and ask Egypt and other countries to terminate the Arab boycott of Israel.[67] In response, Qurie said these points could be the basis of further negotiations and began asking his own series of questions. The questions included, among many others, Israel's view on Arafat's relocation to Gaza; the future of the Palestinian institutions in East Jerusalem; security arrangements in

[64] Interview with Maher El-Kurd (30 January 2025), 7–10.

[65] Qurie, *From Oslo to Jerusalem*, 165; Savir, *The Process*, 35.

[66] Minutes of a Meeting between Abu Ala, Maher El-Kurd and Hasan Asfour with Yoel Singer, Yair Hirschfeld and Ron Pundak. 28 June 1993, Oslo (Fafo) Israel Archives, P-6/5513: 1; Beilin, *Touching Peace* (English ed.), 102–103.

[67] Qurie, *From Oslo to Jerusalem*, 168.

Gaza and Jericho, including the number of Palestinian police officers stationed in Gaza, joint Israeli-Palestinian patrols and the inclusion of international forces; the status of the Agreed Minutes; the status of Qalandia airport; and whether the settlement process would be halted.[68] This was intended as a thinly veiled reprisal for Singer's grilling in the previous meeting. Qurie wrote: 'This interrogation, I confess, was partially in simple retaliation for the catechism to which Singer had previously subjected us.'[69] Qurie also said they agreed to Singer's idea of mutual recognition.[70] Singer responded that he would need to consult on many of the issues. Some, he said, Rabin surely would not like, for example the idea of an international force.[71] Interestingly, Singer and Qurie agreed that a short and general agreement on principles reached within a limited time would be better than 'quibbling over details which would only delay the start of implementation of the interim settlement'.[72] However, it became clear that further negotiations would be necessary, as many issues remained unresolved. When Qurie asked about Palestinian control of land, Singer responded, 'you will not have exclusive control of all the land. There will be land under your exclusive control; a second category under our conclusive control; and a third, where there will be arrangements for cooperation.'[73]

In a show of good faith, the interval between this and the next round of talks was intentionally kept short to demonstrate to the Palestinian delegation that Israel took the Oslo channel seriously.[74]

Ninth Meeting

The Palestinians replaced Maher El-Kurd with Mohammed Abu Koush, an accountant, lawyer and member of the PLO delegation in Geneva.[75] The talks resumed in early July 1993 in the Norwegian village

[68] Israel Archives, P-6/5513; Beilin, *Touching Peace* (English ed.), 103.

[69] Qurie, *From Oslo to Jerusalem*, 167.

[70] Beilin, *Touching Peace* (English ed.), 103.

[71] Minutes of a Meeting between Abu Ala, Maher El-Kurd and Hasan Asfour with Yoel Singer, Yair Hirschfeld and Ron Pundak. 28 June 1993, Oslo (Fafo), Israel Archives, P-6/5513: 18.

[72] Beilin, *Touching Peace* (English ed.), 103.

[73] Minutes of a Meeting between Abu Ala, Maher El-Kurd and Hasan Asfour with Yoel Singer, Yair Hirschfeld and Ron Pundak. 28 June 1993, Oslo (Fafo) Israel Archives, P-6/5513: 27–28.

[74] Abbas, *Through Secret Channels*, 158.

[75] Dr Mohammed Abu Koush was from the economic department of the PLO. See Qurie, *From Oslo to Jerusalem*, 179; Savir, *The Process*, 45; Yair Hirschfeld and Ron Pundak,

of Grefsheim, a hundred kilometres north of Oslo.[76] Here the Israelis showed a complete document, written by Singer, incorporating the ideas and comments of the Palestinian negotiators. This legal document, the DoP, stated that the envisaged Palestinian autonomy would not include East Jerusalem, the Israeli settlements or IDF military zones, and that Israel would remain in charge of the security aspects. The Palestinians insisted on full jurisdiction in the West Bank and the Gaza Strip, but in the accompanying minutes that were drafted by Singer to cover obscure matters, they agreed to exempt the settlements, Israeli visitors to the Occupied Palestinian Territory (OPT) and IDF bases from Palestinian control. The PLO's functional jurisdiction would cover, in the first instance, education, health, tourism, welfare and taxation.[77] A sticking point was Jerusalem. The parties could not reach any agreement on this issue, as the Palestinians wanted the headquarters of their government to be in Jerusalem, with subsidiary offices in the West Bank and Gaza. They insisted that the final status of Jerusalem should not be decided unilaterally and that both parties would preserve the historic, cultural and religious heritage of the city.[78] The Palestinians also posed a series of questions on settlement activities, which Singer was unable to answer.[79]

The DoP would, once signed, produce an immediate interim agreement, with the assurance of discussions to reach a final settlement. Qurie insisted on equalising the status of Jericho and Gaza, ensuring the voting rights of the Palestinians in East Jerusalem and their right to stand for elections, halting settlement building, and the inclusion of some form of arbitration in the accord.[80] At this meeting, the idea of having two signing ceremonies was proposed, one in Oslo between the delegates and one in Washington with representatives of the Israeli government and the PLO. By doing this, the Oslo agreement could also end the deadlocked talks in Washington.[81]

On 9 July 1993, Shimon Peres had a conversation with Dennis Ross. Although he did not explicitly reference the Oslo channel – presuming

Report of a meeting in Norway, 13 July 1993, Israel Archives, P-5/5514 (Hebrew). According to Waage, Qurie found it impossible to work with El-Kurd. See *Peacemaking Is a Risky Business*, 61. Hirschfeld writes (email 29 May 2024) that Qurie was upset that Maher El-Kurd reported to Arafat behind his back.

76 Hirschfeld and Pundak, 'Development of the Norwegian Channel', 4; Qurie, *From Oslo to Jerusalem*, 179; Abbas, *Through Secret Channels*, 159; Beilin, *Touching Peace* (English ed.), 104.

77 Makovsky, *Making Peace with the PLO*, 55.

78 Qurie, *From Oslo to Jerusalem*, 183–184.

79 Ibid., 186–189.

80 Beilin, *Touching Peace* (English ed.), 104–105; Qurie, *From Oslo to Jerusalem*, 179–189.

81 Beilin, *Touching Peace* (English ed.), 104; Abbas, *Through Secret Channels*, 159.

Ross was already aware of its existence – Peres alluded to a preliminary document under development. He described it as a concise, action-oriented framework, deliberately avoiding entanglement in detailed provisions, yet potentially capable of yielding tangible progress on the ground. Peres sought Ross's assistance in mobilising European support for channelling economic aid to the OPT. When Ross inquired whether the initiative pertained solely to Gaza or also included the West Bank, Peres confirmed that both areas were encompassed. Cautious not to divulge too much, Peres's primary aim was to alert the Americans to ongoing developments, so that they would not be caught off guard should the talks culminate in a formal agreement. His reluctance to share further details stemmed from concerns over potential leaks and a lack of complete trust in the American administration.[82]

Tenth Meeting

The next meeting, on 10–12 July 1993, at the isolated Halvorsbøle Hotel, was opened by Qurie, who read aloud a letter from Arafat.[83] It emphasised the importance for Arafat of both allowing his return to Palestinian territory and the early withdrawal of the IDF from Gaza and Jericho. Arafat also wrote that the Palestinians were fully aware of the sensitivity of the Jerusalem issue, which could not be ignored and should be discussed later.[84] Among his demands was the acknowledgement of the relationship between Palestinian institutions in Jerusalem and the future interim Palestinian council.

Beilin described this meeting as the lowest point of the negotiations.[85] Qurie brought twenty-six amendments to the Grefsheim document, aiming to achieve more Israeli concessions. The Palestinians wanted to enlarge the Jericho area to the Jordan River, with potential implications for Palestinian-Jordanian relations. They demanded voting rights for the Palestinians of East Jerusalem in elections for the Palestinian Assembly,

[82] Gil, *Shimon Peres*, 88–89, 93. In June 1993, the US State Department leaked information about the Israeli-Palestinian negotiations to Agence France Presse, which the Norwegians were able to stymie before it made irreparable waves. See Jan Egeland, *A Billion Lives* (New York: Simon and Schuster, 2008), 174. For Peres, the American opposition to the 1987 London agreement with King Hussein was a traumatic experience.

[83] 'Letter from Arafat to the Israeli team in the Norwegian channel', Israel Archives, P-5/5514 (Hebrew); Letter from Arafat-11–7–1993 P-5514–3, https://tinyurl.com/4647hxyz.

[84] Yair Hirschfeld and Ron Pundak, Report of a meeting in Norway, 13 July 1993: 1, Israel Archives, P–5/5514 (Hebrew).

[85] Beilin, *Touching Peace* (English ed.), 105.

their right to stand for elections, a passage between Gaza and the West Bank, and wider responsibilities for the PA.[86] In accordance with UN Resolution 242, the Palestinians pressed the Israelis to withdraw from 'territories' occupied in 1967, create a mechanism during the interim period for repatriating Palestinian refugees, and consider outside arbitration and an international presence in the OPT.[87] The Israelis voiced fierce objections. Qurie responded, 'we have the right to do what you did to us',[88] meaning the right to present demands as Israel did. The negotiations experienced a crisis, as the Israelis responded by nearly breaking off the talks. Formal negotiations ceased. Instead, private talks were held between the negotiators. The parties departed without setting a date for the next meeting,[89] and the Israelis broke off negotiations. Only Savir continued to speak to Qurie. The latter wrote that when he saw Savir's anger, he felt inner satisfaction, as the Israelis were forced to drink from the same cup they had given the Palestinians to drink from before.[90]

At this junction, Johan Jørgen Holst, Mona Juul and Rød-Larsen met with Arafat in Tunis and stressed to him the importance of not allowing the talks to collapse. They emphasised Israeli concessions that would improve the PLO's position. Arafat was pleased with the possibility of territorial handover preceding elections, as well as the proposed creation of a legislative council, as he felt this would increase his own legitimacy as the leader of the Palestinian cause.[91] Holst pressed Arafat to make concessions; otherwise, the negotiations would collapse. He explained to Arafat that Israel would not grant the PLO control over the crossings, nor grant a corridor between Gaza and Jericho.[92] These were essential security matters that Israeli leaders believed were not open to compromise. Holst and his team then provided Peres and Rabin with a detailed handwritten report of their meeting with Arafat.[93]

[86] Qurie, *From Oslo to Jerusalem*, 196–197; Beilin, *Touching Peace* (English ed.), 105; Savir, *The Process*, 38–39; 'The Price of Oslo' (Ep. 2), *Al Jazeera World*.
[87] Savir, *The Process*, 39.
[88] Makovsky, *Making Peace with the PLO*, 60.
[89] Yair Hirschfeld and Ron Pundak, Report of a meeting in Norway, 13 July 1993: 4. Israel Archives, P-5/5514, P-5513–8 (Hebrew), https://tinyurl.com/3h93w9u2.
[90] Qurie, *From Oslo to Jerusalem*, 197.
[91] Beilin, *Touching Peace* (English ed.), 106. See also Andrew S. Buchanan, *Peace with Justice* (Houndmills: Palgrave Macmillan, 2000), 162–220.
[92] Nir Levitan, *Scandinavian Diplomacy and the Israeli–Palestinian Conflict* (London: Routledge, 2023), 54.
[93] Holst's letter to Peres, 16 July 1993, Israel Archives, P–5/5514, https://tinyurl.com/579j79jb; 'The Price of Oslo' (Ep. 2), *Al Jazeera World*.

On 18 July, Peres hosted a lunch for Rød-Larsen, Juul, Savir, Gil, Beilin, Shlomo Gur, Hirschfeld and Pundak at the Laromme Hotel in Jerusalem. Peres clarified that while there could be no compromise on Jerusalem, it was possible to make concessions regarding Gaza and Jericho.[94] It was here that Peres stated for the first time that he was ready to contemplate Arafat and the PLO transferring from Tunis back to the Occupied Territories, on condition that Arafat would not use the title 'President'.[95] In Peres's mind, 'President' meant a state. So, if Arafat was President, then Israel acknowledged that he presided over a state. This, Peres thought, might have serious implications internally, in Israeli public opinion. In addition, Peres wanted to reserve this point as a card in future negotiations and not concede the title without asking Arafat for some concessions.[96] Peres suggested the term *Ra'is* (رَئِيس), – leader, chairman or head in Arabic. This was a petty issue. Later, Arafat called himself 'President'. But at the time, it was perceived as a serious matter.

Another point of contention was Palestinian security. While there could be Palestinian police in Gaza, their number could not be 10,000, as the Palestinians demanded.[97] Peres said he understood the PLO's financial problems and that he was willing to help them. While Israel did not like the PLO, considering the alternative (Hamas), 'we become romantic'.[98] Peres spoke at length about the prospects of massive economic aid to the Gaza Strip, courtesy of the European Community, the World Bank and other international organisations, and the possibility of transforming Gaza into something like Singapore.[99] Peres asked Rød-Larsen to convey a message to Arafat that, firstly, it was impossible to restart each meeting in the negotiation process from the beginning. Israel was unwilling to make further concessions. It had already done more than it wanted. Secondly, Peres asked Rød-Larsen to clarify Israel's caution about Jerusalem. On this issue, Israel could not afford to be 'poetic'. Thirdly, Israel would assist the Palestinians on economic matters. Fourthly, many people had cautioned Israel not to negotiate with Arafat, that he could not be trusted, that he constantly changed his mind. Therefore, Arafat must create credibility. 'He has very little of this

[94] 'Meeting with Larsen at Laromme Hotel (18 July 1993)': 1, Israel Archives, P–6/5514 (Hebrew), https://tinyurl.com/ym7spsty.
[95] Ibid.; Beilin, *Touching Peace* (English ed.), 107.
[96] Interview with Avi Gil (16 January 2025), 21.
[97] 'Meeting with Larsen at Laromme Hotel (18 July 1993)' (Hebrew), 2.
[98] Ibid.
[99] Ibid., 3; Beilin, *Touching Peace* (English ed.), 107–108.

(credibility).'[100] Fifthly, he (Peres) would be willing to meet with Arafat at a later stage, but not at present, as such a meeting must remain secret. Peres feared that news of such a meeting might be leaked.[101]

Another concern was the American response, once they understood the significance of the Oslo channel. Peres explained to Rød-Larsen that Israel wanted the Americans to receive all the credit, but it was concerned that if they became involved too early, they might manage it poorly, 'just as they ruined the agreement with Hussein'.[102] Therefore, Israel wanted to proceed cautiously. Israel would maintain coordination and keep the Norwegians updated, informing them before the Americans were updated. Israel expected the same from Norway.

On 20 July 2023, Holst, Rød-Larsen and Juul met with Arafat. A day later, on 21 July, Holst sent a strictly confidential letter to Peres, urging him to act for peace, as time was running out. Holst wrote: 'Norway's role is that of facilitator, not mediator. We have no special interests or global considerations compelling us to seek particular solutions.'[103] Holst told Peres of his recent meeting with Arafat, where he told Arafat that terror and continued Intifada could jeopardise the peace process. He added that the PLO should establish structures to ensure accountability and control of arms, that Arafat should not press Israel on the issue of Jerusalem and that a substantial economic package for the PLO was doable. Holst then updated Peres on Arafat's reply. Arafat emphasised that the agreement should include Jericho, that the DoP should include 'something about the religious places' and access to them for Jews, Muslims and Christians, and that the PLO accepted the two-state solution. With the DoP, the PLO was no longer committed to the destruction of Israel. Arafat also referred to his discussions with King Hussein concerning a confederation between Jordan and Palestine, with safe passages and economic relations between Jordan, Jericho and Gaza. Furthermore, Arafat wanted the DoP to say at least 'something vague' about Jerusalem and that Arafat needed his own security forces.[104]

Eleventh Meeting

At the next negotiating session, held on 25–26 July at the Halvorsbøle Hotel, some of the amendments proposed by the Palestinians were

[100] 'Meeting with Larsen at Laromme Hotel (18 July 1993)' (Hebrew), 3.
[101] Ibid., 3–4.
[102] Peres–Larsen discussion on 18 July 1993.
[103] Holst's letter to Peres (21 July 1993), 1. Israel Archives, P–6/5514.
[104] Holst's letter to Peres (21 July 1993), 2–3.

integrated,[105] while Qurie proposed some more changes.[106] Both sides tried to close the gaps.[107] The Palestinians agreed that Palestinians living in East Jerusalem should be allowed 'to participate in elections', as Israel wanted, rather than to vote and be elected, as the Palestinians proposed.[108] The PLO delegation proposed establishing an Israeli-Palestinian joint coordination committee to arrange all security matters in Jericho and Gaza. They said that the PLO would be willing to publicly commit to stopping terror and rescinding the Palestinian Covenant paragraphs on violent struggle.[109] However, many significant sticking points still remained. Contested issues included the full implementation of Security Council Resolutions 242 and 338 'in all their aspects', the dissolution of the Israeli Civil Administration, transfer of Israel's military governance to the Palestinians, redeployment of the IDF, Israel's withdrawal from Gaza and Jericho, the refugee problem, control over the crossing points between Gaza and Egypt and between Jericho and Jordan, location of the council's offices and cessation of terrorist activity by the PLO.[110] The Palestinians wanted to discuss 'now' the status of Jerusalem, the rights of refugees and displaced persons, the settlements, security arrangements on the shared borders, borders' location and Palestinian relationships with neighbouring countries. Israel wanted to discuss these issues at a later stage.[111] The PLO demanded 10,000 Palestinian police officers in Gaza and Jericho, Palestinian control of the border crossings, Israel's withdrawal from Gaza within three months, and that the scope of further IDF redeployment would be subject to negotiation.[112] There was also extensive debate about the nature of the insertion of UN Security Resolutions 242 and 338 into the agreement, intact and undiluted.[113] Tension began to build yet again. The Israeli delegation refused to engage with the new demands. Qurie resigned his position theatrically, and the negotiations ceased. However, after half an hour, Qurie asked to meet

105 Abbas, *Through Secret Channels*, 167–169.

106 Qurie, *From Oslo to Jerusalem*, 211–220; Joel Singer, 'Meeting in Norway on 25–26 July 1993', Israel Archives P6/5514 (Hebrew), 1; Abbas, *Through Secret Channels*, 169–170; Savir, *The Process*, 44.

107 Hirschfeld and Pundak, 'Development of the Norwegian Channel', 4.

108 Singer, 'Meeting in Norway on 25–26 July 1993', 2.

109 Ibid., 4.

110 Abbas, *Through Secret Channels*, 171–173; Singer, 'Meeting in Norway on 25–26 July 1993', 3–4.

111 Ibid., 2.

112 Savir, *The Process*, 44.

113 Singer, 'Meeting in Norway on 25–26 July 1993', 2; Beilin, *Touching Peace* (English ed.), 112.

again. The Israeli delegation then offered a compromise deal in which each side would make some concessions. For instance, Israel agreed that 'the future status of displaced Palestinians who were registered on 4th June 1967 will not be prejudiced because they are unable to participate in the elections process due to practical reasons', and that the negotiations on permanent status 'will lead to the implementation of security council resolutions 242 and 338'.[114] On jurisdiction, 'the two sides view the West Bank and the Gaza Strip as a single territorial unit'.[115] The Israelis wanted Palestinian acceptance of this package deal as a precondition for continuation of the negotiations.[116]

At this point, Holst stepped in and proposed that he might serve as a mediator in some capacity, to prevent deadlock or the collapse of talks.[117] It was decided that the permanent settlement would include Resolutions 242 and 338, but without any specific demands. This was a compromise of no practical significance, as the Palestinians conceded that the phrase 'in all their aspects' would be omitted. The two parties agreed that the Palestinians in East Jerusalem could vote, and that the question of standing as candidates in elections would be decided at a later date.[118]

On 28 July 1993, Peres held a meeting with Beilin, Savir, Singer, Pundak, Gil and Gur. Peres said that there was a need to postpone Arafat's return to Gaza, and that the DoP should not mention the PLO. Interestingly, Peres said that he 'does not mind' a Palestinian state, but now he would not be able to 'pass it', and that 'there is also a problem with the Americans'.[119]

Rabin still had misgivings. He had no wish to recognise the PLO and he did not like the idea of Arafat's return to Gaza. He also did not believe that Arafat would sign an agreement with Israel and was interested in pursuing the possibility of striking a deal with Syria.[120] On 2 August, Rabin told Peres that he favoured pursuing the Syrian path. Ross and Martin Indyk preferred that Israel resolve its long dispute with Syria, and Rabin was attentive to the American wishes.[121] However, Rabin's hopes were dashed two days later, on 4 August, when Warren Christopher met with President

114 Singer, 'Meeting in Norway on 25–26 July 1993', 5.
115 Ibid., 6.
116 Ibid., 5.
117 Beilin, *Touching Peace* (English ed.), 113.
118 Singer's comments on a draft of this chapter.
119 Meeting with Peres, 28 July 1993, P-5513–2, Israel Archives (Hebrew), https://tinyurl.com/yeyc8hhy.
120 Discussion with Dan Kurtzer (7 June 2023).
121 Yossi Beilin's written remarks on a draft of this chapter (14 June 2023).

Hafez al-Assad and delivered a message that the gaps between the two sides, Israel and Syria, were unbridgeable.[122] Once Rabin realised that he had no Syrian option, he was determined to move forward with the Oslo path. Rabin's advisor, Itamar Rabinovich, explained that Rabin felt that Israel must move on in the peace process, on any front, Syria or the PLO: 'That was the fundamental decision he made.'[123] And although Rabin saw the flaws in Oslo and never fully trusted Peres, he authorised the continuation of Oslo.

On 6 August, Hirschfeld and Qurie met in Paris. Qurie softened the Palestinians' demands and bridged some of the gaps, especially regarding the Gaza–Jericho aspect of the agreement.[124] Hirschfeld writes that he negotiated with Qurie throughout the entire night to make 'the Palestinian proposal' acceptable. Flying home the next day, Hirschfeld knew an agreement had been reached.[125]

Subsequently, *the twelfth and final round* of the Oslo negotiations took place on 13–15 August 1993 at Borregaard, where the Oslo process started.[126] Negotiations at this stage were primarily aimed at reconciling the remaining points of contention. The Israeli delegation sought to concentrate on a core set of issues, deliberately postponing resolution of more complex matters, such as the precise dimensions of the Jericho enclave, the coordination of border control and the placement of Palestinian administrative institutions. Israel advocated for Jericho to serve as the de facto Palestinian capital during the interim period, while the Palestinians insisted on their right to determine the location of their governing bodies independently. After outlining the unresolved issues, the delegations turned to the question of mutual recognition; however, this discussion failed to yield substantive progress.[127] The issues of Palestinian aspects of jurisdiction, security and Jerusalem remained sticking points.[128] Singer argues that ten issues remained unresolved.[129]

122 Gil, *Shimon Peres*, 87. On 9 February 1993, in a meeting between Rabin and Peres, Peres told Rabin that Assad insisted on Israeli withdrawal to a border line that is ten metres apart from Lake Kinneret and therefore it was better to focus on the Palestinian issue.

123 Raphael Cohen-Almagor, 'Keys for Peace in the Middle East: Interview with Ambassador Itamar Rabinovich', *Israel Affairs*, 25(4) (2019): 713.

124 Report on Hirschfeld meeting in Paris, August 1993, P–5514–3, Israel Archives (Hebrew); Hirschfeld and Pundak, 'Development of the Norwegian Channel', 4.

125 Hirschfeld's comments on a draft of this chapter.

126 Savir, *The Process*, 52.

127 Abbas, *Through Secret Channels*, 174; Beilin, *Touching Peace* (English ed.), 116.

128 Makovsky, *Making Peace with the PLO*, 70.

129 Joel Singer, 'The Talks that Led to the Oslo Accord Culminated in One Dramatic Night – in Stockholm', *Haaretz* (1 July 2025) (Hebrew).

It was unclear whether the talks would succeed or end in failure.[130] The Palestinians agreed that some of their demands could be postponed. While the Israelis continued to insist that the de facto Palestinian capital would be Jericho, the Palestinians preferred not to acknowledge Jericho as the capital. The parties departed with a sense of a continued crisis.[131] Israel insisted on the PLO's recognition of Israel's right to exist in peace and security, mutual commitment to UN Security Council Resolutions 242 and 338, repeal of the sections in the PLO covenant calling for the destruction of Israel, PLO renouncement of terror and ending the Intifada. Israel also continued to insist that Arafat's official title be 'Chairman' and not 'President'.[132] The problem of Arafat's title was not resolved until 1995, when it was agreed that the title 'Rais' would be chosen.

In order to finalise the agreement, Peres and Holst arranged a meeting in Sweden. There, during the night of 17–18 August 1993, Peres and Singer engaged in a marathon series of phone calls with Arafat and other senior PLO officials, with Holst acting as mediator. Over the course of seven hours and nine phone conversations – generously financed by the Swedish hosts – the contours of the final agreement were negotiated. Key understandings were reached, including the incorporation of UN Security Council Resolution 242, provisions for the regulation of border crossings and international supervision of Palestinian elections. Israel agreed to limit its security role primarily to border control, while Arafat accepted continued Israeli military protection for settlements, settlers and Israelis travelling within the territories. A core Palestinian demand – to establish their administrative authority in Jerusalem – was rejected. However, a compromise was reached: existing Palestinian institutions in East Jerusalem would be permitted to continue operating without interference following the agreement's signing.[133] Israel agreed to allow Palestinians access to Muslim and Christian holy sites in Jerusalem. It also yielded to Palestinian demands on jurisdiction, but the Agreed Minutes stipulated that jurisdiction referred only to the specific enumerated powers of transferred civilian authority. Powers that were not mentioned in the document would be agreed upon later.[134] Matters that had not been resolved were left for the final settlement. During that crucial night, Holst was asked to be the go-between on the

[130] Beilin, *Touching Peace* (Hebrew ed.), 131.
[131] Ibid., 133.
[132] Makovsky, *Making Peace with the PLO*, 64.
[133] Beilin, *Touching Peace* (English ed.), 118.
[134] Makovsky, *Making Peace with the PLO*, 70–71.

outstanding issues.[135] He helped with the drafting of messages, refined them and was instrumental in closing gaps between the parties.[136] Still, Norway had only a few carrots and no sticks to influence Israel. It had more capabilities vis-à-vis the Palestinians, but its limitations vis-à-vis Israel disqualified Norway from serving the full influential role of a mediator.

On 20 August, the Norwegians organised a signing ceremony in the presence of Shimon Peres (see Figures 3.1 and 3.2). Uri Savir and Ahmed Qurie initialled the documents, while Holst added his signature as a witness.[137] Peres continued to grapple with the question of how best to integrate the United States into the process. On 23 August, Peres told Holst that he feared American jealousy. Peres suggested that the agreement be presented in Washington.[138]

All this time, the chief Israeli negotiator to the Washington talks, Elyakim Rubinstein, had no idea of the parallel track. In late August

Figure 3.1 Oslo signing ceremony. Sitting left to right: Qurie, Holst and Savir. Photo: Yair Hirschfeld.

[135] Johan Jorgen Holst, 'Reflections on the Makings of a Tenuous Peace', *Brown Journal of World Affairs*, 1(2) (Spring 1994): 9–10.

[136] Waage, *Peacemaking Is a Risky Business*, 134.

[137] Qurie, *From Oslo to Jerusalem*, 247–254. See Abu Ala Speech on signing, 19 August 1993, Israel Archives, https://tinyurl.com/5dapxrhs.

[138] Avi Gil's comments on a draft of this chapter.

Figure 3.2 From left to right: Savir, Singer and Qurie.
Photo: Joel Singer.

1993, he sensed that there was something in the air.[139] Rubinstein called Rabin, who invited him to a meeting in Jerusalem, where the prime minister told Rubinstein about Oslo. I interviewed Rubinstein twenty years later, in 2013, and felt the extent to which he was deeply hurt. In 2018, I met Rubinstein for another discussion, and this time he told me that when Rabin showed him the Oslo document, 'I probably turned white'.[140] Rubinstein maintained that 'it was very painful for me'.[141] He saw no point in continuing the Washington track and, later on, refused the invitation to attend the signing ceremony at the White House.[142]

On 27 August 1993, Peres, Singer, Holst, Rød-Larsen and Juul flew to Port Mugu military base in California to inform Christopher and Ross that an agreement had been finalised and to present them with its text.[143] Both Peres and Holst were unsure how Christopher would react.[144] Peres explained that while Norway had been very helpful, only the United States 'can sell this

139 Interview with Elyakim Rubinstein (28 May 2013), 3.
140 Interview with Elyakim Rubinstein (10 July 2018), 12.
141 Ibid., 13.
142 Interview with Elyakim Rubinstein (28 May 2013), 3.
143 Interview with Itamar Rabinovich (21 July 2017), 6.
144 Interview with Jan Egeland (2 September 2017), 13.

agreement to the world and mobilise the resources necessary to meet the economic needs of the Palestinians'.[145] To have the United States on board, Peres suggested that the DoP be presented as an American-brokered agreement. The Norwegians were not thrilled with this proposition but understood the benefits of the gesture.[146] Christopher listened and asked to consult with President Bill Clinton. Ross thought it was a historic achievement that should be supported. Christopher agreed.[147] While the United States could not present the Oslo agreement as an American product, it agreed to host the signing ceremony at the White House.[148] Having the agreement signed by state dignitaries in the United States benefited not only the Israelis and Palestinians, who hoped to consolidate various ongoing talks, but also Clinton, for whom the Oslo Accords represented a fantastic opportunity for positive press, despite his having had no direct hand in negotiations.[149]

On Peres's return to Israel, a special government session was held to approve the agreement.[150] On 30 August 1993, the Israeli government approved the Oslo Accords after a long and detailed discussion. Sixteen people voted to approve the Accords, two abstained and no one objected.[151] That same day, Holst convened a news conference, where he disclosed that Israel and the PLO had reached a historic breakthrough.[152] On 4 September, Singer, Savir and Qurie met in Paris, where they negotiated an official recognition agreement between Israel and the PLO. It was agreed that Arafat would write a letter to Rabin confirming Israel's right to exist 'in peace and security' while renouncing terrorism and including several other obligations. Rabin would then respond by recognising the PLO. On 9 September, Arafat asked the PLO steering committee for permission to write the letter.[153] Rabin's decision to recognise the PLO was a significant step towards advancing the hope that this would prevent further terrorism and bring about stability, as well as suppressing Palestinian resistance and taking the responsibility for running portions of the conflict-riven territories out of the hands of the Israelis and handing it to the PLO. Those hopes were dashed soon thereafter.

145 Dennis Ross, *The Missing Peace* (New York: Farrar, Straus and Giroux, 2004), 116.
146 Waage, *Peacemaking Is a Risky Business*, 144.
147 Ibid., 117.
148 Beilin, *Touching Peace* (English ed.), 122.
149 Interview with Daniel Kurtzer (6 April 2017), 17.
150 Beilin, *Touching Peace* (English ed.), 125.
151 Protocol of the Israeli government meeting, 30 August 1993, Israel Archives (Hebrew).
152 Alister Doyle, 'Norway Says It Hosted Secret Israel–PLO Talks', *Reuters* (30 August 1993).
153 Mutual recognition letters, 9 September 1993, A412, https://tinyurl.com/msdnbuxa; Beilin, *Touching Peace* (English ed.), 127.

Figure 3.3 1993 Oslo ceremony with Rabin, Clinton and Arafat at the White House. Credit: The William J. Clinton Presidential Library and Museum/NARA.

On 13 September 1993, after much frantic diplomacy, the leaders of the PLO and the Israeli government flew to Washington and signed the Oslo Accords on the White House lawn, under the watchful eyes of President Clinton (see Figure 3.3).[154]

The final text of the Accords represented a major point of progress in the peace process, but it also had serious flaws. The most prominent of these flaws was the decision not to bar the expansion and continued build-up of Israeli settlements in the text of the agreement.[155] The agreement did not stipulate the end of Israeli occupation and, of course, it did not mention the establishment of a Palestinian state alongside Israel. The two-state solution was not on the cards. Only Palestinian autonomy was. In a speech to the Knesset, Rabin declared:

> We view the permanent solution in the framework of the State of Israel which will include most of the area of the Land of Israel as it was under the rule of the British Mandate, and alongside it a Palestinian entity which

[154] Beilin, *Touching Peace* (English ed.), 129; BBC News, '1993: Rabin and Arafat Shake on Peace Deal', https://tinyurl.com/fec4pr2d.

[155] Interviews with Shlomo Ben-Ami (26 June 2013), 1; Yossi Sarid (15 May 2015), 8; Joel Singer (25 March and 5 April 2022).

> will be a home to most of the Palestinian residents living in the Gaza Strip and the West Bank. We would like this to be an entity which is less than a state, and which will independently run the lives of the Palestinians under its authority. The borders of the State of Israel, during the permanent solution, will be beyond the lines which existed before the Six Day War. We will not return to the 4 June 1967 lines.[156]

The very problematic questions of Jerusalem and the Palestinian refugee problem were postponed until the permanent status negotiations. Article V of the Oslo Agreement says: 'It is understood that these negotiations shall cover remaining issues, including Jerusalem, refugees, settlements, security arrangements, borders, relations and cooperation with other neighbours, and other issues of common interest.'[157] Rabin was unwilling to divide Jerusalem. These issues continued to haunt the peace process. They were postponed until the final settlement agreement, as part of the Israeli strategy of focusing on what can be agreed upon, without making significant compromises or highlighting major potentially divisive issues. Although the agreement offered the Palestinians limited self-government and temporarily improved relations with Israel,[158] these key omissions damaged the agreement and would later contribute to its failure. Oslo, argues Ben-Ami, was 'a standing invitation to each of the sides to take steps to establish the nature of the permanent status agreement in its own way'.[159] Ross agrees, saying that the idea of incremental building of foundations, step by step, was what Oslo was supposed to be. But the 'problem with it was, that each side engaged in behaviours that undercut the basic purposes'.[160] While it was impossible to address all the sticky issues at Oslo (e.g., Jerusalem, Temple Mount/Haram al-Sharif, refugees) because it was too early in the process and achieving everything might entail achieving nothing, the Accords should have addressed the issue of settlements, demanding a full stop to them and taking concrete steps to fight spoilers on both sides. Although the Labour government declared that no new settlements would be established and that existing settlements would not be expanded, the government justified settlement expansion on the grounds of 'natural growth'. The Rabin and Peres government facilitated significant settlement growth – 30 per cent in the West Bank, from

156 Rabin speech to the Knesset (5 October 1995), https://tinyurl.com/5empzx87.
157 Oslo I Agreement – Declaration of Principles on Interim Self-government Arrangements, 13 September 1993, www.un.org/unispal/document/auto-insert-180015/.
158 Interview with Hussein Agha (5 April 2019), 22.
159 Interview with Shlomo Ben-Ami (26 June 2013), 3.
160 Interview with Dennis Ross (27 September 2019), 5.

111,600 settlers in 1993 to 144,500 settlers in 1996.[161] In hindsight, Singer regrets following Rabin's and Peres's orders that made it clear that settlements could be built. He says:

> Even though the Oslo agreement did not prevent Israel from continuing to build settlements in the West Bank and Gaza during the transitional period – for which I take the blame, as someone that included this in the agreement, meaning, leaving Israel's hands free to continue to build settlements. I feel that I need to be blamed for that. I mean, I acted according to Peres' and Rabin's instructions, but I did it – Israel took advantage of this open gate, and *accelerated* the building of new settlements and transferring Israelis into the West Bank and Gaza during this period, in a *rush* to create facts on the ground for when the time comes to negotiate a permanent status agreement. Which, of course, created in the Palestinian eyes, the feeling that, look at what is happening here. They are using, or abusing – and I would say this was not a violation of the agreement, but it was a conduct that I think contributed significantly to the fate of the failure of the Oslo agreement.[162]

The agreement was explicitly framed to delineate the limits of the PA's jurisdiction, excluding any authority over Israel, Jerusalem, Israeli military installations outside Palestinian-populated areas and Israeli settlements. Nevertheless, the Palestinian delegation sought to insert a clause in the DoP that would place some form of restraint on Israeli settlement activity in the West Bank and Gaza Strip. Acknowledging that a complete halt to settlement construction was politically unattainable, they proposed a more moderate provision that would reflect limitations in line with Rabin's previously articulated public stance on settlements – statements made independently of the Oslo framework. Rabin had spoken about prioritising certain settlement blocs, curbing expansion and avoiding the establishment of new settlements. The Palestinians hoped to codify a similar sentiment within the formal agreement.

To assess the viability of this addition, Singer consulted directly with Rabin, who categorically rejected the proposal, insisting that while his policy statements on settlements remained a matter of public record, they would not be formalised within the agreement itself. As a concession, he offered to

161 Sivan Hirsch-Hoefler and Cas Mude, *The Israeli Settler Movement: Assessing and Explaining Social Movement Success* (Cambridge: Cambridge University Press, 2021), 49–50.

162 Interview with Joel Singer (5 April 2022), 30–31; Raphael Cohen-Almagor, 'Thirty Years after the Oslo Peace Accords: Interviews with Joel Singer', *Israel Studies*, 29(2) (2024): 20. Marwan Muasher also emphasised the settlements as a key factor in derailing the peace process. Interview on 25 July 2022, 3.

provide the Palestinians with a separate letter affirming his position, but not as an annexe or integral part of the DoP. Faced with Rabin's firm stance, the Palestinian negotiators ultimately acquiesced and abandoned their attempt to include settlement-related language in the Accords.[163]

As for the Temple Mount/Haram al-Sharif (the Noble Sanctuary), this is the third-holiest site in Islam.[164] Jews also assign the Temple Mount great significance. According to Jewish tradition, it is the site where God gathered the dust to create Adam. Jews also believe that, at this site, Abraham attempted to sacrifice his son Isaac to God. The two holiest places in Judaism, the First and Second Temples, stood on the Temple Mount.[165]

According to Jewish tradition, in 1,000 BCE King Solomon built the First Temple on Mount Moriah in Jerusalem.[166] The Temple was the centre of Jewish life for Jews all over the world. To this day, Jews pray facing the Holy Temple. It was destroyed by King Nebuchadnezzar of the Babylonians in 586 BCE, when he conquered Jerusalem.[167] Jerusalem came under the Persian Empire when the Babylonians were defeated by the Persians in 539 BCE. The Jews were allowed to rebuild their Temple in exactly the same place where the First Temple stood. According to Ezra 6:15, the Second Temple was completed about 516–515 BCE, during the time of the Persian King Darius, though many doubt that it could have been rebuilt in only six years.[168] The Temple was rebuilt numerous times, most significantly by King Herod I (the Great). Work continued on the site for another forty-six years and was completed around 63 CE.[169]

163 Cohen-Almagor, 'Thirty Years after the Oslo Peace Accords: Interviews with Joel Singer', 21.

164 Arif al-Arif, *A Brief Guide to the Dome of the Rock and al-Haram al-Sharif* (Jerusalem: Supreme Awqaf Council, 1965); 'Haram al-Sharif', *Encyclopedia of the Modern Middle East and North Africa, Encyclopedia.com* (25 May 2018), www.encyclopedia.com.

165 Hershel Shanks, *Jerusalem's Temple Mount: From Solomon to the Golden Dome* (London: Continuum International Publishing, 2007). For further discussion, see Alona Nitzan-Shiftan, *Seizing Jerusalem: The Architecture of Unilateral Unification* (Minneapolis: University of Minnesota Press, 2017).

166 In the four hundred and eightieth year after the Israelites came out of Egypt, in the fourth year of Solomon's reign over Israel, he began to build the temple. 1 Kings 6.

167 Kings 2, chapter 25: 'In the fifth month, on the seventh day of the month – which was the nineteenth year of King Nebuchadnezzar, king of Babylon – Nebuzaradan, the captain of the bodyguard, a servant of the king of Babylon, came to Jerusalem. He burned the house of the Lord, the king's house, and all the houses of Jerusalem; every great house he burned down.'

168 Tamara Cohn Eskenazi, 'The Destruction and Reconstruction of the Temple', *Bible Odyssey* (2019), https://tinyurl.com/4fw2y4xw.

169 'Rebuilding the Second Temple', *Bible History*, www.bible-history.com/jewishtemple/jewish_templeherods_temple00000006.htm.

Figure 3.4 The Western Wall.
Photo: Raphael Cohen-Almagor.

A mere seven years later, in 70 CE, the Second Temple was destroyed by the Roman army under the command of Titus, following the Jewish revolt. It was never rebuilt.[170] The only remaining part of the Second Temple is the Western Wall, also called the Wailing Wall (see Figure 3.4). It is the Herodian retaining wall surrounding the Temple Mount.[171] Although for Jews it is the most important and holy place in the world, most *halachic* authorities prohibit Jews from praying on the Temple Mount because they could accidentally defile the site.[172]

The thirty-seven-acre plateau on Mount Moriah holds profound religious significance for Judaism, Islam and Christianity. Today, it encompasses two major Islamic landmarks: the Dome of the Rock, a shrine constructed in the late seventh century, and the Al Aqsa Mosque, one of the holiest sites in Islam (see Figure 3.5). Al-Masjid Al Aqsa holds a revered

170 Lawrence H. Schiffman, 'Second Temple', *Bible Odyssey* (2019), www.bibleodyssey.org/en/places/main-articles/second-temple.
171 'Western Wall', *Encyclopedia Britannica*, www.britannica.com/topic/Western-Wall.
172 Yedidia Z. Stern, 'Should Jews Pray on the Temple Mount Today?', *The Israel Democracy Institute* (10 August 2015), https://en.idi.org.il/articles/3951.

Figure 3.5 The Dome of the Rock.
Photo: Raphael Cohen-Almagor.

place in Islamic tradition as a site of worship for numerous prophets and is considered the second mosque ever built, constructed forty years after Al-Masjid Al-Haram in Mecca. The site's historical trajectory bears certain parallels to that of the Jewish Temples; it has witnessed successive cycles of destruction and reconstruction. While early Islamic sources do not detail a Babylonian destruction of Al Aqsa specifically – an attribution that reflects the broader history of the site – the area was subjected to conquest and rebuilding over the centuries. Its history is marked by religious transformations and shifts in political control, reflecting the complex and layered sacred geography of Jerusalem.[173] The mosque was rebuilt after the Muslims conquered the city of Jerusalem in 637. The caliph 'Umar ibn al-Khattab decided to clean up the area and rebuild the Al Aqsa Mosque. In 690, the caliph 'Abd al-Malik of the Umayyad Dynasty rebuilt and enlarged the Al Aqsa Mosque, providing it with a more stable structure.[174]

[173] Masjid Al Aqsa, www.visitmasjidalaqsa.com/islamic-history-of-al-masjid-al-aqsa/.
[174] Firas Alkhateeb, 'The Al-Aqsa Mosque: Through the Ages', *IslamCity* (20 September 2020), www.islamicity.org/11468/the-al-aqsa-mosque-through-the-ages/.

Al-Masjid Al Aqsa did not hold unique prominence in early Islamic practice until the Prophet Muhammad designated it as the first *qibla* – the direction Muslims faced during prayer – prior to the eventual shift towards the Kaʿbah in Mecca. Its enduring sanctity within Islamic tradition, however, stems most profoundly from its central role in the *Isra*ʾ and *Miʿraj* – the Night Journey and Ascension. According to numerous Hadith sources, the Prophet Muhammad was transported miraculously from the Kaʿbah in Mecca to Al Aqsa Mosque in Jerusalem during the night of *Isra*ʾ. He was awakened by the Angel Jibril (Gabriel) and mounted a celestial steed named al-Buraq, described as a white, winged creature. The journey, which would typically take weeks, was completed in a single night. Upon arriving at the site of Al Aqsa, Muhammad led a congregation of prophets who had preceded him in prayer, symbolically affirming his role within the Abrahamic prophetic tradition. From there, he ascended through the seven heavens (*Miʿraj*), encountering various prophets and ultimately reaching the Divine Presence. This event firmly established Al Aqsa's spiritual and theological significance in Islam, rendering it the third-holiest site after Mecca and Medina.[175] The Quran says: 'Glorified be He [Allah] Who did take His servant for a journey by night from Al Masjid Al Haram to Al Masjid Al Aqsa, whose precincts We did bless, in order that We might show him some of Our Signs. Verily He is the All Hearing, All Seeing.'[176]

The Holy Basin, the geographical zone surrounding and including the historic Old City of Jerusalem, is another sticking point (see Figure 3.6). The Holy Basin contains the majority of sites holy to Islam, Judaism and Christianity. At roughly 1–1.2 square miles, it encompasses the Old City and within it the Temple Mount/Haram al-Sharif, the Wailing Wall, the Church of the Holy Sepulchre, the City of David (called Silwan by the Palestinians), Mount Zion and the nearby Christian cemetery, the Kidron Valley where Jesus prayed before his crucifixion, and the Jewish cemetery and the churches on the western slope of the Mount of Olives.[177]

The Holy Basin is also of great importance for Christians because, according to the Gospel of John, Jesus Christ lashed out against the money

175 Masjid Al Aqsa, www.visitmasjidalaqsa.com/islamic-history-of-al-masjid-al-aqsa/.

176 The Quran, Surah Al Isra, 17:1.

177 Menachem Klein, *The Jerusalem Problem: The Struggle for Permanent Status* (Gainesville: University Press of Florida, 2003); Amnon Ramon (ed.), *The Historic Basin of Jerusalem – Problems and Possible Solutions*, The JIIS Studies Series, No. 408 (Jerusalem: Jerusalem Institute for Israel Studies, 2010); Wendy Pullan and Maximilian Sternberg, 'The Making of Jerusalem's "Holy Basin"', *Planning Perspectives*, 27(2) (April 2012): 225–248.

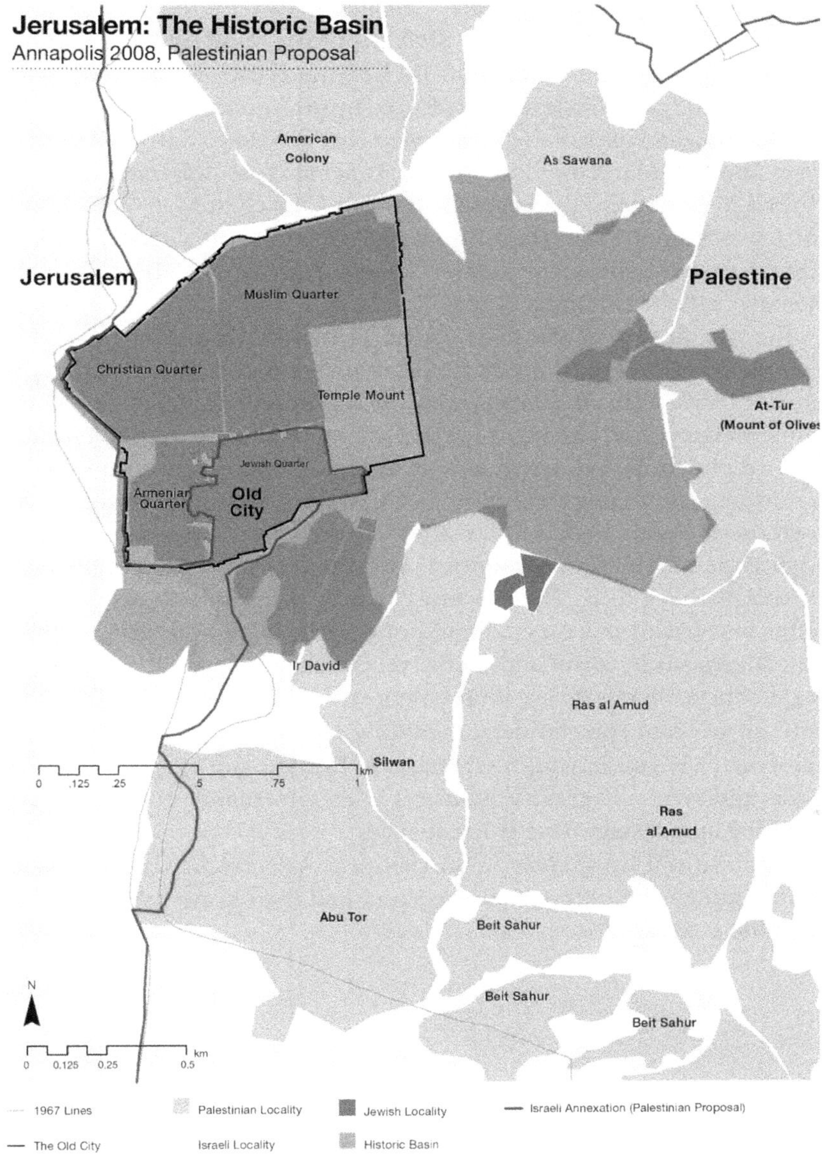

Figure 3.6 The Holy Basin.
Source: Shaul Arieli, www.shaularieli.com/en/maps/color/.

changers on this site and was later crucified a few hundred yards away.[178] In addition to the Church of the Holy Sepulchre, built on the traditional site of Jesus' crucifixion and burial, the Christian holy sites include the Via Dolorosa, the path that Jesus took, forced by the Romans, on the way to his crucifixion; the Tomb of the Virgin Mary, believed to be the burial place of Jesus' mother, Mary; the Church of St Anne, the best-preserved Crusader church in Jerusalem; the beautiful Russian Church of Mary Magdalene; the Church of St Peter; the Church of St Stephen; the Greek Orthodox Church of Viri Galilaei; the Roman Catholic Pater Noster Church; and the Roman Catholic Dominus Flevit Church.

The significance of the Old City of Jerusalem – and particularly the Temple Mount/Haram al-Sharif – cannot be overstated. As the holiest site in Judaism, the location of the Church of the Holy Sepulchre in Christianity and the third-holiest site in Islam, it occupies a unique and deeply contested spiritual and historical space in the Abrahamic traditions. Any viable resolution to the Israeli-Palestinian conflict must treat the site with profound sensitivity and respect, including acknowledging the religious and emotional attachment that Jews, Muslims and Christians have to it. The site must remain accessible to people of all faiths and backgrounds, enabling prayer, reflection and visitation in a manner that is peaceful and inclusive. Crucially, any political arrangement concerning its future must emerge from broad-based consultation with all relevant stakeholders, including religious authorities, political actors and civil society representatives. Given the site's exceptional religious and symbolic gravity, missteps in its governance could have far-reaching and destabilising consequences.

The third and last chapter on the Oslo peace process discusses problems in the implementation of the agreement and then draws important lessons and conclusions.

[178] Joshua Hammer, 'What Is Beneath the Temple Mount?', *Smithsonian Magazine* (April 2011), www.smithsonianmag.com/history/what-is-beneath-the-temple-mount-920764/. See also *Israel Studies Review* 32(1) (Summer 2017), Special Issue: Changing Perspectives on the Temple Mount.

4

Oslo

Implementation, Lessons and Conclusions

If the enemy is inclined towards peace, make peace with them.

~ Al-Anfal: 60.

In 1994, the Nobel Peace Prize was awarded jointly to Yasser Arafat, Yitzhak Rabin and Shimon Peres for their efforts to achieve peace and resolve the Israeli-Palestinian conflict (see Figure 4.1). The Nobel Peace Prize Committee regarded the Oslo Accords as a turning point and 'revolutionary' in the relationship between Israel and the Palestinians.[1] The two parties recognised each other and by that recognition, 'the accords opened up a possible way out of the vicious circle of violence breeding violence, and towards peaceful co-existence'.[2] Furthermore, the Accords led to positive developments on the ground. They 'opened up for a normalization of relations with the entire world', including Arab countries.[3]

Implementation

The Declaration of Principles on Interim Self-Government Arrangements (aka 'Oslo Accords') stipulated that the Palestinian Authority (PA) would assume responsibility for a range of civilian matters, including health, education, social welfare, direct taxation, culture and tourism (see Figure 4.2). The PA would also establish a 'strong police force' to protect Palestinians against internal threats, while Israel would protect against external threats and assume responsibility for the overall security of Israelis.[4]

1 'Award Ceremony Speech', Presentation Speech by Francis Sejersted, Chairman of the Norwegian Nobel Committee, Oslo City Hall, 10 December 1994, www.nobelprize.org/prizes/peace/1994/ceremony-speech/.

2 Ibid.

3 Ibid.

4 Agreement – Declaration of Principles on Interim Self-Government Arrangements (aka 'Oslo Accord'), www.un.org/unispal/document/auto-insert-180015/.

(a)

(b)

Figure 4.1 Nobel Peace Prize certificates of Peres (a), Arafat (b) and Rabin (c). Photos: Raphael Cohen-Almagor.

(c)

Figure 4.1 (cont.)

In October 1993, the United States hosted a donor conference in Washington, DC, that included Sweden, Norway, the European Union, Canada, Japan, Saudi Arabia and the Gulf states. Forty-six countries and international organisations pledged $600 million for the first year to rebuild the Palestinian economy. By late 1998, $4 billion had been given to the cause.[5] Between 1994 and 2017, the United States alone provided the Palestinians with more than $5.2 billion for development in the West Bank and Gaza.[6] Much of these huge sums of money was not spent wisely to meet the targets that the donor governments had set. Inefficient spending and corruption were constant problems.

Also in October 1993, Yair Hirschfeld and Ron Pundak requested that Arafat nominate two Palestinians to work with them on developing a blueprint for a permanent status agreement. In August 1994, they began working with Hussein Agha and Ahmad Khalidi.[7] On 29 April 1994, the Paris Protocol

[5] Edward P. Djerejian, 'War and Peace: The Problems and Prospects of American Diplomacy in the Middle East', *U.S. Department of State Dispatch*, 4(51) (December 1993): 876; Hilde Henriksen Waage, *Peacemaking Is a Risky Business: Norway's Role in the Peace Process in the Middle East, 1993–96* (Oslo: International Peace Research Institute PRIO, 2004), 172.

[6] Congressional Research Service, *U.S. Foreign Aid to the Palestinians* (2018), https://sgp.fas.org/crs/mideast/RS22967.pdf; Dov Lieber, 'How Much Aid Does the US Give Palestinians, and What's It For?', *Times of Israel* (3 January 2018), https://tinyurl.com/yevt4w9y.

[7] Yair Hirschfeld, *The Israeli-Palestinian Peace Process* (Cham: Springer, 2024), 111.

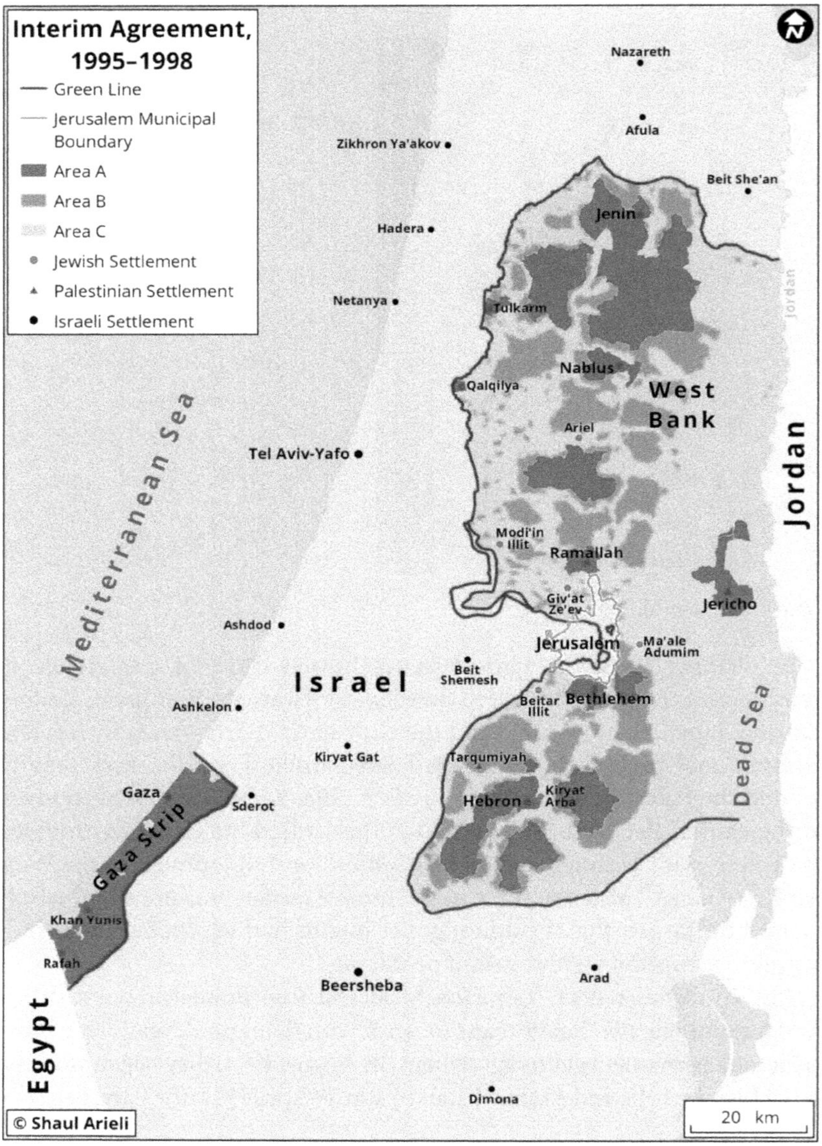

Figure 4.2 Oslo Interim Agreement (1995–1998).
Source: Shaul Arieli, www.shaularieli.com/en/maps/political-arrangements/.

on future economic relations was signed between Israel and the Palestine Liberation Organization (PLO). The Protocol established the interim-period economic relations between the two parties as part of Oslo I, which was signed a few days later. The model established in the Protocol is known as a customs union, the primary characteristic of which is the absence of economic borders between members of the union. The guiding logic was to preserve the economic relations that had existed until then, and to allow the PA to pursue its economic policy and achieve economic growth.[8] The Gaza–Jericho Agreement, known also as the Cairo Agreement, was signed on 4 May 1994, conveying the bulk of the Gaza Strip, 365 square kilometres, and a sixty-five-square-kilometre area encompassing Jericho and its environs to the Palestinians and establishing the independent PA.[9] The Gaza–Jericho Agreement outlined the main areas of PA responsibility. In accordance with the agreement, the Israeli Civil Administration in Gaza and the Jericho area was dissolved, and its powers and responsibilities were transferred to the PA in civilian spheres such as education, nature reserves, housing, social welfare, tourism, postal services, commerce and industry, transportation, health, agriculture, environmental protection and electricity. Personal jurisdiction extended to all persons within the territorial jurisdiction referred to previously, except for Israelis.[10] Palestinian jurisdiction did not include foreign relations, internal security and public order of settlements, the Military Installation Area, Israelis or external security.[11] A Joint Civil Affairs Coordination and Cooperation Committee was established to coordinate between the PA and Israel on civil matters. Other issues to be coordinated were related to infrastructure, questions regarding passage in and to/from the autonomous areas and general contacts between the two sides.[12]

On 25 May 1994, the Israeli army withdrew from Gaza and Jericho. On 1 July 1994, Arafat arrived in Gaza. On 29 August 1994, the Agreement on the Preparatory Transfer of Powers and Responsibilities was signed.[13] This agreement extended Palestinian self-rule. On 26 October 1994, Israel and Jordan signed a peace treaty.[14] Israel's longest border is with Jordan and the

[8] Protocol on Economic Relations between the Government of the State of Israel and the P.L.O., representing the Palestinian people, Paris, 29 April 1994.

[9] Agreement on the Gaza Strip and the Jericho Area, Cairo, 4 May 1994.

[10] Ibid.

[11] Ibid.

[12] Ibid. See C-Span video, https://tinyurl.com/4e88u77b.

[13] Agreement on the Preparatory Transfer of Powers and Responsibilities (29 August 1994), https://tinyurl.com/yc8y92ys.

[14] The Road to the Peace Agreement between Israel and Jordan: September 1993 – November 1994, Israel Archives, https://catalog.archives.gov.il/site/publication/jordan-peace/;

two countries have shared security and economic interests. On 27 August 1995, another agreement setting out the preliminary transfer of authority was signed, covering commerce, employment, industry, gas, fuels, insurance, statistical service, agriculture and local authorities. Israel consented to what became the legitimisation of corruption. When Arafat arrived in Gaza, the immediate concern was to generate income. To accomplish this, Rabin agreed to the establishment of a 'private bank account' and the creation of monopolies on cement, gasoline and other goods. This approach contradicted the promotion of a functioning economy but guaranteed Arafat a monthly income of $20 million. Maher El-Kurd reported this figure in a meeting he had with Hirschfeld in Paris in 1996.[15] In addition, the Palestinian rank and file expected pensions and avoided payment for utilities. Clan interests often prevailed over rational economic considerations. Furthermore, Arafat's control mechanisms and his manipulation of administrative structures fostered a sense of insecurity among his subordinates. His divisive tactics were counterproductive to constructive state-building efforts.[16]

The second Oslo (Oslo II) agreement was signed in Taba on 28 September 1995. This agreement, titled the Israeli-Palestinian Interim Agreement on the West Bank and the Gaza Strip, divided the West Bank, 5,655 km^2, into three areas. Pending a final status accord, the distinct areas were given different statuses, according to their governance and the involvement of the PA. In Area A, the PA had full civil administrative responsibilities, including security, the judicial system, the education system, the municipal governments and the running of other services. Area A is comprised of about 18 per cent of the West Bank and includes eight Palestinian cities and their surrounding areas, including Bethlehem, Jenin, Jericho, Nablus, Qalqilya, Ramallah, Tulkarem and 80 per cent of Hebron. In Area B (22 per cent of the territory), the PA has full civil control, while joint Israeli-Palestinian patrols maintain internal security. This area includes roughly 440 Palestinian villages and their surrounding lands. Consequently, 90 per cent of the Palestinian population became subject to full Palestinian responsibility for about 40 per cent of the West Bank area.[17] Area C makes up 60 per cent of the West

Elyakim Rubinstein, 'For Honour One Has to Work', *Yedioth Ahronoth* (22 October 2024) (Hebrew).

15 I thank Hirschfeld for this information. See also Yair Hirschfeld, 'Meeting with Maher el-Kurd, Paris, January 8, 1996' (8 January 1996), Israel State Archive.

16 Yair Hirschfeld, 'The Oslo Process of Trial and Error Unfolds' (draft paper).

17 The Israeli-Palestinian Interim Agreement (Oslo II), Washington DC (28 September 1995). See also Joel Singer, 'West Bank Areas A, B and C – How Did They Come into Being?',

Bank and includes between 180,000 and 250,000 Palestinians and some 450,000 Israelis.[18] Israel exercises exclusive control of security and civil administrative responsibilities, including planning, construction and law enforcement. The land has largely been allocated to Israeli settlements, military bases and bypass roads.

In the Gaza Strip, the PA had civil and security control over about 70 per cent of the territory, with Israeli military forces controlling the remaining 30 per cent. In 2020, President Donald Trump discussed with Prime Minister Benjamin Netanyahu the annexation of some 30 per cent of Area C, if the latter were to agree to a Palestinian state in Areas A, B and the remainder of Area C.[19]

The division of the West Bank into Areas A, B and C – established under the Oslo II Accord – is disproportionately advantageous to Israel and deeply detrimental to Palestinian interests. Legal scholar Hiba Husseini has argued that the security arrangements embedded in the interim agreement have severely undermined the viability of the West Bank, burdening both Palestinians and Israelis. According to Husseini, these provisions were not the product of good-faith negotiation but were instead imposed unilaterally by Israel to serve its own strategic objectives. Many Palestinians contend that the division into Areas A, B and C was conceived in bad faith, with Area C deliberately reserved for Israeli settlement expansion and the development of a segregated road network. From their perspective, the framework effectively fragmented Palestinian territorial contiguity and obstructed the prospects for statehood. At the same time, Husseini argues that the arrangement has also backfired for Israel by casting it in the role of regional enforcer, obliging it to implement and sustain a complex and costly security regime that exacerbates tensions on both sides.[20]

Israeli military strategist and policy analyst Shlomo Brom agrees. Area C remained in Israeli control in all respects. A situation was created where

International Negotiation, 26 (2021): 1–11; Joel Singer, 'West Bank Areas A, B and C – How Were They Created?', *The Times of Israel* (26 June 2020), https://blogs.timesofisrael.com/west-bank-areas-a-b-and-c-how-were-they-created/.

18 'What Is the Palestinian Authority?', *The Palestinian Center* (16 June 2019), https://gopalestine.org/what-is-the-palestinian-authority/; Joel Singer, 'The Day after in Gaza: This Is How I Proposed to Separate the West Bank to Three Areas', *Haaretz* (28 March 2024) (Hebrew).

19 Noga Kadman, 'As It Is Hers', *B'Tselem* (June 2013) (Hebrew); Lahav Harkov, 'Trump Letter Authorized Israeli Sovereignty in West Bank – Exclusive', *Jerusalem Post* (15 August 2022), https://tinyurl.com/bdzz5t64.

20 Interview with Hiba Husseini (24 December 2024), 21.

Figure 4.3 Rabin and Arafat signing the Israeli-Palestinian Interim Agreement. Photo: Joel Singer.

all the routes in Area C are important to the settlements 'to enable the fabric of their lives'.[21] This is very convenient for the settlers, but it creates an impossible reality. Palestinians who want to go from Nablus to Ramallah have to pass through it, 'like going through the spots of the fur of a leopard and jump from area to area'.[22] The roadblocks create an intolerable reality that might be reasonable for only a very limited time. The situation, however, has been continuing for more than fifty years: 'it's simply an impossible reality that is bad for everyone'.[23] It is also bad because the political right in Israel wants to annex Area C, and most of the Palestinians' agricultural lands are in Area C (see Figure 4.3).

The Oslo II agreement stipulated that a Palestinian Council was to be inaugurated within eighteen months, followed by redeployment by the Israel Defense Forces (IDF) to specified military locations in three gradual phases, each to take place after an interval of six months, and to be completed within eighteen months from the date of the inauguration of the Council. During the redeployment phases, powers and responsibilities

[21] Interview with Shlomo Brom (17 June 2014), 5.
[22] Ibid.
[23] Ibid.

related to territory would be transferred gradually to Palestinian jurisdiction covering the West Bank and the Gaza Strip, except for issues that would be negotiated in the permanent status negotiations.[24] It was understood that at the end of the period, the PA would be in charge of about 75 per cent of the West Bank and Gaza. This would leave Israel in charge of the settlers, and in control of roads leading to and from the settlements and military installations.[25] However, major bones of contention – Jerusalem, refugees and the Temple Mount – were still not addressed.

Implementation of the Oslo Accords was entrusted to army officers. One of the implementers of the agreement, Amos Guiora, said that the implementers found themselves wondering what the drafters intended, as matters were not clarified in the agreement. The drafters of the Oslo agreement did not meet its implementers.[26] Guiora was unsure what the intentions were. For instance, regarding the safe passage between the West Bank and the Gaza Strip, Guiora had to negotiate the agreement from scratch.[27] There were so many issues that had to be addressed. What road system do the Palestinians use? Can they get off the road system? What happens if they have an emergency? Can they work at night? Daytime? What are the restrictions? What is allowed? What is not allowed?[28] Fundamentally, while the Palestinians wanted *free* passage, the Israelis wanted to ensure *safe* passage. It took the Israelis and the Palestinians five years to reach an agreement on this issue alone.

In 1997, Guiora participated in a three-day marathon meeting in Washington, DC, with the Palestinians, during which they hammered out the Safe Passage Agreement. It was hard, taxing, demanding, but successful. It was a breakthrough in the Oslo implementation process. A festive signing ceremony was scheduled for the following week in Jerusalem. At the ceremony, Guiora presented the document to his Palestinian counterpart,

[24] *The Oslo Interim Agreement*, www.mideastweb.org/meosint.htm.

[25] William B. Quandt, 'Israeli-Palestinian Peace Talks', in Tamara Cofman Wittes (ed.), *How Israelis and Palestinians Negotiate* (Washington, DC: US Institute of Peace Press, 2005), 26. See also Nadav Morag, 'Unambiguous Ambiguity: The Opacity of the Oslo Peace Process', *Israel Affairs*, 6(3/4) (2000): 200–220.

[26] Interview with Amos Guiora (10 July 2018), 4–5.

[27] In his comments on a draft of this chapter, Singer wrote: 'The Safe Passages provision of the Oslo Accords (Article X of Annex I of the Interim Agreement) is two page long. Because the parties could not reach agreement on all the aspects of the passage and the leaders wanted to sign the agreement nonetheless, it was agreed to only reduce to writing the agreed principles and continue to negotiate after the signing of the agreement. This was specifically written in the Safe Passage clause (Section 2.a.) Accordingly, it is incorrect that the agreement had to be negotiated "from scratch" rather the negotiations simply continued after the agreement was signed, exactly as the parties agreed.'

[28] Interview with Amos Guiora (10 July 2018), 6–7.

Abdual Rizak Yehiah, with whom he spent three days of negotiations in Washington. To Guiora's complete surprise, Rizak told him: 'I have always known you to be very talented … BUT … I never knew you to be a writer of fiction.'[29] There was a stunned silence. The Israeli delegation walked out of the room. Later, the Israelis learned that when Rizak shared the terms of the agreement with Arafat, the latter objected to the terms. Not for the first time, Arafat had difficulty in accepting a complete agreement that only awaited signatures. He had a tendency to hesitate and raise last-moment reservations, hoping to make further gains beyond those that were agreed upon. After a hiatus, the talks were resumed, and an agreement was ultimately signed. The passage was open for a week or two. Then there was a terror attack, and the safe passage closed and never reopened.

Guiora maintained that the Israelis and the Palestinians came to the implementation meetings with different aims. The Israelis were talking principles; the Palestinians were talking concretely about entry permits. There was a lack of understanding of the other side's agenda.[30] Guiora emphasised the fundamental inequality between the two sides. The Palestinians were still under Israeli occupation and, therefore, in a much weaker position than Israel. He was unsure that the Israeli side fully and consistently internalised this.[31] Guiora concluded that the implementers became responsible for strategic considerations because the architects failed to pay sufficient attention to 'on-the-ground' realities and circumstances. The overwhelming lack of instructions and guidelines meant, in reality, that the implementers became, in many ways, the architects.[32]

Assistance was sought from other parties. Generally, while assistance from third parties is welcome and appreciated, it must be done constructively, paving the road to peace, not blocking it. Norway had been providing financial assistance to the PA in the West Bank and Gaza since the Oslo Agreement was signed in 1993. Since 1999, Norway had held a Representative Office to the Palestinian Authority in Al-Ram, between Jerusalem and Ramallah. This office annually allocated approximately 700 million Norwegian kroner (NOK) for Middle East and Palestinian affairs.[33]

[29] Guiora's written comments on a draft of this chapter (14 June 2023).

[30] Amos N Guiora, 'Negotiating Implementation of a Peace Agreement: Lessons Learned from Five Years at the Negotiating Table', *Cardozo Journal of Conflict Resolution*, 11 (2010): 419.

[31] Ibid., 430.

[32] Ibid., 436; Interview with Amos Guiora (10 July 2018).

[33] 'Bilateral Relations', *Norway in Palestine* (28 February 2017), www.norway.no/en/palestine/norway-palestine/bilateral-relations/.

Endorsing a two-state solution, the money was geared to Palestinian state-building, to help establish the necessary institutions for a viable Palestinian state. The plan was comprehensive and assistance was provided to the major Palestinian ministries. The goals were to improve the education and health systems; to support private sector development, agriculture and renewable energy; and to provide humanitarian aid.[34] These are noble aims, and these large sums of money surely made a positive impact on the lives of Palestinians in the West Bank and the Gaza Strip. Yet repeated concerns were voiced about how the money was spent, where it went and what impact it had. For instance, regarding education, the money was aimed at supporting school building, teacher training and provision of schoolbooks. USAID also sponsored this project. Yet Israel protested time and again that the Palestinian curricula incited hate and violence against Jews.[35] It is counter-peace to sponsor incitement to violence and antisemitic diatribes. In his comments on a draft of this chapter, Hirschfeld wrote that Pundak went to see the Palestinian Director General of the Ministry of Education and suggested to him person-to-person (P2P) cooperation on education; the answer Pundak received was: 'I have one million pupils in the schools. They all hate Israel, so I cannot support any joint P2P activities.'[36]

The United States and Norway also supported the United Nations Relief and Works Agency for Palestine Refugees in the Near East (UNRWA).[37] Israeli critics argue that the money sponsored Hamas terror. Former Head of Mossad Shabtai Shavit estimated that the United States has donated $16 billion to UNRWA. The United States paid 25 per cent of UNRWA's annual budget and the rest of the world the remaining 75 per cent. The United States defines Hamas as a terrorist organisation and Shavit argued that UNRWA is Hamas.[38] In 2018, the UNRWA board in the Gaza Strip had

[34] 'Development Policy and Humanitarian Efforts', *Norway in Palestine* (n.d.), www.norway.no/en/palestine/.

[35] Itamar Eichner, 'European Condemnation of Textbooks – and Criticism of Palestinian Education Minister: "Absolute Scandal"', *Ynet* (6 May 2022) (Hebrew), www.ynet.co.il/news/article/sy6dtczuc; Itamar Eichner, 'Suicide Bombers in Calculus, Stone Throwing in Physics: More Radicalization in Palestinian Textbooks', *Ynet* (12 April 2022) (Hebrew), www.ynet.co.il/news/article/bjtm2wznc#autoplay; Guest contributor, 'For First Time, EU Senior Official Publicly States that Palestinian Textbooks Are "Deeply Problematic", Ahead of EU Parliament Meeting to Discuss Freezing Funds', *Eureporter* (10 September 2021), https://palvision.net/gen/eupalcc.html; Lahav Harkov and Tobias Siegal, 'EU Study Finds Incitement in Palestinian Textbooks, Kept from Public', *Jerusalem Post* (9 June 2021), https://tinyurl.com/f239v5dt.

[36] Discussion with Hirschfeld (7 April 2025).

[37] UNRWA, www.unrwa.org/.

[38] Interview with Shabtai Shavit (2 July 2018), 21–22. Shavit suggests closing UNRWA and transferring its budgets to another UN organisation, the United Nations High

some thirty members, of whom 95 per cent were recognised Hamas members. Furthermore, UNRWA perpetuated the Palestinian refugee problem.[39] In the wake of the 7 October 2023 Hamas terror attack on Israel, Israel cut all ties with UNRWA, due to its links to terror organisations. In 2025, shortly after he was elected to a second presidential term, Trump signed an executive order that prohibited future funding to UNRWA.[40]

The Accords permitted Palestine Liberation Army cadres to arrive in Gaza and to form the embryo of a new police force; however, there was little thinking on practical issues, such as where they were to live, and who would pay their salaries and subsistence. Sir Richard Dalton was the British Consul in Jerusalem from 1993–1997. He said that there were absolutely no arrangements made by the Israelis and the Palestinians or by the United Nations to do this. In 1994, he was heavily engaged in filling a huge gap in the Oslo practical arrangements, which no one had thought about in the run-up to the signature. Dalton cobbled together a last-minute arrangement under which British aid money was provided to meet the salaries of the PA. The United Kingdom had set up and paid for a supervisory organisation to channel payments to the cadres whom Israeli authorities had processed for entry into Gaza and the West Bank. Sacks of money were distributed with the knowledge of the Israelis.[41]

To assist in the Accords' implementation, the UK also administered a programme to provide the Palestinian police with vehicles. The police were supposed to keep order. Order was an Israeli prerequisite for political progress in the peace process, but there was no funding and no provision for this emerging police force to be able to move around. All they had were their guns. The

Commissioner for Refugees (UNHCR). UNHCR is mandated by the United Nations General Assembly to seek international protection and permanent solutions for refugees. It also has the responsibility to supervise the implementation of the 1951 Convention relating to the Status of Refugees by States Parties. Since its inception, UNHCR has solved problems of millions of refugees around the world in many global conflicts. Shavit says that if his recommendation were to be accepted, within two or three years those of the Palestinian refugees who will be recognised as refugees, according to the criteria of the UNHCR, would be dealt with by this organisation. See UNHCR, www.unhcr.org/uk/.

[39] In his comments on a draft of this chapter, Hirschfeld wrote that the UNRWA people planned to hand over the entire organisation to the PA. In 2005 John Ging was nominated as Director General of UNRWA with the task to dissolve it. Then, the 2006 elections and the 2007 Hamas putsch caused UNRWA to reverse the decision. Hamas promised that Ging would leave Gaza in a coffin and launched three assassination attempts against him. Fortunately he survived, but he was replaced. His successors became tools of Hamas's rule.

[40] Executive Order, The White House (4 February 2025), https://tinyurl.com/mr3fuc75.

[41] Interview with Sir Richard Dalton (22 July 2015), 6.

UK, through the Consulate-General in Jerusalem, helped provide them with uniforms, some rudimentary riot control training and equipment.[42]

These problems were exploited by Hamas and the Islamic Jihad. Security problems had further shaken the trust between the PA and the Palestinian people, as well as the fragile trust between Israel and the Palestinians. They especially paved the way for Hamas to enter the scene violently.[43] Arafat resisted Israeli pressures to restrain Hamas and the Islamic Jihad and to restrict, if not destroy, the infrastructure established by these terrorist organisations. The failure to do so put into question the basic underpinnings of the Oslo Accords.[44] Arafat did not wish to be perceived as an Israeli collaborator and thought that he could maintain the duality of the olive branch and the gun simultaneously.

Joel Singer knew how important security was for Rabin. Therefore, this issue was reiterated in the Oslo documents. The 1993 Mutual Recognition Agreement said: 'Accordingly, the PLO renounces the use of terrorism and other acts of violence and will assume responsibility over all PLO elements and personnel in order to assure their compliance, prevent violations and discipline violators.'[45] Article XVIII of the 1994 Gaza–Jericho Agreement, Prevention of Hostile Acts, stated: 'Both sides shall take all measures necessary in order to prevent acts of terrorism, crime and hostilities directed against each other, against individuals falling under the other's authority and against their property, and shall take legal measures against offenders.'[46] It maintained that 'the Palestinian side shall take all measures necessary to prevent such hostile acts directed against the Settlements, the infrastructure serving them and the Military Installation Area, and the Israeli side shall take all measures necessary to prevent such hostile acts emanating from the Settlements and directed against Palestinians'.[47] Article XV, Prevention of Hostile Acts, of the Interim Agreement on the West Bank and Gaza (1995) reiterated the same words. Annex I of the Interim Agreement contained seventy pages of provisions regarding the fight against terrorism.[48]

42 Ibid.

43 Interview with Shlomo Brom (17 June 2014).

44 Israeli Ministry of Foreign Affairs, 'Israel Government White Paper Regarding Palestinian Non-Compliance with Their Commitments and Agreements', *Israel Government White Paper* (20 November 2000).

45 PLO Chairman Yasser Arafat to Israeli Prime Minister Yitzhak Rabin, https://tinyurl.com/2subhjj3.

46 Agreement on the Gaza Strip and the Jericho Area, Cairo, 4 May 1994.

47 Ibid.

48 The Israeli-Palestinian Interim Agreement on the West Bank and Gaza, Annex I, Protocol Concerning Redeployment and Security Arrangements, www.gov.il/en/pages/the-israeli-palestinian-interim-agreement-annex-i.

Yet despite all these agreements, Hamas and the Islamic Jihad inflicted horrendous terror attacks on Israel, one after the other, and the PA, for significant periods of time, did not do what was required to foil them.

Thus, for the Israeli public, the situation was anything but peaceful. A long string of suicide attacks in the heart of Israel's cities, on buses, in bus stations, restaurants, coffee shops and malls, tormented the nation. This agonising wave of terrorism led to deep distrust of the Palestinian partner, internal rivalries within Israel and further radicalisation.[49] Uri Savir argues that the biggest flaw of the Oslo process was the leaders' failure to build public support. The drama of the agreement was insufficient to move both societies towards reconciliation.[50] The spoilers who were opposed to the process created much more drama by staging massive terror attacks. Rabin responded by enforcing closures on the Occupied Palestinian Territory (OPT). The number of days with complete border closure increased from seventeen in 1993 to sixty-one in 1994, seventy-three in 1995 and eighty-two in 1996. Despite the massive economic aid that the PLO received from third parties, the Palestinian economy continued to decline.[51]

Oslo was intended to move the parties to a new path, during which trust would be built. However, witnessing a significant rise in the level of violence against them, the Israelis began to question whether the process was worth so high a price. The PA did not set a monopoly on weapons as its absolute priority. At the same time, the Palestinians, who were led to understand that Israel was willing to concede the West Bank and Gaza and allow them to establish a Palestinian state in both territories, could not understand why Israel was continuously building settlements – if the idea was to give the territory to the Palestinians. They thought Israel had misled them and that its leaders did not really intend to transfer the land to them. As a senior Palestinian said,

> we were ready to compromise and to suffice with 24% of our dream. It is not just our dream. We genuinely believe that it is ours. And we agreed to take only 24%, 25%. And what happened afterwards? From that 24%, you keep on grabbing more and more lands. So, from the very outset, you were not really intending to make peace. You cheated us.[52]

Terrorism and settlement building eroded trust and peace. Disappointed and frustrated, both sides lacked the necessary commitment to abide by the

[49] Raphael Cohen-Almagor, 'The Failed Peace Process in the Middle East 1993–2011', *Israel Affairs*, 18(4) (October 2012): 563–576.

[50] Uri Savir, 'Oslo: Twenty Years After', *Negotiation Journal* (January 2014): 120.

[51] Waage, *Peacemaking Is a Risky Business*, 196.

[52] Interview with Avi Gil (16 January 2025), 15.

terms of the agreement. In the absence of effective arrangements to ensure compliance with the agreement, transgressions became commonplace.

Thus the Oslo process, which started with great hopes and promise, was failing as a vicious cycle of problems hampered its success; corruption and internal rivalries among the Palestinian people, as well, brought about a radicalisation that spurred terrorism.[53] For Hamas, Oslo was both a threat and an opportunity. It was a threat because if Oslo came to fruition, producing peace and a two-state solution, it would negate the very reason for Hamas's existence. But if Oslo failed, its main domestic opponents, Fatah and the PLO, would be completely discredited.[54] Therefore, Hamas sought to derail the peace process. The Israeli public did not think the PLO could stop the terror; the majority thought the government would do better to reinforce security than continue with the peace process.[55]

Ehud Yaari has devoted much of his life to following and scrutinising the Palestinians, specifically Yasser Arafat. Yaari speaks of cooperation between Arafat and Hamas. He argues that Arafat had never considered a long-term compromise, giving up the right of return or divorcing from the 'Armed Struggle'. For him, Oslo was no more than an armistice for a limited period. By 1995, he signalled to Hamas that they could carry out suicide bombings. Arafat's security agencies did not attempt to crush the terrorist attacks. Instead, they arrested suspects and then quickly released them in what came to be known as the revolving door policy.[56] Peace activist Mohammed Dajani similarly writes that Arafat was a disrupter of peace rather than a peacemaker.[57] Arafat, thinking he could extract more compromises from Israel by unleashing violence, remained in 'resistance' mode.

Between 1993 and 2000, thirty-seven suicide bombers blew themselves up in Israel. Although most were identified as members of Hamas, a few were identified as members of a smaller terrorist organisation, Islamic Jihad.[58] From the signing of the Declaration of Principles between Israel

[53] Asher Susser, *The Rise of Hamas in Palestine* (Waltham, MA: Brandeis University Press, 2010); Zinaida Miller, 'Perils of Parity: Palestine's Permanent Transition', *Cornell International Law Journal*, 47 (2014): 331–415.

[54] Interview with Ghaith al-Omari (2 September 2014).

[55] Waage, *Peacemaking Is a Risky Business*, 201.

[56] Ehud Yaari, 'Oslo at 30 – A Personal Perspective', *Fikra Forum* (5 September 2023), https://tinyurl.com/39edbayb.

[57] Mohammed Dajani, 'The Oslo Accords Held Promise; Extremists Derailed Them', *Fikra Forum* (1 September 2023), https://tinyurl.com/3zmrhc28.

[58] Revital Sela-Shayovitz, 'Suicide Bombers in Israel: Their Motives, Characteristics, and Prior Activity in Terrorist Organizations', *International Journal of Conflict and Violence*, 1(2) (2007): 162.

and the PLO on 13 September 1993 to the outbreak of the Second Intifada in September 2000, 269 civilians and soldiers were killed in terrorist attacks in Israel.[59] However, Rabin and Peres were determined to continue with the peace process, striving for peace as if there was no terror, and fighting terror as if there was no peace process.[60] This paradox was doable only in words. In reality, one process came at the expense of the other. Rabin's formula made it possible for Arafat to maintain his olive leaf-and-sword tactics. While Israeli leaders were determined to follow the road to peace, they lost the support of the Israeli public along the way.[61] Great leaders raise their society to their vision.[62] Rabin and Peres failed to do so. Some of those who opposed the Oslo process were as determined as they – to put a stop to the process. Israel had its own violent spoilers. Spoilers derailed the peace process and the vision of a peaceful horizon was tainted with blood.

The Oslo process was dealt a tragic blow by Rabin's assassination on 4 November 1995. With his security credentials and leadership vision, Rabin might have been able to see the process through. Although he did not initiate Oslo, did not like the fact that Peres led the process and did not trust the people involved, with the exception of Singer, Rabin made the Oslo process happen. After Peres was installed as prime minister, he made a drastic mistake by not holding immediate elections. The Americans were of two minds. Some pressed him not to call early elections, because they wanted him to engage quickly with Syria and strike a peace deal with President Hafez al-Assad; others (me included) argued that he should call elections immediately to receive a mandate to govern.[63] The longer Peres waited, the less popular he became. When he finally opted for elections six months later, on 29 May 1996, the gap between him and Likud leader Benjamin Netanyahu had closed. The sympathy that Peres enjoyed as a result of Rabin's assassination had waned. Unremitting Palestinian terror drove the Israeli electorate to vote for a new leader, whose new vision went against the Oslo spirit.

[59] Israeli Ministry of Foreign Affairs, 'Fatal Terrorist Attacks in Israel (Sept 1993–1999)', 24 September 2000, https://tinyurl.com/3pk58yj5.

[60] David Makovsky, *Making Peace with The PLO: The Rabin Government's Road to The Oslo Accord* (Boulder, CO: Westview, 1996), 87.

[61] Raphael Cohen-Almagor, 'Call Terror by Name', *Yedioth Ahronoth* (6 March 1996) (Hebrew); Karin Aggestam, *Reframing and Resolving Conflict* (Lund: Lund Political Studies 108, 1999), 167.

[62] Henry Kissinger, *Leadership: Six Studies in World Strategy* (Milton Keynes: Allen Lane, 2022), xxv.

[63] Dror Moreh's interview with Martin Indyk, *The Human Factor* (2019), chapter 3; discussion with Dan Kurtzer (7 June 2023).

Netanyahu won the elections by a margin of less than 1 per cent. He opposed the Oslo peace process and had little interest, if any, in pursuing the five-year interim plan.[64] Instead of a confidence-building process, there was a confidence-eroding process. Both sides were hesitant about committing to an incremental process. The Likud government believed that Arafat was pursuing a non-committal salami tactic, and that Israel was giving more and more assets to the Palestinians without knowing what the end would be.[65]

Netanyahu's government was installed on 18 June 1996. Unlike under Rabin and Peres, peace was no longer the priority. Netanyahu made security the only priority; he procrastinated and delayed the peace process to the best of his abilities. He wanted to negotiate, but he did not want an agreement.[66] His strategy moved from conflict resolution to conflict management. The conflict was defined in terms of a zero-sum game, where gains on one side entailed losses on the other, and damage control tactics were adopted. Netanyahu had no intention of pursuing peace, notwithstanding the raging terrorism. As he had no trust in Arafat, responsibility for fighting terror reverted to Israel. Branding himself an expert on counter-terrorism, Netanyahu followed his own beliefs that terror should be fought with vigour and that no compromises should be made with terrorists.[67] For the next three years, almost nothing was agreed upon. Final status settlement negotiations, scheduled to take place according to the Accords, did not even start. Steadfastly opposed to paying the price for peace, Netanyahu resisted Palestinian and American pressures. The promised second and third phases of withdrawal and redeployment were long overdue and the settlements continued to expand. According to Ahmed Qurie, of the 130 West Bank settlements that existed when Netanyahu came to office, ninety-three were expanded.[68] This diluted the peace process even more, undermining trust and confidence building. Palestinian frustration grew bitter and the mutual suspicion between Israel and the PA increased. Salam Fayyad thinks that not demanding a settlement freeze in the agreement was a major mistake.[69] Joel Singer and Marwan Muasher agree with him.[70] I concur.

64 Interview with Ghaith al-Omari (2 September 2014), 3. For further discussion, see Ron Pundak, 'From Oslo to Taba: What Went Wrong?', *Survival*, 43(3) (2001): 31–45.

65 Interview with Robert Malley (20 August 2022).

66 Interview with Shlomo Brom (17 June 2014), 9.

67 Benjamin Netanyahu (ed.), *Terrorism: How the West Can Win* (New York: Farrar, Straus and Giroux, 1986).

68 Ahmed Qurie, *Beyond Oslo* (London: I.B. Tauris, 2008), 52.

69 Interview with Salam Fayyad (16 January 2024), 24.

70 Interviews with Joel Singer (5 April 2022), 30–31 and Marwan Muasher (25 July 2022), 3.

In late September 1996, against the advice of Israel's security organisations, Netanyahu exhibited a negligent lack of judgement when he approved the creation of the Hakotel Tunnel, precipitating a wave of violence in Jerusalem and the West Bank. Riots continued for three days, during which at least sixty-two Palestinians died and some 1,600 were injured. Seventeen Israeli soldiers and policemen died and dozens were injured.[71] Under pressure, Netanyahu agreed to the Hebron Agreement, signed in January 1997.[72] The Hebron Agreement divided the city of Hebron into two parts: H1 and H2. Israel retained full security control over its settlement enclaves in downtown Hebron (H2) and over the settlement of Kiryat Arba, just outside the city, and facilitated movement by the settlers and the IDF over the surrounding area. The agreement gave the PA security responsibility for the rest of Hebron (H1), although this responsibility remained closely monitored by Israeli authorities.[73]

To revive the peace process, in October 1998, President Bill Clinton convened a summit at the Wye Plantation near Washington, DC. Israel committed itself to withdraw from 13 per cent of the West Bank within ninety days and to transfer a further 14 per cent of the land under joint Israeli-Palestinian control to the sole control of the PA. The PA also received a transit corridor connecting the West Bank and the Gaza Strip. In return, the PLO agreed to amend its charter, which called for the abolition of the state of Israel.[74] Arafat committed himself, in words, to a policy of zero tolerance of terror and violence.[75]

The Wye River Memorandum was negotiated between Israel and the PA in October 1998, with American mediation (see Figure 4.4).[76] Israel

[71] Yitzhak Mordechai, *For My People and for My Country* (Rishon LeZion: Yedioth Ahronoth, 2022): 357–360 (Hebrew); Eli Kamir, 'Events of the Hakotel Tunnel 1996', *NRG.co.il* (16 April 2002), www.nrg.co.il/online/archive/ART/276/371.html (Hebrew); 'Hakotel Tunnel Riots', *Channel 2*, www.youtube.com/watch?v=dKeMVXFFgs4 (Hebrew); Qurie, *Beyond Oslo*, 22.

[72] Protocol Concerning the Redeployment in Hebron (17 January 1997), https://tinyurl.com/3vp42kht.

[73] Geoffrey Aronson, 'What Was the 1997 Protocol Concerning the Redeployment in Hebron (a.k.a. Hebron Protocol, Hebron Agreement)?', *ProCon.org* (19 May 2008), https://tinyurl.com/pzr8dajb. In 2023, there were some 700 Israeli settlers in Hebron, a city of 160,000 people.

[74] For the first time the PLO recognised Israel's right to exist within the 1967 borders. From the Palestinian standpoint, this amounted to ceding their claim to nearly 80 per cent of British-mandated Palestine. See Quandt, 'Israeli-Palestinian Peace Talks', 16.

[75] 'The Wye River Memorandum', *The American Presidency Project*, www.presidency.ucsb.edu/documents/the-wye-river-memorandum.

[76] The Wye River Memorandum, 23 October 1998, *Israel Ministry of Foreign Affairs*, www.gov.il/en/Departments/General/the-wye-river-memorandum.

Figure 4.4 Arafat, Clinton and Netanyahu, Wye River Memorandum.
Credit: Tim Sloan/Stringer/AFP/Getty Images.

promised to allow construction of an airport in the Gaza Strip. Palestinian Area A was expanded from 3 per cent to 18 per cent, while Area B decreased from 24 per cent to 21 per cent. The Palestinians promised to fight terrorism, collect illegal weapons, prevent incitement to violence, reduce the number of Palestinian police officers and expand security cooperation with Israel.[77] Arafat undertook to review the 1968 Palestinian National Charter and expunge the clauses calling for the destruction of Israel.

In December 1998, the Palestine National Council (PNC) resolved to abrogate the PLO Charter articles calling for the destruction of Israel. The PNC resolution was passed with an overwhelming majority of 504 in favour, fifty-four against and fourteen abstaining. Members of the Popular and Democratic Fronts for the Liberation of Palestine did not participate in the meeting. It was decided to cancel Articles 6, 7, 8, 9, 10, 15, 19, 20, 21, 22, 23 and 30 and to delete specific sections in Articles 1, 2, 3, 4, 5, 11, 13, 14, 16, 17, 18, 25, 26, 27 and 29.[78] Given the importance of the Charter as a founding document of the PLO, and the significant number of changes, one would expect a new, amended Charter to be published soon after;

77 Aggestam, *Reframing and Resolving Conflict*, 199.
78 *The Palestinian Charter*, http://pac-usa.org/the_palestinian_charter.htm.

however, this did not happen. The PLO established committees to amend the language, but in 2000 the Intifada erupted and the issue was neglected. Arafat said the Charter is *caduc*, meaning irrelevant or obsolete.[79]

Both Israel and the PLO had been promised an American economic incentive of $500 million. Israel began a partial withdrawal, as promised, but Prime Minister Netanyahu did not complete his term in office. The Wye Agreement was opposed by some elements in his coalition, and the prime minister's personal behaviour became an issue.[80] On 21 December 1998, the Knesset called for a no-confidence motion and the Netanyahu government came to an end, less than three years after its establishment.

Labour leader Ehud Barak came to power in May 1999. Prime Minister Barak opted for resolving the Syrian option first. As IDF chief of staff, Barak had already pushed for talks with the Syrians, because he believed peace with Syria would mean the end of the wars in the Middle East. Barak also thought the problems with the Syrians were easier to solve than the problems with the Palestinians, which were far more complex.[81] He believed that a peace treaty with Israel's northern neighbour would lead to peace with Lebanon as well and provide additional leverage for resolving the Palestinian issue, as the PA would be put under more pressure to produce results. The Palestinians' options to haggle would be reduced.

Notwithstanding Barak's initial inclination, on 4 September 1999, he and Arafat signed the Sharm El Sheikh Memorandum relating to key agreements, such as the second Oslo agreement, protocols on further transfer of powers and responsibilities, and the Wye River Memorandum. Pertinent issues included the release of prisoners, the work of committees, the Gaza port, safe passage, Hebron and security.[82] On 5 October 1999, the Safe Passage Protocol was signed, relating to the regulation of a passage through Israel, between the Gaza Strip and the West Bank.[83] As mentioned, the passage did not remain open for long. In 2000, President Clinton welcomed Prime Minister Barak and Chairman Arafat to Camp David for a high-stakes peace summit intended to achieve a final resolution to the

79 Rone Tempest, 'PLO's Charter Is Out of Date, Arafat Declares', *Los Angeles Times* (3 May 1989), www.latimes.com/archives/la-xpm-1989-05-03-mn-2470-story.html.

80 William B. Quandt, *Peace Process: American Diplomacy and the Arab–Israeli Conflict since 1967* (Washington, DC: Brookings Institution Press, 2001); Ben Caspit, *The Netanyahu Years* (New York: Thomas Dunne Books, 2017), 157–168.

81 Interview with Ehud Barak, U-BIT: 244 (1997), Fifty Years War, Liddell Hart Archives, King's College, London.

82 1999 Sharm El Sheikh Memorandum, https://tinyurl.com/ywer5kpt.

83 Protocol Concerning Safe Passage between the West Bank and the Gaza Strip, www.un.org/unispal/document/auto-insert-204028/.

Israeli-Palestinian conflict. The summit marked the second major turning point in the peace process, following the initial breakthroughs of Oslo. The Camp David negotiations, the focus of the next chapters, ultimately failed to produce an agreement. In the aftermath, the region descended into renewed violence with the outbreak of the al Aqsa Intifada. This marked the collapse of the Oslo peace process – an ambitious diplomatic initiative that, despite its historic significance, ended prematurely and without resolving the core issues at the heart of the conflict.

Oslo Lessons

The Oslo process stands out as an exceptional episode in the history of international diplomacy. Rarely are academics so centrally involved in high-stakes negotiations, let alone in shaping the trajectory of a major geopolitical conflict. Unlike political figures, who operate within the constraints of electoral constituencies, ideological commitments and partisan agendas, Hirschfeld and Pundak entered the talks unencumbered by formal political affiliations or institutional loyalties. Their approach was grounded in dialogue, mutual understanding and the cultivation of trust. The academics' involvement somewhat balanced the inherent imbalance between Israel, a sovereign state, and the PLO, an aspiring organisation. The fact that the PLO representatives were senior officials, whereas Hirschfeld and Pundak were two academics, blurred the state/organisation imbalance. That imbalance sharpened when Savir and Singer joined the negotiations.

Oslo taught us many lessons:

Leadership is crucial. Oslo happened because Arafat and Rabin needed and wanted an agreement. Rabin, who initially did not want Oslo, did not trust the negotiators and did not want to recognise the PLO, was pushed to embrace Oslo due to Peres's relentless efforts. It is important that both parties, in this case Israel and the Palestinians, want to negotiate and want the negotiation to succeed. The chances of success are then considerably higher than in a situation where one or both parties have no wish to negotiate, as was the case in Camp David 2000, when the Palestinians felt coerced to attend the summit. In Oslo, both parties negotiated in good faith.

Contrary to common wisdom, dreamers can affect reality. Terje Rød-Larsen, Singer, Hirschfeld and Pundak were not official members of their governments. Many people yearn to make a substantive impact on reality, changing it for the better. Very few succeed in doing that. These four people changed the course of history with their vision, daring and hard work. They invested their hearts and souls to bring about peace. Their effort is admirable.

At the same time, a significant difference exists between an academic exercise and a full-fledged peace accord. For the latter, the presence of lawyers, well versed in the construction of legal documents, is indispensable. After Singer's introduction to the talks, the Palestinians were at a disadvantage for not including an experienced lawyer on their team. They did not have the lawyers to give the necessary input as counterparts to Singer. Consequently, Singer dictated the majority of the text.[84]

Oslo yielded results because Israel negotiated directly with the PLO. In the parallel track of Washington, the PLO was absent, and its people therefore thwarted the talks.[85] For many years, Israel tried to get around the PLO: the Village Leagues,[86] Prime Minister Yitzhak Shamir's election plan that barred people in the OPT from voting for Arafat or any other PLO leader;[87] the Madrid Peace Conference; as well as talks in Washington – all those efforts were ultimately futile. In contrast, the PLO wanted very much to see success in Oslo. Equally, it wanted the Washington track to fail. As soon as the PLO was included in Oslo, it made a real difference to the Palestinians. While the Palestinian negotiators in Washington were dogmatic, the Palestinian negotiators in Oslo were pragmatic. Qurie was not familiar with the nuances of the Washington talks and was not committed to them. He was practical, willing to compromise in order to reach a deal.

To reach a deal, there should be healthy communication between the parties. Both parties should be responsive to queries, be active, make counterproposals, be willing to compromise and make concessions, and both need to feel that their basic needs have been met.

An important point of agreement between the two parties was to refrain from offensive terminology and delving into discussions about historical grievances. Qurie wanted to engage with the past in his first meeting with Savir. The latter immediately clarified that that exercise was futile, and that they needed to look forward to the future, rather than delve into the past.[88] El-Kurd proposed not to talk about the past, but about political separation and economic cooperation.[89] Both parties understood that

[84] Interview with Hiba Husseini (24 December 2024), 3.
[85] Interview with Elyakim Rubinstein (28 May 2013), 4.
[86] Yigal Carmon, 'The Story of the Palestinian Village Leagues', *Memri* (September 2016), www.memri.org/reports/story-palestinian-village-leagues.
[87] Jerome M. Segal, 'Shamir's Election Plan: Solvable Problems', *Los Angeles Times* (27 June 1989), www.latimes.com/archives/la-xpm-1989-06-27-me-4262-story.html.
[88] Uri Savir, *The Process* (New York: Vintage Books/Random House, 1999), 15.
[89] Sven Behrendt, *The Secret Israeli–Palestinian Negotiations in Oslo: Their Success and Why the Process Ultimately Failed* (London: Routledge, 2007), 50.

focusing on the past could stifle the talks and bring them to a premature and unsuccessful close.

Creativity and thinking outside the box are required to overcome hurdles. Consider, for instance, the issue of the status of the Palestinians in East Jerusalem. Israel refused to include East Jerusalem in the agreement. The PLO refused to hold elections without the Palestinian East Jerusalemites. Israel suggested that these Palestinians would vote like Palestinians abroad, through an absentee ballot. The PLO refused. Finally, it was Egyptian President Hosni Mubarak who proposed a creative solution: setting up polling stations in East Jerusalem post offices for the duration of the elections. Israelis could claim that the Palestinians were sending their ballots via post, while the Palestinians said that the East Jerusalemites were voting at regular polling stations.[90] Under these arrangements, while most Palestinians of Jerusalem would vote at approximately 170 polling stations situated in the West Bank, approximately 5,000 of Jerusalem's Palestinians were allowed to vote through services provided in five specified post offices inside East Jerusalem.[91]

Israel's insistence on moving forward to close gaps and not acceding to new demands was correct. The usual course of negotiations is that the parties start by presenting maximalist positions and then, following discussions and deliberations, accept compromises that close gaps. The Israelis adhered to this mode of negotiations. The Palestinians, however, moved backward during negotiations and raised new demands. They enlarged the gaps. Consequently, the talks could have failed in the tenth round of July 1993. This tactic, which I call the *accordion tactic*, should be rejected *tout court*, because it is counterproductive. It can result in a lack of trust and stifle the willingness to make compromises.

Small states have a role to play in the Israeli-Palestinian conflict. This is especially true when those nations maintain good relationships with both the Israelis and the Palestinians and are perceived as impartial and sympathetic to both. The good will and good intentions of such players are likely to be appreciated by both parties.

Indeed, the importance of Norway as a facilitator should not be underestimated. Norwegian diplomats were keen to promote themselves as international peacemakers. They made the most of their soft power capabilities.

[90] Uri Savir, *Peace First: A New Model to End War* (San Francisco, CA: Berrett-Koehler Publishers, 2008), 78–79.

[91] Joel Singer, 'Constructive Ambiguity in Middle East Peacemaking', *Israeli-Arab Negotiations 101* (15 October 2020), www.joelsinger.org/constructive-ambiguity-in-middle-east-peacemaking/

Hilde Henriksen Waage argues that from May 1993, Norway became an active mediator.[92] While I would not describe Norway's role as a mediator in the full meaning of the term, especially regarding its ability to affect Israeli decisions, there is no doubt that Johan Jørgen Holst tried to influence the outcome by taking constructive and very positive steps to seal the deal. In an interview, Peres said that the Norwegian role was to soften Arafat.[93] Holst said that the objective was not to persuade, but to offer a detached judgement to both sides. He maintained: 'We paid careful attention to be at the parties' disposal, but never to impose our role on the parties.'[94] Being aware of their limitations, for example the lack of authority and leverage to coerce the parties, they used their physical resources, diplomatic skills, patience and resourcefulness to move the rival parties in the right direction. They were able to gain the trust of both Israel and the PLO. Norway brought the parties together, took care of them, energised them and intervened, when necessary, to keep the process going. Despite all the trials and tribulations, Norway kept the meetings secret. This conduct, over a period of eight months, required commitment, resources and serious diplomacy. It earned Norway international recognition as a credible and skilled peacemaker.

A convivial atmosphere supports the talk. While it is disputed whether informal talks are as important as formal ones, as Savir argues,[95] they are still very important. Establishing connections on a very basic level, as human beings, is important. Personal relationships, building up chemistry, having dinners together, walking together, engaging in relaxed social activities together – all these are important. Dennis Ross thinks personal relationships are crucial, but not because one side or the other is going to sacrifice what they see as their basic needs or interests because they like you or they trust you personally.[96] Ross explains:

> Every negotiation, every mediation, to some extent, involves an effort to get both sides to adjust their behaviour. And adjusting behaviour is the hardest thing to do. And they have to know that when you make promises to them, they can trust it. They have to know, if you are going to make

[92] Hilde Henriksen Waage, 'Champions of Peace? Tools in Whose Hands? Norwegians and Peace Brokering in the Middle East', in Peter Bauck and Mohammed Omer (eds), *The Oslo Accords 1993–2013: A Critical Assessment* (Cairo: American University in Cairo Press, 2013), 33; Waage, *Peacemaking Is a Risky Business*, 107, 119.

[93] Hilde Henriksen Waage, 'Norway's Role in the Middle East Peace Talks: Between a Strong State and a Weak Belligerent', *Journal of Palestine Studies*, 34(4) (2005): 14.

[94] Johan Jorgen Holst, 'Reflections on the Makings of a Tenuous Peace', *Brown Journal of World Affairs*, 1(2) (Spring 1994): 8–9.

[95] Savir, *Peace First*, 104.

[96] Interview with Dennis Ross (27 September 2019), 4.

> a threat, they also have to trust it. That it is real, that it is not a manipulation. So, you have to build, I think you have to build a relationship. Negotiations, you know, you need to reach a point where at the crucial moment, when it becomes clear that, you know, you are kind of at make or break, each side has to trust that the other one, they are saying, 'Look, I can do X, but I cannot do Y.' They have to trust that that is real. So, if you do not have a relationship, they are unlikely to trust that that is real. They are likely to see it as a manipulation. That you are trying to get them to concede something so that you do not have to. So, I think that building personal ties is critical.[97]

At Oslo, from time to time, there was an intermission, often late at night after formal negotiations were over for the day. At such moments, the two sides relaxed, sat together, joked and laughed, essentially relieving the stress and pressure.[98] Humour is a bridge. Ahmed Qurie changed his opinion about Uri Savir after a stroll they had in the woods, just the two of them, when they spoke openly about themselves and their families. Savir told Qurie that every time he was on a mission, he felt ashamed of representing a state occupying the territory of another people. Savir said: 'I wish to live in a democratic country that respects others and is respected by them.' Qurie writes: 'These words changed my earlier assessment of Savir and caused me to revise the impression of him.'[99] Qurie wrote the Afterword to one of Savir's books, saying about Savir: 'His was a character of conviction and integrity, a personality that contributed immensely to a new phase of the relations between Israelis and Palestinians.'[100]

Furthermore, *the two parties need to speak the same language, directly, without interpreters*. At the start of the process, Qurie spoke Arabic, but he soon felt more secure, and all the following discussions were in English.[101] For both delegations, English was a second language, putting both on level ground.

The need for coordination and streamlining is another important lesson. There was no meaningful coordination between the Oslo and Washington negotiation tracks. Once the Oslo channel began to yield tangible results, its primacy became evident, rendering the Washington talks increasingly redundant. Prime Minister Rabin initially envisioned Oslo as a supplementary avenue that would eventually feed into and strengthen the Washington process. However, that expectation collapsed with the arrival

97 Ibid., 4–5.
98 Interview with Joel Singer (25 March 2022), 21; Savir, *The Process*, 31.
99 Ahmed Qurie, *From Oslo to Jerusalem* (London: I.B. Tauris, 2008), 150.
100 Abu Ala, 'Afterword' to Savir, *Peace First*, 213.
101 Yair Hirschfeld, Q&A second round (20 July 2018).

of Savir in Oslo, effectively elevating the status of the backchannel to the level of formal negotiations.

The PLO, which had insight into both diplomatic arenas, quickly recognised Oslo as the more favourable platform, primarily because it granted official recognition to both Yasser Arafat and the PLO – recognition that was absent from the US-led talks. In contrast, the Israeli delegation in Washington remained unaware of Oslo's existence and continued to negotiate in isolation, placing them at a distinct disadvantage. Elyakim Rubinstein and his team proposed ideas that were increasingly misaligned with the positions being developed in Oslo. From the Palestinian perspective, this disconnect was perplexing, if not strategically revealing. The PLO grasped earlier than their Israeli counterparts that Savir's participation in Oslo marked a decisive shift: from that point forward, the Washington process became a diplomatic sideshow.

It should be noted that the Oslo process was hampered by a lack of trust among the Israelis. Rabin did not trust Peres. From 20 April 1993, Rabin oversaw and directed every move of the negotiators.[102] Peres committed to the process fully when his own man, Savir, joined the talks, as he did not appreciate the two academics, Hirschfeld and Pundak. He did not even invite them to the Oslo signing ceremony at the White House, commenting, 'You do not invite the midwife to come to the Brit (male circumcision)'.[103] Gil said that Peres did not trust Hirschfeld and Pundak and regarded them as 'a short bridge, facilitators, to what he wanted'.[104] Peres did not want the academics to receive credit for their work. Peres, as well as Rabin, felt that Hirschfeld and Pundak were too leftist. Rabin and Peres did not want to attach leftism to the agreement, as this would not be helpful for promoting it in Israel.[105] Avi Gil maintained that Hirschfeld was a kind of absent-minded professor and that, at times, it was hard to grasp what he meant. Peres did not like Hirschfeld's academic formulations. Pundak was seen by Peres as too naive: 'Too much on the side of a Mother Theresa way of diplomacy. Trusting people and seeing a kumbaya type of world, if we just take this decision. And Pundak was very pure, very pure. And so, Shimon did not trust his judgment one hundred per cent, because he was, to Shimon's mind, not realistic

102 Hirschfeld's email of 29 May 2024.

103 Yair Hirschfeld Q&A second round (20 July 2018), 3. In his comments on a draft of this chapter, Hirschfeld wrote that Peres was afraid 'we would take away the credit for Oslo from him'.

104 Interview with Avi Gil (16 January 2025), 11.

105 Ibid., 13.

enough'.[106] I mentioned that Rabin berated Hirschfeld and Pundak due to the misinformation that Peres had given to him. Rabin committed himself to Oslo only after he received assurances from Singer, whom he trusted. Lack of coordination and streamlining in the Israeli team, and feelings of distrust, impeded the negotiation process.[107]

Many people maintain that the United States must be involved in peace negotiations between Israel and the Palestinians for them to have any chance of success.[108] Rubinstein said that Israel needs the United States 'to a great extent, in many respects'.[109] Those who believe this see Oslo as proving their case. For them, the agreement was flawed because of the absence of a mediator who could press both sides to make painful concessions. The result was a deficient agreement, which ultimately caused the failure of the peace process.[110] They highlight Camp David 1978, where President Jimmy Carter brokered peace between Israel and Egypt. Carter himself sat with the Israeli and Egyptian negotiators, Aharon Barak and Osama El-Baz, and drafted the peace accord.[111] On the other hand, those who believe that there is no need for the Americans to be involved in direct negotiations between Israel and the Palestinians also perceive Oslo as proving *their* case. The Oslo track had, after all, resulted in accords. Hirschfeld thought that the absence of the United States was a tremendous advantage, although he informed Daniel Kurtzer of the talks and received important advice from him. But, Hirschfeld added, in May 1993, Kurtzer's deputy came to Oslo and 'tried to interfere in the most destructive way you can imagine'.[112] Hirschfeld also thought that the Washington track had failed because the Americans meddled and caused insecurities on both sides.[113] Ehud Barak noted that the absence of the United States from Oslo was an advantage and that all of Israel's successful negotiations

106 Ibid.

107 In his comments on a draft of this chapter, Hirschfeld wrote that the problem was not lack of coordination; the problem was the weakness of leadership to make the necessary concessions – on both sides.

108 Interviews with Stuart Eizenstat (7 July 2022), 13; Pär Nuder (20 August 2019), 28; and Pierre Schori (27 August 2019), 12, among others.

109 Interview with Elyakim Rubinstein (10 July 2018), 20.

110 Singer does not accept this statement. In his comments on a draft of this chapter, Singer wrote that Oslo failed primarily because the PLO failed to live up to its commitments under the agreement, which led to Israel's suspension of its commitments. Singer argues that if both sides had stuck to their commitments the agreement would have succeeded.

111 Raphael Cohen-Almagor, 'Lessons from the Israeli-Egyptian Peace Talks: An Interview with Aharon Barak', *Israel Studies Review*, 34(2) (Autumn 2019): 11.

112 Q&A with Yair Hirschfeld (20 July 2018), 3.

113 Yair Hirschfeld Q&A second round (20 July 2018), 4.

with its Arab neighbours had started out of the public eye and without the Americans. That was the case with the Israel–Jordan peace agreement, as well as the initial stages of the Israel–Egypt peace negotiations.[114] Ahmad Khalidi said that Oslo did not have a filter like the United States, a filter that does not always help because it is biased, tilted in favour of Israel owing to the special relationship between Israel and the United States.[115] Khalidi thinks the PLO should speak to Israel directly.[116]

The United States' involvement can be a blessing or a curse. Its involvement can skew negotiations.[117] The experienced negotiator Robert Malley saw this happening on several occasions in talks involving Israelis and Palestinians. As he described it, when the Americans were in the room, both negotiated with the superpower rather than the other side.[118] The role of the United States as a mediator is most effective – in fact indispensable – during the final stages of a negotiation process, particularly in bridging remaining gaps, facilitating agreement on contentious issues, endorsing the final accord and ensuring its effective execution. Washington's strategic value lies in its ability to mobilise substantial political, economic and diplomatic resources in support of peace implementation. Moreover, US involvement is critical in constructing and sustaining an international coalition that undergirds Israeli-Palestinian agreements. However, it is not essential – nor always desirable – for the United States to be present at the negotiation table from the outset. In the initial stages, direct bilateral dialogue between Israelis and Palestinians, free from external pressures, can foster trust, enable candid exchange and promote ownership of the process.

Critics of Oslo argue that it was anti-democratic, as it was conducted in secrecy, away from the public eye.[119] However, Oslo demonstrated that people of goodwill can shape history and receive support from state leaders

[114] Interview with Ehud Barak (25 May 2022). In 1977, Israeli Foreign Minister Moshe Dayan held secret talks with Egyptian Deputy Prime Minister Hassan Tuhami in Morocco. Another meeting between Israeli and Egyptian senior officials took place in Romania. The United States knew that private talks were taking place but did not know the details. Dayan met with US Secretary of State Cyrus Vance shortly after the meeting with Tuhami but he did not mention it to the Americans. Jackie Headapohl, 'Dayan and Tuhami Engage in Secret Talks', *The Detroit Jewish News* (16 September 2018), https://thejewishnews.com/2018/09/16/dayan-and-tuhami-engage-in-secret-talks/.

[115] Interview with Ahmad Khalidi (5 June 2019), 9.

[116] Ibid.

[117] Interview with Marwan Muasher (25 July 2022).

[118] Interview with Robert Malley (28 July 2022), 7.

[119] Interview with Shabtai Shavit (2 July 2018), 7.

for their initiative. It also showed how important secrecy is when matters are highly sensitive. Savir wrote that mutual public suspicions made public negotiations impossible.[120] Without secrecy, the process likely would have ended prematurely. Attempts at Israeli-Palestinian reconciliation were fiercely opposed both in Israel and in Palestine, which could have toppled the process.

The Oslo track came to fruition because the time was ripe. It was, in Yossi Beilin's terms, 'a meeting of the stars'.[121] The Palestinian leader was at a very low point: he yearned to improve his standing with the Palestinian and international communities and was ready to pay the price. The Israeli prime minister promised an agreement with the Palestinians and wanted very much to deliver it. A group of selfless, dedicated Norwegian facilitators worked hard to bring the parties together. An American president recognised the gift the Norwegians were giving him. He looked to chalk up a major diplomatic achievement and secure a positive legacy, and he was ready to put superpower effort and resources behind the deal. Finally, a supportive international community was not divided, at the time, on this issue by superpower rivalries.

Tor Wennesland also used the stars metaphor, saying that, in Oslo, the stars were in the right position. He meant that the parties were willing to take risks and were able to conclude an agreement. Both believed that they would get more by negotiations than what they had, and what they might give away was less than what they would lose by not taking the deal. The stars were in the right position in Washington as well: Wennesland said that the United States needed to support the process.[122]

Whether it was a good idea to postpone addressing crucial matters to a later stage is debatable. On this issue, we find a plethora of views. Savir,[123] Hirschfeld[124] and Pundak[125] think it was the right thing to do. Martin Indyk, too, thinks that Oslo's incremental approach was right; it just became a victim of events.[126] Ghaith al-Omari thinks Oslo was the best

120 Savir, 'Oslo: Twenty Years After', 118.

121 Interview with Yossi Beilin (13 May 2015), 10.

122 Interview with Tor Wennesland (30 August 2019).

123 Sari Makover-Blikov, 'Architect of the Oslo Accords: "Alone in Yearning for Peace"', *NRG* (17 August 2013) (Hebrew), www.makorrishon.co.il/nrg/online/1/ART2/499/557.html.

124 Yair Hirschfeld, *Track-Two Diplomacy toward an Israeli-Palestinian Solution 1978–2014* (Washington, DC: Woodrow Wilson Center Press and Johns Hopkins University Press, 2014).

125 Ron Pundak, *Secret Channel* (Tel Aviv: Aliyat Hagag, 2013) (Hebrew).

126 Interview with Martin Indyk (9 August 2022), 5

that could have been achieved, given the circumstances of its creation.[127] His opinion is akin to that of Gilead Sher.[128] Both think that Oslo had the correct architecture, considering the climate and the environment in which the process was consolidated. At the same time, they share the belief that the greatest failure of both Israel and the PLO was in the actual implementation of the agreements and arrangements that were reached.[129]

Yossi Sarid was uncritical of Oslo,[130] while Dan Meridor harshly criticised the process and the agreement.[131] Meridor voted against the Accords when the government asked for the Knesset's approval. Kurtzer thought that not including Jerusalem and the settlements was a weakness,[132] while Tzipi Livni and Ziad Abu Zayyad thought this was a mistake.[133] Beilin writes that Rabin did not include the freezing of settlements in the agreement because he thought that including such a statement would be perceived as an Israeli surrender to a Palestinian demand. That, Beilin maintains, was an awful mistake whose consequences linger up to the present.[134] Manuel Hassassian, PLO Ambassador to the UK, said that the Oslo agreement was a dismal failure because it did not address the substantive matters that comprised the issues.[135] The real issues between the PLO and Israel were left to the second stage in the Oslo agreement, in the bilateral relation. That incremental approach killed the Oslo process, 'because we were stuck in the first stage of redeployment and with the change of leadership and characters in Israel; we were stuck in that second redeployment since 1996'.[136] Gamal Helal perceives Oslo as an example of so-called constructive ambiguity, which he thinks should be better termed 'destructive ambiguity'. When things are left unclear and ambiguous, they 'come back and bite you. You can delay honesty in constructive ambiguity, but you cannot end the process and reach an agreement with delaying

127 Interview with Ghaith al-Omari (2 September 2014).
128 Interview with Gilead Sher (26 May 2013).
129 Ibid.; Interview with Ghaith al-Omari (2 September 2014).
130 Interview with Yossi Sarid (15 May 2015).
131 Interview with Dan Meridor (21 May 2013).
132 Interview with Daniel Kurtzer (6 April 2017).
133 Interviews with Tzipi Livni (22 June 2016) and Ziad Abu Zayyad (14 May 2015). For further discussion, see Avraham Sela, 'Difficult Dialogue: The Oslo Process in Israeli Perspective', *Macalester International*, 23 (2009): 105–138.
134 Yossi Beilin's written remarks on a draft of this chapter (14 June 2023).
135 See also Hussein Agha and Robert Malley, *Tomorrow Is Yesterday: Life, Death, and the Pursuit of Peace in Israel/Palestine* (New York: Farrar, Straus and Giroux, 2025), 45.
136 Manuel Hassassian, 'The Peace Process – Where To?', The Ambassador Forum, Middle East Study Group, The University of Hull (20 November 2013).

honesty.'[137] Similarly, Palestinian diplomat Nasser Al-Kidwa argues that the most important lesson learned from the Oslo Accords is the need to reject any provisional agreement that leaves open the issue of a permanent solution.[138]

Most interesting is Beilin's position. He confessed that he 'hated the Oslo agreement'.[139] Beilin explained that the agreement was the fulfilment of the framework agreement between Menachem Begin and Anwar Sadat. If you examine the wording of the agreement, the idea of five years of an interim agreement meant actually never getting to a permanent one. Such piecemeal solutions are proposed to avoid facing up to the tough issues that would be required to nail down a permanent agreement. Beilin also thought that a permanent two-state solution should have been negotiated immediately, rather than waiting five years for another round of elections in Israel, allowing extremists from both sides to thwart efforts.[140] The problem with staged peace is that it unravels at the first step, and the parties never get to the second step. In Beilin's view, it is best to at least have a vision of what the overall structure is and a roadmap for getting to the final stage when a process starts. The parties need to be clear about the conditions and the timetable for moving from one stage to another. As negotiation expert Jonathan Powell argues, 'even if you cannot have one big bang peace agreement that gets you to peace, at least have an overall vision. Otherwise, people will give up at the first step and start arguing about it, before they ever get to the second stage.'[141]

Beilin also 'hated the idea of AB&C',[142] splitting the West Bank into three areas according to the Palestinian population present in them. For Beilin, the idea of following in Begin's footsteps, rather than going directly to a permanent agreement with the Palestinians, was a huge mistake. Beilin thinks that, although it would have been difficult for them, the Palestinians were prepared to sign a permanent agreement. While some of them said the time was not ripe for that, Beilin believes that if Israel had come and said, 'okay, these are the principles for the permanent agreement. We are

137 Interview with Gamal Helal (11 November 2022), 15.

138 Nasser Alkidwa, 'The Oslo Accords: A Closer Look', *The Cairo Review of Global Affairs* (Winter 2019), www.thecairoreview.com/essays/the-oslo-accords-a-closer-look/.

139 Interview with Yossi Beilin (13 May 2015).

140 Yossi Beilin, 'Oslo and Camp David: One and the Same?', *The Cairo Review of Global Affairs* (Winter 2019), www.thecairoreview.com/essays/oslo-and-camp-david-one-and-the-same/.

141 Interview with Jonathan Powell (20 July 2022), 17.

142 Beilin, 'Oslo and Camp David: One and the Same?'

going to the permanent agreement through 4 or 3 years or whatever, you begin to build your own institutions',[143] it would have been very different from just having a general paper which says that in the course of the next five years, the parties will talk about Jerusalem, refugees and other matters.[144] An opportunity was missed.

Implementing the agreement is no less important than reaching an agreement. While security considerations are undoubtedly central to any agreement, a durable and meaningful agreement requires a broader, multidimensional approach. Essential components include confidence-building measures, robust state-building mechanisms and the development of stable political and social institutions within Palestinian society. Equally critical are frameworks for economic coordination and the establishment of a sustainable infrastructure encompassing education, healthcare, social welfare, taxation, agriculture, commerce and industry. Both Israel and Palestine must work to ensure that negotiated principles are effectively translated into concrete outcomes within clearly defined timelines. Protracted implementation processes risk generating disillusionment and eroding mutual trust, particularly when interim outcomes fall short of expectations or when both parties perceive the process as unbalanced or unfulfilled.

The most important lesson is to be aware of violent spoilers and address their challenge. Leaders should not ignore spoilers, because the spoilers might become more adventurous and daring. Spoilers wish to break the rules of the game and, indeed, the game altogether. They will exploit any weakness to do this. Both Israel and the Palestinians did not prepare their people adequately and did not address the spoilers as they should have. Many believe that Yasser Arafat turned a blind eye and tacitly even encouraged spoilers.[145] Arafat flirted with violence for a major part of his life. For him, it was a political tool. He believed in divide and rule, which meant creating many smaller power centres, each with limited authority, while he held overall power. This policy did not help to successfully implement the peace process. Israel allowed Arafat to have as many security forces as

143 Ibid.

144 Ibid.

145 Steven Emerson, 'Hamas, the PLO, and Terrorist Attacks against Israel', United States House of Representatives, House International Relations Committee (12 March 1996), www.investigativeproject.org/documents/testimony/5.pdf; Michael A. Calvo, *The Middle East and World War III: Why No Peace?* (CreateSpace Independent Publishing Platform, 2017); Arie M. Kacowicz, 'Rashomon in Jerusalem: Mapping the Israeli Negotiators' Positions on the Israeli-Palestinian Peace Process, 1993–2001', *International Studies Perspectives*, 6 (2005): 252–273.

he wanted, and he cultivated competition between them in a self-serving rather than a constructive manner. David Makovsky argues that Arafat was willing to use militants like Hamas to advance his goal.[146] The peace process was perceived as decolonisation and not as reconciliation, and violence is justified in fighting decolonisation. Between the signing of the Declaration of Principles on 13 September 1993 and 29 September 2000, 269 persons were killed.[147] Arafat and his people acted against Israel, either actively or passively, instead of cooperating with Israel on security matters.[148] With each casualty, the Israeli public raised more doubts about the peace prospects.

Unlike Arafat, Rabin did not encourage spoilers; however, he failed to recognise their importance. Mistakenly, he dismissed alerts about spoilers and paid the highest price a person could pay: his own life.[149] I tried to warn Rabin via the Legal Advisor to the Government, Michael Ben-Yair, and President Ezer Weizman, without success. On the fateful night of 4 November 1995, a night that many see as the beginning of Oslo's failure just over two years after the signing of the Accords, an Israeli zealot aimed to reverse the trend of history by eliminating Prime Minister Rabin.[150] He saw some success. The Oslo peace process received a major blow.

Conclusion

Terrorist attacks occurred sporadically in 1993 and escalated in 1994, especially after the Baruch Goldstein massacre.[151] Peres suggested that it was time to evacuate the Hebron Tel Rumeida settlement, which, at

146 Interview with David Makovsky (29 July 2022), 17–18.

147 Israeli Ministry of Foreign Affairs, 'Fatal Terrorist Attacks in Israel (Sept 1993–1999)'.

148 Interviews with Joel Singer (5 April 2022), 30; Itamar Rabinovich (21 July 2017), 13; Dennis Ross (27 September 2019), 17; Dan Meridor (20 January 2016), 5; Shabtai Shavit (2 July 2018), 10; Israel Hasson (23 May 2013), 8; Ehud Barak (11 July 2022).

149 Leah Rabin told me that 'we did not think that there was such a danger' to Rabin's life. Rabin received multiple warnings but he refused to change his conduct and way of life. He refused to wear a protective vest. The Rabins simply did not believe that someone might assassin Yitzhak. Discussion with Leah Rabin, Tel Aviv (16 January 1997).

150 Raphael Cohen-Almagor (ed.), *Liberal Democracy and the Limits of Tolerance: Essays in Honor and Memory of Yitzhak Rabin* (Ann Arbor: University of Michigan Press, 2000); Raphael Cohen-Almagor, 'Political Extremism and Incitement in Israel 1993–1995, 2003–2005: A Study of Dangerous Expressions', *Democracy and Security*, 3(1) (2007): 21–43.

151 Ministry of Foreign Affairs, 'Suicide and Other Bombing Attacks in Israel since the Declaration of Principles (Sept 1993)', https://tinyurl.com/2s3fbskm. See also Chronology of Terrorist Attacks in Israel Part V: 1993–1995, compiled by William Robert Johnston, last updated 27 November 2016, www.johnstonsarchive.net/terrorism/terrisrael-5.html.

that time, included fifteen families; however, Rabin was reluctant to confront the settlers.[152] At some point after the festive White House signing ceremony, Arafat decided to continue on two tracks: the Oslo implementation game, but also a drumbeat of violence, which he mistakenly thought would keep the pressure on the Israelis to move quickly on Oslo. This wave of terrorism was the result of dissatisfaction with the Oslo agreement that pushed those opposed to peace, on both sides, to resort to violence.

The decision by both parties to overlook these two significant issues, settlements and terror, is what Shlomo Ben-Ami regards as the main cause of the failure of the Oslo Accords, as such flaws allowed the parties free interpretation, hindering the ability of diplomats to reach a final agreement.[153] For Ben-Ami, the entire history of the years following Oslo was an attempt by each side to create a situation where its own interpretation would win out in the end – Israel through the expansion of the settlements, and the Palestinians through terror. Since the Oslo agreement was so obscure, it posed a standing invitation to both sides to take steps to establish the nature of the permanent status agreement in its own way.[154]

Some Palestinian commentators share similar sentiments, including al-Omari and Hussein Agha. Agha believes that 'Oslo evaded dealing with the core issue', the dispossession of the Palestinians by Israeli settlement activity, and, as a result, failed to provide 'clear ideas about how to resolve it'.[155] To be sure, Palestinian terrorism had a dramatic effect on the Israeli public. The zeal for peace among Israelis eroded.

In 1993, the Palestinians saw Oslo as the starting point for a Palestinian state in the vast majority of the territories, if not all of them. It included East Jerusalem, which would be their capital, and some formula for the resolution of the refugee issue that would be acceptable to the refugees and to the Israelis.[156] The Israeli government and the Israelis at large never bought into that vision. Indeed, Israel and the PLO never agreed on what the endgame would be. Having different endgames in mind proved to be a major problem. The Palestinians thought they had made major concessions by agreeing to a solution that would end the

152 Interview with Avi Gil (16 January 2025), 15 and his comments on a draft of this chapter.
153 Interview with Shlomo Ben-Ami (26 June 2013), 2.
154 Interview with Shlomo Ben-Ami (26 June 2013), 3.
155 Interview with Hussein Agha (5 April 2019), 2.
156 Interview with Ahmad Khalidi (5 June 2019), 32.

Israeli occupation and resolve the return of the Palestinian refugees. The Palestinians accepted Israel as a legitimate state on territory they thought was their own and, in return, they would have their own small, legitimate state on a mere 22 per cent of historical Palestine. But Rabin and Peres did not think in terms of a two-state solution.[157] Rabin had in mind 'autonomy plus' for the Palestinians. The Palestinian leaders knew that, but their people did not. The latter thought the agreement would lead to a state solution. Husseini said:

> The Palestinians were dreaming of statehood. The Palestinians wanted an airport. And they wanted a seaport. And they wanted to travel. And they wanted to have a good life. Good education. They wanted to have a good solid economy. This is what they want. The wellbeing, the welfare of a system that works for them. The Palestinian people are very, very tired. And they are exhausted and feel humiliated all the time.[158]

Agha said that the Israelis did not think in terms of ending the conflict, but rather defusing Palestinian violence. Rabin was concerned about Israel's security.[159] Salam Fayyad argues that the Palestinians should have insisted on precise terminology that explicitly mentions the Palestinian endgame.[160] It was a mistake on their part not to insist on that terminology. However, I doubt Rabin would have agreed to such language.

The agreement deferred the core issues (borders, Palestinian sovereignty, settlements, terrorism, Jerusalem, refugees, the Haram) to a later phase. The two sides did not ignore the issues. They knew these issues were very substantial but thought that it would be better to address them later in the process. They had an overly optimistic view – and critics say not very realistic – of a gradual progression. Agha said Oslo 'opened the door, but it did not really make you aware of what is inside the room. Just opening the door and having all these monsters coming at you from inside the room, is not enough.'[161]

This gradualism stands in contrast to an all-or-nothing approach, by promoting incremental progress rather than immediate, comprehensive resolution. On a practical level, it fosters the emergence of new realities

157 Interviews with Hiba Husseini (24 December 2024), 22 and Shlomo Brom (17 June 2014), 2.

158 Interview with Hiba Husseini (24 December 2024), 24.

159 Hussein Agha, 'Oslo25 | "We Must Liberate Our Thinking from the Oslo Straitjacket": An Interview with Hussein Agha', *Fathom* (August 2018).

160 Interview with Salam Fayyad (16 January 2024), 30.

161 Interview with Hussein Agha (5 April 2019), 22. Mathias Mossberg (interview on 23 August 2019) expressed a similar view.

on the ground, enabling tangible developments in governance, infrastructure and daily life. Politically, gradualism would allow both Israelis and Palestinians to make progress on contentious issues without necessitating the abandonment of core claims or identities. Psychologically, gradualism offers the potential to shift the prevailing discourse from one rooted in conflict and hostility to one framed by reconciliation and mutual understanding. The *lingua franca* may change from a vocabulary of conflict and violence to a vocabulary of peace. Gradualism affects the mindset as things develop and the horizon for conflict resolution becomes clearer. As cooperation expands, trust and hope may gradually take root. Gradualism, however, is not without its drawbacks. In our case, it risks entrenching the status quo, including the continuation of occupation and settlement expansion, and creates openings for spoilers to undermine progress and cast doubt on the process's legitimacy.

Avi Gil thinks that gradualism was a political necessity. The Knesset would not have approved a permanent status agreement. Psychologically, many members of the Knesset were not ready to make the necessary concessions. Gil calls this 'the puppy syndrome'. A man who got a bulldog puppy faced a difficult decision when the puppy was two months old and the puppy had to have its tail docked, a procedure requiring a visit to the vet. The man had grown so attached to the puppy that he was in tears at the thought of it. The vet explained that, while it seemed harsh, the procedure was essential for the puppy's health. To avoid the trauma, the man asked, 'Can't we just cut a little bit at a time?' The vet explained that this would cause repeated pain and bleeding for the puppy, and that it was much better to perform the procedure all at once. This logic, doing what is necessary for the long-term good, reflects a broader idea that humans often struggle with. Sometimes, we have to go directly to the endgame. Gil says: 'We tend to need time to adjust to big ideas, to ease into difficult changes, until wise voices show us that it's the only way forward. It's a reflection of human nature and psychology. Sometimes, we can start a process, but we can't always finish it right away.'[162] Gil thinks the Oslo agreement represented the most Israeli leaders could do at the time: a start to the process, but not its conclusion. It was simply too difficult to fully conclude a deal.

Oslo broke many taboos, leading to the normalisation of Israel's relationship with the Palestinians. It brought about a new reality, where Israel and the PLO opened direct communications. Important joint

[162] Interview with Avi Gil (16 January 2025), 14.

Israeli-Palestinian initiatives and collaborations were established.[163] Oslo also evoked a shared feeling among Jews and Arabs that a basic historic transformation was taking place.[164] As Ehud Olmert observes, 'the very fact that the barrier of direct contacts and recognition between Israel and the PLO was broken was a historical turning point'.[165] While the Oslo Accords failed to culminate in a full peace agreement, they promoted a vision for neighbourly relationships between Israelis and Palestinians to replace the occupier–occupied reality. Ehud Barak said that when peace happens, 'it will become clear that Oslo was a kind of precondition for this whole process, that ultimately had led to a solution'.[166] While the Oslo Accords did not end the Israeli occupation, they did yield significant achievements for Arafat, the PLO and the Palestinians.

- Arafat and the PLO received worldwide recognition. Sa'eb Erekat explained its significance for him, saying:

> I asked to read the agreement. I read the first paragraph and I accepted it. It says the Government of Israel, GOI, and the Palestine Liberation Organisation, PLO, the representative of the Palestinian people, and I saw the term 'Palestinian people' and PLO, and I said I accept. Because in my mind, this is Zionism: Zionist movement in 1897, people with no land, a land with no people; we did not exist, that's number one. Balfour Declaration, we exist, but as subhuman, the white man's burden. Then we became refugees, then we became terrorists, and now, they're telling us we're people, that's it, I accept. I accepted Oslo fully because of this sentence. Because I know this was the major turning point in Zionist and Western thinking. We did not vanish as Palestinians. This was my triumph.[167]

Similarly, al-Omari said that the Oslo process was a historic breakthrough for the Palestinian quest for self-determination. The Palestinians were able to govern themselves in their own territory, the idea of a two-state solution was an international consensus, and diplomatic and institutional pathways were created towards its realisation.[168]

163 Hirschfeld, *The Israeli-Palestinian Peace Process*, 118.

164 Abdel Monem Said Aly, 'The Road to Oslo and Beyond: Prospects for an Arab-Israeli Peace', *Security Dialogue*, 25(1) (1994): 49.

165 Interview with Ehud Olmert (22 February 2019), 1.

166 Interview with Ehud Barak (25 May 2022), 2.

167 Jacob Eriksson, *Small-State Mediation in International Conflicts: Diplomacy and Negotiation in Israel-Palestine* (London: I.B. Tauris, 2015), 111–112.

168 Ghaith al-Omari, 'The Palestinian Authority, a Flawed but Necessary Legacy of Oslo', *Fikra Forum* (7 September 2023), https://tinyurl.com/2uad39jx.

Kurtzer said that the single biggest achievement was to fix the problem of Palestinian representation that had hampered the United States before Oslo.[169] The PLO had never had any dealings with the United States. After Oslo, the United States and the Western world at large began to treat the PLO favourably, providing the PA with significant assistance. According to the Organisation for Economic Cooperation and Development (OECD), over $35 billion in aid money was spent on the West Bank and the Gaza Strip between 1993 and 2016. Of that $35 billion, around $24 billion (70 per cent) was allocated between 2006 and 2016, at an average of $2.2 billion per year. The Palestinians were among the top recipients of non-military per capita aid in the world.[170]

- PLO leaders settled in the West Bank and Gaza.
- Arafat gained partial control over the territories and imposed his leadership on local leaders. Ben-Ami said that Arafat wanted 'to isolate' the local leaders of the territories. 'He hated them.'[171]
- The Oslo Accords paved the way for many donors and international non-governmental organisations (NGOs) to allocate resources to Palestine.[172] The World Bank estimated that the PA received approximately $4.4 billion between 1993 and 2001 from the United States and the World Bank as well as European and Arab countries.[173] The money supported humanitarian and relief operations, as well as development and state-building plans.
- The Oslo Accords assisted in initial steps for Palestinian state-building, enabling a revolutionary movement to begin the process of transformation to an internationally accepted legitimate player. The PA was established. PLO leaders took responsibility for major aspects of the Palestinian people's lives (e.g., internal security, municipal government, education, judicial system, housing, health, communication, tourism, agriculture, sport and culture).[174] It was hoped that this measure would pave the way to a two-state solution.

[169] Interview with Daniel Kurtzer (6 April 2017), 6. Dan Meridor also emphasised this (interview on 21 May 2013, 4).
[170] Alaa Tartir, 'International Aid to Palestine: Time to Change Course', *Middle East Eye* (29 December 2017), www.middleeasteye.net/opinion/international-aid-palestine-time-change-course.
[171] Interview with Shlomo Ben-Ami (26 June 2013), 2.
[172] Nora Lester Murad, 'Humanitarian Aid and the Oslo Process', in *20 Years Since Oslo: Palestinian Perspectives* (Tunis: Heinrich Böll Stiftung, 2013), 74.
[173] Miller, 'Perils of Parity', 369.
[174] Agreement on the Gaza Strip and the Jericho Area, Cairo, 4 May 1994.

- Many new Palestinian NGOs, women's groups, student groups, youth groups, trade unions and businesses emerged.[175]
- After Oslo, Israel and the PA signed the Paris Accords, which include bilateral economic and humanitarian relationships between Israel and the PA.[176]

Oslo also yielded significant achievements for Israel.

- It ended the Intifada.
- It created a legal framework regulating Israeli-Palestinian relations, enhancing Israeli-Palestinian cooperation, including on matters that pertain to security.
- It strengthened strategic cooperation with the United States and Egypt and led to the peace agreement with Jordan. In Washington, there was a joint Jordanian-Palestinian delegation. King Hussein was surprised and offended when he learned about Oslo, having expected to be advised of any significant developments.[177]

Arafat was in Jordan a few days before the Oslo track became public. King Hussein thought that the concerned Arab parties went to Madrid collectively – the Syrians, the Jordanians, the Palestinians and the Lebanese – and that the Arab position would be much stronger if it remained a collective position. If each party were going to find its own agreement, it would weaken the others.[178] Hussein also feared that the agreement might compromise Jordanian interests.[179] Both Ehud Barak and former Deputy Prime Minister of Jordan Marwan Muasher think that Oslo pushed King Hussein to sign a peace treaty with Israel in 1994, after many years of implicit cooperation between the two neighbours.[180] Hussein had been meeting with Israeli leaders in secret for some twenty years. With many of them, including Rabin, the esteem was mutual. Ehud Barak said:

> the Oslo agreements paved the way for the peace with Jordan. I was personally deeply involved in this relationship. I was very close personally to

175 Petter Bauck and Mohammed Omer, *The Oslo Accords 1993–2013: A Critical Assessment* (Cairo: American University in Cairo Press, 2013).

176 Valerie Yorke, *International Agreements with Third Parties* (London School of Economics, April 1998), http://publicintelligence.net/international-agreements-with-third-parties/.

177 Interviews with Marwan Muasher (25 July 2022), 3 and with Shabtai Shavit (2 July 2018), 4.

178 Interview with Marwan Muasher (25 July 2022), 9.

179 Danny Yatom, *The Labyrinth of Power* (Tel Aviv: Contento, 2016), 442, 506; Ali Abunimah, 'Jordan, PLO Clash on Refugee Issue', *Al Jazeera* (24 January 2011), www.aljazeera.com/news/2011/1/24/jordan-plo-clash-on-refugee-issue.

180 Interviews with Ehud Barak (25 May 2022; 21 June 2022; 11 July 2022) and Marwan Muasher (25 July 2022).

> King Hussein, and I do not believe that it would ever have happened without the legitimacy and motivation created by the Oslo agreements.[181]

Muasher explains that King Hussein was a very astute politician. His anger did not last long. He understood that there was a new reality and that he had to deal with it.[182] Soon after Oslo became known, Israel and Jordan agreed on an agenda for the negotiations and then, the next year, arrived at a peace treaty.

Thus, the Oslo process held significant strategic value for Israel, particularly by contributing to the stabilisation of its southern and eastern borders.

- In the aftermath of Oslo, Israel experienced a marked improvement in its international standing. Dozens of states that had previously refrained from formal engagement established diplomatic relations and opened embassies in Israel.
- Israel gained access to international forums and institutions from which it had long been excluded, expanding its global diplomatic and political presence.
- The normalisation trend extended to parts of the Arab world: several Arab states initiated semi-diplomatic missions, while Israel reciprocated in kind.[183]
- A significant portion of the Arab boycott was lifted. New economic opportunities opened, with large international companies opening branches in Israel. Foreign investments began to flow. American, Chinese and Japanese companies were among those that wanted to explore the Israeli market for the first time. New international markets for Israeli goods opened, especially in South-East Asia, increasing exports and enhancing investment opportunities.[184]
- GDP per capita increased from $11,000 in 1990 to $17,000 in 2000.[185]

Many in Israel, particularly those aligned with the political centre and right, view the Oslo Accords as having implicitly legitimised the settlement enterprise. From this perspective, Oslo enabled the entrenchment of

181 Interview with Ehud Barak (25 May 2022), 1.

182 Interview with Marwan Muasher (25 July 2022), 9.

183 Yossi Beilin, 'Beware the Extremists: Lessons from Oslo, Twenty Years On', *Haaretz* (9 September 2013).

184 Ben-Zion Zilberfarb, 'The Israeli Economy in the 1990s: Immigration, the Peace Process and the Medium Term Prospects for Growth', *Israel Affairs*, 3(1) (Autumn 1996): 1–13.

185 David Klein, 'Israel Economic Statistics: The Israeli Economy – 1990–2000', *Jewish Virtual Library* (7 December 2000), www.jewishvirtuallibrary.org/the-israeli-economy-1990-2000.

the Israeli presence in the West Bank, under the guise of a peace process. Conversely, voices from the ideological centre-left regard the Accords' failure to directly address the issue of settlements as a critical omission, one that underscores a deeper societal reluctance to disengage from the occupation. Oslo's ambiguity towards settlements not only reflected internal political constraints but also contributed to the current impasse in the peace process. The ongoing expansion of settlements since the signing of the Accords has, in the eyes of many observers, severely undermined the viability of a two-state solution. Furthermore, the Oslo Accords ultimately failed to produce a permanent status agreement, stemming from a series of structural and procedural flaws inherent in the negotiations themselves. Chief among these was the unusual format of the talks and the reliance on an interim framework, which lacked the binding force and clarity of a final settlement. Compounding these structural weaknesses were significant challenges in implementation, exacerbated by the assassination of Prime Minister Yitzhak Rabin. His death marked a critical turning point, catalysing a political shift within Israel that undermined the continued viability of the Accords.

Oslo remains a distinctive episode in the annals of diplomacy, and its failure is, in part, a reflection of the agreement's unconventional origins. Initially conceived in a semi-academic context, the agreement bore the hallmarks of an improvised and incomplete framework, ill-equipped to resolve the complex and deeply entrenched issues at stake. The peace process was further derailed by mutual shortcomings: Arafat's unwillingness or inability to fully renounce violence and replace violence with tranquil coexistence, and Israel's persistent reluctance to confront contentious issues, such as settlement expansion and the status of East Jerusalem.

Moreover, subsequent talks, intended to address the ambiguities left unresolved by Oslo, failed to deliver. They left critical gaps in the peace framework, which were further aggravated by the deliberate postponement of negotiations on the most sensitive and divisive issues, a strategic decision that ultimately delayed confrontation with the core obstacles to peace.

In the next three chapters, I analyse the second major peace junction – Camp David 2000. I discuss how the peace summit was conceived, the role of the American mediator, and the Israeli, Palestinian and American mistakes that brought about the summit's failure.

5

The Road to Camp David

It is an illusion to believe that one can meet demands for social fairness with violence and military might.

~ Olof Palme

The road to Camp David went through Sweden. Before Olof Palme came to power in 1969, the Palestinians were considered as one component of the Arab–Israeli conflict. Sweden was sympathetic to the Palestinian refugees but still maintained good relations with Israel. Palme, who served as Sweden's prime minister from 1969 to 1976 and again from 1982 to 1986, changed the focus and importance of the Palestinian issue in Swedish foreign affairs. The Palestinians came to be regarded as a nation with legitimate rights of self-determination, and the Palestine Liberation Organization (PLO) was recognised as their representative. Sweden became one of the most critical voices in Europe, if not the most critical, of Israeli policies towards the Palestinians.[1] In 1975, Sweden permitted the PLO to open an office in Stockholm. The Social Democratic Party, led by Palme, became increasingly preoccupied with Middle Eastern affairs.

In 1996, Göran Persson, the leader of the Social Democratic Party, became prime minister. Like Palme, Persson was very interested in Middle Eastern affairs, and like his predecessor, Persson believed that, as a militarily non-aligned country, Sweden must actively work for world peace. However, Persson did not like the pro-Palestinian line that Palme and Sten Andersson had adopted and wanted to move Sweden in a different direction. Unlike Palme and many people in the Swedish Foreign

[1] Jacob Abadi, 'Sweden's Policy toward Israel: Constraints and Adjustments', *Middle Eastern Studies*, 37(2) (April 2001): 33. For discussion on the Swedish–Israeli relationship, see Jacob Eriksson, *Swedish Mediation of the Israeli-Palestinian Conflict: A Study of the Utility of Small-State Mediation and Track II Diplomacy*, PhD thesis (Department of Languages and Cultures of the Near and Middle East, School of Oriental and African Studies, University of London, 2011), chapter 3.

Office, Persson was decidedly pro-Israel. When Ehud Barak was elected prime minister in August 1999, Persson recognised that here was a window of opportunity for Sweden to play a role in the Israeli-Palestinian conflict, given the Swedish Social Democratic party's long-standing relations with Israel and the Labour Party, *and* its close relations with the Palestinians.[2] Persson and Pär Nuder, his chief of staff and state secretary to the prime minister, wished to become involved in assisting the peace process between Israel and the Palestinians, and in supporting Israel. The Swedish channel of communication with Israel moved away from the pro-Palestinian foreign office to the pro-Israeli prime minister's office.

In October 1999, Persson arrived in Israel. This was the first official visit for a Swedish prime minister since Tage Erlander's visit in 1962. It was a good visit.[3] Persson and Barak connected well. Shortly thereafter, Nuder went to Tunis and met with Mahmoud Abbas. Abbas wanted to establish a secret channel for discussion with the Israelis. In Jerusalem, Nuder met with Barak's close advisors, Danny Yatom and Gilead Sher, offering Sweden's services as facilitators.[4] Barak welcomed the idea, but he did not want to negotiate with Abbas's chosen negotiators, Hussein Agha and Ahmad Khalidi. Barak wanted Palestinian officials from the West Bank and Gaza, preferably security people, and mentioned Mohammed Dahlan, head of the Palestinian Authority's (PA) Preventive Security Forces in Gaza. Then Abbas 'went cold'.[5] For a few months there was quiet, but then, in January 2000, the Israelis conveyed the message that they were interested in holding negotiations in Stockholm, and they wanted the Swedes to facilitate secret talks between Israel and the Palestinians.

Like Norway, Sweden is a small state that has no specific interests in the Middle East. Its intentions are to support reconciliation processes in line with principles of international law. As such, Sweden was poised to facilitate communication between Israel and the PA. Nuder travelled to Israel on a Swedish state plane to bring the negotiators back to Stockholm with him.[6] The Israeli representatives were Shlomo Ben-Ami and Gilead Sher.

[2] Interviews with Anders Bjurner (20 August 2019), Ulf Hjertonsson (27 August 2019), Mathias Mossberg (23 August 2019), Pierre Schori (27 August 2019) and Sven-Eric Söder (20 August 2019).

[3] Interview with Pär Nuder (20 August 2019), 2–3; discussion with Anders Lidén (6 October 2023).

[4] Ibid., 2–3.

[5] Raphael Cohen-Almagor, 'History of Track II Peace Negotiations: Interview with Hussein Agha', *Israel Studies*, 26(1) (2021): 55.

[6] Interview with Pär Nuder (20 August 2019), 4.

Gidi Grinstein joined the Swedish channel in the second round of talks. Unsurprisingly, on the Palestinian side, the negotiators were the Oslo people, Ahmed Qurie (Abu Ala) and Hasan Asfour, who were joined by the legal advisor Hiba Husseini. Abbas, who insisted on his chosen negotiators, was not involved, nor were his men Agha and Khalidi. They were invited by Qurie but would not participate without Abbas's authorisation. Khalidi also thought it would be a bad idea for him to sit with an official representative, who would bind him to what he said rather than offer the 'freedom' of an informal exchange.[7]

For many years, Abbas remained convinced that Track II negotiations were preferable to official negotiations. Abbas wanted unofficial people because they could interact freely, and the track could be deniable and non-committing (see Chapter 1). Negotiators are not constrained by official positions. Agha explained:

> If an official goes into a secret channel and says something like, for example, I accept a Palestinian capital in neighbourhoods of East Jerusalem, not the whole of East Jerusalem. Then, that will become our official position; it will be a concession. If an academic says that, it does not bind us, he can play with it and he can see how far you can go.[8]

That was germane to Abbas's logic. He wanted an unofficial track that would prepare the ground and feed the official talks. Barak did not share that logic. He thought such an academic exploration was a waste of time.

The negotiations were held in May 2000, as Barak wanted. The two delegations met at Harpsund, the Swedish prime minister's official residence outside Stockholm. The Swedes – Nuder, Foreign Minister Anna Lindh, Mathias Mossberg (head of policy planning in the Swedish Foreign Office) and John Hagard (head of the Department for Middle East–North African Affairs in the Swedish Foreign Office and former Swedish ambassador to Israel and Tunis) – were outside the room. This was the instruction of Persson, who thought the Swedish should not try to move any party in any direction.[9] They should do nothing beyond facilitation. Sweden provided the venue, transport, accommodation and subsistence.

Israel proposed transferring most of the West Bank and the whole of the Gaza Strip to the Palestinians but retaining three settlement blocs (Gush Etzion, Ariel and the settlements around Jerusalem). Israel proposed

[7] Interview with Ahmad Khalidi (5 June 2019), 18.
[8] Interview with Hussein Agha (5 April 2019), 5. Khalidi said similar things in his interview of 5 June 2019, 17.
[9] Interview with John Hagard (22 August 2019), 2.

that it would continue to be responsible for security in the Jordan Valley for twenty years. Ben-Ami said that the negotiations advanced rapidly towards a solution. Understandings were reached regarding the refugee problem: settling them in different countries and in Palestine, and family unification in Israel, with up to 15,000 people over time. The Palestinians did not agree on numbers but showed a willingness to discuss the issue further. Ben-Ami said that in a follow-up meeting in Jerusalem, Qurie agreed that 4 per cent of the West Bank would remain under Israeli sovereignty.[10] The sensitive issue of Jerusalem was not discussed in that round of talks.[11] The atmosphere in the negotiations was pleasant and both sides demonstrated pragmatism. Ben-Ami thought an agreement was within reach.[12] He told me: 'It was very, very serious negotiation with Abu Ala. Very, very effective.'[13] Interestingly, in my three interviews with Ehud Barak, Barak did not mention Stockholm even once.

In the second round of talks, Dennis Ross and his team visited Harpsund for one day. Unlike the Swedish, they were present in the room to witness the negotiations firsthand. They listened and read the documents prepared by Sher. Qurie did not draft documents.[14] The Americans were impressed by what they saw. Ross was hopeful, because there was an Israeli readiness to accept the 1967 borders and mutually agreed swaps as a principle to resolve border disputes. Abu Ala and Asfour intimated that they were willing to accept certain Israeli settlement blocs.[15] Ross told Nuder that they had never seen a discussion more detailed than the one they witnessed at Harpsund: 'Never had Israeli and Palestinian negotiators on such a high level reached so much on the fundamental issues.'[16]

After two meetings, however, the talks petered out. There was no agreed document. The discussions were very sensitive, and news about the meeting was leaked, which undermined trust between the two parties. Nuder is certain that the Swedish did not leak the information about the meeting. He is unsure whether the Israelis or the Palestinians were responsible for the leak.[17] Ross and Ben-Ami are certain that the leak came from the Abbas camp. Abbas, who wanted to run the backchannel with Agha

10 Ari Shavit, 'The Day Peace Died', *Haaretz* (14 September 2001) (Hebrew).
11 Ibid.
12 Ibid.
13 Interview with Shlomo Ben-Ami (26 June 2013), 14.
14 Interview with Aaron David Miller (12 September 2019), 16.
15 Interview with Dennis Ross (27 September 2019), 8.
16 Interview with Pär Nuder (20 August 2019), 7, 17.
17 Ibid., 5.

and Khalidi, was not interested in seeing Qurie behind the wheel. Ben-Ami said that Abbas 'really did hate Hasan Asfour'.[18] Husseini thinks that Barak leaked the information because he wanted a leaders' summit, with US President Bill Clinton.[19] Hagard thinks that Barak was not ready to discuss the division of Jerusalem. The discussions went too far for Barak's taste, and he did not wish to continue them.[20] Hagard also thinks it was a mistake not to have Abbas on board.[21] Mossberg was not optimistic from the very start because he knew Abbas was not behind the exercise,[22] and he thought this was 'too much of an Israeli-American exercise'.[23]

Over the years, although Abbas held responsibility for the Israeli portfolio within the PLO, his detachment from key negotiations proved detrimental. At the heart of the discord was a fundamental clash between two strategic approaches. Abbas favoured Track II diplomacy – informal dialogue designed to explore ideas and map possibilities – while Israeli Prime Minister Ehud Barak insisted on Track I negotiations involving senior officials with the authority to strike a final deal.

As Barak dictated the moves, Yasser Arafat complied with his terms. As the unhappy Abbas was sidelined, the assumption that it was he who undermined the Harpsund talks is quite plausible.

The Barak–Arafat Relationship

When Ehud Barak came to power, he declared: 'To our Palestinian neighbours, I say in all sincerity: we want to work with your leaders, first and foremost Yasser Arafat, in full partnership and respect, to assure a hopeful, free and prosperous future for the coming generations which will live alongside each other in this land.'[24] Barak dedicated most of his time in office to peace and security. From November 1999 to March 2000, he focused on negotiations with Syria. In his quest for peace with Syria, in January 2000 Barak met with Syrian Foreign Minister Farouq el-Shara'a at the Conference Center in Shepherdstown, West Virginia, near

18 Interviews with Shlomo Ben-Ami (26 June 2013), 14 and Dennis Ross (27 September 2019), 9.
19 Interview with Hiba Husseini (24 December 2024), 31.
20 Interview with John Hagard (22 August 2019), 2–3.
21 Ibid., 16.
22 Interview with Mathias Mossberg (23 August 2019), 18.
23 Ibid., 19.
24 Aharon Klieman, 'Israeli Negotiating Culture', in Tamara Cofman Wittes (ed.), *How Israelis and Palestinians Negotiate* (Washington, DC: US Institute of Peace Press, 2005), 102.

Washington, DC.[25] No breakthrough was achieved, but Syria and Israel continued to engage the United States as a go-between for the two sides. In April and May 2000, Barak was preoccupied with the Israel Defense Forces (IDF) withdrawal from Lebanon. Peace with Syria was his priority. Israel's realpolitik was straightforward: Syria was a much more concrete military threat to Israel. It could force Israel to become involved in a mutually devastating full-scale war. The Palestinians could not do this. While they could disturb the normalcy of daily life in Israel, they could not launch a full-scale war on Israel. Additionally, the Lebanon issue, which had also been ongoing for years, could be resolved once a deal was struck with Syria, as the latter was behind Lebanon's attacks on Israel. Resolving the Syria and Lebanon issues automatically placed the Palestinians in a weaker negotiating position vis-à-vis Israel.

Another factor that influenced Israel's priorities was that Syrian President Hafez al-Assad was battling lethal blood cancer. Barak, who wanted to strike a deal while Assad was still around, shared this logic with Clinton.[26] Barak trusted Assad's ability to deliver and implement a deal, if and when an agreement was signed by the two leaders. Once Barak realised that the Syrian option was closed,[27] he determined to bring the Israeli-Palestinian conflict to an end. Faced with the problems that Yitzhak Rabin and Shimon Peres had postponed to the last stage of the Oslo peace process, Barak did not blink. He was willing to make very tough decisions and to make significant sacrifices, paying a price for peace.

Arafat was relieved to see Barak in office. He hoped that the derailed peace train could be put back on track.[28] Unlike Benjamin Netanyahu, Barak seemed committed to peace and willing to pay a significant price for this precious commodity. Leadership, however, is measured by words *and* deeds. Barak's prioritisation of a peace deal with Syria was most disappointing, even humiliating, for Arafat. The Palestinians understood that Barak wanted to put pressure on them, leaving them without Arab support and undermining their position.[29] They were out of favour, the forgotten minor players, left unnoticed on the pitch amid the major stars. Barak failed to understand that by pursuing the Syrian track, he created

[25] President Clinton Presents Middle East Talks Outline, www.usembassy-israel.org.il/publish/peace/archives/2000/january/me0107b.html.

[26] Interview with Ehud Barak (21 June 2022), 5.

[27] Benny Morris, 'An Interview with Ehud Barak', *New York Review of Books*, 49(10) (13 June 2002), https://tinyurl.com/mrxmbw8p.

[28] Ahmed Qurie, *Beyond Oslo* (London: I.B. Tauris, 2008), 83.

[29] Ibid., 90.

a lot of bad blood between himself and Arafat. Nor did he try to hide his motives.[30] Oblivious to Arafat's misgivings, Barak even shared his logic with the Palestinian leader, expecting him to understand. He explained to Arafat that, regarding Syria, Israel is 'stuck there and I want before Assad dies – it was already known that he has serious blood cancer – and we have a short time with him. And no one knows who will replace him ... I never ignored it. And so, I tried to explain it to him. So, that was the logic.'[31] Barak did not understand that *that* candid explanation did more harm than good. Arafat did not appreciate being second best.

Furthermore, Arafat's hope of seeing a constructive change in Israel's policy regarding the settlements did not materialise. During Barak's term in office, the number of West Bank settlers grew by 12 per cent.[32] His priorities (Syria, Lebanon and then Palestine) disappointed the Palestinians. The trust-building between the sides was deficient, with negative contributions by Barak and Arafat. Arafat did little to convince Barak that he had renounced terrorism and violence.

In addition, Barak's redefinition of the Oslo process came as a blow to the Palestinians. Barak was sceptical about significant aspects of the agreement. He had voiced serious reservations in the government meeting that approved the Oslo agreement,[33] and he continued to do so after his election as prime minister. Barak disliked the asymmetry in the agreement. While Israel had committed to return tangible assets – all of the Occupied Palestinian Territory (OPT), except for settlements and military installations – all the Palestinians had to give in return was promises about the nature of the future relationship. Barak saw a 'very weak logic' for this exchange.[34] The risk was that *after* giving the Palestinians almost all the land, Israel would then have to negotiate the tough issues: borders, security, Jerusalem, refugees' right of return and the finality of the conflict. Barak was convinced that before Israel took the step of giving the Palestinians almost the whole area dictated by any interpretation of the Oslo agreement, it was better to know, 'do we or do we not have a partner for tough decisions about the other issues?'.[35]

[30] Interview with Ehud Barak (21 June 2022), 4–5.
[31] Interview with Ehud Barak (21 June 2022), 5.
[32] Sivan Hirsch-Hoefler and Cas Mudde, *The Israeli Settler Movement: Assessing and Explaining Social Movement Success* (Cambridge: Cambridge University Press, 2021), 51.
[33] Protocol of the Israeli government meeting, 30 August 1993, Israel Archives (Hebrew).
[34] Raphael Cohen-Almagor, 'The Pursuit of Peace with the Palestinians: Interviews with Ehud Barak', *Israel Affairs* (published online 9 March 2023): 12.
[35] Interview with Ehud Barak (21 June 2022), 2.

Barak shifted his focus to the Israeli-Palestinian conflict only after the failed March 2000 Geneva summit between President Clinton and President Assad.[36] By then, Arafat's frame of mind was anything but receptive. He had no wish to abide by Barak's timetable, imposed after the latter's Syrian gambit had failed.[37] Subsequent meetings between Barak and Arafat did little to clear the air between the two leaders.

Before 2000, the Israelis and the Palestinians met many times in Israel, Washington and Stockholm, but they could not conclude a draft agreement. They did not develop positions that could lead to an agreement. According to Barak, his meetings with Arafat were difficult and unproductive. Arafat was uncommunicative and it was impossible to 'create a real warmth' with him.[38] There was no chemistry between the two leaders.[39] Ziad Abu Zayyad said that Barak was arrogant.[40] Hussein Agha said that 'Barak's personal attitude was not very helpful'.[41]

The first Barak–Arafat meeting was on 11 July 1999. The Palestinians expected to obtain a commitment from Barak to immediately implement the long-delayed Israeli forces redeployment. Barak dismissed the idea and the talks disintegrated.[42] The second meeting, on 27 July 1999, was not much better.[43] The Palestinians understood that Barak was very different from Rabin. Their hope of continuing the special relationship established by Rabin and Arafat was dashed.

Despite misgivings, on 4 September 1999, Barak and Arafat signed the Sharm El Sheikh agreement, which included Barak's insistence on concluding 'a Framework Agreement on all Permanent Status issues in five

[36] James B. Foley, State Department Deputy Spokesman, Excerpt from the Daily Press Briefing, Department of State Press Briefing Room, Washington, DC (30 March 2000), www.state.gov/www/regions/nea/000330_foley_excerpt.html.

[37] Ahron Bregman, *Elusive Peace* (London: Penguin, 2005), 65; Robert Malley and Hussein Agha, 'Camp David: The Tragedy of Errors', *New York Review of Books* (9 August 2001), https://tinyurl.com/2s4nskmv.

[38] Interview with Ehud Barak (11 July 2022), 11.

[39] Interview with Ami Ayalon (28 June 2022), 5.

[40] Interview with Ziad Abu Zayyad (14 May 2015), 21.

[41] Interview with Hussein Agha (5 April 2019), 6.

[42] Statement by PM Barak at Joint Press Conference Prime Minister Barak / Chairman Arafat, Israel Ministry of Foreign Affairs Archive; see also Howard Schneider, 'In First Meeting, Barak and Arafat Discuss Peace', *Washington Post* (12 July 1999): A01; Charles Enderlin, *Shattered Dreams: The Failure of the Peace Process in the Middle East, 1995–2002* (New York: Other Press, 2003), 115–116.

[43] Key Points Following the Barak-Arafat Meeting, Israel Ministry of Foreign Affairs Archive 1990–1999.

months from the resumption of the Permanent Status negotiations'.[44] It formulated concrete steps in the implementation of the Oslo Accords; those related to security, transfer of land, prisoner release, safe passage, Hebron, the Gaza seaport and the work of the designated committees. Shortly after the Sharm El Sheikh Summit, Israel released 199 prisoners, and a land transfer of 7 per cent of the West Bank was made from Zone C to Zone B.[45] Both issues, prisoner release and land, were extremely important for the Palestinians. They were tangible achievements that Palestinian leaders could proudly claim as accomplishments and as proof that the Oslo peace process was important and should be backed.

Effective negotiation hinges on clear, respectful communication. For talks to succeed, both sides must speak a common language – politically, diplomatically and even emotionally. Yet this balance was often elusive. Barak had a tendency to lecture, and both he and Arafat leaned heavily on metaphors and issued pointed demands – rhetorical habits that frequently fell flat or caused friction.

One telling moment came in late 1999, when the Norwegians hosted a ceremony in Oslo to mark the sixth anniversary of the Oslo Accords. Barak, Clinton and Arafat were invited as honoured guests. After the official programme, the three leaders retreated to the private residence of Ambassador David Hermelin, the American-Jewish envoy to Norway. It was meant to be an intimate setting for a candid dialogue, but the conversational styles that had long caused tension remained ever-present. Barak told Arafat:

> Look, there is a problem here. It has to be solved, to avoid tragedy for both sides. It will not be solved in heaven. You understand it as well as I do. So, it should be solved by human beings here on earth. We happen to be these two human beings. If we solve it, we made a great change in the history of both peoples. If we do not, our successors will have to tackle the same issues, and without a way to explain why the hell their predecessors did not solve it. The problems will not change. It will be the same jabels [hills] and the same wadis [valleys], the same geography, and the same demography. So, it is not going to change. The only thing that will change is the size of the cemeteries, the graveyards. And I can promise you, that yours will grow faster than ours.[46]

[44] The Sharm el-Sheikh Memorandum on Implementation Timeline of Outstanding Commitments of Agreements Signed and the Resumption of Permanent Status Negotiations, *Jewish Virtual Library*, www.jewishvirtuallibrary.org/jsource/Peace/sharm0999.html.

[45] Qurie, *Beyond Oslo*, 89.

[46] Interview with Ehud Barak (21 June 2022), 10.

Barak maintained that the only way that he could think of it, metaphorically, was to assume that 'both of us now have to jump, to parachute out of this building ... Assume that it is high enough for free parachuting. And we have to dare to jump, in order to solve the problem. But the point is that you have the handle of my parachute, and I have the handle of your parachute. And we have to jump together'.[47] Barak told Arafat, 'your toughest decisions will not be vis-à-vis me or Clinton. Your toughest decisions are facing your own people. And the toughest decisions I have to make are not about you. They are about facing my own people. So, it is only if we are ready to jump together when we know we are lost, if our chutes will not open fast enough'.[48] Barak's lengthy explanations failed to engage Arafat's attention and cognition, and he responded by detouring into his *own* stories. One may assume that Arafat did not appreciate the explicit threat, 'I can promise you, that yours [your graveyards] will grow faster than ours'.

On 21 December 1999, Barak and Arafat met at Mahmoud Abbas's residence. The meeting was so miserable that the two broke off contact for a few weeks.[49] When they met on 17 January 2000 at Yossi Ginossar's house in Kochav Ya'ir, the atmosphere remained strained.[50] Of all the Israelis, the former Shabac senior officer Ginossar communicated best with Arafat, but even he was unable to salvage the meeting. The two leaders met again on 4 and 13 February 2000, but there was no real progress in the negotiations.[51] Arafat and Barak haggled over interim land transfers and over the scheduled withdrawal of Israeli troops from a further 6.1 per cent of the West Bank.[52] In those tense meetings, Barak explained his wishes to Arafat. Barak wanted to push for a final agreement that would resolve the Israeli-Palestinian conflict, once and for all. Arafat wanted Barak to make further concessions before discussing the final status agreement.

In early 2000, the negotiations between Israel and the PLO continued with the blessing of Barak and Arafat, but without their participation. The gaps remained significant. The Palestinians refused Israel's demand that the conclusion of the framework agreement would be regarded as the

[47] Ibid.
[48] Ibid.
[49] Qurie, *Beyond Oslo*, 98.
[50] Ibid., 98–99.
[51] Deborah Sontag, 'Frustrated Arafat and Barak End Session', *New York Times* (4 February 2000), Section A, 3.
[52] Lee Hockstader, 'Arafat, Barak Fail to Hasten Peace Process', *Washington Post* (4 February 2000), A25.

end of the conflict. The Palestinians regarded the framework agreement as only the preliminary stage and had in mind further negotiations on the final status.[53] While Israel wanted to have recognisable, agreed-upon ends, the Palestinians wanted an open-ended list; once the initial list of ends was accomplished, the list could be reviewed and revised to include new items. As the parties distrusted each other, the discussions were fruitless. Barak was frustrated by Arafat's conduct. Arafat had a habit of writing notes on small bits of paper in small Arabic letters and using a pencil, not a pen, when he negotiated. He would refer to promises allegedly given to him earlier, promises that he recorded on those bits of paper. When facing some obstacles, Arafat told Barak, 'but Rabin promised me that this will be an easy thing to solve. We met in private, and I have it in writing, in my small Arabic letters in pencil.'[54] Barak did not take this tactic seriously. Barak knew Rabin well; they had met frequently and exchanged ideas. Barak suspected that many of Arafat's references to these alleged promises from Rabin were exaggerated or untrue, and his trust in Arafat eroded. Arafat was willing to go the extra mile to get what he wanted, and that extra mile, Barak believed, included compromising the truth. Nor did Barak trust Arafat to abide by his promises. Every achievement in the negotiations, every Israeli concession, was used by Arafat as a step towards asking for more concessions. It was very difficult to conduct negotiations when the list of ends continuously piled up.

Another obstacle was Israel's demand for a Palestinian pledge that they would not enter into any political or economic federation with a third party. While the Palestinians agreed not to establish military pacts with a third party, they did not wish to exclude the possibility of other agreements. Indeed, regional economic cooperation can yield benefits to all people concerned, including the Israelis. There were also major differences over borders and Jerusalem. The Palestinians came up with the idea of Jerusalem as an open and undivided city that would serve as the capital of both states. Israel wished to maintain urban Jerusalem, including Ma'ale Adumim and Givat Zeev, under its sovereignty, while the Palestinians would control an equivalent area of villages around the city that would be redefined as the Palestinian capital of Al Quds. Finally, there was the irreconcilable issue of the refugees' right of return to Israel.[55] This was and remains one of the most difficult issues to resolve.

[53] Qurie, *Beyond Oslo*, 103.
[54] Interview with Ehud Barak (11 July 2022), 11.
[55] Qurie, *Beyond Oslo*, 104.

On 24 May 2000, the IDF unilaterally pulled out from South Lebanon, where it had maintained a military presence since the 1982 Lebanon War. Now, Barak was ready to put all his weight behind the Palestinian option. Arafat, however, during the past few months had witnessed Clinton's inability to mediate between Israel and Syria, and Hezbollah's success in ousting Israel from Lebanon. These two impressions did not make Arafat responsive to peace. Quite the opposite.

Pulling out of Lebanon was Barak's major achievement. During Israel's extended presence in Lebanon, it had lost many soldiers. From 6 June to 29 September 1982, 654 IDF soldiers were killed, and four were declared missing in the Battle of Sultan Ya'akov. Another 562 soldiers fell in the war in the Security Strip between October 1982 and the final exit from Lebanon.[56] The price of an Israeli presence in Lebanon was too high.

However, on other matters Barak had little to take pride in. His slim coalition was shaky, and he was unable to resolve internal rivalries. When mapping situations and choosing goals, Barak had a clear strategic vision, but the tactics he employed to reach strategic ends were far less impressive. Politics is all about listening to different people with different opinions, negotiating, manoeuvring and compromising, not only with the other side, but also within your own camp. Here, Barak showed limited ability. Ehud Olmert has said that Barak does not have the necessary emotional and intellectual sensitivities to understand how to operate successfully within the political framework. Although he is a highly intelligent, sophisticated person, this is not enough to succeed in politics. Barak, reflected Olmert, lacks emotional intelligence.[57] The result was a very rocky coalition. Instead of basking in the achievement of the withdrawal from Lebanon with no casualties, Barak found himself engaged in trying to hold his warring coalition together. The differences between the ultra-religious party, Shas, and the civil rights party, Meretz, were irreconcilable. Both were driven by and committed to polar opposites: Shas by religion, Meretz by liberal ideology. Shas aims to instil Jewish law (Halacha) in all spheres of life, while Meretz endorses separation between state and religion and believes in 'live and let live'. In June 2000, Shas resigned from the coalition government.[58] One of the few options that remained for Barak to

[56] Shaul Nagar, '24 May 2020: Twenty Years since the IDF's Departure from Lebanon', *Yad Leshrion* (28 May 2020) (Hebrew), https://yadlashiryon.com/news/28-במאי-2020-עשרים-שנה-ליציאת-צהל-מלבנון/.

[57] Interview with Ehud Olmert (22 February 2019), 17.

[58] Olmert told me the following story: 'Barak was flying on Sunday evening. And on Sunday, at noon, Eli Yishai came to him and asked him, "Look, I am your partner in the coalition.

salvage his coalition was striking a peace deal with the Palestinians – and so, Camp David 2000 was born.

When I interviewed Barak in 2022, he explained that he had received intelligence reports indicating that the situation was about to explode. The Palestinians were planning violent attacks on Israel. Thus, national responsibility dictated that he do whatever he could to avert the threat, and it propelled him to go to Camp David. Barak explained:

> You will not find the real answer, unless you come, look them in the eye, propose something which is probably not everything that they can think of, but they might think. I did not know how ripe the other side is to take decisions, but I was convinced that I have to try. I had total responsibility, because we are heading, for sure, toward a great explosion. And when it happens, you want to be able to answer yourself as to whether it could have been avoided. And you cannot answer yourself why you did not try. What did you have to lose? If you see a ticking bomb, what did you have to lose by trying to dismantle it?[59]

In my long discussions with him, Barak said time and again that he pushed for the summit because he had a responsibility to try and reach a peace deal. Even if the probability was low, he still had to do it, 'because when you bury the people, as a consequence of this, not self-created, but half self-created deadlock, you cannot honestly answer the question, why the hell you did not try to solve it'.[60]

Ami Ayalon, then head of Shabac, confirmed that Israel was well aware of the violence boiling under the surface. He said that the Intifada was not a surprise. The Shabac saw it; it was written on all the walls, in English, in Arabic and in Hebrew. Ayalon warned Barak. He went to see him and told him: 'I believe that at the end of the year, *Israel*, *you*, *we* shall face a very high wave of Palestinian violence.'[61] It was clear to the Shabac that the

Today, you are going to the Sunday cabinet meeting here. And you are going to negotiate at Camp David. What are you going to do there? Can you tell me?" He said, "I can tell you only if you will not share it with Rabbi Ovadia". Yishai said, "Are you crazy? You want me not to share it with my leader? How can you ask that?" And then, at noontime, they called a special emergency session at Rabbi Ovadia's home. And Rabbi Ovadia called me, and asked me to come and advise him what to do. I said, "Look, I can only say this. That as a partner, you are eligible to know what is proposed in negotiations on your behalf." And then they decided on that day, before he was flying to Camp David, to leave the coalition. And they left Barak with 30 members in the coalition.' Interview with Ehud Olmert (6 January 2025), 15.

59 Cohen-Almagor, 'The Pursuit of Peace with the Palestinians: Interviews with Ehud Barak', 39.

60 Interview with Ehud Barak (11 July 2022), 24.

61 Interview with Ami Ayalon (28 June 2022), 2–3. See also Ami Ayalon, *Friendly Fire: How Israel Became Its Own Worst Enemy* (Lebanon, NH: Steerforth Press, 2020), 169.

Palestinians would use violence after the summer of 2000. Gidi Grinstein said that the Palestinians were already preparing for the Intifada from March or April 2000, before Camp David.[62]

In an earlier interview, Barak said that during the year following his election as prime minister, he had some twenty hours of talks with Arafat on six or seven occasions. The negotiation teams had met for hundreds of hours. There was nothing more to learn.[63] Barak thought that the time was ripe to seal a deal.

While Barak was keen to have a peace summit, this was not the case for the Palestinians. Arafat explicitly told the Americans that the Palestinians were not ready and that they needed more time for preparations.[64] The Camp David papers highlight the Palestinians' repeated warnings that a summit was premature.[65] The situation was not ripe. On 15 June 2000, at his meeting with Clinton, Arafat said: 'I would not wish to attend a summit that has not been prepared well enough to succeed. You will blame me for its failure.'[66] Clinton responded: 'Come over, and if it fails, we will not blame you.'[67] The Americans pushed hard for a summit. Clinton agreed that whether there was a deal or not at the end of the peace summit, Arafat would get the third redeployment of Israeli forces.[68] This meant that redeployment was not an incentive for Arafat to come to Camp David, as he would get it anyway.

The Palestinians were doubtful about Israel's intentions, as the settlements continued growing. Israel still controlled the majority of the West Bank and established checkpoints limiting Palestinian freedom of movement. Furthermore, Israel did not abide by its promises of a safe passage between the West Bank and Gaza, the opening of a Palestinian airport and seaport, and the release of prisoners. The Oslo process, which started with great hopes and promise, was failing, and Barak did not restore a feeling of confidence in the Palestinians. He was unable to establish a good relationship with Arafat similar to the 'peace of the brave' that Arafat shared with Rabin. The Palestinians thought that Barak and Clinton would use

62 Interview with Gidi Grinstein (21 May 2013), 16.

63 Raviv Druker, 'Olmert, Abu Mazen and Barak on the Peace Process', *HaMakor* (17 November 2015).

64 Bregman, *Elusive Peace*, 81–82.

65 Akram Hanieh, 'The Camp David Papers', *Journal of Palestine Studies*, 30(2) (2001): 75–97.

66 Qurie, *Beyond Oslo*, 161.

67 Ibid. On the eve of the Camp David Summit, Arafat sent Clinton a position paper detailing his vision of the solution.

68 Interviews with Rob Malley (28 July 2022), 14 and Salam Fayyad (19 January 2024), 2.

the peace summit to press the Palestinians for concessions they did not want to make, and their suspicions were not without foundation. Indeed, Barak planned to use Clinton to exert pressure on the Palestinians to force them into accepting a deal. Barak believed that Arafat understood that if he did not respond positively to Clinton, a concrete price would have to be paid – and it would be exacted from *him*.[69] Barak's special relationship with Clinton encouraged Barak to think that Clinton would not press him to make concessions he dreaded. He trusted Clinton to pull the chestnuts out of the fire for him. The Palestinians were aware of this arrangement and Israel's expectations.

Clinton

While the Palestinians were very reluctant to come to Camp David, Bill Clinton was the strongest American proponent for the summit.[70] He liked Barak and believed Barak was a man for big occasions. According to Dennis Ross, from the moment that Israel withdrew from Lebanon, Barak wanted a summit immediately. Ross persuaded Clinton that they, the Americans, did not know enough, and that they needed to know more, to have a better sense of whether there was any chance of success for a summit. So, the Americans held out for six weeks. During that period, Barak pushed Clinton to convene a summit. He told Clinton: 'I am willing to come to Camp David and finalise the deal with the Palestinians.'[71] Barak, who had direct phone communication with Clinton and did not have to pass through the usual channels that could filter him, called upon Clinton to gamble. Clinton wanted to believe that Barak was serious in his pledge to offer the Palestinians an unprecedented deal.

In June 2000, the Israelis provided the Americans with detailed papers that included bridging ideas, hinting at the points on which Israel was willing to make concessions.[72] One document included all the issues on which there was agreement, in Israel's opinion, in the light of negotiations that had been held previously. A second document included all the points where, in Israel's opinion, it was possible to reach an agreement through

69 Interview with Ehud Barak (11 July 2022), 16.

70 Interview with Dennis Ross (27 September 2019), 12.

71 Raphael Cohen-Almagor, 'Israeli-Palestinian Negotiations through the Eyes of Gamal Helal', *Israel Journal of Foreign Affairs*, 17(2) (2023): 159–174.

72 Shlomo Ben-Ami, *Prophets without Honor: The 2000 Camp David Summit and the End of the Two-State Solution* (Oxford: Oxford University Press, 2022).

aggressive mediation. A third document included issues requiring leaders' decisions.[73]

Barak presented his ideas to the Americans, which included an independent, sovereign, contiguous Palestinian demilitarised state with a police force. Israel would annex five major settlement blocs near the Green Line: the Shaked, Hinanit and Rihan blocs in northern Wadi Ara; the Kedumim, Ariel, Alfei Menashe, Beit Aryeh, Hasmonaim, Givat Ze'ev and Neve Horon bloc; Ofra, Beit El, Mitzpeh Yeriho (Jericho) and Ma'ale Adumim; Gush Etzion; and the Carmel and Eshkolot bloc in the southern Hebron Hills. The annexed area encompassed 15 per cent of the West Bank and 85 per cent of the settlers. The Jordan Valley, which constitutes 20 per cent of the West Bank, would remain under Israeli control. In the future, if there were sustained peace, it would be transferred to the Palestinians. The PA would control 65 per cent of the West Bank and all of the Gaza Strip. Jerusalem would remain united in Israel. There would be no right of return for the Palestinians.[74]

The Americans were familiar with Israel's positions far more than they were with the Palestinian positions, as the Israelis cooperated with them regularly. The Palestinians, who hardly ever wrote anything down, revealed very little.[75] All the Americans had was information provided verbally by Sa'eb Erekat, Arafat's trusted advisor; Mohammed Dahlan; and Mohammed Rashid, also known as Khaled Salam, Arafat's trusted finance officer. Those conversations were not nearly as detailed as what was received from the Israelis.[76]

While the Americans did not have a similar Palestinian position paper, they knew that the gaps between the Israeli and the Palestinian positions were wide. According to Ross, Clinton would say, 'look, we may not succeed, but we ought to look like we died trying'.[77] Ross met with Dahlan and Rashid several times before Camp David and, based on those discussions, he felt a deal was within reach. Ross was hopeful.[78] Clinton convened a meeting with his advisors and went around the room, asking for the opinion of each person present. They all felt that they ought to try, even though they did not know the Israelis' or the Palestinians' bottom lines, and they were not sure whether they would be

[73] Interview with Gidi Grinstein (21 May 2013), 13.
[74] Danny Yatom, *The Labyrinth of Power* (Tel Aviv: Contento, 2016), 574.
[75] Interview with Gidi Grinstein (21 May 2013), 13.
[76] Interview with Dennis Ross (27 September 2019), 13.
[77] Ibid., 12.
[78] Ibid., 10–11.

able to construct sufficient bridges to overcome differences.[79] This was a very high-stakes decision.

Reflecting on that meeting, American negotiator Robert Malley explained Clinton's thinking: Barak had been lobbying for some time for a heads-of-state meeting, saying that he could only put forward his final proposals at such a meeting, and that the Palestinians needed to be put before 'a true black-and-white-deal-or-no-deal moment'.[80] Barak told Clinton that the negotiations could become serious only at a summit, where everything he had to gain and everything he had to lose would be made clear to Arafat. Malley maintained that there was some hesitation on the American side, particularly after the Shepherdstown experience, and Clinton's meeting with Assad in Geneva. But at the end of the day, the conclusion was reached that 'things were deteriorating in the Palestinian territories anyway'.[81] This summit was going to be the last opportunity. Clinton wanted the summit, and everyone in the room agreed to go for it.

Malley further explained that at that point, the Americans had been trying long enough to negotiate between the Israelis and the Palestinians, including the Stockholm process. Now there was an impasse, and Barak and Arafat were not prepared to move forward. The feeling in the American camp was: 'Let us go to Camp David and try to force the issue … it was smarter to try to force a resolution with a prime minister who was very bold, ambitious, so that he was prepared to go very far to reach a deal.'[82]

American negotiator Aaron David Miller was also present at that crucial meeting. He recalled that everybody said the same thing. Clinton must convene a summit because, if he did not, no one would understand why. In a sense, it was the end of an era. Both King Hussein and Prime Minister Rabin, who had been deeply involved in the Palestinian issue, were dead. Clinton truly cared about the matter at hand and wanted to leave his mark. The Americans also received warnings from their security agencies that violence might erupt if a peace deal was not signed. Miller said that in hindsight, what he should have said was:

> Mr. President, I realize what I am going to say will upset you. And as a consequence, you may decide that I should not participate in this process.

[79] Ibid., 12.
[80] Interview with Robert Malley (20 August 2022), 1.
[81] Ibid.
[82] Interview with Rob Malley (28 July 2022), 15.

> But listen to what I am going to tell you. You should not go to Camp David. Or, if you do go, you should understand that you cannot succeed. This must be one of several high-level summits, between now and the end of your term.[83]

But instead, he said what everybody else in the room did.

The Composition of the Israeli and Palestinian Delegations

Barak was the head of a minority government at a very important historical crossroads, and Gilead Sher said that the politics could have been conducted more intelligently. Sher thought that Meretz, Barak's natural partner in the government, had to be represented at Camp David.[84] Meretz's leader, Yossi Sarid, told Barak not to go to Camp David. Sarid was convinced that the deal was not ready and had no chance of success. Primarily, the issue of Jerusalem remained wide open.[85] Barak explained to Sarid that he would reach an agreement in five minutes. Sarid described the conversation: 'One meeting and it's done, because he's [Barak] going with grand ideas. I wasn't exactly amazed as to their quality. He's going with grand ideas, this is the last chance.'[86] Sarid told Barak that he was mistaken and that it was not worth going to Camp David at that time, that he needed to prepare better to improve the chances for success. But Barak was deeply convinced that his plan was ripe and right. Sarid knew Barak was arrogant,[87] and now he had a further insight: 'I already knew him better by then, and now I understood that I was dealing with a psychopath.'[88] By this, Sarid meant that Barak was dangerously delusional, a person whose self-confidence trumped his better judgement and led him to recklessness. Sarid thought Barak lacked the requisite conscience to acknowledge the damage caused by his misperceptions of his own capabilities and of the situation.

Sarid was Barak's primary partner, especially on matters of peace. Weeks before the summit, Barak invited him to travel with him to Camp David. Every time Barak saw Sarid, he said: 'So have you already prepared? Are you ready? Have you packed?'[89] However, when it was

[83] Interview with Aaron David Miller (12 September 2019), 5.
[84] Interview with Gilead Sher (26 May 2013), 10.
[85] Interview with Yossi Sarid (15 May 2015), 27.
[86] Ibid.
[87] Ibid.
[88] Ibid.
[89] Ibid.

announced that the delegation was set to leave in a matter of days, Sarid did not receive any concrete details. While he himself had no great enthusiasm for the trip, his Meretz associates thought it was inconceivable that the party would not be represented at such an important meeting. Peace was an essential component of Meretz's *raison d'être*. Sarid thought, correctly, that he would not be invited in the end, especially as he had advised Barak not to go. Sarid also understood that Barak wanted to give the delegation a centre-right character and, therefore, he invited people who were not identified with the Israeli left. Speaking about himself, Sarid said, 'Yossi Sarid wasn't good for him there'.[90] Sarid understood that, as the leader of Meretz, 'it was a delegation of bad angels. A delegation of defeatists'.[91] Although he did not call Barak, Sarid thought he deserved an explanation.

The delegation was scheduled to leave on Sunday, 9 July 2000. Two days earlier, on Friday, Sarid received a phone call from the prime minister's office, inviting him to meet Barak on the following day. After twenty minutes of idle talk, Barak told Sarid: 'You know that I wanted you to come with us. I told you so several times. I still do very much, but it can't be helped.'[92] Sarid inquired why it could not be helped and was surprised by Barak's answer: 'There are no more beds available at Camp David.'[93] What Barak meant to say was that each delegation had a fixed number of delegates; instead, he told Sarid: 'Listen, there are rooms there, we're in pairs, there will be a pair in each room, and there are no more beds available.'[94] Sarid, who was known for his cynicism and sharp humour, replied: 'Look, if a bed is a problem, to tell you the truth, I have a folding bed at home. I can bring the folding bed.'[95] Barak tried to clarify that the Americans allocated the Israelis only twelve representatives.[96] Then Sarid decided to be serious and told Barak how disappointed he was by the prime minister's

[90] Ibid., 28.
[91] Ibid.
[92] Ibid, 30.
[93] Ibid.
[94] Ibid.
[95] Ibid.
[96] Interestingly, in his book Barak mentions only ten people: Barak, Danny Yatom, Shlomo Ben-Ami, Amnon Lipkin-Shahak, Elyakim Rubinstein, Gilead Sher, Gidi Grinstein, Shlomo Yanai, Dan Meridor and Israel Hasson. See Ehud Barak, *My Country, My Life: Fighting for Israel, Searching for Peace* (New York: Macmillan, 2018), 355. In his comments on a draft of this book (1 July 2025), Sher wrote that initially, the US hosts allocated nine persons per delegation, the heads (Barak and Arafat) included. Grinstein, an indispensable aide, was creatively added as the 'delegation administrative secretary'.

reasoning.[97] Sarid said that he and Barak would continue to work together as heads of parties and partners in the government, 'but in regard to everything concerned with relations beyond the formal relations between a prime minister and one of his ministers – today, they're finished'.[98]

Barak knew that his peace offering to the Palestinians would alarm some segments of the Israeli population. Rabin was assassinated for less. Barak wanted to show that he had a wide government, with diverse views and opinions. To pass the judgement of the Knesset and the public, right-wingers must be included in the delegation.[99] Barak opted for people like David Levy, Dan Meridor and Elyakim (Ely) Rubinstein, among others.

Barak had appointed Levy to serve as minister of foreign affairs, in the hope that, in due course, Levy would support the peace agreement. Barak wanted Levy to come along to Camp David, not so much to help with the negotiations, but for political reasons. After all, Levy served most of his political career in the right-wing Likud ranks. A few days before the summit, Levy told Barak that he did not intend to travel with him to Camp David. Levy's relationship with Barak was problematic. Levy did not know what concessions Barak intended to make, as Barak had not shared his vision with his cabinet. Levy suspected that the concessions would be beyond what he could accept. In addition, he did not speak English and believed that he would be at a great disadvantage in a summit where the *lingua franca* would be English.[100]

Barak wanted someone from Shas, the Sephardi-religious political party – again, not for the sake of negotiations or for improving the chances for a successful resolution, but for political reasons. Shas refused. Barak wanted Natan Sharansky, a *bon ton* figure in Israeli politics, known

97 Sarid said: '"Listen, Ehud, I'm a minister in your government. This isn't a private matter of yours or mine. Therefore, I'd expect, if you were looking for an excuse – is that the best excuse you could find? You couldn't find something more –", I said to him, "Let me suggest one to you. For example, if you'd say tell me: The configuration of the delegation isn't comfortable for me, for public reasons, for reasons of public opinion. I'm not sure that I'd respect such a consideration, but I'd at least respect your candour. You could say 'I want people around me –'". I'm not sure that I'd burst with joy upon hearing this explanation, but at least I could say, the man's telling the truth.' Interview with Yossi Sarid (15 May 2015), 30.

98 Ibid.

99 Interview with Ehud Barak (21 June 2022), 9.

100 Raviv Drucker Blog, 'If Levy Intends to Make Dramas – Let Him Not Come to Camp David' (2020) (Hebrew), drucker10.net/חרקירי/פרק-14-אם-לוי-מתכוון-לעשות-דראמות-שלא?utm_campaign=shareaholic&utm_medium=email_this&utm_source=email.

for his rightist political views, but Sharansky refused as well.[101] Barak did not look for people to agree. He looked for people who could help him sell a success or a failure.

Former Likud member Meridor met with Barak a few hours before Sarid on Saturday, 8 July. The meeting lasted about two hours. For Meridor, the invitation came out of the blue. He was genuinely surprised.[102] At that time, Meridor was a member of the Centre party and chairperson of the Knesset Foreign Affairs and Defence Committee. The six-person Centre party was part of Barak's coalition. Meridor was perceived by Barak to be a moderate, liberal-right politician with whom he could cooperate.[103] In his bold language, Barak exhorted: 'There is an iceberg. We are going to crash it.'[104] Barak and Meridor agreed that Meridor could oppose the peace agreement if he were uncomfortable with the details, but he would not be allowed to leave the summit in protest.[105]

Rubinstein was also invited to Camp David at the last minute, 'a day or two before the conference'.[106] Barak invited Rubinstein as, in his mind, he would succeed in the same place where Menachem Begin succeeded in 1978. Barak knew that a key figure at the first peace summit with Egypt was the legal advisor to the government at that time, Aharon Barak.[107] In 2000, Rubinstein held that same position. He was also at the first Camp David and was an expert on the refugee issue. Barak perceived Rubinstein as an honest man who would not leak sensitive information from the summit, and who might oppose the deal that Barak wished to offer but would not go against it. Rubinstein was known to be a quintessential civil servant; although he did not voice political opinions in public, 'it was not a secret that he is a right-winger', Barak said.[108] Because Meridor and Rubinstein were last-minute invitees, and because Barak liked to keep all the cards to himself, both were unfamiliar with the details of possible solutions to all

[101] Natan Sharansky spent nine years in Soviet prisons before he was allowed to immigrate to Israel. He was embraced by the Israeli establishment and became quite a successful politician, and later Chairman of the Jewish Agency for Israel. www.jewishagency.org/executive-members/natan-sharansky-0.

[102] Interview with Dan Meridor (20 January 2016), 7.

[103] Interview with Ehud Barak (21 June 2022), 9.

[104] Interview with Dan Meridor (21 May 2013), 11.

[105] Raviv Drucker Blog, 'If Levy Intends to Make Dramas – Let Him Not Come to Camp David'.

[106] Interview with Elyakim Rubinstein (28 May 2013), 6.

[107] Raphael Cohen-Almagor, 'Lessons from the Israeli-Egyptian Peace Talks: An Interview with Aharon Barak', *Israel Studies Review*, 34(2) (Autumn 2019): 1–32.

[108] Interview with Ehud Barak (21 June 2022), 9.

the problems. On the flight to Camp David, Rubinstein complained that he had no idea what the Israeli stance on the refugee issue was. He was briefed then and there.[109]

Ehud Olmert told me that Barak also asked him to participate in Camp David. Olmert was then mayor of Jerusalem. According to Olmert, Barak told him that he planned to reach an agreement on a comprehensive basis, including Jerusalem, and that Jerusalem would be the most sensitive issue. Barak believed that if Olmert were standing next to him on the lawn of the White House when he announced what he had agreed on Jerusalem, he would be more likely to convince the Israeli public to accept such an agreement. Olmert naturally inquired what Barak intended to propose about Jerusalem, and Barak replied that he could not tell him what he had in mind. Olmert was not prepared to accept the invitation on such vague terms.[110] Like Levy, he refused the offer.

This story is interesting given that, at the time, Olmert was one of the leaders of Likud. Even more interesting was Barak's reaction when I inquired whether he had approached Olmert to join his delegation before he approached Meridor, which was my understanding from my communications with Olmert. I thought Barak had wanted a right-winger to negotiate on Jerusalem. Both Olmert and Meridor are intelligent men. Both could assist in convincing the public of the need for concessions in Jerusalem. First, Barak tried Olmert. When the latter refused, Barak opted for Meridor. Barak, however, denied issuing such an invitation to Olmert and said that he had consulted several people about Jerusalem. Olmert was one of them, as it was important to know what the mayor of Jerusalem thought about possible solutions for the city. Apparently, there was some misunderstanding. While Olmert believes that Barak *did* invite him to the summit, Barak maintains that such an invitation was not issued.[111]

109 Raviv Drucker Blog, 'If Levy Intends to Make Dramas – Let Him Not Come to Camp David'.

110 Raphael Cohen-Almagor, 'Lessons from Peace Negotiations: Interview with Ehud Olmert', *Israel Affairs*, 27(6) (2021): 8–10.

111 Cohen-Almagor, 'The Pursuit of Peace with the Palestinians: Interviews with Ehud Barak', 23–24. In a personal communication on 25 August 2023, Olmert reiterated that Barak did invite him to Camp David. In my third interview with him, Olmert raised this issue at the conclusion of the interview, when I asked him whether he wanted to add something. Olmert said: 'You know, I recall our previous interview when I told you that Barak called me and asked me to come to Camp David. And Gili Sher is the one who told me that he advised Barak to do it. I did not invent it. And I wrote that in my book, and there was no comment about it years and years and years ago. I do not know now why Barak is trying to deny it. This is rubbish. When he asked me to come, I said to him, "Why do you need

Barak needed sharp people with vast experience. Barak's spokesperson, Gadi Baltiansky, suggested inviting Yossi Beilin, but Barak rejected the idea.[112] I asked Barak why he did not invite Shimon Peres to join him at Camp David. Barak seemed surprised by my question. It seems that the thought did not cross his mind. Barak said he did not think Peres could be of any help. I explained that Peres was the elder statesman of the government and, therefore, he seemed to be one who could assist in delicate negotiations. Barak agreed that Peres was, indeed, the elder statesman. But Barak was very close to Peres's arch-rival, Yitzhak Rabin, and witnessed what really happened between Peres and Rabin for all those years. These episodes did not evoke any appetite to involve Peres in the peace talks he had in mind. Furthermore, Barak said he was very close to King Hussein, and he was aware of what had happened between Peres and King Hussein, alluding to the 1987 London Document that exploded in Hussein's face.[113] Hussein held Peres responsible for that failed episode, and the relationship between the two leaders soured. So, from Barak's experience, 'it was a bad idea to put Shimon Peres into such a summit', when 'you really want to make clear that you know what you are doing. Namely, that you will have an opportunity to put to the test the need to take a tough decision.'[114] Barak did not trust Peres and suspected that Peres would not accept his leadership and might leak information from the negotiations.

An interesting figure at Camp David was Yossi Ginossar. A controversial former Shabac agent who became a businessman upon his forced resignation, Ginossar utilised his connections in the OPT to establish a close relationship with Arafat. Rabin used him as a special channel to the Palestinian leader. As the Palestinians insisted on Ginossar's presence at Camp David,[115] Ginossar was part of the American headcount. Barak said: 'We did not have a place for him, we did not see a reason to have one. It was known that Ginossar was very close to Arafat, probably too close to

me there?" I was mayor of Jerusalem at the time. He said, "If I will reach an agreement on Jerusalem, I want you to stand next to me and support it". I said, "How do I know if I will support it? What are you going propose about Jerusalem?" And he refused to tell me. So I said, "I am not going"'. Interview with Ehud Olmert (6 January 2025), 13.

112 Interview with Gadi Baltiansky (25 January 2016).

113 In 1987, Hussein was upset when Peres could not deliver Israeli support for a secret agreement the two had signed in London. The Hussein–Peres Agreement (London Document), 11 April 1987, https://tinyurl.com/3u83ewxe. See also Mordechai Gazit, *Israeli Diplomacy and the Quest for Peace* (London: Routledge, 2002).

114 Cohen-Almagor, 'The Pursuit of Peace with the Palestinians: Interviews with Ehud Barak', 20.

115 Interview with Ehud Barak (21 June 2022), 8.

Arafat.'[116] Barak argues that, officially, Ginossar was not part of the Israeli delegation; however, Grinstein writes that Barak brought along Ginossar to serve as a go-between for him and Rashid.[117]

The composition of the Palestinian delegation was problematic due to the sour relationships between its members. It was split into factions with different and distinct positions, all trying to compete for Arafat's attention, while Arafat was in a realm of his own.[118] Mahmoud Abbas, one of the co-founders of Fatah, was secretary general of the PLO Executive Committee and held the Israeli file in the PLO. He saw himself as the most knowledgeable person in the delegation about the conflict and the holder of the keys to its resolution. Ahmed Qurie, the speaker of the Palestinian Legislative Council, had gained a reputation as a skilled negotiator following the successful Oslo talks. Sa'eb Erekat, the minister of local government, was the closest advisor to Arafat. Both Qurie and Erekat had aspirations that Abbas did not appreciate. Hasan Asfour, the minister of state and head of the PLO Negotiations Department, had been in Oslo and also regarded himself as a skilled negotiator. Mohammed Dahlan, the chief of preventive security in Gaza, had developed good relationships with the Americans and the Israelis, which Abbas did not like. Asfour was Abbas's chief of staff, but the two had fallen out over issues following the 1998 Wye agreement, which led to demonstrations outside Abbas's villa in Gaza. Dahlan failed to quell the situation, and Abbas later learned that Asfour was among those leading the crowd.[119] Mohammed Rashid, an economic advisor, had also developed good relationships with the Americans and the Israelis, especially with Ginossar, with whom he also had financial dealings.[120]

Minister of Information and Culture Yasser Abed Rabbo was one of Arafat's closest advisors; many Palestinian foreign missions, mostly secret, were assigned to him. Abed Rabbo had his own ideas about how to advance the negotiations. The rest of the Palestinian delegation were all keen Arafat loyalists: Minister of Planning and International Cooperation Nabil Sha'ath, Advisor to the Chairman Akram Haniya (Hanieh), Chief of Staff Nabil Abu Rudineh and Assistant to the Chairman Yousef Abdallah.

116 Interview with Ehud Barak (11 July 2022), 12.

117 Gidi Grinstein and Ari Afilalo, *(In)Sights: Peacemaking in the Oslo Process Thirty Years and Counting* (Jerusalem: Gefen, 2023), 230.

118 Qurie, *Beyond Oslo*, 210, 227, 326–327.

119 Clayton E. Swisher, *The Truth about Camp David: The Untold Story about the Collapse of the Middle East Peace Process* (New York: Nation Books, 2004), 205.

120 Interview with Yitzhak Mordechai (19 December 2024), 17.

American Mediation

The Palestinians did not perceive the Americans as impartial mediators. The United States is a powerful player, with leverage and the ability to drive the process forward, but successful mediation also requires impartiality and credibility. In 1974, Secretary of State Henry Kissinger was able to succeed in his mediation between Israel and Egypt because he was perceived as an objective, fair broker between the two sides. Kissinger was able to maintain a balanced view regarding their competing interests. The same can be said of President Jimmy Carter and his successful mediation at Camp David in 1978.[121] But there was no such perception of the American broker prior to Camp David 2000. The Palestinians believed the Americans had coordinated their negotiation plans with the Israelis, and their suspicions were valid. Aaron David Miller confessed: 'Not only did we consistently coordinate our positions with the Israelis, showing them our negotiating texts first – a practice I might add the Palestinians had come to expect – but we saw the issues largely from Israel's point of view. I remember how impressed we all were when we learned that Barak was willing to concede 80% of the West Bank.'[122] The Americans did not recognise that 80 per cent was a far cry from what the Palestinians wanted, and that a deal could not be reached based on this figure. The Palestinians' inability to trust President Clinton undermined his position and his ability to relay information effectively to both sides.

The three delegations arrived at the summit quite stressed. The Americans knew that there was a lot to do and that the gaps between the two sides were wide. Clinton had a lot at stake. He wanted the summit to succeed, perceiving it as the single most important topic near the conclusion of his presidency. The Americans were well aware that signing a peace deal was also the single most important matter for Barak and his coalition government. Clinton wanted to support Barak, seeing his own interests and Barak's as in sync.

The Israelis were stressed because several political parties (United Torah Judaism, Shas, Yisrael B'Aliyah and National Religious Party) had withdrawn from the coalition. Barak's coalition now included only forty-two Knesset members (MKs) out of 120. Barak lost a vote of no confidence in his government (54:52) on 9 July 2000, just before leaving for

[121] For further discussion, see Jacob Bercovitch (ed.), *Resolving International Conflicts: The Theory and Practice of Mediation* (Boulder, CO: Lynne Rienner, 1996).

[122] Aaron David Miller, 'How Not to Host a Summit', *Foreign Policy* (10 July 2012).

Washington.[123] The government survived because the opposition did not receive the required majority vote of sixty-one or more.

The Palestinians were stressed because they thought the summit was an American-Israeli trap. The Americans tried to ease their fears, but the Palestinians only came because Clinton put so much pressure on Arafat that he eventually succumbed. However, they were not enthusiastic. There was no feeling that the wings of history were hovering above Camp David. One reads Qurie's depiction of the day of their arrival at the summit and understands that the Palestinians did not think they were about to solve the Israeli-Palestinian conflict. Qurie feared that they were in for 'gruelling days'.[124] When their State Department driver got lost in the Maryland countryside on the way to Camp David, the Palestinians joked that this was a bad omen for the conference: 'We had lost our way even before the talks began!'[125] Camp David looked to them like 'a well-guarded citadel',[126] manned by 'squads of formidable armed marines'.[127] Officials and protocol personnel welcomed them and then 'shepherded' them to their accommodation.[128]

The Americans agreed to host the peace summit, although the prescriptions for failure were clearly inscribed. They decided to ignore the clear signs. They knew that it would be difficult to make peace when there was little trust between the two sides, and when Barak did not have public support.[129] They were aware that he was racing against time, as his government seemed unsustainable, and that the Palestinians had been forced to come to the summit. Still, they wanted to go ahead and try.

The Americans did not invite other Arab countries to the summit, even though Arafat always said that he needed to consult Arab leaders on crucial matters. They thought this would be unwise, because the Arabs would be negative and the Palestinians would hide behind the Arabs. Moreover, the Israelis would feel they were battling on several fronts

123 Knesset no-confidence vote, 10 July 2000, *C-SPAN*, www.c-spanvideo.org/program/158184-1; 'Israeli PM Survives No-Confidence Vote', *The Guardian* (10 July 2000), www.guardian.co.uk/world/2000/jul/10/israel2.

124 Qurie, *Beyond Oslo*, 174.

125 Ibid.

126 Ibid.

127 Ibid.

128 Ibid.

129 Beilin writes that during the last week before the Camp David Summit he met with a Palestinian central figure who thought that the summit was destined to fail because not enough had been done in practical areas, and the atmosphere between the two sides was not positive. See Yossi Beilin, *The Path to Geneva* (New York: RDV Books, 2004), 152.

concerning *all* Arab-occupied territories. The focus might shift from the Palestinian track to the Syrian and Lebanese tracks. Therefore, inviting other parties to Camp David was not even in the cards.[130]

Conclusion

Despite the Oslo promise, the 1990s were difficult years. Israel was continuously attacked by suicide terrorists. Israeli leaders mistrusted the Palestinians, first and foremost Yasser Arafat, perceiving Israel's security as the highest priority and the PLO as an enemy, not a partner for peace. At the same time, the settlements continued to grow. Israel controlled Gaza and the majority of the West Bank, and it established checkpoints limiting Palestinian freedom of movement.

Some fascinating accounts explain the complexity of the situation as the parties resolved to meet at Camp David.[131] These and my interviews reveal inherent problems in the search for peace in the Middle East. These problems are explored and analysed in the next two chapters. The analysis focuses primarily on the three central figures, whose leadership shortcomings contributed to the failure of the Camp David Summit: Ehud Barak, Yasser Arafat and Bill Clinton. I contend that all three bear significant responsibility for the summit's disappointing outcome. The gaps between the Israeli and Palestinian positions were simply too vast to be bridged within the constrained two-week time frame allotted by the American mediators. At the heart of the impasse was the

[130] Interview with Gamal Helal (11 November 2022), 28.

[131] Shlomo Ben-Ami, *Scars of War, Wounds of Peace* (London: Phoenix, 2005) and *A Front without a Rearguard* (Tel Aviv: Yedioth Ahronoth, 2004, Hebrew); Bill Clinton, *My Life* (New York: Knopf, 2010); Martin Indyk, *Innocent Abroad* (New York: Simon and Schuster, 2009); Daniel C. Kurtzer, *Negotiating Arab-Israeli Peace: American Leadership in the Middle East* (Washington, DC: United States Institute of Peace Press, 2008) and *The Peace Puzzle: America's Quest for Arab-Israeli Peace, 1989–2011* (Ithaca, NY: Cornell University Press, in Collaboration with the United States Institute of Peace, 2013); Malley and Agha, 'Camp David: The Tragedy of Errors'; Robert Malley and Hussein Agha, 'A Reply to Ehud Barak', *New York Review of Books*, 49(10) (13 June 2002); Dan Meridor, 'Camp David Diaries', *Haaretz* (29 July 2011) (Hebrew); Aaron David Miller, *The Much Too Promised Land: America's Elusive Search for Arab-Israeli Peace* (New York: Bantam, 2008); Morris, 'An Interview with Ehud Barak'; Qurie, *Beyond Oslo*; Dennis Ross and Gidi Grinstein, with a reply by Hussein Agha and Robert Malley, 'Camp David: An Exchange', *New York Review of Books* (20 September 2001); Dennis Ross, *Missing Peace: The Inside Story of the Fight for Middle East Peace* (New York: Farrar, Straus and Giroux, 2004); Gilead Sher, *The Israeli-Palestinian Peace Negotiations, 1999–2001: Within Reach* (London: Routledge, 2006).

issue of Jerusalem, particularly its religiously significant sites. The summit ultimately failed because neither side was willing – or politically able – to make the painful concessions necessary for a historic compromise. Even in the final moments of negotiation, the Palestinian leadership insisted on the partition of Jerusalem and full, unconditional sovereignty over the Temple Mount – positions the Israeli delegation could not accept in full. This mutual rigidity underscored the depth of mistrust and the enduring complexity of the conflict.

6

The 2000 Camp David Peace Summit

> The future of mankind must rest upon the foundation of mutual understanding amongst all nations and that aggressive nationalism must be overcome.
>
> ~ Albert Einstein

The Summit

In accordance with the 'no surprise' policy between the United States and Israel, the Americans informed Ehud Barak of their intentions. On the evening of 12 July 2000, Barak, his close confidant Danny Yatom, Shlomo Ben-Ami, Amnon Lipkin-Shahak, Yossi Ginossar, Shlomo Yanai, Elyakim Rubinstein, and Dan Meridor met. Barak told them the Americans would present their paper on the following day.[1]

Gidi Grinstein divides the summit into four phases. The exploratory and organisation phase was from 11–15 July, when the Americans met with the two delegations and explored agreements and gaps. The peak of the summit was from 16–19 July, when the Israeli teams presented what they perceived as ground-breaking ideas that would enable an agreement. President Bill Clinton was in Japan from 20–22 July, and Barak waited for his return. Lastly, from 22–25 July, desperate attempts were made to convince Yasser Arafat to sign an agreement, but he refused.[2]

The summit began with a plenary session in which the three leaders, Clinton, Arafat and Barak, delivered speeches. This was followed by the allocation of tasks to the delegates. During the first week, Barak formed his negotiation teams: Ben-Ami, Lipkin-Shahak and Yanai on borders, Lipkin-Shahak and Yanai on security, Yatom and Meridor on Jerusalem (later Gilead Sher replaced Yatom), and Rubinstein and Grinstein on refugees.[3]

1 Dan Meridor, *Camp David 2000* (personal diary, Hebrew), 5.

2 Gidi Grinstein and Ari Afilalo, *(In)Sights: Peacemaking in the Oslo Process Thirty Years and Counting* (Jerusalem: Gefen, 2023), 232.

3 Meridor, *Camp David 2000*, 9.

Sher took part in all negotiation teams, except refugees.[4] Later, other people (e.g., Israel Hasson, Reuven Merchav,[5] Oded Eran[6]) joined the negotiations. On the Palestinian side, Ahmed Qurie, Sa'eb Erekat, Mohammed Dahlan and Hasan Asfour were to negotiate borders;[7] Qurie and Dahlan were to negotiate security; Erekat and Abed Rabbo were to discuss Jerusalem; and Mahmoud Abbas (Abu Mazen) was to negotiate the refugee issue together with Nabil Sha'ath, Abed Rabbo and Akram Haniya (Hanieh).

The first few days went according to Barak's plans. He believed that progress would be made only under pressure, and that nothing meaningful would happen before Clinton's departure for Japan. After the president returned, Arafat would be forced, under pressure from Clinton, to decide whether he would accept Barak's deal or not.[8]

13 July

The Americans proposed a working paper. Here they followed the Jimmy Carter model of putting together a draft that they would keep revising.[9] The United States delegation aimed to employ the 'one-text procedure', a negotiation method in which the mediator plays an active, guiding role in shaping a mutually acceptable agreement. Under this approach, the mediator drafts a single text and presents it to both parties for review and feedback. Areas of disagreement are identified and systematically addressed through iterative revisions. The process employs a range of techniques – clarifying ambiguous language, refining proposals, introducing new ideas, postponing contentious issues and, when necessary, enlisting the support of third parties to provide additional insight or data.

This method is designed to lower tensions, foster mutual trust and gradually bridge divides by shifting the focus from positional bargaining to problem-solving. The success of the 'one-text procedure' was exemplified during the creation of the Camp David Accords in September 1978. At that summit, the American delegation, acting as mediator, drafted a proposal to which neither Israel nor Egypt was initially bound. Through constructive critique and continuous refinement, over the course of thirteen days and twenty-three iterations, a final text emerged that both parties

[4] Communication with Gilead Sher (22 October 2023).
[5] Former Director General of the Ministry of Foreign Affairs.
[6] A senior diplomat in the Ministry of Foreign Affairs.
[7] Ahmed Qurie, *Beyond Oslo* (London: I.B. Tauris, 2008), 191.
[8] Grinstein and Afilalo, *(In)Sights*, 235.
[9] Interview with Dennis Ross (21 October 2019), 20.

were prepared to endorse. The procedure proved effective in limiting the number of unresolved issues, easing adversarial dynamics and paving the way for a historic agreement through focused, incremental progress.[10]

This time, Dennis Ross introduced a twelve-page document, which was a variant of the paper discussed in Sweden entitled 'Israeli-Palestinian Framework Agreement on Permanent Status'. The paper was designed to present broad principles on all the issues and identify the gaps between the Israelis and the Palestinians. Border changes would require land swaps. On refugees, the formula was 'reconciling the Palestinian need for the refugees to have the right of return with Israel's need to control admission to its territory'.[11] On Jerusalem, the idea was to suggest practical arrangements.[12] William Quandt argues that the drafting on Jerusalem was 'careless'.[13]

Ben-Ami thought the American paper was reasonable and recommended that Barak accept it as the basis for negotiation. Barak, however, together with some other members of the delegation, wanted to introduce changes in the document. In fact, Barak thought there was no need for an American paper and wanted to have direct talks with the Palestinians.[14] He thought the draft went beyond what he could convince the Israeli people to accept.[15] Jerusalem was the main issue. The American proposal stated outright that there would be two capitals, one Israeli and the other Palestinian, within the city of Jerusalem.[16] Barak wanted the document to state: 'Jerusalem will be an open city, undivided, placed under Israeli sovereignty.'[17]

The Palestinians rejected the American text as well.[18] Ross added a word in his own handwriting before the draft was shown to the Palestinians,

10 Lawrence Wright, *Thirteen Days in September* (London: Oneworld, 2014); Roger Fisher and William Ury, *Getting to Yes: Negotiating Agreement without Giving In* (London: Random House, 1991), 121–122.

11 Shlomo Ben-Ami, *Prophets without Honor: The 2000 Camp David Summit and the End of the Two-State Solution* (Oxford: Oxford University Press, 2022), 59.

12 Interview with Dennis Ross (27 September 2019), 19.

13 William B. Quandt, *Peace Process: American Diplomacy and the Arab-Israeli Conflict since 1967* (Berkeley: University of California Press, 2005), 367; Clayton E. Swisher, *The Truth about Camp David: The Untold Story about the Collapse of the Middle East Peace Process* (New York: Nation Books, 2004), 265–272.

14 Interview with Shlomo Ben-Ami (26 June 2013), 6.

15 Interview with Ehud Barak (11 July 2022), 16.

16 Ehud Barak, *My Country, My Life: Fighting for Israel, Searching for Peace* (New York: Macmillan, 2018), 359.

17 Charles Enderlin, *Shattered Dreams: The Failure of the Peace Process in the Middle East, 1995–2002* (New York: Other Press, 2003), 193.

18 Aaron David Miller, 'How Not to Host a Summit', *Foreign Policy* (10 July 2012). See also Daniel C. Kurtzer, Scott B. Lasensky, William B. Quandt, Steven L. Spiegel and Shibley Z. Telhami, *The Peace Puzzle* (Ithaca, NY: Cornell University Press, 2013).

which confirmed what Arafat suspected all along: that the United States and Israel were colluding against him.[19] Clinton was reluctant to 'jam' the Israelis. Ironically, his refusal contributed to stalled talks and the summit's ultimate failure. The paper, which was meant to give the summit a sense of direction, was invalidated by both parties. The Americans did not insist on having it as the groundwork for discussions; instead, they withdrew it altogether. The entire strategy that the Americans had developed for the summit was undone. They continued to coordinate with Israel, aiming to obtain concessions from the Israelis and then take them to the Palestinians.

14 July

Yatom and Meridor met with Erekat and Abed Rabbo for the first round of talks on Jerusalem. Meridor said that Israel would not concede its sovereignty on any part of Jerusalem. At most, discussion of the transfer of religious and other functional responsibilities and arrangements to the Palestinians in East Jerusalem was possible.[20] The Palestinians perceived the appointment of Meridor to the discussions on Jerusalem as rigid.[21] They rejected the Israeli offer, insisting on full Palestinian sovereignty over East Jerusalem. Erekat suggested that Barak and Arafat discuss this sensitive issue between them;[22] however, the two leaders never negotiated directly.

As for the refugee issue, Israel refused to take responsibility for their plight. The Palestinians sensed that Barak did not want to deal with the issue at all.[23] The gaps between the two sides were enormous. The Palestinians wanted Israel to accept hundreds of thousands of refugees; Israel agreed to family reunifications of 5,000 people.[24]

The Americans presented a bridging paper, which the Palestinians rejected as 'Israeli in full', especially as regards a so-called Palestinian acceptance of a 'municipal solution' for Jerusalem and the Abu Dis-as-capital idea.[25] The Palestinians drafted a response and presented it

19 Quandt, *Peace Process*, 368.
20 Meridor, *Camp David 2000*, 9.
21 Ibid.
22 Ibid.
23 Interview with Ghaith al-Omari (2 September 2014), 15.
24 Interview with Ely Rubinstein (10 July 2018), 19.
25 Akram Hanieh, 'The Camp David Papers', *Journal of Palestine Studies*, 30(2) (Winter 2001): 87.

to Secretary of State Madeleine Albright, showing that the American paper distorted their positions and contradicting the United States' own positions on Jerusalem. The American response was quick. Clinton told Arafat that the paper was 'null and void'.[26]

15 July

Clinton decided to simply appear and listen to one of the negotiation sessions. As a consequence, the summit lost a major Palestinian player. Ben-Ami presented the Israeli positions, with maps. Qurie responded with a general speech about 1967, international legitimacy and so forth. He also wanted to take with him the Israeli map, in order to consult his colleagues who were not present.[27] The Israelis refused the request. Clinton, who was in the room to 'observe', told Qurie that he would understand if Qurie did not like the Israeli map, but that he could not simply reject it without clarifying his position. Clinton asked Qurie to put forward his own map. Qurie refused; he felt cornered and dug in his heels even further. Gamal Helal told Clinton: 'Mr. President, it is time to be tough.'[28] Clinton lost his temper.[29] He lashed out at Qurie, shouting: '"Sir, this is not the [UN] Security Council, this is not the General Assembly. You can give your lectures there, but don't waste my time. I have a lot at stake here as well."'[30] Clinton continued: '"A summit's purpose is to have discussions that are based on sincere intentions and you, the Palestinians, did not come to this summit with sincere intentions."'[31] Clinton left the room in anger, together with the American mediators.

Qurie explained his position by saying that Clinton wanted the Palestinians to engage in a debate that would have culminated in the imposition of the entire Israeli plan on them. He thought that Clinton had 'an extreme bias' in favour of the Israeli position. Thereafter, Qurie wrote, 'we were dumbstruck when the American leader turned angrily on us, directing at us, and at me in particular, a long and hostile diatribe about our

26 Ibid.
27 Ben-Ami, *Prophets without Honor*, 68.
28 Raphael Cohen-Almagor, 'Israeli-Palestinian Negotiations through the Eyes of Gamal Helal', *Israel Journal of Foreign Affairs* (2023): 12.
29 Interview with Dennis Ross (21 October 2019), 24.
30 Shlomo Ben-Ami, *2000 Camp David Summit: Daily Diary* (July 2000), www.jewishvirtuallibrary.org/jsource/Peace/benamidiary.html.
31 Ibid.; Ben-Ami, *Prophets without Honor*, 67–68; Martin Indyk, *Innocent Abroad* (New York: Simon & Schuster, 2009), 310; Swisher, *The Truth about Camp David*, 274–275.

lack of willingness to engage with the other side'.[32] Qurie was 'astonished and totally shocked' that Clinton blamed him personally for the failure of the summit, especially as he did so in public and in front of the Israeli delegation.[33] Qurie planned to leave, 'never to return'.[34] He was deeply hurt. Despite Arafat's pleading, he refused to participate in the negotiations and the dinner later that day. Clinton's rushed intervention had negative implications for the summit and for the peace process.

The discussions revealed that Jerusalem might be a crucial problem. The Palestinians wanted Al Quds as their capital in East Jerusalem, including the Haram al-Sharif/Temple Mount. Barak invited Israel Hasson to join the delicate talks. Barak also gave Meridor reading material on possible solutions to the Jerusalem problem, highlighting the solution that spoke of dividing the city. Meridor remained unconvinced. He repeated his uncompromising views to Clinton.[35] In a late evening meeting of the Israeli delegation, Barak said that the summit might fail due to a lack of agreement on Jerusalem.[36] It became apparent to at least some of the participants that no agreement would be reached at Camp David.[37] The Palestinians explained that they had made their concessions by acceding to an Israeli presence in 78 per cent of historic Palestine. Now it was Israel's turn to make concessions. At first, the Israeli delegation thought there was leeway in the Palestinian starting points. Now, some realised that the Palestinian starting and ending points were the same.

Clinton asked Arafat and Barak to choose two trusted negotiators each and provide them with a mandate to brainstorm ideas for twelve hours. Arafat chose Erekat and Dahlan. Barak chose Ben-Ami and Sher.[38] This reminds us of Carter's conduct at Camp David in 1978, when Carter requested that Anwar Sadat and Menachem Begin choose one representative of their respective delegations to draft an agreement.

16 July

Arafat told Clinton he was willing to concede to Israel between 8 and 10 per cent of the West Bank. He said that he would leave it to Clinton to

[32] Qurie, *Beyond Oslo*, 197.
[33] Ibid.
[34] Ibid., 198.
[35] Meridor, *Camp David 2000*, 11–12.
[36] Ibid., 13.
[37] Interview with Gidi Grinstein (21 May 2013), 12.
[38] Enderlin, *Shattered Dreams*, 205.

resolve the issue of the land swap (the exchange of territories), and that he was also prepared to let Clinton decide on security arrangements, provided that an international force would be part of the solution.[39] In a letter to Clinton, however, Arafat made it clear that no agreement would be signed unless the issues of Jerusalem and the refugees were resolved.[40]

After the rejection of the first American paper, the American legal advisor Jonathan Schwartz was tasked to prepare an I-and-P paper, that is, a paper noting the Israeli and Palestinian positions on core concerns. But this tactic became too cumbersome, and the Americans backed off from that exercise as well. In the following days, Clinton tried to move the negotiations forward by resorting to 'shuttle diplomacy', relaying questions between Arafat and Barak. He also tried to exert pressure on Barak, demanding that he make substantial concessions on Jerusalem.[41] Ross, on his part, created a backchannel between Ben-Ami and Lipkin-Shahak on the Israeli side and Dahlan and Mohammed Rashid on the Palestinian side, hoping to see some positive movement in the negotiations; however, this effort, too, was not very helpful.[42] Clinton proposed that Barak and Arafat negotiate directly, but both refused.[43] Barak had no desire for a dialogue with Arafat, and the latter knew it. Barak wanted the summit so that Clinton would negotiate for him.

Then Ben-Ami, Sher, Erekat and Dahlan met, and the Israelis improved their offer. Their so-called red lines continued to shift. On Jerusalem, they proposed that the outer envelope of Arab neighbourhoods (Dalat el-Barid, Al-Sawahreh, Semiramis, Kalandia, Kufr Akab, Beit Hanina, Shuafat, Umm Tuba and part of A-Ram) would be under Palestinian sovereignty. The inner envelope would be under functional autonomy, the 0.9 square kilometre Old City under a special regime and the Temple Mount under a perpetual Palestinian trusteeship. Ben-Ami and Sher also improved the territorial proposal, reducing the areas for annexation to 12 per cent.[44] Erekat and Dahlan rejected the proposal, as they knew Arafat would not agree to it. Qurie later learned about the meeting and saw it as an attempt

[39] Ari Shavit, 'The Day Peace Died', *Haaretz* (14 September 2001) (Hebrew).
[40] Hanieh, 'The Camp David Papers', 87.
[41] Meridor, *Camp David 2000*, 21.
[42] Interview with Dennis Ross (27 September 2019), 19.
[43] Swisher says that also on 16 July, when Clinton convened Arafat and Barak for a dinner, Barak ignored Arafat, who looked humiliated. Swisher, *The Truth about Camp David*, 282.
[44] Enderlin, *Shattered Dreams*, 211. Swisher argues that the meeting was on 17 July. See Clayton E. Swisher, *The Truth about Camp David*, 283–284. Qurie writes that the meeting took place on 15 July. Qurie, *Beyond Oslo*, 200.

to exclude him from the negotiations.[45] This is an indication of the bad relations and lack of comradeship within the Palestinian delegation.

17 July

Qurie describes this day as 'the day of Jerusalem'.[46] Clinton met with Arafat and proposed that the Palestinians annex the Muslim and Christian Quarters of Jerusalem, while Israel would annex the Armenian and Jewish Quarters, as well as the Haram al-Sharif. The UN Security Council and Morocco would delegate to the Palestinian Authority (PA) 'custodial rights', enabling it to administer the Islamic Holy Places. Palestinian sovereignty would be declared in the outlying neighbourhoods, and 'a special regime' would be instituted for the inner neighbourhoods (Musrara, Wadi al-Juz, Shaykh Jarrah, Ras al-Amud, al-Tur, Suwwana and Salah al-Din), where Palestinians would have functional jurisdiction.[47] Abbas told Albright how dissatisfied he was with the American position, and that 'any agreement without Jerusalem would endanger Arafat's life'.[48] The Palestinians were convinced that these were Israeli ideas, and further proof that the Israelis and the Americans were coordinating their moves behind the backs of the Palestinian delegation.[49] The Israeli delegation tasked the Americans to do their haggling for them.

In the afternoon, the Israeli delegation convened to discuss Jerusalem. Each member of the delegation expressed his opinion about this sticking point. The meeting lasted a few hours and ended without a formal conclusion. The general tenor was to make an historic concession.[50] Meridor and Rubinstein, however, remained convinced that Jerusalem should not be divided – the minority position.

18 July

Barak sent Ben-Ami and Sher to advance the talks. Sher argues that no concessions were made, as it was a negotiation exercise with no binding or enforceable outcome. They reiterated Israel's willingness to concede full Palestinian sovereignty over two Arab neighbourhoods in East Jerusalem.

[45] Qurie, *Beyond Oslo*, 200.
[46] Ibid., 204.
[47] Hanieh, 'The Camp David Papers', 88.
[48] Enderlin, *Shattered Dreams*, 215.
[49] Ibid.
[50] Grinstein and Afilalo, *(In)Sights*, 165, 239.

An international force was to take over responsibility in the Jordan Valley, with Israel retaining control over part of it for a long period (ten to fifteen years). All concessions were conditional upon reaching a full-fledged Framework Agreement on Permanent Status on all core contentious issues.[51] Ben-Ami and Sher suggested that the Palestinians would control some 90 per cent of the West Bank. The Palestinian negotiators, Erekat and Dahlan, took notes and asked questions, but made no counteroffer,[52] which the Israelis found very frustrating.

The Americans submitted a proposal according to which Israel would annex 8 per cent of the settlement blocs in the West Bank and, in return, give up 2 per cent in other areas; the future of East Jerusalem would be decided over the next two years, the Palestinians would be the custodians of the Temple Mount and both sides would agree to end the conflict. Security arrangements and the refugee issue were not mentioned.[53] While the Israelis agreed to the paper in principle as a basis for continued negotiations, Arafat rejected it. He did not want to postpone the Jerusalem issue. Granting the Haram al-Sharif a status similar to that of diplomatic missions was not enough, as Israel would still be the sovereign. Nor would raising the Palestinian flag over the Haram al-Sharif revoke Israeli sovereignty. Arafat also rejected the idea of Israel's annexation of the Armenian and the Jewish Quarters and recognising that the Arab neighbourhoods outside the walled city, such as Sheikh Jarrah, Wadi Al Jawz, Shufat and Beit Hanina, would remain under Israeli sovereignty.[54] Angrily, Arafat told Clinton that Ross was working for the Israelis, not for the Americans.[55] At 2:00 am, Arafat delivered a letter to Clinton stating that the latter's proposals contradicted the fundamental principles of the peace process as established by the United States. Arafat referred to his previous letter of 16 July, which outlined the only acceptable bases for negotiation.[56] He reiterated that *his* red lines were absolute.

Ginossar, who knew Arafat well and received information from the Palestinian delegation, said that Arafat was interested only in one thing: Jerusalem. He needed some form of sovereignty in the Old City.[57] By

51 Sher's comments on a draft of this book (30 July 2025).
52 Barak, *My Country, My Life*, 364–365.
53 Meridor, *Camp David 2000*, 22–23.
54 Qurie, *Beyond Oslo*, 212.
55 Enderlin, *Shattered Dreams*, 232.
56 Swisher, *The Truth about Camp David*, 284.
57 Gidi Weitz, 'Meridor's Diaries: Last Minutes of Dialogue', *Haaretz* (30 July 2011) (Hebrew).

having a grip on Jerusalem, Arafat would establish a long-lasting legacy that would be deeply appreciated by the Palestinians and the Muslim world at large. Clinton asked Arafat: 'Have you anything to offer in return for what Barak is offering? If you have not, we shall leave here empty-handed.'[58] Arafat remained adamant. This demonstrates just how remote the American agenda was from that of the Palestinians. Clinton thought that leaving empty-handed was bad news for the Palestinians, whereas they thought they could achieve more at a later stage. Arafat repeated what he had said to Clinton, that the differences between the Palestinian and the Israeli sides were too wide to bridge.[59] Frustrated, Barak ordered the Israeli delegation to pack their suitcases, a ploy Sadat had resorted to at the 1978 Camp David Summit. In both peace summits, none of the sides left Camp David unilaterally.

One delegate did leave. Abbas left the summit to attend his son's wedding. As the other constructive negotiator, Qurie, had disengaged after Clinton's outburst, the Israelis were left with Dahlan and Rashid as the only potential deal-makers.[60] However, they could not push Arafat to make the necessary concessions.

19 July

Barak wrote Clinton a letter explaining the summit's failure, attacking Arafat and thanking Clinton for his efforts.[61] The Palestinians were also ready to leave. Arafat suggested continuing the negotiations later. From the very start, Arafat wanted to postpone and delay. Clinton could assess the situation and, if he thought it would be useful, convene another summit. Clinton rejected the suggestion.[62] He knew that Barak objected to the idea of having a series of summits. Arafat told Clinton: 'A billion Muslims will never forgive me if I do not succeed in obtaining full sovereignty over East Jerusalem. I have no authority to make any concession in this respect. This issue is not for me personally to decide; rather it relates to the whole Muslim world.'[63] Clinton pleaded with both Arafat and Barak to stay in Camp David and wait for him to return from the G7 talks in Okinawa.

[58] Qurie, *Beyond Oslo*, 200.
[59] Ibid., 161.
[60] Grinstein and Afilalo, *(In)Sights*, 240.
[61] Meridor, *Camp David 2000*, 24.
[62] Hanieh, 'The Camp David Papers', 90.
[63] Qurie, *Beyond Oslo*, 216.

Arafat and Barak agreed. One of the Palestinians remarked: 'Our detention has just been extended for another few days!'[64] The Palestinians felt coerced into being at Camp David, and they certainly did not have any sense of urgency to seal a deal.

According to Akram Hanieh, Clinton spent much of 18 and 19 July on the telephone with Arab leaders, trying to convince them to pressure Arafat. Clinton told them that progress had been made on all the issues, and that extremely generous offers had been made by Israel concerning Jerusalem, which Arafat had rejected. Clinton asked the Arab leaders to call Arafat and ask him to accept the offers so that peace could be achieved or, failing that, to encourage Arafat to sign an agreement postponing the Jerusalem issue.[65] The Arab leaders, however, disappointed the Americans. Some never returned Clinton's calls, while others expressed support for the Palestinian position. From the first day of the summit, Arafat had kept Arab and international leaders informed about what was going on; he had instructed Nabil Sha'ath to brief Arab leaders about the situation daily.[66] The experienced Arafat pre-empted Clinton's efforts to exert pressure on him via third parties.

20 July

The summit was reaching an impasse and momentum had stalled. President Clinton temporarily departed for Japan to fulfil his G7 obligations, leaving Secretary of State Madeleine Albright to steward the negotiations in his absence. Both the Israeli and Palestinian delegations were reluctant to make any meaningful concessions without Clinton's direct involvement, and their reluctance effectively sidelined Albright's efforts. When she called for a face-to-face meeting between Barak and Arafat, Barak declined. Prior to Clinton's departure, Barak had made it clear that no substantive progress would occur in the president's absence. While he did not prohibit informal discussions among his delegation or dialogue with the Palestinians or American mediators, the summit, in effect, was placed on hold. Barak did not let negotiations move forward 'because, if they rejected moving in the presence of the American president, no way that they will move in his absence'.[67] Barak maintained: 'I loved

[64] Hanieh, 'The Camp David Papers', 91.
[65] Ibid., 89.
[66] Ibid.
[67] Interview with Ehud Barak (11 July 2022), 20.

Madeleine, I highly appreciated her. But she does not have the gravitas or the capacity to move it.'[68] At dinner the same day, Barak avoided Arafat, did not shake his hand and made no effort to exchange courtesies.[69] Arafat, who carefully guarded his honour and cared a great deal about his dignity, was humiliated in front of the three delegations.[70] For the following two nights, Barak ate his meals in his cabin. He had no wish to continue business as usual, signalling that everything was normal, when it was not.[71] Instead, he wanted to project that it was crisis time and wait for Clinton's return.

The same day, the Palestinians produced a paper on the refugee issue, according to which Israel would be required to take responsibility for the problem and resolve it. Refugees would be entitled to resettle in Israel and/or receive compensation for their property and suffering at the hands of Israel.[72] All refugees would be compensated, those who chose to return and those who did not. The Absentee Treasurer created in Israel in 1949 to administer refugee money would be responsible for the compensation. Host countries should also be compensated. An international fund could be established, but the fund would only be responsible for part of the compensation.[73] The Israelis refused these substantial demands relating to the refugees' right of return to Israel.

In a meeting between Yanai and Dahlan on security, Yanai explained that Israel's heartland was between Tel Aviv and Hadera, where 85 per cent of the population resided. To defend them, Israel needed strategic depth and intelligence. Therefore, Israel had to have troops in four or five locations in the Jordan Valley, and three early warning stations situated in elevated areas. Movement to and from those areas would be via three specific routes. Israel also needed control over the Israel/West Bank airspace. The Palestinians could have civilian air control, and air movement would be coordinated between Israel and the PA. Furthermore, Palestine would

68 Ibid.

69 Qurie, *Beyond Oslo*, 223, 274; Gilead Sher, *Just beyond Reach* (Tel Aviv: Yedioth Ahronoth, 2001) (Hebrew), 200; Enderlin, *Shattered Dreams*, 241.

70 Shimon Peres said that he always communicated with Arafat with tact. On sensitive matters, especially when he disagreed with Arafat, he would wait for personal meetings, never challenging Arafat in front of other people. Shimon Peres and Robert Littell, *For the Future of Israel* (Baltimore, MD: Johns Hopkins University Press, 1998), 109, 126.

71 Interview with Ehud Barak (11 July 2022), 20.

72 Meridor, *Camp David 2000*, 28–29.

73 Abu Mazen's speech at the meeting of the PLO's Palestinian Central Council, 9 September 2000, *United Nations*, www.un.org/unispal/document/auto-insert-204899/.

be demilitarised and only have a police force that would establish internal security. No foreign army would be allowed into the Palestinian state, and no military agreements between Palestine and other countries could be signed.[74] The Palestinians objected to most of those demands, and no agreement was reached.

21–22 July

This was a relatively relaxed weekend. On Friday and Saturday, Rubinstein, Meridor and Eran discussed the refugee issue with their Palestinian counterpart negotiators, Sha'ath, Abed Rabbo and Hanieh. There was no progress. The two sides failed to bridge the gaps and reach any agreement. The Palestinians refused to discuss compensation separately from the refugee right of return.[75] Hiba Husseini explained that language is important. The Palestinians spoke of the principle of the right *of* return, not right *to* return. They wanted recognition of their right of return to Palestine – not to historic Palestine; and 'Palestine' would be defined in the agreement between the two sides.[76]

At another meeting relating to Jerusalem, the Palestinians asked that the Israeli settlement areas of Pisgat Ze'ev and Gilo be handed over to them, while the Israelis laid claim to the Holy Basin (primarily the Western Wall and the Temple Mount). In a loaded and hostile atmosphere,[77] no agreement was reached.

Albright wanted to do something constructive and decided to visit Barak. Alerted that she was on her way, he thought that either Clinton had not told her what they had agreed (to do nothing), or that he *had* told her, but she decided to try to approach him anyway.[78] Barak had maintained strict isolation and wished not to be disturbed.[79] So, to avoid her, he went jogging. Barak felt that there was somehow a 'broken telephone', and 'that Albright was not told that we [Clinton and Barak] agreed that we would not meet'.[80] Fundamentally, Barak did not trust Albright to deliver.

[74] Israeli Presentation: Security, Camp David, translated from Dahlan's notes (20 July 2000).
[75] Meridor, *Camp David 2000*, 29.
[76] Interview with Hiba Husseini (24 December 2024), 33.
[77] Qurie, *Beyond Oslo*, 226.
[78] Interview with Ehud Barak (11 July 2022), 20.
[79] Danny Yatom, *The Labyrinth of Power* (Tel Aviv: Contento, 2016) (Hebrew), 665.
[80] Raphael Cohen-Almagor, 'The Pursuit of Peace with the Palestinians: Interviews with Ehud Barak', *Israel Affairs* (published online 9 March 2023): 60.

23 July

Arafat complained to CIA Director George Tenet: 'Where is Barak? Why won't he meet with me or talk to me?'[81] Abbas, who was away for four days, returned from his son's wedding and joined the negotiations on the refugee issue. There was no progress.[82] Abbas, who ever since the Stockholm talks had believed that the peace process would not succeed, did not engage.[83] Clinton returned from Japan that afternoon and joined the dinner. Barak, who also attended, spent most of his time with Chelsea Clinton and ignored Arafat.[84] To his delegation, Barak seemed revitalised. He told his people that if Arafat were to accept Clinton's proposals, he would extend even further his boundaries of compromise on Jerusalem, as well as on other core issues, and reach an historic agreement.[85] Following the dinner, Clinton discussed security matters throughout the night. Sher and Yanai represented Israeli interests, while Qurie and Dahlan represented those of the Palestinians. The Israelis wanted to have patrols in the Jordan Valley, three early warning stations in the West Bank, five Israeli 'supplies bases' in the Jordan Valley to be used by the Israel Defense Forces (IDF) in emergencies, and inspection of all goods imported to the demilitarised Palestinian state. The Palestinians objected to the presence of any Israeli soldier on their territory, including in the Jordan Valley and at the crossing points, as such a presence would infringe on their sovereignty. They were prepared to provide security guarantees and to accept American or international troops in these areas.[86]

Clinton made some bridging proposals, but the gaps between the two parties on the significant issues remained enormous and unbridgeable. For instance, on the refugee issue, the Palestinians demanded the right of every Palestinian refugee to return home in accordance with UN Resolution 194. The refugees in Lebanon would be the first to return to their rightful homes in the Galilee. The Palestinians wanted to delineate a timetable, including the numbers of refugees, for the return of all refugees who might wish to exercise the right of return and to institute a compensation regime. The Israelis reiterated their well-known position: Israel is not responsible for the Palestinian refugee problem and does not

[81] Enderlin, *Shattered Dreams*, 244.
[82] Meridor, *Camp David 2000*, 33–34.
[83] Interview with Ahmad Khalidi (5 June 2019), 18.
[84] Meridor, *Camp David 2000*, 35.
[85] Ben-Ami, *Prophets without Honor*, 91.
[86] Hanieh, 'The Camp David Papers', 94; Qurie, *Beyond Oslo*, 233.

recognise the Palestinian right of return. 'We are prepared to allow the return of several thousands of persons spread over several years under a "family reunification" program and for "humanitarian reasons." We are ready to discuss an international compensation fund that would also allocate compensation for Jews "expelled" from Arab countries.'[87] As a counter-proposal, the Israeli delegation raised the issue of the 700,000 Jews forced to flee from the Arab world.[88] If the Palestinians asked for decisions on their 1947–1948 Nakba refugees' right of return and compensation, Israelis asked for compensation for those Jewish refugees.

Interestingly, Gamal Helal argued that the refugee issue was not substantive, and that it was 'a phony issue'.[89] The Palestinians, Arab leaders and the Israelis knew it. It was used by the Palestinians to get what was important to them: 100 per cent of the territories, including East Jerusalem.[90] The Americans had prepared a comprehensive package to put an end to the problem.

> So, the idea that there was a problem is a lie. It is an absolute lie. It was not a problem. But, did we reach a conclusion on that? I would say no. Why? Because this was a card in the hands of the Palestinians that they were not willing to give up until they got what they wanted. And what they really wanted was the territories and an acceptable arrangement in East Jerusalem.[91]

24 July

Dahlan told Ginossar that they were unhappy with Clinton's bridging proposals.[92] Still, Ben-Ami wrote that there was some progress on specific issues. Dahlan did not object to Israeli early warning stations, provided there was a symbolic American presence in addition to an Israeli presence. Qurie did not entirely reject the Israeli Air Force's use of Palestinian airspace, on the condition that it did not affect their commercial flights.[93]

As Clinton was pushing for an agreement, extensive talks were held. Ross indicated that there were some positive movements on the Palestinian side. On borders, the Palestinians presented Sher with a

[87] Hanieh, 'The Camp David Papers', 94.
[88] Interview with Elyakim Rubinstein (10 July 2018), 2.
[89] Cohen-Almagor, 'Israeli-Palestinian Negotiations through the Eyes of Gamal Helal', 4.
[90] Interview with Gamal Helal (11 November 2022), 9.
[91] Interview with Gamal Helal (11 November 2022), 11.
[92] Meridor, *Camp David 2000*, 36.
[93] Ben-Ami, *Prophets without Honor*, 94.

map outlining their suggestions for the settlement blocs.[94] According to Meridor, Ross informed the Israelis that the Palestinians had agreed to Israeli sovereignty in the Jewish neighbourhoods of East Jerusalem and from 8 to 10 per cent of the West Bank that included the settlement blocs. Arafat also accepted Clinton's proposals on the refugee issue and security.[95] Disagreement remained on the questions of Jerusalem and the Holy Places.[96] To bring the summit to a successful end, Israel would have to make substantial concessions on Jerusalem and the Holy Basin.

25 July

On the last day of the summit, Clinton proposed that the outer area around Jerusalem would be under Palestinian sovereignty; the Temple Mount would be under Israeli sovereignty, but in Palestinian trusteeship. This was in accordance with the Ben-Ami and Sher proposal of 17 July. Clinton also proposed Palestinian sovereignty in two quarters of the Old City, the Muslim and the Christian. There was also a possibility of postponing the debate on Jerusalem for three years. Tenet tried to persuade Arafat to accept Clinton's proposals, but to no avail. Arafat refused them all,[97] maintaining that they were short of what he wanted and not significantly different from prior proposals. Arafat was committed to Jerusalem and the Holy Places. For him, there could not be peace with Israel if Israel retained sovereignty on the Temple Mount, and if the Palestinians did not get 100 per cent of the West Bank and Gaza. In a letter to Clinton, Arafat reiterated his demand for sovereignty over the Muslim and Christian sites in Jerusalem: 'Any imposition of Israeli sovereignty over any Islamic or Christian Holy Places will be rejected by Muslim and Christian Arabs as well as Muslims and Christians at large.'[98] Time and again, Arafat reiterated that no peace deal could be concluded without resolving the Jerusalem question and issues surrounding the Holy Places. He was willing to meet again later for further discussions, but he was unwilling to

[94] Ibid.

[95] I doubt all those 'agreements' were granted. On the border issue, Arafat apparently was willing to concede more than other members of his negotiating team. According to Qurie, while they were willing to agree on territorial exchange of 1.5 to 3 per cent, Arafat in a one-to-one meeting with Clinton agreed to 8 to 10 per cent territorial exchange. See Qurie, *Beyond Oslo*, 201.

[96] Meridor, *Camp David 2000*, 39.

[97] Hanieh, 'The Camp David Papers', 96; Shavit, 'The Day Peace Died'.

[98] Qurie, *Beyond Oslo*, 226.

finalise a deal without addressing these vital concerns. To resolve them, there was a need for innovation and thinking outside the box. Other ideas should have been aired different from those that had been proposed and repeatedly rejected.

The disillusioned and hugely disappointed Clinton told Arafat: 'You might as well go now. You are not negotiating, not making any offers. They [the Israelis] are moving forward but you are not. You think you should get a medal for saying they can have the Jewish Quarter.'[99] Arafat responded: 'I can wait two, twenty, even a hundred years until a man comes who can liberate Jerusalem.'[100] This statement illustrates the different concepts of time in the Western and Arab worlds. In the West, people think in terms of their lifetimes, their children's lifetimes and their grandchildren's lifetimes. In the Arab world, people are prepared to wait generations to see their ambitions fulfilled. Timewise, Arafat was far more patient than Barak and Clinton.

At noon, Clinton delivered a statement and spoke to journalists. He said, 'Prime Minister Barak showed particular courage, vision, and an understanding of the historical importance of this moment', while 'Chairman Arafat made it clear that he, too, remains committed to the path of peace'.[101] Clinton maintained that 'progress was made on all fronts, that significant progress was made on some of the core issues', but Jerusalem 'remains the biggest problem'.[102] No agreement could be signed. It was a gloomy end to a sad and stressful summit.

Barak's Proposal

There is a great deal of controversy as to what Israel proposed. Hussein Agha and Robert Malley said that there was no Israeli offer and that nothing was stated in writing. Ideas were aired and presented as American ideas.[103] There was nothing at Camp David that was clearly from Barak. Agha said it was 'a total joke! Nobody took the offers seriously; they were vague, conditional and deniable.'[104] I asked Barak

[99] Ibid., 242.
[100] Ibid., 243.
[101] Remarks on the Middle East Peace Summit and an Exchange with Reporters 25 July 2000, *Administration of William J. Clinton, 2000 / July 25*, 1454.
[102] Ibid., 1456.
[103] Robert Malley and Hussein Agha, 'Camp David: The Tragedy of Errors', *New York Review of Books* (9 August 2001), https://tinyurl.com/2s4nskmv.
[104] Interview with Hussein Agha (5 April 2019), 24.

why he refused to put his proposal in writing. He explained that he wanted to put the proposal in writing *after* the Palestinians agreed to it. According to Barak, the Palestinians were fully aware of the proposal, as it was conveyed to them orally. Barak said: 'We know what happens with written documents. They become a kind of position, and that is the kind of *escalier*, over which they climb from place to place, without ever making any decision.'[105] Barak thought Arafat was ready to make only tactical compromises that would serve as a springboard to demand further concessions. Mutual distrust hampered the negotiations. With Barak reluctant to put his proposal in writing, it was unclear which discussions reflected actual proposals, much less if there was a Barak proposal that Arafat rejected.

Barak was thinking in historical terms. He addressed Palestinian demands with a proposal along the following lines (see Figure 6.1):[106]

- Evacuation of 91 per cent of Judea and Samaria, and 100 per cent of the Gaza Strip.[107] Gilead Sher says that, unofficially, Israeli negotiators talked about annexation of 7.5 per cent, meaning that the Palestinians would get 92.5 per cent.[108]
- Accepting the idea of transferring pre-1967 Israeli territories to PA control, in exchange for blocs of settlements in the territories to be annexed by Israel.
- Annexing the 9 per cent of the West Bank with the most Jewish settlers.[109] The modifications of the 1967 borders meant that Israel would have incorporated 80 per cent of the settlements.[110]

105 Interview with Ehud Barak (11 July 2022), 17.

106 Interviews with Ehud Barak (21 June 2022, 11 July 2022), Gilead Sher (26 May 2013), Dan Meridor (21 May 2013, 20 January 2016), Shlomo Ben-Ami (26 June 2013), Gadi Baltiansky (25 January 2016), Israel Hasson (23 May 2013) and Gidi Grinstein (21 May 2013). See also Benny Morris, 'An Interview with Ehud Barak', *New York Review of Books*, 49(10) (13 June 2002), https://tinyurl.com/mrxmbw8p; Malley and Agha, 'Camp David: The Tragedy of Errors'. Barak speaks of 92 per cent of the West Bank, Malley and Agha of 91 per cent.

107 Some argue that Israel offered 86 per cent because the offer excluded the No Man's Land near Latrun, East Jerusalem and the Dead Sea. See Jeremy Pressman, 'Visions in Collision: What Happened at Camp David and Taba?', *International Security*, 28(2) (2003): 16–17. Shaul Arieli (interview 11 November 2024) said that Barak proposed 89 per cent of the West Bank.

108 Interview with Gilead Sher (2 February 2024), 10.

109 Alan Dowty, *Israel/Palestine* (Cambridge: Polity, 2012), 228; Qurie, *Beyond Oslo*, 268.

110 *From Oslo to Camp David to Taba: Setting the Record Straight*, Featuring Dennis Ross, Margaret Warner, and Jim Hoagland, The Washington Institute for Near East Policy (8 August 2001).

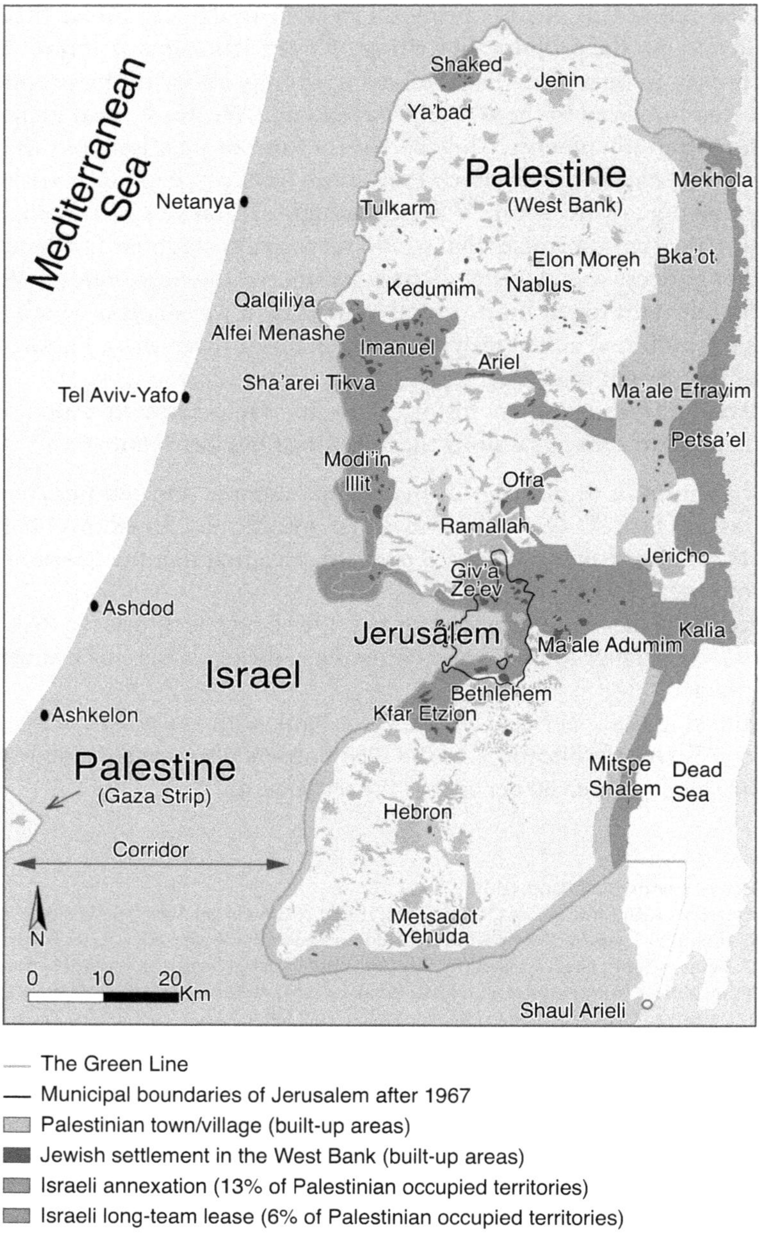

Figure 6.1 Camp David 2000: the Israeli proposal.
Source: Shaul Arieli, www.shaularieli.com/en/maps/color/. Note that this was the map that Israel presented to Clinton. Barak and Sher speak of different numbers but these were not backed by official maps.

- Exchange of land between Israel and the PA: in return for keeping some major clusters of settlements, Israel would concede territories in the Jordan River Valley.[111] Pressman argues that the exchange would amount to 1 per cent of the West Bank.[112]
- Division of Jerusalem and acknowledgement of Al Quds as the Palestinian capital.[113] Jewish areas outside Jerusalem's municipal boundaries would be annexed to the city, including such population centres as Givat Ze'ev, Ma'ale Adumim and Gush Etzion. The outer envelope of Arab areas around Jerusalem would come under Palestinian sovereignty, including Abu Dis, El-Azaria, Beit Jala, Anata and Al-Ram. Arab neighbourhoods inside Jerusalem's boundaries, such as a-Tur (also spelt Al-Tur or At-Tur), would either be annexed to Al Quds or granted extensive self-rule. The Old City would be divided. The Muslim and Christian Quarters would have autonomy under formal Israeli sovereignty, while the Western or Wailing Wall area, the City of David, and the Jewish and Armenian Quarters would remain under Israeli rule.[114] For the first time, there was an Israeli suggestion to divide Jerusalem.[115]
- Palestinian permanent custodianship over the Haram al-Sharif, although allotting a small site on the Temple Mount for Jewish prayers.[116] Neither party would have sovereignty on the Temple Mount.[117]
- Acceptance of the establishment of a Palestinian state.
- Return of refugees to the prospective Palestinian state, but with no 'right of return' to Israel, and a massive aid programme, sponsored

[111] Yigal Carmon and Aluma Dankowitz, 'Camp David and the Prospects for a Final Settlement, Part I: Israeli, Palestinian, and American Positions', *Memri* (3 August 2000), https://tinyurl.com/4cxbmrwy.

[112] Pressman, 'Visions in Collision', 17.

[113] Al Quds (spelled also Al Kuds) is the Arab name of Jerusalem.

[114] Barak's Proposal to Divide Jerusalem, Information Regarding Israel's Security (n.d.), https://iris.org.il/divided-jerusalem/.

[115] Yossi Beilin, *The Path to Geneva* (New York: RDV Books, 2004), 164.

[116] Carmon and Dankowitz, 'Camp David and the Prospects for a Final Settlement, Part I'. See also Swisher, *The Truth about Camp David*, 284; William B. Quandt, 'Israeli-Palestinian Peace Talks', in Tamara Cofman Wittes (ed.), *How Israelis and Palestinians Negotiate* (Washington, DC: US Institute of Peace Press, 2005), 33. Arafat said: 'I can't betray my people. Do you want to come to my funeral? I'd rather die than agree to Israeli sovereignty over the Haram al-Sharif … I won't go down in Arab history as a traitor.' Omar M. Dajani, 'Surviving Opportunities', in Tamara Cofman Wittes (ed.), *How Israelis and Palestinians Negotiate* (Washington, DC: US Institute of Peace Press, 2005), 64.

[117] Grinstein and Afilalo, *(In)Sights*, 167.

by the international community, to facilitate the refugees' rehabilitation.[118] Israel refused to accept moral, judicial or political liability for the creation of the refugee problem or its resolution. Freilich argues that Israel agreed to the return of 'tens of thousands of Palestinian refugees'.[119]
- A humanitarian framework for family reunions, allowing some refugees to return to pre-1967 Israel, as well as to the Palestinian state.[120]

Barak considered his proposal generous. He was certain that he was offering the Palestinians the most anyone would offer.[121] He believed this package would compel Arafat to sign a historic peace agreement and bring the Israeli-Palestinian conflict to a definitive close. Barak assumed that a comprehensive offer, however painful, would be more attractive to the Palestinians than a partial or temporary alternative. Crucially, he made this offer contingent on a mutual and public declaration marking the formal end of the conflict.

The American delegation shared Barak's view that the proposal was generous; however, their assessment of what was necessary to secure peace fell significantly short of Palestinian expectations. The gap between what the Israelis and Americans saw as a bold compromise and what the Palestinians deemed an acceptable resolution proved too wide to bridge.

The Palestinian Position

The Palestinians were not prepared to accept Israel's moral legitimacy. For them, land was not being given to them but was being justly returned to them.[122] They viewed the Israeli proposal as fundamentally inadequate. In their eyes, it fragmented Palestine into four disconnected cantons, encircled by Israeli-controlled areas, and undermined the territorial contiguity essential for a viable state. They sought the full extent of the West Bank and Gaza Strip – amounting to just 22 per cent of historic Palestine – which they considered the minimal basis for a just solution. Any further erosion of this land was, to them, unacceptable. If Israel

118 Morris, 'An Interview with Ehud Barak'; Malley and Agha, 'Camp David: The Tragedy of Errors'.

119 Charles D. Freilich, *Zion's Dilemmas* (Ithaca, NY: Cornell University Press, 2012), 165.

120 Carmon and Dankowitz, 'Camp David and the Prospects for a Final Settlement, Part I'.

121 Interviews with Ehud Barak (25 May 2022, 21 June 2022, 11 July 2022), Uzi Dayan (26 July 2017), Gidi Grinstein (21 May 2013) and Dan Meridor (20 January 2016).

122 Malley and Agha, 'Camp David: The Tragedy of Errors'.

insisted on retaining the three major settlement blocs, the Palestinians demanded a land swap of equal size and value to preserve the integrity of their prospective state.

The Palestinians demanded East Jerusalem but were willing to concede Israeli sovereignty over the Jewish Quarter, the Wailing Wall and the Jewish neighbourhoods.[123] They contested Israel's wish to maintain control over much of the Jordan Valley and most West Bank settlements, arguing that those settlements disrupt Palestinian contiguity. They would not agree that Palestinian territory would include settlements, bypass roads, checkpoints and roadblocks.[124] Lack of territorial contiguity undermines sovereignty and viability and runs counter to both Palestinian *and* Israeli best interests.

The Palestinians insisted that Israel bore responsibility for creating the refugee problem.[125] They sought the full implementation of UN Security Council Resolutions 242 and 338, as well as General Assembly Resolution 194, on the refugees. They would not have agreed to anything less. Resolution 242 of 22 November 1967 calls for the withdrawal of the IDF from territories occupied in the 1967 war; the 'termination of all claims or states of belligerency'; and 'respect for and acknowledgment of the sovereignty, territorial integrity and political independence of every State in the area and their right to live in peace within secure and recognised boundaries free from threats or acts of force'. The resolution also affirms the necessity of guaranteeing freedom of navigation through international waters and resolving the refugee problem.[126] UN Security Council Resolution 338 of 22 October 1973 calls upon all parties concerned to implement Security Council Resolution 242.[127]

In turn, Section 11 of Resolution 194 holds that:

> refugees wishing to return to their homes and live at peace with their neighbours should be permitted to do so at the earliest practicable date and that compensation should be paid for the property of those choosing not to return and for loss of or property damage which, under

[123] Ibid.

[124] Stephen Zunes, 'The United States and the Breakdown of the Israeli-Palestinian Peace Process', *Middle East Policy*, 8(4) (December 2001): 70.

[125] Robert Malley and Hussein Agha, 'A Reply to Ehud Barak', *New York Review of Books*, 49(10) (13 June 2002), https://tinyurl.com/4cfxzbnj.

[126] Resolution 242 of 22 November 1967, https://peacemaker.un.org/sites/peacemaker.un.org/files/SCRes242%281967%29.pdf.

[127] U.N. Security Council Resolution 338 of 22 October 1973, https://peacemaker.un.org/sites/peacemaker.un.org/files/SCR338%281973%29.pdf.

> principles of international law or in equity, should be made good by the Governments or authorities responsible.[128]

The resolution further instructs the Conciliation Commission 'to facilitate the repatriation, resettlement, and economic and social rehabilitation of the refugees and the payment of compensation, and to maintain close relations with the Director of the United Nations Relief for Palestine Refugees and, through him, with the appropriate organs and agencies of the United Nations'.[129]

On security, some progress was made. While the Palestinians demanded that Israel's defensive arrangements should not jeopardise Palestinian sovereignty, they were prepared to make another concession, allowing three Israeli early warning sites.[130] However, this was a small achievement in a sea of disagreement and, later, the Palestinians retracted their agreement.

Analysis

Ehud Barak became Israel's prime minister after a mere four years in politics. From his position as IDF Chief of Staff, the most decorated soldier in Israel's army was parachuted into the highest echelons of politics. Barak's self-esteem and confidence were high.[131] He thought he could single-handedly resolve all issues in one crucial summit, control negotiations and determine their outcome. Barak was determined to achieve Israeli-Palestinian peace, with the help of President Clinton. He thought he could succeed where others had failed, relying on his own boldness and commitment,[132] unconvinced that this was not enough in peace negotiations.

From the very start, Arafat believed it would not be possible to strike a deal at Camp David. The gaps were simply too wide. Throughout the summit, Arafat's right-hand man, Abbas, was an absent participant. Abbas did

128 UN General Assembly Resolution 194, www.un.org/unispal/wp-content/uploads/2016/06/ARES194III.pdf.

129 Ibid.

130 Yanai spoke of three warning posts at Nablus on Mount Eibal, at the village of Al-Tayibeh near Ramallah, and in the south of the Hebron region. See also *From Oslo to Camp David to Taba: Setting the Record Straight.* Arieli (interview on 11 November 2024) argues that only one of the three warning stations was important.

131 Discussions with Gad Yaacobi (2004–2006); interviews with Shlomo Brom (17 June 2014), 16 and Yossi Sarid (15 May 2015), 27.

132 Cohen-Almagor, 'The Pursuit of Peace with the Palestinians: Interviews with Ehud Barak', 36; Interviews with Gidi Grinstein (21 May 2013) and Gadi Baltiansky (25 January 2016).

not like the conduct of the Israelis and Americans before and during the summit. He went back to Ramallah for four days during the summit to attend his son's wedding, a clear signal to the Israelis and the Americans of Arafat's thinking. On his way to the wedding, Abbas met Agha at London's Heathrow Airport, where he showed Agha a piece of paper in his own handwriting that summarised the Israeli and American positions and Abbas's conclusion: 'They are not serious.'[133]

The Palestinians and the Israelis did not negotiate according to the same set of rules, and the differences between them were striking. The Israelis assumed that once an issue was agreed upon, it was closed, and it was time to move on to other issues. The Palestinians, in contrast, would pocket agreements on specific issues and, later on, return to those same issues and ask for more concessions.[134] Three years earlier, Abbas reflected on Palestinian negotiation tactics, explaining that Arafat always strove to increase his demands, as he saw this as 'his right as a negotiator'.[135] The Palestinians resorted to these tactics throughout the Oslo peace process,[136] frustrating the Israelis and undermining trust.

Arafat's negotiating style, incompatible with the standard Western style of negotiation, left Barak cautious and suspicious. Kimhi, Even and Post, in their psychological profile of Arafat, write that his conduct at the negotiating table was characterised by the creation of crises in true 'Oriental bazaar' style, 'creating bargaining sessions in which the party with the better combination of craft and fortitude wins'.[137] They maintained:

> Arafat does not place great importance on authenticity. He has a natural dramatic ability, of which he makes extensive use. With great skill, he adapts his style of speech and his message to his target audience. He uses repetition and exaggeration (some of which he apparently believes with all his heart). He often uses body language, along with euphemistic language and hints, to say what he is prevented from stating openly. He is able to lie without batting an eye.[138]

133 Interview with Hussein Agha (5 April 2019), 7.
134 Interviews with Ghaith al-Omari (2 September 2014), Shlomo Ben-Ami (26 June 2013) and Gidi Grinstein (21 May 2013).
135 Interview with Abu Mazen (23 October 1997) U-BIT 867, Fifty Years War, Liddell Hart Archives, King's College, London.
136 Ron Pundak, *Secret Channel* (Tel Aviv: Aliyat Hagag, 2013) (Hebrew); Uri Savir, *The Process* (New York: Vintage Books/Random House, 1999).
137 Shaul Kimhi, Shmuel Even and Jerrold Post, *Yasir Arafat: Psychological Profile and Strategic Analysis* (Herzliya: The Interdisciplinary Center, 2002), 35.
138 Ibid., 6.

Shimon Peres understood this, saying that the 'art of negotiation is creativeness even more than bargaining'[139] – but Peres was not invited to Camp David.

The Israeli Delegation

Both delegations were problematic. Not only did the Israelis and the Palestinians want different things, but people *within the delegations* wanted different things. Both delegations lacked coherence. Throughout the summit, the aspirations of the two sides remained far too wide to be bridged.

Barak knew that Jerusalem and the refugee question would feature prominently in the negotiations. As mentioned, for the delicate issue of Jerusalem, he assigned Dan Meridor and Danny Yatom (the latter was later replaced by Gilead Sher). Barak wanted a hardliner to negotiate this most important issue, one who would not flinch or compromise, and he got what he wanted. Meridor remained loyal to his fundamental belief that there could be no compromise on Jerusalem, that it must remain undivided and under Israeli sovereignty. He was not prepared to discuss the status of Jerusalem, and Barak expected Meridor to oppose any substantive concessions on Jerusalem. By assigning negotiations on Jerusalem to Meridor, Barak conveyed a clear message to Arafat and, at the same time, guaranteed the failed outcome. Barak also invited Elyakim Rubinstein to the summit, in the full knowledge that he, too, was opposed to any suggestion of dividing Jerusalem. Assigning Rubinstein to negotiate the refugee problem assured tough and long negotiations on this issue as well. Still, Barak trusted him.[140]

Barak invited Meridor and Rubinstein, in particular, to the summit with an eye to internal Israeli politics as well. He valued their intelligence and independent thinking – qualities he felt were lacking among other members of the Israeli delegation. He hoped that the two would show pragmatism. By including them, Barak ensured that perspectives from the political centre and right were genuinely represented, favouring their voices over those of figures such as Yossi Sarid and Yossi Beilin, who were more closely aligned with the left. A poll conducted during the summit revealed that 60 per cent of the Israeli public viewed Meridor's presence at Camp David as important, indicating the trust he commanded and the strategic value of

[139] Peres and Littell, *For the Future of Israel*, 121.
[140] Interview with Ehud Barak (21 June 2022), 12.

his inclusion.[141] Barak was well acquainted with Meridor and regarded him as a person of quality and integrity who had a very profound understanding of politics, security and strategy. Barak trusted both him and Rubinstein not to go behind his back and leak anything, unlike Shimon Peres, 'who tried any of these bypasses'.[142] Of Meridor, he said he is 'an honest man, with different views than mine, who is worth listening to'.[143]

Barak believed that in order to take historic steps, it was crucial to sincerely engage those with opposing viewpoints, listen openly and then chart a decisive course. He understood that broad political support would be necessary to secure support for the painful compromises he anticipated. At the time, public consensus in Israel was that Jerusalem should not be divided. After listening to every person in the delegation, Barak was ready to break with this consensus. If respected figures such as Meridor and Rubinstein could be persuaded of the need for such concessions, Barak reasoned, their endorsement would lend greater credibility and weight to any agreement. Moreover, at the end of the day, he would have to make tough decisions, and he trusted them to accept whatever he decided, without trying to torpedo the agreement.

Barak told me that he came to the negotiations with an open mind.[144] He either had no clear ideas about the extent to which he was willing to manoeuvre, or he lacked coherence in transmitting his ideas to all members of the Israeli delegation. When they accepted Barak's invitation, neither Meridor nor Rubinstein knew Barak's frame of mind and the extent of what he was prepared to concede. They remained unconvinced of Barak's vision during the course of the summit, maintained their hardline positions and did not endorse his concessions.

It was interesting to interview Meridor, Sher, Ben-Ami and Rubinstein on these substantive issues. Ben-Ami thought it was unwise to appoint Meridor to represent Israel in the Jerusalem negotiations.[145] It was impossible to reach a compromise with Meridor at the helm. Ben-Ami told Barak that there would not be any movement with Meridor. Understanding the political motivations that drove Barak to invite Meridor to the summit,

141 Raviv Drucker Blog, 'If Levy Intends to Make Dramas – Let Him Not Come to Camp David' (2020) (Hebrew), drucker10.net/חרקירי/פרק-14-אם-לוי-מתכוון-לעשות-דראמות-שלא?/utm_campaign=shareaholic&utm_medium=email_this&utm_source=email.

142 Interview with Ehud Barak (21 June 2022), 11.

143 Cohen-Almagor, 'The Pursuit of Peace with the Palestinians: Interviews with Ehud Barak', 22.

144 Interview with Ehud Barak (21 June 2022), 23.

145 Interview with Shlomo Ben-Ami (26 June 2013), 12.

Ben-Ami told Barak: 'In the end, your base is the left. You have no other base.'[146] Ben-Ami maintained: 'Someone from the right won't give you, won't try to accommodate the Palestinians, which is necessary for the purposes of this negotiation. A right-winger – put him on security matters.'[147]

Conversely, Sher thought that Meridor's nomination for the Jerusalem talks was sensible, as Meridor is deeply rooted in Jerusalem. Sher said Meridor accepted the line dictated by Barak.[148] On the refugees issue, however, Sher thinks there was 'an unfortunate choice of people' by both the Palestinian and Israeli delegations.[149] The negotiations on refugees were 'very badly and very lousily managed'.[150] In Sher's opinion, Sha'ath, Abbas, Rubinstein and Grinstein were not the best composition of a team to resolve a deep problem;[151] they were unable to close the gaps. The delegations drifted further away from a solution.

Barak's seriousness about the refugee question, or lack thereof, is reflected in the preparations for the summit. Rubinstein, who, like Meridor, received a last-minute invitation, acknowledged that the preparations were not serious. He had only two days to collect information and write a detailed position paper.[152] It is difficult to comprehend how Barak, a leader renowned for his meticulous attention to detail, could entrust the negotiation of two of the most sensitive and complex issues – Jerusalem and the right of return for Palestinian refugees – to envoys just days before the summit. These were not marginal concerns; they lay at the heart of the Israeli-Palestinian conflict. Yet there was no comprehensive strategy in place, no clearly defined objectives, no detailed implementation framework and no contingency plans should the talks falter. For matters of far less gravity, months of rigorous preparation are typically standard. In this case, the absence of groundwork was glaring. The warning signs were unmistakable, and the writing was on the wall.

The Palestinian Delegation

The Palestinian delegation was riddled with intrigue and tensions, and above all the delegates there was Arafat, who relished and implemented

146 Ibid., 13.
147 Ibid.
148 Interview with Gilead Sher (26 May 2013), 11.
149 Ibid., 13.
150 Interview with Gilead Sher (2 February 2024), 10.
151 Ibid.
152 Interview with Elyakim Rubinstein (28 May 2013), 6.

a divide-and-rule policy. Arafat played Abbas, Qurie, Erekat and Abed Rabbo one against the other.[153] His power was based on a neo-patrimonial game of offering privileges while playing one group against the other and creating a sense of insecurity among his senior employees.[154] Kimhi, Even and Post identified Arafat's need to manipulate people and to 'divide and conquer'.[155] When underlings fought each other, they could not fight against him, and so he ensured that Abbas and Qurie would always be at odds.[156] Qurie competed with Abbas, and Abbas believed that Qurie went behind his back in Stockholm.[157] Both were well aware of Arafat's deep reluctance to attend the Camp David Summit. They understood that Arafat did not believe a deal could be reached on terms acceptable to him, and that he had no intention of yielding to external pressure. Operating under this assumption, both Abbas and Qurie adopted positions that were not only unconstructive but also at times actively obstructive. This shift in posture helps explain why Qurie appeared markedly different from the pragmatic negotiator the Israelis had engaged with during the Oslo talks.

The political climate had changed dramatically. In 1993, Arafat was driven by a sense of urgency and opportunity; he sought a deal as a means of securing political legitimacy and addressing the dire circumstances of the Palestinian people. By 2000, however, that urgency had diminished. The Palestinian leadership no longer approached the negotiations with the same resolve or commitment to compromise. The altered strategic calculus made meaningful progress at Camp David all the more elusive.

Arafat brought with him his loyal yes-men: Akram Hanieh, Nabil Abu Rudineh, Nabil Sha'ath and Yousef Abdallah. Sa'eb Erekat, who was Arafat's negotiator, also competed with Abbas and Qurie.[158] At times, he

[153] Interview with Hiba Husseini (24 December 2024), 30.

[154] In his comments, Hirschfeld wrote that throughout the 1990s, Arafat kept different warlords within a semi-feudal structure, for example, Dahlan's security people controlled the income from the Karni crossing, Jibril Rajoub from the Allenby Bridge and the jewel trade. Arafat played one against the other. It took Salam Fayyad to change the system in the spring of 2004 and pay the salaries of security people directly to their bank accounts rather than in cash (Fayyad's comments on 30 June 2025). Then, following the Roadmap of 2003, the United States Security Coordinator was created and helped prepare a functioning system of Israeli-Palestinian security cooperation, which still functions today.

[155] Kimhi, Even and Post, *Yasir Arafat: Psychological Profile and Strategic Analysis*; Shaul Kimhi and Shmuel Even, 'Yassir Arafat: Behavioral and Strategic Analysis', *Social Behavior and Personality*, 31(4) (2003): 368. See also Danny Rubinstein, 'The Palestinian Version of Divide and Rule', *Haaretz* (30 June 1995): B3.

[156] Interview with Ghaith al-Omari (2 September 2014), 20.

[157] Ibid., 20.

[158] Interview with Hiba Husseini (24 December 2024), 30.

and Abed Rabbo were invested in the negotiations, trying to move things forward.[159] Another group included the younger guards, Mohammed Rashid, Mohammed Dahlan and Hasan Asfour, who served as opposition to Abbas. The Americans dealt with those who were prepared to deal with them; they wished to hear more flexible positions. Although aware of the tension existing between Abbas and the two young lions, Dahlan and Rashid, the Americans believed that the latter two could play a constructive role.[160] Unsure of the extent to which they reflected Arafat's views, and what political power they had to move the negotiations in a positive direction, the Americans presumed that Arafat had brought them to Camp David for a reason, and that he had empowered them to talk.[161] Abbas and Qurie did not like the warming relations between the Americans and their Palestinian rivals. They wanted to exit the summit unscathed, retaining their senior positions.[162] Thus, the atmosphere in the Palestinian delegation was not congenial or friendly, and Arafat thrived on such tensions.

The American and Israeli approach to the negotiations was strikingly out of touch with the internal dynamics of Palestinian politics. Abbas, a key figure with a deep understanding of the issues and significant political influence, was sidelined, both at Stockholm and, even more conspicuously, at Camp David. Rather than engaging with him directly, the Americans and Israelis chose to interact with other Palestinians, effectively marginalising him at a critical juncture. President Clinton further compounded the problem by publicly humiliating Qurie, another senior negotiator. This dismissive treatment not only alienated key Palestinian interlocutors but also severely weakened the negotiating framework. By undermining Abbas and Qurie, the Americans and Israelis also undermined the prospects for a successful agreement.

Barak

There is no doubt in my mind that Barak wanted to strike a deal with Arafat. He wanted to bring the Israeli-Palestinian conflict to an end. However, he lacked understanding of what was required to bring Arafat to sign such a deal. As generous as his proposal was, it was insufficient. Barak

[159] However, Gamal Helal argued that Yasser Abed Rabbo and Sa'eb Erekat were not constructive. Interview with Gamal Helal (11 November 2022), 30.
[160] Interview with Rob Malley (28 July 2022) 24.
[161] Ibid., 43.
[162] Interview with Ghaith al-Omari (2 September 2014), 18.

also lacked the personal skills to negotiate peace with Arafat. He might have been more successful with another Palestinian leader with whom he could have established a rapport. With Arafat, Barak was unable to establish a personal connection; instead, he tasked Clinton to do so. Like Ben-Ami, Barak believed that a dialogue with Arafat would not be fruitful. Before the summit, he had had some twenty hours of talks with Arafat, in six or seven separate meetings which were not very productive.[163] Striking a peace deal is difficult when personal connection is lacking and when the leaders do not like each other.

Most of my interviewees believe that Barak's demeanour did a disservice to Israeli interests. His arrogance and deficient human relations were certainly of no help in reaching the desired end.[164] Gilead Sher reports repeated criticism of Barak by members of the Israeli delegation for dictating terms to the Palestinians.[165] At the same time, Sher said that the personal relationship between Barak and Arafat, with all its importance, 'wasn't really critical and, in my opinion, would not have influenced the results even one iota'.[166] Barak's attitude played into Arafat's hands, as it was easier for him to reject his proposals *tout court*. Ami Ayalon said Barak is 'super-intelligent. Really, brilliant.'[167] But he is missing the human factor. Ayalon told Barak:

> You are playing chess with yourself. Now, the joke is, when you finally meet a partner to play with … you are trying to convince him that he is making mistakes. But he is playing his game, and it is different from yours. You are telling him, 'Look, but I planned for you a different set of actions.' *It is unbelievable!* You are not playing with yourself. He is a partner … and his goal is different from yours. You have to accept it.[168]

Furthermore, as Barak tends to be suspicious of everyone around him, he compartmentalises.[169] His mode of operation is to manage advisors

[163] Raviv Drucker, 'Olmert, Abu Mazen and Barak Refer to the Political Process', *HaMakor* (17 November 2015).

[164] Interview with Ziad Abu Zayyad (14 May 2015), 21.

[165] Sher, *Just beyond Reach*, 194–212. See also Gilead Sher, *The Israeli-Palestinian Peace Negotiations, 1999–2001: Within Reach* (London: Routledge, 2006).

[166] Interview with Gilead Sher (26 May 2013), 11.

[167] Interview with Ami Ayalon (28 June 2022), 10.

[168] Ibid., 11. Interestingly, Gadi Baltiansky resorted to the same metaphor, saying that Barak negotiated with himself. 'Barak played chess with himself. He thought, okay, here are my positions. If only I have a secret plan that I will tell nobody, nobody will know about it. But when I'm alone in the shower, I tell myself that I will be willing to make those five extra concessions. If worse comes to worse, and there's no, then I will do two more concessions. And then he plays by himself.' Interview on 25 January 2016, 12.

[169] Discussions with Gad Yaacobi (2004–2006).

directly and independently from one another; according to his philosophy, each should know only the issues within his own expertise. Only Barak had the full picture; the others worked in silos, on a need-to-know basis.[170] Unlike Camp David in 1978, in 2000 there were very few meetings in which the entire Israeli delegation participated. Rubinstein, who shared a room with Yanai, did not speak to him about security issues (Yanai's remit) or about the refugee issue (Rubinstein's remit). Rubinstein said: 'We weren't even supposed to brief each other, as far as I remember.'[171] In this way, Barak achieved what he wanted: to be the only person who knew the entire picture and who had full control of the direction of the negotiations. This was characteristic of Barak. Former head of Mossad Efraim Halevy stated that Barak kept all his civil service subordinates 'at arm's length', did not confide in them and created an atmosphere of mistrust between himself and them, and also among themselves.[172] At Camp David, Barak's managerial style vis-à-vis the Israeli delegation was questionable. Information was not shared with the whole delegation; different people knew different things, instructions changed often and consequently, at times, delegates contradicted one another.

Arafat

Arafat was familiar with the Israeli framework for peace. He knew the Israelis would not be willing to make the sacrifices he wanted, and he was unwilling to make significant concessions. As far as he was concerned, the Palestinians had already made enough concessions. Throughout the summit, Arafat was passive and allowed his negotiators to make insufficient concessions. Arafat accepted the idea of land swaps of equal size and value for settlement annexation that did not exceed 2 per cent.[173] He was unwilling to forgo the refugees' choice between the right of return or compensation, as stipulated in UN Resolution 194. Arafat understood that the refugee question 'could not upset the demographic balance in Israel but not at the price of giving up the right of return',[174] as well as the importance of the Jewish Quarter in the Old City, the Wailing Wall and

170 Grinstein and Afilalo, *(In)Sights*, 41.
171 Interview with Elyakim Rubinstein (28 May 2013), 8.
172 Efraim Halevy, *Man in the Shadow* (London: Phoenix, 2007), 151.
173 Abu Mazen's speech at the meeting of the PLO's Palestinian Central Council, 9 September 2000, United Nations, www.un.org/unispal/document/auto-insert-204899/.
174 Sophie Claudet, 'Camp David, One Year Later: Old Myths and New', *Jerusalem Quarterly*, 13 (Summer 2001), www.palestine-studies.org/en/node/78058.

cemeteries for Israel, but he was unprepared to narrow the Palestinian claim for sovereignty in East Jerusalem. Arafat was ready to compromise on security as he understood the sensitivity of the issue for Israel. The Palestinians agreed, in principle, on Israeli early warning stations and joint patrols in specific areas and for specific lengths of time, but these concessions were not enough to close a deal. The Palestinians insisted on full sovereignty over the Jordan Valley.[175] Arafat's main goal was to leave the summit without losing face while maintaining relationships with the United States. He sought an escape route, rather than a resolution of the conflict.

As the summit progressed without a meaningful breakthrough, the Israeli negotiators grew visibly strained. The mounting pressure was palpable. Barak felt acutely the weight of political expectations and the urgency of delivering a tangible result to the Israeli public. In contrast, Arafat remained composed, unhurried by any comparable political constraint. While Barak was racing against time, Arafat was playing for time.

Barak approached the summit with a now-or-never mindset, that this was a fleeting window of opportunity. Arafat understood that Israel's structural vulnerabilities – its demographic trajectory, societal sensitivity to human casualties and deep internal divisions – could be strategically advantageous over the long term. His patience was not simply a tactic but a long-term asset to be cultivated.[176]

Arafat was also aware of Barak's political needs, of the limited support that the latter enjoyed in the Knesset. He was unconcerned about Barak's election prospects. Barak, a politician in a democracy, aroused little sympathy and appreciation from Arafat. At one point, Arafat told Shimon Peres: 'Democracy! My God, who has invented it? It is so tiring ... You have to go from one meeting to another.'[177] Arafat cared only about his own political interests, and similarly, Barak did not care about Arafat's needs and constraints. Barak pressed him to decide on issues, such as the Haram al-Sharif, that concerned not only the Palestinians but also Muslim countries, without understanding that Arafat did not think he could take upon himself such responsibility.

At the same time, dignity and honour were immensely important to Arafat. Analysing his personality, Kimhi, Even and Post argued that Arafat was so sensitive about his honour that he would halt important political

175 Shlomo Yanai, Security Presentation – Summary (n.d.).
176 Kimhi and Even, 'Yassir Arafat: Behavioral and Strategic Analysis', 369.
177 Peres and Littell, *For the Future of Israel*, 117.

processes if he felt that he did not receive the honour he deserved.[178] He viewed himself as the reincarnation of Saladin, who redeemed Jerusalem from the infidel Crusaders in the twelfth century,[179] and as a legendary leader of the Palestinian people whose character and life encapsulate and symbolise the Palestinian strife and struggle. In Arafat's mind, his personal honour and Palestinian honour were one and the same. Martin Indyk argues that if Arafat had felt respected by his Israeli counterparts, he would have been more likely to respond positively. 'His dignity was more important to him than gaining an advantage in a negotiation.'[180] Disrespecting him and disputing his authority made Arafat angry.[181]

Because of his passivity, Arafat was perceived by both the Israelis and the Americans as a leader who lacked strategic thinking, who was caught in deep-seated suspicions of them, who was unwilling to seize the moment and perceive peace as a game changer. As a leader, if he truly wanted peace, they expected him to initiate, air ideas, push an agenda and be creative. This was not the case with Arafat. During the fifteen days of the summit, he himself never raised a single constructive idea, although his negotiators did. Ross said that the only new idea he raised at Camp David was that the Holy Temple was located not in Jerusalem, but in Nablus.[182] This was hardly helpful.

Arafat refused to recognise that the Temple Mount is an historical, holy place for Jews, that it was the centre of Jewish life during biblical times and in the Hasmonean and Herodian periods. Gamal Helal said the Palestinians made a huge mistake by not recognising the holy status of the Temple Mount. 'In fact, Arafat said the Temple Mount was in Nablus, then in Northern Yemen, and then Saudi Arabia.'[183] Ross initially humoured Arafat, because he thought he was joking. Ross said: 'Careful, Mr. Chairman, because then the Israelis will claim Nablus.'[184] When Arafat went through a whole explanation that the Temple Mount was in Nablus, Ross responded by saying: 'If you continue to say something that

178 Kimhi, Even and Post, *Yasir Arafat: Psychological Profile and Strategic Analysis.*

179 Ben-Ami, *Prophets without Honor*, 9.

180 Indyk, *Innocent Abroad*, 116.

181 Kimhi and Even, 'Yassir Arafat: Behavioral and Strategic Analysis', 365.

182 Dennis Ross' Interview to Brit Hume, Fox News (21 April 2002), https://havurahshirhadash.org/interview-with-dennis-ross/.

183 Swisher, *The Truth about Camp David*, 305. Arafat came with the idea that Solomon's Temple had really been in Yemen. At some point, during the forty-year journey in the desert, the Israelites took a wrong turn and ended up in Yemen. See Sari Nusseibeh, *Once Upon a Country: A Palestinian Life* (London: Halban, 2009), 426.

184 Interview with Dennis Ross (21 October 2019), 31.

we all know is untrue, the president will never take anything you say seriously again.'[185] Arafat did not discuss it anymore, but he also did not compromise on his demand for sovereignty over the area. It was easier for him to insist on having sovereignty over the Haram, believing that the Jews had no true stakes there.

There are diverse opinions as to what Arafat actually wanted. I asked Ziad Abu Zayyad whether Arafat wanted peace, and he replied: 'Yes, I had many private talks with Arafat; I know him very closely. I know him very well. He came here, and he wanted to settle. He wanted a solution, but things did not develop the way he wanted.'[186] Salam Fayyad said he was close to Arafat and knew him well, as he spent many hours with him and communicated well with him. Fayyad has no doubt that Arafat wanted peace, until the eruption of the Second Intifada.[187] He argued unequivocally that Arafat wanted a two-state solution: Israel and a Palestinian state on the territory occupied in 1967.[188] Maher El-Kurd and Asfour had similar thoughts.[189] Hiba Husseini explained that Arafat wanted several things: statehood, peace and a two-state solution, the glory of ending the conflict and remaining an honorary figure of Palestinian nationalism. Arafat was not ready to compromise too much, because he feared he would be dubbed a traitor.[190]

Hussein Agha also thinks Arafat was a peacenik.[191] Arafat believed there was an opportunity to strike a deal with Rabin, but Rabin was murdered by people who opposed the idea of peace. In Arafat's mind, after Rabin, no Israeli leader would go for peace. Rabin's example would be vivid in their minds: he was assassinated only because he wanted peace. Arafat believed this deeply.[192] Benjamin Netanyahu strengthened this belief because his conduct showed little readiness to comply with the Oslo agreements. Nor did Barak calm Arafat's qualms. I asked Agha whether Arafat would have signed a deal if Barak would have given him everything he wanted. Agha responded: 'Yes, even if he did not give him everything he wanted. If it had

185 Ibid. See also Cohen-Almagor, 'Israeli-Palestinian Negotiations through the Eyes of Gamal Helal', 8.
186 Interview with Ziad Abu Zayyad (14 May 2015), 12.
187 Interview with Salam Fayyad (19 January 2024), 3–4.
188 Ibid., 3.
189 Interviews with Maher El-Kurd (30 January 2025), 17–19 and Hasan Asfour (19 February 2025), 7.
190 Interview with Hiba Husseini (24 December 2024), 7–8, 11, 12.
191 Interview with Hussein Agha (5 April 2019), 15.
192 Ibid., 17.

most of what he wanted, he would have signed.'[193] Arafat wanted a state and a capital in East Jerusalem. This was what he was meant to present to the Palestinian people as the culmination of their struggle: an independent state with a capital in Jerusalem for the first time.[194] Having Jerusalem would be a monumental, historical achievement. For Jerusalem and the Haram, Arafat was willing to make a principled compromise on the refugee issue.

Herbert Kelman thinks that Arafat made a strategic decision to strike a deal with Israel and opted for a two-state solution.[195] Arafat was able to persuade many of the Swedish members of the Sten Andersson camp of the sincerity of his wishes for peace. To my question as to whether Arafat wanted peace, Pierre Schori, former Secretary General of Sweden's Foreign Ministry, answered in the positive: 'Peace is for the brave', Arafat said.[196] Annika Söder and Sven-Eric Söder, former State Secretaries for Sweden's Foreign Ministry, answered this question with the exact same word: *Absolutely!*[197] Mathias Mossberg thinks Arafat 'definitely' wanted peace, and that he supported a two-state solution.[198] Svein Sevje, Norwegian Ambassador to Israel, thought Arafat wanted peace, because he made very tough concessions.[199] Richard Dalton thought Arafat was sincere in his peace negotiations.[200] In contrast, Pär Nuder, who did not belong to the Andersson group, thought Arafat was an obstacle and a destructive force. 'You never knew where Arafat was', Nuder said.[201] John Hagard thinks Arafat was not eager enough for peace.[202]

Ghaith al-Omari thinks that Arafat was fully invested in the Oslo process, but after Rabin's assassination, he lost faith in the process.[203] In answer to my query about what Arafat wanted at Camp David, al-Omari said 'I actually don't know'.[204] This statement is astonishing coming from

193 Ibid., 28.
194 Ibid.
195 Herbert C. Kelman, 'The Israeli-Palestinian Peace Process and Its Vicissitudes', *American Psychologist*, 62(4) (May–June 2007): 292.
196 Interview with Pierre Schori (26 August 2019), 6.
197 Interviews with Annika Söder (23 August 2019), 14 and Sven-Eric Söder (20 August 2019), 17.
198 Interview with Mathias Mossberg (23 August 2019), 23–24.
199 Interview with Svein Sevje (1 September 2019), 3.
200 Interview with Richard Dalton (22 July 2015), 26.
201 Interview with Pär Nuder (20 August 2019), 20–22.
202 Interview with John Hagard (22 August 2019), 18–19.
203 Interview with Ghaith al-Omari (2 September 2014), 10–11.
204 Ibid., 11. Gadi Baltiansky also does not know what Arafat wanted. Interview on 25 January 2016, 10.

a member of the Palestinian delegation. Analysing Arafat's personality, Kimhi, Even and Post said that Arafat was unpredictable because his manner of thought and conduct was not customary, and his intentions were hard to read.[205] Al-Omari said that Arafat was very pragmatic, but he did not have any vision. If he were to get a peace deal on terms that he believed would be acceptable to his people, he would have taken it. But 'we were more interested in avoiding a trap, than we were in actually, reaching a deal'.[206] The Palestinians avoided a trap but soon found themselves in a far more complicated situation.

I asked Shlomo Ben-Ami whether Arafat wanted peace. He replied that he was not sure. Ben-Ami said that negotiating with Arafat was like picking mercury with a folk. Arafat had an enigmatic personality that made the art of negotiation very difficult.[207] He would only converse in metaphors, slogans and catchwords, making fruitful dialogue impossible.[208] Gidi Grinstein, Brig. Gen. (res.) Udi Dekel, Gilead Sher and Elyakim Rubinstein, on the other hand, are quite certain that Arafat did not wish for peace.[209] Grinstein thinks Arafat did not want to put an end to the conflict and to the claims. He did not want peace. He wanted, to use the language of Hamas, a *hudna*, which means a temporary 'truce' or 'armistice' as well as 'calm' or 'quiet'. It is sometimes translated as 'ceasefire'.[210] For a *hudna*, Arafat had very broad support from the Palestinian public. For peace – he did not, so he was prepared for all sorts of long-term intermediate arrangements.[211] That is to say, Arafat intended to make *tactical* compromises, but not a *principled* compromise that would solve the conflict once and for all. Those critical of Arafat mention that on 10 May 1994, in Johannesburg, Arafat delivered a speech in which he declared: 'The Jihad will continue and Jerusalem is not for the Palestinian People.

[205] Kimhi, Even and Post, *Yasir Arafat: Psychological Profile and Strategic Analysis*.

[206] Interview with Ghaith al-Omari (2 September 2014), 12.

[207] Interview with Shlomo Ben-Ami (26 June 2013); Ben-Ami, *Prophets without Honor*, 9.

[208] Shlomo Ben-Ami, 'So Close and Yet So Far: Lessons from the Israeli-Palestinian Peace Process', *Israel Studies*, 10(2) (Summer, 2005): 73.

[209] Interviews with Gidi Grinstein (21 May 2013), Udi Dekel (17 June 2014), Gilead Sher (26 May 2013) and Elyakim Rubinstein (28 May 2013).

[210] A particularly famous early *hudna* was the Treaty of Hudaybiyyah between Muhammad and the Quraysh tribe. See Definitions, https://tinyurl.com/y3rnf37j.

[211] Interview with Gidi Grinstein (21 May 2013), 5. The founder of Hamas, Sheikh Ahmed Yassin, offered a ten-year *hudna* in return for complete Israeli withdrawal from all occupied territories and the establishment of a Palestinian state in the West Bank and Gaza. Yassin said that a *hudna* can be renewed for thirty, forty or one hundred years and does not mean recognition of Israel. There is no limit to how many times a *hudna* can be renewed.

It is for all the Muslim Uma, all the Muslim Uma. You are responsible for Palestine and for Jerusalem before me.'[212] This is in the spirit of the *hadith* (a report of the sayings, actions, approvals or characteristics of the Prophet Muhammad), which instructs: 'Whoever takes a piece of the land of others unjustly, he will sink down the seven earths on the Day of Resurrection.'[213]

Dekel believed Arafat wanted Palestinian legitimacy and recognition of their rights, with no vision for a comprehensive peace.[214] Sher said there was no agreement because Arafat was not ready to reach an agreement. He was compelled to go to Camp David against his will and felt trapped.[215] Avi Gil thinks that the Oslo peace process reflected contradictory sentiments for Arafat: on the one hand, an historic compromise that would enable Palestinian self-determination and, on the other hand, a stage in the grand plan to bring about the destruction of Israel.[216] Israel Hasson analysed the Camp David process in terms of the Islamic *Tzumud*, which means stubbornness and determination, viewing unfolding events in the light of an unyielding historical ethos in which Muslim believers eventually prevail.[217] Sir John Jenkins, former British Consul General, Jerusalem, thinks Arafat was an irredentist, a person advocating the restoration to their country of any territory formerly belonging to it. Jenkins was unsure whether Arafat had reconciled himself to the prospect of peaceful coexistence with Israel.[218] Ariel Sharon thought Arafat wanted a Palestinian state instead of the state of Israel.[219] Critics of Arafat argue that he was unwilling to go down in history as the Palestinian leader who relinquished the vision of a Palestine stretching from the Jordan River to the Mediterranean Sea. For Arafat, fully accepting Israel's legitimacy was not just politically fraught. It was ideologically and emotionally untenable.

212 Arafat's Speech in Johannesburg, May 10, 1994, www.textfiles.com/politics/arafat.txt. Critiques also argue that in this speech, Arafat compared the Oslo Accords to the Hudaybiyyah peace treaty of 628 CE, which the Prophet Muhammad made with the tribe of Quraish, giving him time to build his force. Two years later, Muhammad attacked the Quraish and conquered Mecca. Arafat's statement, however, is open to contrasting interpretations. See the Treaty of Hudaybiyyah, www.qtvtutor.com/treaty-of-hudaybiyyah/.

213 See Sunnah.com, https://sunnah.com/bukhari:2454.

214 Interview with Udi Dekel (17 June 2014), 2.

215 Interview with Gilead Sher (26 May 2013), 13.

216 Avi Gil, '20 Years to Arafat's Death: In His Dreams He Saw an Olive Leaf Alongside the Destruction of Israel', *Haaretz* (18 November 2024) (Hebrew).

217 Interview with Israel Hasson (23 May 2013), 31.

218 Raphael Cohen-Almagor, 'Analysis of the PLO and Hamas: Interview with Sir John Jenkins', *International Dialogue*, 14 (2024).

219 Gilad Sharon, *Sharon – The Life of a Leader* (New York: Harper, 2011), 460.

The conflict, after all, is not rooted solely in the events of 1967, but also in the deeper historical wounds of 1947 and 1948. As a leader with a profound sense of history, Arafat was acutely aware of the legacy he would leave behind. He did not want to be remembered as the man who capitulated under pressure, or who made irrevocable concessions that future generations might view as betrayal.

Many of the American peace negotiators are also very critical of Arafat. Aaron David Miller said that Arafat did not come to Camp David to make a deal. He came because he had to, due to the pressures on him, and he only sought to survive.[220] Similarly, Daniel Kurtzer and Robert Malley explained that Arafat did not come to the summit intending to reach an agreement. The best that could have been expected from Arafat was a continuation of the process – perhaps another summit in September, another in October, and then a closing summit that would wrap things up before the American administration left office. But Arafat was not going to reach an agreement at Camp David. The Palestinians were in a defensive mode, fending for themselves against immense American pressure.[221] They were not in a creative mode, trying to find solutions to problems. Dennis Ross said that Arafat wanted to manage the conflict. He could do limited deals, but not a whole deal that required him to say 'no more conflict, no more claims, no more grievances'. Arafat never foreclosed options.[222] Indyk wrote that Arafat always chose a path that 'secured his survival to fight another day, rather than make the decisions that would secure the interests of his people'. Arafat 'chose to let history's horse gallop past his window'.[223] Quite a few horses passed his window. None convinced Arafat to invest in peace more than in 'resistance'.

Avi Gil said that Arafat had an enigmatic personality and that there are four ways to understand Arafat. The first is that Arafat wanted peace but felt, at a certain point, that Israel was deceiving him. The second possibility is that, from the very outset, Arafat did not want peace, but he saw it as part of his stages policy aiming to destroy Israel. Arafat always wanted to destroy Israel and went to Oslo as a stage in a process. The third option is that Arafat wanted peace when he went to Oslo, but he regretted that decision because he realised he would be remembered in the annals of Palestine and Islam as the one who destroyed the

[220] Interview with Aaron David Miller (12 September 2019), 8.
[221] Interviews with Daniel Kurtzer (6 April 2017) and Rob Malley (28 July 2022).
[222] Interview with Dennis Ross (27 September 2019), 14.
[223] Indyk, *Innocent Abroad*, 375.

Palestinian dream and recognised the Jewish presence in the Holy Land. The fourth option is that he was insane, that he was not normal or consistent. Arafat could pursue peace and the destruction of Israel at the same time.[224]

Clinton

Bill Clinton was enthusiastic and industrious, full of good intentions to solve the conflict. He said: 'Even if we cannot succeed … we have got to make the effort.'[225] While the Americans had a great many good intentions, they were short on 'honesty, clarity, and good analysis'.[226] Clinton exhibited several traits associated with superforecasters. He was relentless, intelligent, pragmatic, reflective and committed to self-improvement and updating his beliefs. He approached problems with openness and a deep desire to make progress. However, he lacked key attributes that define truly exceptional forecasters. Clinton struggled to accurately anticipate the outcomes of his team's decision-making and fell short in thinking probabilistically or seeing situations through a 'dragonfly eye' – the capacity to integrate diverse perspectives. He was neither particularly cautious nor humble in his assessments. He paid insufficient attention to the cognitive and emotional biases that can distort judgement, and he often miscalculated the delicate balance between overreacting and underreacting to new information. Clinton sometimes vacillated between overconfidence and hesitation, between rashness and restraint, making it difficult for him to recalibrate effectively as new evidence emerged. Unlike superforecasters, who treat mistakes as learning opportunities and value nuanced reasoning, at times Clinton appeared driven more by conviction than by careful probabilistic thinking. Where superforecasters elevate the capabilities of those around them and seek out constructive dissent, Clinton's leadership style occasionally obscured competing viewpoints rather than embracing them (see Chapter 1).

In their 15 June meeting, Clinton pledged to Arafat not to blame him if the peace summit failed.[227] This was an unnecessary shackle, for this promise decreased his leverage over Arafat. Clinton made another mistake at the end of the summit, when he did not abide by his explicit

[224] Interview with Avi Gil (16 January 2025), 21–22.
[225] Interview with Dennis Ross (27 September 2019), 13.
[226] Miller, 'How Not to Host a Summit'.
[227] Qurie, *Beyond Oslo*, 161.

promise and blamed Arafat for the summit's failure. Kurtzer and Lasensky argue that promising no blame may have encouraged Arafat not to invest in the negotiation process, as he assumed there would be no negative consequences for him. 'The blame card is a key element of U.S. influence in the peace process and should not be withdrawn preemptively unless major concessions are offered.'[228] It was a mistake to publicly blame Arafat for the failure after the summit. Kurtzer rightly said that even if Arafat bore the lion's share of responsibility for failure, once the Americans assigned blame to him, they effectively declared that the process was over, or that it had reached a point where it could not go further.[229] Instead of assigning blame, the Americans should have conveyed the message that the two sides had narrowed some differences, but that unresolved issues remained and the two sides were determined to iron them out, to devise a solution and sign a peace treaty. Indyk explains that Clinton was worried about Barak's political survival. He thought it was important to help him by blaming Arafat.[230] But blaming Arafat publicly took the wind out of his sails and the sails of the entire peace process.

Furthermore, Clinton's leadership was ineffective and even destructive. As the president of the United States, Clinton was also the leader of the free world. He should not have taken upon himself the role of an ordinary negotiator. The task should have been left to his assistants. It is one thing to mediate between leaders; it is quite another to involve oneself in the work of delegations. Presidential prestige requires detachment and the discipline to know when and how to intercede, and with whom to negotiate. Clinton should not have walked into the negotiation room and bluntly taken sides. He humiliated Qurie in front of his own delegation, as well as the Israeli delegation. Qurie did not succumb to the American president, because he knew his limits as a negotiator. Arafat would not have accepted the American dictates and would have only reprimanded him for succumbing to pressure. Qurie felt that President Clinton overstepped his authority by launching a personal attack on him, and so, on 15 July 2000, Qurie lost faith in the process.[231] Clinton's explosive exchange with him damaged the summit greatly.

[228] Daniel C. Kurtzer and Scott B. Lasensky, *Negotiating Arab-Israeli Peace* (Washington, DC: US Institute of Peace Press, 2008), 70.

[229] Raphael Cohen-Almagor, 'Israel–PLO Peace Process: Interview with Ambassador Daniel Kurtzer', *Israel Studies*, 24(3) (2019): 144.

[230] Interview with Martin Indyk (9 August 2022), 12.

[231] Qurie, *Beyond Oslo*, 194–201.

Ted Widmer was Clinton's speech writer. I asked him how the president's conduct could be explained. Widmar said that Clinton was complicated, brilliant, a great politician, well organised, competent, incredible in relating to people, that he had an incredible memory and was charming and mercurial. Clinton thought he could use his charming personality to convince people to do what he wished them to do. He was often successful, but when he was not his big personality could erupt. Clinton did not always know how to control his temper.[232]

The American president must see the big picture and speak directly to leaders, intervene with authority and tell them his expectations. Clinton knew details and worked around the clock, but he became too involved. He became so accessible that the delegations took him for granted.[233] Ben-Ami said:

> The president is supposed to be the one who sits, who plays golf. Which, by the way, he did do. To play golf and sit, and people came to him for the big decisions. And then he sits with his people and tells them things, and says to them, look, now, after we've heard both sides, let's present the historical bridging proposals to them. And it didn't happen.[234]

I asked Kurtzer whether Clinton could have put more pressure on Arafat and Barak at Camp David. Kurtzer answered, 'yes, of course', provided that the pressure is applied relentlessly.[235] This was the problem, as Clinton was unable to do so.[236] Ross explained that Clinton does not have the personality to exert pressure beyond a certain point. He is a very empathic person. He would learn everything and then marry his understanding of the details with his capacity for empathy. This is an extraordinary gift. Ross argues that nobody has such an ability to the extent that Clinton has. But he was unable to issue threats in support of his demands and stick to them.[237] Once threats are not followed by action, they become meaningless.

Barak thought that with Clinton's endless efforts, he would return to Israel as a victor, as the person who brought an end to the Israel-Palestinian conflict. Instead, he returned home empty-handed, with no

[232] Interview with Ted Widmer (27 September 2015).
[233] Aaron David Miller, 'Memorandum to the President: Thinking through an Israel–Palestinian Initiative', in Daniel C. Kurtzer (ed.), *Pathways to Peace* (New York: Palgrave Macmillan, 2012), 143.
[234] Interview with Shlomo Ben-Ami (26 June 2013), 8.
[235] Interview with Daniel Kurtzer (6 April 2017), 19.
[236] Interview with Dennis Ross (27 September 2019), 35.
[237] Interview with Dennis Ross (21 October 2019), 35.

peace treaty. Clinton did not wish to press hard, especially not on the Israelis. He was reluctant to confront Barak. Ross explained that this was needed to get results. With regard to Arafat, Clinton was unable to push him to compromise. Barak told Clinton that he needed someone like Jim Baker, who never raised his voice, always talked calmly, but still 'you felt that the whole clout of America is behind him. And he never threatened. He would say, it is up to you, but it is your fate that is hanging in the balance.'[238] Barak maintained that 'even when [Clinton] flushed red and was extremely angry', Arafat did not feel that his anger was really consequential, 'that if he does not respond to it, there is a concrete price to be paid, and it will be exacted from him'.[239] Sher said that Clinton did not put his whole weight and energy behind pushing Barak and Arafat to reach an agreement. Clinton's leadership was sparingly presented: 'His personal leadership vis-à-vis each of the two leaders was doled out with a measuring spoon.'[240] Al-Omari said: 'Barak was not an easy person, Arafat was not an easy person, and the Americans I think were too sensitive to the concerns and to the quirks of both leaders in ways that did not make them very effective negotiators.'[241]

Furthermore, the days when Clinton was absent from the summit were wasted. Barak did not think Albright was capable of closing a deal. Grinstein said that Albright was very weak, 'a lightweight' who was unable to make a difference.[242] Bill Quandt also does not regard Albright as a strong leader.[243] Miller maintained: 'Madeleine was not going to deliver. I love Madeleine [but she] was not going to move the ball with Arafat. Only the president could do that.'[244] The summit's failure shows that this statement was mere wishful thinking. Clinton failed to deliver.

The Refugee Question

Elyakim Rubinstein, who led Israel's delegation in the official Washington negotiations with the Palestinians in 1993, arrived at Camp David with familiar ideas, many of which had already failed to produce meaningful

[238] Interview with Ehud Barak (11 July 2022), 15; discussions with Aaron David Miller (October–November 2008).
[239] Interview with Ehud Barak (11 July 2022), 16.
[240] Interview with Gilead Sher (26 May 2013), 7.
[241] Interview with Ghaith al-Omari (2 September 2014), 29.
[242] Interview with Gidi Grinstein (21 May 2013), 17.
[243] Interview with Bill Quandt (11 September 2019), 28.
[244] Interview with Aaron David Miller (12 September 2019), 14.

progress. The refugee issue, one of the most emotionally charged and politically complex topics, remained a major sticking point. At Camp David, Rubinstein faced Mahmoud Abbas who remained inflexible, viewing Rubinstein's proposals as recycled and unresponsive to core Palestinian concerns. From the Palestinian perspective, Israel's insistence on drawing a parallel between Palestinian refugees and Jewish refugees from Arab countries was deeply problematic. Abbas viewed the comparison as not only irrelevant but also disingenuous. In Palestinian eyes, the Nakba – the mass displacement of Palestinians in 1947–1948 – was a direct result of Israeli actions, for which Israel bore full responsibility. By contrast, they rejected any notion that Palestinians were accountable for the plight of Jewish refugees from Arab lands. This fundamental disconnect undermined trust and reinforced the perception that Israel was not prepared to engage seriously with the Palestinian narrative or the depth of the refugee tragedy.[245] If Israel was seeking compensation, it should demand it of the relevant Arab countries. The Palestinians had nothing to do with this. Indeed, while the issue of the Jewish refugees is an important part of the *Arab*-Israeli conflict, it is separate from the specific *Palestinian*-Israeli conflict and should not be integral to the latter conflict resolution process.

Abbas saw the appointment of Rubinstein as a clear signal that Barak had no intention to address the Palestinian concern about refugees.[246] Al-Omari thinks that Barak simply did not wish to address the refugee question. Barak took risks when it came to the issue of Jerusalem and when it came to borders. These were the issues he focused on. He did not want to open the refugee issue as well, preferring to leave it for a later point in time. According to al-Omari, the first time the refugee issue was examined in a meaningful way was only later, in Taba. At that point, Yossi Beilin was the Israeli negotiator, and it is unclear to what extent Beilin was reflecting Barak's views, and how much he was speaking his own mind.[247] But even then, at Taba, the Israeli proposal was far from what the Palestinians perceived as a just solution.

I asked Barak about the issue of the Jewish refugees, and his answer was most revealing. Barak said that raising this issue was a tactical card. Because the Palestinians voiced absurd ideas about the Palestinian right

[245] Discussion with a senior Palestinian diplomat, London (17 February 2014).
[246] Swisher, *The Truth about Camp David*, 324.
[247] Interview with Ghaith al-Omari (2 September 2014), 15.

to return to Israel, Israel raised the idea of compensation for Jewish refugees – tackling one absurdity with another. Barak said:

> It is very usual, I know it from other discussions I have had, that if one side proposes something that sounds absurd, then the second side puts forward another thing which is absurd, with the understanding that both sides understand that, now that they have proposed this, they can write down that they proposed their starting positions ... They started the negotiations with the right of return which, under the Palestinian interpretation, relates to everyone, anyone, whoever, whenever he wants, he can come. That is absurd and they know that it is absurd. And they did not propose it in order to negotiate, but in order to put it on record.[248]

By raising this absurd demand, the Israelis caused the Palestinians to think that they were not serious, that they were not keen to find a solution. While the hurdle of the Jewish refugees could potentially be overcome with the financial assistance of the international community, primarily of the United States, the Palestinian demand that Israel agree to settle at least 200,000 refugees in the Galilee was a non-starter. Qurie insisted that without Israel's agreement to this demand, no solution was viable. Israel could not have agreed to this, said Rubinstein.[249] The Palestinian demands made the discussion untenable. 'Israel was not crazy enough' to agree to the return of 200,000 or up to a quarter of a million refugees from Lebanon to the Galilee.[250] From an Israeli perspective, this was a prescription for suicide.

Some of my American interviewees said that Rubinstein had no interest in resolving the refugee issue in a way that considered any of the Palestinian sensitivities. The Americans floated all kinds of numbers, including 100,000 over ten years, but none of this was serious.[251] Throughout the 2000–2001 negotiations, the Palestinians underestimated the degree to which Israelis associated even a theoretical Palestinian right of return with the prospect of the end of Israel as a Jewish state. The Israelis, on their part, have always belittled the seriousness of the Palestinian demand.[252] Like Helal, for the Israelis, the refugee issue was often seen less as a matter of justice and more as a negotiating tool. While they were prepared to show some flexibility on the principle and acknowledge, in a limited and

248 Interview with Ehud Barak (21 June 2022), 13.
249 Interview with Elyakim Rubinstein (28 May 2013), 7.
250 Ibid.
251 Interview with Aaron David Miller (12 September 2019), 22.
252 Hussein Agha and Robert Malley, 'A Solution Is Possible Now', *The Guardian* (29 March 2002).

symbolic way, the right of return, they sought precision and constraint in its application, particularly regarding the number of refugees who might actually return to Israel. Israel was willing to entertain a carefully worded reference to the right of return, provided it was paired with language that made it clear that there was no blanket right for all Palestinian refugees to resettle within Israel's borders. Recognising the right in principle, they argued, did not equate to full implementation in practice. Moreover, Israeli leaders refused to accept historical responsibility for the refugee crisis. From their perspective, the 1947–1949 civil war and the broader Arab-Israeli conflict were defensive and justified. As such, no Israeli prime minister had, up to that point, expressed regret or offered an apology for the displacement of Palestinians. This position reflected a deep-rooted belief that acknowledging moral culpability would undermine the legitimacy of Israel's founding and fuel future demands.

I asked Ehud Olmert whether, when he was prime minister, he studied the reasons for the Nakba. Olmert replied that he did not do specific research about the matter. He is familiar with the research conducted by Israeli scholars which, in his view, provides 'a balanced picture: that there were some cases where Jews forced Arabs out of their homes and, in many cases, they volunteered to do it themselves. What were the proportions between those who volunteered and those who were forced, I do not know to say.'[253]

When Palestinians speak of the right of return, a lot of emotions are involved. The solution should be not only practical. The Palestinians need Israeli acknowledgement of what happened in 1947–1949 and the role the Israelis played in the Nakba. Most of the Israeli and American delegations failed to internalise the emotional meaning of the refugee issue for Palestinians.

The ever-practical Barak proposed that the Palestinians would not give up the right of return, and that Israel would not accept the right of return. Both sides would agree on what would happen on the ground. Barak did not want to acknowledge Israeli responsibility for the Nakba.[254] He thinks the Palestinians were ready to agree to a number, 'probably 100,000 or 200,000' refugees,[255] under the title of the right of return. But first, he proposed agreement on practical arrangements, without any admission

[253] Interview with Ehud Olmert (24 April 2019), 6.

[254] Interview with Ehud Barak (21 June 2022), 15.

[255] Interview with Ehud Barak (21 June 2022), 14. There is quite a difference between 100,000 and 200,000 refugees.

of guilt or responsibility. The Palestinians refused and no agreement was reached. Still today, Barak remains oblivious to Palestinian sentiments. For him, symbolic statements are mere words, whereas he offered a concrete plan. The cultural divide between the two parties remains wide.

After Camp David, some Palestinians conceded, off the record, that Arafat was willing to accept a limited right of return within the symbolic structures of family reunification if the Palestinians received recognition of that right and a viable state, with Palestinian sovereignty over East Jerusalem and the Haram al-Sharif.[256]

Jerusalem and the Haram al-Sharif/Temple Mount

These were the two most challenging sticking points. The question of sovereignty over the Haram al-Sharif/Temple Mount was, and remains, one of the most emotionally charged and intractable issues in the Israeli-Palestinian conflict. Both parties lay claim to the site on deep historical and religious grounds. Anyone familiar with the entrenched positions of both Palestinians and Israelis regarding Jerusalem and the Temple Mount prior to the Camp David Summit could have anticipated the clash of irreconcilable expectations. The lack of sustained, preparatory dialogue on these core issues left the negotiators ill-equipped to confront them within the summit's compressed time frame.

For the Palestinians, Israel's proposals fell far short of their aspirations. They could not accept a vision of East Jerusalem in which only selected Arab neighbourhoods, including parts of the Old City, would be transferred to Palestinian sovereignty. Nor were they satisfied with only custodial rights over the Haram al-Sharif. Arafat demanded full Palestinian sovereignty over East Jerusalem, including Al Quds as their capital, and complete control over the Haram al-Sharif – an area sacred to Muslims, Jews and Christians alike. On the Israeli side, Barak was willing to make significant and painful concessions, but not to the extent demanded by the Palestinians. His position was shaped by competing pressures – from his delegation, from the Clinton administration and, most crucially, from his reading of Israeli public opinion. Barak was acutely aware of the political costs of offering too much. While he believed that bold moves were necessary, he also knew that ideas too far ahead of public sentiment could cost him the premiership. Arafat, for his part, appeared to believe that by

[256] Swisher, *The Truth about Camp David*, 281–282.

stalling and holding out, he could extract more favourable terms, but this strategy clashed with Barak's urgent need to return home with an agreement he could sell to a sceptical public.

President Clinton invested considerable time and energy in trying to resolve the impasse, eventually floating a proposal to divide sovereignty: Palestinian sovereignty above ground, where the mosques stand, and Israeli sovereignty below, where the ancient Temple once stood. Though innovative, the idea was received by the Palestinians as both offensive and absurd. To them, it symbolised not compromise, but condescension and denial of their full and equal claim to one of Islam's holiest sites. Ultimately, the Temple Mount debate laid bare the wide chasm not just between the sides, but also between their fundamental narratives and expectations. The failure to adequately prepare for this confrontation before the summit proved to be a decisive factor in its unravelling.[257] Arafat responded angrily, asking Clinton whether he would ever agree that someone else be sovereign over territory beneath the streets of Washington.[258] Arafat said: 'The Palestinian leader who will give up Jerusalem has not yet been born. I will not betray my people or the trust they have placed in me. Don't look to me to legitimize the occupation!'[259] He told Clinton: 'I am not only the leader of the Palestinian people; I am also the vice president of the Islamic Conference. I also defend the rights of Christians. I will not sell Jerusalem.'[260]

Ghaith al-Omari explained that Arafat was a devout Muslim and a pragmatist. Arafat thought if he did not get the Haram, the peace pact 'will not sell among the Palestinians and it certainly will not sell among the Arabs'.[261] Arafat felt that Jerusalem was not something for the Palestinians to give. 'If the Saudis are not on board, if the Moroccans are not on board, if the OIC (Organisation of Islamic Cooperation)[262] is not on board, then it's not for the Palestinians to give.'[263]

[257] Abu Mazen, 'If We Were to Meet Again in Camp David We Would Take the Same Positions', *Al Ayyam* (Memri) (30 July 2001) (Hebrew), https://tinyurl.com/ytybpkyb.

[258] Nusseibeh, *Once Upon a Country*, 426.

[259] Swisher, *The Truth about Camp David*, 304–305.

[260] Ibid., 327.

[261] Interview with Ghaith al-Omari (2 September 2014), 25.

[262] The Organisation of Islamic Cooperation (OIC) is the second-largest intergovernmental organisation after the United Nations, with a membership of fifty-seven states in four continents. The OIC is the collective voice of the Muslim world. Its aim is to safeguard and protect the interests of the Muslim world. See www.oic-oci.org/page/?p_id=52&p_ref=26&lan=en.

[263] Interview with Ghaith al-Omari (2 September 2014), 25.

As the talks progressed, Israel agreed to relinquish sovereignty over the Muslim and Christian parts of the Old City of Jerusalem. Israel offered a form of Palestinian custodianship over the Haram al-Sharif/ Temple Mount, but Arafat insisted on sovereignty.[264] The Palestinians wanted the internationalisation of Jerusalem and the implementation of UN Resolution 181 declaring Jerusalem as a *corpus separatum*, a Latin term referring to a city or region that is given a special legal and political status.[265] For the first time, the Palestinians recognised that the Wailing Wall, the Jewish Quarter of the Old City and the Jewish neighbourhoods of East Jerusalem would be part of Israel.[266] Significant as this concession might be, the Israelis rejected the Palestinian demands on Jerusalem.

Settlements

On 14 September 1999, at a meeting in Ma'ale Adumim, Barak stated that it would remain

> part of the State of Israel and part of Greater Jerusalem forever ... We, the new government, will continue to strengthen the State of Israel and its hold on the Land of Israel, and we will continue to strengthen Ma'ale Adumim ... Every tree you plant, every house you build is part of the State of Israel forever. Period. We are not going to move settlements of 25,000 people whom the Rabin government and all governments nurtured. You are part of Greater Jerusalem! ... You will be part of the State of Israel in every permanent arrangement.[267]

On 27 September, the Israeli Housing Ministry reported that, during its first three months in office, the Barak government authorised construction of 2,600 new housing units in the West Bank.[268] Barak continued to develop settlements in the West Bank throughout his time in office. True, he ordered fifteen of the forty-two unauthorised settlements constructed after the Wye accord to be dismantled, but this was insufficient. The PA was dismayed by Barak's conduct. Inattentive to its protests, he was far

264 Quandt, 'Israeli-Palestinian Peace Talks', 33.

265 United Nations General Assembly Resolution 181 (29 November 1947), www.yale.edu/lawweb/avalon/un/res181.htm.

266 Beilin, *The Path to Geneva*, 160; *From Oslo to Camp David to Taba: Setting the Record Straight*; Malley and Agha, 'A Reply to Ehud Barak', 46.

267 Geoffrey Aronson, 'Settlement Monitor', *Journal of Palestine Studies*, 29(2) (Winter 2000): 137.

268 Ibid., 138.

more attentive to the settlers' demands. West Bank settlements continue to be a major obstacle on the road to peace.

Security

This was the main Israeli consideration. Life in Israel is constantly challenged by violence and terror. The unresolved Israeli-Palestinian conflict fosters an abnormal reality. Wars erupt frequently (1948, 1956, 1967, 1973, 1982, 2006, 2023), and the Palestinians manifest their resistance to the Israeli occupation by resorting to violence and terror. It was important for Israel that Palestine be a demilitarised state, with only a 'strong' police force. It was also important for Israel that there were no foreign armies or military forces on Palestinian soil, and no alliances with other states which are hostile to Israel. After extensive negotiations, Israel insisted on having *two* early warning stations, situated in agreed-upon locations in the Palestinian area. The Palestinians agreed to these conditions.[269] No agreement was reached on Israel's right, in an emergency situation, to deploy forces on Palestinian land without prior consent by the Palestinians, but just by notification of Israel's intention. The parties also could not agree on who would define what an emergency situation is. In addition, no agreement was reached regarding the Israeli military presence along the Jordan Valley: for how long, what kind of presence, what composition of forces and what would be the gradual phasing out of this deployment of Israeli forces.[270]

Critical security concerns, such as the threat of spoilers, the role of Hamas, monopoly over weapons and the need for decisive action against terrorism, were insufficiently addressed in the Camp David negotiations. For Israel, these issues were foundational, not peripheral. Without credible Palestinian cooperation to curb violence and dismantle terror organisations, Israeli willingness to make painful concessions on borders, refugees and Jerusalem was significantly eroded.

Barak went to Camp David with the stated goal of preventing an eruption of violence. Yet, despite the urgency of that objective, the summit was consumed almost entirely by high-stakes issues of final status: borders, Jerusalem, Holy Places and refugees. As a result, little progress was made in developing concrete, enforceable mechanisms to address security threats on the ground, leaving a dangerous vacuum. Although the Israeli delegation

[269] Interview with Gilead Sher (2 February 2024), 1.
[270] Ibid.

believed they had reached a set of understandings at Camp David, within weeks – by August 2000 – the Palestinians walked back those understandings. They claimed that what Israel considered agreed-upon terms were, in fact, never formally accepted.[271] This retraction, coupled with the absence of clear plans to neutralise violent actors and prevent internal spoilers, cast a long shadow over the summit's outcomes. It also revealed a deeper structural flaw: the process had not fully reckoned with the security realities that would shape, and potentially derail, any future agreement.

Prisoner Release

This is a concrete issue that troubles Palestinians a great deal. When Israel releases prisoners, this is perceived as a real achievement for the Palestine Liberation Organization (PLO). It brings prisoners home, reuniting them with their loving families. As a measure of goodwill, this can be an important card. At Camp David, the parties discussed the principle that all prisoners should be freed once there is a permanent status agreement, a finality to all claims and an end of conflict.[272] Many families have one or more of their members in Israeli prisons.

Conclusion

After the closing exchanges, given their reluctance to accept any further proposals, the Palestinians were relieved to leave. They did not feel comfortable at Camp David. All they wanted was to go home and escape the American and Israeli pressures. Qurie wrote in his book: 'We felt like prisoners released from a sentence that had endured for two apparently endless weeks.'[273] The absent participant, Abbas, used similar terminology.[274] Qurie maintained: 'We had the sensation of having made good our

[271] Ibid.

[272] Ibid., 12.

[273] Qurie, *Beyond Oslo*, 248.

[274] Abbas said: 'It was a trap on every scale, from beginning to end, and we escaped it. No one has ever been subjected to pressure [like this] that was put on us. Imagine that you can't talk to anyone and you can't go out. Once, I went out with brother Abu Ala, to talk to the counselors. A commotion broke out. We only left for fifteen minutes. How did you get out? from where? why? All these questions were addressed to us. There were wire fences, police and army. And we went out in coordination with the American security, probably without them receiving approval from the upper echelons. The whole time we stayed at Camp David isolated and under siege.' 'Abu Mazen, "If We Were to Meet Again in Camp David We Would Take the Same Positions"'.

escape from a trap that had been set for us with much care and premeditation.'[275] This statement is very revealing. The Israelis felt they were in a historic place, similar to the signature of the peace treaty with Egypt. Now, they hoped to sign another peace treaty that would shape the future of Israel and the region for the better. The Palestinians, however, were more interested in escaping the role assigned to them by the United States and Israel. Jerusalem provided the perfect pretence for them and their line of defence vis-à-vis their own people, the Arab world and the international community at large.

Strangely, Arafat did not sense that, after the summit, the future would be bleaker for the Palestinians. A few hours after his return from Camp David, he hosted a dinner at his office. He was happy and optimistic. He thought things went well at Camp David, and that Israel and the PLO had agreed on 90 per cent of the issues. He said: 'We reached great, great progress. We were even negotiating about the Armenian Quarter and the Old City of Jerusalem.'[276] Two points were still subject to further negotiations. The main issue was that of sovereignty over the Haram al-Sharif. There was also the refugee issue – how many would return to Israel? As for the Temple Mount, Arafat said, 'I cannot decide. We cannot decide. We need to consult mainly with the Saudis, the Egyptians and the Jordanians.'[277] About the refugees, Arafat was willing to compromise. In the coming weeks, in late July, Arafat planned to travel to Egypt, Saudi Arabia and Jordan. In August, there would be another meeting in Camp David, followed by a final meeting in mid-September. That would commemorate the signing of the Oslo agreement in September 1993.[278] In his view, the summit had not failed. Israel and the PLO would sign the final agreement in September. El-Kurd said Arafat was shocked and surprised to hear from Ehud Barak that 'everything was now coming to a standstill. Everything was rejected.'[279] Until his final days, whenever Arafat and El-Kurd talked about Camp David, Arafat was going crazy with this. What happened? Why?, Arafat wondered.[280]

[275] Qurie, *Beyond Oslo*, 248. Throughout his book, Qurie reiterates that the Americans were not an impartial broker; they sided with the Israelis, presenting their views as American views. They exerted pressure only on the Palestinians while expressing sympathy for the Israelis.

[276] Interview with Maher El-Kurd (30 January 2025), 17.

[277] Ibid.

[278] Ibid.

[279] Ibid., 19.

[280] Ibid.

In the immediate aftermath of Camp David, Israel launched a public diplomacy campaign aimed at shaping the narrative of failure. Arafat was cast as the chief culprit, blamed for intransigence and for squandering a historic opportunity. This blame game, far from being constructive, revealed Barak's short-sightedness. With upcoming elections already looming large in his mind, his focus shifted from peacemaking to political survival. Despite repeatedly asserting that he had 'no partner' on the Palestinian side, Barak nonetheless continued to engage with Palestinian representatives after the summit. This contradiction underscored the complexity of the moment. Barak was torn between domestic political calculations and a lingering belief that diplomacy had not yet run its course.

For Israel and the United States, Camp David ended in bitter disappointment, a failed gamble that left them questioning the very feasibility of peace. For the Palestinians, however, the conclusion of the summit came with a sense of relief. They had resisted pressure to compromise on core principles without the guarantees they deemed necessary.

The next two chapters explore the enduring lessons of Camp David: what went wrong, why it failed and how it shaped the trajectory of Israeli-Palestinian relations in the wake of the Oslo process. What began in hope ended in disillusionment, leaving a legacy that continues to inform negotiations to this day.

7

Camp David

Lessons

And if two factions of the Believers get to fight, make them reconcile ... And put justice to work. Surely, Allah loves those who do justice.

~ Al-Quran Surah: 9

Lessons

Timing

Convening the Camp David Summit was a mistake. It was ill-timed and ill-conceived. Ehud Barak took very high risks, because the timing was not right and the situation was not ripe for an agreement. For a conflict to be ripe for negotiation, the parties must see themselves as caught in a painful stalemate, and they must find a way to improve their condition. This was not the case for Yasser Arafat, who believed he could achieve more at a later point. Arafat decided to come to the summit because he thought he would lose more by not coming.[1] He explicitly said that the Palestinians were not ready, and that they needed more time for preparations.[2] Too many difficult issues were on the table, and the lack of preparation made room for fears, suspicions, prejudices and insecurities to grow. The Americans issued the invitations, despite Israel's refusal to carry out its earlier commitments and despite Arafat's plea for additional time to prepare. This only reinforced the sense of an American-Israeli conspiracy in Arafat's mind.[3] He was well aware of the special relationship between the United States and Israel and between Bill Clinton and Barak. Camp David was their game, not his.

[1] Interviews with Ziad Abu Zayyad (14 May 2015), Shlomo Brom (17 June 2014) and Ghaith al-Omari (2 September 2014).

[2] Interview with Shlomo Ben-Ami (26 June 2013), 3.

[3] Robert Malley and Hussein Agha, 'Camp David: The Tragedy of Errors', *New York Review of Books* (9 August 2001), https://tinyurl.com/2s4nskmv.

Making peace in a pressure cooker when there is little trust between the two sides is precarious.[4] Barak was racing against time, as his government was facing serious challenges and seemed unsustainable. The possibility of failure was clear – and ignored.

The pressure took its toll. Barak, who by nature is not very friendly, became a loner in the secluded camp, poring over the Israeli public opinion surveys that were regularly fed to him.[5] He became dependent on the process, and his vulnerabilities were exposed to the Palestinians. While Arafat did not have to deal with democratic political pressures, Barak was preoccupied with weighing different scenarios that might help him rescue his political future.

The Americans knew that the gaps between the two sides were wide. They also knew that Arafat never decided anything except one minute before midnight and that, to his mind, Camp David was only one more step in the process. They opted for a summit so as not to waste the opportunity. They saw the choice as not having a summit or having a summit at the wrong time.[6] They did not correctly assess the implications of a resounding failure.

Dennis Ross wanted to postpone the summit to late summer so that the negotiating teams could narrow the gaps, but his view was rejected.[7] Testing his own leadership, Clinton decided to risk going ahead with the summit. He accepted Barak's timetable, despite Israel's failure to carry out earlier commitments and its continued settlement building, and despite Palestinian terrorism. Clinton's personal participation in the negotiations, despite his good intentions and tremendous efforts, was not constructive. Like Jimmy Carter at Camp David in 1978, Clinton demonstrated remarkable perseverance and a genuine grasp of the parties' needs and interests. Unlike Carter, however, he could not close the gaps between the adversaries and deliver the historic peace agreement he so fervently pursued. His energetic and sincere leadership could not

[4] Beilin writes that, during the last week before the Camp David Summit, he met with a Palestinian central figure who thought that the summit was destined to fail because not enough was done in practical areas, and the atmosphere between the two sides was not positive. See Yossi Beilin, *The Path to Geneva* (New York: RDV Books, 2004), 152.

[5] Interview with Shlomo Ben-Ami (26 June 2013), 5. See also Clayton E. Swisher, *The Truth about Camp David: The Untold Story about the Collapse of the Middle East Peace Process* (New York: Nation Books, 2004), 332.

[6] Interview with Dennis Ross (27 September 2019), 10.

[7] William Quandt, *Peace Process: American Diplomacy and the Arab-Israeli Conflict since 1967* (Berkeley: University of California Press, 2005), 367.

overcome the structural mistrust, asymmetry and hardened positions that pervaded the summit.

Furthermore, Clinton rushed the negotiations. Nearing the end of a troubled and controversial second term, he wanted to be remembered for something other than the Monica Lewinsky scandal.[8] The final year of a presidency is arguably the least opportune time to broker a major peace agreement. The president becomes increasingly vulnerable, pressed for time, distracted by the urgency to cement a legacy, and more susceptible to external and internal pressures. The desire to secure an historic breakthrough can lead to haste, rather than strategic patience. This urgency often undermines careful diplomacy by forcing timelines, overpromising outcomes or trying to push parties beyond what they are prepared to concede.

Abstruseness of Purpose

Both sides lacked a clear vision about their respective endgames and how to get there. They did not clarify their intentions to their counterpart. Most of the time, the Americans were not fully aware of the two parties' exact intentions and endgames. The Palestinians, whose willingness to make concessions leading to peace was unclear, complained about Israel's lack of clarity. Ghaith al-Omari said that Barak 'was a disaster' to negotiate with. There was a lot of back and forth, and while 'most of his team was unauthorised to negotiate, he himself was not very available'.[9] Indeed, even the Israeli delegation did not know Barak's bottom lines.

Procedural problems surfaced during the talks and hampered substantive negotiations.[10] The Israelis came with detailed maps and ideas, and with concrete demands and demarcations. The Palestinians did not have a mapping expert at Camp David. For much of the negotiations, when the Israelis asked to see the Palestinians' maps, they refused to reveal them, limiting themselves to only an outline of general principles. The Palestinians did not wish to close off opportunities to achieve more and demand more at later stages.[11] This incremental policy is a double-edged

8 From mid-1995 to 1997, Lewinsky was involved in an extramarital sexual relationship with President Bill Clinton. See Biography, Monica Lewinsky, www.biography.com/people/monica-lewinsky-21292085.

9 Interview with Ghaith al-Omari (2 September 2014), 33.

10 Interview with Udi Dekel (17 June 2014), 3.

11 Ahmed Qurie, *Beyond Oslo* (London: I.B. Tauris, 2008), 223. See also Ahmed Qurie, *Peace Negotiations in Palestine* (London: I.B. Tauris, 2015).

sword, because it undermines trust. Banking on future possibilities at the expense of securing tangible gains in the present can be counterproductive, as 'a bird in the hand is worth two in the bush'. The Hebrew equivalent is: 'A bird in the hand is worth two in the tree.' Future gains may be not only uncertain, but also inaccessible. In diplomacy, as in life, chasing the ideal can sometimes mean forfeiting the achievable.

The Israelis' approach to the negotiations was that they required mutual compromise. To them, diplomacy was the art of meeting halfway – although defining the midpoint was open to interpretation. They came to the summit expecting genuine concessions from the Palestinian side that would reflect a shared responsibility in reaching a historic agreement.

The Palestinians, however, viewed the negotiations through a fundamentally different lens. From their perspective, Israel's proposals were merely a starting point, not a compromise. They believed that their own historical sacrifices in 1947–1948 and 1967 had already exacted a heavy toll. Israel, as the stronger party, was expected to continue making concessions. For the Palestinians, the negotiations were not about mutual give and take, but about pressing for maximum gains without equivalent concessions. This deep asymmetry in expectations shaped the entire summit and contributed to its ultimate breakdown.

Lack of Resolve

Neither Israel nor the Palestine Liberation Organization (PLO) came to Camp David fully prepared to pay the steep price a lasting peace demanded. Barak was determined to end the conflict, but he remained constrained, both mentally and politically. He was unwilling to overcome Palestinian objections by offering a deal they could not refuse, especially on the most sensitive issues. He sought peace, but on terms largely defined by Israel's red lines. Arafat wanted peace, but on his own terms, too. The critical difference between them was that Barak was ready to make meaningful and painful concessions, while Arafat was either unwilling, unable or both to go beyond symbolic gestures. In the end, both were captives of their own political limitations and visions, leaving the promise of peace just out of reach.

Elyakim Rubinstein said that the sides need leadership, people who 'can lift the yoke and can do something'.[12] In his opinion, Anwar Sadat and Menachem Begin were such leaders. 'Barak was ready. He is a courageous

[12] Interview with Elyakim Rubinstein (10 July 2018), 17.

person. You may criticise him here and there, but Arafat was not.'[13] Barak was ready to declare the end of the conflict, something that Arafat did not care to do. 'Arafat was not going to finish the refugee problem, to say that this is the end of the conflict, I am shaking your hand and we, if you fulfil the agreement, I fulfil it and that is it. He was not there.'[14]

Success at Camp David required Israel to make significant concessions on Jerusalem and the Temple Mount. Arafat could have compromised on other issues, but not on Jerusalem. On Jerusalem, Arafat's view was principled. He was unwilling to receive less than what he asked for: sovereignty in the eastern part, including the Haram. Arafat wanted to be remembered as the father of the Palestinian revolution, the founder of Palestine, and the leader who returned Jerusalem, with its Holy Places, to the bosom of the Arab world, Muslim and Christian. This would assure Arafat an eternal place of honour among Arab leaders.[15] He believed that if he were to compromise over Jerusalem and the Haram, his own people would kill him.[16] Barak's inability to compromise on these two issues provided Arafat with an exit route from the summit. Shlomo Ben-Ami said he heard Arafat telling Mahmoud Abbas: 'Leave me alone you and your refugees.'[17] That is, Arafat did not consider the refugees as the primary problem. For him, the core issue was Jerusalem. Salam Fayyad, however, said that the very last words Arafat said to him before he died was to remember his brothers in Lebanon.[18]

Lack of Preparation

The parties – Israel, the PLO and the US – came to the summit with impossibly wide differences between the sides.[19] My interviewees testified that nobody arrived at Camp David fully prepared. Quoting James Baker, Aaron David Miller said: 'Prior preparation prevents poor performance.'[20]

13 Ibid.

14 Ibid.

15 Shaul Kimhi, Shmuel Even and Jerrold Post, *Yasir Arafat: Psychological Profile and Strategic Analysis* (Herzliya: The Interdisciplinary Center, 2002); Shaul Kimhi and Shmuel Even, 'Yassir Arafat: Behavioral and Strategic Analysis', *Social Behavior and Personality*, 31(4) (2003): 367.

16 Interview with Svein Sevje (1 September 2019), 22.

17 Interview with Shlomo Ben-Ami (26 June 2013), 8.

18 Interview with Salam Fayyad (19 January 2024).

19 Interviews with Aaron David Miller (12 September 2019), 4 and Yossi Sarid (15 May 2015), 27.

20 Interview with Aaron David Miller (12 September 2019), 12.

Prior to the summit, in June 2000, the Israelis had provided the United States with information that included their positions on all contentious issues, where there were agreements and disagreements between Israel and the Palestinians, and possible solutions to debatable concerns. Gidi Grinstein claims that the Palestinians did not provide any draft proposals. According to him, the Palestinians *never* provided any proposal in writing.[21] This claim is not altogether correct. While the Palestinians were passive *most* of the time, they were not passive *all* the time. Drawing on the Israeli documents, the Americans should have put the delegations to daily tasks from the very first day. When they failed to do so, it became clear to Grinstein and other negotiators after a few days that there would be no agreement.[22] The question was not what kind of deal would be struck, but how Israel would exit the summit, and who would bear responsibility and blame for the failure.

Furthermore, different members of the delegations had different levels of understanding of the issues at hand. In the Israeli delegation, Dan Meridor and Rubinstein were invited at the last minute. Barak invited Meridor in the eleventh hour, on 8 July 2000. Rubinstein said: 'I did not know what Barak is going to do. What are his intentions, in terms of the "give". I only know that if you are going to a peace conference, you are going to try to get results.'[23] Interestingly, the US Department of State Archives mention only seven members of the Israeli delegation: Prime Minister Ehud Barak, Minister of Internal Security Shlomo Ben Ami, Minister of Transportation and Tourism Amnon Lipkin-Shahak, Attorney General Elyakim Rubinstein, Chief of Staff Maj. Gen. (Ret.) Danny Yatom, Chairman of the Negotiating Team Gilad [sic] Sher,[24] and Head of Security Team Shlomo Yanai.[25] The United States delegation included fifteen people,[26] while the Palestinian delegation numbered

[21] Interview with Gidi Grinstein (21 May 2013), 13.

[22] Ibid., 16.

[23] Interview with Ely Rubinstein (10 July 2018), 3.

[24] Should be Gilead Sher.

[25] 'Official Delegations', US Department of State Archives, https://1997-2001.state.gov/regions/nea/summit_delegation.html

[26] The President, Secretary of State Madeleine Albright, Chief of Staff John Podesta, Assistant to the President for National Security Affairs Samuel Berger, Assistant to the President and Press Secretary Joe Lockhart, Deputy Chief of Staff Maria Echaveste, Special Middle East Coordinator Dennis Ross, US Ambassador to Israel Martin Indyk, US Consul General in Jerusalem John Herbst, Special Assistant to the President and Senior Director for Near East and South Asian Affairs NSC Bruce Riedel, Deputy Special Middle East Coordinator, Department of State Aaron D. Miller, Special Assistant to the President for Arab–Israeli

twelve.[27] The Israeli delegation, like the Palestinian, was allocated twelve participants.

The Israelis prepared detailed documents on most issues, thinking that most issues were ripe for agreement with the Palestinians,[28] but there was no preparatory meeting of the entire Israeli delegation. Problems were reflected in the work of the delegation and internal divergences of opinion. Negotiators who were closer to Barak enjoyed accessibility to him (notably Yatom, Lipkin-Shahak Sher and Ben-Ami), while others were more remote. Two problems emerged: the delegates' level of understanding of Barak and what he was willing to concede varied, and they did not speak in one voice. In this respect, Barak's circumstances were manifestly different than those of Menachem Begin in 1978. Barak aspired to a consensual agreement that would reflect the rainbow of Israeli public opinions, not realising that at *that* junction, such an aspiration was bound to conflict with the necessity of making tough decisions. In essence, Barak opted for hardline negotiations over pragmatic reconciliation.

While the Oslo peace process was based on gradualism, Barak arrived at the Camp David Summit with an 'all or nothing' approach in mind, and he convinced Clinton to adhere to the same thinking. There was no alternative plan in the event of failure or exhaustion of the negotiations without results. It was ambitious binary thinking, 1 or 0. Sher and Ben-Ami advised Barak to narrow the gaps through additional negotiation, but Barak stuck to his all-or-nothing plan.[29] Neither the Israelis nor the Americans had a safety net so that all would not be lost if and when the original plan failed.

A year before Camp David, the government of the United Kingdom initiated and funded the Negotiations Support Unit for the Palestinians in Ramallah. The project was intended to enable Palestinian negotiators to develop policies based on international law, to engage with peaceful initiatives and to provide legal skills for negotiation with Israeli interlocutors. It

Affairs and Director for Near East and South Asian Affairs NSC Rob Malley, Deputy Legal Adviser, Department of State Jonathan Schwartz, Deputy Assistant Secretary, Near Eastern Affairs, Department of State Toni Verstandig, and Senior Advisor, Department of State Gemal Helal.

27 Yasser Arafat, Mahmoud Abbas, Ahmed Qurie, Yasser Abed Rabbo, Nabil Sha'ath, Sa'eb Erekat, Hasan Asfour, Akram Haniya (Hanieh), Mohammed Dahlan, Mohammed Rashid, Nabil Abu Rudineh and Yousef Abdallah.

28 Interview with Gidi Grinstein (21 May 2013), 1; Shlomo Brom argues that at Camp David the Israelis called experts from the Jerusalem Institute for Israel Studies to come to the summit to help with negotiations. Interview with Shlomo Brom (17 June 2014), 16.

29 Gidi Grinstein and Ari Afilalo, *(In)Sights: Peacemaking in the Oslo Process Thirty Years and Counting* (Jerusalem: Gefen, 2023), 225.

comprised dozens of permanent legal, policy and communications advisors in a negotiation support unit, and more than fifty external consultants. John Jenkins argues that there were excellent professional lawyers on the staff, able to produce detailed briefs and maps.[30] Still, the Palestinians arrived at Camp David without senior lawyers and map experts. Outside Camp David, they had specialist lawyers who advised them on issues such as water and economics, but they did not have a senior legal negotiator who could advise them on matters pertaining to borders and international law. This reflected their lack of confidence in the American ability to close a deal. Ghaith al-Omari, a lawyer, was a junior participant who was brought to Camp David when the Palestinians realised they did not have anyone in their delegation who could draft documents. Hiba Husseini, another lawyer, was outside Camp David. When the Palestinians realised they also did not have anyone who had mapping abilities, they brought in Samih Al-Abed to fill the lacuna.[31] Given that two of the core issues were, and still are, borders and security, this is *most* puzzling.

I asked Hiba Husseini to explain the logic. Husseini said that the Palestinian leadership 'wanted to have the big boys there, and lawyers were seen as support. Technical experts were seen on an as-needed basis only, because then they were still discussing the principles, not the text itself. They would call on the team when they needed it.'[32] Husseini thinks this was not a good policy, and when she expressed her opinion to that effect, her superiors' reply was, 'well, we do not need you right now'.[33]

As for the Americans, the negotiators were unfamiliar with all the details of possible solutions to problems. They did not know whether Israel and the PLO were in the same ballpark and did not come prepared with fallback positions. The briefing papers for Clinton and Madeleine Albright were very succinct. Rob Malley said:

> I think we had a lot of ideas. We had worked very closely with some Israelis in ECF, the Economic Cooperation Foundation. You know them, Nimrod Novik and Hirschfeld and Boaz Carmi. So, we worked with them. We worked with outside experts, who were giving us ideas all of the time. We tried to come up with different scenarios. So, in that sense, yes, that kind of preparation. Where we were not prepared, as I said, is we did not have a clear … vision. What do we think this could end like? What is an ending

[30] Interview with John Jenkins (9 December 2022), 15.

[31] Interview with Ghaith al-Omari (2 September 2014), 17; Qurie, *Beyond Oslo*, 223; Gilead Sher, *Just beyond Reach* (Tel Aviv: Yedioth Ahronoth, 2015) (Hebrew), 201.

[32] Interview with Hiba Husseini (24 December 2024), 4.

[33] Ibid., 5.

> that we think both sides might be able to accept, and what will we do to get there? And what will we do if we are not able to get there? In that sense, I do not think we were sufficiently prepared. But I do not want to engage in self-flagellation, that we got everything wrong. I am very critical, but that is my nature ... If there was no deal, it is a collective failure, but it is a failure that redounds very heavily on the US. And so, I think we need to take our share of blame. And we should have had a clear sense of the objective, of how we were going to get there and what we would have done if we did not.[34]

PLO Ambassador to London explained that the Americans were not structurally prepared for this summit.[35] He thought the Camp David Summit was rushed and ill-prepared. The summit should have convened only after clearing the way and making adequate preparations for reaching tough decisions on issues of contention. For instance, Arafat could not have decided alone on the future of the Haram. He needed to consult with and receive the consent of Muslim leaders. Because there were already substantial gaps between Israel and the PLO, inviting another Arab country (Egypt, Jordan) would have made the negotiations even more complicated, as each country had its own stakes. The Americans should have laid better groundwork and pressed Arafat *prior* to the summit to get certain assurances from Arab stakeholders; they also failed to secure coherent and verified assurances from Arafat himself. Similarly, Sher thinks the Americans should have obtained mutual guarantees from each of the sides regarding the core issues. He thinks this was possible.[36] Grinstein thinks the Americans dealt with the principles but did not know the details about the refugees, the area and the security arrangements.[37] One would have expected Clinton to obtain this data before he committed to the Camp David gambit.

Shifting Red Lines

James Baker emphasised the importance of knowing the opponent's red lines.[38] The Palestinians showed little flexibility throughout the summit, and the Israelis kept changing their red lines. The lack of preparation and multiple voices created the problem of shifting red lines. Israel would

[34] Interview with Rob Malley (28 July 2022), 17.
[35] Discussion with PLO ambassador (20 November 2013).
[36] Interview with Gilead Sher (26 May 2013), 6.
[37] Interview with Gidi Grinstein (21 May 2013), 9.
[38] Carnegie Connects: Aaron David Miller in Conversation with The Honorable James A. Baker, III (29 September 2021).

say, 'this is the most we can do', Arafat would say 'no', and soon enough, yesterday's red line became obsolete. Red lines became pink, making absolutely final offers hardly credible. The Palestinians realised that rejection yielded positive results. They regarded the negotiations as an inconsequential bazaar,[39] while the Americans, who defended yesterday's red lines, lost their reliability. Gadi Baltiansky said that Israel invented fake red lines. On Jerusalem, for example, Israel promised that it would be united forever under Israeli sovereignty, 'blah, blah, blah. Now, it's fake. We don't ... really want Kalandia, Kafr 'Aqab, and Shuafat, right?' Still, the Israelis insisted that 'Jerusalem should be united forever under Israeli sovereignty'.[40]

Malley asserted that the shifting red lines put the Americans in a bad light because they followed whatever the Israelis told them. The Americans would convey a message from the Israelis that this was the most they could do, and the following day, Israel would compromise further. Consequently, the Palestinians thought the Americans were just useless messengers.[41] Palestinian trust in both the Israelis and the Americans eroded quickly.

Trust is the cornerstone of any successful negotiation. Without it, suspicion colours every move, and intentions are doubted at every turn. The Israeli delegation at Camp David was viewed by the Palestinians as overly calculating and manipulative, reinforcing an atmosphere of mistrust. As the summit dragged on without tangible progress, the Israeli negotiators grew visibly tense. Pressure mounted with each passing day. The Palestinians, by contrast, remained largely unmoved, refusing to be bound by Israeli or American timelines.

Barak's strategy – to create, with US backing, a pressure-cooker environment that would force Arafat into making concessions – ultimately failed. While the Israelis approached negotiations with methodical precision and analytical rigour, they were often left in the dark about their own leader's bottom lines. Barak deliberately withheld key information, issuing conflicting instructions at different stages. His tendency to centralise control and play his cards close to his chest undermined the cohesion of his own team and blurred the clarity needed for effective diplomacy.

Barak defended this negotiation tactic by saying 'Arabs need negotiations. They needed to see that there is progress. They need to see you

[39] Interviews with Shlomo Brom (17 June 2014), 18; Ghaith al-Omari (2 September 2014), 24 and Hussein Agha (5 April 2019), 6; Aaron David Miller, 'How Not to Host a Summit', *Foreign Policy* (10 July 2012).

[40] Interview with Gadi Baltiansky (25 January 2016), 12.

[41] Interview with Rob Malley (28 July 2022), 21.

moving through it. It is the only way to expect from *them*.'[42] Negotiations are time-consuming. Barak believed he was well equipped to conduct them. He said that, except for Moshe Sharett,[43] he did not know of any other prime minister who could read Arabic, read Ibn Khaldun,[44] know what Arkan al Islam is,[45] or recite the Surah Al-Fatihah by heart.[46] Barak testified that he spent many years studying Arab thinking.[47] While knowledge of language, religion and literature is certainly an asset, it is important to utilise this knowledge to establish a rapport with one's counterpart – something Barak could not do. Furthermore, there are other, no less important keys for successful negotiations with the Palestinians (see Chapter 11). Barak chose the tactic of shifting red lines, believing it was the most appropriate way to deal with them.

A key lesson from Camp David is the danger of prematurely invoking red lines. Negotiators must use that term with precision, integrity and restraint. Declaring a position as final or non-negotiable should carry real weight; otherwise, the credibility of the negotiating process erodes. Israel weakened its negotiating posture by labelling certain concessions as the absolute maximum, only to stretch those boundaries later. Once a line is red, it must remain firm; otherwise, it signals to the other side that further pressure might yield greater concessions. This ambiguity undermined trust and strategy. Why would the Palestinians accept today's offer if they believed that rejecting it would lead to a better one tomorrow? All three delegations recognised this dynamic, and it dulled the urgency of compromise. Without clear and consistent communication, negotiations lose authenticity and effectiveness.

Lack of Coordination

Some members of the Israeli delegation told the Palestinians to ignore certain red lines, telling them that *that* was not where Israel intended to

42 Interview with Ehud Barak (11 July 2022), 13.

43 Moshe Sharett was Israel's second prime minister, from 1954 to 1955.

44 Ibn Khaldūn, in full Walī al-Dīn ʿAbd al-Raḥmān ibn Muḥammad ibn Muḥammad ibn Abī Bakr Muḥammad ibn al-Ḥasan Ibn Khaldūn (born 27 May 1332, Tunis, died 17 March 1406, Cairo, Egypt), the greatest Arab historian, who developed one of the earliest non-religious philosophies of history, contained in his masterpiece, the *Muqaddimah* ('Introduction'). See *Britannica*, www.britannica.com/biography/Ibn-Khaldun.

45 The pillars of Islam: Muslim creed, prayer, charity, fasting during Ramadan and pilgrimage to Mecca.

46 The Opener, the first surah (chapter) of the Quran, consisting of seven phrases.

47 Interview with Ehud Barak (11 July 2022), 13.

end up. This totally ruined Barak's posture vis-à-vis Arafat and created an unhealthy dynamic that undermined the talks.

Barak appointed Sher and Meridor to lead the talks on Jerusalem, an arrangement that caused him embarrassment. When he told the Palestinians one thing, Sher would tell them the opposite.[48] Sa'eb Erekat spoke of two municipalities in Jerusalem, one Israeli and the other Palestinian. Meridor responded by insisting on one municipality and sole Israeli sovereignty over Jerusalem. To Meridor's surprise, Sher agreed with Erekat, suggesting two municipalities, an Israeli one in West Jerusalem and a Palestinian one in Abu Dis, a Palestinian village in the West Bank, bordering Jerusalem.[49] Ben-Ami went further than he was instructed to by Barak, suggesting that Beit Hanina, Sur Baher and Shuafat would be partially transferred to Palestinian sovereignty. They would be part of Al Quds, the capital of Palestine. Barak was quick to inform Clinton that Ben-Ami and Sher had gone beyond what he could live with.[50] These contradictory messages and lack of coordination hampered negotiations, demonstrating to the Palestinians that the situation within the Israeli camp was complex, with no clear consensus or leadership. This lack of seriousness and professionalism did little to establish trust and confidence in Israel and its positions.

Meridor, however, thinks the summit failed not because of Jerusalem, but because of the refugee issue.[51] No great progress was achieved on this issue either. Meridor explained that Israel expected that when the Palestinians had a state, all their claims and aspirations would be vested in the land that would be theirs, in the State of Palestine, not in Israel. In other words, 'we don't resolve just the '67 issue, but the '48 issue, which was the source of all the conflict'.[52] The Palestinians were expected to give up the idea that 1948 could be reversed somehow, and that refugees would have a right to settle in Israel. Meridor's views failed to strike a chord with the Palestinians.

Both Barak and Arafat failed to pick the right people to move the negotiations on refugees forward. The more they talked, the further away the teams were from a solution. Meridor's view, however, that the summit failed due to the refugee issue is exceptional. Most of my

48 Interview with Dan Meridor (21 May 2013), 12.

49 Dan Meridor, *Camp David 2000* (personal diary, Hebrew), 11.

50 Danny Yatom, *The Labyrinth of Power* (Tel Aviv: Contento, 2016), 618–621.

51 Interview with Dan Meridor (21 May 2013), 13.

52 Interview with Dan Meridor (20 January 2016), 2.

interviewees – Israelis, Palestinians and Americans – think that Jerusalem and the Temple Mount were the major obstacles. Furthermore, in his diary, Meridor wrote that Arafat accepted Clinton's proposals on the refugee issue.[53]

Deficient Human Relationships

The best negotiation situations are those among equals.[54] It has been argued that efficient negotiations are impossible in asymmetric situations. Some minimal equality between the parties is required, otherwise the stronger party has an undue advantage.[55] In a situation of an asymmetric power relation between the negotiating sides, as is the case between Israel and the PLO, the powerful side must calm the anxieties and qualms of the weaker side by demonstrating understanding of, respect for and generosity towards the other's interests and concerns.[56] Israeli leaders should have been sensitive to the Palestinians' concerns that their notable weaknesses would be exploited. They should have made an effort to calm the Palestinians' anxieties. Instead, they did the exact opposite.

When leaders act under duress, they lack goodwill. The Israelis thought they could compel the Palestinians to make concessions. Arafat understood; he felt no goodwill to resolve the conflict. Quite the opposite. He went to Camp David with the sense that the Israelis, with American support, aimed to corner him.[57] Arafat was determined to do everything possible to defy Barak.[58]

Much has been said about the tenuous and problematic relationship between Barak and Arafat. Prior to Camp David, Barak kept Arafat waiting while he went off and pursued 'the other woman', the Syrian track, which caused a lot of bad blood. When Israel missed out on the Syrian deal, Clinton and Barak began chasing Arafat, and Camp David came about. However, Barak did not abide by the Oslo II agreement. He did not release prisoners and was reluctant to transfer land to the Palestinians

53 Meridor, *Camp David 2000*, 39.

54 Mona Fixdal, *Just Peace: How Wars Should End* (Houndmills: Palgrave, 2012), 35–38.

55 Ibid. See also Mona Fixdal (ed.), *Ways Out of War: Peacemakers in the Middle East and the Balkans* (Houndmills: Palgrave, 2012).

56 Karin Aggestam, 'Mediating Asymmetrical Conflict', *Mediterranean Politics*, 7(1) (2002): 69–91; D. Quinn, J. Wilkenfeld, K. Smarick and V. Asal, 'Power Play: Mediation in Symmetric and Asymmetric International Crises', *International Interactions*, 32(4) (2006): 441–470.

57 Interview with Ghaith al-Omari (2 September 2014), 17.

58 Interview with Martin Indyk (9 August 2022), 13.

Figure 7.1 Barak, Clinton and Arafat.
Credit: The White House/Handout/Hulton Archive/Getty Images.

as agreed.[59] He thought that the Oslo formula was flawed and wanted to receive tangible assets for tangible assets. Consequently, the relationship between Arafat and Barak was already considerably damaged.

Although Camp David was regarded as a peace summit, the two leaders never met for a session of serious negotiation, what Itamar Rabinovich calls a 'meeting of the minds' (see Figure 7.1).[60] Barak had tea with Arafat only once, at Birch, Arafat's cabin, but no specific political issues were discussed.[61] The trilateral meetings between Clinton, Arafat and Barak were not effective and did not yield a breakthrough.

Many of my interviewees noted that Barak lacks emotional intelligence. Israel Hasson said that 'with Ehud Barak, the gap between his intelligence and his emotional intelligence is wide enough so that you can pass the Sixth Fleet through it'.[62] Baltiansky said that Barak does not understand

[59] Charles Enderlin, *Shattered Dreams: The Failure of the Peace Process in the Middle East, 1995–2002* (New York: Other Press, 2003), 135–172.
[60] Raphael Cohen-Almagor, 'Keys for Peace in the Middle East: Interview with Ambassador Itamar Rabinovich', *Israel Affairs*, 25(4) (2019): 702.
[61] Akram Hanieh, 'The Camp David Papers', *Journal of Palestine Studies*, 30(2) (Winter 2001): 93.
[62] Interview with Israel Hasson (23 May 2013), 13.

the importance of personal chemistry and small talk, and that negotiations are not a zero-sum game. Barak is 'very smart, very knowledgeable and he's not good at negotiations'.[63]

Ben-Ami writes that Barak was inept at addressing the sensibilities of both friends and rivals, and he lacked the intuitive tactile sense that makes a great politician.[64] Gad Yaacobi said Barak enjoys talking much more than listening.[65] Barak was condescending,[66] and he lacked the patience and diligence necessary for dealing with Arafat, who exhausted people with his ambiguous, unclear formulations and his conduct while speaking. Dealing with Arafat was difficult,[67] and Barak felt he had better things to do than play audience for Arafat's meandering talk. Arab leaders and American negotiators who dealt with him felt the same.[68] Few were able to penetrate and establish rapport with Arafat. One of those who was able to do so was Yossi Ginossar.

Barak is a business-like person. He does not like to waste time in empty conversation. Fayyad said that the first time he met Barak, the latter opened the meeting by asking: 'What can I do for you?' Fayyad thought this was rude and arrogant.[69] Barak does not think negotiations are about emotions.[70] He did not invest in building a connection with Arafat; for Barak, Arafat was a business partner. Each must offer things the other needs. Barak saw no need to get to know Arafat as a person or to open himself up to Arafat – Barak did not open himself up to people in his *own* delegation. He was there to fulfil a historic role, to bring peace to Israel. He was not there to strike up friendships, certainly not with Arafat.

Arafat felt neither respected nor understood by Barak and did not like him personally. The Israeli leader's style alienated him, and the harder the Israelis pushed, the more resolute Arafat became in his refusal to yield. Attempting to win his goodwill, the Israelis relied on arguments that carried little weight with Arafat: coalition politics, electoral timelines and the pressures of a democratic system. These considerations, while critical to

63 Interview with Gadi Baltiansky (25 January 2016), 13.
64 Shlomo Ben-Ami, *Prophets without Honor: The 2000 Camp David Summit and the End of the Two-State Solution* (Oxford: Oxford University Press, 2022), 7–8.
65 Private conversation.
66 Shlomo Ben-Ami, 'So Close and Yet So Far: Lessons from the Israeli-Palestinian Peace Process', *Israel Studies*, 10(2) (Summer, 2005): 72.
67 Interview with Shlomo Ben-Ami (26 June 2013); Ben-Ami, *Prophets without Honor*, 9.
68 Interview with Gamal Helal (11 November 2022), 21.
69 Interview with Salam Fayyad (16 January 2024), 17.
70 Interview with Ehud Barak (11 July 2022), 13.

them, meant nothing to Arafat. He was not about to compromise on core issues – Jerusalem, the Haram al-Sharif and refugees – because of Barak's political constraints. Nor did he feel obligated to help Barak succeed; if anything, their strained relationship hardened his stance. Arafat, said Gamal Helal, had 'zero intention to do anything or to give anything to the Israeli prime minister, who was not even willing to sit down with him'.[71]

As the prospects of a peace deal became more remote, so did Barak. He found spending time with Arafat, even at the dinner table, difficult. Barak explained that speaking with Arafat was not productive and that Arafat was not communicating. 'I cannot create a real warmth [with Arafat], but I never hurt him. I always showed respect to him. I never raised my voice. I never scorned him. I never pretended to know more or do more.'[72]

True, Barak never derided Arafat verbally; however, he patronised him.[73] There is a famous photo in which Barak is pushing Arafat into Clinton's cabin at Camp David while Clinton waits in anticipation (see Figure 7.2). Arafat did not like to be pushed around. His psychological profile showed that independence was extremely important to him, that he needed to feel in control of any situation, and that he did not like accepting authority.[74] In many respects, this photo is very symbolic.

Arafat's psychological profile also speaks of his need for control; he always wanted to have the last word in every argument.[75] My Camp David interviewees noted that Barak's negativity towards Arafat was noticeable. He tried to avoid Arafat to the best of his ability, which was sometimes difficult at a small place like Camp David.[76] Helal criticised Barak's conduct by saying, in bilateral meetings, 'is that the conduct of somebody who really wants to reach peace? By refusing even to meet with Arafat one-on-one?'[77] Helal said that Arafat was insulted, as were the Americans, 'because we invited the two sides to Camp David, based on what Ehud

71 Interview with Gamal Helal (11 November 2022), 30.

72 Interview with Ehud Barak (11 July 2022), 11.

73 Interviews with Tzipi Livni (22 June 2016), 1 and Shlomo Brom (17 June 2014), 16.

74 Kimhi, Even and Post, *Yasir Arafat: Psychological Profile and Strategic Analysis*; Kimhi and Even, 'Yassir Arafat: Behavioral and Strategic Analysis', 365.

75 Kimhi, Even and Post, *Yasir Arafat: Psychological Profile and Strategic Analysis.*

76 Olmert said: Sa'eb Erekat told the story that one day, he and Arafat were sitting on the terrace of the bungalow where they stayed in Camp David. And Barak was walking not far on the road, strolling with one of his assistants. At some point, they noticed that if they would continue walking, they have to come close enough to Arafat to stop by and say hello. So, Barak turned around and moved away. Erekat said, 'He did not even want to just say good morning to us'. Interview with Ehud Olmert (22 February 2019), 14.

77 Interview with Gamal Helal (11 November 2022), 24.

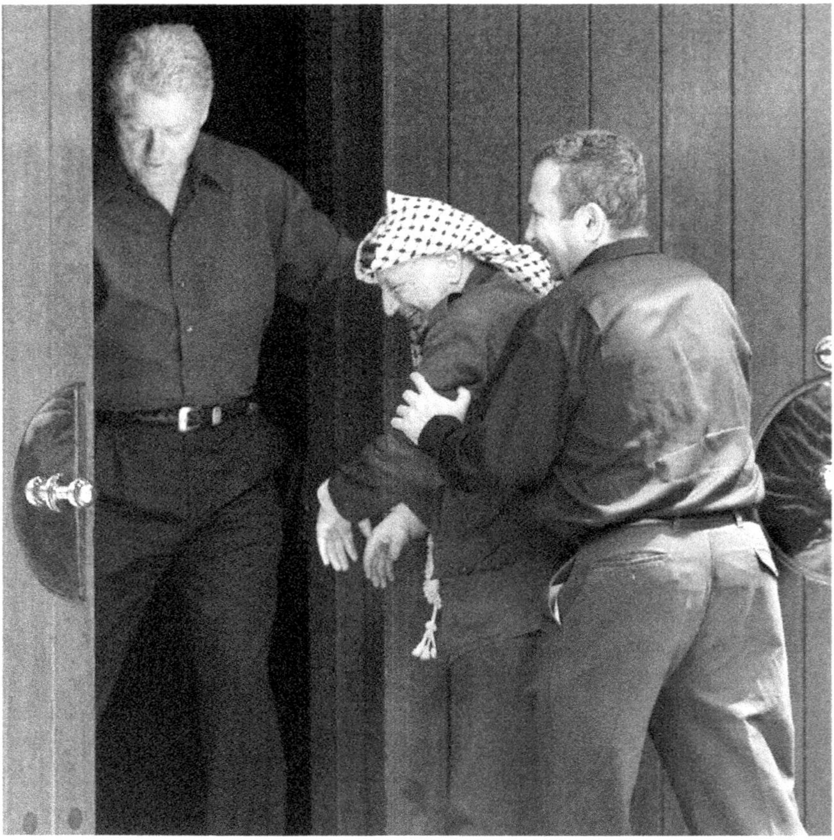

Figure 7.2 Clinton, Arafat and Barak.
Credit: Stephen Jaffe/Staff/AFP/Getty Images.

Barak told us'.[78] The Americans were surprised by Barak's conduct: 'We did not learn from Shepherdstown or from Geneva. We always gave the Israelis the benefit of the doubt.'[79] Barak failed to keep his promises in Shepherdstown and Geneva, and he failed to keep his promises at Camp David. Surely Clinton did not know that he was to do *all* the bargaining himself. Barak's aloof behaviour is not the expected code of conduct in a diplomatic summit convened to resolve conflicts.

[78] Raphael Cohen-Almagor, 'Israeli-Palestinian Negotiations through the Eyes of Gamal Helal', *Israel Journal of Foreign Affairs* (published online 1 December 2023), 12.
[79] Ibid.

Indeed, the fact that the two leaders did not meet for concrete talks is strange. Why convene a summit, bringing the two leaders together in the presence of the American president, and not meet with your partner for talks? In this respect, it was a curious summit. To justify his questionable conduct, Barak notes that Begin and Sadat hardly met at the 1978 summit. This is true, and it is also true that the 1978 summit nearly failed. Senior people in the Egyptian delegation opposed the agreement due to the bad relationship between the Israeli and Egyptian leaders.[80] The drama continued at that summit until the very last moment.

Robert Malley and Hussein Agha criticised Barak's insensitive generalisations, misconceptions and derogatory depictions of Palestinian culture.[81] In an interview with Benny Morris, Barak described the Palestinians as people who 'are products of a culture in which to tell a lie ... creates no dissonance. They don't suffer from the problem of telling lies that exist in Judeo-Christian culture. Truth is seen as an irrelevant category. There is only that which serves your purpose and that which doesn't. They see themselves as emissaries of a national movement for whom everything is permissible. There is no such thing as "the truth".'[82] On several occasions, at critical moments of the summit, Barak's advisors urged him to speak directly with Arafat, but he refused, even though he knew that Arafat was the only leader in the Palestinian delegation who was able to make difficult decisions. Yossi Ginossar was the man for special missions. He met with the Palestinians more than any other member of the Israeli delegation and was very cognisant of their thoughts and sentiments. He pleaded with Barak several times to meet Arafat, as did other members of the Israeli and Palestinian delegations (Yatom, Ben-Ami, Sher, Lipkin-Shahak, Yanai, Grinstein, Yasser Abed Rabbo), but Barak refused. He did not trust Arafat.[83] Barak did not wish to reveal his cards to Arafat; he thought the latter would simply stockpile this information for future haggling.

80 Raphael Cohen-Almagor, 'Lessons from the Israeli-Egyptian Peace Talks: An Interview with Aharon Barak', *Israel Studies Review*, 34(2) (Autumn 2019): 1–32; discussion with Nabil Elaraby (31 October 2019); Mohamed Ibrahim Kamel, *The Camp David Accords: A Testimony* (Abingdon: Routledge, 1986), 313–382.

81 Robert Malley and Hussein Agha, 'A Reply to Ehud Barak', *New York Review of Books*, 49(10) (13 June 2002): 46, https://tinyurl.com/4cfxzbnj.

82 Benny Morris, 'An Interview with Ehud Barak', *New York Review of Books*, 49(10) (13 June 2002); Arie Kacowicz, 'Rashomon in the Middle East: Clashing Narratives, Images, and Frames in the Israeli-Palestinian Conflict', *Cooperation & Conflict*, 40(3) (2005): 343–360.

83 Dan Meridor, 'Camp David Diaries', *Haaretz* (29 July 2011) (Hebrew); interviews with Dan Meridor (20 January 2016), Shlomo Ben-Ami (26 June 2013) and Gidi Grinstein (21 May 2013).

Ron Pundak thought that Barak's approach to negotiation facilitated the summit's failure. His arrogance, his single-mindedness, his historical viewpoint, his belief that only he understood the 'big picture' – all these factors failed him as he attempted to impose his operating style on Arafat, who was unwilling to accept dictates.[84] Ben-Ami agrees, writing that Barak's condescending attitude towards Arafat was unhelpful.[85] Similarly, psychoanalyst Emanuel Berman said that Barak alienated the Palestinian negotiators. His arrogance and impatience, his inability to take into account their sensitivities and vulnerabilities, and his pushing for a final solution by giving deadlines all backfired.[86]

I mentioned Clinton's verbal attack on Ahmed Qurie that led the latter to disengage. In his book, Qurie criticised Barak for his 'irrational behavior' when he locked himself in his cabin later in the summit, while he considered his own similar conduct appropriate and justified.[87] Both Barak's and Qurie's conduct did little to advance the talks to a positive conclusion. The summit was a political and psychological failure.

Lack of an Effective Mediator

The Americans were not effective. There was no continuous follow-up, no daily tasks, no reporting as to progress on each issue, no binding agenda. The Palestinians did not think the American negotiators could maintain a balanced view regarding the competing interests of the two parties. Nabil Sha'ath said that Ross and Martin Indyk were pro-Israeli, partial and biased, and they 'sometimes defended Israel much more than the Israeli delegates did'.[88] Mohammed Dahlan viewed Ross, Indyk and Albright as especially unhelpful due to their pro-Israeli bias and 'advanced negative attitudes toward Palestinians'.[89]

The Americans failed to create a convivial atmosphere at Camp David. Such an atmosphere is instrumental to successful negotiations. The atmosphere at Camp David was always very tense. It was tense because Barak

[84] Ron Pundak, 'From Oslo to Taba: What Went Wrong?', *Survival*, 43(3) (2001): 40; Jerome Slater, 'What Went Wrong? The Collapse of the Israeli-Palestinian Peace Process', *Political Science Quarterly*, 116(2) (Summer 2001): 180–181.

[85] Ben-Ami, 'So Close and Yet So Far', 72.

[86] Clare Pointon, 'Therapists and the Israel-Palestine Conflict: Clare Pointon Talks to Emanuel Berman', *Counselling and Psychotherapy Journal* (*CPJ*) (July 2003): 13–15.

[87] Qurie, *Beyond Oslo*, 201, 223.

[88] Swisher, *The Truth about Camp David*, 148.

[89] Ibid., 151.

was depressed, because he secluded himself, because he was anxious about what would be said in Israel.[90] While he downplayed the role that polls had played in his decision-making, others argued that he was always studying opinion polls, while his coalition in Israel was falling apart.[91] The atmosphere was also tense because the Palestinians were divided and stressed. They did not want to be there. Their personal rivalries were noticeable, encouraged by Arafat's divisiveness, and by the Americans who were pressing for constructive, positive thinking in the Palestinian delegation.

Reflecting on Camp David, Malley said the Americans did not have a plan for the summit, and they lacked clarity about their role.[92] Miller said: 'The Israelis and Palestinians came very prepared to Camp David – the problem was, we didn't.'[93] I agree with the last part of this statement. The American negotiation team included many experts on Israel, but none on Palestine. Many of the American delegates were familiar with the Jewish-Israeli way of life, thinking and values. Very few were familiar with the Palestinian-Muslim way of life, thinking and values. Furthermore, the Americans did not invest enough in presenting themselves as a credible broker.[94] Akram Hanieh writes that the Americans were not even brokers. They aligned themselves with the Israeli delegation.[95] Influential American negotiators aligned themselves with the Zionist national movement. No American delegate aligned himself with the Palestinian national movement. Arafat called the American team 'The Four Rabbis', referring to Ross, Dan Kurtzer, Miller and Indyk, and complained about them.[96] Husseini said the Palestinians did not trust the Americans because there were so many Jews in their delegation. They hesitated to have an open discussion with the Americans. Husseini maintained:

> I hope the US will learn more, if they want to become a more honest broker. You have a lot of Americans with a Jewish background, American Jews, on the team. They bring their prejudices with them, and that weakens

[90] Interviews with Shlomo Ben-Ami (26 June 2013), 5 and Gamal Helal (11 November 2022), 29. Barak denied he was depressed. See Raviv Drucker, 'Olmert, Abu Mazen and Barak Refer to the Political Process', *HaMakor* (17 November 2015).

[91] Barak denied that polls were important. See Ibid.

[92] Interview with Rob Malley (28 July 2022), 15.

[93] Swisher, *The Truth about Camp David*, 264; Discussions with Aaron David Miller (October–November 2008).

[94] Discussions with Aaron David Miller (October–November 2008).

[95] Hanieh, 'The Camp David Papers', 92.

[96] Interview with Avi Gil (16 January 2025), 3.

> their ability to be neutral and to resolve the issue. There has to be more of a balance. The mediation, I remember Wye River, and I remember other meetings that were taking place in Washington with Aaron Miller and Dennis Ross and others. And the chats. And we were always kind of, not outnumbered, but undermined. 'Oh, this is very difficult. Let us leave it until later on. This is, no, I really recommend that you do not touch this issue.' There is always, not intimidation, but always asking the Palestinians to be more compromising. Or not to raise an issue.[97]

At Camp David, there was no clear strategy for achieving results once the talks began, and the Americans lacked internal consensus about the core issues. The United States shifted its own team around during the summit, signalling to the parties that their delegation was incoherent and disorganised.[98] They neglected what had already been achieved in Stockholm, even though Ross was present in Stockholm and was aware of the progress that was made. At times, the Americans appeared ignorant of the history and complexities of the conflict. They undermined the importance that the Palestinians assigned to UN resolutions and paid little attention to the principles of international legitimacy.[99] When it came to Israel, the Americans had a reasonably clear sense of what concessions might be on the table, but the Palestinian position remained opaque. Arafat was guarded, unwilling to reveal his bottom lines. As a result, the US mediators were left in the dark, unable to accurately assess how wide the gaps truly were, or whether they could realistically be bridged. This lack of clarity severely undermined their ability to steer the negotiations towards a workable compromise.

Barak continually said he wanted to go to a summit because he felt that only in the hothouse of a summit could significant decisions be made. He did not want any discussions in advance, lest they erode Israeli positions.[100] The Americans did not press him to reveal his true red lines and pledged to him a 'no surprise' policy. The principle of no surprise basically forced the United States to discuss and consult with the Israelis about what they would like to do. In and of itself, this is a shackle that the United States has imposed on itself to continuously enjoy Israel's trust.

Too often, Israeli points were presented as American ideas. A senior Palestinian negotiator said: 'We never felt that the American team was

[97] Interview with Hiba Husseini (24 December 2024), 28–29.

[98] Daniel C. Kurtzer and Scott B. Lasensky, *Negotiating Arab-Israeli Peace* (Washington, DC: US Institute of Peace Press, 2008), 53.

[99] Qurie, *Beyond Oslo*, 258.

[100] Interview with Dennis Ross (27 September 2019), 8.

playing a fair game ... we always felt that there ... [was a] division of labor between the Israelis and the American teams ... The Israelis ... were using some Americans as a vanguard ... to explore our position and to see what extent we are ready to compromise or to concede.'[101] The Palestinians' suspicions were valid: Miller said the Israelis saw the American negotiating texts first.[102]

Kurtzer testified: 'It's only a problem when the U.S. bends too far. Aaron Miller called the United States "Israel's lawyer", which meant we were bending over too far. When the Palestinians say that they were hearing things directly from the Israelis, and then they would hear the same things from us, but only worse – what were we doing? Why were we pretending to be a mediator?'[103] Indyk disagreed, saying that there were times when it might look like the United States was advocating Israel's position, but not as Israel's lawyers. Rather, these were attempts to see if the United States could bridge differences. 'And if we could not, then we had to go back to the Israelis and try to get something more out of them. But that was precisely the role that the Palestinians expected us to play.'[104]

As mentioned, to make things worse, the Americans caused the estrangement of Abbas and Qurie from the process. Already in the lead-up to the summit, the Americans alienated Abbas. Dennis Ross and Gamal Helal orchestrated a meeting between Mohammed Dahlan, Abbas's chief rival, and National Security Advisor Sandy Berger at the White House. The Americans were captivated by Dahlan's charisma. As head of the Palestinian Preventive Security, Dahlan had developed a close working relationship with the CIA, earning their trust and admiration. His growing rapport with US officials raised alarm bells for Abbas, who increasingly suspected that Washington was grooming Dahlan as Arafat's eventual successor. Camp David only deepened his suspicions.

The Americans sought to exploit the divisions within the Palestinian team, working with those who showed willingness to negotiate. Dahlan, Mohammed Rashid and, at times, Erekat wanted to get it done, so the Americans worked with them. The Americans felt that Abbas, Qurie

101 Kurtzer and Lasensky, *Negotiating Arab-Israeli Peace*, 61.

102 Discussions with Aaron David Miller (October–November 2008); Miller, 'How Not to Host a Summit'. See also Aaron David Miller, 'Memorandum to the President: Thinking through an Israel-Palestinian Initiative', in Daniel C. Kurtzer (ed.), *Pathways to Peace* (New York: Palgrave Macmillan, 2012), 135–155.

103 Raphael Cohen-Almagor, 'Israel–PLO Peace Process: Interview with Ambassador Daniel Kurtzer', *Israel Studies*, 24(3) (2019): 144–145.

104 Interview with Martin Indyk (9 August 2022), 9

and Abed Rabbo were disinterested and so did not invest in them.[105] The Americans did not carefully assess the implications of bringing some people closer at the expense of others, or what ability Dahlan and others actually had to influence Arafat when people like Abbas were resisting that influence. The matrix of influence on Arafat by his close associates remained unclear.

Hasson said that both Qurie, the architect of the Oslo Accords who was constructive and forthcoming then, and the pragmatic Abbas objected to reaching an agreement.[106] Thus, the reluctant Arafat was supported by his two most senior advisors in not wishing to make major concessions, making the work of peacemaking more arduous. Ben-Ami asked Abbas after the summit why they were unable to reach an agreement, and Abbas's answer was, 'because you're not negotiating with the right people'.[107]

A vicious circle was created. Abbas and Qurie were not really invested in the summit, not with their hearts and minds. The Americans spoke with the Palestinians who were willing to invest in the summit. They pampered them, in the hope that they would persuade Arafat to make a deal.[108] Dahlan and Rashid, however, were not popular among the other Palestinian representatives. Arafat, untroubled by personal rivalries in his own camp, did not try to resolve them. Witnessing the Americans courting the 'Young Guard', Abbas, like Qurie, disengaged even further from the negotiations.[109] Of the three senior Palestinians, Arafat, Abbas and Qurie, the Americans managed to alienate two. They knew they were alienating Abbas and Qurie but pressed on, thinking it would be possible to reach a deal without them.

I wondered to what extent Arafat would have been able to reach an agreement without the support of people like Abbas and Qurie. The majority of my interviewees thought it was possible, because Arafat called the shots. A few disagreed. Agha, who worked closely with Abbas, and Israeli senior security officer Hasson thought it was impossible, while Ahmad Khalidi thought it would have been very difficult for Arafat to move forward without Abbas. Agha explained that Arafat could not make a final deal without Abbas, because he did not know the issues. Arafat knew the general themes; he counted on Abbas for details. Abbas had the file, 'had the studies, had piles of files on Jerusalem, on borders, on security, on

105 Interview with Dennis Ross (27 September 2019), 14, 21. At times, Abed Rabbo did engage with the Israelis.
106 Interview with Israel Hasson (23 May 2013), 11–12.
107 Interview with Shlomo Ben-Ami (26 June 2013), 14. Ross wanted Barak to meet with Abbas and Qurie, but Barak refused. Interview with Dennis Ross (21 October 2019), 22.
108 Interview with Aaron David Miller (12 September 2019), 15.
109 Martin Indyk, *Innocent Abroad* (New York: Simon & Schuster, 2009), 311.

refugees'.[110] Hasson said that Arafat was unable to make decisions of historic magnitude without the support of his senior people. He needed to be convinced that he was making the appropriate concessions. When I asked Hasson directly whether Abbas constrained Arafat, Hasson answered: 'Wow! You can't even imagine how much.'[111] In his capacity as deputy head of the Shabac, Hasson was well versed in internal Palestinian politics.

Khalidi explained that Arafat was a man of consensus. 'All the big other Abus were either killed or assassinated by the Israelis or by somebody else. So, he, Arafat *needed* these two [Abbas and Qurie] to lean on.'[112] Arafat needed them to be on his side, especially when he had to make historical decisions. After Qurie took offence at what he perceived as Clinton's personal attack on him, he spent most of his time touring the lawns of Camp David in a golf cart.[113] Qurie had arrived at Camp David in an unenthusiastic mood after Sweden, as he felt that Arafat was not invested in the peace process.[114] The encounter with Clinton shut him down.

Need for a Guiding Paper

The Americans should have insisted on presenting a draft document, even if it required modifications, to steer the negotiations, much like the effective approach taken at Camp David 1978. Withdrawing the draft was a critical misstep that undermined their credibility as mediators and weakened the entire negotiation process. The American plan for the summit unravelled in the first days, leaving the talks adrift. There was no clear framework or guiding compass, resulting in directionless dialogue that went nowhere.

As mediator, the Americans should have had their document on board, following it step by step and building momentum. Ben-Ami writes that at Camp David, the US looked like a diminished and humbled superpower, unable to assert its will.[115] The host, who was supposed to set the reference and the rules of engagement, had relinquished its role. Ben-Ami

110 Interview with Hussein Agha (5 April 2019), 10–11. See also Jacob Eriksson, *Small-State Mediation in International Conflicts: Diplomacy and Negotiation in Israel–Palestine* (London: I.B. Tauris, 2015), 194.

111 Interview with Israel Hasson (23 May 2013), 10.

112 Interview with Ahmad Khalidi (5 June 2019), 18–19.

113 Ari Shavit, 'The Day Peace Died', *Haaretz* (14 September 2001) (Hebrew).

114 Interview with Dennis Ross (27 September 2019), 11.

115 Shlomo Ben-Ami, *Scars of War, Wounds of Peace* (London: Phoenix, 2005), 263. See also Aaron David Miller, *The Much Too Promised Land: America's Elusive Search for Arab-Israeli Peace* (New York: Bantam, 2008), chapter 8.

wondered: 'Why are you panicking? It is two Middle Eastern tribes fighting with each other. You're the kings of the world. The Americans panicked.'[116]

Ben-Ami thought that Israel should accept the paper as the basis for negotiation, while Barak's position clung to what Ben-Ami calls 'a stupid mantra that Israelis repeat even today. No, no. Direct talks. We'll conduct direct talks with the Palestinians. We don't need an American paper. We'll reach an agreement with the Palestinians.'[117] I agree with Ben-Ami that this expectation was unrealistic at Camp David, and that the withdrawal of the paper was a colossal blunder. Barak was unrealistic in what he expected from the Palestinians. While he was facing mounting political pressure to offer substantial concessions in order to survive in office by reaching an agreement, the Palestinians were not prepared to make similarly significant concessions. With the suspicion prevailing between the two sides, both were likely to oppose any paper that the other side suggested, thus the need for a third-party proposal.

End of Conflict

Barak demanded that there be a joint declaration concerning the end of the conflict: no more claims, and peace would prevail. He strove for an agreement declaring 'the end of the conflict and finality of all mutual claims'.[118] Ben-Ami notes that both the Israeli and American delegations aired plans for interim or partial settlements,[119] but they came late and were rejected outright by the Palestinians, who wanted to leave the Camp David pressure cooker.

Given the circumstances, whether Barak's demand was reasonable and doable is questionable. Bercovitch and Gartner's *International Conflict Management* dataset suggests that high-intensity and protracted conflicts are unlikely to end in a full-scale agreement, mediated or not, and that any agreement reached is likely to be limited and short-lived.[120] As argued,

[116] Interview with Shlomo Ben-Ami (26 June 2013), 7.

[117] Ibid., 6.

[118] Interview with Ehud Barak (21 June 2022), 15.

[119] Ben-Ami, 'So Close and Yet So Far', 78.

[120] J. Bercovitch and S. Gartner, 'Is There Method in the Madness of Mediation? Some Lessons for Mediators from Quantitative Studies of Mediation', *International Interactions*, 32(4) (2006): 329–354. See also D. Carment, Y. Samy and S. El Achkar, 'Protracted Conflict and Crisis Mediation: A Contingency Approach', in J. Bercovitch and S. S. Gartner (eds), *International Conflict Mediation: New Approaches and Findings* (London: Routledge, 2009), 216–239.

the two sides did not trust each other at Camp David. Arafat preferred a gradual approach, seeking to address issues step by step, rather than being forced to resolve everything at once. He advocated for a series of meetings to build momentum over time. In protracted conflicts, the most effective path to peace often involves a sequence of small, trust-building agreements that gradually foster goodwill and pave the way for a comprehensive settlement. Rather than convening a high-stakes summit prematurely, it is wiser to hold such a gathering only after the bulk of the gaps have been bridged – at which point leaders and mediators come together to make the final push towards lasting peace.

Henry Kissinger won the Nobel Peace Prize for his astute diplomacy. He laid the foundations for the Israeli-Egyptian peace. Kissinger recognised that, throughout history, leaders have been tempted to use their influence and power to end conflicts, but their zeal often led to more wars. Pushing too hard for peace may break the process. Kissinger called this 'the paradox of peace'.[121] He believed in an incremental approach that would ameliorate conflict and enable parties to come to terms with each other. In 2000, the Palestinian Authority was still in the midst of its state-building process, without sufficient governing institutions and without a corresponding yearning to bring the conflict to an end, as Barak wished. The Palestinians felt that Israel did not support them in their efforts to meet the requirements for statehood. The situation was not ripe for replying positively to what they perceived as excessive Israeli demands.

Conclusion

The Camp David Summit collapsed for a multitude of reasons: poor timing, broken communication, conflicting expectations and sharply diverging interests. It was plagued by a lack of mutual respect and courtesy, transparency deficits and the absence of truly impartial, honest mediation. The mediator struggled to control the agenda, while both parties engaged in counterproductive negotiation tactics. Most critically, neither side was willing to pay the steep price that genuine peace demands. All these factors doomed the summit to failure.

Barak conspired with Clinton to bring Arafat to Camp David, to press him and push him into a corner, to force him to make a deal. I use the

[121] Martin Indyk, 'How Would Kissinger Solve the Israel–Hamas War Today? Incrementally', *Washington Post* (30 November 2023). See also Martin Indyk, *Master of the Game: Henry Kissinger and the Art of Middle East Diplomacy* (New York: Knopf, 2021), 569.

word ‘conspire’, a strong term that Indyk used when he described what happened at the peace summit.[122] Indyk said:

> Clinton and Barak agreed to shlep Arafat to Camp David and to present him with what *we* regarded – we, being the US and Israel – as a far-reaching offer and expect him to accept it. Or, as Barak said, unmask him for being unwilling to do the deal. And it was a mistake, it was a very big mistake, for which Israel and the Palestinians paid a very high price.[123]

In hindsight, the deal could not have been reached, because Arafat did not get what he wanted: sovereignty over the Temple Mount, East Jerusalem and 100 per cent of the West Bank. The rest, including refugees, could have been resolved, but those three issues remained unsolvable. Barak, who was prepared to make many bold and unprecedented concessions, was unwilling to go *that* far. He thought that, with Clinton’s help, he could extort a deal from Arafat. He was wrong.

Barak overestimated Clinton’s diplomatic prowess and underestimated Arafat’s unyielding resolve. Instead of assigning blame, it is more productive to speak of shared responsibility. Israel, the PLO and the US all bear responsibility for the resounding failure. Rather than culminating in a breakthrough, the Oslo peace process unravelled.

Perhaps it was too much to expect from Arafat, whose life was defined by struggle, to willingly bring the conflict to a close. Having devoted decades to resistance, he may not have known how to navigate a post-conflict reality. Yet he was willing to gamble on confronting a more hardline Israeli leadership. This high-stakes risk, compounded by the toxic relationship between Arafat and Barak, made any other outcome unlikely.

Arafat recognised Barak’s desperation to secure an agreement and knew that failure would send Barak’s party back to the opposition benches. Arafat simply had to reject each Israeli offer and play a patient waiting game to extort concessions. Meanwhile, Israel and the United States failed to press for a meaningful Palestinian counter-proposal. In the end, Palestinian stubbornness paid off. Israel’s sense of urgency and the intense self-imposed pressure led their negotiators to repeatedly extend concessions, ultimately undermining their own position.

Arafat’s negotiating style was defined by relentless manoeuvring until the very last moment, always pushing to extract maximum concessions. At Camp David, he said ‘NO’, true to his brinkmanship strategy: never agree, if patience can yield more. His approach was clear: push the process

122 Interview with Martin Indyk (9 August 2022), 12.
123 Ibid.

further, apply relentless pressure, advance his agenda through tactical compromises and undermine his opponent's concerns.

Arafat played the role of the difficult negotiator, voicing complaints to both the Israelis and the Americans about his own constraints, and anything else that suited his purpose. He cultivated a reputation as an *enfant terrible*, all while subtly probing Barak's vulnerabilities, manipulating circumstances and biding his time. The plan was to wear down Barak, who, under mounting pressure and political insecurity, would be compelled to offer more.

Arafat tolerated terror attacks as leverage to raise the stakes and turned a blind eye to spoilers within his ranks. He exploited Barak's desire to remain prime minister, knowing that his struggle for political survival would force him to yield to further concessions. Although Barak did improve his offer at Taba, the foundation for a binding, lasting agreement remained fragile at best.

The next chapter analyses the events that took place after Camp David, including the al Aqsa Intifada, the Clinton Parameters, the Taba peace talks, the 2001 elections in Israel and the 2002 Arab Peace Initiative (API).

8

Post Camp David Summit

> The Palestinian people have a political identity and a just demand for national self-determination. As long as they are denied this right, the conflict will not be resolved.
>
> ~ Olof Palme

After the failed summit, the Israelis went all over the world in an organised campaign to tell what happened at Camp David; its slogans were 'We offered, they refused' and 'Israel had no partner'.[1] In effect, from a certain stage of the negotiations at Camp David, it was a battle for public opinion, for a story that would explain what happened at the summit. Ehud Barak strove to turn the tables on Yasser Arafat, convincing Bill Clinton to break his explicit promise to Arafat that he would not blame him.[2] Soon, Barak was facing what he had dreaded: Palestinian violence on a large scale. When relationships break, the attractiveness of violence as a means to exert pressure and improve the chances of reaching at least some of the desired ends grows. Jibril Rajoub, a Palestinian political leader, senior Fatah official and long-time figure in Palestinian security and sports administration, stated:

> When there is progress in the peace process, security cooperation with Israel allows the PA [Palestinian Authority] to take action against militant radical groups. Then, any act of terror only puts sticks in the wheels of a forward movement. However, when there is stagnation in the peace process, security cooperation is seen by our people as a means to prolong occupation. We are perceived to be collaborators with the enemy, similar to the position of General Haddad of South Lebanon, whose collusion with Israel would then turn him into a traitor in the national Lebanese perception.[3]

[1] Interview with Gidi Grinstein (21 May 2013), 15.
[2] Ibid., 16.
[3] Rajoub as cited in Yair Hirschfeld, The Oslo Process of Trial and Error Unfolds (draft paper).

Emotions are especially high when the subject is the Temple Mount. In Israel, the threat to Israeli sovereignty over the site only served to increase the yearning for the Temple Mount and for the ideal of re-establishing the Temple in some religious circles. Since the signing of the Oslo Accords and the debate over sovereignty in the Holy Basin, there has been a strong counter-reaction, demanding that Jews enter the site and create facts on the ground.[4] Some have used the Temple Mount as a political card to advance their own partisan agenda.

The al Aqsa Intifada

In September 2000, Ariel Sharon decided to visit the Temple Mount. Prime Minister Barak felt he could not stop the visit. Violence erupted,[5] and many people, including Israelis, Americans and Palestinians, believe that Arafat fomented it. Relying on Israeli intelligence, Ehud Olmert argued that Arafat instigated, motivated, organised and financed the Intifada.[6] Barak reiterated that the Intifada was planned well before Camp David, and that the summit's failure was not its cause. When Event B happens after Event A, it does not necessarily mean that A caused B. Barak said: 'The fact that the cock crows early in the morning and then the sun rises, does not mean that the cock causes the sun to rise.'[7] Once the peace summit failed, the eruption of violence was expected. Yair Hirschfeld is convinced that the Intifada was launched by Arafat as a short-term act to

[4] The Temple Mount Faithful Movement campaigns for Jewish prayer rights and legal recognition on the Mount. They perceive the site of the First and Second Temples as central to Jewish prophecy and identity, advocate for rebuilding the Third Temple and aim to rebuild it as part of messianic fulfilment. Once fringe, the movement has gained mainstream traction in recent years. The Temple Institute was founded by Rabbi Yisrael Ariel. It focuses on preparing for the Temple's reconstruction through research and education. See Mordechai (Motti) Inbari, 'The Role of the Temple Mount Faithful Movement in Changing Messianic Religious Zionists' Attitude toward the Temple Mount', in Leonard J. Greenspoon (ed.), *Next Year in Jerusalem: Exile and Return in Jewish History* (West Lafayette, IN: Purdue University Press, 2019), 247–264. Beyadenu – Returning to the Temple Mount is an Israeli nonprofit focused on promoting awareness of the Temple Mount and its heritage within Jewish communities worldwide. Beyadenu offers professional, guided tours of the Temple Mount. See their website, https://beyadenu.org/en/who-we-are/; Motti Inbari, 'Religious Zionism and the Temple Mount Dilemma – Key Trends', *Israel Studies*, 12(2) (2007): 29–47.

[5] Joel Greenberg, 'Sharon Touches a Nerve, and Jerusalem Explodes', *New York Times* (29 September 2000), https://tinyurl.com/yuan8brh.

[6] Interview with Ehud Olmert (22 February 2019), 16.

[7] Interview with Ehud Barak (11 July 2022), 2.

renew negotiations in a way that was acceptable to Arafat.[8] Uzi Dayan and Dennis Ross also think Arafat was behind the al Aqsa Intifada.[9] Believing that anything others can do, he can do better, Arafat wanted to drive Israel out of the Occupied Palestinian Territory, just as Hezbollah drove the Israel Defense Forces from Lebanon. The use of terror and violence would compel Israel to accept his demands. Imad al-Faluji, Minister of the Palestinian Executive Authority in charge of Post and Telecommunications, confirmed that the Intifada was planned and triggered by Arafat. Sharon's visit to Al Aqsa Mosque was merely the last straw.[10] Arafat's widow, Suha, said that her husband asked her to remain in Paris because he was about to start an Intifada.[11] According to a French TV interview with Suha Arafat, Arafat planned the Second Intifada, which was very costly to both Israel and Palestine. Records confiscated from his compound show that he funded the Fatah-linked Al Aqsa Martyrs' Brigades, which launched terror attacks in Israel. Hamas co-founder Mahmoud Zahar said that Arafat encouraged his militant group to launch its own attacks.[12] Zahar said that Hamas and Islamic Jihad leaders met with Fatah and PA officials daily.[13] Mamdouh Nofal, one of Arafat's advisors, further explained that the Intifada was not a mass movement distinct from the PA or a spontaneous eruption. The reverse was the case. It began based on a 'decision from above by the Authority before it turned into popular activity'.[14] The decision was made immediately after Sharon visited Al Aqsa. The political and security bodies of the PA convened to decide how to react. Arafat, explained Nofal, viewed Al Aqsa as the 'detonation point of the status quo that would suffice to ignite a conflagration not only on Palestinian soil but would also impact the situation outside the boundaries of Palestine'.[15] Decisions were made that dealt with practical preparations, and security measures for

8 Hirschfeld's comments on a draft of this book.
9 Interviews with Uzi Dayan (26 July 2017), 36 and Dennis Ross (27 September 2019), 15.
10 Michael A. Calvo, *The Middle East and World War III: Why No Peace?* (CreateSpace Independent Publishing Platform, 2017), 178–179.
11 Jonathan D. Halevi, 'The Palestinian Authority's Responsibility for the Outbreak of the Second Intifada: Its Own Damning Testimony', *Jerusalem Viewpoints*, 594 (March–April 2013): 1–14.
12 Ben Birnbaum, 'The End of the Two-State Solution: Why the Window Is Closing on Middle-East Peace', *The New Republic* (11 March 2013), https://tinyurl.com/3umuky4r.
13 Matthew Levitt, *Hamas* (New Haven, CT: Yale University Press, 2006), 15.
14 Halevi, 'The Palestinian Authority's Responsibility', 9.
15 Ibid. For a contrasting view, see Clayton E. Swisher, *The Truth about Camp David: The Untold Story about the Collapse of the Middle East Peace Process* (New York: Nation Books, 2004), 389.

the mosque were reinforced by bringing in additional guards and issuing directives to the security apparatuses to enter Al Aqsa and defend it.

Dan Meridor does not think that Arafat actually ran the Intifada, but he gave it his general blessing in his inciting speeches. And he could have stopped it.[16] Gadi Baltiansky argues that the Intifada started with Hamas and continued with competition among the Palestinians. This was Marwan Barghouti's tragic mistake. Barghouti, the leader of Tanzim, a Fatah-affiliated militant group, wanted to show Hamas that his organisation was stronger than Hamas, and the situation escalated. The Intifada was not planned by Arafat, but he did not stop it and his people actually encouraged and participated in it.[17]

The George Mitchell Report that studied the Intifada concludes:

> we have no basis on which to conclude that there was a deliberate plan by the PA to initiate a campaign of violence at the first opportunity or to conclude that there was a deliberate plan by the GOI [Government of Israel] to respond with lethal force. However, there is also no evidence to conclude that the PA made a consistent effort to contain the demonstrations and control the violence once it began, or that the GOI made a consistent effort to use non-lethal means to control demonstrations of unarmed Palestinians.[18]

Shlomo Ben-Ami contends that Arafat did not initiate or plan the Intifada, but he encouraged the violence and indicated a return to violence if Camp David failed.[19] Hiba Husseini said that the Palestinians were revolting against the continuing state of affairs and the lack of progress in the peace process. Soon, Arafat gave the green light: 'He rode the wave of the violence, and he gave the green light for the al Aqsa Brigades.'[20]

I asked my interviewees about Arafat's attitude to violence and terror. Hussein Agha responded that Arafat was of two minds about it. If there was progress on the diplomatic front, Hamas would not be allowed to disturb it; but if there was no progress, he would resort to violence as leverage.[21] Avi Gil argued that Arafat could dream two dreams in one night. In

16 Interview with Dan Meridor (20 January 2016), 27.

17 Interview with Gadi Baltiansky (25 January 2016), 18.

18 Senator George Mitchell Report. Sharm El Sheikh Fact Finding Committee, Excerpts (8 May 2001).

19 Shlomo Ben-Ami, 'So Close and Yet So Far: Lessons from the Israeli-Palestinian Peace Process', *Israel Studies*, 10(2) (Summer 2005): 80.

20 Interview with Hiba Husseini (24 December 2024), 10.

21 Raphael Cohen-Almagor, 'History of Track II Peace Negotiations: Interview with Hussein Agha', *Israel Studies*, 26(1) (2021): 63; Interview with Hussein Agha (5 April 2019), 23.

one, he was concluding the peace process, signing a permanent peace with Israel and receiving a second Nobel prize. In the second dream, Arafat was throwing all the Jews into the sea and liberating Palestine from the river to the sea. Arafat would wake up in the morning cognisant of both dreams, and untroubled by contradictions in his thinking. Gil concluded that for us, it is very difficult to grasp such a person, but it may be that this was Arafat.[22]

Ghaith al-Omari said that Arafat dealt with security as a commodity to be used as a negotiating tool every now and then,[23] and that Arafat looked at violence as a way of reshuffling the deck – that when politics started getting stagnant, he should engage in some violence. At the beginning of the Second Intifada, Arafat looked at things and said, 'okay, let me remind the Israelis what would happen if there is no progress'.[24] John Jenkins said that Arafat approved of violence if it brought closer the prospect of a Palestinian state.[25] Two people who claim to have been close to Arafat, Ziad Abu Zayyad and Salam Fayyad, said similar things. Abu Zayyad maintained that Arafat supported violent resistance, but not terrorism. Abu Zayyad said: 'Resistance should be between armed people … Arafat was against … acts of terror. I know how much furious and upset he was, every time they told him that a bus exploded.'[26] Fayyad said that during the 1990s, Arafat *did* try to stop Hamas's terror, but things changed after Camp David 2000.[27] In a 2002 *New York Times* article, Arafat wrote: 'I condemn the attacks carried out by terrorist groups against Israeli civilians. These groups do not represent the Palestinian people or their legitimate aspirations for freedom. They are terrorist organizations, and I am determined to put an end to their activities.'[28]

Dennis Ross asserts: 'Arafat's greatest travesty as a leader is that he did nothing to delegitimize those who used violence against the Israelis.'[29] Sari Nusseibeh wrote that, in 2002, he went to Arafat to warn him of the 'coming apocalypse'. While Arafat did not dispatch suicide bombers, any more than he personally pocketed bribes, he failed to do all he could to root out the problem because he was unable to recognise the 'evil the bombers were

[22] Interview with Avi Gil (16 January 2025), 21–22.
[23] Interview with Ghaith al-Omari (2 September 2014), 1.
[24] Ibid., 6.
[25] Interview with John Jenkins (9 December 2022), 12.
[26] Interview with Ziad Abu Zayyad (14 May 2015), 12.
[27] Interview with Salam Fayyad (19 January 2024), 5.
[28] Yasir Arafat, 'The Palestinian Vision of Peace', *New York Times* (3 February 2002).
[29] Dennis Ross, *The Missing Peace* (New York: Farrar, Straus and Giroux, 2004), 776.

causing'.[30] Nusseibeh maintained: 'It is a certain kind of craziness not to recognize a pattern, especially a debilitating one like repeatedly shooting yourself in your own foot.'[31] Similarly, Manuel Hassassian spoke about the negative impact of the militarisation of the Intifada. Arafat was wrong to pursue violence instead of political means through negotiations.[32] He did nothing to stop the violence and did some things to inflame it, including signalling to people under his command to take part in it. Violence did not strike Arafat as being totally immoral.

The Palestinian Intifada dealt a devastating blow to the Israeli peace camp, and the hope for peace was shattered. More and more Israelis lost whatever trust they had in Arafat, believing in Barak's 'no partner' statements. They also lost confidence in Barak's ability to restore security. To their minds, Barak was deluded in going to Camp David and lost face dealing with Arafat's manoeuvring. The country needed a strong leader who would not be misled by Arafat, and who would show the Palestinians that violence does not pay. It was time for a change. Barak paid a personal political price for his high-stakes politics. The idea of peace was replaced by refocusing on Israel and its needs. Moral introspection about the occupation, and its toll on both Palestinians and Israelis, was pushed aside. Peace was no longer seen as a realistic pursuit, but rather as a luxury Israel could no longer afford.

The Clinton Parameters

In December 2000, in a meeting with the Israeli and Palestinian delegations at the White House, President Clinton introduced his proposal for Israeli-Palestinian peace. This proposal came to be known as the Clinton Parameters.

Clinton's proposal laid down the framework and foundations for a peace agreement. It did not delve into details; instead, it set the basis for further deliberations and probing. According to the Parameters, Israel would evacuate the entire Gaza Strip and around 95 per cent of the West Bank and compensate the Palestinians for the annexation of 80 per cent of the settlement blocs by a 1–3 per cent land swap, plus a permanent safe

30 Sari Nusseibeh, *Once Upon a Country* (London: Halban, 2007), 476.

31 Ibid.

32 Discussion with Manuel Hassassian (20 November 2013). Yossi Beilin argues that Abbas criticised Arafat, saying to him: 'You are not going to win. So, you are actually paying a huge price in our young generation, and you are not creating a situation which will make it easier to get back to the peace process.' Middle East Study Centre Annual Lecture, University of Hull (19 October 2022), 3.

passage between the West Bank and Gaza. The borders to be drawn would maintain Palestinian contiguity and attempt to minimise annexed Israeli areas and their effect on Palestinian life.[33]

The Clinton Parameters proposed that for security purposes, the Israeli presence would remain in fixed locations in the Jordan Valley, under the authority of an international force, for a maximum period of thirty-six months, and that Israel would maintain three facilities in the West Bank with a Palestinian liaison presence. The State of Palestine would be a 'non-militarized state',[34] but it would have a strong Palestinian security force and an international force for 'border security and deterrent purposes'. Whenever Israelis wish to lessen security threats by opposing the idea that their adversary will have a military force, they propose the adversary having a *strong* security force, as opposed to a (regular) military force.[35]

On Jerusalem and the Holy Places, President Clinton proposed that 'Arab areas are Palestinian and Jewish ones are Israeli',[36] and that the Palestinians would have sovereignty over the Haram and the Israelis over the Western Wall. Palestine and Israel would have shared functional sovereignty over the issue of excavation under the Haram and behind the Wall. Mutual consent would be required before any excavation could take place.

President Clinton's Parameters were quite elaborate on the sticky issue of the refugees. He distinguished between the declarative aspects of the problem and the practical aspects involved in addressing the issue. As for the former, Israel would acknowledge the moral and material suffering caused to the Palestinian people because of the 1948 war, and the need to assist the international community in addressing the problem. As for the latter, an international commission would be established to implement a just and fair solution, including compensation for the refugees' suffering, their resettlement and rehabilitation. Clinton said that the United States 'is prepared to lead an international effort to help the refugees'.[37] He further postulated that the guiding principle should be that 'the Palestinian state would be the focal point for Palestinians who choose to return to the area without ruling out that Israel will accept some of these refugees'.[38] The

33 The Clinton Parameters, 'Clinton Proposal on Israeli-Palestinian Peace', White House (23 December 2000), https://tinyurl.com/bdftv3kk.
34 Ibid.
35 Raphael Cohen-Almagor, 'Lessons from the Israeli-Egyptian Peace Talks: An Interview with Aharon Barak', *Israel Studies Review*, 34(2) (Autumn 2019): 9.
36 The Clinton Parameters.
37 Ibid.
38 Ibid.

refugees would have five choices for resettlement: the State of Palestine; areas in Israel being transferred to Palestine in the land swap (part of the newly founded State of Palestine, thus there is not much difference between this and the first choice); rehabilitation in host countries; resettlement in a third country; and admission to Israel 'consistent with Israel's sovereign decision'.[39]

The Clinton Parameters represented the most just and fair proposal to solve the conflict up to that time. While it was not perfect,[40] Clinton tried to find constructive compromises between the two sides, taking their best interests on board. I believe many of the Parameters can still serve as the basis for resolving the conflict. Sadly, while both parties expressed reservations, the Israeli government accepted the proposal and the Palestinians rejected it. In January 2001, Fatah issued a document explaining its rejection of the Clinton Parameters. Instead of perceiving them as a springboard for detailed negotiations, the Palestinian response dismissed them with multiple objections, wasting another golden opportunity for a breakthrough. The Palestinians contended that the American proposal was vague, unclear and lacked the backing of effective international implementation guarantees. The proposal was not accompanied by a map, and the Palestinians were worried that Palestinian contiguity would not be preserved. The proposal 'provides Israel with control over large swaths of land, rendering the Palestinian state unviable and lacking direct access to international borders'.[41] The Palestinians believed Clinton was far more concerned about Israeli interests than Palestinian interests. The very recognition of Israeli 'settlement blocs', deemed illegal by the international community, subordinated Palestinian interests to those of the Israelis. Inter alia, the Palestinians asked for clarifications as to which settlements Israel intended to annex, which lands were meant to be swapped and whether Israeli sovereignty would include the entire Western Wall or only the Wailing Wall. They insisted that compensation for those who would not return should be made from Israel's Custodianship of Absentee Property,[42] and they voiced concerns about their water rights.

39 Ibid.

40 For a critique of the Parameters, see Stephen Zunes, 'The United States and the Breakdown of the Israeli-Palestinian Peace Process', *Middle East Policy*, 8(4) (December 2001): 70–73.

41 Official Palestinian Response to the Clinton Parameters (and letter to international community), Remarks and Questions from the Palestinian Negotiating Team Regarding the United States Proposal (1 January 2001), https://tinyurl.com/3rth5sk2.

42 Shlomo Ben-Ami, *Prophets without Honor: The 2000 Camp David Summit and the End of the Two-State Solution* (Oxford: Oxford University Press, 2022), 162.

On security, the American proposal spoke of permitting Israel to maintain three early warning stations for at least ten years. The Palestinians contended that Israel requires no more than one early warning station in the West Bank to satisfy its strategic needs, and that maintenance of stations at current locations near Ramallah and Nablus and in East Jerusalem 'will seriously inhibit Palestinian development'.[43] They also asked for detailed clarifications to ensure that Israel's security needs would not encroach on Palestinian sovereignty.

On Jerusalem, the Palestinians argued that the formulation 'Arab areas are Palestinian and Jewish areas are Israeli' was far too simplistic, as it ignored the new neighbourhoods Israel had built in the eastern part of the city, resulting in Palestinian islands within the city, separated from one another, while Israel would maintain contiguity.[44] The Palestinians proposed granting Jerusalem the status of an Open City, with free access for all.

On refugees, the Parameters denied what the Palestinians perceive as their fundamental right of return, presented as the core of the Arab-Israeli conflict. The Palestinians argued that the Parameters adopted the Israeli position and denied the refugees the freedom of choice to decide where to resettle: 'Recognition of the right of return and the provision of choice to refugees is a pre-requisite for the closure of the conflict.'[45] Furthermore, they argued, the American proposal 'fails to provide any guarantee that refugees' rights to restitution and compensation will be fulfilled'.[46]

The 2001 Taba Peace Talks

Immediately after the failure of the Camp David Summit, Barak announced that Israel had no partner in peace. Yet, a few days after the summit, Shlomo Ben-Ami, Gilead Sher and Israel Hasson on the Israeli side, and Sa'eb Erekat, Mohammed Dahlan, Ghaith al-Omari and Akram Hanieh on the Palestinian side, resumed negotiations.[47] A few months later, Barak made a last-ditch attempt to strike a deal with the Palestine Liberation Organization (PLO),

[43] Official Palestinian Response to the Clinton Parameters (and letter to international community), Remarks and Questions from the Palestinian Negotiating Team Regarding the United States Proposal (1 January 2001).

[44] Ibid.

[45] Ibid.

[46] Ibid. See also Amnon Aran, *Israeli Foreign Policy since the End of the Cold War* (Cambridge: Cambridge University Press, 2021), 246–251; 'Palestinians Reject Clinton Deal', *MailOnline* (21 January 2001), https://tinyurl.com/ycmh6h78.

[47] Interview with Gilead Sher (26 May 2013), 8.

demonstrating a willingness to give the Palestinians even further concessions. At the 22–28 January 2001 talks in Taba, Egypt, the Israeli negotiating team included two 'doves', committed to peace, who were not invited to Camp David: Minister of Justice Yossi Beilin and Meretz party leader Yossi Sarid. The negotiations revolved around four themes: security, borders, Jerusalem and refugees. On security, Shlomo Yanai presented a list of weapons that the Palestinians should not have.[48] The Israeli and Palestinian negotiators, Mike Herzog and Dahlan, argued about Israel's right to deploy forces in the Jordan Valley during emergencies. Herzog emphasised that such potential incidents are very rare, and that Israel would withdraw its forces once the emergency was over. Dahlan rejected Israel's concern as undermining Palestinian sovereignty. The Palestinians were unwilling, as a matter of principle, to allow anyone to fight on Palestinian soil. This included Israel and all other countries, including Arab countries. Bluntly, Dahlan asserted that Israel was unable to free itself from its occupier mentality. 'Later', Dahlan said in bitter sarcasm, 'you'll say you need five locations for emergencies, two roads for access, 500 soldiers on a permanent basis. I know you and can anticipate your demands. Generally speaking, you need to change your attitude.'[49] Indeed, security should not serve as a façade for continued Israeli occupation. While there is much truth in what Dahlan said, the Palestinians, as well, must change their attitude and commit to peace wholeheartedly.

Omar Dajani asked whether Israel would take action against hostile forces if they were to enter Jordan and pose an existential threat to Israel. Herzog answered in the positive. Then Dajani asked whether Israel had an agreement with Jordan relating to such a situation. Herzog replied that it did not. Dajani queried why, then, Israel was making such an impossible demand from the Palestinians.[50]

Both parties agreed to devise protocols establishing an international presence in the Jordan Valley and at the early warning stations. Israel agreed that Palestine would have sovereignty over its skies, and that Palestinian rights in the field of civil aviation would be observed. The parties also agreed to establish a safe corridor between Beit Hanun in the northern Gaza Strip and Al-Khaleel (Hebron).[51]

[48] Security Session, Permanent Status negotiations, Taba (26 January 2001). Minutes prepared by the Negotiations Support Unit of the PLO Negotiations Affairs Department. Confidential.

[49] Security Session, Permanent Status negotiations, Taba (25 January 2001). Minutes prepared by the Palestinian delegation. Confidential.

[50] Ibid.

[51] Ahmed Qurie, *Beyond Oslo* (London: I.B. Tauris, 2008), 323–324.

Israel demanded the right to annex 8 per cent of the West Bank, of which 2 per cent would be on lease, incorporating Jewish settlements that accounted for some 80 per cent of the settlers. Israel was prepared to give Palestine the equivalent of 6 per cent of land contiguous with the rest of Palestine in the West Bank and along the Gaza Strip, which would become part of Palestine. The Palestinians proposed that Israel annex 3.1 per cent (according to Qurie, between 2 and 3 per cent)[52] and consented to annexation consisting of three settlement blocs, amounting to 4 per cent. Thus, the disagreement concerned approximately 110 square kilometres (see Figure 8.1).[53]

The issue of percentages was tricky. The Israeli mapping expert Shaul Arieli admitted that Israel manipulated the Palestinians over time. Israel was the one that determined how to calculate percentages. Sometimes, Israeli negotiators referred only to the West Bank. Sometimes they also included Gaza. Sometimes they included Jerusalem, and sometimes they did not. The land area of the West Bank has been growing because the Dead Sea is drying up, but Israel paid no attention to this. In his preparations for managing the negotiations, Arieli devised a formula, where the West Bank was 5,860 square kilometres and Gaza was 363 square kilometres. Later, the Palestinians understood this issue better and, at Annapolis, an agreement was reached that no matter what, the Palestinian state would ultimately span 6,205 square kilometres. This included the West Bank, Gaza and East Jerusalem, as well as half of the no-man's land in Latrun.[54]

The two sides agreed that Jerusalem would be an open city and the capital of two independent states, and that the Arab neighbourhoods would become part of Palestine.[55] However, Ben-Ami said that the sides were unable to resolve four issues about Jerusalem: the Temple Mount, the Mount of Olives, the four quarters of the Old City and the Western Wall.[56] Beilin wrote that the issue of sovereignty over the Holy Places remained for further probing, with internationalisation as a possible solution.[57]

[52] Ibid., 306, 320.

[53] Yossi Beilin, *The Path to Geneva* (New York: RDV Books, 2004), 246–247; Ron Pundak, 'From Oslo to Taba: What Went Wrong?', *Survival*, 43(3) (2001): 44. See also Ron Pundak and Shaul Arieli, *The Territorial Aspect of the Israeli-Palestinian Final Status Negotiation* (Peres Centre for Peace, September 2004) (Hebrew), 31–37.

[54] Interview with Shaul Arieli (11 November 2024), 7.

[55] Qurie, *Beyond Oslo*, 323–324.

[56] Interview with Shlomo Ben-Ami (26 June 2013), 16.

[57] Beilin, *The Path to Geneva*, 246. See also Israeli Position on Three Main Points at Taba Talks (21 January 2001).

Figure 8.1 Taba: Israeli and Palestinian proposals.
Source: Shaul Arieli, www.shaularieli.com/en/maps/negotiations/.

Figure 8.1 (cont.)

Ahmed Qurie wrote that the Palestinians demanded the dismantling of the settlements Ma'ale Adumim and Givat Ze'ev, saying that the first 'is choking us and preventing us from getting to Jerusalem from the east' while the second 'closes off Jerusalem from the north'.[58] Israel was willing to negotiate the Palestinian right of return, repatriation and relocation, which it had declined to discuss at Camp David.[59]

At Taba, agreement on issues of territory, settlements and borders seemed within reach. However, there were two other major problems. Elections for the office of Israel's prime minister were coming in a few days, on 6 February 2001, so the timing was wrong. In an interview with Clayton E. Swisher, Amnon Lipkin-Shahak was very explicit, explaining his opinion on Taba: 'Taba was bullshit. Taba was an election exercise – don't trust nothing! Taba was not aimed to reach an agreement. Taba was aimed to convince the Israeli Arabs to vote! [for Barak].'[60] In addition, the compromises that both sides were willing to make were not enough. The Palestinians insisted on Israeli acceptance of the right of return and on having the sole sovereignty over the Temple Mount.[61] As before, Israel refused to budge on those important issues.

At Camp David and at Taba, various figures for the number of refugees to be allowed to return to Israel were discussed. The highest figure mentioned by Palestinians was 150,000 refugees a year over a ten-year period, for a total of 1.5 million. At times, the Palestinians had spoken of between 100,000 and 800,000 refugees.[62] Ben-Ami proposed that Israel would admit no more than 15,000 refugees, and that even this number would be spaced over twenty years.[63] He further suggested that hundreds of thousands of refugees would return to the swap areas, to those areas of Israel proper that would become part of the Palestinian state. This idea was rejected by the Palestinians because it did not allow for the refugees' free choice of where to settle in Israel.[64] According to Asher Susser, Israel informally proposed the return of 40,000 refugees over five years, but no agreement was reached on any numbers.[65] Martin Indyk said that, in

58 Qurie, *Beyond Oslo*, 307, 310.
59 Israeli Response RE Refugees, The Taba Proposals and the Refugee Problem, www.mideastweb.org/taba.htm.
60 Swisher, *The Truth about Camp David*, 403.
61 Benny Morris, 'An Interview with Ehud Barak', *New York Review of Books* (13 June 2002), https://tinyurl.com/mrxmbw8p.
62 Jeremy Pressman, 'Visions in Collision: What Happened at Camp David and Taba?', *International Security*, 28(2) (2003): 32; Ben-Ami, 'So Close and Yet So Far', 75.
63 Shlomo Ben-Ami, *A Front without a Rearguard* (Tel Aviv: Yedioth Ahronoth, 2004) (Hebrew), 142–143, 372, 440; Qurie, *Beyond Oslo*, 239.
64 Ben-Ami, *A Front without a Rearguard*, 447.
65 Asher Susser, *Israel, Jordan and Palestine* (Waltham, MA: Brandeis University Press, 2012), 56. See also Joel Peters, 'Israel and the Palestinian Refugee Issue', in Elizabeth G. Matthews

Taba, the parties came closer in relative terms, but in absolute terms, the gap between Israel and the PA was not closed.[66]

The Palestinians could not have asked for a more congenial Israeli negotiator than Sarid, yet even he said, 'we cannot bear the burden of negotiation on our own, and neither can you. If you expect all the concessions needed to reach a solution to come from us, then I think our task will be impossible. We have to share the burden.'[67] Qurie responded: 'We made huge concessions in Oslo. We gave up all claims to the territory that was occupied by Israel before 4 June 1967 including West Jerusalem.'[68] While Israel was thinking in 1967 terms, the Palestinians were thinking in 1947 terms. Their gap between their respective objectives remained too wide to be bridged.

Taba was a despairing attempt to reach an agreement just before Barak was to leave the prime minister's office, with little hope of return. He assembled all the 'doves' to negotiate peace, but even this Dream Team (for the Palestinians) was unable to strike a deal. Their additional concessions were insufficient in the eyes of the Palestinians, who at that point were not interested. Qurie told Hasson that nothing would come of it. Hasson warned him that the results would be bloodshed, the dismantling of the Israeli peace camp and the rise of Hamas.[69] The Palestinians remained unmoved, Barak's desperate move failed and Hasson was correct in his predictions.

I asked Ben-Ami what prompted Barak and him to try another round of negotiations when it should have been clear to them that there would be no time to implement an agreement, even if the Palestinians were willing to reach one. Ben-Ami responded that, on 24 December, the Israeli government approved the Clinton Parameters, 'and we went to negotiate at Taba, to close the details of the agreement based on the Clinton Parameters. Of course, there was also a political assumption that there would be a breakthrough here.'[70] If there were a breakthrough, then it would bring Barak a victory in the elections. Sarid said (quoting Barak): 'I sent Yossi Sarid and Yossi Beilin to Taba so that they themselves would be convinced that there's no one to talk to. That was the intention.'[71] This is a *very* curious reason to convene a peace summit, but, apparently, it was the case. When she negotiated the

(ed.), *The Israel-Palestine Conflict* (London: Routledge, 2011), 29; Pressman, 'Visions in Collision', 31.

66 Martin Indyk, *Innocent Abroad* (New York: Simon and Schuster, 2009), 372.

67 Qurie, *Beyond Oslo*, 313.

68 Ibid.

69 Interview with Israel Hasson (23 May 2013), 6.

70 Interview with Shlomo Ben-Ami (26 June 2013), 13.

71 Interview with Yossi Sarid (15 May 2015), 31.

Figure 8.2 Barak at the Knesset.
Credit: AFP/Stringer/Getty Images.

Annapolis process, Tzipi Livni asked Barak for the maps discussed at Taba. Barak replied that Taba was 'just an experience'.[72] It was not part of the peace process. Barak wrote that the only reason he decided to engage in the talks was 'to have other ministers in the Israeli government, or, to convince other ministers that there is no hope for peace with the other side'.[73]

According to Sarid, everything was collapsing. It was clear that Barak's political career was over, and that Meretz was going down with him. Taba, said Sarid, 'was a desperate and pathetic last-minute effort to try to save something. And it may be that I thought then that I could help somehow, in the restoration of the ruins. It was quite a harebrained thought.'[74] Indeed, the odds of success at Taba were close to nil. Barak had lost public support, including much of the support of his own base (see Figure 8.2).

Fundamentally, Arafat and Barak were not flexible enough. They could not establish a constructive partnership. Arafat turned to violence. Barak was out of favour in Palestine and Israel. The Palestinians had no trust in him. The Israelis were unwilling to pay the heavy price of human life in

[72] Interview with Tzipi Livni (22 June 2016), 2.
[73] Ibid.
[74] Interview with Yossi Sarid (15 May 2015), 31.

return for an abstract and unrealisable peace. Indeed, terror and the peace process cannot live together. Terror and peace are a zero-sum game. One comes at the expense of the other.

The 2001 Israeli Elections

Barak's coalition, which began to disintegrate before Camp David, continued on the same trajectory after the summit. He lost the support of most of the parties in his coalition and the trust of many members of his own party. Shootings became routine news items, as did snipers, bombings, cars driven into crowds and savage murders. On 6 February 2001, elections were held in Israel, and Arafat's arch-enemy, Ariel Sharon, won with a significant majority of 62.4 per cent. This was the first time that special elections had been called only for the prime minister's office. Barak received only 37.6 per cent of the vote. His campaign was negative: why is Sharon bad for Israel? In fact, there was hardly anything positive to say about Barak's administration. His main achievement, the withdrawal from Lebanon, was insufficient for winning the election. It did not address the real issue at hand: restoring security to daily life. More than 1,000 Israeli civilians were killed during the Intifada and many more were injured. On the Palestinian side, more than 3,000 were killed and many more were injured.[75] After Benjamin Netanyahu's failure to convince the public of the desirability of his objectives, Barak came in, certain he could change things for the better. He pushed the process too rapidly, forcing it, believing it would gain momentum and, in the end, the leader who came into office as Mr Security faded away. Arafat, who lived in a world of his own, did not realise this was the end of an era. While Barak and Arafat had a few 'cold meetings', Prime Minister Sharon refused to meet Arafat in person. His contempt for the Palestinian leader was loud and clear.

The Arab Peace Initiative (API)

In 1998, King Hussein of Jordan began thinking about broadening the scope of engagement with Israel, involving Arab countries. He presented his ideas to the Americans, but they were busy with the Wye River talks, and then King Hussein fell ill. When King Abdullah came to power, he wanted

[75] Ben-Ami, *Prophets without Honor*, 123; David A. Jaeger and M. Daniele Paserman, 'The Cycle of Violence? An Empirical Analysis of Fatalities in the Palestinian-Israeli Conflict', *IZA Discussion Paper* No. 1808 (October 2005); BBC, 'Intifada Toll 2000–2005', *BBC.com* (8 February 2005), http://news.bbc.co.uk/1/hi/world/middle_east/3694350.stm.

to revive his father's initiative. The 11 September 2001 attack on the United States delayed matters, but a few months later, Crown Prince Abdullah's peace initiative became public.[76] The Jordanians never expected the Saudis to lead such an initiative, but they welcomed their involvement.[77]

In March 2002, the Arab League Summit was held in Beirut. Extensive discussions were held about the Saudi initiative. The Saudis wanted the text to be simple and general, saying full peace for full withdrawal. It was a general principle, without loading the text with details. Other Arab states, particularly Syria and Lebanon, did not accept the general idea and wanted a more detailed document. They wanted it to mention UN Resolution 194, the refugee right of return – and particularly the return of the Palestinian refugees in Lebanon to Israel. Extensive negotiations ensued to come up with a text that would be acceptable to all. The final text was a compromise that all the Arab countries were ready to work with.

The Arab Peace Initiative (API) called upon Israel to affirm full withdrawal from all the territories occupied since 1967, including the Syrian Golan Heights, to the 4 June 1967 lines, as well as the remaining occupied Lebanese territories in the south of Lebanon. It further required Israel to agree to a just solution to the Palestinian refugee problem, in accordance with UN General Assembly Resolution 194.[78] Israel should acknowledge refugee rights in principle, while the determination of those rights would be decided by direct negotiations between Israel, the PLO and other relevant countries, that is, countries that would agree to the resettlement of refugees in their territory. The refugees would be able to choose from several options for their resettlement.

The API also speaks of the acceptance of the establishment of a sovereign independent Palestinian state on the Palestinian territories occupied since 4 June 1967 in the West Bank and Gaza Strip, with East Jerusalem as its capital. The Arab countries, on their part, would 'consider the Arab-Israeli conflict ended, and enter into a peace agreement with Israel, and provide security for all the states of the region'.[79] This text was approved unanimously by every Arab state, without reservation.

[76] Thomas L. Friedman, 'An Intriguing Signal from the Saudi Crown Prince', *New York Times* (17 February 2002).

[77] Interview with Marwan Muasher (25 July 2022), 4. See also Marwan Muasher, *The Arab Center: The Promise of Moderation* (New Haven, CT: Yale University Press, 2008); Raphael Cohen-Almagor, 'The Role of the Arab World in the Palestinian-Israeli Conflict: Interview with Marwan Muasher', *Israel Affairs*, 29(5) (2023): 864–894.

[78] UN General Assembly Resolution 194, www.unrwa.org/content/resolution-194.

[79] Text of Arab peace initiative adopted at Beirut summit, https://tinyurl.com/2aytxcrh.

The API aimed to give Israel, as the strong party, needs that the weak party, the Palestinians, could not give Israel on their own. Therefore, the API is about a wide Arab-Israeli peace. In the context of this comprehensive peace, Arab countries would establish normal relations with Israel. They would boost Israel's economy to a new level. Economic synergies between Israel and twenty-two Arab countries could be created, and Israel would receive oil supplies at a preferred tariff. New job markets would open in Arab and Muslim countries. By offering Israel economic incentives, as well as peace and security guarantees that the Palestinians alone could not offer, Israel would be prepared, in return, to make very difficult concessions regarding Jerusalem and the withdrawal from all occupied territory. Marwan Muasher explained that the Arabs were ready to do four things. Firstly, they would offer Israel collective peace agreements with every Arab country, those that shared borders with Israel and those that did not. Secondly, the Arab world would offer Israel security guarantees by every Arab state. Thirdly, in return for withdrawal from all occupied territories, Arab states would not claim Jaffa, Lod, Haifa or any other Israeli city inside the 1967 borders (see Figure 8.3). Fourthly, Arab states were ready to solve the refugee problem.[80]

In the same period, the UN Security Council passed Resolution 1397, which was premised on a vision of a region where two states, Israel and Palestine, live side by side within secure and recognised borders. It demanded the immediate end of all acts of violence, including all acts of terror; called upon the Israeli and Palestinian sides and their leaders to resume negotiations on a political settlement; and expressed support for the efforts of the Secretary-General and others to assist the parties in their efforts to stop violence and resume the peace process.[81]

While Arafat saw the initiative as a strong platform for achieving a comprehensive peace, Hamas objected to it. In their worldview, no Arab state should normalise its relations with the Zionist entity. As for Israel and the United States, they were not enthusiastic.[82] The Israelis were not ready to make such deep concessions to their neighbours. Sharon was aware of the Initiative when it was in the making in late 2001, but he did

[80] Interview with Marwan Muasher (25 July 2022), 1–2; 'Arab Peace Initiative: Full Text', *The Guardian* (28 March 2002), www.theguardian.com/world/2002/mar/28/israel7.

[81] UN Security Council Resolution 1397 (12 March 2002), https://tinyurl.com/mr2nrbnj.

[82] Elie Podeh, 'Israel and the Arab Peace Initiative, 2002–2014: A Plausible Missed Opportunity', *Middle East Journal*, 68(4) (Autumn 2014): 587; Charles Enderlin, *The Lost Years* (New York: Other Press, 2007), 133–134. See also Elie Podeh, *Villa in the Jungle?* (Jerusalem: Carmel, 2025) (Hebrew), 220–224, 252–256.

— Pre-1967 lines (the "Green Line")
Israel
Territories occupied by Israel during the 1967 war

Figure 8.3 Territories occupied by Israel during the 1967 war.
Source: Shaul Arieli, www.shaularieli.com/en/maps/negotiations/.

not want to make the substantial concessions it required. Withdrawal of Israel to the 1967 borders was inconceivable.[83] Shimon Peres said that while 'Israel views positively every initiative aimed at arriving at peace and normalization' and, in this respect, the significant Saudi initiative is important, it is bound to fail if terrorism is not stopped. Peres added that 'the details of every peace plan must be discussed directly between Israel and the Palestinians, and to make this possible, the Palestinian Authority must put an end to terror'.[84]

The timing of the Initiative was not right. It coincided with a horrible terrorist attack on the eve of Pesach (Passover), when Jews traditionally gather to recite its story from the Haggadah, over a festive meal, the Seder. The Passover holiday is one of the most cherished and important events on the Jewish calendar, similar in its importance to the American Thanksgiving and the Christian Christmas Eve. On 27 March 2002, a Hamas suicide bomber murdered twenty-nine Israelis and wounded 150 others who were gathered at the Park Hotel in Netanya for the Seder meal. Families were eradicated. Israel was deeply shaken. Discussions about peace were out of touch, unrealistic.[85] The Israelis felt that what they wanted was separation, a divorce, not peace with the Palestinians, who crossed every line with their terror. The Sharon government launched *Operation Defensive Shield* (*Homat Magen* in Hebrew) against the PA, aimed at uprooting terrorism and isolating Arafat.

In June 2003, Israel also embarked on a large building project: a separation barrier, aimed at separating most of the West Bank from areas inside Israel.[86] The 'fence' (as Israel calls it; others call it the 'wall') was deemed necessary to block terrorists from entering Israel. Indeed, the fence/wall has proved a security success story. The facts are conclusive. Before it was erected, the average number of terrorist attacks was twenty-six per year. Since its partial construction, the number has dropped to three to zero per year, as Israel was able to foil every suicide bombing originating from the northern West Bank and, specifically, from the cities of Nablus and Jenin, which were infamous for exporting suicide bombers. However, almost the

83 Gilad Sharon, *Sharon – The Life of a Leader* (New York: Harper, 2011), 447.

84 'Response of FM Peres to the decisions of the Arab Summit in Beirut-28-Mar-2002', Ministry of Foreign Affairs (28 March 2002), https://tinyurl.com/yvyf4vy7.

85 Between April 1993 and May 2005 there were 164 suicide attacks. I thank Arie Perliger for this information. See also Raphael Cohen-Almagor, 'An Israeli's Shift from Peace Activist to War Backer', *Washington Post* (31 March 2002), B1; Roei Mendel, 'Decade to Operation Defensive Shield', *Ynet* (30 March 2012), www.ynet.co.il/articles/0,7340,L-4210103,00.html.

86 'Israel Begins Construction of Fence on West Bank Border', *cnn.com* (19 June 2003).

entire fence/wall passes inside Palestinian territory. Many Palestinians found themselves living between this new barrier and the Green Line.[87] According to Human Rights Watch, 85 per cent of the barrier is constructed in such a way that it confiscates Palestinian land, cuts off thousands of Palestinians from their agricultural lands and isolates 11,000 Palestinians. It is estimated that the barrier cuts off at least 9 per cent of Palestinian territory (see Figure 8.4).[88] Because of its route through Palestinian living space, dozens of gates have been established to enable the daily movement of farmers to their lands, students and teachers to their schools, and businessmen and merchants to their places of work. As a practical matter, it severely limits Palestinians' freedom of movement.

Against this violent background, the API did not receive the attention it deserved, and the frustrated Palestinians moved on to a new form of terror – rocket attacks on southern Israel. Years later, Shabtai Shavit told me:

> I think the API needs to be the main component of the peace process. Why? Because the API originated from Saudi Arabia, the wealthiest, strongest and most influential country among the moderate Arab states. Saudi Arabia wrote it and passed it to the Arab League whose 22 Arab states subsequently adopted it. I decided to take the initiative seriously the first time I read it. Why? Because it's very short. Every line is black and white – there's no type of sophistry with commas, brackets or legal terminology. It's simple. We demand such and such from you, and we will give you such and such in return. And there will be peace *inshallah*. Not only peace, but peace with the entire Arab world, and an additional 30 Muslim countries. I'm trying to imagine – and it's difficult – what diplomatic relations such as these would mean. But the initiative promises that the entire Muslim world will recognise the State of Israel and establish full diplomatic relations with us. Just think about the economic significance of such a thing; what it would give to the state.[89]

As for the United States, in the wake of the 11 September attacks on the US, President George W. Bush was preoccupied with the War on Terror and the war in Afghanistan. Condoleezza Rice wrote that the API 'was a bold proposal and could have been an important point of departure

[87] Uri Ben-Eliezer, *Old Conflict, New War* (New York: Palgrave, 2012), 174–193; Eyal Hareuveni, 'Disturbed Life', *B'Tselem* (October 2012) (Hebrew).

[88] Human Rights Watch, 'Israel and Palestine', *World Report 2023*, www.hrw.org/world-report/2022/country-chapters/israel-and-palestine-0.

[89] Raphael Cohen-Almagor, 'Interview with Former Head of Mossad Shabtai Shavit', *Fathom* (January 2019), https://tinyurl.com/ffy7zj3j. For further analysis, see Kobi Michael, *Arab Peace Initiative – Is It a Historical Opportunity?* (Jerusalem: Jerusalem Institute for Israel Studies, 2007) (Hebrew).

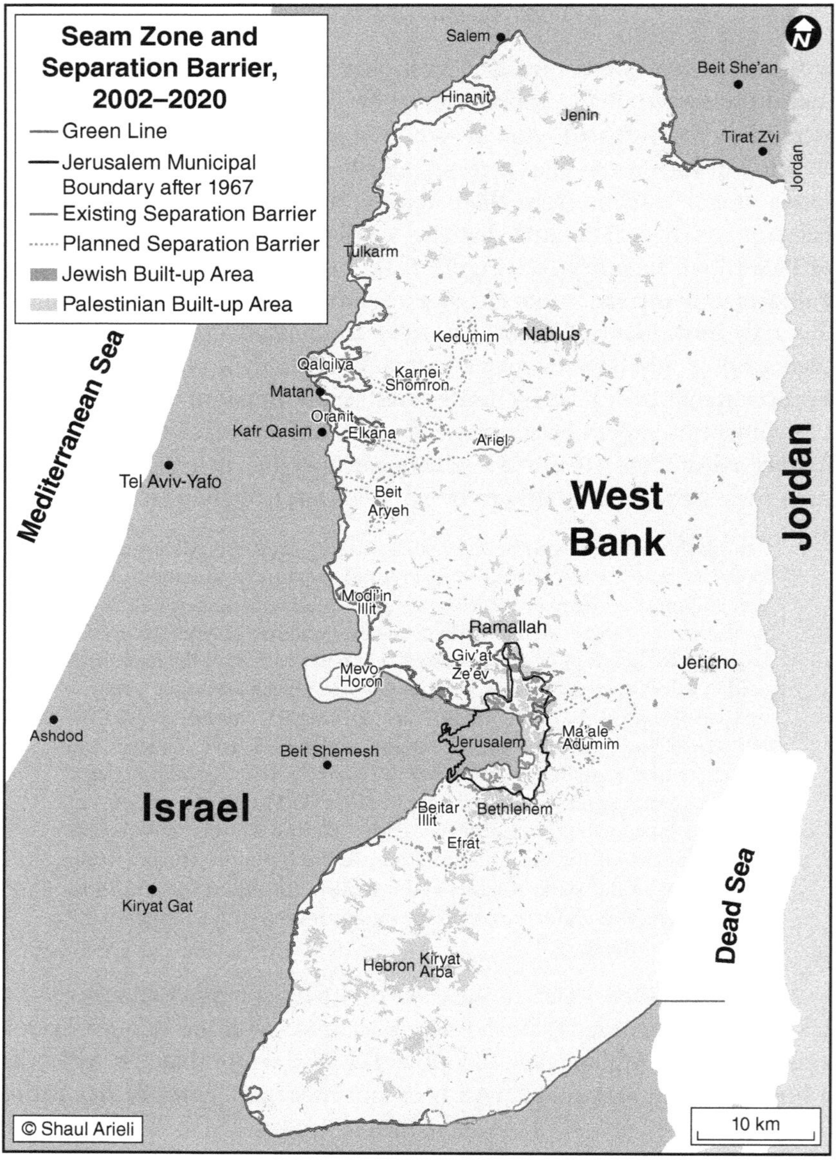

Figure 8.4 The Seam Zone and the Separation Barrier.
Note: The Seam Zone refers to the area in the West Bank that lies between the 1949 Green Line (the armistice line between Israel and Jordan) and the Israeli separation barrier. This zone was created when the barrier was constructed inside the West Bank, not along the Green Line, effectively enclosing certain areas and separating them from the rest of the West Bank.
Source: Shaul Arieli, www.shaularieli.com/en/maps/negotiations/.

for negotiations', but its timing 'could not have been worse'.[90] Jenkins remarked that this kind of agreement needs to come at the end of a peace process, rather than the beginning. And you cannot simply say 'take it or leave it'.[91] Elliott Abrams was critical because the Initiative was a 'take it or leave it' offer that presented 'unacceptable' demands: complete withdrawal to the Green Line, and unqualified Palestinian right of return.[92] The Bush Roadmap for Peace in the Middle East of 30 April 2003 included a statement about 'Arab state acceptance of full normal relations with Israel and security for all the states of the region in the context of a compressive Arab-Israeli peace',[93] but the focus was on the Israeli-Palestinian conflict. I will discuss the Roadmap in more detail in the next chapter. Gamal Helal explained that while the original intention was good, the API tried to achieve too much instead of focusing on the Palestinians.[94] In 2008, Livni asked the Egyptian and Jordanian foreign ministers whether the API was negotiable. They replied that it was. Livni wanted to negotiate with them, but they referred her to the Palestinians, saying that they would accept and support any decisions made by the Palestinians.[95] Olmert was ready to accept the API as the framework for negotiations with the Palestinians.[96] Note, however, that he used the word '*framework*', not the word *basis* for negotiations.

Conclusion

In 2022, when I interviewed Barak, he believed that when the Israeli-Palestinian conflict is eventually solved, 'you will need a magnifying glass to see the difference between what was on the table at Camp David and what will be agreed upon in the end'.[97] Barak discounted what was offered at Taba, which exceeded his Camp David offer, as well as Olmert's offer during his negotiations with Abbas, to be discussed infra.

90 Condoleezza Rice, *No Higher Honor: A Memoir of My Years in Washington* (New York: Simon and Schuster, 2011), 136.
91 Interview with John Jenkins (9 December 2022), 29.
92 Elliott Abrams, *Tested by Zion: The Bush Administration and the Israeli-Palestinian Conflict* (New York: Cambridge University Press, 2013), 29.
93 Road Map, https://ecf.org.il/media_items/577; Bureau of Public Affairs, 'Roadmap for Peace in the Middle East: Israeli/Palestinian Reciprocal Action, Quartet Support', Washington, DC (16 July 2003), https://2001-2009.state.gov/r/pa/ei/rls/22520.htm.
94 Interview with Gamal Helal (11 November 2022), 13.
95 Interview with Tzipi Livni (22 June 2016), 3.
96 Interview with Ehud Olmert (22 February 2019), 19.
97 Interview with Ehud Barak (21 June 2022), p. 16.

The consequences of the failed peace process were brutal for Israel and the Palestinians. It would take years for the two parties to return to the negotiation table. The next two chapters analyse the third important peace junction, which took place after both Israel and the PA had seen a change in leadership: Ehud Olmert in Israel and Mahmoud Abbas in the PA. To date, Olmert's proposal is the most generous offer ever made to the Palestinians by a serving Israeli prime minister.

9

Annapolis Peace Process

It is always easier to fight for one's principles than to live up to them.

~ Alfred Adler

The third most significant junction in the history of the peace process between Israel and the Palestine Liberation Organization (PLO) relates to Ehud Olmert and his efforts to strike a deal with the Palestinians, led by Mahmoud Abbas. Abbas said that the most serious negotiations between Israel and the Palestinians took place when Olmert was in office.[1] This chapter documents the events that brought about meaningful negotiations between the new Palestinian and Israeli leaders following the departure of Yasser Arafat and Ariel Sharon. It discusses Sharon's disengagement from Gaza, summarises Arafat's contribution as his life came to an end, and explains the events that brought about new leadership in Israel and the Palestinian Authority (PA). New leadership brings new thinking, new promises and new opportunities. Menachem Begin engaged with Egypt soon after he became prime minister and, two years later, signed the peace accords with Anwar Sadat. Yitzhak Rabin signed the Oslo Accords one year after he became prime minister for the second time. With the introduction of Olmert and Abbas, hopes emerged for renewed efforts to reach a peace agreement. Subsequently, I discuss the Annapolis Conference. George W. Bush assembled impressive representatives from many countries, and the conference was festive and well organised. Its effectiveness in yielding peace, however, is questionable.

Sharon's Disengagement Plan

In February 2004, Prime Minister Sharon announced a bold plan to dismantle Israeli settlements in the Gaza Strip and evacuate approximately

1 Raviv Drucker, 'Olmert, Abu Mazen and Barak Refer to the Political Process', *HaMakor* (17 November 2015).

7,500 residents. This move revived the long-dormant 'Gaza First' initiative originally proposed by Shimon Peres in the mid-1980s but never implemented. Sharon's disengagement plan was a strategic evolution of that idea, aiming not only to relocate settlements and military installations in Gaza but also to withdraw from a handful of villages in Samaria, West Bank. Sharon believed Israel had no viable Palestinian partner committed to peace and deemed the ongoing stalemate detrimental. His plan sought gradual disengagement as a pragmatic step to reduce friction between Israelis and Palestinians, enhance Israel's security and stabilise Israel's political and economic landscape.[2]

The plan was coordinated with the Americans. Olmert told me that he met with Dan Kurtzer in 2004 and asked for his opinion about the disengagement plan. Kurtzer had suggested that it should be done with Arafat's cooperation, not unilaterally, something Sharon was unwilling to do. Sharon intended to disengage unilaterally, as he did not believe he could achieve meaningful cooperation with Arafat, whom he deeply distrusted. As the toll – in blood and money – was too high, Sharon made a strategic decision that Israel could no longer support those settlements. While the American administration preferred a coordinated withdrawal, it did not oppose the unilateral move.[3] In his letter to Sharon of 14 April 2004, Bush wrote that his plan was a 'bold and historic initiative that can make an important contribution to peace'.[4] Bush commended Sharon's efforts and promised his continued support. Sharon thought it was in Israel's best interest to disengage from Gaza, regardless of the Palestinian position on the issue. Israel needed to secure its future.[5] The rationale for the disengagement plan was:

A) The stalemate is damaging; to break the stalemate, the government must act unilaterally.
B) The plan acknowledges the demographic reality necessitating a reconsideration of Israel's presence in Gaza.
C) The plan aims to provide better security for Israel and improve its diplomatic relations and economy.

[2] Disengagement Plan – General Outline (15 April 2004); Ariel Sharon's letter to George W. Bush (14 April 2004).
[3] Phone conversation with Ehud Olmert (26 February 2022).
[4] George W. Bush's letter to Ariel Sharon (14 April 2004).
[5] 'Sharon: The Disengagement Has Started; We Will Leave Gaza by the End of 2005', *Ynet* (6 June 2004) (Hebrew), www.ynet.co.il/articles/0,7340,L-2927949,00.html.

D) Friction between Israelis and Palestinians should be lessened. (Sharon promised that there would be no Jews in Gaza by the end of 2005.[6])
E) The military, whose presence in the Gaza Strip had cost many soldiers' lives to defend a few thousand settlers, will be pulled back.

Sharon knew that the die-hard settlers in Gaza would oppose his plan but thought their opposition could be overcome. The Gaza Strip does not have any holy Jewish components and is not emotionally fraught with religious significance, as are Judea and Samaria. Thus, evacuating settlements in Gaza is very different from evacuating settlements in Judea and Samaria. Disengagement was necessary due to demographics – there were 7,500 Jewish settlers in Gaza, which was densely populated with more than 1.2 million Palestinians – and because of continued Palestinian attacks on Israel Defense Forces soldiers.

Originally, Sharon intended to evacuate seventeen settlements in the West Bank. Under pressure, he backed down and revised his plan to include only four settlements.[7] The Americans dissuaded him from implementing a large evacuation in the West Bank because they feared internal resistance in Israel. They doubted Sharon's ability to successfully evacuate a large number of West Bank settlements as well as those in Gaza.[8] They believed that, politically, it would be easier to evacuate Gaza and preferred that option. They did agree to the evacuation of the four West Bank settlements, however, as an indication of potential future moves.[9]

The Sharon plan was considered more practical than Bush's 'Roadmap', which would be difficult to implement in the light of the fundamental lack of trust between Israel and the PLO.[10] Sharon's plan to disengage from Gaza enjoyed the support of large circles in Israel, left and right. While critics of the plan saw it as a victory for the Palestinians and incited negative opinion against Sharon,[11] he believed that pulling out of Gaza was to Israel's advantage. Israel did not want or need Gaza.

6 Sharon's Disengagement Plan – Full Text, *Miftah* (3 May 2004), www.miftah.org/Display.cfm?DocId=3655&CategoryId=10.
7 Interview with Ehud Olmert (22 February 2019), 26.
8 Nadav Shragai, 'Former Officials Reveal: How Close Israel Was to Another Disengagement', *Israel Hayom* (2 August 2020) (Hebrew), www.israelhayom.co.il/article/786169.
9 Interview with Ehud Olmert (24 April 2019), 3.
10 Raphael Cohen-Almagor, 'Breaking the Deadlock: The Gaza First Plan', *The Baltimore Sun* (18 December 2003).
11 Raphael Cohen-Almagor, 'Political Extremism and Incitement in Israel 1993–1995, 2003–2005: A Study of Dangerous Expressions', *Democracy and Security*, 3(1) (2007): 21–43.

Figure 9.1 Ariel Sharon.
Credit: David Silverman/Contributor/AFP/Getty Images.

On 6 June 2004, the Israeli cabinet approved Sharon's disengagement plan by a vote of fourteen to seven (see Figure 9.1). However, Sharon lost his majority in the Knesset and was left with only fifty-nine Members of the Knesset (MKs) out of 120.

The Labour Party assured Sharon that it would back him as long as he pursued the Gaza disengagement plan. On 26 October 2004, the Knesset approved a resolution to dismantle all Israeli Gaza settlements, evacuate their residents and withdraw all army troops. Sharon's disengagement plan was approved by a vote of sixty-seven to forty-five, although almost half of the Likud members and most of its traditional allies in the ultranationalist and religious parties did not support the motion. Sharon received support from the more dovish opposition parties.[12] On 16 February 2005, the Knesset enacted into law a bill to implement the withdrawal from Gaza. Fifty-nine MKs were in favour, forty were against and five abstained. Public opinion polls showed large support for the Gaza Plan.[13]

[12] John Ward Anderson, 'Sharon Wins Vote for Gaza Pullout', *Washington Post* (27 October 2004), https://tinyurl.com/4srhj77v.

[13] Uri Ben-Eliezer, *Old Conflict, New War* (New York: Palgrave, 2012), 197.

Years later, in 2019, Olmert reflected on the disengagement plan, saying it was the right decision. It was wrong to hold Gaza under siege, 'rid ourselves of any responsibility for the growing bitterness of the people who suffer from a terrible standard of living and a terrible quality of life, and put all the blame on the terrorists' actions'.[14] While I condemn Palestinian terrorism and argue that Israel should fight it, I also contend that Israel should not assume that the vast majority of Palestinians support terror. Israel failed to distinguish between the broad Gaza population and Hamas. Israel needed to enable the Gazans to separate themselves from the terrorist atrocities and to improve their living conditions, but it did not. Israel permitted the Gazans to have electricity for four to six hours a day. It did not transfer to them the funds that they were supposed to receive, or it transferred them through Hamas. I agree with Olmert, who said that Israel needed to show the Gazans that Hamas is not the only broker that can deliver.[15] Israel's policies wrongly and unjustly affected a population that was caught between a rock and a hard place.

The disengagement from Gaza was carried out in August 2005 amid a highly emotional atmosphere marked by widespread protests and demonstrations. Despite these tensions, most confrontations between settlers and soldiers were non-violent. Although the withdrawal was not coordinated with the PA, the Palestinians assumed responsibility for the Gaza Strip once the evacuation was complete. By then, Abbas had taken leadership of the PA and communicated to Sharon his commitment to govern Gaza, as well as his expectation of a subsequent Israeli withdrawal from the West Bank. Sharon, however, rejected these terms and proceeded with the unilateral withdrawal.

This decision significantly weakened Abbas's standing among Palestinians, and Hamas capitalised on his diminished authority. Sharon appeared willing to accept Hamas's eventual takeover of Gaza as a preferable alternative to negotiating a comprehensive peace deal with the PA. The events of 7 October 2023 starkly revealed the grave miscalculations behind this assumption. That day marked one of the most traumatic moments in Israel's history and should be solemnly memorialised.

Olmert and Hussein Agha think it would not have been possible for Israel to coordinate with the PA on the withdrawal. Olmert said that if Israel had entered into negotiations with the PA about a possible pullout from Gaza, without a doubt, the PA would have added conditions and the process 'would get into a messy negotiating process that, in the end, will

14 Interview with Ehud Olmert (22 February 2019), 20.

15 Ibid.

blow up and it will not take place. So, we will not have a disengagement and would be blamed for not having it.'[16] Agha agreed that the only way Israel could withdraw from Gaza was unilaterally, saying: 'I do not believe in coordination. If you are coordinating, you are negotiating. Until today, you will be negotiating like in other issues; until today you will still be in Gaza.'[17] Olmert and Agha believe that Sharon's disengagement plan was the only possible way to leave Gaza.

Yasser Arafat: 1929–2004

On 11 November 2004, Arafat's life came to an end. He fell ill and was rushed to Paris for treatment, but the physicians were unable to save him. Arafat died in the hospital.[18]

Arafat wrote that the Palestinians have a vision of peace. It is a peace based on the complete end of the occupation and a return to Israel's 1967 borders, and the sharing of Jerusalem as one open city and as the capital of two states, Palestine and Israel. It is a warm peace between two equals enjoying mutually beneficial economic and social cooperation.[19] Yet Arafat's world vision was one of struggle. His psychological profile showed a strong need to strive and overcome.[20] In his modest way of life, in his dress and in his public speeches, struggle transformed from a means to an end into an end in itself. Arafat symbolised the Palestinian revolution and struggle. This was his life's mission. In his own eyes, Arafat was a 'counter-revolutionary' and a 'freedom fighter', a historical leader who dedicated his life to the Palestinian people. Before his marriage, Arafat used to say that he was married to the Palestinian revolution. On one occasion, Arafat said that *he* was the Palestinian revolution, and that there would be 'no other symbol for the revolution in my lifetime'.[21] He was far less a statesman who could achieve peace via reconciliation with his enemy. Arafat was unable to shift wholeheartedly from being a man of

16 Ibid., 21.

17 Interview with Hussein Agha (5 April 2019), 36.

18 El-Kurd argues that Israel is responsible for Arafat's death. He maintains that 'there was a famous meeting between Sharon and Avi Dichter. He was the head of Shabac at that time, I think. And on a hot mic, Avi Dichter said, "We need to get rid of Arafat". And Sharon said, "Yes, we need to get rid of him". They were caught on a hot mic. And everyone heard it, including Arafat.' Interview with Maher El-Kurd (30 January 2025), 36.

19 Yasser Arafat, 'The Palestinian Vision of Peace', *New York Times* (3 February 2002).

20 Shaul Kimhi, Shmuel Even and Jerrold Post, *Yasir Arafat: Psychological Profile and Strategic Analysis* (Herzliya: The Interdisciplinary Center, 2002).

21 Ibid.

Figure 9.2 Arafat, Peres and Rabin at the Nobel Prize ceremony.
Credit: AFP/Stringer/Getty Images.

struggle to a man of peace. He still wore his uniform when he attended the Oslo Accords signing ceremony at the White House, and the Nobel Peace Prize ceremony in Oslo (see Figure 9.2).

When Arafat arrived in Gaza in 1994 after years in Tunis, he smuggled weapons and terrorists in his convoy.[22] Groups under his influence or direct command, such as Fatah, Force 17, the Tanzim and the Al Aqsa Martyrs' Brigades, were responsible for more than 1,500 terror attacks, including shootings, bombings and assassinations.[23] During the al Aqsa Intifada, Fatah carried out terror attacks against Israeli civilians in collaboration with Hamas and the Islamic Jihad.[24] In 2002, the Al Aqsa Martyrs'

[22] Yair Hirschfeld, *The Israeli-Palestinian Peace Process* (Cham: Springer, 2024): 104; Nadav Shragai, 'Step by Step: The History of Arafat's Deception in the Oslo Accords', *Israel Hayom* (2 September 2023) (Hebrew), www.israelhayom.co.il/magazine/hashavua/article/14553744; Leon Sverdlov, 'Former Shin Bet Head: Arafat Smuggled Terrorists in His Mercedes', *Jerusalem Post* (5 September 2019), https://tinyurl.com/5n72ce9c.

[23] Sean Durns, 'Background: Tanzim', Committee for Accuracy in Middle East Reporting and Analysis (5 September 2017), www.camera.org/article/backgrounder-tanzim/.

[24] Numerous attacks between 2001 and 2004 are recorded in 'Yasser Arafat's Timeline of Terror', Committee for Accuracy in Middle East Reporting and Analysis (13 November 2004), www.camera.org/article/yasir-arafat-s-timeline-of-terror/.

Brigades, a military offshoot of Arafat's Fatah movement, decided to join Hamas and Palestinian Islamic Jihad in targeting Israeli civilians. The Al Aqsa Martyrs' Brigades claimed responsibility for a series of terror attacks that killed dozens of people and wounded many more.[25] The head of Tanzim, Marwan Barghouti, was arrested by Israel, stood trial and was convicted of five murders. He was sentenced to five life terms in prison and is still in an Israeli prison.[26] In January 2002, Israel intercepted a ship called the Karine-A, which was loaded with fifty tons of weapons and ammunition. The PA had paid Iran $15 million for those weapons.[27] As president of the PA, chairman of the PLO and a widely recognised leader of the Palestinian people, Arafat bore responsibility for the terror attacks and for Karine-A. Thus, he never truly rejected the option of an armed struggle, to be replaced with a vision of diplomacy and conflict resolution measures. It is questionable whether he had a vision of two states, Israel and Palestine, living side by side, in peace. The normal and the abnormal were fused in his worldview. Tranquillity seems not to have featured in his vision.

Winning an argument with the swing of a hammer is more compelling than a lengthy exchange of opinions. It is also a thousand times more destructive. Enchanted by the image of resistance, Arafat failed to understand how destructive it was. Violence was an important tactical tool to be used to exert pressure and improve his bargaining position. Throughout his negotiations with Israel, Arafat tried to hold the olive branch *and* the sword. He embraced diplomacy and armed struggle at the same time,

[25] In January 2002, a suicide attack in Jerusalem killed an elderly man and wounded forty other people. In March 2002, a suicide bombing in a Jerusalem café killed eleven Israelis and wounded more than fifty. In March 2002, a suicide bombing in Jerusalem killed three Israelis. In April 2002, a suicide bombing at a marketplace in Jerusalem killed six people and injured 104 more. In November 2002, a shooting spree at a kibbutz in northern Israel killed five Israelis, including two children, and wounded seven more. In January 2003, a suicide bombing in Tel Aviv killed twenty-three people and injured about 100 more. In January 2004, an attack on a bus in Rehavia, Jerusalem, killed eleven people. In March 2004, two suicide bombings at a checkpoint at the Port of Ashdod killed ten people. This was a joint operation with Hamas. See Al-Aqsa Martyrs Brigade, Council on Foreign Relations, www.cfr.org/backgrounder/al-aqsa-martyrs-brigade; James Bennet, 'Suicide Bombers Attack Israeli Port; Talks Called Off', *New York Times* (14 March 2004).

[26] 'Who Is Marwan Barghouti, the Most Senior Palestinian Prisoner?', *The National* (21 December 2023), https://tinyurl.com/3mybptrx.

[27] Amos Harel, 'Hezbollah Paid for Karine A, PA Paid for Arms – Army Source', *Haaretz* (1 February 2002); 'Iran and the Palestinian War against Israel: Implications of the *Karine-A* Affair', The Washington Institute for Near East Policy (26 February 2002), https://tinyurl.com/275d4waf.

failing to understand that one comes at the expense of the other. He never prioritised ensuring that the PA would have a monopoly on weapons. Hamas, the Islamic Jihad, the Popular Front for the Liberation of Palestine (PFLP) and groups under his control carried weapons. In Chapter 4, I mentioned an agreement that Arafat signed in which he committed to take all measures necessary to prevent acts of terrorism,[28] but he did not keep his word. Whenever he thought it would be advantageous to gain something by undermining previous commitments, he had no qualms about doing so. Agreements were not binding, and commitments were made to be broken – if, to his mind, there was a good reason. Deals were signed if not signing was a worse alternative, but he did not feel bound by them anyway. Arafat had a sense of ownership of resistance, and no such sense regarding the Oslo Accords.

In October 1996, Arafat stated at a rally near Bethlehem: 'We know only one word – jihad. jihad, jihad, jihad. Whoever does not like it can drink from the Dead Sea or from the Sea of Gaza.'[29] In March 1997, four years into the Oslo peace process, in a speech to Arab League foreign ministers in Cairo, Arafat said: 'I now see the walls of Jerusalem, the mosques of Jerusalem, the churches of Jerusalem. My brothers! With blood and with spirit we will redeem you, Palestine! Yes, with blood and with spirit we will redeem you, Palestine!'[30] In April 1997, he declared: 'We know only one word: jihad, jihad, jihad. When we stopped the Intifada, we did not stop the jihad for the establishment of a Palestinian state whose capital is Jerusalem. And we are now entering the phase of the great jihad prior to the establishment of an independent Palestinian state whose capital is Jerusalem.'[31] In April 1998, in a statement published in the official PA newspaper, *Al-Hayat Al-Jadeeda*, Arafat was quoted as saying: 'O my dear ones on the occupied lands, relatives and friends throughout Palestine and the diaspora, my colleagues in struggle and in arms, my colleagues in struggle and in jihad ... Intensify the revolution and the blessed Intifada ... We must burn the ground under the feet of the invaders'.[32] Instead of consistently perceiving peace and reconciliation as keys to Palestinian

[28] The 1993 Mutual Recognition Agreement; the 1994 Gaza–Jericho Agreement; the Interim Agreement on the West Bank and Gaza (1995).

[29] Jeffrey F. Addicott, 'Using a Civil Suit to Punish/Deter Sponsors of Terrorism: Connecting Arafat & the PLO to the Terror Attacks in the Second Intifada', *St. John's Journal of International & Comparative Law*, 4(2) (2014): 99.

[30] 'In the Words of Arafat', *New York Times* (4 August 1997).

[31] Ibid.

[32] 'Yasser Arafat's Timeline of Terror'.

self-determination, Arafat opted for jihad. His leadership was built on the idea of a relentless and uncompromising struggle against Israel.

In July 2001, the US Congress condemned the PA for using children as soldiers and 'inciting children to acts of violence and war'.[33] An official Israeli report from May 2002 found that 'Arafat was personally involved in the planning and execution of terror attacks. He encouraged them ideologically, authorised them financially and personally headed the Fatah Al Aqsa Brigades organization.'[34] Similarly, during the same period, the US Congress passed the Arafat Accountability Act, declaring that 'Yasser Arafat and the forces directly under his control are responsible for the murder of hundreds of innocent Israelis and the wounding of thousands more since October 2000'.[35]

For Arafat, Palestinian spoilers were a tool. He understood that Israel is very sensitive to human life and believed that by exerting terror, he could achieve more. He never relinquished the option of terror. Instead, he turned a blind eye to it; he tolerated it.[36] When the peace option did not progress in the way he wanted, Arafat turned to violence.[37] Until his last day, he did not understand that terror has a dramatic effect on the psyche of the Israeli public, making it question its resolve to make peace with a violent enemy. Arafat derided democracy and was unable to understand how important democratic mechanisms in Israel are, that leaders in a democracy cannot ignore their people, and that their responsibility to their people is crucial when they undertake peace initiatives. Shlomo Ben-Ami says that Arafat never conveyed a clear message of peace and reconciliation to the Israeli public.[38] His words and actions blocked the road to peace, led to Sharon's election victory and, eventually, also brought about Arafat's own miserable isolation in his Ramallah headquarters.

The failure of the Camp David 2000 high-stakes summit unleashed tragic consequences. Arafat and Barak never forged a productive working

33 H.CON.RES.202 (27 July 2001).

34 'The Involvement of Arafat, PA Senior Officials and Apparatuses in Terrorism against Israel: Corruption and Crime', Israel Ministry of Foreign Affairs (6 May 2002), www.gov.il/en/pages/the-involvement-of-arafat-pa-senior-officials-in-terrorism.

35 H. R. 4693, 107 Congress, Arafat Accountability Act, To hold accountable the Palestine Liberation Organization and the Palestinian Authority, and for other purposes. In the House of Representatives (9 May 2002), www.congress.gov/bill/107th-congress/house-bill/4693/text.

36 Interview with Hiba Husseini (24 December 2024), 8, 14. See 'Comprehensive Listing of Terrorism Victims in Israel', *Jewish Virtual Library*, https://tinyurl.com/ne9y6kmx.

37 Discussion with Yair Hirschfeld (7 April 2025).

38 Shlomo Ben-Ami, *Scars of War, Wounds of Peace* (London: Phoenix, 2005), 215.

relationship and squandered a rare opportunity to resolve the conflict. Barak's political future hung precariously in the balance – a fact Arafat was well aware of but seemingly indifferent to. While he invested in the Intifada, he showed little commitment to Camp David, failing to grasp that its collapse would usher in a new Israeli leadership with a starkly different vision for the Israeli-Palestinian relationship. Instead, Arafat clung to the belief that he could work with – and around – any Israeli leader, regardless of the changing tides.

Ben-Ami believes that Arafat was very egocentric and was haunted by megalomania.[39] Ben-Ami further writes that, for Arafat, brinksmanship had no brakes; it was the art of bringing both the Palestinian people and the Israeli people to the edge of the abyss and beyond.[40] Time and again, he miscalculated. Arafat miscalculated the extent to which he could extort concessions from the Israelis. He miscalculated his ability to control the violent flames he fanned. He miscalculated his ability to simultaneously conduct peace negotiations and violent campaigns against the Israelis. Shimon Peres said that Arafat did not submit to the discipline of history. He did not feel himself obligated by facts. Arafat did not allow himself to be controlled or confused by facts, which were real only if they fit his worldview. He created his own interpretation of facts. In Peres's terms, Arafat was 'a master of the facts, not a slave to them'.[41] Arafat did not feel that he had to be concerned with details. Whenever the facts disturbed his plans, he either ignored them or changed them, even retrospectively. Dennis Ross writes that all Arafat did at Camp David was 'to repeat old mythologies and invent new ones, like, for example, that the Temple was not in Jerusalem but in Nablus'.[42] Ross argues that for Arafat, as leader of the Palestinians, ending the conflict meant ending himself. Like Peres, Ross believes that Arafat was unable or unwilling to confront history and mythology.[43]

In Chapter 6, I provided a plethora of views regarding what Arafat truly wanted, ranging from those who were certain that Arafat wanted peace

[39] Interview with Shlomo Ben-Ami (26 June 2013), 10.

[40] Ben-Ami, *Scars of War*, 277.

[41] Shimon Peres and Robert Littell, *For the Future of Israel* (Baltimore, MD: Johns Hopkins University Press, 1998), 109.

[42] Dennis Ross and Gidi Grinstein, with a reply by Hussein Agha and Robert Malley, 'Camp David: An Exchange', *New York Review of Books* (20 September 2001), https://tinyurl.com/2du8uy53. At the same time, Ross writes that he is not 'one who believes that Chairman Arafat is against peace in principle'.

[43] Dennis Ross, *Missing Peace: The Inside Story of the Fight for Middle East Peace* (New York: Farrar, Straus and Giroux, 2004), 758. See also Gilead Sher, *The Israeli-Palestinian Peace Negotiations, 1999–2001: Within Reach* (London: Routledge, 2006).

to those who were certain that he did not. In Chapter 8, I discussed at some length Arafat's attitude to violence and terror. I never met Arafat. I am inclined to think that he lacked the ability to think analytically and allowed circumstances to control him rather than controlling them. His worldview was shaped by dreams, myths, truths, half-truths and lies. Consequently, I think those who argue that Arafat never wholeheartedly wanted peace are correct. He did not want the peace that Israelis had in mind: full commitment to reconciliation and total rejection of violence. People who speak about peace have France and Germany, Sweden and Denmark in mind. This was not Arafat's vision. He played games in his mind and with others. When Israel told Arafat that Marwan Barghouti was involved in terror activities, Arafat asked Sa'eb Erekat: 'Who is this man, Barghouti?'[44]

I believe Arafat was willing to accept coexistence with Israel – at least for a limited time. His ultimate goal was a sovereign Palestinian state with Jerusalem as its capital and the Haram under Palestinian control. To achieve these core aims, he was prepared to make significant concessions. The most notable of these was a willingness to forgo the Palestinian right of return, which he recognised as unrealistic. Arafat also understood the inherent vulnerabilities of a future Palestinian state, squeezed geographically between Israel and Jordan and divided between the West Bank and Gaza. Its greatest assets would be Jerusalem and the Haram, sites of immense international and Muslim significance. Securing them would firmly place Palestine on the global stage.

I think Arafat might have accepted a compromise on the Haram's status – agreeing that it would not be under full Palestinian sovereignty but governed under a legal framework acceptable to both Palestinians and Israelis. However, the collapse of the Camp David Summit, followed by the eruption of the bloody Intifada, sidelined Arafat as a viable partner for peace.

Despite decades of violence and terror, the occupation persists, and few Palestinians have embraced non-violent resistance. One of those who has is Dr Mubarak Awad, founder of the Palestinian Centre for the Study of Nonviolence in Jerusalem. Awad advocated for Israeli soldiers to refuse service in the Occupied Palestinian Territory – a threat Israel could not ignore, leading to his deportation to the United States in 1988. There, he established Nonviolence International, dedicated to promoting peace education and non-violent strategies for resolving political

[44] Interview with Avi Gil (16 January 2025), 22.

and social conflicts.[45] Following Mahatma Gandhi, Awad sought to resolve conflict and overcome it with love and uncompromising adherence to truth. Like Gandhi, Awad preached that resistance via non-violent methods is the most effective way to resist occupation. Sadly, he failed to persuade the Palestinian leaders and the public to follow in Gandhi's footsteps.

Arafat's abilities manifested in destroying rather than building, creating obstacles to peace rather than removing them. When the 2000 Intifada broke out, Arafat rode the tiger. He encouraged the Second Intifada as another instrument to pressure Israel and harvest political gains.[46] Throughout the 2000–2001 negotiations, the Israelis, for their part, belittled the seriousness of the Palestinians' demands.[47] Mutual distrust brought about a very troubled reality, leaving much to be desired for both Israelis and Palestinians. Arafat gained world recognition as the sole representative of the Palestinian people, but he wasted opportunities to lead his people to freedom and statehood.

New Leadership

In November 2004, President Mahmoud Abbas pledged to his predecessor, and to all listeners, that he was committed to the right of return and to the establishment of an independent Palestinian state with Jerusalem as its capital.[48]

On 9 January 2005, a new era began in Palestinian politics. Abbas was elected chairman of the Palestinian National Authority (PNA), with 62 per cent of the vote,[49] on a platform of non-violence and ending the conflict through direct negotiations with Israel. It was a landslide victory, reflecting the support of Palestinians who trusted Abbas to continue with the peace talks with Israel. He was elected to serve four years, yet he

[45] Mubarak Awad, Nonviolence International, www.nonviolenceinternational.net/mubarak_awad; 'Mubarak Awad on Nonviolence', *Peace Magazine*, 31(1) (January–March 2015); Mubarak E. Awad, 'Non-Violent Resistance: A Strategy for the Occupied Territories', *Journal of Palestine Studies*, 13(4) (Summer 1984): 22–36.

[46] Interview with Maher El-Kurd (30 January 2025), 35; Matti Steinberg, *In Search of Modern Palestinian Nationhood* (Tel Aviv: Moshe Dayan Center, 2016), 121–134.

[47] Hussein Agha and Robert Malley, 'A Solution Is Possible Now', *The Guardian* (29 March 2002).

[48] Dore Gold and David Keyes, 'What if Bush Invited Sharon and Abu Mazen to Camp David?', *Jerusalem Viewpoints*, 526 (January 2005), https://tinyurl.com/pn4ppz4t. President Abbas is also known by the name Abu Mazen.

[49] Salam Fayyad's comments on a draft of the book (17 July 2025).

remained in office for many more. Even before the 2005 election results were made public, Ariel Sharon called Abbas to congratulate him.[50] Sharon was very happy to see Abbas in office instead of his bitter rival Arafat. Abbas, at least publicly, always expressed his aversion to violence. Hamas and Islamic Jihad, however, have no intention of ceasing their terror, and Abbas has been incapable, or unwilling, to disarm them.

In February 2005, Abbas and Sharon held talks in Egypt. The two leaders agreed to a truce: ceasing all acts of violence against Israelis and Palestinians everywhere. Sharon also decided to pull back Israeli troops from Jericho, Bethlehem, Ramallah, Tulkarm and Qalqilya over the following three weeks, and to stop the arrests and assassinations of Palestinians if they agreed to cease violent activity.[51]

On 21 November 2005, Sharon reached a breaking point with the internal strife plaguing the Likud party. He felt that senior Likud members wished to undermine him, his ability to govern and the plans he had in mind for Israeli society. Many Likud parliamentarians opposed the disengagement plan from Gaza. Confident in his ability to lead beyond Likud's confines, Sharon announced his departure from the party he had helped build. He took with him several key allies and established Kadima – Hebrew for 'Forward' – a new centrist party aimed at reshaping Israel's political landscape. The move drew broad support, attracting prominent figures such as Shimon Peres and Haim Ramon, the former head of the Histadrut (Israel's General Federation of Labour), signalling a realignment in Israeli politics with Sharon at its helm.

At the end of 2005, the al Aqsa Intifada continued to linger and exact lives. Hiba Husseini explains that the general mood among Palestinians, a mood that has been fostered over and over, is that Israel understands the language of violence, but not the language of peace. 'And we the Palestinians, are hurting, so we want to hurt the Israelis. We have pain, the Israelis should have pain. So, this is the revenge quid pro quo that was ongoing all the time. Sad. But these are the elements that were working along those lines.'[52] As Husseini describes the psychology of the conflict, the Palestinians do not accept the occupation. They do not accept what the Israelis are doing to the Palestinians. They want to separate from Israel, but Israel does not let them live in peace, nor has Israel returned their land

[50] Charles Enderlin, *The Lost Years* (New York: Other Press, 2007), 253.

[51] Steven Erlanger, 'Urging New Path, Sharon and Abbas Declare Truce', *New York Times* (8 February 2005).

[52] Interview with Hiba Husseini (24 December 2024), 9.

to them. So, the Palestinians resist.[53] During the period 2000–2005, the Intifada claimed 1,064 Israeli victims, of whom 745 (70 per cent) were civilians; another 7,462 Israelis were wounded, of whom 5,212 (70 per cent) were civilians. On the Palestinian side, 3,729 Palestinians were killed and nearly 25,000 wounded; less than one-third of them were actively involved in violence.[54] Oslo seemed to leave a very limited legacy of peace.

On 4 January 2006, Sharon suffered a severe cerebral haemorrhage and fell into a state of prolonged unawareness.[55] Condoleezza Rice said that Sharon intended to do more than the Gaza disengagement. 'I had a conversation with Sharon on his farm that he wanted to keep going after Gaza', she said.[56] Ehud Olmert confirmed that Sharon had further West Bank withdrawals in mind: 'There's no question.'[57]

A day after his stroke, Sharon was replaced by his deputy, Olmert. Olmert had in mind even grander plans to resolve the Israeli-Palestinian conflict, which included the West Bank in addition to Gaza. He had pushed in that direction as Sharon's deputy, but Sharon opted for an incremental process as he felt that rushing the process was unwise. Now, Olmert could implement his own agenda. At the Herzliya conference later that month, Olmert stated his plans. He said that demography is important, and that to maintain a Jewish majority, Israel must relinquish its control over the West Bank and the Gaza Strip. If Israel wishes to maintain itself as a Jewish democracy, it must make difficult choices. The two-state solution, one Jewish and another Palestinian, and resolving the refugee issue by absorbing them fully in a Palestinian state are a necessity. Olmert declared: 'We are interested in neighborly relations which are good, productive, and progressive. We support the establishment of a modern, democratic Palestinian state which respects civil rights, and is economically prosperous. Their welfare is our welfare, their well-being is our well-being, their stability is our stability.'[58] Olmert reiterated the same views in my conversations with him.

While Israel was heading towards moderation, the Palestinians opted for violence. On 25 January 2006, elections were held for the Palestinian

[53] Ibid., 10.
[54] Ben-Eliezer, *Old Conflict, New War*, 213.
[55] For discussion of this condition, see Raphael Cohen-Almagor, 'Some Observations on Post-Coma Unawareness Patients and on Other Forms of Unconscious Patients: Policy Proposals', *Medicine and Law*, 16(3) (1997): 451–471.
[56] Ben Birnbaum, 'The End of the Two-State Solution: Why the Window Is Closing on Middle-East Peace', *The New Republic* (11 March 2013), https://tinyurl.com/ycyuwhdw.
[57] Interview with Ehud Olmert (22 February 2019), 26.
[58] Vice Prime Minister Ehud Olmert's Speech at the Herzliya Conference 24 January 2006, www.imra.org.il/story.php?id=28275.

Legislative Council (PLC), the legislature of the PNA. This was the first election to the PLC since 1996. Knowing the American aspirations for democratisation everywhere, Abbas said what was expected of him: that if Hamas were prohibited from participating, he would not conduct the elections.[59] Olmert said that Bush emphasised the importance of Hamas's participation in the elections.[60] Hasan Asfour argues that Abbas conceded to Hamas's participation under American pressure. The Americans also instructed him not to present Hamas with any preconditions for participation.[61] According to Asfour, Abbas wanted to cancel the elections but was forced to hold them and to include Hamas. Asfour opines that the Americans and the Israelis wanted to weaken the PA. Therefore, they let the Palestinians experience democracy in action. The final results showed that Hamas's political party, the Change and Reform List, had won with seventy-four seats. As Fatah won only forty-five seats, Hamas had the majority of the 132 seats and could form a government on its own.[62] The Bush administration, which had pushed for the elections, had relied on erroneous sources and estimates. This was not the result it had expected. Hosni Mubarak criticised the Americans for their miscalculation and for the risks they took in their quest for democratisation, saying, 'what kind of democracy did he [Bush] get in Gaza? And what kind of democracy will we have in Egypt, if he will continue to defend the rights of the Muslim Brotherhood?'[63] The Americans were so detached from reality that they had not prepared for Hamas's victory. Such a victory was unthinkable for them.[64]

I think it was a mistake to allow Hamas to participate in the elections before it accepted the Oslo principles. Israel has limitations on freedom of election. Not every party is allowed to run, and some parties are disqualified if they oppose the credo of Israel as a Jewish democracy.[65] Similarly,

[59] Interview with Ehud Olmert (24 April 2019), 3.

[60] Ibid.

[61] Interview with Hasan Asfour (18 February 2025), 13. Asfour said: 'What is the meaning of that? Why was Hamas allowed to compete? Why were no preconditions presented for standing for elections?'

[62] Bjorn Brenner, *Gaza under Hamas* (London: I.B. Tauris, 2022), 35; Mapping Palestinian Politics, https://ecfr.eu/special/mapping_palestinian_politics/legislative-elections-2006/; Scott Wilson, 'Hamas Sweeps Palestinian Elections, Complicating Peace Efforts in Mideast', *Washington Post* (27 January 2006), https://tinyurl.com/4atd7uuj.

[63] Interview with Ehud Olmert (24 April 2019), 4.

[64] Elliott Abrams, *Tested by Zion: The Bush Administration and the Israeli–Palestinian Conflict* (New York: Cambridge University Press, 2013), 163.

[65] Raphael Cohen-Almagor, 'Disqualification of Political Parties in Israel: 1988–1996', *Emory International Law Review*, 11(1) (1997): 67–109; Raphael Cohen-Almagor, 'Disqualification

Palestine should introduce some qualifications to its elections law to ensure that terrorist bodies that are opposed to the peace process are not allowed to participate in elections. Hamas wants to destroy the peace process. It should have been treated not as a legitimate political actor but as a rogue terrorist organisation. The attack on 7 October 2023 showed Israel and the world how ruthless its leaders are. Israel cannot permit a Hamas-run state to border its territory. The attack of 7 October is a painful lesson that should never be forgotten.

Olmert led an interim government until 28 March 2006, when elections for the 17th Knesset were held and he was elected prime minister of Israel. He formed a government with Labour, Shas and the Gil parties. The Yisrael Beiteinu party joined the government later. Olmert declared his intention to exhaust all possibilities to resolve the Israeli-Palestinian conflict, and that he intended to work closely with Abbas.[66] Soon, however, his peace plans were shelved, as they were replaced by war plans. I will discuss the Hezbollah–Israel War, also known as the Second Lebanon War or the 2006 Lebanon War, in Chapter 10.

On 8 February 2007, Hamas and Fatah agreed to share power. On 17 March 2007, a new Fatah–Hamas unity government was formed under the leadership of Hamas's Ismail Haniyeh. However, tensions between Fatah and the Islamist Hamas were simmering, and on 9 June 2007, Hamas seized control of Gaza, routing Fatah forces and killing more than 100 people. Hamas, in collaboration with the Muslim Brotherhood movement in Jordan, Egypt and other parts of the Middle East, and with the support of Iran, Qatar, Syria, Lebanon, Yemen, Libya, Sudan and other countries, gained absolute control of the Gaza Strip. Gaza became the central hub of terror attacks on Israel. Hamas, the PLO and Israel have since been engaged in a continued power struggle, derailing the peace process.

On 14 June 2007, Haniyeh was dismissed by President Abbas, who appointed Salam Fayyad as prime minister. Fayyad, considered a moderate who could contribute positively to the peace process, was not directly involved in negotiations with Israel.[67] Abbas assumed this responsibility, taking full control of negotiations. While Hamas intensified its rocket attacks on Israel, Abbas was ready to continue negotiating with Olmert, who was focused on resolving the conflict. Negotiations between Abbas

of Lists in Israel (1948–1984): Retrospect and Appraisal', *Law and Philosophy*, 13(1) (1994): 43–95.

[66] Enderlin, *The Lost Years*, 273.

[67] Interview with Salam Fayyad (19 January 2024), 2.

and Olmert began in December 2006 and continued until September 2008. They will be the focus of Chapter 10.

The Annapolis Conference

The idea of an international conference was raised by Condoleezza Rice in May 2006, during Olmert's first visit to Washington as prime minister. The Americans proposed an international umbrella to help promote negotiations between Abbas and Olmert. Olmert agreed in principle to Rice's idea, provided that the forum would supplement and support the bilateral process he wanted to pursue with Abbas (see Figure 9.3). Olmert thought: 'Why not? I don't care. It is a good platform for an international event that will portray Israel as a peace pusher.'[68] The Israel–Hezbollah War delayed the process until November 2007.

The Israeli delegation submitted a new demand: recognition of Israel as a Jewish state. Whether this was necessary or productive is doubtful.

Figure 9.3 Olmert, Bush and Abbas.
Credit: Chip Somodevilla/Staff/Getty Images.

[68] Raphael Cohen-Almagor, 'Lessons from Peace Negotiations: Interview with Ehud Olmert', *Israel Affairs*, 27(6) (2021): 1177.

Arafat had explicitly recognised Israel as a Jewish state.[69] Quoting Arafat, Agha said that the Palestinians 'accepted that openly and officially in 1988 at our Palestine National Council' and remained completely committed to it. Thus, the refugee problem needed to be solved in a way that would not change the Jewish character of the state. That was 'clear and obvious'.[70] Agha maintained that in Palestinian political literature, Israel has always been referred to as *aldawla alyahudiyya* (the Jewish state) or *aldawla ali'briyya* (the Hebrew state). The definition of Israel became an ideological issue only when it became a demand of the Israeli team in the Annapolis process.[71]

In November 2007, the Palestinian drafting team issued a memorandum on the issue of recognising Israel as a Jewish state, which said: 'Recognizing Israel as a "Jewish State" would be an explicit recognition of Israel's demographic objections to the right of return. This would make it legally and practically harder to insist on recognition in principle for the right of return and negotiating the implementation of that right with Israel'.[72] Furthermore, such recognition would legitimise systematic discrimination of Israeli Palestinians. The Palestinians argued that such a characterisation is an internal issue, and that no such provision was included in the peace treaties that Israel signed with Egypt and Jordan. They maintained that within Israel, the Palestinians reject it, while Orthodox and secular Jews have different interpretations of the term 'Jewish state'. Therefore, the memorandum concluded that Israel should not be recognised as a Jewish state.[73]

I concur with the argument that the characterisation of Israel as a Jewish state is fundamentally a matter of internal governance and national identity, rather than a prerequisite for international recognition or peace agreements. This is evidenced by the fact that neither the 1979 Egypt–Israel Peace Treaty nor the 1994 Israel–Jordan Peace Treaty included any requirement for recognition of Israel as a 'Jewish state'. Both Egypt and Jordan recognised Israel's right to exist as a sovereign state, without prescribing its internal character.

69 Yasser Arafat: The PNC Recognises Israel as a Jewish State, www.youtube.com/watch?v=eZkx8zQ5H9g.

70 Hussein Agha, 'Oslo25 | "We Must Liberate Our Thinking from the Oslo Straitjacket": An Interview with Hussein Agha', *Fathom* (August 2018).

71 Ibid.

72 Palestinian drafting team, Memorandum RE: The Precondition of Recognizing Israel as a 'Jewish State' (13 November 2007).

73 Ibid.

Palestinian recognition of Israel as a Jewish state should not be conflated with the endorsement of any form of discrimination against Arab citizens of Israel, as the Palestinians argued. Indeed, many states that define themselves in religious or national terms – such as the United Kingdom, which has an established Church – continue to uphold minority rights within democratic frameworks. Recognition of Israel's Jewish character, therefore, need not imply an erosion of civil or political rights for non-Jewish citizens.

Linking Israel's identity as the world's only Jewish state with the Palestinian demand for a 'right of return' is problematic and politically untenable. Historical parallels make this evident. It is inconceivable that countries such as Poland or Iraq would allow the mass return of Jewish populations who fled or were expelled in the twentieth century, along with their descendants. While discussions about compensation and historical justice are legitimate, the prospect of a wholesale return to former homes, now inhabited by others, is widely regarded as incompatible with contemporary political and demographic realities. No modern state is expected to accept an influx of individuals that could fundamentally alter its national identity or demographic balance. Israel is no exception. The mass return of Palestinian refugees and their descendants would not merely redress a historical grievance; it would radically transform the character of Israel, undermining its foundational ethos as a Jewish and democratic state. The continued insistence by Palestinian leadership on the right of return is therefore not simply a humanitarian or legal demand. It is perceived by many Israelis as a denial of Israel's right to exist in its current form. The specific number of returnees, in this context, is less important than the principle itself, which appears to reject the legitimacy of Israel as a Jewish Zionist state. So long as this fundamental rejection persists, Israeli leaders will remain sceptical of Palestinian intentions and commitment to a negotiated two-state solution.

On 27–28 November 2007, the Bush administration hosted a grand peace conference at the Naval Academy in Annapolis. In addition to representatives from the United States, Israel and the PLO, there were also representatives of the Quartet,[74] the United Nations, the World Bank, the International Monetary Fund (IMF), the Arab League and some forty countries (see Figure 9.4). It was a celebratory occasion. In his speech, Olmert said that negotiations would be based on previous agreements

[74] The Middle East Quartet mediators include the United Nations, European Union, United States and Russia.

Figure 9.4 Annapolis.
Credit: Saul Loeb/Stringer/Getty Images.

between Israel and the Palestinians, UN Security Council Resolutions 242 and 338, and the Bush administration Roadmap. Olmert did the right thing, voicing empathy for the Palestinians' anguish and recognising Palestinian suffering, which still lingers. He said:

> I know that this pain and deprivation is one of the deepest foundations that fomented the ethos of hatred towards us.
>
> We are not indifferent to this suffering. We are not oblivious to the tragedies you have experienced. I believe that in the course of negotiations between us, we will find the right way, as part of an international effort in which we will participate, to assist these Palestinians in finding a proper framework for their future, in the Palestinian state which will be established in the territories agreed upon between us. Israel will be part of an international mechanism which will assist in finding a solution to this problem.[75]

At the same time, priority was given to establishing security. The Israeli and Palestinian security services were instructed to work together. The Roadmap directed that the Palestinians should take immediate steps to ensure security, and that the PA would have a monopoly on weapons. The

[75] Ehud Olmert's Address at the Annapolis Peace Conference (27 November 2007), *Jewish Virtual Library*, https://tinyurl.com/yxaht42u.

PA would confiscate illegal weapons and consolidate its security authority, which would be 'free of association with terror and corruption'.[76] Israel would cease its anti-Palestinian actions, including deportations, attacks on civilians, confiscation of property, demolition of Palestinian homes and property, and the destruction of Palestinian institutions and infrastructure. Israel would also lift curfews and ease restrictions on the movement of goods and people.[77]

The Roadmap involved other stakeholders in ensuring security. The Quartet would establish formal monitoring mechanisms, ensuring that both parties act constructively, per the Roadmap. Arab states were instructed to cease support for terror groups, and donor states were instructed to deliver financial support only through the Palestinian Ministry of Finance's Single Treasury Account.[78] As the PA consolidated its position, the Israeli army would withdraw from the West Bank, and the Israeli government would take appropriate measures aimed at improving the humanitarian situation in Palestinian areas, dismantling settlement outposts established after March 2001 and freezing all settlement activity ('including natural growth of settlements').[79]

Concurrently, the Roadmap stipulated that the Palestinians would engage in institution-building processes. They would draft their constitution, 'based on strong parliamentary democracy and cabinet with the empowered prime minister, for public comment/debate' and on 'genuine separation of powers'.[80] An interim prime minister or cabinet 'with empowered executive authority/decision-making body' would be installed.[81] An independent Palestinian election commission would be established, and elections would be held for Palestinian institutions.

Phase II of the Roadmap aimed at establishing an independent and democratic Palestinian state based on tolerance and liberty, with provisional borders and 'attributes of sovereignty'. A new constitution would facilitate and lead to a permanent status settlement. Civil institutions would be reformed and enjoy the support of the Quartet and the

76 A Performance-Based Roadmap to a Permanent Two-State Solution to the Israeli-Palestinian Conflict (30 April 2003).

77 Ibid.; 'Framework for Mideast Peace Talks Set at Conference', *New York Times* (27 November 2007).

78 A Performance-Based Roadmap to a Permanent Two-State Solution to the Israeli-Palestinian Conflict (30 April 2003).

79 Ibid.

80 Ibid.

81 Ibid.

international community. Phase II would begin after the Palestinian elections and would end with the creation of a Palestinian state with provisional borders in 2003.[82]

Phase III of the Roadmap aimed at further consolidation of Palestinian reform and the stabilisation of institutions, 'sustained, effective Palestinian security performance, and Israeli-Palestinian negotiations aimed at a permanent status agreement in 2005'.[83] The process would be supported by convening international conferences. Efforts would be made to reach a comprehensive Arab-Israeli peace, in which Arab states would accept Israel as a member of the region and establish full normal relations with it. All states of the region would ensure security for all.

These were high tolls to pay. Bush's Roadmap for Peace suffered from a fundamental structural weakness: the absence of robust and enforceable monitoring mechanisms. While the document outlined a phased approach to resolving the Israeli-Palestinian conflict and stipulated reciprocal obligations for both parties, it failed to establish an independent body with the authority to verify compliance or enforce accountability. Although the Roadmap nominally assigned the Quartet (the United States, the European Union, the United Nations and Russia) a consultative role in the creation of a formal monitoring mechanism, this provision was never meaningfully implemented. In practice, the Quartet was sidelined, largely due to the United States' reluctance to empower it with real oversight capabilities. Washington preferred to retain unilateral control over the peace process and resisted ceding authority to a multilateral framework that might constrain its diplomatic flexibility or subject Israeli and Palestinian actions to international scrutiny.

As a result, violations of the Roadmap's provisions – by both sides – went unpunished and, in many cases, unaddressed. There was no impartial adjudicative body to assess breaches or impose corrective measures, nor was there a credible enforcement mechanism to deter non-compliance. The lack of accountability severely undermined the credibility of the process and allowed the parties to interpret and apply the Roadmap selectively, contributing to the eventual stagnation and erosion of the plan.

The Annapolis talks covered the core issues, intending to end all grievances between the parties. Israel and the PA reached a joint understanding in which they agreed to engage in negotiations, with a view to concluding a peace treaty by the end of 2008. The parties agreed to develop a joint

[82] Ibid.
[83] Ibid.

work plan and address all issues. It was agreed that Abbas and Olmert would negotiate directly, and that a steering committee would be established to oversee the work of expert teams to discuss the environment, water, the economy and many more issues. Tzipi Livni and Ahmed Qurie agreed that the formation of expert committees to study each issue separately was the best way to move forward.[84] The committees would be headed by Israeli and Palestinian lead representatives,[85] Udi Dekel and Sa'eb Erakat, respectively.

After the festivities of the international conference, three routes of negotiations between Israel and the Palestinians were established. The idea was to strive for a final solution status while upholding the Roadmap. Every step was conditioned on progress in implementing the Roadmap. Concurrent with direct negotiations between Abbas and Olmert, there were negotiations between Livni and Qurie, and between Israeli and Palestinian teams headed by Dekel and Erekat. This rather complex structure of negotiations was the result of political constraints. Both Abbas and Olmert were forced to acknowledge domestic politics.

Abbas appointed Qurie to head the Palestinian peace team. Initially, Olmert was unhappy; he wanted control over the negotiations, and he wanted to conduct them with the Palestinian leader. Abbas explained his political constraints, saying: 'I need him because of political reasons. He is very strong politically and I need him on my side.'[86] Olmert still had reservations and thought that Qurie and his own party colleague and political rival, Livni, would only delay the negotiations. In Olmert's view, Qurie was committed to the process while he, Olmert, wanted peace, not process. Olmert thought Livni and Qurie would haggle endlessly over insignificant issues. He wanted concrete results and believed that these could be achieved only by direct talks between him and Abbas. Then, Olmert and his advisors devised a solution: Livni and Qurie were given the titles of chief negotiators, but the true negotiations would take place elsewhere. Olmert explained: 'Okay. So let us send Tzipi to sit with him because they fit each other. She likes to negotiate every small item which is unimportant, unnecessary and he can do it. Let them do it.'[87] Livni, elated to

[84] Meeting between Ahmed Qurie, Sa'eb Erekat, Salah Ilayan, Tzipi Livni, Tal Becker and Alon Bar. Minutes, Jerusalem (27 January 2008).

[85] George J. Mitchell and Alon Sachar, *A Path to Peace* (New York: Simon and Schuster, 2016), 102; Abrams, *Tested by Zion*, 256.

[86] Cohen-Almagor, 'Lessons from Peace Negotiations: Interview with Ehud Olmert', 1177–1178.

[87] Ibid., 1178.

receive the nomination, was unaware that the serious negotiations would be between Olmert and Abbas.[88] Olmert said dismissively that Livni and Qurie were appointed to deal with *narishkeit* [Yiddish: foolishness, trivialities].[89]

In Chapter 10, I discuss the peace process that followed the Annapolis Conference. It was very elaborate in its composition but still relied heavily on the two leaders, Olmert and Abbas. Olmert was the engine behind the talks. He was willing to put his political capital at stake and make substantial concessions. I question whether the formula of direct negotiations between the two leaders was the right one to achieve what Olmert yearned for: peace between Israel and the PA.

[88] Interview with Ehud Olmert (22 February 2019); Drucker, 'Olmert, Abu Mazen and Barak Refer to the Political Process'.

[89] Interview with Ehud Olmert (22 February 2019), 28.

10

Peace within Reach

Swerve from evil and do good, seek peace and pursue it.

~Psalms 34

Despite Prime Minister Ehud Olmert's demonstrable willingness to reach a comprehensive peace agreement – evidenced by his offer of far-reaching and, by many accounts, unprecedented concessions – he ultimately failed to secure Palestinian Authority (PA) President Mahmoud Abbas's assent to a final deal. This outcome reflects not a singular misstep, but a confluence of structural, political and contextual factors that collectively undermined the prospects for success.

This analysis explores the multiple reasons behind the collapse of the 2008 negotiations. These include the suboptimal structure of the talks, characterised by the absence of binding frameworks and enforceable timelines; deep-seated internal political rivalries within both the Israeli and Palestinian leaderships; and the ongoing expansion of Israeli settlements, which continued to erode Palestinian confidence in the peace process. Olmert's decision to engage in two military campaigns during his tenure, against Hezbollah in Lebanon (2006) and Hamas in Gaza (2008–2009), further complicated his credibility as a peace partner. Moreover, his declining political legitimacy, exacerbated by multiple corruption investigations, severely weakened his authority both at home and abroad. On the Palestinian side, long-standing doubts about Israel's willingness, or ability, to follow through on long-term commitments fostered a deep mistrust that hindered Abbas's capacity to make politically costly compromises. While Olmert may have entered the negotiations with genuine intent, the interplay of internal and external pressures, institutional dysfunction and mutual mistrust ultimately rendered the process untenable.

The Dekel–Erekat Expert Teams

Olmert explained the Dekel–Erekat track by saying that, while this steering committee was very important, it was not a committee that was supposed to make peace. The committee was designed to complement all the other elements of the negotiation process. Once a peace treaty was formulated and an agreement reached on the most essential issues – Jerusalem, the Holy Places, refugees, borders and settlements – *then* there would be a need to tackle all the other aspects that the Dekel–Erekat committee addressed. Olmert contended that the committee was 'on the framework, on the periphery. The heart of the negotiations was conducted by two guys only. Abu Mazen and myself. If anyone tells you anything else, he is not telling the truth. And you ask Abu Mazen – he will verify what I say.'[1]

Udi Dekel and Sa'eb Erekat headed twelve expert professional committees that discussed different aspects of the peace agreement. There were 300 meetings about procedures. A format was established for the permanent status arrangement. Periods for negotiation and implementation were set. An infrastructure for the meetings was established from the bottom up.[2] The meetings were secret and quiet, away from the media and the public eye. Dekel and Erekat identified nineteen themes that a comprehensive peace accord should include: a preamble, general provisions, borders, settlements, security issues, refugees, Jerusalem, water, safe passage arrangements between Gaza and the West Bank, environment, economic relations, state-to-state and infrastructure arrangements, legal relations, people-to-people issues, implementation of the agreement, coordination and conflict resolution, finality of claims, prisoners and final clauses.[3] As always, the top priority was to ensure Israel's security.[4] Dekel did not have permission to discuss Jerusalem.[5] Samih Al-Abed, the PA's map expert, told Dekel that he could not progress in the talks without Jerusalem on the table, but the issue of Jerusalem and the adjacent settlements, such as Ma'ale Adumim, was reserved for Olmert and Abbas.[6]

1 Interview with Ehud Olmert (22 February 2019), 29.
2 Interview with Udi Dekel (17 June 2014), 5.
3 George J. Mitchell and Alon Sachar, *A Path to Peace* (New York: Simon and Schuster, 2016), 104.
4 E.g., Minutes from Security Session, 28 February 2008; Summary Minutes from Security Meeting, 6 May 2008; Minutes of Security Meeting, 2 July 2008, in Clayton E. Swisher, *The Palestine Papers* (Chatham: Hesperus, 2011), 121–132, 151–159, 187–193.
5 Minutes of Security Meeting, 2 July 2008; Gregg Carlstrom, 'The Biggest Yerushalayim', *Al Jazeera* (23 January 2011), www.aljazeera.com/news/2011/1/23/the-biggest-yerushalayim.
6 'A Glimpse into the Negotiation Room', *Al Jazeera* (26 January 2011), www.aljazeera.com/news/2011/1/26/a-glimpse-into-the-negotiation-room; Clayton Swisher, 'Erekat's Solution for the Haram', *Al Jazeera* (22 January 2011), www.aljazeera.com/news/2011/1/22/erekats-solution-for-the-haram.

Olmert said – prior to Annapolis *and* in Annapolis – that 'we are ready to accept the Arab Peace Initiative as the framework for negotiations with the Palestinians on the issues involved',[7] as well as the Roadmap. The expert professional committees sought to implement the Bush Roadmap of 30 April 2003, aiming to get a final status agreement. The Roadmap stipulated that the Palestinian leadership would issue an unequivocal statement 'reiterating Israel's right to exist in peace and security and calling for an immediate and unconditional ceasefire to end armed activity and all acts of violence against Israelis anywhere. All official Palestinian institutions end incitement against Israel.'[8] On its part, Israel's leadership would issue an 'unequivocal statement affirming its commitments to the two-state vision of an independent, viable, sovereign Palestinian state living in peace and security alongside Israel' and 'calling for an immediate end to violence against Palestinians everywhere. All official Israeli institutions end incitement against Palestinians.'[9] Dekel said that Israel offered the Palestinians a final arrangement package and asked the Palestinians to present one of their own. The Palestinians did not agree to the Israeli package. Both sides thought that the other side should do more, and although the Israelis later improved the deal that was put on the table, the Palestinians never agreed to any final status arrangement. They always felt that the Israeli offers were insufficient, thinking that they themselves had already made enough concessions. Erekat considered the Palestinian demands reasonable and their concessions significant: 'Israelis want the two-state solution but they don't trust [us]. They want it more than you think, sometimes more than Palestinians. What is in that paper gives them the biggest Yerushalayim in Jewish history, symbolic number of refugees return, demilitarised state … what more can I give?'[10] Dekel, however, contended that 'Israel exposed its soft spots and received nothing'.[11] Major issues remained unresolved, waiting for both leaders to address them.

Livni–Qurie Negotiations

Olmert's chief negotiator was also his chief political rival, Tzipi Livni. When I interviewed each of them, they did not hide their mutual dislike.

7 Interview with Ehud Olmert (22 February 2019), 19.

8 A Performance-Based Roadmap to a Permanent Two-State Solution to the Israeli-Palestinian Conflict (30 April 2003).

9 Ibid.

10 Carlstrom, 'The Biggest Yerushalayim'; Swisher, 'Erekat's Solution for the Haram'.

11 Interview with Udi Dekel (17 June 2014), 5.

Figure 10.1 Livni, Qurie and Rice.
Credit: Bloomberg/Contributor/Getty Images.

Their animosity reminded me of the Yitzhak Rabin–Shimon Peres relationship. Politics makes strange bedfellows. At times, politics brings together very different people who are forced to work together as a result of the political power they have garnered. The Livni–Qurie negotiations included extensive meetings during which the parties systematically negotiated various issues without reaching a breakthrough, exactly as Olmert envisaged. After nearly a year of negotiations, Livni and Ahmed Qurie had made little progress (see Figure 10.1). The parties agreed that Palestine would not have a military force, but they argued over terminology. Livni spoke of a demilitarised Palestine and Qurie spoke of it being 'limitedly militarized'.[12] Livni and Qurie did not agree on the timeline for Israel's withdrawal or on the number of weapons permitted for Palestine. The Palestinians wanted an international force to replace the Israel Defense Forces (IDF). Livni said that certain types of international presence might be accepted, but not an international force with military functions.[13]

12 Meeting between Ahmed Qurie, Sa'eb Erekat, Salah Ilayan, Tzipi Livni, Tal Becker and Alon Bar. Minutes, Jerusalem (27 January 2008). In Swisher, *The Palestine Papers*, 108–113.

13 'Current P/I Positions Reflecting Discussion up to November 1, 2008', www.jewishvirtuallibrary.org/jsource/arabs/PalPaper110208b.pdf.

In January 2008, Hamas breached a section of the border with Egypt near the Rafah crossing by detonating explosives. On 4 February 2008, Qurie and Livni met with their delegations. Qurie said that Hamas's conduct was a victory for the organisation and suggested that Israel reoccupy the Philadelphi Corridor, the eleven-kilometre-long border between Gaza and Egypt. As Israel has enclosed Gaza from all other directions, the Philadelphi Corridor was the lifeline for the Gaza Strip and for Hamas's activities, including terrorism. Qurie said: 'Hamas must not feel that it's achieving daily victories.'[14] Qurie wanted Israel's help in ousting Hamas and instating the PA in Gaza. Livni asked whether Hamas wanted to establish a state in Gaza, and Qurie answered in the affirmative. Hamas, Qurie said, wanted to apply Islamic Shari'a law and 'export their regime to neighboring countries'.[15] Erekat stated: 'I can't stand Hamas.'[16]

In May 2008, Livni and Qurie tried again to resolve the issue of security. Livni repeated the Israeli dictate that Palestine should be demilitarised. The Palestinians would not have an army or an air force, but they would have 'strong police' to maintain law and order. Erekat questioned whether the IDF would be present in Palestine. Livni responded: 'We don't see ourselves in the territory except for limited cases, like early warning stations and the Jordan Valley.'[17] Israel wanted to be present at the border. Erekat then asked: 'Can I choose where I secure external defence?' and Livni responded: 'No … in order to create your state you have to agree in advance with Israel – you choose not to have the right of choice afterwards. These are the basic pillars.'[18] This was not a negotiation between equals, and Israel enjoyed asserting its dominance.

Livni agreed to land swaps in principle; however, Livni and Qurie did not agree on the nature of those swaps, ratio, quality and location.[19] Qurie objected to the Israeli annexation of all the major settlement blocs. He agreed that Israel could annex some Jewish neighbourhoods in East Jerusalem and some parts of the Etzion bloc, south-west of Jerusalem. In a trilateral meeting with US Secretary of State Condoleezza Rice on 15 June 2008, Qurie said: 'We proposed that Israel annexes all settlements in Jerusalem except Jabal

14 Ali Abunimah, 'Cutting Off a Vital Connection', *Al Jazeera* (25 January 2011), www.aljazeera.com/news/2011/1/25/cutting-off-a-vital-connection.

15 Ibid.

16 Ibid.

17 Alastair Crooke, 'The Limits of Autonomy', *Al Jazeera* (25 January 2011), www.aljazeera.com/news/2011/1/25/the-limits-of-autonomy.

18 Ibid.

19 Mitchell and Sachar, *A Path to Peace*, 105.

Abu Ghneim (Har Homa). This is the first time in history that we make such a proposition; we refused to do so in Camp David.'[20] Qurie conceded part of the predominantly Arab East Jerusalem neighbourhood of Sheikh Jarrah in return for land swaps.[21] On 30 June 2008, in his meeting with Livni, Qurie insisted on discussing Jerusalem, saying: 'Jerusalem is part of the territory occupied in 67. We can discuss and agree on many issues relating to Jerusalem: religious places, infrastructure, municipal function, economic issues, security, and settlements. However, the municipal borders for us are 67. This is the basis, and this is where we can start.'[22] Livni refused. Erekat specified the settlements that the PA was willing to concede: French Hill, Ramat Alon, Ramat Shlomo, Gilo, Talpiot and the Jewish Quarter in Jerusalem's Old City. Those areas included some 120,000 settlers. Erekat did not mention other major East Jerusalem settlements, such as Pisgat Ze'ev and Neve Ya'akov, but, implicitly, the Palestinians conceded that these settlements would also remain part of Israel.[23] Qurie, however, refused to concede the Ma'ale Adumim and Giv'at Ze'ev settlements near Jerusalem, Efrat in Gush Etzion, and the Ariel and Kedumim settlements in the northern West Bank, because they divided the West Bank.[24] Qurie suggested that Ma'ale Adumim would remain under Palestinian sovereignty as proof that Israel and Palestine can coexist and cooperate. Livni dismissed the ideas as unrealistic.[25] Rice said that no Israeli leader would ever cede Ma'ale Adumim. Qurie replied that no Palestinian would agree to Israeli sovereignty over Ma'ale Adumim, and Rice concluded that without this concession, there would not be a Palestinian state.[26]

In their meeting of 8 April 2008, Qurie told Livni: 'In light of these circumstances and these unrealistic propositions, I see that the only solution is a bi-national state where Moslems, Christians, and Jews live together.'[27] The Palestinians need to consider the future of their diaspora and the

[20] Carlstrom, 'The Biggest Yerushalayim'; Ian Black and Seumas Milne, 'Israel Spurned Palestinian Offer of "Biggest Yerushalayim in History"', *The Guardian* (23 January 2011), https://tinyurl.com/577payvm.

[21] Black and Milne, 'Israel Spurned Palestinian Offer'.

[22] Swisher, 'Erekat's Solution for the Haram'.

[23] Carlstrom, 'The Biggest Yerushalayim'.

[24] Ibid.; Meeting between Ahmed Qurie, Sa'eb Erekat, Salah Ilayan, Tzipi Livni, Tal Becker and Alon Bar. Minutes, Jerusalem (27 January 2008); Juan Cole, 'Pressman: One Leaked Document on the Annapolis Process', *Informed Comment* (26 January 2011), https://tinyurl.com/2n66c5w3.

[25] Carlstrom, 'The Biggest Yerushalayim'.

[26] Ibid.

[27] Cole, 'Pressman: One Leaked Document'.

future of the Palestinians in the Occupied Territories. They must navigate between them. Therefore, from their point of view, the one-state solution would be acceptable and possible.[28] For Israel, however, the one-state solution is synonymous with the end of the Zionist project. Israel would cease to be the only Jewish state in the world. I cannot conceive of any government in Jerusalem agreeing to that.

Livni and Qurie barely discussed Jerusalem, recognising that this thorny and complicated issue should be the last on the agenda. Livni said that Olmert promised the ultra-Orthodox parties in the government that Jerusalem would not be addressed until the end of the negotiations.[29] Different representatives aired different figures and suggestions. Livni spoke about the annexation by Israel of 7.3 per cent of the West Bank, and that discussions on land swaps be postponed to a later stage.[30] She asked whether the Palestinians would hold a referendum concerning the agreement, and Qurie answered in the affirmative.[31] As for the refugees, Livni said that Israel would not agree to UN Resolution 194 and that no Israeli official would support the refugees' return to Israel. She said that many people in the world were ready to help resolve the issue.[32] Erekat said: 'The Palestinians need to know that 5 million refugees will not return.'[33] Qurie thought this issue could be resolved provided the Arabs were part of the solution. Qurie said they had engaged with countries that would host the refugees.[34] Jordan and Syria were mentioned as two countries that wished to do so.

Interestingly, when I asked Livni what the obstacles were in her negotiation with Qurie, she replied, 'time'. She explained that the negotiations stopped when Israel launched its military campaign against Hamas in Gaza, and then later, Benjamin Netanyahu was elected.[35] I asked whether

[28] Discussions with Palestinians 2024–2025.

[29] Interview with Tzipi Livni (22 June 2016), 9.

[30] Shaul Arieli, *A Border between Us and You* (Tel Aviv: Miskal Publishing – Yedioth Books, 2021), 243.

[31] Meeting between Ahmed Qurie, Sa'eb Erekat, Salah Ilayan, Tzipi Livni, Tal Becker and Alon Bar. Minutes, Jerusalem (27 January 2008).

[32] Amira Howeidy, 'PA Relinquished Right of Return', *Al Jazeera* (24 January 2011), www.aljazeera.com/news/2011/1/24/pa-relinquished-right-of-return; Gregg Carlstrom, 'Qurei to Livni: "I'd Vote for You"', *Al Jazeera* (24 January 2011), www.aljazeera.com/news/2011/1/24/qurei-to-livni-id-vote-for-you.

[33] 'The Palestine Papers, Day 2: Population "Swaps" and the Right of (No) Return', *Al Jazeera* (24 January 2011), https://tinyurl.com/4mmzhkzj.

[34] Meeting between Ahmed Qurie, Sa'eb Erekat, Salah Ilayan, Tzipi Livni, Tal Becker and Alon Bar. Minutes, Jerusalem (27 January 2008); Howeidy, 'PA Relinquished Right of Return'.

[35] Interview with Tzipi Livni (22 June 2016), 8.

the two parties agreed on the settlements. Livni replied that they did not decide which settlement blocs would be part of Israel.[36] She mentioned that the Palestinians conceded that Jews may reside in Palestine as Palestinian citizens and voiced concern that their presence might provoke violence, forcing Israel to intervene. No agreement was reached.[37] I asked about Palestinian refugees, and Livni said that some progress had been made in discussions about the international mechanism that would compensate the refugees, but that no agreement was reached.[38] I inquired as to whether the parties agreed to the unification of families and humanitarian provisions for the Palestinians. Livni replied that she did not discuss those issues. Olmert did.[39] Livni was unwilling to make any concessions regarding refugees. This was always an issue on which she was unwilling to compromise. Her principled viewpoint was strikingly different from Olmert's, and far more stubborn. One wonders how much time is needed to resolve all those issues. I suspect time was not the only, or even the major, factor. Livni's stubbornness was matched by Qurie's.

Abbas–Olmert Negotiations

Abbas and Olmert had thirty-six meetings.[40] This was quite an investment. The negotiations, initiated by Olmert, were one on one. At first, Abbas was hesitant. He cancelled the initial meetings, one by one, until Olmert persuaded him by appealing to the human factor. A meeting was scheduled at Olmert's home, and his wife, Aliza, had prepared a meal. When Abbas called to cancel at the last minute, Olmert told him: 'How do you, why do you do it? You want to insult me? You want to hurt me, okay, that I understand. But why do you have to insult my wife?'[41] That worked. Abbas arrived at Olmert's home, and the negotiations began. Olmert did not want anyone else in the room. He certainly did not want the Americans. He told me: 'We needed the Americans only when we did not want to negotiate. Then the Americans felt that they needed to intervene to force us into the process. But in *my* time, there was no such need, because I was absolutely committed to carry on from day one.'[42] With

36 Ibid., 9.
37 Ibid., 11.
38 Ibid., 9. See also Howeidy, 'PA Relinquished Right of Return'.
39 Interview with Tzipi Livni (22 June 2016), 9.
40 Interview with Ehud Olmert (24 April 2019), 4.
41 Interview with Ehud Olmert (22 February 2019), 27.
42 Ibid.

Figure 10.2 Abbas and Olmert.
Credit: Mandel Ngan/Staff/Getty Images.

time, mutual trust was built. Abbas and Olmert found each other to be serious and trustworthy negotiating partners (see Figure 10.2).

Abbas and Olmert reached important agreements on security. They agreed on a set of security parameters that included the demilitarisation of the prospective Palestinian state, the creation of a robust Palestinian police force capable of maintaining internal order and combating terrorism, and the strategic deployment of international forces in sensitive areas. Specifically, the proposed arrangements envisioned an international presence at critical junctures: border crossings, within Jerusalem, along key transportation corridors and at two Israeli early warning stations to be located within Palestinian territory. These measures were intended to address Israeli security concerns while respecting Palestinian sovereignty.

A notable divergence in Olmert's approach from that of his successor, Netanyahu, was his position on the Jordan Valley. Contrary to the prevailing consensus among many Israeli policymakers, who view the Jordan Valley as a vital strategic buffer, Olmert did not consider an ongoing Israeli military presence in the area essential for national security. Instead, he was open to entrusting security responsibilities in the Jordan Valley to NATO or a similarly capable international force, reflecting a more flexible and multilateral approach to security arrangements. This framework illustrated Olmert's readiness to depart from maximalist Israeli security doctrines in favour of pragmatic, internationally supported mechanisms.[43]

Rice agreed with King Abdullah of Jordan on a NATO international force stationed on the other side of Jordanian border that would block the passage of people from one side to the other.[44] With these forces and in cooperation with Palestinian security forces, Olmert was confident that Israel could deal effectively with challenges posed by spoilers wishing to undermine peace and normalisation between Israel and Palestine. In an interview in November 2012, Abbas said he agreed with Olmert on all security concerns.[45] They agreed that Palestine would not have a military. Abbas said, 'we don't want an air force or tanks or rockets'.[46] This was an important concession.

The refugee issues remained a stumbling block. Here, there were two issues: Israeli recognition that it bears responsibility for the Nakba, and that a certain number of refugees would be allowed to resettle in Israel. Concerning the first matter, Israel refused to either apologise for its conduct in the 1947 civil war and the 1948 war or to take responsibility for creating the refugee problem. Ehud Barak had wanted to evade these issues, and Olmert did not improve much on his offer. Olmert could not offer an apology because, according to him, 'what we call the creation of the State of

[43] Ibid., 38. Abbas and Olmert did not delve into the details of which countries would be represented in the international force.

[44] Interview with Ehud Olmert (24 April 2019), 7; Raphael Cohen-Almagor, 'Lessons from Peace Negotiations: Interview with Ehud Olmert', *Israel Affairs*, 27(6) (2021): 1186.

[45] Arieli, *A Border between Us and You*, 311–312.

[46] Ethan Bronner, 'Olmert Memoir Cites Near Deal for Mideast Peace', *New York Times* (27 January 2011), www.nytimes.com/2011/01/28/world/middleeast/28mideast.html.

Israel, they call the Nakba'.[47] This interpretation of the term 'Nakba' prohibits Israeli politicians from apologising for Israel's conduct in 1947–1948. The Palestinians lost their homeland, while Israel gained its homeland. The loss of one was the other's gain. It is possible to limit the understanding of the term, however, to the eviction of people from their homes and to the creation of a refugee problem. With this interpretation, Israel could acknowledge wrongdoing and take responsibility for its actions.

Olmert rejected the Palestinian right of return but was ready to make a humanitarian gesture, which was deemed insufficient for the Palestinians.[48] He proposed that Israel would accept 1,000 refugees a year, for five years, within the framework of the Arab Peace Initiative – but not based on UN Resolution 194, which acknowledges the Palestinian right of return. That meant 5,000 refugees, on an individual humanitarian basis. Olmert said: 'And if he came to me and said, not one thousand every year in five years, but four thousand every year in five years, I would have signed it on the spot, but he did not come back to me with this.'[49] Olmert spoke of 20,000 to 25,000 refugees, saying, 'that is more or less what I think I could acquiesce to'.[50] He thought that Abbas had agreed *in principle* and was 'very close' to accepting his proposal.[51] Abbas told Olmert that the Palestinians did not want to change the nature of the Jewish state and that he, Abbas, thought that no refugee would come to Israel. According to Olmert, Abbas told him: 'Do not worry. No one will come anyway. What we need to do is to compensate them financially.'[52] Abbas said: 'On numbers of refugees, it is illogical to ask Israel to take 5 million, or indeed 1 million. That would mean the end of Israel.'[53] Then why do the Palestinians insist on their right of return?

Olmert and Abbas discussed the establishment of an international fund that would support the refugees and provide compensation for both Arab *and* Jewish refugees who were uprooted from their homes as a result of wars.[54] However, various sources quote Abbas as saying different and contrasting things. According to one, Abbas said he could not tell four

47 Interview with Ehud Olmert (24 April 2019), 5.
48 Kevin Peraino, 'Olmert's Lament', *Newsweek* (12 June 2009).
49 Cohen-Almagor, 'Lessons from Peace Negotiations: Interview with Ehud Olmert', 1181.
50 Interview with Ehud Olmert (24 April 2019), 5.
51 Ibid.
52 Cohen-Almagor, 'Lessons from Peace Negotiations: Interview with Ehud Olmert', 1182.
53 Ian Black and Seumas Milne, 'Papers Reveal How Palestinian Leaders Gave Up Fight over Refugees', *The Guardian* (24 January 2011), www.theguardian.com/world/2011/jan/24/papers-palestinian-leaders-refugees-fight.
54 Interview with Ehud Olmert (24 April 2019), 7.

million people that only a few thousand of them could return home.[55] Yet another contends that Abbas was willing to accept a compromise of 40,000 to 60,000 refugees.[56] Tzipi Livni, I reiterate, refused to discuss numbers. She opposed giving in on this issue in principle, saying that if Israel were to agree even to accept *one* refugee, she would not sign the peace treaty.[57] The issue of the refugees remained unsettled.

Olmert spoke of the establishment of a Palestinian state with its capital in East Jerusalem.[58] The former mayor of Jerusalem was willing to split the city, in accordance with the Clinton Parameters: the Jewish Jerusalem would be Israeli and the Arab Jerusalem would be Palestinian.[59] Olmert proposed that the Jewish part of Jerusalem would continue to be the capital of Israel, including areas built after the 1967 Six-Day War. These areas include the neighbourhoods of Gilo, Ramot, Neve Yaakov, Pisgat Ze'ev and Armon HaNatziv. The Palestinian areas in East Jerusalem, including Shuafat, Beit Hanina, Sheikh Jarrah and Isawiya, would be part of the Palestinian capital. The Holy Basin, 'which will be defined accurately on the map, will be administered by a trust of five nations and trusted by the United Nations Security Council with specific provisions that will be accepted and defined'.[60] The five nations would be the United States, Israel, Palestine, Saudi Arabia and Jordan. It would be open for all believers, and no party would have sovereignty over it. Rather, 'it will be under God's sovereignty'.[61] The five-nation committee would not have the ability to force either Israel or Palestine to accept an agreement.[62] Olmert explained:

> The Holy Basin is holy to the Jewish people, but it's holy to hundreds of millions of Muslims as well. And how about the Christians? After all, the

[55] Natasha Mozgovaya, 'Condoleezza Rice's Biography', *Haaretz* (25 October 2011) (Hebrew).
[56] Ben Birnbaum, 'The End of the Two-State Solution: Why the Window Is Closing on Middle-East Peace', *The New Republic* (11 March 2013), www.newrepublic.com/article/112617/israel-palestine-and-end-two-state-solution#.
[57] Cohen-Almagor, 'Lessons from Peace Negotiations: Interview with Ehud Olmert', 1182; Elliott Abrams, *Tested by Zion: The Bush Administration and the Israeli-Palestinian Conflict* (New York: Cambridge University Press, 2013), 262.
[58] Aluf Benn, 'Haaretz Exclusive: Olmert's Plan for Peace with the Palestinians', *Haaretz* (17 December 2009), https://tinyurl.com/nrd3t2a3; Ehud Olmert interview to Stephen Sackur, *BBC HARDtalk* (2009).
[59] On 23 December 2000, President Clinton published his parameters for peace. See www.un.org/unispal/document/auto-insert-203898/.
[60] Cohen-Almagor, 'Lessons from Peace Negotiations: Interview with Ehud Olmert', 1180. See also Gregg Carlstrom, 'The "Napkin Map" Revealed', *Al Jazeera* (23 January 2011), www.aljazeera.com/news/2011/1/23/the-napkin-map-revealed.
[61] Cohen-Almagor, 'Lessons from Peace Negotiations: Interview with Ehud Olmert', 1180.
[62] Swisher, 'Erekat's Solution for the Haram'.

> Church of the Holy Sepulchre is the holiest site in the Christian world,[63] more than the Vatican. So rather than force exclusive Israeli sovereignty, why not let people of different faiths run their own various sites and worship their God? That shouldn't be an obstacle to a reasonable political settlement.[64]

Abbas accepted Olmert's plan to place the most sensitive part of the capital, the Holy Basin, under the control of a five-nation consortium.[65]

Olmert went beyond the offers that Israel had made at Taba. In large part, his proposed annexation to Israel of settlement blocs corresponds to the route of the security fence. Olmert wanted to annex West Bank areas that are home to 75 per cent of the Jewish population of the territories (at that time about 413,000 Israeli settlers).[66] According to *Al Jazeera*, Abbas proposed an unprecedented land swap, offering to allow Israel to annex all the settlements in East Jerusalem.[67] Through land swaps and safe passage between the West Bank and the Gaza Strip, Olmert was, in effect, offering the equivalent of 100 per cent of the West Bank. His proposal included the evacuation of dozens of settlements and all IDF forces from the Jordan Valley, the eastern Samarian hills and the Hebron region. In return for the annexation to Israel of Ariel, Beit Aryeh, the Gush Etzion bloc of settlements and settlements adjacent to Jerusalem, including Ma'aleh Adumim, Har Homa and Givat Zeev, Olmert proposed transfer of territory to the Palestinians in the West Bank, as well as a safe-passage route from Hebron to the Gaza Strip. It would remain part of the sovereign territory of Israel, but there would be no Israeli presence.[68] The settlements that would be evacuated include Ofra, Beit El, Elon Moreh, Kiryat Arba and the Jewish community in Hebron.[69] Included in the territories that Olmert proposed to transfer to the Palestinians, in return for the settlement blocs, were areas in the Beit She'an Valley near Kibbutz Tirat Tzvi, near Har Adar, in the Judea Hills near Nataf and

[63] The site of the Church has been recognised since the fourth century as the location where Jesus died, was buried and was resurrected.

[64] Tal Kra-Oz, 'The Last Dove: An Interview with Ehud Olmert', *Fathom* (February 2020), https://fathomjournal.org/the-last-dove-an-interview-with-ehud-olmert/.

[65] Bronner, 'Olmert Memoir Cites Near Deal for Mideast Peace'; Birnbaum, 'The End of the Two-State Solution'.

[66] Ehud Olmert, *In First Person* (Tel Aviv: Yedioth Ahronoth, 2018) (Hebrew), 838; 'From Olmert's Book: "Closer Than Ever to an Agreement in Principle"', *Globes* (27 January 2011) (Hebrew), www.globes.co.il/news/article.aspx?did=1000618622.

[67] Carlstrom, 'The "Napkin Map" Revealed'.

[68] Interview with Ehud Olmert (22 February 2019), 35; Olmert, *In First Person*, 838.

[69] Benn, 'Haaretz Exclusive'.

Mevo Betar, in Lachish and the Yatir Forest, and the Gaza envelope. This would have transferred 327 square kilometres from within the Green Line to the future Palestinian state.[70] Olmert proposed that the future border between Israel and the Gaza Strip would be adjacent to kibbutzim and moshavim such as Be'eri, Kissufim and Nir Oz, and that their fields would be given to the Palestinians. Abbas had reservations, but he neither accepted nor rejected the proposal. On 7 October 2023, these kibbutzim were destroyed in the Hamas terror attack.

In November 2008, Olmert arrived in Washington for the last time before leaving the prime minister's office. Astonishingly, despite the disagreements and the short period of time that remained for him in office, he was still optimistic. Olmert ignored his political and legal problems and the Palestinian disagreements. The settlements were still a crucial stumbling block. The Palestinians insisted that only 1.9 per cent of the West Bank be annexed to Israel, including the Jewish Quarter of the Old City.[71] Erekat said that the negotiations were 'poisoned' due to Israel's continued settlement building. Although during the Olmert government (2006–2008) the number of housing units constructed in settlements decreased by 50 per cent compared with the Sharon government (2001–2005), from 9,694 to 4,976, it still continued.[72] Erekat contended that 60 per cent of his negotiations with Israel during the Annapolis process concerned the settlements. He said that Olmert 'was not committed to stopping settlement activity. I'm not going to say he was lying. But he was playing games with us.'[73] Livni conceded that settlement building had been the policy of the Israeli government for a long time.[74] She said: 'We have distinctions between blocs of settlements and individual settlements. Some are not even in our interest to expand',[75] although others were.

One of the main controversies was the Ariel and Kedumim settlement bloc, rooted deep in the West Bank. To annex this area, Israel must retain a long finger of territory in the northern West Bank. Ariel has a population

70 Avi Issacharoff, 'Olmert: "I Am Still Waiting for Abbas to Call"', *The Tower* (24 May 2013), https://tinyurl.com/2a8ve3eb; Raviv Drucker, 'Olmert, Abu Mazen and Barak Refer to the Political Process', *HaMakor* (17 November 2015).

71 Arieli, *A Border between Us and You*, Maps 22, 25.

72 Sivan Hirsch-Hoefler and Cas Mudde, *The Israeli Settler Movement: Assessing and Explaining Social Movement Success* (Cambridge: Cambridge University Press, 2021), 98.

73 Peraino, 'Olmert's Lament'.

74 Seumas Milne, 'Palestinian Leaders Weak – and Increasingly Desperate', *The Guardian* (23 January 2011), https://tinyurl.com/mvdnjhc9.

75 Ian Black and Seumas Milne, 'Palestinian Negotiators Accept Jewish State, Papers Reveal', *The Guardian* (24 January 2011), https://tinyurl.com/yna7jt6m.

of 25,000 people and is the home of Ariel University, with some 16,000 students. Another controversy relates to the Latrun enclave, an area of some forty-six square kilometres, which Israel and Jordan failed to agree upon in their 1949 armistice agreement. Israel regards this territory as part of the country and has established several settlements there.[76]

Olmert said that Ariel was not a bone of contention and that it did not prevent the agreement.[77] He suggested the construction of a tunnel under Ariel, enabling the Palestinians to commute from east to west without a significant detour. Olmert believed that, politically, he could not propose the evacuation of Ariel.[78] He said he wanted to give the Palestinians 94.2 per cent of the West Bank and a highway between the West Bank and Gaza. The Palestinians demanded 100 per cent of the West Bank. I questioned Olmert about the percentages he mentioned. What was the actual size of the settlement blocs? How many settlers lived in them? How many settlers lived outside the blocs? How many Palestinians lived in the territories that Israel would annex? Olmert did not remember all these details by heart. This is understandable, as the interviews were conducted many years after the talks. Olmert did say that the number that 'we really need and that we can give in return in swaps is 4.2%' and that he inflated the percentage that would be retained by Israel to 5.8 per cent to leave 'a certain margin' for negotiations.[79] He estimated that there would be some 80,000 Israeli settlers who would need to be resettled.[80] Most of them (50,000–60,000) could be relocated in the major settlement blocs that would remain in Israeli hands: Ma'ale Adumim, Givon, Givat Ze'ev, Ariel and Gush Etzion.[81] Olmert did not know how many Palestinians resided in the 5.8 per cent that would be Israel's. He was willing to absorb them.[82]

According to Olmert, the main disagreement related to Har Homa, which the Palestinians insisted be part of their territory.[83] Ariel and Maale

[76] Arieli, *A Border between Us and You*, 245.

[77] Interviews with Ehud Olmert (24 April 2019), 9, (6 January 2025), 2; Cohen-Almagor, 'Lessons from Peace Negotiations: Interview with Ehud Olmert', 1183.

[78] Interview with Ehud Olmert (6 January 2025), 2.

[79] Cohen-Almagor, 'Lessons from Peace Negotiations: Interview with Ehud Olmert', 1184.

[80] Interview with Ehud Olmert (24 April 2019), 5.

[81] Ibid.; Cohen-Almagor, 'Lessons from Peace Negotiations: Interview with Ehud Olmert', 1185; 'From Olmert's Book'.

[82] Interview with Ehud Olmert (22 February 2019), 35–38. According to other sources, Olmert's last proposal to Abbas was that Israel would retain 6.5 per cent of the West Bank, give the Palestinians land equal to 5.8 per cent and 0.7 per cent safe passage to Gaza. See Abrams, *Tested by Zion*, 287; Arieli, *A Border between Us and You*, Map 21.

[83] 'From Olmert's Book'.

Adumim, as well, posed a problem. While Abbas refused to include them in Israel, he welcomed American bridging proposals.[84] Because of his willingness to consider such proposals, Olmert was confident that Abbas would have agreed to Israel retaining sovereignty over three population centres in exchange for swaps – Ariel, the surroundings of Jerusalem and Gush Etzion.[85]

In his proposal for a territory swap, Olmert rejected suggestions previously raised involving the transfer of the eastern Lachish hills to the Palestinians (see Figure 10.3). He decided, instead, to establish communities there for evacuees from the Gaza Strip. He also showed a preference for giving the Palestinians agricultural land rather than the transfer of the Halutza sands near the Egyptian border.[86] In addition to these comprehensive and sweeping land exchanges, there was also an offer for Palestinian sovereignty over Al Aqsa and large swathes of East Jerusalem.

Negotiations between the two parties continued until Olmert's indictment on corruption allegations forced him to resign. Abbas, said Olmert, did not reject his comprehensive proposal, but he was hesitant about the borders and the land swaps that Olmert proposed. On 16 September 2008, Olmert showed Abbas a map outlining the territory in his proposal; however, disagreements remained. Abbas agreed to hand over only 1.9 per cent of the West Bank to Israel, far less than the 6.3 per cent that Olmert proposed.[87] Abbas said it would be possible to exchange territory of a certain percentage, 'on the condition that the territory that we'd receive in exchange would be equal in size and identical in character'.[88]

In Chapter 8, I explained that the percentage issue was tricky. Instead of discussing percentages of territory, parties should use detailed maps and decide exactly where the border will be. They should name towns and villages and agree on the territories to be included. The negotiators resorted to percentages during the negotiations on Oslo B, on the interim agreement and on areas A, B and C. Gilead Sher did not think this was a good method. He suggested: 'Let us talk systemically and schematically on

84 Bronner, 'Olmert Memoir Cites Near Deal for Mideast Peace'.

85 Cohen-Almagor, 'Lessons from Peace Negotiations: Interview with Ehud Olmert', 1183.

86 'C2. Aluf Benn, Ehud Olmert's Plan for Peace with the Palestinians, Ha'aretz, 17 December 2009 (Excerpts)', *Journal of Palestine Studies*, 39(3) (2010): 206–208, www.jstor.org/stable/10.1525/jps.2010.xxxix.3.206.

87 Issacharoff, 'Olmert: "I am still waiting for Abbas to call"'; Cohen-Almagor, 'Lessons from Peace Negotiations: Interview with Ehud Olmert', 1180.

88 Drucker, 'Olmert, Abu Mazen and Barak'.

Figure 10.3 Annapolis, 2008 Israeli proposal.
Source: Shaul Arieli, www.shaularieli.com/en/maps/negotiations/. Arieli argues this is the map that Olmert had presented to Abbas.

what the principles are, and then the percentages will derive from that.'[89] The Palestinians, however, said, 'look, you have 78% of British Mandatory Palestine. We have 22%. We need to make sure that at least that is what we get.'[90] When I spoke with the Palestinians, they said one of the issues that stopped them from signing an agreement was the fact that they did not fully understand what those percentages meant. Those percentages were contested, and they did not fully comprehend them.

When Abbas asked Olmert to give him the map he had drawn, Olmert agreed, provided that Abbas sign a comprehensive peace agreement that would settle the conflict once and for all. Abbas, who is not an expert on maps, said he wanted to consult with his people. Olmert believed that direct, bilateral negotiations with Abbas would solve problems, but this intimate style of negotiation is not for everyone. Abbas was not prepared to commit, and Olmert refused to give him the map. He told the Palestinian leader that he could take notes and consult with his experts. Olmert refused to give Abbas the map because he thought the latter might use it in the future as a springboard to demand further concessions from Israel.[91] Abbas said a Palestinian map expert would study the proposal 'even tomorrow',[92] and that he would get back to Olmert, but he never did. A year later, in 2009, Abbas said: 'All I know is that the state of Israel should exist solely within the 1967 borders.'[93]

Olmert sent Ron Pundak to Abbas, to ask him what changes to the agreement he wanted to introduce. When Pundak returned empty-handed, Olmert decided to pursue the concept of 'coordinated multilateral unilateralism', allowing progress towards creating a two-state solution under fully coordinated, bilateral conditions, with optimal regional and international support.[94] Unfortunately, in September 2008, Olmert's political career came to an end, as did the intense peace negotiations.[95] Livni succeeded him as leader of Kadima, and in elections in 2009, the party won by a margin of one seat (twenty-eight) over Netanyahu's Likud (twenty-seven). She was unable to form a coalition, and Netanyahu became prime

89 Interview with Gilead Sher (2 February 2024), 8.
90 Ibid.
91 Cohen-Almagor, 'Lessons from Peace Negotiations: Interview with Ehud Olmert', 1181.
92 Drucker, 'Olmert, Abu Mazen and Barak'.
93 Arieli, *A Border between Us and You*, 157.
94 Yair Hirschfeld's communication (18 December 2024).
95 According to Yair Hirschfeld, *The Israeli-Palestinian Peace Process* (Cham: Springer, 2024), 185, Olmert planned Israeli unilateral steps that would lead to a two-state solution, but he ran out of time and the plan did not materialise.

minister, while Olmert fought to clear his name in court. In March 2014, after a long legal proceeding, Olmert was convicted of bribery and sentenced to eighteen months in prison. He began his term in February 2016 and was released in July 2017.

Although Udi Dekel tried to convince Netanyahu to maintain the twelve expert professional committees, the new prime minister was not enthusiastic. As for the Palestinians, they believed that Netanyahu had no interest in continuing the Annapolis process. Trust was non-existent, and the Annapolis peace process came to an end.

Wars

The peace process was hampered greatly by violence. By the end of 2008, the winds of war were blowing strongly. The main Palestinian spoilers, Hamas and the Islamic Jihad, terrorised Israel. They launched rocket and mortar attacks from Gaza, orchestrated infiltration operations and carried out terrorist shootings that targeted Israeli civilians and security personnel. The Americans were briefed by the Israelis and the Palestinians about the situation; at every meeting, the Israelis told the Americans that a massive incursion into Gaza was pending.[96] Olmert, who was elected on a clear and explicit peace plan, and in whom the Israeli peace camp was strongly invested, led Israel to two wars in three years: the July–August 2006 Israel–Hezbollah war,[97] and the subsequent intense military operation against Hamas.[98]

On 12 July 2006, Hezbollah launched a coordinated cross-border attack against two IDF patrols along the Israeli-Lebanese frontier. The assault was accompanied by a barrage of rocket fire targeting civilian areas in northern Israel. The initial attack resulted in the deaths of three Israeli soldiers and the capture of two others. In the immediate aftermath, an Israeli tank, dispatched as part of a rescue mission, struck a landmine approximately six kilometres inside Lebanese territory, resulting in the deaths of four more IDF soldiers. In response, Israel initiated a large-scale

96 Abrams, *Tested by Zion*, 260.

97 See Raphael Cohen-Almagor and Sharon Haleva-Amir, 'The Israel–Hezbollah War and the Winograd Committee', *Journal of Parliamentary and Political Law*, 2(1) (2008): 113–130.

98 See National Security Law Report, *American Bar Association* 31(1) (January–February 2009); Israeli Politics, http://almagor.blogspot.com/2010_01_31_archive.html; http://almagor.blogspot.com/2010_04_25_archive.html; On the Goldstone Report, http://almagor.blogspot.com/2010_04_04_archive.html.

military operation targeting Hezbollah's infrastructure across southern Lebanon, employing heavy artillery and armoured units. Israel's air force conducted extensive airstrikes aimed at degrading Hezbollah's military capabilities, restricting the militants' mobility and preventing the transfer of the abducted soldiers deeper into Lebanese territory – thus averting a potential hostage stand-off or prolonged captivity. These measures, however, were both retaliatory and temporally insufficient. By the time the strikes commenced, Hezbollah had already moved the captured soldiers beyond the reach of immediate Israeli recovery efforts. The ensuing escalation marked the beginning of the 2006 Lebanon War, intensifying the hostilities between Israel and Hezbollah and entrenching a broader regional conflict.

On the evening of 12 July 2006, Prime Minister Olmert convened the Israeli government to decide on a response. The government determined that the attack had created a new situation on the northern border, and that Israel had to take decisive action to 'exact a price' and restore deterrence.[99] Olmert rejected Hezbollah's demand to release Lebanese and Palestinian prisoners in exchange for the captured soldiers. That night, Israel responded with airstrikes, targeting bridges in central Lebanon and Hezbollah positions along the border. Hezbollah retaliated on 13 July 2006, launching Katyusha rockets that killed two people and injured a few others.

The Israeli–Hezbollah war concluded on 14 August 2006 with the implementation of UN Security Council Resolution 1701.[100] Over the course of the thirty-four-day conflict, 155 Israelis were killed, thirty-six of them civilians killed as a result of Hezbollah rocket fire.[101] A total of 119 IDF soldiers were killed in Israel and Lebanon. Hezbollah launched 3,970 rockets, averaging 120 per day, causing significant damage and casualties.[102] Many of the rockets hit buildings, causing damage and costing lives. The north of Israel came to a standstill. Hundreds of thousands of residents left their homes to move beyond the rockets' range. About 2,000 people

99 Steven Gutkin, 'Crisis Allows Israel to Pursue Strategic Goals', *nbc.com* (14 July 2006), www.nbcnews.com/id/wbna13847803.

100 Security Council SC/8808, 'Security council calls for end to hostilities between Hizbollah, Israel, Unanimously adopting resolution no. 1701 (2006)' (11 August 2006), https://press.un.org/en/2006/sc8808.doc.htm.

101 '155 Victims of War in the Northern War', *Ynet* (14 August 2006) (Hebrew), www.ynet.co.il/articles/0,7340,L-3288289,00.html.

102 Sharon Rofe-Ofir and Hanan Grinberg, 'Rear-Area Headquarters: Returning to Normal in all the Northern Settlements', *Ynet* (14 August 2006), www.ynet.co.il/articles/0,7340,L-3291201,00.html. Arieli argues that forty-four Israeli civilians died. Arieli, *A Border between Us and You*, 153.

were injured, and many suffered from shock and anxiety. The cost of the damage exceeded five billion shekels. On the Lebanese side, casualty estimates vary. Hezbollah claimed about 250 of its fighters were killed, while Israel estimated 600 Hezbollah casualties. A UN official put the number at 500, and Lebanese sources also estimated that up to 500 Hezbollah fighters died, with another 1,500 injured. According to the Commission of Inquiry on Lebanon, 1,191 Lebanese civilians were killed and 4,409 were injured.[103] According to Harel and Issacharoff, over 1,000 Lebanese lost their lives, almost half of them civilians.[104] Other reports estimated the Lebanese death toll to be 1,300.[105]

During the war, protests erupted in Israel, primarily among reserve soldiers and journalists. Prominent figures such as the writers A. B. Yehoshua, Amos Oz and David Grossman – who lost his son in the war – called for a shift from military to political solutions, urging the government to avoid escalating the conflict. After the war, widespread criticism of government decisions ensued. Many called for a national inquiry into the events of the war and demanded the resignations of the key figures responsible: Prime Minister Olmert, Defense Minister Amir Peretz and Chief of Staff Dan Halutz. The Israel-Hezbollah war brought to light Israel's weaknesses and undermined Olmert's image as a peacenik in the eyes of the Palestinians.

On 27 December 2008, in response to increasing rocket barrages from Gaza, Israel launched *Operation Cast Lead* against Hamas, a twenty-two-day military assault on the Gaza Strip. The ferocity of the attack was severe, killing some 1,400 Palestinians, most of them civilians.[106] According to Olmert, Hamas did not fight back. They did not have operational tunnels; they were 'just running away'.[107] The IDF took over the northern part of Gaza, and Olmert wanted to extend the operation to try to completely eliminate Hamas from Gaza. He wanted to take the Philadelphi Corridor and Rafah and then, advancing from the south, squeeze and rid Gaza completely of Hamas. However, his political partners at the time – Barak,

[103] Con Coughlin, 'Teheran Fund Pays War Compensation to Hizbollah Families', *Telegraph* (4 August 2006), https://tinyurl.com/4jsb79zp; Cohen-Almagor and Haleva-Amir, 'The Israel-Hezbollah War and the Winograd Committee'.

[104] Amos Harel and Avi Issacharoff, *34 Days: Israel, Hezbollah, and the War in Lebanon: The Second War in Lebanon* (Houndmills and New York: Palgrave Macmillan, 2008), ix.

[105] Arieli, *A Border between Us and You*, 153.

[106] 'Operation Cast Lead', Institute for Middle East Understanding (4 January 2012), https://imeu.org/article/operation-cast-lead.

[107] Interview with Ehud Olmert (6 January 2025), 4.

Livni and others – were against it.[108] The UN called on Israel to open Gaza's borders to allow for reconstruction work to begin. The conflict had caused significant destruction in the Gaza Strip, with thousands of homes destroyed and infrastructure heavily damaged.

Olmert had proven that he had no qualms about using military force if and when necessary. He regretted the opportunity Israel missed in late 2008 to destroy Hamas due to internal pressure on him from political and military leaders who opted for restraint. Olmert said: 'I think that we missed the opportunity to destroy Hamas in Gaza in *Operation Cast Lead* because at that time Barak and Gabi Ashkenazi and others were not prepared to carry on Cast Lead to the end.'[109] Ashkenazi was IDF Chief of Staff.

These two wars and corruption allegations brought about the premature end of Olmert's term in office. He left behind a very different legacy from the one he had in mind when he assumed his responsibilities.

Analysis

I asked Olmert about the significance of the Annapolis Conference. He said that Annapolis had set a time framework, which was important, and in addition it recognised that there was a genuine, serious and credible process taking place.[110] Olmert started negotiations with Abbas in December 2006. Annapolis took place in November 2007. Hiba Husseini explains that Annapolis was important because it came after years of Intifada. It was held against the backdrop of changing Israeli politics, with the Kadima party at the helm. It was and still is important to keep negotiating, until Israel and the Palestine Liberation Organization (PLO) iron out all the issues.[111]

The construction of the Annapolis process was complex and not all that coherent. The first layer of the expert committees, headed by Dekel and Erakat, was important because they discussed most of the serious matters. These discussions informed the Annapolis process and supported it but were insufficient to bring the conflict to a close. They could not discuss Jerusalem, which is at the very heart of the conflict. The Palestinians continued to insist on Jerusalem in all negotiations. The Israelis believed the

108 Ibid.
109 Interview with Ehud Olmert (22 February 2019), 39.
110 Ibid., 28.
111 Interview with Hiba Husseini (24 December 2024), 34.

Palestinian contention that resolving the Jerusalem question was *sine qua non* to resolving the conflict. Olmert reserved the issue for himself.

The second layer, Livni–Qurie, was a political necessity, and naturally Livni assigned it great importance. Olmert did not. It was clear to me that Olmert underestimated those negotiations, allowing them to take place to offload Livni, whom he perceived as an unfortunate political liability. As prime minister, Olmert called the shots and made the crucial decisions, notwithstanding what Livni wanted.

Abbas was certainly committed to the process. He established a good rapport with Olmert. The two leaders appreciated each other and enjoyed each other's company; otherwise, they would not have met thirty-six times. But the deal that Olmert offered, as generous as it was, was not enough to satisfy Abbas, and he would not sign an agreement. Husseini thinks Abbas was afraid that he would be giving up too much in terms of territory.[112] Furthermore, Olmert's political and legal difficulties undermined his credibility. Abbas doubted that the time was ripe for an agreement.

Negotiations were not conducted on an equal footing. Olmert did not go to Ramallah even once; most of their meetings were conducted in Olmert's surroundings, where he was comfortable. As the leader of the State of Israel, Olmert was the senior of the two. Bilateral negotiations suited him, and Abbas acceded to Olmert's dictate. Ultimately, it does not seem that these kinds of encounters suited Abbas.

I asked Olmert about these two issues. Olmert explained that security was a problem. Abbas never asked to host a meeting. Prior to the only meeting that they scheduled in Jericho, they received an alert from the Shabac that two of Abbas's bodyguards intended to assassinate Olmert during his visit. The two were arrested for conspiracy to commit a crime by Abbas's security. Olmert went ahead with the visit and had this single meeting with Abbas in Palestinian territory, but about 3,000 soldiers and police officers secured the road to Jericho. It was a major security operation, a major headache. Olmert asked Abbas: 'Listen, we do not need this. What do you think?' Abbas agreed.[113] According to Olmert, having negotiations in Palestinian territory, and alternating between Jericho, Ramallah and Jerusalem, was not important to Abbas.

Regarding the bilateral negotiations, Olmert thought this was the only way he could have progressed. There were other committees, such as Livni's and Dekel's, but to sign a deal, Olmert believed one-on-one

[112] Ibid., 16.

[113] Interview with Ehud Olmert (6 January 2025), 1.

meetings were very important. He said that after the first meeting, which was held in his private residence, Abbas told him that whatever the Palestinians knew about negotiations with Israelis until then, from now on it would be very different. Olmert was able to break the ice, and he did not get the impression that this style of negotiation did not suit Abbas or made him uncomfortable.[114]

Olmert has been in politics since the age of twenty-one. He was confident in his ability to conduct peace negotiations alone with Abbas. He knew the material inside out and thought that with charm and respect, they would make an historic breakthrough. He believed that he alone could strike a peace deal and assumed the burden of negotiations on himself. He took full responsibility for the outcome. If he succeeded, the entire achievement would be his. If he failed, the entire responsibility for the failure would be his. Olmert thought that Abbas had similar experience, knowledge and self-confidence, was equipped to negotiate one on one, and was also prepared to take sole responsibility for the outcome. On this, Olmert was wrong. While Abbas was certainly experienced, he lacked the confidence, vision and drive that Olmert had. On previous occasions, he preferred to send Hussein Agha and Ahmad Khalidi to negotiate on his behalf. Tony Blair writes that experienced leaders are confident. Their experience makes them believe that they know more than they actually do, which is risky, of course. Blair's advice for leaders is to surround themselves with experts.[115] Not only did Olmert refuse to do so, but he also attracted criticism from his own camp, especially from Livni, who wished to be in the negotiation room. While Olmert always invited her to the luncheons that preceded the negotiations, she was never included in the serious conversations with Abbas. Left outside, she became a bitter spoiler (see Figure 10.4).

Olmert did not think that in real time, inside the room, he needed advice from experts or colleagues. However, experts can underscore contributing factors that politicians might ignore. Leaders need experts not only on specific issues such as borders, Jerusalem, the Holy Basin, refugees and security, but also on conflict resolution, on negotiation, decision-making processes, on getting the right results. Olmert still believes he had the knowledge, political experience and strategic judgement to guide the process towards a successful outcome. His perception, however, is open to

114 Ibid., 2.

115 Tony Blair, *On Leadership: Lessons for the 21st Century* (London: Hutchinson Heinemann, 2024).

Figure 10.4 Livni and Olmert.
Credit: Pool/Pool/Getty Images.

serious criticism, particularly in the light of the complex realities and ultimate outcome of the negotiations. Self-assurance is an essential quality, but only to an extent. Abbas certainly needed experts on his side. While I do not argue that Abbas necessarily would have signed an agreement, the 16 September 2008 meeting might have ended differently if experts had been present, or in an adjacent room for immediate consultation.

I asked Olmert about the use of percentages in the territorial discussions. His reply was that the territorial issue was very clear and that there was no room for misunderstandings. Olmert referred to 4 or 5 per cent that would remain Israeli territory, which included 82 per cent of the settlers. The remaining 18 per cent could have stayed wherever they were, subject to the Palestinian state and with Israeli citizenship, or they could opt to leave. I spoke about Shaul Arieli's view that there was a discrepancy between what Israel perceived as a percentage and what the Palestinians perceive as a percentage (see Chapter 8). Olmert reiterated that this was not an issue. At Annapolis, the issue was clarified. The Palestinians understood that Olmert insisted only on retaining the key settlement blocs, and that they would be compensated for the 5 per cent with land swaps of the same size and the same quality.[116]

In general, Israeli leaders do not wish to provide the Palestinians with documents because they believe they will become the basis for the next round of negotiations. That is, while the Israelis perceive the documents as the final offer, the Palestinians view them as a fertile ground for asking for more concessions. The Palestinians, on their part, argue that Israel refuses to give them maps and other important documents because it wishes to ensure deniability. Israel is not prepared to commit to certain borders because it continues to build settlements in the West Bank. Israel wants to continue to deprive Palestine of its rightful land.[117]

Abbas did not respond to Olmert's proposal, and the negotiations ended. Abbas did not say yes, and he did not say no. He never replied. I asked Olmert why he thinks Abbas decided not to decide. Olmert replied that it takes a certain type of character to make such a historical decision, to end the conflict, to make peace with a bitter foe. Olmert said: 'Not everyone is emotionally capable of taking [such a decision] lightly. It requires a certain inner strength which does not come automatically.'[118] The gravity of this historical decision might have been 'just too big for one person to be able to assume'.[119] This statement reinforces my thinking that bilateral negotiations were an ill-suited formula. Furthermore, Olmert's political vulnerability was certainly a factor. Livni, Barak and others told Abbas not to sign because Olmert was a lame duck and was facing serious criminal investigations. Maher El-Kurd argues that Abbas did not sign because Condoleezza Rice ordered him not to do so. 'She told him to wait for the election. She ordered him not to sign. She is to blame for that.'[120] Hasan Asfour made a similar argument, saying that Rice pressured Abbas not to sign and that the Americans forbade Abbas from continuing negotiations with Olmert.[121] Olmert mentioned Livni and Barak as two people who undermined his position and were destructive forces in the peace process, dissuading Abbas from signing a peace pact with Israel because they did not believe Olmert could deliver his side of the deal. Olmert was very blunt in his assessment of his colleagues. There is not much appreciation

116 Interview with Ehud Olmert (6 January 2025), 3.
117 See Al Jazeera Investigates – The Palestine Papers, Day 1 (23 January 2011).
118 Interview with Ehud Olmert (24 April 2019), 8.
119 Ibid., 9.
120 Interview with Maher El-Kurd (30 January 2025), 42.
121 Interview with Hasan Asfour (18 February 2025), 10.

or respect between these leaders.[122] One wonders whether, later on, Livni and Barak regretted their conduct.

Erekat confirmed that the Palestinians received those warnings, saying that it was meaningless to sign anything with Olmert because his political career was over.[123] Israeli society was divided, and Olmert did not enjoy public support or have the ability to deliver a deal. Perhaps Abbas, like Yasser Arafat before him, did not wish to be the Palestinian leader who made the historical decision of conferring legitimacy on Israel and its right to exist in what many Palestinians perceive as their territory, 'from the river to the sea'.

Olmert was unsure whether Abbas's fear of his *own* opposition was a factor. This issue was never prominent in their negotiations,[124] but Hamas and other extremist spoiler groups were very much opposed to such a deal. The Palestinians did not have a shared view on ending the conflict. Abbas believed that Mohammed Dahlan wanted to assassinate him,[125] and that a peace agreement with Israel would only encourage him to carry out his plan. Abbas, unable to deliver the plan, would be embarrassed. Olmert believes that when Abbas failed to sign the peace proposal, he made the greatest mistake of his life.[126] I agree. Even if, in the light of his predicament, Olmert could not deliver, the Palestinians still would have had an agreement, signed by an Israeli prime minister, that included unprecedented concessions which no other prime minister, before or after Olmert (as of this writing), had ever proposed. The offer was important for both sides; it would have been a historic milestone in the Israeli-Palestinian conflict, a point of departure for future negotiations and, perhaps, a deal that could have materialised into a two-state solution. Of course, there would have been obstacles to resolve and disagreements to settle, but the situation on the ground might have changed drastically.

Had the agreement been signed, it would have been a transformative moment for the Palestinians, providing an internationally recognised framework for the establishment of a sovereign Palestinian state. Such recognition, particularly from Israel and other key international actors, would have conferred on the Palestinian leadership both legitimacy and

[122] Interviews with Ehud Olmert (22 February 2019, 24 April 2019) and Tzipi Livni (22 June 2016).

[123] Drucker, 'Olmert, Abu Mazen and Barak'.

[124] Interview with Ehud Olmert (24 April 2019), 8.

[125] Interview with Ehud Olmert (22 February 2019), 31.

[126] Cohen-Almagor, 'Lessons from Peace Negotiations: Interview with Ehud Olmert', 1179–1180.

the opportunity to initiate a robust state-building process. With appropriate institutional support, international aid and cooperation from Israel, the PA – under the aegis of the PLO – could have moved towards consolidating its governing authority. This would have included establishing effective mechanisms for law and order, achieving a monopoly on the legitimate use of force, and laying the foundations for a sustainable and independent economy. Most significantly, it would have offered the Palestinian people a tangible alternative to the ongoing cycle of conflict and paved the way for political stability, economic development and a new trajectory, grounded in sovereignty and self-determination.

Unlike superforecasters, Olmert and Abbas did not have what it takes to reach an agreement. Superforecasters work in teams and are willing and able to admit to error and to change the course of action when necessary. They are also committed to belief-updating and self-improvement. Olmert and Abbas did not have what it takes to reach an agreement. While the Olmert–Abbas talks were the most significant attempt to peacefully resolve the Israeli-Palestinian conflict to date, the two leaders were not sufficiently pragmatic to bridge the gaps between them and reach a historic agreement that could have changed the Middle East for the better.

Conclusions

Annapolis was intended to push the parties forward, with the blessing of the international community. It set a time framework and conferred international recognition on 'a genuine, serious, credible process' that was taking place.[127] Annapolis contributed to the peace process; however, the construction of the three channels was problematic. Neither Livni nor Qurie knew exactly what was transpiring between Olmert and Abbas, as the two leaders did not brief them.[128] Indeed, Olmert went beyond what Livni had suggested.

The Abbas–Olmert negotiations represented a significant effort to resolve the Israeli-Palestinian conflict. They made progress on some issues, but the time was not ripe for a resolution. The negotiations were hindered by the ongoing violence and political challenges that both Olmert and Abbas faced, as well as internal divisions. The two wars did not help make Olmert a popular leader in Israel, nor a credible partner for

[127] Ibid., 1178.

[128] Interview with Tzipi Livni (22 June 2016); Black and Milne, 'Israel Spurned Palestinian Offer'.

peace in the eyes of the Palestinians. Furthermore, during Olmert's time as prime minister, settlement building in East Jerusalem and parts of the West Bank continued,[129] poisoning the atmosphere between the sides and undermining any peace offer he made. Olmert admitted that Israel had failed to uphold its promise to halt construction in the settlements.[130] The fact that he faced corruption charges further undermined his ability to deliver. Abbas had no wish to be humiliated by signing an agreement that would not be fulfilled by Olmert's successor.

Ehud Olmert brought to the negotiation table a wealth of political experience and a long-standing reputation for boldness and acumen. From the early stages of his career, Olmert demonstrated an assertive and independent streak. As a young Knesset member, he publicly called for the resignation of Herut party leader Menachem Begin due to repeated electoral defeats. He built his political profile by championing campaigns against organised crime. By 2006, Olmert had accumulated the political confidence and institutional authority to lead high-stakes negotiations with the Palestinians – an endeavour he not only accepted but actively sought. His ambition to establish his legacy as a peacemaker was clear.

Olmert's decision to centralise negotiations and act as the sole principal negotiator on the Israeli side imposed a parallel structure upon Mahmoud Abbas, who was thereby expected to shoulder comparable responsibility on behalf of the Palestinian side. While this unilateral structuring of the negotiation framework suited Olmert's leadership style, it did not align with Abbas's more cautious and consensus-driven approach. He was averse to bearing such weight alone, reflecting both internal political constraints and his own leadership disposition. This asymmetry had significant implications for the negotiation process. Ultimately, Abbas declined to accept Olmert's far-reaching proposal. Several core issues remained unresolved, chief among them borders, the status of settlements, refugees and Jerusalem. Abbas's refusal stemmed from a combination of factors: substantive reservations about the offer itself, doubts regarding Olmert's political capacity to implement an agreement (particularly in the light of his legal troubles) and a strategic inclination to postpone decisions in the hope of more favourable conditions in the future. Unlike Israeli leaders, who operate under the pressure of electoral cycles, Palestinian leadership, lacking comparable mechanisms of political accountability, has often exhibited a lesser sense of urgency.

129 Black and Milne, 'Israel Spurned Palestinian Offer'.
130 'Olmert: Israel Failed Its Settlement Promise', *NBC News* (4 January 2008).

Thus, although Olmert's offer was arguably the most generous presented by any Israeli prime minister, it fell short of core Palestinian aspirations. As Udi Dekel has noted, the Palestinian right of return remains a foundational narrative and a deeply embedded expectation among Palestinians, one that Abbas simply could not renounce. Likewise, his refusal to recognise Israel as a Jewish state was rooted in the perception that such recognition would delegitimise Palestinian claims and compromise the rights of Palestinian citizens of Israel, as well as those in the broader diaspora.[131] Even if he wanted peace, these issues were too big for Abbas to resolve alone. Abbas did not say yes because he thought the Palestinians might get a better offer in the future. He did not say no because he did not wish to be perceived as an obstacle to peace, a convenient target for blame. Therefore, he said nothing and left things up in the air, to be resolved in the future.

Olmert and Abbas's failure to reach a final status agreement had far-reaching and deeply consequential effects on both the Israeli and Palestinian political landscapes. In Israel, the political fallout contributed to the collapse of the centrist Kadima party, which had spearheaded the peace efforts. This vacuum paved the way for the return of Benjamin Netanyahu to the premiership in 2009, and a significant shift in Israeli policy away from negotiation and towards a more security-focused, status quo-oriented approach. Under Netanyahu's leadership, the peace process stagnated and the expansion of Israeli settlements in the West Bank accelerated, further complicating the territorial basis for a two-state solution.

On the Palestinian side, Abbas's failure to secure an agreement undermined his credibility and weakened the legitimacy of the PA. His inability to deliver tangible political achievements deepened public disillusionment and fostered perceptions of ineffectiveness and political paralysis. Abbas turned inward, avoiding bold political initiatives and becoming increasingly detached from his constituents. This power vacuum allowed Hamas, which had been designated a terrorist organisation by the US, the European Union and other countries, to gain both political and military strength, particularly in Gaza.

The enduring occupation, the steady growth of settlements and repeated cycles of violence further eroded prospects for peace. Popular frustration on both sides contributed to a radicalisation of political discourse. Violent resistance gained traction among some Palestinians, and hardline policies became more mainstream in Israeli politics. In this deteriorating climate, the vision of a two-state solution, once the cornerstone of international

131 Interview with Udi Dekel (17 June 2014), 2.

diplomacy, was increasingly marginalised. As support for alternative frameworks, including confederal or one-state models, grew, so too did scepticism about their feasibility or desirability, leaving the conflict more entrenched and intractable than ever.

In the next part of the book, I offer practical suggestions for conflict resolution, outlining the keys to successful negotiations, mediation and facilitation, and then exploring possible solutions to the Israeli-Palestinian conflict. Following the superforecasters model, it is argued that negotiators must have certain crucial qualities, including abilities to communicate, analyse, assert their best position, get along with people and evoke the interest of their counterparts, so they can appreciate their standpoint. Another desirable skill is persuasion. Good negotiators need to know how to present their argument in the best possible way, appeal to their interlocutor's reason and empathy, and explain complicated matters in language that their disputant understands. In negotiations, the greatest achievement is winning – with no apparent losers.

I present what skills and qualities negotiators, mediators and facilitators should have, what they should do and what they should refrain from doing. Inter alia, it is argued that negotiators, mediators and facilitators must set clear, realistic aims, prioritise the most important issues and highlight positives. Negotiators and mediators should be bold when necessary in order to reach important decisions; they should seek to bridge gaps through innovation, rhetoric and imagination. Specifically, as regards a peace summit, I recommend what should be done prior to, during and after the summit. In the last chapter, I outline my proposal for resolving the Israeli-Palestinian conflict.

PART II

Practical Suggestions

11

Keys to Successful Negotiations, Mediation and Facilitation

We are stronger when we listen, and smarter when we share.

~ Rania Al-Abdullah

This chapter aims to outline the keys to successful negotiations, mediation and facilitation. Its insights are the result of many years of research and peace activity. The writing has benefited greatly from the interviewees' perspectives. I believe these insights will be useful when another opportunity to resolve the conflict presents itself. With these insights, it is hoped that the opportunity will not be missed.

Conducting successful negotiations requires considerable skill and preparation. While leaders may think that their involvement is crucial to the extent that their mere presence in the room will yield success, this perception is simplistic. Success in negotiations increases when negotiators undergo comprehensive training in diplomacy. Negotiators must be assisted by specialists for specific issues. The team should include lawyers, military professionals, mapping experts, historians, sociologists, psychologists, political scientists and media specialists. While all these experts cannot and should not be in the negotiation room, they should be accessible and ready to support the negotiations as they proceed. One person, intelligent and capable as this person may be, will probably not possess all the qualities needed for success.

The negotiation environment also plays a vital role in shaping outcomes. Those responsible for organising and facilitating peace talks should provide a setting conducive to focus, emotional stability and productive dialogue. Informal settings, social activities and personal connections can humanise the process, reduce tensions and build interpersonal trust. Providing negotiators with opportunities to bring spouses, as at Camp David in 1978 with President Jimmy Carter and his wife, Rosalynn, can offer emotional support and enhance resilience during high-stress moments. Recognising the psychological dimension of negotiations is essential to navigating the crises that inevitably arise.

Failure, while always a risk, must not be normalised or treated lightly. Both parties must enter negotiations with a shared understanding that while setbacks may occur, abandonment of the process cannot be an option. Crises are not signs of collapse but expected features of protracted negotiation on very complicated matters and must be managed, not feared.

No single negotiation framework guarantees success. The Israeli-Palestinian conflict, like other lingering disputes, may be addressed through a range of mechanisms, and flexibility is key. The conflict may be resolved by means of various negotiation options, agreed to between the parties as the best choice to pursue. If one option fails, the parties may adopt another. The possibilities may include direct negotiations between leaders, as was the case between Ehud Olmert and Mahmoud Abbas; direct negotiations between representatives of the leaders (Oslo); direct negotiations between delegations (Israel–Jordan); negotiations between leaders or their representatives with mediators (Camp David 1978); or negotiations between delegations with mediators (Camp David 2000).

Fisher and Ury,[1] Kelman[2] and Zartman[3] argue that negotiators should recognise and understand emotions, theirs and their counterparts. They should build a working relationship. Empathy is fundamental in any process of conflict resolution. Negotiators should try to put themselves in the other side's place; show them that they appreciate their efforts; and deal with them as human beings and with the problems on their merits. Empathic responsiveness is paramount, especially in asymmetrical negotiations such as the Israeli-Palestinian conflict. Israelis and Palestinians, who feel threats to their existence as people, have developed powerful emotions that permeate discussions.

[1] Roger Fisher and William Ury, *Getting to Yes: Negotiating Agreement without Giving In* (London: Random House, 1991).

[2] Herbert C. Kelman, *Resolving Deep-Rooted Conflicts* (London: Routledge, 2020); Herbert C. Kelman, 'The Political Psychology of the Israeli-Palestinian Conflict: How Can We Overcome the Barriers to a Negotiated Solution?', *Political Psychology*, 8(3) (1987): 347–363; Herbert C. Kelman, 'Acknowledging the Other's Nationhood: How to Create a Momentum for the Israeli-Palestinian Negotiations', *Journal of Palestine Studies*, 22(1) (Autumn 1992): 18–38; Herbert C. Kelman, 'Some Determinants of the Oslo Breakthrough', *International Negotiation*, 2 (1997): 183–194; Herbert C. Kelman, 'The Israeli-Palestinian Peace Process and Its Vicissitudes', *American Psychologist*, 62(4) (May–June 2007): 287–303.

[3] I. William Zartman, *Negotiation and Conflict Management: Essays on Theory and Practice* (London: Routledge, 2007); I. William Zartman, *Ripe for Resolution* (New York and Oxford: Oxford University Press, 1989).

Fisher and Ury advise focusing on principles and interests, not on positions. The Egyptian-Israeli peace treaty at Camp David in 1978 demonstrates the usefulness of looking behind positions, which in this instance were incompatible. Israel insisted on keeping at least part of Sinai; Egypt insisted on receiving every inch of it. Any compromise was unacceptable. Looking at their respective *interests* made it possible to find a solution.

The Fisher and Ury negotiation model includes the following instructions.[4]

- Formulate concrete and actionable demands. Clearly articulate your interests in tangible terms, avoiding vague or abstract formulations. Recognise and respect the legitimacy of the other side's concerns; underestimating their interests can lead to impasse and undermine mutual trust.
- Tackle the problem without blaming the people. Listen to the other side with respect, show them courtesy, express your appreciation for their time and effort, and emphasise your concern with meeting their basic needs.
- Explore multiple options before reaching agreement. Encourage the generation of diverse, creative solutions through collaborative brainstorming. Postponing premature commitment allows parties to consider a range of alternatives that may better satisfy the core interests of both sides.
- Prioritise clear and effective communication. Communication failures often hinder progress in negotiations. These failures typically arise from three core issues: (1) interlocutors talking past each other or failing to establish a shared vocabulary; (2) insufficient attention paid to what is being communicated; and (3) misinterpretations stemming from ambiguity, cultural differences or poor phrasing. Language, when used skilfully, can serve as a powerful bridge. When mismanaged, it can become a barrier to mutual understanding.
- Ground agreements in objective criteria. Anchor the terms of any agreement in fair, independent standards such as international law, precedent or empirical data. Objective benchmarks enhance legitimacy, reduce bias and make the outcome more acceptable to all parties.
- Avoid threat-based tactics. Refrain from using coercive threats as a primary negotiation tool. While threats can sometimes communicate urgency, they often provoke resistance and escalate tensions.

[4] Fisher and Ury, *Getting to Yes*.

If employed, they must be communicated with credibility and clarity, but ideally, negotiators should explore alternative means of conveying their positions and consequences without resorting to adversarial rhetoric.

First, I outline the qualities that negotiators, mediators and facilitators should cultivate. Note that leaders may play a role as negotiators (Shimon Peres, Abbas, Olmert) and as mediators (Carter, Bill Clinton). Subsequently, I discuss what negotiators, mediators and facilitators should *not* do. Finally, I discuss what interlocutors should do before, during and after the summit. While every conflict is different, characterised by factors that may shift and dramatically affect the recipe for success, still, from history and the vast experience of people who have been directly involved in peace processes, we can deduce some basic principles and parameters that are important for successful negotiations.

Basic Qualities

Negotiators, mediators and facilitators should demonstrate certain basic qualities.

Be Intellectually Curious, Empathetic and Humble

Genuine interest is encouraged. It helps to avoid clashes and anchor a common purpose. Like superforecasters,[5] negotiators, mediators and facilitators should be intelligent and curious, able to approach negotiations with a sense of humility, acknowledging the complexity of predicting future events and the potential for error. Curiosity is productive and contagious. It makes the relationship warmer. When one party shows curiosity, the other becomes curious as well. Negotiators become more invested. Like superforecasters, talented negotiators are committed to continuous learning and self-improvement. They look to progress in the negotiations and move the dialogue forward.

Constructive interpersonal relationships and sustained rapport between negotiators, particularly at the leadership level, are vital components of successful peace diplomacy. When a relationship is grounded in mutual deference and trust, adversaries are often more willing to

[5] Philip E. Tetlock and Dan Gardner, *Superforecasting: The Art and Science of Prediction* (London: Random House, 2015), 191.

accommodate one another's needs and display sensitivity to each other's political and psychological constraints. This form of engagement encourages a shift from zero-sum thinking to more cooperative frameworks.

Effective negotiations require more than the exchange of logical arguments or the advancement of self-interested positions. Parties must strive to understand the underlying motivations, priorities and lived experiences of their counterparts. This includes grasping their cultural narratives, historical myths, collective fears, national ethos and long-term aspirations, whether rooted in objective realities or deeply held perceptions. Engaging with one another on this level enables negotiators to humanise their counterparts and fosters an atmosphere conducive to empathy and creativity. Purely analytical discourse, while essential, is insufficient. Human beings are not machines; they bring to negotiations a complex emotional landscape shaped by personal histories, communal identities and psychological needs. Alongside rational deliberation, parties must establish what might be termed a 'heartful' connection – a capacity to engage one another with emotional intelligence and moral imagination.

To foster such a connection, interlocutors should deliberately highlight shared values, mutual interests and overlapping goals. Common ground, whether in terms of basic needs, aspirations for peace or visions for the future, provides a platform from which trust and cooperation can be built. One practical approach involves trying to visualise positions from the perspective of the other and asking future-oriented questions: where do you hope to be one year from now? What is your vision for your people? What are you prepared to do to realise that vision? Can we achieve it together?

As the more powerful actor in the Israeli-Palestinian conflict, Israel possesses a greater capacity to offer material and symbolic gestures of goodwill. A posture of generosity, whether through tangible assistance or rhetorical empathy, need not be interpreted as weakness. On the contrary, such gestures often resonate deeply and can catalyse reciprocal engagement. Acts of kindness, when sincerely offered, are rarely dismissed.

Negotiations inevitably encounter moments of stagnation. Emotions may flare, and progress may halt. At such junctures, empathy is not a liability but a strategic necessity. Importantly, empathy does not entail surrendering one's core interests; rather, it signals recognition of the other's legitimate concerns and emotional truths. Many aspects of conflict, particularly in prolonged and identity-driven disputes, are not reducible to rational calculations alone. Addressing the emotional and symbolic dimensions of a conflict is therefore essential to any sustainable resolution.

A case in point is the issue of Jerusalem. The symbolic weight of Jerusalem renders negotiations especially fraught, as it invokes passions that transcend conventional diplomacy. Here, an appreciation for the emotional and spiritual stakes involved is as crucial as technical expertise or legal analysis. Without acknowledging these layers of meaning, any proposed resolution risks falling short of the legitimacy required for implementation. The history, religion, nationalism, patriotism and sensibilities that are not altogether rational weigh hard on the participants. In a conversation with a member of the American peace team at Camp David, Dan Meridor said, 'I understand intellectually what you are saying, but emotionally, I cannot entertain it. It is just impossible for me.'[6] Palestinians also express similar sentiments. Interlocutors should express understanding of each other's feelings and state of mind.

Meir Ben-Shabbat, who headed the Israel National Security Council, said that in the Middle East, negotiations are not driven solely by interests, and that a great deal of importance is assigned to sentiment. For him, sentiments played a major role in striking the normalisation accords between Israel and Morocco.[7] In contrast, during the peace negotiations at Camp David, when Ehud Barak explained his political constraints, as the leader of a very shaky coalition government, to Yasser Arafat, Arafat was not even interested in listening, let alone empathising with him (see Chapter 7).

Be Creative

Effective negotiation requires more than adherence to established frameworks or conventional thinking. Negotiators should cultivate a spirit of creativity, encouraging participating teams to explore novel ideas and consider out-of-the-box solutions. Such intellectual openness fosters innovation and encourages the discovery of previously unexamined pathways towards agreement. A resolute commitment to achieving a constructive outcome is essential. To this end, negotiators must be prepared to employ flexible and inventive strategies when attempting to bridge substantive divides.

6 Background information with a member of the American delegation (17 August 2022), 10; interviews with Dan Meridor (21 May 2013; 20 January 2016).

7 Barak Ravid, *Trump's Peace* (Rishon LeZion: Yedioth Ahronoth, 2022) (Hebrew), 304.

In moments of apparent deadlock or impasse, the ability to generate imaginative alternatives becomes indispensable. Rather than retreating into entrenched positions, effective negotiators view crises as opportunities to reframe issues, introduce new variables or redefine the structure of discussion, injecting momentum back into stalled talks and moving parties closer to mutually acceptable outcomes.

Be Honest and Clear

Honesty and clarity are crucial. Gamal Helal says that the first step in negotiations is to make it clear why the parties are engaged in negotiations, what they intend to achieve and what principles will guide the discussions.[8] At Oslo, one of the major problems was that while the Palestinians wanted an independent state, the Israelis were pursuing the idea of Palestinian autonomy in the Occupied Palestinian Territory. The two parties were negotiating about different things, leading to misunderstanding and mistrust. In the end, the Israelis pursued their settlement project and the aggrieved Palestinians responded with violence and terror.

Be Cautious and Non-deterministic

Like superforecasters,[9] negotiators, mediators and facilitators should understand the value of compromise and be pragmatic and cognisant of the value of checking thinking for cognitive and emotional biases. Capable negotiators, mediators and facilitators understand the value of *not* saying an unqualified 'no'. As much as possible, they should leave room for continued engagement.

Demonstrate Goodwill

Successful conflict resolution fundamentally depends on the presence of goodwill between the parties involved. Without a genuine willingness to engage in constructive dialogue and a shared commitment to ending hostilities, the conflict is likely to persist indefinitely. For an agreement to be attainable, the parties must perceive that reaching a settlement will align with their self-interest and offer tangible benefits. This motivation

[8] Interview with Gamal Helal (11 November 2022), 5.
[9] Tetlock and Gardner, *Superforecasting*, 191.

is critical, as peace processes invariably require substantial compromises and sacrifices that affect multiple dimensions of societal and individual life. The parties must be convinced that the prospective agreement will significantly enhance their collective well-being and quality of life. In essence, they have to envision a future that is demonstrably superior to the present reality, a future characterised by stability, security and improved human conditions. Only when the parties believe that peace will yield a more promising and sustainable future can they be expected to commit wholeheartedly to the difficult and often protracted task of negotiation and reconciliation.[10]

Sometimes interlocutors engage in negotiations to deflect pressure. An external power pressures them to engage, and they go through the motions without any real motivation to resolve the conflict. Under such circumstances, the likelihood of success is not great. The Oslo process materialised into the Accords because both parties wanted to negotiate, and both wanted to reach an agreement. This was also the case at Camp David in 1978. Conversely, one of the reasons for the Camp David 2000 failure was that the Palestinians did not believe the time was ripe for a deal and did not even want to attend the summit. Leaders should feel that they will lose more by not negotiating; otherwise, they will stall and wait.

Be Fair and Reasonable

Deliberations should be fair and reasonable. 'Fair' means that considerations are not deceitful, that there is no hidden, sinister agenda, and that negotiators do not aim to deceive their opponent.[11] Fairness also requires that each side has ample opportunities to affect the discussions. 'Reasonable' refers to the quality of being 'as much as is appropriate or fair'.[12] The terms 'rational' and 'reasonable' are nearly synonymous; each derives from the Latin word *ratio*, meaning reason.[13] Reasonable decision-makers consider alternatives, estimate consequences and weigh advantages and disadvantages. Following John Rawls's theory of justice, the concept of reasonableness includes a strong moral aspect,

[10] Interview with Sven-Eric Söder (20 August 2019).

[11] In his comments on a draft of this chapter, Dan Kurtzer wrote that negotiators will not normally reveal their ultimate aims. Their 'hidden agenda' might not be 'sinister', but it will remain hidden so that nothing is given away prematurely.

[12] The Oxford Dictionary, https://en.oxforddictionaries.com/definition/reasonableness.

[13] Michele Mangini, 'Toward a Theory of Reasonableness', *Ratio Juris*, 31(2) (2018): 216.

where people act fairly, pursue cooperation and assume others do the same.[14] In Rawls's framework of justice as fairness, members of society value agreements, balance conflicting interests and seek fair and reasonable compromises (see Chapter 1).

Shlomo Brom argued that during the Oslo peace process, when it came to territorial arrangements, the Israelis 'quite jerked' the Palestinians around. Brom admitted: 'We deceived them.'[15] The Israelis took advantage of their own expertise, which, at that time, the Palestinians lacked.[16] The Palestinian delegation did not have a lawyer who could match Joel Singer's legal skills, nor did they have mapping experts. The Israelis exploited the Palestinians' shortcomings.

Be Focused

Negotiators should remain focused on the most important issues and avoid issues that are trifles. A good practice before going into a meeting is to write down what negotiators want to accomplish, and what outcome they wish to achieve by the end of the day. This will sharpen their focus on what to do during the meeting.

Be Well Argued

Negotiators should avoid petty arguments. Argumentation does not increase the quality of one's reasoning. In fact, more arguments only dilute the power of one's strong points. Negotiators should employ just their cogent arguments.

Be Realistic

Negotiators should know their limitations and acknowledge the constraints posed by reality. They should not try to round the square. One must differentiate between aspirations and realistic goals. This also applies to mediators. During his shuttles between Israel and Egypt, Henry Kissinger effectively explained the politics and constraints of each side to the other.[17]

14 John Rawls, *Political Liberalism* (New York: Columbia University Press, 1993), 49.
15 Interview with Shlomo Brom (17 June 2014), 4.
16 Interview with Hiba Husseini (24 December 2024), 3.
17 Edward R. F. Sheehan, 'How Kissinger Did It: Step by Step in the Middle East', *Foreign Policy*, 22 (Spring 1976): 3–70.

Effective negotiation requires a clear-eyed assessment of capabilities and constraints. Overreaching or striving for outcomes that exceed what can realistically be achieved can derail even the most well-intentioned diplomatic efforts. Overambition, even when driven by normative aspirations, often undermines pragmatic progress by creating expectations that cannot be met.

For years, Israeli and Palestinian negotiators continued to approach the territorial questions of the West Bank and Gaza as a unified issue, despite the transformative impact of Hamas's violent takeover of Gaza in 2007. This event fundamentally altered the internal landscape of the Palestinian polity. However, the peace process largely ignored this development, maintaining the fiction of political unity between the Palestinian Authority (PA) in the West Bank and Hamas in Gaza. The Palestine Liberation Organization (PLO) remained committed to a framework that defined the future Palestinian state as encompassing both territories, despite Hamas's explicit rejection of the Oslo framework and its exclusion from the negotiations.

Olmert accepted this position, endorsing the notion of territorial continuity between the West Bank and Gaza. Yet this approach failed to account for the internal Palestinian political fragmentation, rendering the implementation of any agreement increasingly implausible. For much of the Israeli public, long before 7 October 2023, the prospect of territorial withdrawal from the West Bank, under conditions of political instability and without credible guarantees against a Hamas takeover, provoked serious security concerns. The peace deal was not attractive to the Israeli public. The fear that the West Bank could become a forward base for Iranian-backed militancy, akin to the situation in Gaza, significantly undermined domestic support for the peace process.

In this context, a more effective strategy would have acknowledged the limitations imposed by intra-Palestinian divisions and tailored negotiations accordingly. Realism, grounded in a sober understanding of the political and security environment, is essential. Negotiators should recognise when idealistic aspirations must yield to the constraints of practical feasibility. Sustainable agreements are built not only on shared goals, but also on mutual recognition of political, structural and societal limits.

Be Cognisant of Differences

It is essential to recognise that Israel and the PLO are asymmetrical actors in both political structure and international status. Israel is a fully sovereign, recognised state with established institutions, a robust economy and a powerful army. In contrast, the PLO, although internationally acknowledged as the representative of the Palestinian people, does not govern a fully sovereign state and operates within a fragmented and constrained political framework. The PA, which exercises limited self-rule in parts of the West Bank, functions under authoritarian conditions, lacking many of the institutional checks and balances characteristic of democratic governance. The disparities in population size, military capacity, economic resources and global diplomatic standing further underscore the structural imbalance between the parties. Both Israeli and Palestinian leaders are acutely aware of these asymmetries, which shape the strategic calculations, expectations and leverage each side brings to the negotiation table. Understanding and addressing this imbalance is critical for designing fair and effective negotiation frameworks that account for the relative capacities and constraints of each actor.

Furthermore, in cross-cultural negotiations, the two parties should invest time in building relationships and getting to know one another, aiming to understand how interlocutors think and identify perception gaps. They should identify cultural differences, as well as their common ground despite these differences. The values of dignity, honour and respect are of great importance to both parties, especially the Palestinians. Their concepts of time, however, are different. In Arabic-speaking Islamic culture, time is understood as an interplay between two dimensions: earthly existence, bounded by birth and death, and eternal heavenly existence (*dahr*), which has no end. These realms are interconnected, influencing each other in distinct ways. Divine guidance, rewards and retribution flow from the heavenly to the earthly, while human faith, religious duties and rituals extend from the earthly towards the heavenly. Because a believer's time is not restricted and shares in eternity, eventually God will provide an intervening event.[18] Israeli culture is more secular; it focuses on the earthly. Israelis wish to make the intervention themselves, here and now. Patience is a highly esteemed virtue in Islamic culture, particularly within Arabic-speaking communities, where it is emphasised and valued to a far greater degree than in Western cultures. Israelis and Palestinians frame their arguments differently. Israelis are direct; they pride themselves on speaking to the point, speaking *dugri*. They do not like to beat around the bush.

[18] Ilai Alon and Jeanne M. Brett, 'Perceptions of Time and Their Impact on Negotiations in the Arabic-Speaking Islamic World', *Negotiation Journal*, 23(1) (2007): 55–73.

This direct discursive form is one of the traits of the *sabra*, the 'new Jew', in contrast to the diaspora Jew, who must always take note of their non-Jewish, majoritarian environment. Israelis usually speak their minds and, albeit unintentionally, come off as rude to those who have never encountered them before.

In contrast, Palestinians' discursive style is indirect; they tell stories and use metaphors. It takes them time to reach the point. Their style of argumentation is circular, coming from different directions before they address an issue. This was very noticeable during my interviews. The longest interviews I conducted were with Palestinians, who sat with me for three, four or five hours, at times in one session.[19] In dealing with the Palestinians, Israelis must exhibit patience. Barak's impatience with Arafat did a disservice to Israeli interests.

Know How to Move the Discussion Forward

Negotiators and mediators should know how to facilitate discussion, appreciate timing, raise sensitive issues with caution and pose open-ended questions that start a conversation, rather than closing it. Negotiations require time, the ability to elucidate and have an exchange. In Arab culture, slow movement is appreciated. Annoyance at the slow pace of negotiations does not help, and it casts the impatient interlocutor in a negative light.[20]

Be Adaptable

Like superforecasters,[21] negotiators, mediators and facilitators should be able to adjust and be open to doubt, to revise and rephrase. Conclusions should be considered tentative and open to testing, with the aim of improving them. Capable negotiators, mediators and facilitators are also willing to admit errors and change course when necessary. Tetlock and Gardner think the most important quality is the degree to which people are committed to belief updating and self-improvement. In their terms, these are perpetual beta people.[22]

[19] Interviews with Ziad Abu Zayyad (14 May 2015), Ghaith al-Omari (2 September 2014), Hussein Agha (5 April 2019), Ahmad Khalidi (5 June 2019) and Salam Fayyad (16 January 2024; 19 January 2024).

[20] Uri Sagie, *The Frozen Hand* (Tel Aviv: Miskal, 2011) (Hebrew), 81–82.

[21] Tetlock and Gardner, *Superforecasting*, 191.

[22] Ibid., 192.

Be Respectful

Negotiators should relate to each other as fellow humans. Mutual respect is a must. They should remain positive and respectful, despite disagreements. They should remain focused on the topics they wish to resolve, treating each other with dignity, which generates trust. Being respectful is a key to establishing rapport between opponents. Praising and honouring Palestinian negotiators is important.[23] Having *chemistry* between negotiators is at least a plus, if not critical. Uri Savir wrote that he was fortunate to have Ahmed Qurie as his counterpart because they understood one another as 'two human beings, each representing a different cause'.[24] Savir maintained that building personal relationships reveals that both sides are human. Dennis Ross thinks that having such chemistry is 'critical', not because one side or the other is going to sacrifice what they see as their basic needs, or because they like their interlocutors personally or trust them. Every negotiation, however, involves an effort to get both sides to adjust their behaviours. 'And adjusting behaviour is the hardest thing to do.'[25]

Ross supported his contention with an example. At Wye River, he introduced the Syrian ambassador to Washington, Walid Muallem, to Savir. It was the first time they had met and it was important that they establish a personal relationship.[26] They had to believe in each other. Ross said to them: 'I am going to leave you alone. I do not even want you to talk about the substance. I just want you to talk about who you are. About your families. About why you are here. What do you hope to achieve and why? What do you hope for your kids? I want you to get to know each other.'[27] And then Ross left the room. The meeting between Muallem and Savir lasted two and a half to three hours. Clearly, it was a good meeting. Similarly, the walk in the woods that Savir and Qurie took in May 1993, during the Oslo peace process, on Terje Rød-Larsen's suggestion, broke the ice between the two and led to fruitful negotiations.[28] Qurie wrote that that personal conversation 'changed my earlier assessment of Savir, and caused me to revise the impressions of him I had

[23] Sagie, *The Frozen Hand*, 85.

[24] Uri Savir, 'Oslo: Twenty Years After', *Negotiation Journal* (January 2014): 118.

[25] Interview with Dennis Ross (27 September 2019), 4. See also interview with Francesco Motta (1 April 2022), 17.

[26] Between December 1995 and February 1996, the United States hosted talks between Israel and Syria at the Aspen Institute Wye River Conference Center.

[27] Interview with Dennis Ross (27 September 2019), 5.

[28] Ahmed Qurie, *From Oslo to Jerusalem* (London: I.B. Tauris, 2008), 149–150.

gained at first, especially when he had opened the first session of negotiations the day before with such stubbornness'.[29]

Not all Israelis had the foresight to treat the Palestinians as equals. The opposite is true. The Israelis had a tendency to look down on the Palestinians, an attitude that did not help the negotiations.[30] Shlomo Brom said that most of the time during the negotiations, the attitude of the Israeli side towards the Palestinians was the attitude of Shabac handlers.[31] Of course, personal relationships are not the only or the major ingredient for success, but they are certainly an important factor. The Palestinians' lack of motivation may be at least partly due to the Israeli attitude, which alienated them from the process.

Several Palestinian, Israeli and American delegates commented on the disrespectful way Barak treated Arafat. Barak maintained that he always respected Arafat. He never raised his voice, scorned Arafat or 'pretended to know more or do more'.[32] But he ignored Arafat again and again and avoided his company. Even when they were seated next to each other, Barak spoke with other people. Arafat was not oblivious to Barak's conduct, which was, of course, insulting.

In his defence, Barak reiterated that sharing a meal with Arafat would not have made him more receptive to his ideas.[33] Shlomo Ben-Ami also finds it difficult to believe that Arafat would have conceded the Temple Mount had Barak had coffee with him. Ben-Ami found this suggestion laughable.[34] At the same time, Ben-Ami acknowledged that the atmosphere at Camp David was sour.[35] Akram Hanieh remarked that Barak was unable to establish an effective working relationship with Arafat. Aside from two meetings with Clinton on the first and last days of the summit, Arafat and Barak met, but did not engage, at official dinner parties hosted by Clinton. On one occasion, Barak initiated a visit to Arafat's lodgings and had tea with him, but no specific political issues were discussed. No other meeting took place between the two leaders.[36]

29 Ibid., 150.
30 Interview with Shlomo Brom (17 June 2014), 3. See also Sari Nusseibeh, *Once Upon a Country* (London: Halban, 2007), 430; Uri Savir, *The Process* (New York: Vintage Books, 1998), 215–216.
31 Interview with Shlomo Brom (17 June 2014), 2.
32 Interview with Ehud Barak (11 July 2022), 11.
33 Ibid.
34 Interview with Shlomo Ben-Ami (26 June 2013), 5.
35 Ibid.
36 Akram Hanieh, 'The Camp David Papers', *Journal of Palestine Studies*, 30(2) (Winter 2001): 93.

Figure 11.1 Begin and Sadat.
Credit: Sahm Doherty/Contributor/Getty Images.

True, there were huge hurdles to overcome, and sharing coffee and baklava with Barak would not have moved Arafat to make significant concessions on Jerusalem. And while a positive attitude would not necessarily yield a positive result, I believe a negative attitude made negative results more likely.

Barak discounted the human factor. He reminded me that Menachem Begin hardly met with Anwar Sadat at Camp David in 1978.[37] It is true that Sadat and Begin did not have a warm relationship at the peace summit. Ben-Ami argues that Sadat despised Begin.[38] He could not stand Begin's over-legalistic attitude to issues. Still, they were able to see beyond personality issues and reach an agreement (see Figure 11.1).

Be Able to Explain

Effective negotiations depend not only on the substantive outcomes reached at the table, but also on the clarity and transparency with which those involved articulate their positions, both to each other and to

[37] Interview with Ehud Barak (11 July 2022), 12.
[38] Interview with Shlomo Ben-Ami (26 June 2013), 5.

their respective constituencies. Interlocutors must communicate their interests, needs and underlying motivations with precision and sincerity. Explaining *what* is needed and *why* it is needed facilitates mutual understanding, reduces misperceptions and fosters trust between negotiating parties.

Equally important is the parallel process of domestic communication. Political leaders engaged in negotiations must provide their publics with a coherent narrative: why they are negotiating, the objectives they seek to attain, the outcomes they have achieved and the nature and rationale behind any concessions they have made. This explanatory process is not merely an exercise in public relations; it is a democratic imperative. Leaders are accountable to their constituencies, and legitimacy in peace processes often hinges on public comprehension and consent.

In pluralistic societies, where public opinion can shape or constrain diplomatic action, cultivating broad-based support requires consistent and persuasive messaging. Even in more centralised or authoritarian contexts, leaders must contend with influential stakeholders, internal factions and national narratives that demand justification. In short, all actors in a negotiation, state or non-state, operate within political ecosystems that require them to justify their actions to some form of audience. Communication and explanation are not ancillary to negotiation; they are integral to its success and sustainability.

Be Relentless and Reflective

Like superforecasters,[39] negotiators, mediators and facilitators should be determined and persistent in their search for solutions. They should be comfortable with uncertainty and willing to test and refine their predictions.

Be Open-Minded, with Dragonfly-Eyed Ability

Like superforecasters,[40] negotiators, mediators and facilitators should be open to diverse views and perspectives. This helps them avoid cognitive and emotional biases. They should value diverse opinions and be able to synthesise them. Negotiators and mediators who are not the leaders themselves receive instructions from their leaders. They should understand and evaluate different views. Granted, they would rarely be 'open' to those

[39] Tetlock and Gardner, *Superforecasting*, 154–155.
[40] Ibid., 216.

views unless they comport with their instructions; still, they can explain and fill knowledge gaps, highlight the importance of certain sensitivities and be effective in their messages to various stakeholders.

Be Ready to Pay the Price

This refers to leaders. Will in itself is insufficient. Genuine leadership in peace negotiations requires a willingness to bear the political and personal costs that often accompany meaningful compromise. Peace is rarely achieved without significant sacrifice, and those who aspire to broker it must demonstrate more than rhetorical commitment. Declarations of intent, absent concrete actions or readiness to make unpopular concessions, amount to little more than performative gestures.

For peace to be credible and sustainable, leaders must exhibit moral courage and political resolve, particularly when the decisions required are likely to provoke opposition from key segments of their constituencies. This involves a readiness to expend political capital, risk public backlash and, in some cases, jeopardise their own hold on power. In such moments, leadership is measured not by the ability to reflect popular sentiment, but by the capacity to shape and lead it towards a vision of a more stable and just future.

Indeed, history shows that transformative peace agreements are seldom forged without principled risk-taking. Leaders must rise above the pressures of short-term political gain to pursue the long-term interests of their societies, understanding that the dividends of peace, though hard-won, are ultimately far more enduring than the costs required to secure them.

Kahneman and Tversky argue that decision-makers tend to attach greater importance to prospective losses than to prospective gains, even when these are of equivalent magnitude. The implication is that parties in a dispute will prove reluctant to trade concessions and accept gambles unless the payoffs are very favourable. Interlocutors should weigh short-term advantages as well as long-term advantages; otherwise, they may be stuck in the status quo. Kahneman and Tversky argue that as the disadvantages of alternatives to the status quo are weighted more heavily than the advantages, a strong bias exists in favour of the status quo.[41] This tendency hampers the chances of achieving peace.

[41] Daniel Kahneman and Amos Tversky, 'Conflict Resolution: A Cognitive Perspective', in Kenneth Arrow, Robert H. Mnookin, Lee Ross, Amos Tversky and Robert Wilson (eds), *Barriers to Conflict Resolution* (New York: W. W. Norton, 1995), 45–60.

Basic Behaviours

Negotiators, mediators and facilitators should take a number of actions.

Do the Homework

Thorough preparation is an essential prerequisite for effective negotiation. All parties, whether negotiators or mediators, must engage in rigorous preparatory work ahead of each meeting, equipping themselves with a deep and nuanced understanding of the issues at stake. Mastery should extend beyond general principles and overarching frameworks to include detailed knowledge of facts, figures, precedents and historical timelines. Such precision enables negotiators to identify when a counterpart misstates information, through incorrect data, misquoted figures or inaccurate chronologies – not necessarily as a sign of ill intent, but as a result of the complexity of protracted conflicts. Recognising that human error is inevitable fosters a more constructive atmosphere where mistakes can be corrected in good faith rather than viewed as deliberate misrepresentations.

In addition to factual mastery, effective negotiators must understand their counterpart's worldview, as well as their own predispositions. Cognitive, cultural, religious and ideological biases inevitably shape perceptions and judgements, often erecting barriers to resolution. A critical component of preparatory work is identifying and acknowledging these biases – not to eliminate them, which is unrealistic, but to manage and mitigate their impact. Such awareness also extends to recognising the structural and situational constraints under which both sides operate, including domestic political pressures, institutional limitations and broader societal influences.

Preparation, in this comprehensive sense, enhances sensitivity to the intricacies of the conflict and promotes greater understanding and realism at the negotiation table. It lays the groundwork for more responsive and adaptive dialogue and significantly increases the likelihood of meaningful progress.

Some of my interviewees highlighted the fact that senior negotiators arrived at the negotiation table without the necessary understanding of the issues.[42] One reason for the failure of Camp David 2000 was

[42] Interviews with Gidi Grinstein (21 May 2013), Israel Hasson (23 May 2013), Martin Indyk (9 August 2022), Dennis Ross (27 September 2019; 21 October 2019) and Aaron David Miller (October–November 2008; 12 September 2019).

the last-minute invitations that were issued to Meridor and Elyakim Rubinstein. Both came to the summit unprepared. Rubinstein writes that only when he arrived at Camp David was he assigned to negotiate the refugee issue and he needed to improvise quickly, gathering information by making urgent phone calls, inter alia to his wife, who worked at the Attorney General's Office.[43] Prime Minister Barak should have invited them early, assigned them specific tasks and enabled them to study the material carefully, so that they could come to the negotiation table fully prepared.

Interlocutors should be familiar with the history of the conflict, and of places, events and outcomes. In the Israeli-Palestinian conflict, negotiators should master maps and know important details: borders, Jerusalem neighbourhoods, the number of people in certain cities and areas, the implications of suggested plans for people and the number of people affected by each plan. What are the likely patterns if option A is preferred? Option B? Option C? What are the implications of the status quo? Negotiators should eliminate or at least reduce the chance of surprising arguments.

For instance, instead of speaking about the percentage of territory that would remain in Israel, speak in square kilometres about the territory of each settlement and the roads to them, as well as to security zones and installations; explain why these are needed, and for what period of time. Then discuss the territory that Israel would give the Palestinians, in square kilometres, its location and fertility. What are the water resources there? Ensure that the deal is just and fair to both sides so as to avoid future grievances.

According to the PLO, the West Bank area is 5,737 square kilometres. Every 1 per cent amounts to approximately fifty-seven square kilometres. However, the Israeli position was that the disputed territory of the West Bank amounted to 5,428 square kilometres, and that every 1 per cent amounts to approximately fifty-four square kilometres.[44] Consequently, the gap between the Israeli and Palestinian positions ahead of Camp David was 1,124 square kilometres, or 20 per cent of the PLO's territorial aspirations.[45] This is a substantial gap that cannot be resolved if the two sides continue to speak in contested percentage terms.

[43] Elyakim Rubinstein, 'Critical Policy Decisions – Wishes versus Reality: Memoirs of a Participant Witness', lecture delivered in May 2024.

[44] Gidi Grinstein and Ari Afilalo, *(In)Sights: Peacemaking in the Oslo Process Thirty Years and Counting* (Jerusalem: Gefen, 2023), 97.

[45] Ibid.

Interlocutors should learn from the experiences of successful and unsuccessful negotiations. Jonathan Powell thinks that having people who have worked on previous successful negotiations can be useful. These are people who can say 'last time this happened, we found this and that useful'.[46] In Northern Ireland, the South Africans were quite influential. They took the different parties in the Northern Ireland conflict to South Africa and explained how the negotiations took place there. They introduced them to all the planners. They provided people from Northern Ireland with an opportunity to talk to each other *there*, in South Africa, in a way they could not have at home. Subsequently, Powell took some of the lessons from that experience to Colombia and Spain for negotiations in those parts of the world.[47] Powell was never asked to advise and support the Israeli-Palestinian negotiations. Tony Blair offered his help to Prime Minister Ariel Sharon, based on his experience in Northern Ireland. Sharon replied: 'How kind of you to come, when you have got so many problems at home, to try and help us with our problems. We really appreciate it.'[48] In other words, thank you, but no thank you. Mind your own business. Unsurprisingly, Sharon proceeded not to listen to a word Blair said.

Negotiators should master the ins and outs of the two Camp David peace summits, understand the differences between them and be able to explain to themselves why 1978 ended with a peace treaty, while the 2000 summit failed and was followed by another Intifada and violence. In contrast to 1978, Camp David 2000 was not well prepared. Each party lacked an understanding and appreciation of the other's value system and sense of justice. They did not care about the other's constraints, and the mediator was unable to serve as a bridge. Entrenched positions remained entrenched, and after a few days, it became clear that peace was beyond reach.[49]

Effective negotiation requires interlocutors to undertake a thorough and systematic analysis of the situation, beginning with a clear distinction between declared positions and underlying interests, both their own and those of their counterparts. While positions are often shaped by public expectations, political constraints or strategic posturing, true interests reflect the core needs, concerns and objectives

46 Interview with Jonathan Powell (20 July 2022), 11.
47 Ibid.
48 Ibid.
49 Interview with Gidi Grinstein (21 May 2013), 13.

that a party seeks to fulfil. All members of the negotiation team must internalise this distinction, avoiding the common error of conflating surface-level demands with foundational priorities. Only with this clarity can negotiators develop cogent arguments and articulate respectful, well-reasoned counterproposals that address the other party's concerns while advancing their own interests.

Mutual preparedness is also critical to maintaining equilibrium at the negotiation table. When one party is significantly better prepared than the other, a cognitive and strategic imbalance emerges. Even if the more prepared side refrains from exploiting its advantage, the asymmetry can undermine trust and respect. The less prepared party may experience feelings of inferiority, frustration or resentment, while the better prepared side may, consciously or not, project impatience, superiority or disdain. Such dynamics risk derailing the negotiation, replacing cooperation with suspicion or defensiveness.

Given the stakes involved in peace negotiations, often including existential concerns and long-standing grievances, dialogues demand diligent preparation, intellectual discipline and anticipatory thinking. Preparation must include scenario planning, in which negotiators consider a range of potential developments, particularly the possibility that their initial proposals will be rejected. Crafting a draft peace agreement should be part of this exercise, not as a rigid endpoint, but as a framework to stimulate discussion and explore viable alternatives. Negotiators must be ready to pivot and adapt to counter-offers and proposals that differ from their expectations while remaining anchored in their core interests. This flexibility, grounded in painstaking preparation, significantly enhances the prospects for a constructive and outcome-oriented negotiation process.

Listen

Negotiators (especially leaders) like to talk, because then they are in control and at the centre of attention. They set the tone and the agenda. Meaningful conversation, however, requires a balance between talking and listening. Negotiators must be present and invested in the conversation. They should be open to understanding their opponent fully and *not* occupy their mind with preparing a response while others are talking. Listening is very different from hearing. Most of us are born with a sense of hearing. It is a capacity that we take for granted unless we lose it. Listening is a capacity that must be cultivated. Leaders who pontificate, who are interested only in what they say and who fail to listen, are less likely to generate goodwill in their interlocutor, who is then less likely to make meaningful concessions. Buddha said: 'If your mouth is opened, you are not learning.'[50] For a successful negotiation, you cannot have people who just talk and are unwilling to listen. We were given one mouth and two ears for a very good reason. We should get the message.

Listeners should be attentive and focused, able to nudge the discussion to where they want it to go. Israelis should be patient and respectful and understand the Palestinian discursive style. Barak, lacking the patience to listen to Arafat's stories and convoluted argumentation, refused to listen to him.[51] This did not play out well. Arafat perceived this as a sign of disrespect. His willingness to strike a deal eroded with time because he felt that Barak had dishonoured him.[52] Barak's hopes and expectations of resolving the conflict without meeting Arafat were dashed.

True listening requires the ability to open oneself to learning, although it does not mean accepting. At the very least, however, negotiators who listen better understand the reasons for disagreements. Interpersonal communication practices, such as active listening and direct eye contact, can be helpful, especially when one's counterpart holds a very different worldview. While these skills do not assure a smooth process, they can pave the way to a better understanding of each other.[53]

Listening requires paying close attention to what the other party is saying. This is why it is important that in each delegation, one person has the designated role of listener. The listener should not be preoccupied with anything else; he/she does not negotiate. The listener is there to fathom the underlying interests of the other side and convey his/her thoughts to his/her team. Listening takes effort and energy. Dean Rusk said the most valuable element of diplomacy in general was the ability to listen with discernment.[54]

Attentive and empathetic listening is foundational to any successful negotiation. Without it, communication becomes a mere exchange of words, devoid of resonance or impact. Statements pass one another without registering, let alone anchoring in mutual understanding. For dialogue to be meaningful, interlocutors must engage not only with their own

50 Guatama Buddha Quotes, *Goodreads*, https://tinyurl.com/2972drha.

51 Interview with Ehud Barak (11 July 2022).

52 Interviews with Hussein Agha (5 April 2019), Ami Ayalon (28 June 2022), Israel Hasson (23 May 2013) and Martin Indyk (9 August 2022).

53 Jeffrey R. Seul, 'Mediating Across Worldviews', in Catherine Turner and Martin Wählisch (eds), *Rethinking Peace Mediation* (Bristol: Bristol University Press, 2021), 203–226, at 208.

54 Dan Kurtzer's comments on a draft of this chapter.

narratives, grievances and objectives, but also with the concerns and perspectives of the other side. A central premise of conflict resolution theory is that durable agreements are only possible when each party recognises that its own needs cannot be fully addressed in isolation; mutual responsiveness is essential. This requires a willingness to adopt a relational mindset, where the resolution of one's problems is intrinsically linked to an understanding of the other's challenges. Genuine progress is achieved not by asserting unilateral demands, but by demonstrating an openness to the other party's reality, its constraints, fears and aspirations. Such openness fosters trust and creates space for reciprocity, increasing the likelihood of creative problem-solving. Thus, negotiators must approach the process with a dual awareness: of their own core interests and of the equally valid interests of their counterparts. Only through this reciprocal attentiveness can the groundwork be laid for a mutually beneficial and sustainable agreement.

Negotiate in Good Faith

Interlocutors should come to the negotiation table in good faith, removing obstacles that are important to their counterpart and refraining from augmenting obstacles. Kant wrote: 'No peace treaty is valid if it was made with mental reservations that could lead to a future war.'[55] For Hiba Husseini, Aharon Barak and Avi Gil, negotiating in good faith is the key, the most important point. Husseini says that knowing that there is a genuine will to reach an agreement is important. It is imperative to make a genuine and serious effort to reach an agreement that will have a lasting effect.[56] Jonathan Schwartz commented that in Camp David 2000 Israel often controlled information about an issue under negotiation (e.g, water resources). Israel considered this part of its bargaining leverage; however, withholding key information gives rise to suspicion and, perhaps, inflated demands by the other side. It also undermines the idea that the parties will work in good faith post-agreement to implement provisions. This does not mean that negotiators should reveal all the information uniquely available to their side, but it is a step that should be considered wherever possible.[57]

[55] Immanuel Kant, *Toward Perpetual Peace* (Jonathan Bennett edition, 2017), 1.

[56] Interview with Hiba Husseini (24 December 2024), 19; Raphael Cohen-Almagor, 'Lessons from the Israeli-Egyptian Peace Talks: An Interview with Aharon Barak', *Israel Studies Review*, 34(2) (Autumn 2019): 1–32. See also James K. Sebenius, *Kissinger the Negotiator* (New York: Harper, 2018), 224.

[57] Jonathan Schwart's comments on a draft of this chapter.

Create a Conducive Environment

Facilitators should create the most conducive environment possible in which the parties feel comfortable, and where the stress of negotiations can be mitigated. Pär Nuder spoke of the need to create an environment between the parties where they can step out of their professional roles and speak to each other as human beings with families.[58] The atmosphere should be beneficial for people to open up, rather than shut down. There should be opportunities, such as mealtimes, to develop personal relationships. Leisure activities for the delegations should be planned so the people can get to know one another in their day-to-day capacities, not only as professional negotiators.

Negotiations are about human relations. Simple positive steps yield a positive atmosphere and goodwill in which the other is viewed as a human being whose aspirations are similar to one's own. The closer you can come to each other, the easier it is to connect and understand each other's core issues. When interlocutors create an atmosphere where they can put all the cards on the table, they come closer to finding solutions.

When Singer negotiated the 1995 Interim Agreement with Sa'eb Erekat, he always made a point of alternating the location for their bilateral meetings between Erekat's office in Jericho and a hotel in Tel Aviv. When they met in Cairo, they always stayed in separate hotels. There, Singer most often met Erekat at his hotel. Singer thought that this gesture would bear fruit and, indeed, notwithstanding Erekat's normally aggressive manner of talking with other interlocutors (Israeli and American alike), he was always very cordial with Singer. When Singer retired from the Israeli Foreign Ministry, Erekat held a farewell party for him in his Jericho home.[59]

I mentioned the sour atmosphere at Camp David 2000. The atmosphere was always very tense, for several reasons. Lack of direction and the bad chemistry between Barak and Arafat affected the mood.[60] When Clinton was away at the G7 conference, Barak isolated himself. People thought he was depressed. Opinion polls from Israel did not reassure him, and he was anxious about his political survival, about what was being said about him and the peace summit. He was also constantly concerned about possible leaks. Barak explained that if the Palestinians refused to move forward in the presence of the American president, there was no

[58] Interview with Pär Nuder (20 August 2019), 14.
[59] Joel Singer's comments on a draft of this chapter.
[60] Interview with Israel Hasson (23 May 2013), 10.

way they would move forward in his absence.[61] Furthermore, from early on, the Israelis understood that the Palestinians were not interested in the summit's success. This understanding did not improve their mood. And the atmosphere was bad also because of the bad relationships between some of the Americans and some of the Palestinians (see Chapters 6 and 7). Abbas and Qurie, who were considered more moderate than Arafat, were alienated from the summit. Although they supported the Oslo process, mentally, they were not at Camp David. They were absent participants. To a large extent, this was the Americans' doing.

After consulting with the leaders, organisers of meetings should consider inviting leaders' spouses to join them if they deem such invitations beneficial and believe they would make a positive contribution towards the summit's success.

Clarify Needs and Ambitions

Each side has certain ambitions and desires – things it would be *nice* to have. These desires should be differentiated from *needs* – things that the parties *have* to have and on which they cannot compromise. Each side should clarify its own needs and desires to itself and then convey them to the other party, delivering a clear message about the bread-and-butter issues, without which there cannot be an agreement. Fisher and Ury argue that the most powerful interests are basic human needs, including security, economic well-being, a sense of belonging, recognition and control over one's life.[62]

Generally speaking, people seek to secure a good future for themselves and their children. Specifically, this means satisfying the need for food and housing, securing a job, having sufficient drinking water for the community, and the right to education and health. Increasingly, this also includes concern for the environment. By reaching agreements regarding these shared needs, the parties can create a shared reality that would be better than the separate realities that each party may strive to achieve on its own.[63]

[61] Interview with Ehud Barak (11 July 2022), 20.

[62] Fisher and Ury, *Getting to Yes*, 49–50.

[63] Gerald Echterhoff, E. Tory Higgins and John M. Levine, 'Shared Reality: Experiencing Commonality with Others' Inner States about the World', *Perspectives on Psychological Science*, 4 (2009): 496–521; Gerald Echterhoff and E. Tory Higgins, 'How Communication Shapes Memory: Shared Reality and Implications for Culture', in Gun R. Semin and Gerald Echterhoff (eds), *Grounding Sociality* (New York: Psychology Press, 2011), 115–146.

We should understand what Israelis and Palestinians truly want. The Israelis want security. The Palestinians want freedom.[64] A peace agreement should provide a foundation for both; otherwise, it is doomed to fail.

Appreciate Balance and Nuance

Like superforecasters,[65] negotiators, mediators and facilitators understand the importance of striking a balance between under- and overreacting to evidence, between under- and overconfidence, and between prudence and decisiveness. Capable negotiators, mediators and facilitators appreciate the nuances in data and understand that the more degrees of uncertainty they can distinguish, the better their forecasts are likely to be.

Understand Not Only Their Own Constraints, but Also the Other Party's Constraints

It takes two to tango. Coordination and planning are paramount. In the context of Israeli-Palestinian negotiations, where there exists a pronounced asymmetry of power, the responsibility falls primarily on the stronger party, Israel, to exercise sensitivity and restraint. Israel must remain cognisant that assuming a dominant role in shaping the agenda, tactics and logistical framework of the talks may be perceived as overbearing or coercive by the Palestinian side, thereby undermining trust and goodwill.

To foster a more balanced and constructive environment, Israel should actively seek to mitigate power imbalances by ensuring that the procedural aspects of the negotiations, including the choice of venue,

64 William Ury was tasked to mediate between two giant companies that had a multibillion-dollar dispute. He met with the CEO of one company and asked him: what do you want? The CEO said: 1.5 billion worth of shares, ability to execute projects, etc. Then Ury said: OK. But what is it that you REALLY want? The CEO reflected for a while and then said: freedom. I want my freedom back. The dispute was so bitter that the two companies could not function. Each CEO only stifled the other. Once Ury understood the underlying motive of the first CEO, he went on to meet the second CEO and proposed that the two rivals strike an agreement that has at its base two overarching principles: freedom and dignity, ensuring that the managers respect each other. Then he brought the two rivals together. They sat with their teams for three days, at the end of which they signed a seventy-page agreement that ended a years' long rivalry and dispute that sabotaged both the Brazilian and the French economies. William Ury, 'The Art of Negotiation', YouTube, www.youtube.com/watch?v=sajCKwxXG_g&t=3116s.

65 Tetlock and Gardner, *Superforecasting*, 158.

logistical arrangements, scheduling and overall setting, are acceptable and accessible to both parties. By promoting equity in these foundational elements, the negotiation process can proceed on a more inclusive and respectful footing, increasing the likelihood of meaningful engagement and durable outcomes.

Kissinger thought that, generally speaking, heads of state should meet only if they know the outcome, because they are people with strong egos. If negotiations fail, it means the end of talks.[66] If an Israeli leader decides to go solo and bear responsibility for the negotiations, he/she must understand that by this decision, s/he dictates that the Palestinian leader go solo, too. That leader, however, may not be equipped with the leadership traits necessary to assume such a responsibility. Moreover, both parties have not only intellectual problems but also political problems and constraints. These considerations should be taken very seriously.

Appreciate Teamwork

Like superforecasters,[67] negotiators, mediators and facilitators frequently operate in collaborative teams, leveraging their diverse expertise and complementary skill sets to enhance the effectiveness and strategic depth of the negotiation process.

Learn from Mistakes

Instead of justifying or excusing their errors, negotiators, mediators and facilitators, like superforecasters, should seek to understand where they went wrong to improve their future forecasts.[68]

Have Stamina and Grit

Facilitators, negotiators and mediators should be determined to keep the negotiations going, notwithstanding problems and unfolding dramas. There is rarely a negotiation worth doing that does not require all-day and all-night exhausting meetings. In both Camp David 1978 and 2000, leaders threatened to leave. At Oslo, Qurie threatened to leave. Notwithstanding the threats, the Palestinian and Israeli teams stayed and continued the

66 Sebenius, *Kissinger the Negotiator*, 216.
67 Tetlock and Gardner, *Superforecasting*, 201–204.
68 Ibid., 221.

negotiations. The staying power and stamina of the people concerned, their ability to think clearly and to remain focused despite sleep deprivation, is tremendously important.[69] Grit refers to the 'passionate perseverance of long-term goals, even in the face of frustration and failure'.[70]

Be Tactical

Negotiators should begin with relatively easy topics upon which they can reach an agreement, find common ground and build on agreements to move forward. Only then should they negotiate more controversial and complex issues that are the sticking points in the conflict.

Behaviours to Avoid

Negotiators, mediators and facilitators should avoid certain behaviours.

Expecting Others to Be Like Them

We are the products of our upbringing, our history, our environment. These factors shape us differently, leading us to adopt different conceptions of the good, motivations and desires. Negotiators should not assume that others have the same abilities and qualities that they themselves have. People are different, and negotiators should appreciate the differences.

Arafat told the Israelis and the Americans, when they pressed him to make concessions, that if he did this or that, he would be killed. In response, Ehud Barak told him that Sadat was assassinated because of his attempts to make peace with Israel; Yitzhak Rabin was assassinated because he was ready to make peace with you; I, Barak, am in a riskier situation than you are, and I am willing to take the risk.[71] This argument did little to convince Arafat. The fact that Barak was bold and brave did not mean that someone else was similarly bold and brave. Some leaders are willing to sacrifice their lives for certain ends, while others would never be willing to put their lives at risk.

Moreover, the issue was not only life or death. It had to do with shame, an issue that was foreign to Barak. For Arafat, dying with honour was preferable to living with shame. Dying with shame was unthinkable. If he

[69] Interview with Stuart Eizenstat (7 July 2022), 1–3.
[70] Tetlock and Gardner, *Superforecasting*, 182–187.
[71] Interview with Ehud Barak (11 July 2022), 23.

were to sacrifice Jerusalem, he would be considered a traitor by people in the Muslim world – or so Arafat thought. They might assassinate him. In his eyes, the thought that he would give up Palestinian territory, including Jerusalem, lose honour and be assassinated was something he was unable to consider. Standing firm on Jerusalem would earn him great honour and respect; therefore, for Arafat, Jerusalem was also a personal matter, the source of how he would be remembered. His legacy.

Showing Weakness

Interlocutors should know what issues and concerns may evoke responsiveness and what issues they should avoid when trying to arouse sympathy. Generally speaking, accentuating weakness does not evoke understanding. Arafat used to complain that he did not have money, that he needed the support of everyone, that he was in a risky, weak position. This did not help the Palestinian cause.[72] Barak pleaded with Arafat to understand his political constraints, the complexity of his coalition, with its many diverse opinions, and that working in a democratic environment is different from Arafat's own situation. Arafat was unimpressed. He found democracy tiring,[73] and he was unsympathetic to Barak's predicament (see Chapters 6 and 7). Both leaders showed very little empathy for the weaknesses of the other. Parties should highlight their strengths, not their weaknesses.

Trying to Resolve Issues that Are Currently Insoluble

Instead, these should be deferred to a later stage. In Oslo, the parties did not wish to address issues that were of interest to them, knowing full well that they constituted serious obstacles for their counterpart. They decided to leave permanent status open-ended and delay decisions on these issues for five years.

Closing Options

Negotiators and mediators should leave options open. It is not prudent to close options prematurely. It was not prudent for Barak and Clinton

[72] Shaul Kimhi, Shmuel Even and Jerrold Post, *Yasir Arafat: Psychological Profile and Strategic Analysis* (Herzliya: The Interdisciplinary Center, 2002).

[73] Shimon Peres and Robert Littell, *For the Future of Israel*: (Baltimore, MD: Johns Hopkins University Press, 1998), 117.

to blame Arafat at the end of the Camp David Summit, only to return to him soon after to resume negotiations.

Losing Their Temper

Negotiators should not turn negotiations into a personal fight. They should not raise their voices or insult their interlocutors. Conversation is *not* a shouting contest. One's voice may be louder than the other's but that 'victory' is unlikely to bring a solution closer. When conversation becomes destructive and not constructive, negotiators should strive to find new ways to advance the conversation calmly, by seeking common purposes that will anchor the relationship and give substance to the discussion, paving the way for further exploration of matters that unite and positively shape the future. Negotiators should have the ability *not* to react immediately to what they perceive as provocation, but to take a breath and think before crafting a counter-argument. They should remain focused and put their anger aside. Clinton's loss of temper at Camp David harmed the summit greatly (see Chapters 6 and 7).

In his comments on a draft of this chapter, Daniel Kurtzer writes that James Baker used anger as a very effective tactic with both the Israelis and the Palestinians. He did not 'lose his temper', but he exhibited annoyed anger as a means of getting them to focus. Negotiators would benefit from taking professional acting classes.[74]

Attacking Their Counterpart

The last thing that negotiators and mediators want is to shut down the conversation. There is a need to distinguish between personalities and topics; negotiators, mediators and facilitators must not alienate interlocutors. They should respond to their arguments. Personal attacks only push the attacked out of negotiations.

There is much bad blood between Israel and the PLO. It may be the case that the interlocutors do not like each other. Negotiators may know each other from a previous period, when they fought each other. Rabin initially did not want to come to the White House Oslo ceremony, because he could not bear the thought of shaking Arafat's hand. Sharon sent his son Omri to meet Arafat. As personal histories can constitute obstacles

[74] Daniel Kurtzer's comments on a draft of this chapter.

to moving forward, it is important to evaluate and analyse issues at face value, notwithstanding the person who presents the topics.

Indeed, when personalities become the subject of discussion, there is a greater likelihood that people will take offence and stop listening or cooperating. They may then refuse to engage with the person who offended them. Negotiators do not wish to alienate their counterparts, as this would undermine and derail the process. They have a mutual interest in engaging and overcoming complications. The art of statesmanship is to leave room for negotiations, not to leave the room.

Lying and Tricking

Lies are self-defeating. Lying corrupts negotiation, undermines it and can destroy what has been achieved and the potential for a successful resolution. Baker said categorically: never lie. Lies never stay secret. If you lie, your opponent will lose confidence. You won't be able to negotiate with him.[75] Aharon Barak remarked: 'If you trick a party, if one of the parties does not conduct the negotiations openly and tries to trick the other party, the negotiations will not hold water. At some point, the other party will find out what went on. He will lose trust and he will not comply.'[76] Once trust is betrayed, negotiations are damaged, sometimes beyond repair.

Against human inclinations, negotiators should try not to exaggerate facts. They should not use empty words and make promises they cannot fulfil. Unfulfilled pledges erode confidence. Consider Israel's 'red lines' argumentation at Camp David 2000 (see Chapters 6 and 7). In negotiations, when the red lines of one side constantly shift, it would be imprudent for the other side to agree to something that can be achieved later for a better deal. Israel Hasson asked Barak to clarify the Israeli red lines but did not receive a response.[77] Consequently, the tactics of the Israeli negotiation team were viewed with suspicion and invited attempts to test them. Because the Israelis wanted to reach an agreement more than the Palestinians did, they made more and more concessions. Seeing this, the Palestinians had little or no incentive to be flexible. Why should they? Israel would continue to compromise.

***

75 Carnegie Connects: Aaron David Miller in Conversation with The Honorable James A. Baker, III (29 September 2021).

76 Interview with Aharon Barak (8 July 2018), 1.

77 Interview with Israel Hasson (23 May 2013), 19.

After bridging gaps as much as possible, the last stage of the negotiations relates to the hard sticking points. When interlocutors believe they have reached agreements on most issues, and all that is left are a *few* obstacles, they may decide that the most problematic challenges should be discussed and negotiated during a final peace summit. Camp David 2000, I should note, never reached this point. Arafat thought of having another summit.

Preferably, leaders should participate personally in negotiations only at a critical moment, when interlocutors are facing a significant obstacle that they are unable to remove, or when negotiations reach the end stage, and what remains are two or three sticking points that must be concluded by the leaders. Then, a peace summit can be convened with the leaders' participation. Let me discuss things that should be done before the peace summit, during the summit and after the summit.

Before the Peace Summit

Bridging Gaps

Both sides should have a realistic assessment of the situation and the chance for success. The deal must look doable. If the gaps between the parties before arriving at the negotiation table are too wide, the likelihood of a successful deal at the table is slim. Therefore, interlocutors who truly wish to resolve the conflict between them should aim to bridge the gaps by extensive communication directly or through third parties, making constructive bridging proposals, showing readiness to compromise, engaging in thinking outside the box to make that which looks unachievable achievable, and being positive.

Both sides should identify the main issues they wish to discuss and agree on them. Assuming that pre-summit negotiations had settled the majority of the issues, including mutual recognition, settlements, refugees, security, Palestinian sovereignty, relationships with Gaza, the Palestinian economy, Israel–Palestine relationships, prisoners and water, negotiators will be assigned to discuss the stickiest issues: borders, land swaps, Jerusalem and the Holy Places.

The summit planners will prepare a guiding paper for each issue that must be accepted by both delegations. Because months of preparation are invested in these papers, both parties should know what to expect. There will not be any surprises. The papers will offer compromises where gaps between the two sides were flagged.

Location

Both sides should agree on the summit location. Preferably, it should be at a neutral, historical place that all parties respect and where they will feel comfortable, possibly one of the King of Morocco's guest houses. Francesco Motta, chief of the Asia Pacific and MENA branch at the UN in Geneva, remarked:

> The discussions have to take place in a place of trust. That people feel secure, that they feel that they can speak freely. That they can feel that there are not going to be ramifications or politicization, and there is a structure in place for those talks and discussions to take place in a very frank and honest way that is non-inhibitory, in the sense that people are going to be as straightforward as possible, in terms of their interests and their demands.[78]

The Delegation

Leaders who assemble the delegations should think carefully about who is likely to develop workable and original ideas. Negotiators may come to the table with all the good intentions in the world, but if they lack the skills to negotiate, they may fail. The composition of the delegation is extremely important. It should be a professional, experienced team and include people who have mastered the material inside and out.

One member of the negotiation team should assume the role of a devil's advocate, an individual unafraid to raise doubts, challenge assumptions, pose critical questions and introduce unconventional perspectives. This role is essential for ensuring thorough scrutiny of all proposals, fostering a deeper understanding of the implications, trade-offs and potential consequences of each option under consideration. The presence of a devil's advocate strengthens analytical rigour and guards against groupthink. Ultimately, such internal critique enhances the quality of decision-making, reinforcing the indispensable value of collaborative teamwork.

Use of Experts

The delegation should be supported by a team of experts. Ghaith al-Omari said that using professional negotiators is key to successful negotiations.[79] These individuals must possess a comprehensive understanding

78 Interview with Francesco Motta (1 April 2022), 1.
79 Interview with Ghaith al-Omari (2 September 2014), 30.

of the substantive issues, historical context, political dynamics, psychological dimensions and the potential solutions on the table. They must be attuned to the emotional weight and symbolic significance that certain issues carry for each side.

In addition to political figures or their representatives, the delegation should include legal experts to draft and interpret agreements, military and security specialists to address issues of demilitarisation and defence, and technical experts who can contribute specialised knowledge relevant to matters such as borders, water, infrastructure or refugees. Historians can provide crucial insights into the evolution of the conflict, grounding present negotiations in an informed understanding of the past. Experienced negotiation practitioners bring strategic acumen and procedural expertise, helping navigate the dynamics of give and take.

The inclusion of psychologists can prove especially valuable in recognising the limits of purely rational deliberation. They can illuminate the emotional undercurrents shaping negotiators' behaviour and offer guidance on how to defuse tensions and reframe deadlocks through creative, non-traditional interventions. Imaginative ideas, those that may not be strictly political or legal, can open new avenues when conventional approaches falter.

Even the most well-informed politicians may lack the tactical finesse required to present arguments persuasively, gauge the appropriate timing for compromise or judge when to pause versus when to press forward. They may need support in knowing when to use visual aids, maps or multimedia, and when to rely on rhetoric alone. An expert-led, coordinated team helps ensure that each element of the negotiation is handled with precision, insight and strategic coherence.

At Camp David 1978, Aharon Barak, the Israeli government's legal advisor, brought the negotiations to a successful conclusion. Barak is a master of phrasing. His legal expertise and sharp mind, full of innovative ideas, were praised by all who were at Camp David.[80] Barak enjoyed Begin's full confidence and therefore felt able to air his ideas.

In 1993–1994, Israel's chief negotiator at the peace talks with Jordan, Elyakim Rubinstein, was aided by an array of experts on different issues who fed ideas into the process. Rubinstein was full of praise when he described their role.[81]

[80] Cohen-Almagor, 'Lessons from the Israeli-Egyptian Peace Talks: An Interview with Aharon Barak'.

[81] Interview with Elyakim Rubinstein (15 February 2021), 9.

At Camp David 2000, Rubinstein was invited in his capacity as the government's legal advisor. Ehud Barak wanted to copy the success of Rubinstein's predecessor at Camp David 1978. Rubinstein's task, however, was mainly to negotiate the refugee issue, which is a very different role than the one assigned to Aharon Barak at the first Camp David Summit.

Yuval Rotem, former Director General of the Israeli Ministry of Foreign Affairs, thinks that negotiators should use experts, and that failure to do so is a major shortcoming. At times, issues are so complicated that negotiators need information, as well as fresh ideas and concepts. Rotem thinks it is useful to bring people of faith, philosophers and experts on certain issues to the table 'to enable the negotiators just to think differently or in a wider way'.[82] Rotem mentioned the issue of Jerusalem as an example, where such people can provide complementary support to the politicians if and when they put Jerusalem on the agenda.

Agenda

The daily agenda should be clear to both sides. Both sides should know what they are required to discuss and, no less importantly, what *not* to discuss. They should also decide on the dates; Israel and Palestine should agree on the length of the summit. To build confidence, negotiators should start with relatively easy subjects and then move on to more complex concerns. This means that the Palestinians and Israelis would agree that nothing is agreed until everything is agreed, because they do not want to be pushed into a process that signs off on easy and less complicated matters but never gets around to addressing existential issues.

Language

Communicating directly, without translation, creates an immediate connection. Communication via translators is cumbersome. It hinders the flow of conversation. Interlocutors may hope that a message was delivered accurately, but there is also a chance that something was missing during the translation. The delay caused by translation gives interlocutors more time to think, but translation changes the rhythm. Yair Hirschfeld said that in Oslo, at the very beginning of the negotiations, Qurie spoke Arabic. He may not have trusted his own language abilities, or perhaps he did not trust the Israelis, thinking they might exploit his

[82] Interview with Yuval Rotem (11 January 2021).

language limitations. As soon as he felt more secure in himself and in his counterpart, he resorted to English, and from then onwards all the discussions were in English.[83] The phrase 'lost in translation' refers not only to the content of the discussion, but also to building a connection between the discussants.

Mediation

Interlocutors should decide whether they wish to negotiate directly or through a mediator. If they opt for a mediator, the identity of the mediator should be acceptable to both parties. Mediation should not be enforced or coerced.

Powers like Russia and China cannot serve as mediators. In the foreseeable future, I cannot think of a scenario in which Israel may agree to accept them as potential mediators. The European Union is hardly an option, as it is too divided to assume this role. The United States should take part as a mediator if the stakeholders believe it is necessary, as the US is the only power that has leverage over both Israel and Palestine. Stuart Eizenstat, former US Deputy Secretary of the Treasury, argues that leverage is tremendously important. The leverage can be military, economic or political influence over the country. It may involve military threats and economic sanctions. Therefore, the American ability to exert leverage is critically important;[84] however, the US is not an impartial mediator.

I have pointed out that the Israeli-Palestinian conflict is asymmetrical. In asymmetrical conflicts, the mediator can play a constructive role by counterbalancing the stronger side, but the US has emboldened and supported the stronger side, Israel. Its favouritism towards Israel antagonises the Palestinians, who feel at a disadvantage, having to counter not only Israeli arguments but also American pressure in support of these arguments. Kurtzer argues that during the 1990s, the American relationship with Israel was an asset, because they could use that relationship to help Israel make hard decisions by providing a soft landing, a safety net and off-the-table benefits. But such support is constructive only when the US does not go overboard. If it supports Israel without expecting anything in return, and without demanding that Israel take risks for peace, there

[83] Yair Hirschfeld, interview in writing (20 July 2018).
[84] Interview with Stuart Eizenstat (7 July 2022), 1–3.

is no incentive for Israeli leaders to move forward. In Kurtzer's language, the US should not 'bend too far'. It should not become 'Israel's lawyer'.[85]

The US can make the last push for an agreement. It can provide guarantees and assets that few others can provide. The US can also apply meaningful penalties, if needed. Aaron David Miller thinks that building peace between Israel and the Palestinians requires an effective third party that is prepared to apply ample amounts of honey and ample amounts of vinegar.[86] In his mind, only the US can do this.

Having said that, one should note that all the major breakthroughs in the Arab-Israeli conflict have occurred without American foreknowledge. In 1977, when Moshe Dayan showed up at the State Department in October to brief the Americans, they were stunned by the fact that he had been meeting secretly with Hassan Tuhami, Sadat's deputy prime minister.[87] In September 1977, Tuhami met Dayan in Morocco, and this meeting led to Sadat's trip to Jerusalem in November 1977. The Americans knew about the Oslo meetings, but they thought they were a discussion channel, not a decision-making channel. The American peace team did not think much about Oslo, despite the reports that Kurtzer wrote.[88] Furthermore, the Israeli-Jordanian peace was negotiated directly between the two parties, who were committed to the process and to the end result. Both King Hussein and Prime Minister Rabin wanted peace, and they ensured that all hurdles were removed. Note that leverage is not always a function of size. Sometimes smaller countries, such as Saudi Arabia, can have leverage if they exercise their negotiating positions well. However, Saudi Arabia can assume this role only if it enjoys the trust of both Israel and Palestine.

If Israel and Palestine decide to have a mediator in the talks, the keys to successful mediation are having leverage, the ability to find common ground, to devise confidence-building between the mediator and the interlocutors and between the parties themselves, and to set realistic aims and follow them. The mediator must be well informed and prepared, with good communication skills, diplomatic ability and experience. It must provide suitable conditions for interaction, address both parties' fears, be respectful of both parties, have public support, prioritise what it wants to achieve, be aware of spoilers and be present until the end of negotiations.

85 Interview with Daniel Kurtzer (6 April 2017), 19.
86 Interview with Aaron David Miller (12 September 2019), 2.
87 Ibid.
88 Discussion with Daniel Kurtzer (16 August 2022).

The Peace Summit

Negotiations are neither a boxing match nor a war aimed at defeating the opponent. Negotiators do not wish to clash, subdue their opponent or conquer it. Rather, they want to establish a common ground upon which progress in negotiations can be made.

Timing

Both sides should feel that the status quo is not acceptable and yearn for change. They should feel that the time is ripe to strike a deal and that stalling is not in their best interest. Itamar Rabinovich calls it a balance of pain and reward.[89] Interlocutors who arrive at the negotiation table with serious intentions should believe that there is some commonality in the outcome, although they may start from divergent positions. Still, at some point, their positions may sufficiently overlap.

As interlocutors look at the situation, at the negotiation and at the desirable outcome, they would normally be motivated either by the price of continuing the status quo, or by the rewards of changing it. Is time on my side or against me? The parties should feel that time is not on their side, and that they should conclude now, rather than wait.[90] Sven-Eric Söder argues that ripeness is key. The time needs to be right.[91] Ripeness creates a situation where analysis leads each party to believe that it should have an agreement, rather than not.

Tom Phillips, former British Ambassador to Israel, argues that leaders must have the skill to spot exactly when negotiations might be fruitful. Leaders should be able to detect the moment when a deal is possible with relatively moderate people on the other side, recognising that missing such an opportunity means that increasing violence is inevitable, and that hardliners on both sides will gain ground, making negotiations and compromise more and more difficult. In the Israeli-Palestinian context, there is a particular need to see the timing issue in a wider international context, particularly with American electoral cycles and the overall international position. Timing is also related to the region – spotting the moment when the stars are aligned in a way that ensures maximum regional support for forward movement.[92]

[89] Interview with Itamar Rabinovich (21 July 2017), 1.
[90] Raphael Cohen-Almagor, 'Keys for Peace in the Middle East: Interview with Ambassador Itamar Rabinovich', *Israel Affairs*, 25(4) (2019): 699–725.
[91] Interview with Sven-Eric Söder (20 August 2019), 9.
[92] Tom Phillips's comments on a draft of this chapter.

Camp David 2000 was cursed by bad timing. President Clinton was about to complete eight years in the White House. Ehud Barak was facing elections that were likely to end his time in the prime minister's office. It was difficult to enter momentous talks when two of the three leaders were about to leave office, while the third, Arafat, did not even want to attend the summit and did so only because the American president exerted pressure on him to attend.

Rubinstein spoke about the relatively little-discussed chapter of the Israeli peace negotiations with Lebanon that were sabotaged by the Syrians. He was reminded of it when I asked him about ripeness. In Rubinstein's view, the conditions at that time were not ripe for an agreement. He was working seriously on the Lebanese file during 1982 and 1983 with Joel Singer. The assassination of Bashir Gemayel in September 1982 was a major setback.[93] However, determined to start a new chapter with Lebanon, Israel pursued negotiations with Amin, Bashir's brother.[94] On 16 May 1983, an agreement was officially signed, but the Syrians killed it. Rubinstein said: 'The Lebanese would like to have the agreement, but the Syrian big brother, big enemy, big something, killed it.'[95] The situation for Lebanon was not ripe.

On 6 March 1984, Lebanon formally declared the agreement 'null and void'. Immediately thereafter, Syrian President Hafez al-Assad telephoned Gemayel and praised his decision as a 'victory for the Lebanese people, Syrian people and the Arab nation'.[96]

Unity

To foster honesty, clarity and coherence in negotiations, it is essential that delegations present a unified front in both their objectives and messaging. Internal cohesion not only strengthens a delegation's position but also enhances its credibility in the eyes of the other party. Leaders should ensure that all members of their negotiating team are thoroughly briefed on substantive issues, strategic goals and acceptable parameters for compromise.

[93] Bashir Gemayel (1947–1982) was elected president of Lebanon by the Parliament in August 1982 and Bashir was assassinated ten days before he was due to take office. *Brittanica*, www.britannica.com/topic/Gemayel-family#ref92463.

[94] Amin Gemayel was elected president of Lebanon a week after Bashir died. *Brittanica*, www.britannica.com/topic/Gemayel-family#ref92463.

[95] Interview with Elyakim Rubinstein (10 July 2018).

[96] Thomas L. Friedman, 'Lebanese Cabinet Formally Cancels Pact with Israel', *New York Times* (6 March 1984), https://tinyurl.com/44bac5ma.

Conversely, internal fragmentation, whether intentional or incidental, can prove detrimental. A divide-and-rule approach within a delegation may serve narrow political purposes, but in the context of high-stakes diplomacy, it undermines the negotiation process itself. Disunity within a delegation signals weakness, fosters ambiguity and creates room for miscommunication and mistrust. Moreover, visible divisions are often seized upon by opposing parties, who may exploit them to derail progress or extract concessions.

In the Oslo negotiations, when Uri Savir was in Norway, he had to negotiate with Qurie and with Shimon Peres as well. Savir also found himself negotiating with Joel Singer as to how and what to present to Rabin, and with Peres when they were back in Israel.[97] Peres had to negotiate with Rabin, to decide what to negotiate and what not to negotiate. All this was necessary to establish a clear line of argumentation that was acceptable to the leaders and to the negotiators.

At Camp David 2000, the Palestinian delegation was very divided. Gamal Helal spoke of foot-dragging, delays and internal competition.[98] This was partly Arafat's doing, as he always believed in divide and rule. It was also due to personal rivalries and competition between actors, and because the negotiators wanted different things and had different aims. While Mohammed Dahlan and Mohammed Rashid were willing to negotiate, Qurie was 'basically there in order to create impediments and to make sure nothing is going to happen'.[99] Nor did the Israeli delegation always speak in one voice. Meridor said it was strange when Gilead Sher came with him to the meeting about Jerusalem on the first day, and they presented two different views about Jerusalem.[100] Kurtzer wrote that Israeli negotiators fought and argued among themselves and in front of others. He saw this firsthand in the 1979–1982 autonomy talks, when three Israeli ministers constantly fought in front of the Americans.[101] Coordination and unity of opinion are fundamental.

Trust

I have mentioned trust several times. Israeli leaders who sincerely wanted peace and who were committed to peace suspected Arafat,

97 Interview with Avi Gil (16 January 2025), 1.
98 Interview with Gamal Helal (11 November 2022), 26.
99 Ibid., 30.
100 Interview with Dan Meridor (20 January 2016), 10.
101 Kurtzer's comments on a draft of this chapter.

who provided ample reasons not to trust him. On 10 May 1994, Arafat delivered a speech at a mosque in Johannesburg, calling on the Muslim nation to embark on jihad for Jerusalem and maintaining that he did not consider the Oslo agreement more significant than the agreement between the Prophet Muhammad and the tribe of Quraysh (also spelt Koraish). Caliph Omar refused to continue the agreement and considered it a low-level one, although Muhammad had agreed to it. The agreement with Quraysh allowed Muhammad to pray in Mecca, which was under Quraysh control, for ten years. When Muhammad grew stronger two years later, he abrogated the agreement, slaughtered the tribe of Quraysh and conquered Mecca. Arafat said that now he agreed to the Oslo agreement; however, the Palestinians will 'continue our way to Jerusalem, to the first shrine together and not alone' and they are 'in need of you as Moslems, as warriors of Jihad [in Arabic, Mujaheddin]'.[102]

Negotiations are successive trust-building steps. Essentially, there are two kinds of trust. The first is the trust that the parties will abide by their word, whatever one party tells the other party, especially if they put words on paper. And when negotiators make a counter-offer and concessions, they must trust that their interlocutor is not going to suddenly shift, take their offer and pull back on their pledge. A second kind of trust concerns the ability to *deliver* commitments. Negotiators should have an element of trust that what is being offered is something that can be delivered by the government that person is representing. King Hussein lost trust in Peres when the latter failed to deliver on their London agreement.[103] Trust is built when parties see that promises are not empty and that the other party is committed to implementing the agreement, one step at a time.

Working trust can develop only if interlocutors think the other side has a genuine interest in making peace. Each side needs to convince the other that they are there for *strategic*, not merely tactical, reasons. Similarly, both sides should believe that concessions are genuine, stemming from mutual recognition of each other's rights and interests, and leading to constructive solutions. Commonalities should be emphasised. With this process, trust will slowly be built, and upon it, it should be possible to erect bridges, reach understandings and move forward. Without trust, it is much more difficult to have a constructive process. James Baker said

[102] 'Arafat's Johannesburg Speech', Information Regarding Israel's Security, https://iris.org.il/arafats-johannesburg-speech/.

[103] Center for Israel Education, London Document, Agreement between Israel and Jordan on an International Peace Conference (2024), https://tinyurl.com/3cr9wsx5.

that if you can establish relations with your opponent, you have a better chance to find a way to an agreement.[104]

Kelman argues that the development of mutual trust is essential in efforts to resolve conflict and transform the relationship between enemies into stable cooperation. In deep-rooted, lengthy conflicts, such as the Israeli-Palestinian conflict, the conditions for creating trust are, by definition, elusive at best.[105] Arabs and Israelis have been shedding each other's blood for over a century. Their common assumption is that their rival wishes to harm them, until evidence is produced to the contrary. They perceive their interests in polar opposition to those of their enemy and analyse the situation in zero-sum game terms: their enemy's gains come at the expense of their own interests. Given the violent history and high level of mutual suspicion, the adversaries will come to the negotiation table only out of necessity, when they believe that it is in their own best interest to end the conflict.

Trust is essential, especially when interlocutors conduct secret negotiations. Maintaining secrecy is critically important, as was the case in Oslo, and contributes to building trust.[106] Leaking can undermine the process and bring it to an end. This was the case in Stockholm. All those involved in negotiations should trust that no one will leak offers that have been made to the media, as this might be extremely destructive (see Chapter 5). In Oslo, Savir said the trust he established with Qurie helped them 'transcend suspicion'.[107] In the Israel–Syria Shepherdstown talks, a draft prepared by Jonathan Schwartz was leaked to the Lebanese press during the discussions; though each page said 'nothing is agreed until everything is agreed', the exposure of Syria's tentative acceptance of certain normalisation provisions before securing the return of the entire Golan Heights doomed the talks.[108] During sensitive and high-stakes negotiations, details must remain in the room until leaders decide to release the information. If sensitive details are leaked, the constituencies at home will

[104] Carnegie Connects: Aaron David Miller in Conversation with The Honorable James A. Baker, III (29 September 2021).

[105] Kelman, *Resolving Deep-Rooted Conflicts*, 171.

[106] In his comments on a draft of this chapter, Mervyn Frost writes that in the run-up to the negotiations that ended apartheid, the ANC leadership together with a very high-level group of South African politicians met in secret in an African state to discuss the past, present and future of South Africa. Without this initial secret round of diplomacy, Frost doubts that the new South Africa would ever have been born. Rotberg, however, begs to differ.

[107] Savir, 'Oslo: Twenty Years After', 118.

[108] Jonathan Schwartz's comments on a draft of this chapter.

put pressure on the parties to change the agenda and parameters of the agreement, while spoilers will push to derail the process altogether.

Trust is particularly important in the Israeli-Palestinian conflict because it is an asymmetrical conflict. Both sides are fully aware of this, and we have seen both Israel and the PLO exploit this asymmetry for their own purposes. Israel often dictated moves to the Palestinians, and the Palestinians presented themselves as needy and deserving of special consideration. The Palestinians asked for more resources and appealed to the moral obligations of Israel. They referred to international law and international conventions. The PLO has repeatedly emphasised the applicability of the Fourth Geneva Convention regarding the occupation, as well as different UN resolutions.[109] Palestinian leaders found it difficult to make decisions because they wished to consult other parties that had a say in the conflict. This need for consultation and affirmation of Arab and other players was perceived by Israel as a delaying tactic and deficient leadership. The Palestinian leadership was seen as dragging its feet and being incapable of making a decision. This perception undermined their ability to trust the other party.

Rapport is crucial, especially at make-or-break junctions, when the parties explain: 'Look, I can do X, but I cannot do Y.' The other side must trust that that is real. If negotiators do not have a relationship, they are unlikely to do so. Ross thinks that building personal ties is critical. He maintains: 'A relationship is not like a light switch, where you flip it and you have got it. You have to develop it, you have to prove yourself over time. But still, trying to create that personal connection, I think, is crucial in any negotiation or mediation.'[110]

Trust does not presuppose friendship, goodwill or even sympathy between rival interlocutors. It can develop slowly between enemies.[111] Developing a sense of trust and confidence in one's interlocutor does not mean that negotiators are going to become personal friends, but interlocutors should develop, over time, something other than stilted, across-the-table negotiation. They should develop confidence-building skills.

Many of my interviewees think that trust is very important.[112] Lack of trust leads to reticence to brainstorm in private talks or to put anything

[109] Karin Aggestam, 'Mediating Asymmetrical Conflict', *Mediterranean Politics*, 7(1) (2002): 71.
[110] Interview with Dennis Ross (27 September 2019), 5.
[111] Kelman, *Resolving Deep-Rooted Conflicts*, 178.
[112] Interviews with Udi Dekel (17 June 2014), Gilead Sher (26 May 2013), Dennis Ross (27 September 2019), Ely Rubinstein (15 February 2021), Yuval Rotem (11 January 2021),

down in writing, and to mutual accusations over leaks and other hindrances.[113] Muasher spoke of the need to build trust so that both sides feel that the end result is a win–win situation.[114] Ehud Olmert said trust is essential.[115] Martin Indyk agreed, saying 'it is a *sine qua non*'.[116] Indyk explained that the relationship between Abbas and Benjamin Netanyahu was very toxic. Their mutual distrust made it impossible to negotiate. Indyk also mentioned the need to establish trust between peoples. Palestinians do not believe that the Israelis will ever agree to a withdrawal that will lead to a viable contiguous Palestinian state. Israelis do not believe that they have a partner for peace, that the Palestinians will ever be willing to end the conflict and accept an end to claims. Here, distrust is fundamental to the difficulties of the situation and makes peace a remote dream.[117]

Similarly, Jonathan Powell thinks that building trust between negotiating parties is 'absolutely fundamental'. Negotiations are *highly* political acts. It is all about whether the parties can build enough trust to stop fighting each other. Powell did not want to be friends with the Irish Republican Army leaders Gerry Adams[118] and Martin McGuinness,[119] but he needed to build trust with them so that they would make concessions because they knew they could trust him to try and work in good faith to get to reach an agreement.[120] Pär Nuder and Sven-Eric Söder argue that successful mediation and facilitation are built on trust, and that these have to be at the parties' request.[121] Yair Hirschfeld accentuated the importance of trust-building, saying that he had built trust with the Palestinians for thirteen years, especially after Faisal Husseini was released from prison in January 1989.[122] The basic idea that guided

Gamal Helal (11 November 2022), Stuart Eizenstat (7 July 2022), David Makovsky (29 July 2022), Alistair Burt (22 April 2022) and Francesco Motta (1 April 2022); conversations with Salam Fayyad (5 December 2023) and Avi Gil (16 January 2025); Yair Hirschfeld Q@A (20 July 2018; 15 July 2018); Prince Khalid Q&A (8 May 2024).

113 Jonathan Schwartz's comments on a draft of this chapter.

114 Interview with Marwan Muasher (25 July 2022), 21.

115 Interview with Ehud Olmert (22 February 2019), 13.

116 Interview with Martin Indyk (9 August 2022), 10.

117 Ibid., 11.

118 Gerry Adams, *Before the Dawn: An Autobiography* (Dublin: Brandon, 2017).

119 Henry McDonald, *Martin McGuinness: A Life Remembered* (Newtownards: Blackstaff Press, 2017).

120 Interview with Jonathan Powell (20 July 2022), 13.

121 Interviews with Pär Nuder (20 August 2019), 19 and Sven-Eric Söder (20 August 2019), 11–13.

122 Faisal Husseini was one of the most prominent Palestinian nationalist figures in East Jerusalem and the leading local representative of the PLO in the West Bank during the

him was to be reliable: 'You say what you can deliver, and what you cannot.'[123] In his comments on a draft of this book, Hirschfeld wrote that it is important to create complete reliability in what negotiators promise and what they reject. Interlocutors must be able to deliver what they commit to achieve and should retain tight red lines. During the first phase of the Oslo negotiations, it was acutely important to maintain trust, because the meetings were not official. Hirschfeld maintained direct contact with Qurie and updated him on Jerusalem's reactions. Qurie later said that this was a decisive trust-building move.[124]

Very few interviewees discounted trust. Yossi Beilin thinks an agreement can be made without trust, but with guarantees. Negotiators do not need to trust each other, but they must communicate and clarify their positions.[125] Hussein Agha said: 'I do not want trust. Any agreement based on trust is going to be a flawed agreement. You have to build an agreement despite the mistrust; in spite of the mistrust.'[126] Ami Ayalon said that 'if you create confidence, trust, you will have much more flexibility'.[127] But Ayalon maintained that 'trust between political leaders is something that I find … almost impossible'.[128] According to Ayalon, what negotiators need are good cards.

Robert Malley thinks trust can be overstated:

> You know you cannot trust the other side, because the other side is out to get you and you are out to get them. *But*, at some point you have to trust that what they are telling you they can deliver, and that they mean it. It does not mean that you trust the intentions of the other side, but there has to be a modicum of belief that what is being said is not going to be withdrawn the next day. And that you can actually deliver. So, call it trust if you want, but the trust has a connotation that I would hesitate to use, because each side is trying to gain an advantage over the other. So, you do not trust that the other side is trying to do you good.[129]

Kurtzer agrees with Malley, arguing that parties in a conflict distrust each other at every stage of the conflict and assume that the other side

First Intifada. Israel placed him under administrative detention in 1987. In early 1989, Yitzhak Rabin decided not to renew Husseini's detention order.

123 Interview in writing with Yair Hirschfeld (15 July 2018).
124 Interview in writing with Yair Hirschfeld (20 July 2018).
125 Yossi Beilin, Middle East Study Centre Annual Lecture, University of Hull (19 October 2022), 26.
126 Interview with Hussein Agha (5 April 2019), 29.
127 Interview with Ami Ayalon (20 July 2022), 4.
128 Interview with Ami Ayalon (28 June 2022), 12.
129 Interview with Robert Malley (28 July 2022), 52.

'is trying to screw them'.[130] Kurtzer would rather build a strong agreement, with assurances, monitoring, accountability and the like, rather than rely on trust.

Mitigation of Inequalities

The Israeli-Palestinian conflict stretches beyond Israel and Palestine. Palestinian leaders are reluctant to sign a deal on their own. They feel the need to consult leaders of interested Arab nations and are constrained by their weaknesses. Qurie told Gil: 'Look. Territories, you can negotiate with us. Borders, you can negotiate with us. Refugees, we are not enough. You need the Arab world, because they are there. And they have claims in that regard.'[131] To resolve the question of the Haram and the Holy Basin, the Muslim world needs to be involved.

Therefore, the concluding summit should involve other Arab leaders, first and foremost the leaders of Egypt and Jordan, who have high stakes in the conflict. Whether they like it or not, they are involved in it. Instead of delaying because no Palestinian leader will move forward without consultation, Egyptian and Jordanian leaders should be active participants in the resolution of the conflict.

Support of the Significant Other Countries

The regional environment must be favourable, especially from the Palestinian point of view. At some point, other Arab states that have normal and peaceful relationships with Israel should be involved in the discussions with Israel's consent, per its understanding that certain issues cannot be decided only by Israel and Palestine. Israel must understand that support for concessions on issues that are considered all-Arab, not just Palestinian, requires Arab endorsement. Any Palestinian leader would like to have Arab assurance when deciding the future of Jerusalem or the refugee question. The terms of engagement should be clarified and decided between the parties.

Use of Threats

Negotiators should know that when people make promises to them, they can trust them. While credible commitments are necessary for effective

[130] Kurtzer's comments on a draft of this chapter.
[131] Interview with Avi Gil (16 January 2025), 7.

bargaining, threats as a strategic tool should be approached with great caution. In asymmetric conflicts, overt threats often exacerbate power imbalances and foster resentment, especially when one party perceives the other as exploiting its superior position. In the Israeli-Palestinian context, threats tend to sour the atmosphere, reinforce mutual suspicion and entrench adversarial mindsets. Rather than facilitating agreement, they frequently deepen polarisation and inhibit constructive engagement.

Before issuing a threat, the threatening side should be ready to execute it and understand the likely consequences. The threat should support the side that makes it in achieving its long-term ends. The party that issues a threat should understand that threats may lock them into a certain course of action that can backfire. Threats may also push the threatened party into a stubborn position as it does not wish to lose face. Instead of defusing tensions, threats can aggravate them. Therefore, threats should come at a later stage, when all alternatives have been exhausted. They should be real, calculated and meaningful. They should be commensurate with the end that the party wants to achieve and should not be made in vain.

In mediated negotiations, it is often preferable to allow mediators to convey messages carrying implicit pressure, thereby preserving the rapport between the primary interlocutors and reducing direct antagonism. Ultimately, the goal of negotiations is to reach mutual agreement through dialogue, persuasion and empathy – not coercion. Whenever possible, parties should prioritise cooperative strategies and seek a 'yes' through constructive engagement rather than threat-based escalation.

Mutuality

Each side should determine whether negotiations are genuine. That is, are they mutual or only one-sided? If a party, or both parties, think that the negotiations are one-sided, that they have come to the table genuinely prepared to make concessions while the other side is operating for ulterior motives, without any real urgency and desire to reach peace, then the will to complete the deal will be eroded and, with it, the likelihood for success.

Ownership

Leaders should own the process and have a sense of accountability for the results. Aaron David Miller said that people do not wash rental cars, because human nature is such that we care only about what we own. Interlocutors should protect their own negotiation.[132] Successful negotiations take place when the parties want to reach a peace deal, are ready to make difficult and painful compromises, and have a sense of ownership. Leaders should be invested in the peace process, drive it forward and put their weight behind it, even when their political capital may be at risk. Great leaders are those who have the ability to assess complicated situations, consolidate efforts to address challenges and lead by example.

Use of Fall-Back Positions

When negotiations are stuck, interlocutors should resort to their Plans B, C and D. There is no point in pressing the same buttons time and again, only to face another failure. A well-known truism is that it is insane to do the same thing over and over again and expect different results. At a certain point, it is important to decide to move on and try something else. At Camp David 2000, Barak had no Plan B. When Plan A failed, he was quick to blame Arafat and argue that Israel had no partner. This is no Plan B. Rubinstein says that Barak was ill-prepared on the issue of Jerusalem. He did not have well-crafted alternative plans, nor had he determined what concessions he could make to move forward.[133]

After the Peace Summit

Signing a peace treaty is a significant milestone, but it certainly is not the final step. After the pomp and celebration, the hard work of peacebuilding begins.

Process

After the peace summit, meetings between the parties should continue. The parties should continue to engage, discuss development and resolve problems. Complications are likely to emerge. Sustained communication is key to their successful resolution.

Continue the Trust-Building

The challenge is to maintain trust in an environment that is fraught with suspicion. During the implementation process, the two sides will come to

[132] Interview with Aaron David Miller (12 September 2019), 1.
[133] Interview with Elyakim Rubinstein (10 July 2018), 4.

know each other as human beings. They will learn to acknowledge their similarities, accentuating commonalities, rather than the differences that divide them. If people do not trust each other, if they think that the other party deceives, resorts to lies and is fundamentally dishonest, they will be reluctant to implement the treaty. If one believes that a treaty is not worth the paper on which it is written, because the other party is not abiding by it, the zeal for peace will be eroded. This happened after the signing of the Oslo Accords. Both Israel and the PLO became disenchanted as the Israeli settlements continued to grow, together with Palestinian terrorism. Both the Palestinian and Israeli publics lost their desire for peace. The Palestinians continued living under Israeli occupation, while the Israelis suffered, living under the constant shadow of terror that hit them at bus stops, on buses, in shopping malls, coffee shops, bars and restaurants. Both parties felt that Oslo was not achieving what it was meant to achieve.

Provide Explanations

Everyone needs an explanation. Leaders have a constituency or a public that they need to address. Leaders need to engage with their political constituencies, not ignore them. This is especially true in democracies, but it is also true in non-democratic societies. Sometimes, needs can be addressed in a practical, discrete forum, but not so easily in a public forum. So, the parties have to figure out how they can frame what is being done in a way that each side can accept.

Suppress Spoilers

Spoilers are those actors who have no interest in mitigating the conflict in any way. Instead, they want to intensify the flames, escalate problems and make things worse. Spoilers are intent on introducing new challenges with the aim of derailing the peace process.

Some people do not trust the other party and do not believe that the peace agreement is genuine. Some do not trust their own government, thinking that its actions put the nation at unacceptable risk. Some are unwilling to pay the price for peace, a price that, for them, seems extravagant and unjustified. Because successful peace negotiations may yield a very different reality, not only in Israel and Palestine, but also in the Middle East at large, and spoilers dread that new reality, they may become more desperate and resolute in their attempts to bring the peace process to a halt. We should learn from experience and never underestimate spoilers' ability to derail peace.

Both Israeli and Palestinian leaders put themselves in harm's way when they tried to put a stop to a century and a half of bloodshed. Yitzhak Rabin ignored the threats on his life and, by his dismissive attitude, made himself vulnerable to attack. On 4 November 1995, a Jewish zealot assassinated Rabin and derailed the peace process. The process was not yielding the results that the parties hoped for, and now it was damaged beyond repair. The assassin's plan worked. Rabin's assassination was a national trauma and should serve as a constant warning. In 2023, Israel suffered another trauma – 7 October took Israel and Palestine to a new level of violence, pain and trauma.

Israel has tried different modes of engagement and negotiation with political extremists and terrorists: tactical (aimed at dealing with practical concerns), direct engagement, and indirect or backchannel negotiations via mediators. Some Israeli leaders believed it was possible to reach some kind of deal with Islamist fundamentalist movements, such as Hamas and the Islamic Jihad, which are religious-ideological movements that wish to see the destruction of Israel. While I am reluctant to say movements never change, regarding them I have little hope or belief that they are capable of significant change. They may make tactical concessions, but there is very little likelihood that they would be willing to compromise over principles. Their *raison d'être* is based on violent jihad. The events of 7 October 2023 clarified their true intentions. It is in Israel's interest to deal with the more moderate elements in Palestine that abhor Muslim fundamentalism. Israel and Palestine should develop mechanisms for collaboration in order to see that spoilers fail. They should sanction spoilers and employ travel bans and asset freezes when appropriate. A monopoly on weapons should be kept. Violence should be met by the necessary apparatuses. Neither Israel nor Palestine can afford to have multiple armed militias that challenge Palestinian and Israeli authorities and resort to violence to undermine sovereignty and the peace process. By creating a system of accountability, the Israeli government and the PA can prevent spoilers from disrupting the peace process. Egypt, Jordan, Saudi Arabia and other moderate Arab countries can assist in targeting spoilers' financial and logistical support networks and reduce spoilers' operational capabilities. Qatar cannot be allowed to continue its dangerous brinkmanship policy of presenting itself as a moderate country that supports American interests in the region and, at the same time, be a major sponsor of terrorism. Effective border controls are essential for stopping cross-border infiltration of people, weapons, money and criminal activity. Furthermore, spoilers should be excluded from the international community, which should speak for peace and against the enemies of peace. Both Israel and Palestine should invest in long-term solutions via education designed to cultivate a peaceful environment of tolerance, coexistence and reconciliation, accentuating the need to erect defence mechanisms against spoilers at home and away.

Updated Contingency Plans

While the parties would like to see their agreements executed as planned, they should have alternative plans in the event that the leading plan becomes obsolete. Costly months are wasted when parties must reckon with developments that obstruct their policies. Contingency plans should be available and immediately put in place when agreed policies fail. I mentioned the implementation problems in the Oslo peace process. Amos Guiora said that the Israeli implementers were learning what needed to be done on the job, creating their own ground rules, and were often in the dark as to what was expected of them.[134] Contingency plans needed to be invented out of the blue, without sufficient thinking and a full understanding of advantages and risks. Comprehensive and detailed planning is essential for a successful peace process.

Timeline

A clearly defined and mutually agreed-upon timeline for implementation is critical. The parties must establish precise operational guidelines that delineate the responsibilities of implementers, specifying what actions are required, the manner in which they are to be carried out and the time frames and locations for their execution. Clarity, coordination and accountability are crucial in translating negotiated agreements into sustainable realities.

Dispute Resolution and Monitoring Mechanisms

To ensure effective and accountable implementation, a peace agreement must incorporate robust mechanisms for dispute resolution, monitoring and enforcement. Implementation is often the Achilles heel of peace processes, and without a credible system to manage compliance, the sustainability of any accord is jeopardised.

[134] Interview with Amos Guiora (10 July 2018), 8–12.

A central feature of this system should be the establishment of an impartial monitoring and oversight body, mandated to assess whether the parties are adhering to the terms of the agreement. This body should be empowered not only to identify violations, but also to recommend and, where agreed, enforce proportionate responses. Its authority must be clearly outlined in the treaty, including procedures for adjudicating disputes, mechanisms for verifying compliance and protocols for responding to breaches.

In deeply divided or asymmetric conflicts, international or third-party involvement may be necessary to lend credibility and neutrality to these mechanisms. External actors can help insulate the process from domestic political pressures and provide technical expertise, logistical support and diplomatic leverage. By embedding a clear framework for monitoring, accountability and dispute resolution, peace agreements become not merely aspirational documents, but operational instruments for managing long-term conflict transformation.

Accountability is critical to maintaining the legitimacy of the peace process. Violations must carry consequences, both to deter future infractions and to reassure the parties and their publics that commitments are meaningful. Sanctions or corrective measures, calibrated to the severity and nature of the breach, should be predefined in the agreement. These may range from diplomatic and economic measures to the temporary suspension of benefits granted under the agreement. Crucially, enforcement must be consistent, transparent and devoid of bias.

Conclusion

To achieve peace, several preconditions are imperative. Both leaders should critically reflect on the other's interests and on the moral framework and understanding of justice underlying those interests. Both parties must understand what motivates the other and what its endgame is, given present constraints. Both parties should reflect on and understand the other party's interests in accordance with the value system and culture of that party, *not their own.* At the same time, they should endeavour to explain their own interests and value system to their rival. The role of the mediator in this process is significant. The mediator needs to support the parties in dispute in reflecting on their declared interests in the light of their moral frameworks and their understanding of the concept of justice. The mediator is tasked to bring the parties together to clarify their interests and moral frameworks. Improved mutual understanding gives each party an opportunity to explain its case in more depth and helps the participants see beyond their stereotypes of others. Thus, movement from entrenched positions can become possible.[135]

Once the parties are fully appreciative of the value systems, aims and constraints of their rivals and perceive peace as their strategy, leaders must be equally committed to bringing peace to their people and be willing to pay the necessary price. Peace is a precious commodity. As such, it comes with a price that will demand painful sacrifices from both sides. Furthermore, leaders should have a shared belief that the time is ripe for peace.

Interlocutors should familiarise themselves with the art of negotiations and have the skills required for successful negotiations. Negotiators should understand the psychology and aims of their interlocutors. They should have a full assessment of the personal and political motivations of the other party, of the parties' willingness to pay a price and make painful, genuine concessions before going into peace negotiations. Interlocutors should strive for a win–win situation. Negotiations cannot be successful when one party feels that their needs are not met. An enforced peace agreement will not last.

Negotiations are not a competition, and there is no need to prove to anyone that you are the smartest person in the room. This is not the goal of negotiations. The negotiator should not be the centre of attention; there is no need for negotiators to bolster their identity and ideology by constantly talking. Constantly talking is a sure way to lose one's counterpart, and negotiators are unlikely to appreciate a speaker's self-driven stream of words that pays little attention to them. Negotiators should engage, reflect, ponder and think about what the other is saying. They should unfold and analyse the message.

In the next chapter, I review some proposals for settling the Israeli-Palestinian conflict and then outline what I perceive to be the preferred, just proposal for resolving the conflict.

[135] Gerald Midgley and Luis A. Pinzón, 'Systemic Mediation: Moral Reasoning and Boundaries of Concern', *Systems Research and Behavioral Science*, 30 (2013): 607–632.

12

Resolving the Israeli-Palestinian Conflict

Possible Solutions

> They shall beat their swords into ploughshares, and their spears into pruning hooks; nation shall not lift up sword against nation, neither shall they learn war any more.
>
> ~ Isaiah, II:4

Installing peace and ending one of the bloodiest and most complex conflicts in human history is not a quick fix. It does not resemble a 100-metre run. Rather, it is an excruciating marathon. It demands foresight, resilience, determination and concessions. Good starting points are the Clinton Parameters,[1] the Geneva Accords[2] and the New York Declaration on the Peaceful Settlement of the Question of Palestine and the Implementation of the Two-State Solution.[3] These documents lay the foundations for resolving the contentious issues. It has been persuasively argued that a sustainable and just peace between Israel and Palestine can be achieved only under a specific confluence of conditions, all of which are necessary, although none is sufficient on its own. These include the emergence of an Israeli leader resolutely committed to peace and prepared to incur the political and strategic costs required to achieve it; the presence of a Palestinian leader with an equivalent level of commitment and readiness to make difficult compromises; the capacity of both leaders to persuade their respective constituencies of the necessity and urgency of peace, mobilising public support and fostering a shared vision of a post-conflict future; and a mutual recognition by both leaders that the current moment is ripe for resolution, and that delaying an agreement is not only counterproductive but also contrary to their long-term national interests. The absence of any one of these conditions is likely to prolong the conflict and defer the hope for peace. Only when

1 The Clinton Parameters, www.peacelobby.org/clinton_parameters.htm.
2 The Geneva Accord, https://tinyurl.com/5fb4jwcm.
3 A/CONF.243/2025/1/Add.1, 6 August 2025, https://tinyurl.com/4tvkevmf.

all are present can a genuine breakthrough occur, offering both societies a tangible horizon of reconciliation.

First, I briefly present some of the proposals that have been suggested by scholars and decision-makers. Some of them are manifestly unjust. Some people see only themselves and disregard others. I am not one of them. To be sustainable, the solution must be just, reasonable and doable, a solution that respects the right of independence and self-determination of both Israel and Palestine. Destructive solutions, aiming to install Israel at the expense of Palestine, or Palestine at the expense of Israel, are self-destructive and fundamentally unjust. They are mentioned, but I do not intend to give them much scope. We should be aware of them and recognise their inherent flaws. Subsequently, I present what I consider the most preferred solution to the conflict.

To approach this challenge with fairness and conceptual clarity, the philosophical framework of John Rawls's 'veil of ignorance' offers a valuable normative tool. By imagining decision-makers situated behind a veil of ignorance – unaware of their future identity as either Israeli or Palestinian, Jew or Muslim – this method seeks to neutralise biases arising from entrenched religious, ethnic or national affiliations. In doing so, it encourages the formulation of principles that would be considered just and acceptable, irrespective of one's communal identity. Individuals behind the veil are assumed to possess conceptions of the good but are unaware of the specific social positions they will occupy once the veil is lifted. This uncertainty compels the construction of arrangements that are equitable, durable and conducive to coexistence. Guided by this commitment to justice and mutual recognition, the proposed resolution must reflect genuine compromise – balancing historical grievances, present-day realities and future aspirations. Only a solution crafted with these considerations in mind can offer both Israelis and Palestinians a path forward that is not only politically sustainable, but also ethically sound.

Auguste Comte said, 'Demography is Destiny'.[4] While demography is not the only factor and is not necessarily the decisive factor, undoubtedly it is very important. The demographic factor influences the trajectory of societies. The number of Jews and Palestinians between the Jordan River and the Mediterranean Sea is almost equal. As of December 2024, the Israeli population was 10.07 million; 76.9 per cent (7.707 million) were Jews, while 21 per cent (2.104 million) were Arabs.[5] The State

[4] The Socratic Method, https://tinyurl.com/3nz72n85.

[5] Israel Central Bureau of Statistics (Hebrew), https://tinyurl.com/yb52rat8.

of Palestine's 2025 population is estimated at 5.59 million people.[6] The Israeli-Palestinian conflict is about two peoples who have justified claims over the same small piece of land.

Israeli occupation is harmful to both the Palestinians and Israel. The United Nations has passed dozens of resolutions denouncing the Israeli occupation and the settlements and supporting Palestinian self-determination. I have mentioned UN Resolutions 242 and 338. In addition, Resolutions 252, 267 and 476 regarding the status of Jerusalem,[7] Resolution 465 regarding the settlements,[8] and Resolutions 607 and 608 calling upon Israel to refrain from deporting any Palestinian civilians from the Occupied Palestinian Territory (OPT)[9] – all postulate that the acquisition of land via military means is inadmissible and that Israeli expropriation of land and properties, including those that changed the legal status of Jerusalem, are invalid. Resolution 3236 speaks of the right to Palestinian national sovereignty and independence, calling for the Palestinian right of return and the restitution of the refugees' properties.[10] Resolution 2787 reaffirms 'the inalienable right of all peoples in particular those of … the Palestinian people to freedom, equality and self-determination and the legitimacy of their struggles to restore those rights'.[11] Resolutions 58/292,[12] 76/150,[13] 77/208[14] and 78/192[15] hold that the Palestinian people have the right to self-determination and that Israel has the obligations of an occupying power. Resolution 67/19 explicitly affirms the Palestinian right to

[6] Worldometer, State of Palestine Population, www.worldometers.info/world-population/state-of-palestine-population/.

[7] UN Resolution 252 (1968), https://digitallibrary.un.org/record/90754?ln=en&v=pdf; UN Resolution 267 (1969), https://digitallibrary.un.org/record/90766?ln=en&v=pdf; UN Resolution 476 (1980), https://digitallibrary.un.org/record/25616?ln=en&v=pdf.

[8] UN Resolution 465 (1980), https://tinyurl.com/y8k35dzz.

[9] UN Resolution 607 (1988), http://unscr.com/en/resolutions/607; UN Resolution 608 (1988), http://unscr.com/en/resolutions/608.

[10] UN Resolution 3236 (1974), www.un.org/unispal/wp-content/uploads/2016/05/ARES3236XXIX.pdf.

[11] UN General Assembly Resolution 2787 (6 December 1971), www.refworld.org/legal/resolution/unga/1971/en/34713.

[12] UN General Assembly 58/292, https://documents.un.org/doc/undoc/gen/n03/512/04/pdf/n0351204.pdf.

[13] UN General Assembly 76/150, www.un.org/unispal/wp-content/uploads/2022/01/GARES.A.RES_.76.150_161221.pdf.

[14] UN General Assembly 77/208, www.un.org/unispal/wp-content/uploads/2023/01/A.RES_.77.208_281222.pdf.

[15] UN General Assembly 78/192, https://documents.un.org/doc/undoc/gen/n23/424/72/pdf/n2342472.pdf.

self-determination in an independent state within the 1967 borders.[16] Resolution 2334 holds that the borders between Israel and Palestine are those of 1967 and asserts that no party can impose border modifications by settlement expansion.[17]

Resolving the Israeli-Palestinian conflict necessitates a cooperative framework in which both Israel and the Palestinian Authority (PA) actively engage with one another. Despite its institutional shortcomings, the PA remains a preferable interlocutor for Israel compared with more radical and violent Palestinian factions. From a strategic and security standpoint, the preservation of the PA is in Israel's interest; its collapse would likely create a vacuum that could be filled by less moderate, less accountable and potentially more destabilising actors.

Over the years, Israel and the PA have established mechanisms of coordination across a range of administrative and security matters, demonstrating that pragmatic engagement is not only possible but also beneficial. This foundation of functional cooperation should be expanded, particularly in areas of mutual interest such as security coordination, economic development, civil infrastructure and public health. Israel should take proactive steps to strengthen these collaborative frameworks, especially with Palestinian actors who are committed to non-violence, coexistence and a negotiated resolution to the conflict. Bolstering such partnerships contributes not only to stability, but also to the gradual cultivation of trust between the two societies.

The disintegration of the PA would be a strategic setback for both parties. It would effectively revert the conflict to a more volatile phase, without any guarantee that a successor entity would be more capable of governing effectively or implementing future agreements. Such a collapse would severely undermine the already fragile prospects for peace. Accordingly, constructive elements within both Israeli and Palestinian societies must work to disrupt the cycle of violence that has repeatedly derailed peace efforts. This requires a principled commitment to dialogue, mutual recognition and non-violence. One important step in this direction would be the promotion of democratic processes within the Palestinian political system, particularly through the facilitation of elections in the West Bank. These elections should be open

[16] Resolution adopted by the General Assembly on 29 November 2012, 67/19. Status of Palestine in the United Nations, https://docs.un.org/en/A/RES/67/19.

[17] Sonia Boulos and Xavier Abu Eid, 'Recognizing Palestinian Statehood; Some Critical Comments', *Security Context* (25 April 2024), https://tinyurl.com/3ycxd348.

exclusively to parties that recognise Israel's right to exist, renounce violence and commit to upholding the principles of democratic governance and peaceful negotiation.

Empowering moderate voices and institutionalising democratic norms within Palestinian society would provide Israel with a credible and legitimate negotiating partner while simultaneously reinforcing the internal accountability of the Palestinian leadership. For peace to be viable, both parties must engage not only with each other, but also with their own societies, to ensure that the path to reconciliation is both inclusive and durable.

Proposals to Resolve the Israeli-Palestinian Conflict

First Option: Decide Not to Decide – Maintaining the So-Called Status Quo

This approach is most attractive to politically passive leaders, risk-averse actors and those unwilling or unable to make bold strides towards a negotiated peace. However, such a stance fundamentally undermines efforts to achieve a just and durable resolution to the Israeli-Palestinian conflict. It does not constitute a genuine solution but rather perpetuates an unjust status quo. By legitimising a prolonged occupation – an arrangement widely regarded in international law and moral discourse as untenable – this approach sustains the very conditions that fuel ongoing hostility and human suffering.

Crucially, the so-called status quo is a misnomer. In reality, no static condition exists. The status is continuously disrupted by both parties. On one side, Israel has steadily expanded its territorial control, often through settlement activity in the West Bank, eroding the territorial contiguity necessary for a viable Palestinian state and deepening Palestinian disenfranchisement. On the other side, radical Palestinian factions, such as Hamas and the Palestinian Islamic Jihad, both of which are designated as terrorist organisations by the United States, the European Union and other international actors, persist in rejecting Israel's right to exist. These groups are ideologically committed to Israel's destruction and are prepared to pursue that objective across generations, regardless of the human cost.

Such spoilers on both sides render the notion of a sustainable status quo illusory. What exists instead is a fragile and volatile arrangement, vulnerable to repeated eruptions of violence. Maintaining this unstable equilibrium risks not only undermining future prospects for peace, but also entrenching deeper cycles of mistrust, radicalisation and violence. Without a proactive commitment to a negotiated settlement based on mutual recognition, justice and compromise, the region is likely to experience recurring escalations, further distancing both peoples from the hope of a peaceful and equitable future.

Second Option: Palestinian Autonomy

Menachem Begin's autonomy plan of 1977 guided the 1978 Camp David talks. Begin did not wish to see the establishment of a Palestinian state alongside Israel. He was willing to grant the Palestinians limited administrative rights and abilities. Later, Yitzhak Rabin adopted the same formula during the Oslo peace process.

Begin's plan was summarised in a 26-point document titled 'Self-Rule for Palestinian Arabs, Residents of Judea, Samaria and the Gaza District, Which Will Be Implemented Upon the Establishment of Peace'.[18] The aim was to establish self-rule for Palestinians in the West Bank and Gaza as a permanent solution. The plan focused on personal, not territorial, autonomy. The elected Palestinian government would manage administrative affairs, but not the land. The territory would remain Israeli. The key elements of the plan were the following: administrative autonomy for Palestinians in the West Bank and Gaza would be established; an eleven-member administrative council would be elected to oversee eleven civilian governmental functions; Israeli military governance would be abolished, but Israel would still maintain security forces in the territories; an administrative council would supervise local police, while Israeli forces would handle public order; legislative power would be granted to a joint Palestinian-Israeli-Jordanian committee, which would decide laws unanimously; and Israeli settlers would be permitted to settle in the West Bank and the Gaza Strip, with sovereignty left unresolved. The administration of the Holy Places of the three religions in Jerusalem would be decided later. A special proposal 'will be drawn up and submitted that will include the guarantee of freedom of access to members of all faiths to the shrines holy to them'.[19] These principles would be reviewed after five years, without specifying the review process or involving other parties.[20]

[18] Self–rule for Palestinian Arabs, Residents of Judea, Samaria, and the Gaza District, Jerusalem, 28 December 1977, www.palquest.org/en/historictext/9646/begins-autonomy-plan.

[19] Ibid.

[20] Joel Singer, 'Developing the Concept of Palestinian Autonomy', *The Cairo Review of Global Affairs* (Winter 2019), www.thecairoreview.com/essays/developing-the-concept-of-palestinian-autonomy/.

This plan is unjust. Israel made very small and insufficient concessions. The plan gives Israel full control over the OPT and gives the Palestinians very little. The plan denies their self-determination and rights as a people. It preserves Israel's best interests, at the expense of the Palestinians. One may assume that all parties behind the veil of ignorance would reject the plan, as no party would wish to be the permanent subject of a military occupation.

Third Option: One-State Solution

The post-Zionist version of the one-state solution is also known as the State-of-all-its-citizens solution. All Palestinians will become Israeli citizens, with full citizenship rights. The principle of proportionality would apply, prescribing equitable representation across the political spectrum and fair distribution in civil service activities and appointments, as well as in the allocation of public funds. With one homeland for both Israel and Palestine, the one-state solution is said to do away with the conflict over history and mutual legitimisation and also resolve some of the stickiest points in the conflict. Israel and Palestine could maintain their 'right of return' without it being at the expense of the other; Israeli settlers could remain where they are, and Jerusalem could truly become the accepted capital of a unitary Arab-Jewish state.[21] The guiding model is South Africa, 'where a deeply divided society embarked on a path of truth and reconciliation to forge a new national identity. But the unique circumstances of Israel-Palestine demand tailored solutions developed through inclusive dialogue'.[22] As the birth rate among Arabs exceeds that of the Jews, with time Jews will become a minority in Israel, which means the end of Zionism.[23] Israel would forgo its clear Jewish identity as the home for all Jewish people. Only a small minority of Israeli Jews are willing to accept such a vision.

One-state rhetoric advances the aim of an equitable, pluralistic, democratic state incorporating Jewish Israelis and Arabs in a single state, without favouring either community. In practice, this language is one of undisguised hostility and delegitimisation of Israeli Zionists and

[21] Ahmad S. Khalidi, 'A One-State Solution', *The Guardian* (29 September 2003), www.theguardian.com/world/2003/sep/29/comment.

[22] Samer Elchahabi, 'Shifting the Paradigm: The One-State Solution as a Path to Peace', Arab Center (14 December 2023), https://tinyurl.com/2s3v3bt7.

[23] Ariella Azoulay and Adi Ophir, *The One-State Condition*, Stanford Studies in Middle Eastern and Islamic Societies and Cultures (Stanford, CA: Stanford University Press, 2012).

their national project.[24] The option is unjust, and one that most Israelis would reject. While a significant segment of Israelis are secular, the majority of them support the need for maintaining Israel as the Jewish Homeland, the only Jewish state in the world. Such a solution would not be consensual; it would be coerced and enforced on Jewish Israelis. One of the lessons of the Holocaust, which is a permanent shadow in the lives of Jews, is that they must have a state of refuge, if and when antisemitism becomes unbearable. The one-state solution would end the Jewish state.

Fourth Option: Annexation of Area C of the Oslo Accords

Area C, which constitutes the majority of the West Bank (3.3 million dunam), is under Israeli control. The PA is responsible for education and health for the Palestinian population in Area C, but Israel remains responsible for the infrastructure. The Palestinians are not allowed to build in 70 per cent of Area C. Indeed, the majority of this territory is not built up. Some 30 per cent is designated for military training, and 14 per cent for parks. According to Peace Now, in 2024, 14 per cent of the West Bank population was Jewish. There were 478,600 settlers living in the West Bank, in 146 settlements and 224 outposts.[25]

Leaders of the Jewish Orthodox right-wing parties propose that Israel annex Area C, including all settlements and an estimated 180,000–300,000 Palestinians.[26] The remaining scattered patches of land would remain under Palestinian authority.[27] The Palestinians in this expanded Israel would not become Israeli citizens; they would continue living under occupation. The Palestinians have no reason to accept such a 'solution' and would reject it with force and violence.

Likud governments have aimed to increase the Israeli presence in Area C, effectively delineating only 40 per cent of the West Bank for

24 Asher Susser, *Israel, Jordan and Palestine* (Waltham, MA: Brandeis University Press, 2012), 143.

25 Peace Now Statistics (2024), https://peacenow.org.il/en/settlements-watch/settlements-data/population.

26 'Area C', *B'Tselem* (2024), www.btselem.org/topic/area_c.

27 David E. Rosenberg, 'The Man Leading Israel's Not-So-Quiet Annexation of the West Bank', *Foreign Policy* (26 June 2024), https://tinyurl.com/37bmkket; see also Ben Birnbaum, 'The End of the Two-State Solution: Why the Window Is Closing on Middle-East Peace', *The New Republic* (11 March 2013), www.newrepublic.com/article/112617/israel-palestine-and-end-two-state-solution#.

the PA and granting the Palestinians the ability to govern their lives in Areas A and B, without recognising their national rights and aspirations. Simply put, the struggle is over land. Israel has aimed to create facts on the ground and to expand its territory at the expense of the Palestinians. The Palestinians would not accept this. For them, their big sacrifice was made in 1948, when they were left with only 22 per cent of historic Palestine. To give up 60 per cent of the 22 per cent is a difficult pill to swallow. Israeli facts (i.e., settlements) on the Palestinian land of the West Bank could be sustained either through a solution agreed to by both sides, or through violence. As it is hard to envisage Palestinian consent to this sacrifice without ample compensation, the reality of Israeli expansion is likely to yield even more violence and blood.

Such a 'solution' would have widespread repercussions for Israel, Palestine, Jordan and the rest of the Middle East. Annexation would make Israel an island in itself and subject further generations of Israelis to endless cycles of violence. It would encourage more Israelis to seek personal tranquillity by emigrating from the country. Those who have the option of working abroad would weigh the pros and cons of continued life in their beloved home country, overshadowed by the constant presence and fear of violence, or relocating, establishing a new life, new connections and identity in a new country, free of such fear, one of peace and tranquillity.

Should Israel proceed with the annexation of Area C in the West Bank, it could trigger a significant demographic and geopolitical shift with far-reaching consequences. Such a move would likely precipitate the displacement of large segments of the Palestinian population, whether through coercive measures or indirect pressures, resulting in a substantial influx of refugees into neighbouring Jordan.

This would place the Hashemite Kingdom in a profound moral and political quandary. Given Jordan's complex demographic composition, where a significant proportion of the population is of Palestinian origin, the government would face intense domestic and regional pressures. It could not simply close its borders without incurring political costs. The absorption of a large number of displaced Palestinians would strain Jordan's already fragile economy and social infrastructure, undermine internal stability and exacerbate political tensions. The ripple effects would likely destabilise the country's internal order and could jeopardise the 1994 Israel–Jordan peace treaty, which remains a cornerstone of the regional security architecture. Moreover, such a development would not occur in a vacuum; it would invite the attention and intervention of regional actors and global powers, who would view the situation as a threat to regional stability and international norms.

The resulting crisis could catalyse the emergence of a radically different Middle East, one characterised not by greater security and cooperation, but by heightened volatility, polarisation and antagonism. The long-term consequences of such a trajectory may run counter to Israel's strategic interests, eroding the relative regional stability from which it has historically benefited. In this context, unilateral annexation not only poses a moral and legal challenge but also risks unleashing a chain of destabilising events with unpredictable and potentially severe ramifications.

An unjust variation on this theme is the 2020 Trump plan, which recognises Israel's sovereignty over Jerusalem and all West Bank settlements (see Figure 12.1). It would enable Israel to annex some 30 per cent of the West Bank, with no land swaps. It holds that the establishment of Palestine would be deferred for years and would be subjected to Israeli and American discretion.[28] The Palestinians were not consulted and, unsurprisingly, rejected this very skewed plan that ignores Palestinian interests almost completely and aims to assure maximum Israeli interests.

Fifth Option: Federation

The Federation plan, advocated by the Federation Movement, presents a new approach to the Jewish-Arab/Palestinian conflict.[29] The Federation Movement seeks to promote regional stability and prosperity. In the federative system, members' entities do not have much political power, given the fact that sovereignty is exclusively vested in the federation (federal state). Membership is mandatory, and participating states lose part of their authority. The major authority of a federation is a central government that governs member states. It makes all decisions regarding foreign policy, national security, the military and diplomacy. The Federation plan calls for a transformation of Israel's system of governance into a federal government, similar to arrangements in the US, Canada, Switzerland and twenty-five other countries. Israel would be divided into cantons which would enjoy a large degree of independence in managing their affairs. The PA would be disbanded by consent, and Israeli rule would be applied to all parts of the country, including the OPT. The Jewish residents of the West Bank would remain in their settlements. All Palestinians residing in the

[28] Ishaan Tharoor with Ruby Mellen, 'Trump's "Deal of the Century" Is No Deal at All', *Washington Post* (28 January 2020).

[29] *The Federation Plan: The Founding Document*, www.federation.org.il/index.php/en/the-federation-plan.

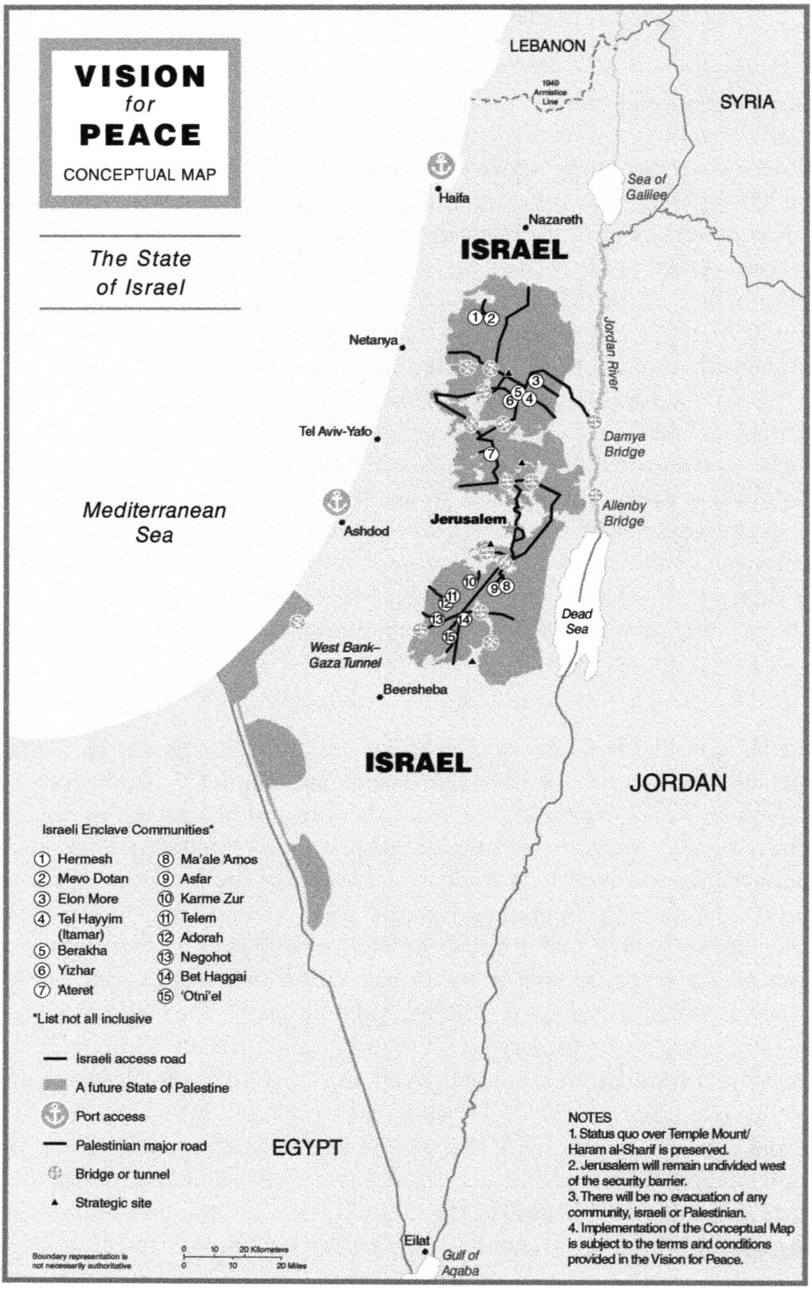

Figure 12.1 Trump Vision Map.

Note: For the text of the plan, see White House, *Peace to Prosperity: A Vision to Improve the Lives of the Palestinian and Israeli People* (January 2020), https://tinyurl.com/53nxme8m.

Credit: US government employee, Public domain, via Wikimedia Commons.

West Bank who wish to receive full Israeli citizenship would receive it. The Israeli Federation would not include the Gaza Strip.[30]

In my view, because of the wide asymmetry of the two entities, Israel and Palestine, it is unthinkable that Palestinians would agree to this solution.[31] This solution does not fully respect the right to Palestinian self-determination. The majority of Israeli Jews are also not likely to accept this proposal.[32]

Sixth Option: Confederations

A confederation is a union of sovereign states created by a treaty (*foedus* in Latin) and manifesting itself as a single state, with each part of the confederation retaining self-governance. Central competence is confined to defence, security and foreign affairs. Confederation enables each party to retain its own set of principles and distinct characteristics so as to secure peace and security through power sharing. Unlike a federation, a confederation maintains maximum authority for the individual states and minimal authority for the shared government.

There are several options:

1. Palestine with Jordan (West and East Banks of the Jordan River), to be discussed in detail *infra*. To recall, this was Qurie's dream.[33]
2. Palestine with Egypt (Gaza and the West Bank). Discussions with senior decision-makers in Egypt and other countries clarified that this proposal is impractical. Since 1967, the Egyptians have tried very hard to avoid any responsibility for the Gaza Strip. Financially, Egypt has enough burdens. Politically, it is troubled by the Muslim Brotherhood and does not need to add Hamas to the mix.
3. Jordan, Palestine and Egypt. This is Hasan Asfour's idea. He wants this confederation in order to prevent Israel from using the pretence of security issues to undermine Palestinian sovereignty.[34] Essentially, Asfour is suggesting only a very limited confederation, a security confederation to protect Palestine. I doubt that 'confederation' is the

[30] Ibid. See also Riccardo Bocco and Nigel Roberts, *An Israeli/Palestinian Federation: An Alternative Approach to Peace* (Geneva: Geneva Graduate Institute, November 2024).

[31] Daniel Bar-Tal, 'Is a Confederation between Israel and Palestine with Jordan a Viable Arrangement?', *World Affairs* 185(4) (2022): 737–765, https://doi.org/10.1177/00438200221128026.

[32] Raphael Cohen-Almagor, 'Is Israel a Liberal Democracy?', *The Cairo Review of Global Affairs* (December 2024), www.thecairoreview.com/essays/is-israel-a-liberal-democracy/.

[33] Yossi Beilin, *Touching Peace* (London: Weidenfeld & Nicolson, 1999) (English ed.), 83.

[34] Interview with Hasan Asfour (18 February 2025), 20.

right term to use here. Security alliance is the right term. Palestine would be dependent on the Egyptian and Jordanian armies.

4. Jordan, Palestine and Israel. Shimon Peres raised this proposal in a meeting with King Hussein on 28 August 1974. He proposed creating three political entities – Israel, Jordan and the PA – governed by Israel and Jordan. The PA would include both Gaza and the West Bank and would be completely demilitarised. The three entities would compose one economic unit and be open to the free movement of ideas, people and commerce. Hussein rejected the proposal *tout court*, because, at that time, he did not wish to forgo the West Bank.[35] This solution does not do justice to the Palestinians. It ignores their right to self-determination. This might be an option, after establishing a confederation between Palestine and Jordan and resolving the Gaza problem. For his part, Mahmoud Abbas said he would agree to a trilateral confederation that includes Israel.[36] If peace and tranquillity become the norm, Israel might consider joining the Palestinian-Jordanian confederation.[37]
5. Palestine with Israel: *The Holy Land Confederation*. This idea was proposed by Hiba Husseini and Yossi Belin. It suggests a confederative framework of cooperation between two independent states, Israel and Palestine, which includes joint authorities and enterprises. There would be two separate parliaments, governments and judicial systems, at least in the beginning. There would be free movement between them, and Jerusalem would be an open city and the capital of both states. Jewish settlers in the West Bank would be allowed to choose to relocate to Israel or become permanent citizens of Palestine while remaining Israeli citizens. An equal number of Palestinian citizens would be allowed to reside in Israel as permanent residents and remain Palestinian citizens. During the first thirty months of the arrangement, Israel would prepare its full withdrawal from the area which would eventually be the Palestinian state. The Palestinian state would comprise more than 95 per cent of the West Bank and would be fully compensated for the small area remaining in Israel. Compensation would include areas around the Gaza Strip, the Judean Desert and

[35] Avi Shlaim, *Lion of Jordan* (Or Yehuda: Kinneret, Zmora-Bitan, 2009) (Hebrew), 333.
[36] Hani Hazaimeh, 'Why Jordan Rejects a Confederation with Palestine', *Arab News* (4 September 2018), www.arabnews.com/node/1366951/middle-east.
[37] Alon Ben-Meir, 'The Case for an Israeli-Palestinian-Jordanian Confederation: Why Now and How?', *World Affairs*, 185(1) (2022): 9–58.

the Valley of Springs. After these thirty months, the two states would confederate. There would be advisory bodies on all issues that ministries deal with, such as health, agriculture and environment.[38]

This kind of arrangement could work if the parties share a sense of unity that would neutralise communal differences, and if there is sufficient trust between the communities. A poll conducted in July 2024 shows that 64 per cent of the Israeli population thought that Israel should strive to instil a political agreement that would result in a Palestinian state and normalisation with Arab countries.[39] Israelis yearn for tranquillity. To fathom what living in Israel and Palestine is like, one needs to try thinking about one's life without tranquillity. Both Israel and Palestine have known never-ending cycles of violence.

Polls' results fluctuate a great deal. The situation is dense and tense. Given the hatred, suspicion and hostility between Israelis and Palestinians, the Husseini–Belin proposal is no more than wishful thinking. Trust and goodwill between the two sides are low. Neither Israelis nor Palestinians are enchanted by the proposition of a shared reality. The analogy used by Beilin and Husseini is the European Union, but the reality is far from the present relationships between France, Spain and Germany. Life is beset by violence and terror, mutual incitement and hostility.

Abba Eban said:

> Not for one single moment in 24 hours of any day do these two peoples, the Israelis in the area defined as sovereign areas by our parliament, and the Palestinians in the West Bank in Gaza, share a single common experience, a sense of common origin, common hope, common tongue, common faith, common aspiration. There does not exist upon the surface of the inhabited globe any two communities between which there is a lesser flow of common destiny and aspiration.[40]

I would say that Israelis and Palestinians share painful memories of wars and terrorism, with conflicting interpretations and understanding of the same historical events that make agreement about what happened extremely difficult, if not impossible. Israeli society is very

[38] Yossi Beilin et al., *The Holy Land Confederation as a Facilitator for the Two-State Solution*, https://ecf.org.il/media_items/1538; Hiba Husseini and Yossi Beilin, 'An Israeli-Palestinian Confederation Is the Best Path to Peace', *Foreign Policy* (23 May 2022), https://foreignpolicy.com/2022/05/23/israeli-palestinian-confederation-peace/.

[39] aChord poll, No. 33 (Jerusalem, July 2024) (Hebrew).

[40] Abba Eban, 'Prospects for Peace in the Middle East', Landon Lecture (29 January 1990), www.k-state.edu/landon/speakers/abba-eban/transcript.html.

much the product of the Zionist narrative, which celebrates much of what Palestinians abhor. Similarly, Palestinian society is the product of its national liberation narrative, fighting to regain independence and sovereignty. There is very little of the positive that connects the two people. They do not study the same history, do not sing the same songs, do not pray the same prayers, do not wish to live together and do not share a common vision for the future.

Even Uri Avneri, of the Israeli far left, acknowledged that it takes 'quite a stretch of the imagination to believe that Israelis and Palestinians will come together, serve in the same army, enact the same laws, and pay the same taxes. One wonders how such a state would function.'[41]

6. Palestine with Israel, Egypt and Jordan. This would create a New Middle East. Sadly, this is a far-fetched reality. The factors separating these countries outweigh those that might unify them. With the high level of distrust between the parties, this solution is aspired to in stages. First, the Palestinian challenge must be resolved. Only then could the parties move forward to a more comprehensive framework.

   In terms of viability, undoubtedly some form of confederation will better serve the Palestinians' interest. However, at present, Jordan, Egypt and Israel have no wish to rush to establish such a confederation. This option can become realistic only when there is peace, trust and goodwill among all concerned nations, three ingredients which must be strengthened.

Resolving the Israeli-Palestinian Conflict: The Proposal

Next I outline the parameters for resolving the Israeli-Palestinian conflict. The solution includes several stages.

1. There is a need to rebuild Gaza and install a new order. It is a delicate task to re-establish Gaza from the ashes. This is also in Israel's interest and its responsibility, which it should not ignore. It must be part of the solution, but it cannot do it on its own. It must have partners: the Arab nations, the PA, the US, the UN, Egypt, Saudi Arabia, the Gulf countries, and other countries that have the goodwill and interest to re-establish Gaza.[42] Alternatively, if Donald Trump's 'ownership'

[41] Susser, *Israel, Jordan and Palestine*, 215.

[42] See Gilead Sher and Samih Al-Abed, 'A Framework for Middle East Security, Peace, and Normalization', Working paper, Rice University's Baker Institute for Public Policy, 2024.

proposal over Gaza of February 2025 holds water, then the United States will have to clear tens of millions of tons of debris and make Gaza, as Trump suggested, into the 'Riviera of the Middle East'.[43]

2. Renew constructive cooperation between Israel and the PA on all matters, including civilian and economic.
3. Marginalise Hamas, the Islamic Jihad and other terrorist factions, and dismantle their arms. The aim is to include the major terrorist organisation, Hamas, in the Palestine Liberation Organization (PLO) under certain conditions and with the consent of the PLO. Hamas is the main challenge.
4. Insist on democratic elections in the West Bank. Only parties committed to peace that recognise Israel's right to exist and are committed to fighting terror and violence would be allowed to participate.
5. Two-state solution.
6. Confederation between Palestine in the West Bank and Jordan.
7. Gaza will be part of the confederation, if and when its authorities agree to resolve the conflict via peaceful means and accept the principles outlined later. Discounting Hamas and hoping for the best is not an option. Zealots and terrorists should be put in check, preventing them from derailing the peace process, as they have done so effectively up to now.

Two-State Solution

In 1936, against the background of the Arab Revolt, the British Mandate in Palestine established the Peel Commission, headed by Lord William Peel, to investigate the reasons for the unrest. After close examination of the situation in Palestine, the Peel Commission proposed the partition of Palestine. The basic principle was to separate Jews from Arabs. The British proposed an exchange of land and populations between the two future states, Jewish and Arab, as an essential step to complement their delineation of the border. A small part of Palestine (including Jerusalem) would remain under the supervision of the British Mandate.[44]

On 29 November 1947, the United Nations reached a similar conclusion: the way to solve the Arab-Israeli conflict was via partition and the

[43] Ishaan Tharoor with Sammy Westfall, 'Trump's Plan for Gaza Is a Nonstarter, but It Reflects a Stark Reality', *Washington Post* (6 February 2025).

[44] Shaul Arieli, *A Border between Us and You* (Tel Aviv: Miskal Publishing – Yedioth Books, 2021), 180–185.

establishment of an Arab state alongside a Jewish state. This resolution, like the Peel Report, was rejected by the Arabs, who refused to recognise the establishment of a Jewish state in Palestine.

In December 2012, two independent public opinion polls showed near-identical results: two-thirds of Israelis supported a peace deal creating a Palestinian state the size of the West Bank and Gaza, with its capital in East Jerusalem.[45] Subsequent polls showed considerable support for a two-state solution. The terror attack of 7 October 2023 inflicted a major blow to peace prospects and the vision of the two-state solution. Still, a third of Palestinians supported a two-state solution; nearly half of respondents, in both the Gaza Strip and the West Bank, believe that the most vital goal for the Palestinian people should be an 'Israeli withdrawal to the 1967 borders and the establishment of a Palestinian state in the West Bank and the Gaza Strip with East Jerusalem as its capital'.[46] A public poll conducted in September 2025 among West Bank Arabs showed that 52 per cent supported a two-state solution, 28 per cent supported a single Palestinian state between the Jordan River and the sea without Jews, while 16 per cent supported a single bi-national democratic state.[47]

The key to ensuring Israel's long-term survival is its integration into the Middle East. And the key to Israel's integration is resolving its conflict with the Palestinians. Without peace, violence is inevitable. As President Barack Obama said in his historic speech in Jerusalem on 21 March 2013:

> Given the demographics west of the Jordan River, the only way for Israel to endure and thrive is through the realization of an independent and viable Palestine … And given the march of technology, the only way to truly protect the Israeli people is through the absence of war – because no wall is high enough, and no Iron Dome is strong enough, to stop every enemy from inflicting harm.[48]

Security must be at the centre of any agreement. Former military intelligence chief Amos Yadlin explained that, as long as there are adequate security provisions in place, such as a demilitarised Palestinian state,

45 Birnbaum, 'The End of the Two-State Solution'.

46 Palestinian Center for Policy and Survey Research, Press Release: Public Opinion Poll No (92) (12 June 2024), https://pcpsr.org/en/node/980.

47 Swords of Iron Survey: Palestinian Public Opinion in the West Bank, INSS Survey, 15 October 2025, https://tinyurl.com/mr3acth6.

48 'Barack Obama's Speech in Jerusalem – Full Text', *The Guardian* (21 March 2013), www.guardian.co.uk/world/2013/mar/21/barack-obama-speech-jerusalem-text.

early warning stations, Israeli control of the West Bank's airspace and electromagnetic spectrum, and an effective international force in the Jordan Valley, Israel's security will be assured.[49] Israel's insistence on security does not exclude peace with the Palestinians. Quite the opposite. Assuring Israel's security necessitates peace, but it must be a just peace, or it will not be sustainable. As President Obama maintained:

> It is not fair that a Palestinian child cannot grow up in a state of her own, and lives with the presence of a foreign army that controls the movements of her parents every single day. It is not just when settler violence against Palestinians goes unpunished. It is not right to prevent Palestinians from farming their lands; to restrict a student's ability to move around the West Bank, or to displace Palestinian families from their homes. Neither occupation nor expulsion is the answer. Just as Israelis built a state in their homeland, Palestinians have a right to be a free people in their own land.[50]

In his bold speech, Obama called upon the people of Israel: 'Only you can determine what kind of democracy you will have. But remember that as you make these decisions, you will define not simply the future of your relationship with the Palestinians – you will define the future of Israel as well.'[51] President Obama recalled what Prime Minister Sharon said: 'It is impossible to have a Jewish, democratic state and at the same time to control all of Eretz Israel. If we insist on fulfilling the dream in its entirety, we are liable to lose it all.'[52] Israel cannot maintain its place in the democratic world if it continues to control the lives of millions of Palestinians. A zero-sum game exists between democracy and occupation. One comes at the expense of the other.

Ehud Barak,[53] Ehud Olmert,[54] Ami Ayalon,[55] Itamar Rabinovich,[56] Avi Gil,[57] Sven-Eric Söder,[58] Stuart Eizenstat,[59] Aaron David Miller[60] and many others think a two-state solution is the most just solution.[61]

49 Birnbaum, 'The End of the Two-State Solution'.
50 'Barack Obama's speech in Jerusalem – full text'.
51 Ibid.
52 Ibid.
53 Interview with Ehud Barak (21 June 2022), 17.
54 Interview with Ehud Olmert (6 January 2025), 8.
55 Ami Ayalon, 'Outline of an Israeli-Palestinian Permanent Peace' (2022).
56 Interview with Itamar Rabinovich (21 July 2017), 9.
57 Interview with Avi Gil (16 January 2025), 24.
58 Interview with Sven-Eric Söder (20 August 2019), 21.
59 Interview with Stuart Eizenstat (7 July 2022), 17.
60 Interview with Aaron David Miller (12 September 2019), 27.
61 Ayalon, 'Outline of an Israeli-Palestinian Permanent Peace'.

Hussein Ibish, a former Senior Fellow at the American Task Force on Palestine, described by Miller as 'the most clever Palestinian I have ever met', observes that the abandonment of a two-state agenda will give way to a campaign of non-violent resistance, boycotts and sanctions that will eventually bring Israel to its knees.[62] I have been campaigning for a two-state solution since 2012, and I have explained the reasons why this solution is fair and just in several articles, which the reader is welcome to read.[63] I believe that peace is a precious commodity and, therefore, requires both parties to pay a high price for its achievement. The peace deal should be attractive to both Israel and Palestine, equally. It cannot be one-sided, enforced or coerced.

At present, it is impossible to see the two rivals sitting together and reaching a comprehensive agreement that will settle all disputes and declare an end to hostilities. There is too much anger, suspicion and bad blood between them. Trust and goodwill between Israel and the PA are vital and sorely needed commodities to pave the way to the negotiation table.

As has been said, the two primary obstacles to a successful implementation of any peace treaty are the expansion of Israeli settlements and Palestinian terrorism. Historically, neither issue has been adequately or consistently confronted in previous rounds of negotiations, resulting in a cycle of mistrust, delegitimisation and violence that has entrenched the status quo.

The settlement project had a modest beginning. In 1967, there were 1,500 settlers. Through the years, all Israeli governments have supported and expanded it, preferring to increase Israeli control and territory at the expense of making a sincere attempt to resolve the conflict. While I do not doubt the good intentions of Barak and Olmert, neither of them halted the project. Settlements were expanded as new settlers joined. To achieve peace, the trajectory must be reversed. Israeli settlements constitute a major obstacle to peace.

The expansion of settlements undermines the territorial contiguity necessary for the establishment of a viable Palestinian state and signals a

[62] Hussein Ibish, interview with Jeffrey Goldberg in *The Atlantic* (3 November 2009).

[63] Raphael Cohen-Almagor, 'Two-State Solution – The Way Forward', *Annual Review of Law and Ethics*, 20 (2012): 381–395; Raphael Cohen-Almagor, 'Breaking the Israeli-Palestinian Deadlock – Two State Solution', *Global Education Magazine: International Day of Peace* (21 September 2014): 58–63; Raphael Cohen-Almagor, 'Suggestions for Israeli-Palestinian Agreement', *New Directions* (*Kivunim Hadashim*), 30 (June 2014) (Hebrew): 144–159; Raphael Cohen-Almagor, 'In Support of Two-State Solution', *Youth Law Journal* (12 November 2018), www.theylj.co.uk/in-support-of-two-state-solution/.

de facto annexation policy that contradicts the spirit of a negotiated two-state solution. The use of terrorism by Palestinian actors has not only inflicted harm and fear on Israeli civilians but has also severely eroded Israeli public support for compromise and bolstered security-oriented, hardline political positions. This has created a political and psychological climate deeply resistant to progress, and unless these impediments are meaningfully and comprehensively addressed, through enforcement, international guarantees and reciprocal commitments, the negotiation process will remain stalled. It will be impossible to resolve the most contentious and emotionally charged final status issues, including the status of Jerusalem, the administration of holy sites, the delineation of permanent borders and the resolution of the Palestinian refugee question.

Israel and the PA are either unwilling or unable to stop settlement growth and acts of terror and violence. What is required is the involvement of third parties in the conflict, to shoulder efforts to tackle these issues, closely coordinating their constructive trust-building steps. They should include the US and perhaps members of the Arab League.[64] The PA is too weak and fragile to address the conflict successfully with its very modest means. It needs the assistance, legitimacy and capabilities of major powers that have some vested interest in resolving the conflict. Up to now, the US has been unable to deliver the goods on its own, and the Arab League cannot carry the burden alone. But coordinated efforts by the US and the Arab League may prove successful.

In an atmosphere that is not derailed by settlement build-up or terror, further constructive steps can be made. Granted, there will be spoilers on both sides. Settlers will try to create facts on the ground and terrorists will continue their attempts to throw both parties into another round of violence. Israel and the PA must take firm stands against such spoilers; explicit and unequivocal condemnation and firm action are needed. No shred of legitimacy should be conferred on them; both parties must clearly state that they are intent on embarking upon a renewed journey towards peace. There are many possibilities for agreements, such as on the allocation of water resources,[65] the slow but steady release of prisoners and the evacuation of isolated Israeli settlements.

64 See the Arab Peace Initiative 2002.

65 For further discussion, see Hillel Shuval, 'Is the Conflict over Shared Water Resources between Israelis and Palestinians an Obstacle to Peace?', in Elizabeth G. Matthews (ed.), *The Israel-Palestine Conflict* (London: Routledge, 2011), 93–113; Amjad Aliewi, Enda O'Connell, Geoff Parkin and Karen Assaf, 'Palestine Water: Between Challenges and Realities', in Elizabeth G. Matthews (ed.), *The Israel-Palestine Conflict*, 114–138.

Significant changes in the Israeli and the Palestinian education programmes should be introduced, emphasising good neighbourly relations, pluralism, diversity, acknowledging differences of culture and religion – all with the utmost respect for one another's traditions – and using these traditions as levers for tranquil coexistence.[66]

The peace agreement should include the following elements.

Palestinian sovereignty – to be declared and respected in the West Bank. As long as Hamas controls Gaza and is committed to the destruction of Israel, the accord will be restricted to the West Bank. The hope is that if the agreement is sustained, pressure will be exerted on Hamas to change its ways, or strong opposition to Hamas will emerge in Gaza, supporting Israel's efforts to suppress Hamas and forcing Hamas out of positions of power. Then it will be possible to think of a Palestinian state that also encompasses Gaza. For many years, this has been no more than wishful thinking.

Mutual recognition – Israel shall recognise the State of Palestine. Palestine shall recognise the State of Israel.[67]

Mutual diplomatic relations – Israel and Palestine shall immediately establish full diplomatic relationships with each other, installing ambassadors in the capitals of the respective partner.

Capital – each state is free to choose its own capital. If peace and quiet prevail, and the relationship between Israel and Palestine is normal, free of terror and violence, the two parties may consider making Jerusalem a shared city, an open city, a truly multicultural city, where all people enjoy the same rights equally – one that would serve as a model of successful normalisation.

Jerusalem – the Palestinians want the internationalisation of Jerusalem and the implementation of UN Resolution 181, declaring Jerusalem as a *corpus separatum*, a Latin term referring to a city or region which is given special legal and political status.[68] This issue should be addressed and settled during final status negotiations.

[66] See Daniel Bar-Tal, 'Challenges for Constructing Peace Culture and Peace Education', in Elizabeth G. Matthews (ed.), *The Israel-Palestine Conflict*, 209–223; and Salem Aweiss, 'Culture of Peace and Education', in Elizabeth G. Matthews (ed.), *The Israel-Palestine Conflict*, 224–246.

[67] Livni and Netanyahu unnecessarily compounded a complex conflict by insisting on Palestinian recognition of Israel as a Jewish state. This issue can be resolved by diplomacy of words.

[68] United Nations General Assembly Resolution 181 (29 November 1947), www.yale.edu/lawweb/avalon/un/res181.htm.

Those supporting the division of Jerusalem argue that what is Palestinian will come under the territory of the new capital, Al Quds. The Israeli capital would include West Jerusalem and the adjacent Israeli settlements. To maintain Palestinian contiguity, Israel may be required to give up some of the settlements around Arab Jerusalem.

According to the vision of two capitals, an Israeli one and a Palestinian one, Al Quds would include East Jerusalem and the adjacent Palestinian land and villages, including Al-Sawahreh, al-Tur, Beit Hanina, Beit Zafafa, Isawiya, Jabel Mukaber, Kufr Akab, Shaykh Jarrah, Sharafat, Shuafat, Silwan, Sur Baher, Umm Tuba and Wadi al-Juz. Sheikh Jerrah would be administered jointly. The Palestinians would agree that Israel has sovereignty over the Jewish Quarter and the Wailing Wall section of the Western Wall.[69]

I agree with Gilead Sher that dividing the Old City into two-and-a-half quarters for the Palestinians and one-and-a-half quarters for Israel is a bad idea.[70] Whoever thinks it is possible to separate the quarters, installing Israeli sovereignty over the Jewish and Armenian Quarters, and Palestinian sovereignty over the Muslim and Christian Quarters, should visit the Old City and see how impractical this is. The quarters mesh and are inseparable. At Camp David 2000, there was a suggestion to treat the Temple Mount as *corpus separatum*. I suggest that the entire Holy Basin come under a special regime, a *corpus separatum*, which controls and manages the area, rather than its being divided by the parties. The Old City will be open to all faiths, under international custodianship. There will be Israeli-Palestinian cooperation in providing municipal services to both populations. While the existing arrangements and responsibilities of the religious authorities will continue on most matters, the special regime will be responsible for security, the maintenance of the sites, archaeological activity, city planning and heritage preservation. This means that the special regime will have its own police service, that only this service will be allowed to bear weapons and that the chief of the police would be neither Israeli nor Palestinian.[71] This arrangement would require international dispute resolution mechanisms to resolve misunderstandings and contrasting interpretations of procedures.

69 Palestinian non-paper, ‘Palestinian Vision for the Outcome of Permanent Status Negotiations Based on the Arab Peace Plan’ (12 June 2002).

70 Interview with Gilead Sher (22 February 2024), 7.

71 Jerusalem Old City Initiative, *Proposals for the Old City of Jerusalem* (Windsor: University of Windsor, 2010), 16–20.

Temple Mount/Haram al-Sharif – the Temple Mount is part of the Holy Basin. It is important to Islam, Judaism and Christianity. Muslims believe that the Prophet Muhammad ascended to heaven from the Haram al-Sharif.[72] I think the idea that the Palestinians would be sovereign above the ground and Israel would be sovereign under the ground is not workable and quite impracticable.

The Americans developed a proposal allowing the Palestinians to have a diplomatic presence in the Haram. Palestine would not acquire *sovereignty* over any part of the Temple Mount, but it would have a diplomatic presence. Palestinians could live and stay there.

On 31 March 2013, a Jordanian-Palestinian agreement was signed between the PA and Jordan, entrusting King Abdullah II with the defence of Muslim and Christian holy sites in Jerusalem.[73] In the future, while Jordan may be a party to any agreement concerning the site, a broader arrangement would be welcomed. As agreed by Abbas and Olmert, it may come under the control of a five-nation consortium comprising Palestine, Israel, Jordan, Saudi Arabia and the United States.[74] The Waqf will continue its administration. Jews will enjoy the right of access. Excavation for antiquities may be undertaken only with the full agreement of both sides. Similarly, alterations to the historical structures and foundations can be made only with the consent of both sides.

Borders – these should be reasonable and logical for both sides. Former military intelligence chief Amos Yadlin explained: 'Having a border is the best security arrangement.'[75] Settling the conflict would give Israel greater international legitimacy to fight terrorism and enable it to deal with the more serious emerging threat from Iran. Israel would withdraw to the Green Line, evacuate many settlements and resettle settlers in other parts of the country.

At Camp David 2000, the Israeli proposal infringed on Palestinian contiguity.[76] Ariel, Shilo, Petza'el, Ma'ale Adumim and Kalia chop up Palestinian territory, and Israel insisted that they remain in Israel. A few months later, at Taba (January 2001), the Israeli proposal was far more

72 Arif al-Arif, *A Brief Guide to the Dome of the Rock and al-Haram al-Sharif* (Jerusalem: Supreme Awqaf Council, 1965); 'Haram al-Sharif', *Encyclopedia of the Modern Middle East and North Africa, Encyclopedia.com* (25 May 2018).

73 'Analysts: Jerusalem Deal Boosts Jordan in Holy City', Ma'an News Agency (3 April 2013).

74 Interview with Ehud Olmert (22 February 2019), 31.

75 Birnbaum, 'The End of the Two-State Solution'.

76 Arieli, *A Border between Us and You*, Map 21.

reasonable and considerate, allowing Palestinian contiguity;[77] however, the Palestinians insisted on more Israeli concessions.[78] The gaps between the parties also remained wide in Annapolis.[79] Israel should insist only on what is absolutely *necessary*, not on what is desired.

The Security Barrier – creates a political reality. It should be adjusted to establish a mutually agreed border. After five years of a lasting peace, Israel may consider dismantling the barrier. True peace is an effective security barrier.

Security – both Israel and Palestine must take all necessary measures to ascertain that their citizens live free of fear for their lives. Security is equally important for both Israelis and Palestinians. Palestine and Israel shall base their security relations on cooperation, mutual trust, good neighbourly relations and the protection of their joint interests.[80]

Israel takes security very seriously, for very good reasons. Dismantling all terror organisations and the demilitarisation of Palestine are non-negotiable as far as Israel is concerned. This was agreed upon in 1995. Also agreed upon were joint Israeli-Palestinian patrols along the Jordan River, the installation of early warning posts and the establishment of an international observer force to ensure implementation of the agreed security arrangements.[81] This international observer force would be temporary, until both parties feel that it is no longer required. The early warning posts will be periodically visited by Israeli security officers, but they will not be permanently present on Palestinian soil. If there is a need for a permanent presence, this will be entrusted to an agreed-upon third party. Shaul Arieli thinks that one warning post is sufficient.[82]

Sa'eb Erekat conceded that the Palestinians would not have an army, air force or navy.[83] Palestine would not be permitted to make military alliances or cooperation agreements with countries or movements hostile to Israel. Both parties must collaborate to fight terror. The Palestinian notion of having an international force in Palestine to replace Israeli forces is contested. The sovereignty of Palestine should be respected as much as possible; it is

77 Ibid., Map 22.
78 Ibid., Map 23.
79 Ibid., Maps 26–27.
80 The Geneva Accord.
81 Yossi Beilin, *The Path to Geneva* (NY: RDV Books, 2004), 169.
82 Interview with Shaul Arieli (11 November 2024).
83 Seumas Milne, 'Palestinian Leaders Weak – and Increasingly Desperate', *The Guardian* (23 January 2011), https://tinyurl.com/mvdnjhc9.

required to enforce law and order in Palestine and ensure that Israel's security remains intact. An arbitration committee should be installed to receive and adjudicate parties' concerns regarding infringements of their security.

A Palestinian non-paper says:

> Neither Palestine nor Israel will participate in military alliances against each other, or allow their territory to be used as a military base of operation against each other or against other neighbours. No foreign troops may be stationed in the territory of either state unless otherwise specified in the permanent status agreement or subsequently agreed to by the two parties. Palestine and Israel's respective sovereignty and independence will be guaranteed by formal agreements with members of the international community.[84]

Terrorism and violence – zero tolerance in this sphere. Both parties will work together to curb violence. Both parties will see that their citizens on both sides of the border reside peacefully. Zealots and terrorists – Palestinians and Jews – will be severely penalised for any violation of the peace.

In the past, the Palestinians failed to understand the gravity of terrorism and accepted it as part of life. Nabil Sha'ath said: 'The option is not either armed struggle or negotiations. We can fight and negotiate at the same time, just as the Algerians and the Vietnamese had done.'[85] Democracies, however, see things differently. On this issue, there should be no compromise.

Settlements – there will be a complete freeze on settlement building. Israel, with the help of the international community, will offer incentives to settlers to resettle in other parts of Israel, preferably in the Galilee in the north, and in the Negev in the south. The international community will resolve to set up a special fund to incentivise settlers to buy houses and settle in these parts of Israel if they so wish. The aim is to decrease friction between Israelis and Palestinians in the West Bank.

The future of the major settlement blocs – Ma'ale Adumim, Givat Ze'ev, Gush Etzion and Modi'in Illit – which account for approximately 70 per cent of the Jewish population in the West Bank and for less than

[84] Palestinian non-paper, 'Palestinian Vision for the Outcome of Permanent Status Negotiations'.

[85] Shlomo Ben-Ami, *Scars of War, Wounds of Peace* (London: Phoenix, 2005), 240. Yossi Beilin tells the story of the Taba talks, during which two Israelis were murdered in Tulkarem. The Palestinians, he writes, expressed their shock at the murder, but they found it difficult to understand why 'we always play into the hands of those who want to sabotage the talks'. Beilin, *The Path to Geneva*, 243.

2 per cent of its size, will be discussed. Some of them, possibly all of them, may be annexed to Israel upon reaching an agreement with the PA on the exchange of territory that will be equal in size.[86] The city of Ariel in the West Bank is the most difficult needle to thread (see later discussion). Palestinian territorial contiguity would be maintained and created via high-fly connecting roads and tunnels. Border adjustment along the 1967 Green Line must be kept to a minimum and be reciprocal. At the Taba talks, the Palestinians presented a map in which Israel would annex 3.1 per cent of the West Bank and transfer to the PA other territories of the same size.[87] Beilin said the Palestinians were willing to concede to Israeli annexation of three settlement blocs of at least 4 per cent of the West Bank.[88] Prime Minister Olmert offered President Abbas a similar or even slightly better deal, but Abbas did not reply positively.

Egyptian President Anwar Sadat thought of turning the West Bank over to the United Nations Emergency Force (UNEF), established after the 1956 Suez crisis, for a period of five years, during which the Palestinians would enjoy self-determination. He proposed that the Gaza Strip become the main weight of a Palestinian state, to which he would give part of the Sinai, including Rafah and Yamit. The West Bank should be given the option of independence or becoming a confederation with Jordan.[89] These ideas should be discussed and explored.

Ariel – Ariel is a major problem. Gidi Grinstein thought there was no option but to vacate Ariel. He said this was also the opinion of former IDF Chief of Staff Amnon Lipkin-Shahak.[90] Beilin maintained that in 2002 he met with Lipkin-Shahak, who said:

> I know you, politicians. You are always trying to find compromises which are not workable. For the time being, the compromises work and then you are happy. And I suspect that you will insist on annexing Ariel. I am telling you, if you intend to demand Ariel as part of Israel, I am out. And I need you to promise me that this will not be the demand of our delegation to the Geneva Initiative.[91]

86 For pertinent maps, see www.geneva-accord.org/mainmenu/static-maps/. See also West Bank 'Settlement Blocs', Peace Now, http://peacenow.org.il/eng/content/west-bank-%E2%80%9Csettlement-blocs%E2%80%9D.

87 Beilin, *The Path to Geneva*, 239.

88 Ibid., 246.

89 Seth Anziska, *Preventing Palestine: A Political History from Camp David to Oslo* (Princeton, NJ: Princeton University Press, 2018), 96.

90 Interview with Gidi Grinstein (21 May 2013), 25.

91 Yossi Beilin, Middle East Study Centre Annual Lecture, University of Hull (19 October 2022), 12.

Beilin reassured Lipkin-Shahak that the Geneva Initiative did not include Ariel and questioned why this was Lipkin-Shahak's precondition. Lipkin-Shahak explained: 'As a military person, I cannot defend Ariel if it is part of my country, because it is like a balloon with a rope. In order to get to Ariel, which is in the middle of the northern part of the West Bank, you have to ensure that the military can go there, and that the military will be responsible for this area. We cannot defend Ariel. So, it should be evacuated and we should not demand it.' Beilin concurred, arguing that Israel cannot assure the security of Ariel and cannot assure the security of the settlements, once it leaves the area and the Palestinians remain.[92]

Another less favourable option is to relocate Ariel. After Camp David, Ariel was discussed internally by the Israeli delegation in Taba. Lipkin-Shahak, clearly troubled by the Ariel dispute, suggested that Ariel be relocated and reconstructed in one of the areas adjacent to the 1967 lines. He said there was no use 'having a finger poking in the eyes of the Palestinians and disrupting the contiguity of the Palestinian state with 20 or 20-some kilometers into their territory'.[93] If and when there is political will to resolve the conflict and recognition of the need for a viable Palestine, Israel can devise relocation and compensation schemes in support of Ariel settlers (see Figure 12.2).

Ariel presents a potential test case for peaceful coexistence and shared sovereignty within a broader framework of conflict resolution. As part of a forward-looking initiative, Palestinians could be granted the right to purchase property and reside in Ariel, fostering integration rather than segregation. Concurrently, Israeli residents preferring not to remain in a mixed community could be provided with state-supported options for voluntary resettlement elsewhere in Israel, ensuring that their personal choices are respected and facilitated. Those choosing to remain in Ariel would do so with a clear commitment to the city's transformation into a symbol of coexistence, mirroring, in some respects, the pluralistic ethos of cities such as Haifa. Central to this vision is the role of Ariel University, a prominent academic institution in the region. Building on its existing inclusion of Arab Israeli students, the university could expand its mission by opening its doors to Palestinian students from the West Bank and, ultimately, to students from across the broader Middle East. This would position Ariel University as a hub of regional academic

[92] Ibid.

[93] Interview with Gilead Sher (2 February 2024), 5.

Figure 12.2 A map of Israel and the Palestinian Occupied Territory.
Source: NPR.

exchange, fostering intercultural dialogue, mutual understanding and the development of a truly international academic community. Such an initiative would not only serve as a confidence-building measure in the peace process but also provide an example of coexistence grounded in shared civic space, equal access to education and respect for diversity. If successful, Ariel could offer a replicable model for other contested areas, where cooperation replaces confrontation and integrated communities replace divided enclaves.

Prisoners – this issue is one of the most sensitive and important matters for the Palestinian people. The PA appointed a special minister for prisoner affairs. My Arab interviewees emphasised the importance of prisoner release time and again, while most of the Israeli interviewees hardly mentioned it. The Israelis addressed this issue only when I raised it. The prisoners are central to all of the Palestinian organisations, their supporters, and their social and national bases.[94] Jonathan Schwartz wrote in his comments that no issue was more important, in his experience, to the Palestinian public than prisoner releases;[95] every family suffered under the Israeli practice of widespread imprisonment without due process, and prisoner releases symbolised progress by their negotiators. It was not the practical effect of wage-earning Palestinians being unavailable to their families, but the image of the occupier detaining significant numbers of the Palestinian community, that had to be addressed. Israel has obvious security concerns, but committing to a process of prisoner releases and fulfilling that commitment could serve its interests. Unlike most Israeli leaders, Olmert was forthcoming in understanding this. When Abbas asked him to release 500 prisoners, Olmert said he was willing to release even 900 prisoners.[96]

An especially worrisome concern is the issue of administrative detention. This issue was raised by the Palestinians several times. For instance, in a meeting of a Palestinian delegation headed by Sufian Abu Zaideh, Minister for Prisoner Affairs, and an Israeli delegation, headed by Minister of Justice Tzipi Livni, the Palestinians pointed out that administrative detention decrees were renewed automatically without any substantive judicial review. The Palestinians argued that following interrogation, prisoners should stand trial in a court of law, be sentenced or be released. Palestinian delegate Qaddura Faris maintained that 'all

[94] Sufian Abu Zaida, 'Palestinian Prisoners from Oslo to Annapolis', in Peter Bauck and Mohammed Omer (eds), *The Oslo Accords 1993–2013: A Critical Assessment* (Cairo: American University in Cairo Press, 2013), 135–146.

[95] Jonathan Schwartz's written comments (20 November 2024).

[96] Raviv Drucker, 'Olmert, Abu Mazen and Barak Refer to the Political Process', *HaMakor* (17 November 2015).

administrative prisoners must be released if they are not sentenced'.[97] In reality, some of those prisoners have been detained for four and five years. This cannot be considered fair and reasonable.

At the end of June 2024, the Israel Prison Service (IPS) was holding 3,340 Palestinians in administrative detention.[98] The power to use administrative detention was established during British rule under the Defence (Emergency) Regulations, 1945. When Israel gained independence in 1948, a state of emergency was declared and these regulations became Israeli law. After the 1967 Six-Day War, military orders were issued allowing the use of these regulations in the West Bank and the Gaza Strip. Israel began using administrative detentions as a security measure against the Palestinian population and occasionally targeting Jews involved in activities posing a threat to national security. In 1979 and 1980, procedures for administrative detention within the Green Line borders and the OPT were changed. The Defence Regulations were replaced by the Emergency Powers (Detention) Law, 5739–1979, allowing the minister of defence to detain individuals for up to six months. Extensions of the detention period required court approval. This law only applies to Israeli citizens not living in the OPT. In the OPT, detention orders are issued under different provisions, such as the Security Ordinance and the Administrative Detention Order. In 1982, Attorney General Yitzhak Zamir clarified that the power of detention in these territories is granted to a military commander.[99]

Administrative detention is widely regarded as a practice that undermines fundamental principles of justice, due process and the rule of law. A coercive and exceptional measure, it permits the deprivation of liberty without formal charges or a fair trial and is more commonly associated with authoritarian governance than with liberal democracies. In democratic societies committed to the protection of civil liberties and the integrity of legal institutions, individuals must be afforded the right to a transparent judicial process in which they can confront evidence and mount a defence. Reliance on security assessments, particularly those issued by the defence minister without the presentation of substantiated, reviewable evidence, raises serious legal and ethical concerns. It not only circumvents judicial scrutiny but also erodes

[97] Negotiation on Prisoners Release, meeting notes (8 May 2005).

[98] 'Statistics on Administrative Detentions in the Occupied Territories', *B'Tselem* (2 September 2024), www.btselem.org/administrative_detention/statistics.

[99] Raphael Cohen-Almagor, 'Administrative Detention in Israel and Its Employment as a Means of Combating Political Extremism', *New York International Law Review*, 9(2) (1996): 1–25.

public confidence in the justice system. If individuals are suspected of committing criminal acts, the appropriate response should be to initiate legal proceedings in accordance with established criminal law, requiring the state to present admissible evidence and adhere to procedural safeguards. Resorting to administrative detention, in lieu of due legal process, risks normalising a practice that is antithetical to democratic norms and can lead to arbitrary and indefinite incarceration, thereby weakening the very foundations of justice and accountability. Military courts are not objective, certainly not at a time of war. A military judge told me that he authorises the vast majority of administrative detention applications.[100]

Administrative detention should not be used en masse. While security is important, it should not justify the use of inhumane measures such as administrative detention. Democracy should focus on protecting individual freedoms and rights while maintaining security.

As an act of goodwill and part of the trust-building process, Israel should release some agreed-upon prisoners. With time, as trust grows between the two sides, all security prisoners will return home.

Refugees and their right of return – the refugee question is a major concern for both Palestine and Israel. For Palestinians, this issue is about their history, justice and fairness. For Israelis, it is a debated issue. Many Israelis are unwilling to claim responsibility for the Palestinian tragedy and most object to the right of return, as it would mean the end of Zionism. However, Israeli leaders should acknowledge that the refugee issue is of great importance to the Palestinians. They cannot and should not dismiss it as a mere negotiation card. Yasser Arafat said that the Palestinians seek a fair and just solution to the refugee problem. He maintained that the Palestinians understand Israel's demographic concerns; however, Arafat wrote, 'just as we Palestinians must be realistic with respect to Israel's demographic desires, Israelis too must be realistic in understanding that there can be no solution to the Israeli-Palestinian conflict if the legitimate rights of these innocent civilians continue to be ignored'.[101]

On his deathbed, Arafat called Salam Fayyad. Fayyad could not understand most of what Arafat murmured incoherently, but one sentence

100 Discussion with a military judge (15 September 2024).

101 Yasir Arafat, 'The Palestinian Vision of Peace', *New York Times* (3 February 2002).

was clear: 'Take care of your brothers in Lebanon.'[102] This was the last conversation between the two, and Arafat's last words. It is the last memory Fayyad has of Arafat and, for him, it was a powerful statement.[103]

The issue is the most difficult to resolve, as the original refugee population of an estimated 700,000–750,000[104] has grown to 5.9 million Palestine refugees who are eligible for the United Nations Relief and Works Agency for Palestine Refugees in the Near East (UNRWA) services. Nearly one-third of registered Palestine refugees, more than 1.5 million individuals, live in fifty-eight recognised Palestine refugee camps in Jordan, Lebanon, Syria, the Gaza Strip and the West Bank, including East Jerusalem.[105] UNRWA's role in resolving the refugee problem is debatable. This UN organisation is not looked upon with favour by the Israeli establishment. UNRWA is separate from the main UN organ established to tackle the refugee problem worldwide, the Office of the United Nations High Commissioner for Refugees (UNHCR).

UNHCR is a global organisation dedicated to saving lives, protecting rights and building a better future for forcibly displaced communities. It was established in 1950, in the aftermath of the Second World War, to help the millions of European refugees. In 1951, the United Nations enacted the Convention and Protocol Relating to the Status of Refugees, also known as the Refugee Convention.[106] According to this Convention, the permanent solution for refugees is, first and foremost, to return to their country of nationality when it is safe to do so and they no longer fear persecution. If this is impossible, refugees should be able to integrate into the first state of refuge or relocate and resettle in another state. Article 1D of the Refugee Convention excludes protection or assistance of people who have already received assistance from a UN agency. It states: 'This

[102] Interview with Salam Fayyad (19 January 2024), 12.

[103] In his comments on a draft of this book, Fayyad wrote (30 June 2025): 'For context only, and not necessarily requiring any adjustment, I would note that one reason I felt those words were powerful was that they were the last he said to me, and, according to Suha Arafat (his wife) who was with him at the time of the call, they were his very last words because after the call with me the phone fell from his hand and he went into a coma.'

[104] According to one estimate, 280,000 refugees fled to the west of the Jordan River, later annexed to the Kingdom as the West Bank; 70,000 fled to the Hashemite Kingdom of Jordan, 200,000 fled to the Gaza Strip, 97,000 to Lebanon, 75,000 to Syria and 4,000 to Iraq. Jalal Al Husseini, 'Jordan and the Palestinians', in Myriam Ababsa (ed.), *Atlas of Jordan: History, Territories and Society* (Amman: Presses de l'Ifpo, 2014), 230–245.

[105] Palestine Refugees, UNRWA, www.unrwa.org/palestine-refugees.

[106] Convention and Protocol Relating to the Status of Refugees, www.unhcr.org/media/convention-and-protocol-relating-status-refugees.

Convention shall not apply to persons who are at present receiving from organs or agencies of the United Nations other than the United Nations High Commissioner for Refugees protection or assistance.'[107]

One such exception concerns the Palestinian refugees. The term 'Palestinian refugees' predates UNHCR and the Refugee Convention. After the UN passed, on 29 November 1947, the partition resolution (number 181) dividing Palestine into two states, one Jewish and the other Arab,[108] a civil war erupted in Palestine between the Arabs, who rejected the partition idea, and the Jews, who accepted it. When the State of Israel was declared in May 1948, following the departure of the British Mandate from Palestine, a whole-encompassing war erupted between the newly founded Israel and several Arab armies that invaded Israel. As a result of that fierce war, hundreds of thousands of Arabs lost their homes and became refugees. This is what the Palestinians term the 'Nakba', or catastrophe. UNRWA was established as a subsidiary organ of the United Nations General Assembly in December 1949 and became operational on 1 May 1950 to address their plight. Article 11 of the 1948 UN Resolution 194 holds that

> refugees wishing to return to their homes and live at peace with their neighbours should be permitted to do so at the earliest practicable date, and that compensation should be paid for the property of those choosing not to return and for loss of or damage to property which, under principles of international law or equity, should be made good by the Governments or authorities responsible.[109]

Furthermore, Resolution 302 of the UN General Assembly recognises that 'continued assistance for the relief of the Palestine refugees is necessary to prevent conditions of starvation and distress among them and to further conditions of peace and stability, and that constructive measures should be undertaken at an early date with a view to the termination of international assistance for relief'.[110] This means that UNRWA was supposed to exist for a few years, provide the refugees' basic needs and promote their integration in host countries. The expectation was that UNRWA would resolve the refugee problem. It was not supposed to last forever.

107 Ibid.

108 UN RES 181 The Partition Plan, https://tinyurl.com/45uthzyh.

109 UN Resolution 194, Article 11 (11 December 1948), https://tinyurl.com/mr7dmw5y.

110 General Assembly Resolution 302, A/RES/302 (IV), 8 December 1949, www.unrwa.org/content/general-assembly-resolution-302.

In the context of the former Mandate of Palestine, Palestinian refugees received humanitarian assistance from UNRWA and the legal protection of the then United Nations Conciliation Commission for Palestine (UNCCP). Arab states, except Jordan, used Article 1D of the Refugee Convention to exempt themselves from assuming responsibility for Palestinian refugees. All of them, with the exception of Jordan, did not want Palestinians who had sought refuge in their territory after 1948 to become permanently integrated into their communities. Palestinians were stranded in refugee camps in the West Bank, Gaza, Lebanon, Syria and Egypt. Palestinian refugees do not have a country of nationality. Their former homes in the State of Israel do not exist. The Mandate of Palestine no longer exists. All this has created a highly complex legal problem.[111]

In 2005, the newly appointed director-general of UNRWA, John Ging, was given the mandate to dissolve UNRWA and transfer its tasks to the PA. After the Hamas victory of 2006, the decision was reversed. Under Ging's leadership, major action was taken to fight internal corruption, teach human rights and allow Palestinian youth to seek an education so that they could become prosperous members of their society instead of turning into self-sacrificing terrorists, as the Hamas leadership wanted them to do. Three assassination attempts put an end to Ging's leadership in Gaza. The UN relocated him to New York, and his successors became completely dependent on Hamas.[112]

UNRWA continued to carry out health and education programmes, organised municipal services in recognised refugee camps and issued identity cards for stateless Palestinians.[113] Undoubtedly, this is very important work; however, since Hamas took over Gaza in 2007, Israel voiced grave reservations regarding its operations. UNRWA had become extremely politicised. In order to deliver humanitarian services, food, healthcare and education on the massive scale that UNRWA provides for Palestine refugees, it must employ a large number of Palestinians. In Gaza, many of them were Hamas members or had some affiliation with it. Francesco Motta said this was unavoidable.[114]

There was evidence that Nahed Attalah, UNRWA's director of food supplies for Gaza Strip refugees, used UN vehicles to transport arms,

[111] Interview with Francesco Motta (1 April 2022), 31.

[112] I thank Yair Hirschfeld for this information. Communication on 18 December 2024.

[113] Anne Irfan, 'Whose Agency? UNRWA and the Palestinian Refugees in History', in Pietro Stefanini (ed.), *UNRWA at 70: Palestinian Refugees in Context* (London: Palestinian Return Centre, 2020), 23.

[114] Interview with Francesco Motta (1 April 2022), 38.

explosives and other weaponry in support of Hamas's terror activities.[115] Senior Israeli security people told me that UNRWA serves Hamas's interests. I was surprised when Shabtai Shavit bluntly told me in July 2018 that UNRWA is Hamas.[116] After Hamas's tragic attack of 7 October 2023, Israel argued that UNRWA staff took an active part in the attack and used its facilities to carry out their terror operations. The UN responded by saying that nine UNRWA staff would be sacked due to their involvement in the 7 October 2023 terror attacks against Israel.[117] However, the Israeli authorities believed the problem was far more endemic and refused to cooperate further with the UN organisation. A UN Watch report holds that UNRWA has cultivated a troubling alliance with Hamas, Palestinian Islamic Jihad and other designated terrorist groups. This covert relationship has enabled these organisations to exert significant influence over the operations and policies of a UN agency that employs 30,000 staff and manages an annual budget of $1.5 billion, largely funded by Western nations.[118] In late 2024, an Israeli bill was passed banning the agency's activities in Israel.

For many years, Israel has wished to dismantle UNRWA, believing the organisation has become part of the Palestinian problem. Not only has it failed to resolve the refugee problem, but Israel claims that UNRWA sustains the problem. Now, there is an opportunity to bring its operation to an end. However, the Palestinian refugees need support, of course, if not by UNRWA, then by another country or organisation. The previously mentioned Article 1D of the Refugee Convention holds: 'When such protection or assistance has ceased for any reason, without the position of such persons being definitively settled in accordance with the relevant resolutions adopted by the General Assembly of the United Nations, these persons shall ipso facto be entitled to the benefits of this Convention.'[119] It is time to shift responsibility for Palestinian refugees to UNHCR. Much is dependent on the United States to make this happen. The institutions and programmes through which UNHCR

115 Matthew Levitt, *Hamas* (New Haven, CT: Yale University Press, 2006), 95.

116 Interview with Shabtai Shavit (2 July 2018), 21.

117 'UN Completes Investigation on UNRWA Staff', *UN News* (5 August 2024), https://news.un.org/en/story/2024/08/1152841.

118 UN Watch, *The Unholy Alliance: UNRWA, Hamas, and Islamic Jihad* (December 2024), https://tinyurl.com/2usp2fpr.

119 Article 1D of the 1951 Convention relating to the Status of Refugees, https://tinyurl.com/3fj96msf. See also Raphael Cohen-Almagor, 'Israel Moves to Redefine UNRWA: Controversial Bill Passes Preliminary Reading – Opinion', *Jerusalem Post* (27 June 2024).

would discharge its mandate must not become Hamas or Hamas-like. It would be futile to replace one faulty organisation with another.

The United Nations has addressed the Palestinian refugee issue many times. The UN General Assembly has adopted numerous resolutions acknowledging Palestinians' rights as a people under the UN Charter, including their 'right of return' to their homes pre-1947–1948. The UN has reiterated the refugees' right of return in many resolutions, including Resolution 2649 of 30 November 1970, recognising the Palestinian right to self-determination;[120] Resolution 2672C of 8 December 1970, which echoed that right;[121] Resolution 3089(D)(3) of 7 December 1973, declaring that 'the enjoyment by the Palestine Arab refugees of their right to return to their homes and property … is indispensable for the achievement of a just settlement of the refugee problem and for the exercise by the people of Palestine of its right to self-determination';[122] and Resolution 3236 of 22 November 1974, in which the General Assembly added the right to national independence and sovereignty to the right of self-determination.[123]

Israel and the PA have been arguing endlessly about this issue as a matter of principle. What must be done is twofold: first, Israel must recognise that it has a shared responsibility with the Palestinians to solve the problem. Israel must honestly confront history, refute myths and acknowledge the role it played in the creation of the refugee problem. Second, there is a need to identify the population, establish the numbers and, after mapping the refugee population, conduct a survey among them that would include the following options:

- return to Israel
- return to the West Bank
- return to the Gaza Strip
- emigrate to third countries that would commit to absorbing a certain quota (an appeal will be made to countries that receive immigration on a regular basis to participate in this settlement effort)
- remain where they are.

In 2003, Khalil Shikaki conducted three major surveys among Palestinians in refugee camps in the West Bank, Syria, Lebanon and

120 UN Resolution 2649 (30 November 1970), www.worldlii.org/int/other/UNGA/1970/28.pdf.
121 UN Resolution 2672C (8 December 1970), https://tinyurl.com/yu9r5dba.
122 UN Resolution 3089 (7 December 1973), https://tinyurl.com/ucptmn98.
123 UN Resolution 3236 (22 November 1974), www.un.org/unispal/wp-content/uploads/2016/05/ARES3236XXIX.pdf.

Jordan. He surveyed a sample of 4,506 refugees, asking them, at the start of the poll, whether they were ready to give up the right of return. The overwhelming majority of the refugees, more than 95 per cent, insisted on maintaining the 'right of return' as a sacred right that can never be given up. However, in the same poll, only 10 per cent said they wished to return to Israel and become (or not become) an Israeli citizen. Thirty-one per cent preferred to stay in the Palestinian state that will be established in the West Bank and Gaza Strip and receive fair compensation for property taken over by Israel and for other losses and suffering. Twenty-three per cent preferred to receive Palestinian citizenship and return to designated areas inside Israel to be swapped later on with Palestinian areas as part of a territorial exchange and receive any deserved compensation. Seventeen per cent preferred to receive fair compensation for property, losses and suffering and to stay in a host country, receiving its citizenship or Palestinian citizenship. Thirteen per cent refused all options, and 5 per cent had no opinion.[124] In other words, the vast majority of the sample wished to feel they were part of the land. Realistically, they understood that they could not go back to the places they had left.[125]

Olmert discussed the refugee issue with Abbas. He quoted Abbas as saying: 'I need a gesture from you in regard to the refugees. None of them will want to come [return] anyway.'[126] Olmert and Abbas agreed that an international fund should compensate the refugees.

A new poll among refugees should be conducted to understand their wishes. Refugees will be able to settle in Palestine and other countries. Unification of families should be allowed in Israel under an annual limited quota. The Palestinians themselves understand that a massive refugee return to Israel cannot be allowed; this dream should be abandoned. When Abbas was asked whether he wished to return to Safed, where he was born, he replied: 'It's my right to see it, but not to live there.'[127] I suspect that Abbas's view reflects that of many Palestinians who seek recognition, apology and compensation, not the right of return. Israel should recognise the Nakba, acknowledge Palestinian suffering and arrange to compensate the 1947–1948 refugees and their descendants. Research

124 Results of PSR refugees' polls in the West Bank/Gaza Strip, Jordan and Lebanon (January–June 2003), https://pcpsr.org/en/node/493.

125 Leadership Seminar with Marwan Muasher (8 May 2024), 10.

126 Drucker, 'Olmert, Abu Mazen and Barak Refer to the Political Process'.

127 Birnbaum, 'The End of the Two-State Solution'.

shows that symbolic gestures that express respect for a rival party and its core values may open the door to dialogue.[128]

An international tribunal of reputable historians and international lawyers, including equal representatives of Israel and Palestine, will determine the level of compensation. If needed, Israel and Palestine may establish an international relief fund to which humanitarian countries wishing to see the end of the conflict contribute. I believe that between Israel, Europe, the Muslim world, North America and other countries of goodwill, the required funding can be secured. The United Nations and the World Bank may also be approached. A Palestinian non-paper from May 2000 suggested that Israel, the PLO, the United Nations and the host countries establish an International Commission to administer the relocation process and compensation. An international fund will be established under the supervision of the committee and the World Bank. The fund will verify and evaluate the claims.[129]

Jonathan Schwartz remarked that when Israeli negotiators insisted that 'Jewish refugees' be covered in an agreement with the Palestinians as well, the Palestinian response was 'why us', since Israel did not demand that of Egypt and Jordan. John Kerry was prepared to organise an international effort to find compensation, independent of an Israeli-Palestinian agreement. For Palestinian refugees, the US was ready to organise an international effort to find homes and compensation, which would only require Israel's support consistent with its demand that it control any returns to Israel and the financial contributions it had agreed upon.[130]

Languages – starting in primary school, Arabic would be a mandatory language for pupils to study in Jewish schools. Similarly, Hebrew would be a mandatory language for pupils to study in Palestinian schools. Language is the most important bridge between different cultures and nations. Israelis would master Arabic to the same extent that they presently master English; Palestinians would master Hebrew as their second language.[131]

128 Scott Atran and Robert Axelrod, 'Reframing Sacred Values', *Negotiation Journal* (July 2008), 242.

129 'Framework Agreement on Permanent Status', Non-paper draft for brainstorming and discussion purposes only (21 May 2000).

130 Jonathan Schwartz's written comments (20 November 2024). See also Vincent Fean interview (24 March 2016), 2–6.

131 Bhikhu Parekh commented that there is no reason why all Palestinian children should learn Hebrew. Israeli Palestinians should, but he does not see why this should be a requirement for all Palestinian Arabs. I think that requiring the children of both societies to learn

Education – Israel and Palestine would institute a shared curriculum on good neighbourly relations, understanding cultures and religions, respect for others and not harming others. This education programme would commence from the kindergarten level and continue in primary and high schools. For every age group, vital concepts for understanding the other would be studied. Israeli-Palestinian projects would be instituted in which children work together to achieve certain shared tasks. The next generation must build trust, replacing prejudice with knowledge and awareness regarding similarities and differences between the two peoples. A culture of tolerance, care and compassion will replace hatred and incitement.[132] This programme is critical for establishing peaceful relationships, respect and trust between the two parties.

Incitement – both sides must purge the atmosphere of bigotry, racism, incitement and hate on both sides of the fence/wall, including a close study of the education curricula in the PA and Israel. The contents of schoolbooks must be reviewed.[133] The media should be utilised to promote messages of peace, tolerance and liberty.

Water – the UN secretary-general has said that Palestinians 'have virtually no control' over water resources in the West Bank, with 86 per cent of the Jordan Valley and the Dead Sea under the de facto jurisdiction of settlement regional councils.[134] Israel and Palestine should seek a fair solution that would not infringe on the rights of either side and would assure that the Palestinian people will have the required water supply for sustenance and growth.[135]

Economic agreements – Israel and Palestine should actively explore and pursue avenues for economic cooperation, with the objective of fostering mutual benefit, optimising shared resources and coordinating efforts across sectors. Such collaboration not only offers pragmatic

both Arabic and Hebrew is vital for facilitating connections between the two communities, for promoting understanding of one another's cultures and for decreasing animosity and fear.

132 For further discussion, see Jay Rothman, *From Confrontation to Cooperation* (London: Sage Publications, 1992).

133 See Bar-Tal, 'Challenges for Constructing Peace Culture and Peace Education'; Aweiss, 'Culture of Peace and Education'.

134 Briefing: Beyond the E-1 Israeli settlement, *IRIN* (18 March 2013), www.un.org/unispal/document/auto-insert-206673/.

135 For further discussion, see Shuval, 'Is the Conflict over Shared Water Resources between Israelis and Palestinians an Obstacle to Peace?'; and Aliewi et al., 'Palestine Water'.

advantages but also serves as a foundation for building trust and interdependence. Israel, with its advanced economy and global ties, can play a critical role in the development of a sustainable and independent Palestinian economy. In parallel, Palestine can facilitate Israel's integration into the broader Middle East region, advancing economic, industrial, cultural and tourism-based relations between Israel and the Arab and Muslim worlds.

This reciprocal vision recognises that the 'economy of peace' may demand levels of investment comparable to those of the 'economy of war'. However, unlike the destructive and regressive outcomes of conflict, peace-oriented economic cooperation is inherently constructive, generating prosperity, stability and long-term regional resilience.

The Abraham Accords, signed in 2020 between Israel and the United Arab Emirates, Bahrain, Morocco and Sudan, marked a significant shift in regional dynamics. While the Accords yielded important economic and diplomatic dividends, they should not be viewed as a substitute for resolving the Israeli-Palestinian conflict. Notably, Israel's decision to suspend its annexation plans in the West Bank underscores the potential of diplomatic engagement to moderate hardline policies; however, the Accords did not address core issues of justice, sovereignty and self-determination for the Palestinian people. Rather than enabling the indefinite continuation of the occupation, the Abraham Accords should serve as a platform for demonstrating that Arabs and Israelis can, through dialogue, reconcile their differences and reach equitable agreements. For this potential to be realised, Palestinians must be brought into the process in a meaningful way. The inclusion of Palestine in the spirit and substance of regional normalisation is essential to ensure that these agreements promote not only economic gain, but also political justice and human dignity.

As additional states join the framework of cooperation inaugurated by the Abraham Accords, positive momentum towards regional peace can emerge. This growing web of relations can exert normative and diplomatic pressure on all parties to uphold peace-oriented commitments and refrain from actions that undermine reconciliation. Ultimately, sustained economic and diplomatic engagement, grounded in mutual recognition and respect, offers a viable path towards a just and lasting resolution of the Israeli-Palestinian conflict.

Fishing – this issue pertains to Gaza. Israel and Palestine would enjoy fishing rights in their respective territorial waters.

International commerce – Israel and Palestine would be free to conduct international commerce as they see fit. To develop trust between the two parties, some level of transparency about logs of commerce would be agreed and memorandums of understanding signed by the parties.

Tourism – Israel and Palestine would coordinate efforts to promote tourism to the region, collaborating with neighbouring countries to facilitate cultural and religious experiences unique to the region.

Communication and media – mutual channels of communication would be opened on television, radio and the internet. The channels would broadcast in two or three languages: Arabic, Hebrew and, possibly, English. Communication and language are important for the development of good neighbourly relations.

End of conflict – a critical distinction must be drawn between the *end of conflict* and the *end of claims*. While a formal declaration marking the end of the conflict is both necessary and symbolically significant, it is neither reasonable nor justifiable to expect a comprehensive declaration signalling the end of all claims. The term 'claims' encompasses not only core, high-profile issues, such as borders, refugees and Jerusalem, but also a wide range of subsidiary matters, including individualised grievances and demands for compensation or restitution.

Requiring the Palestinians to forgo all present and future claims as a condition of agreement would impose an undue burden on them and disregard the ongoing nature of implementation-related concerns. For example, issues such as compensation for Palestinian refugees involve complex legal, moral and logistical questions that may require adjudication over time. Declaring an end to all claims would prematurely close the door on these legitimate concerns and may appear as a denial of justice. Furthermore, from a political and symbolic perspective, it is unrealistic to expect Palestinians to renounce claims tied to matters of national identity and religious heritage, such as those related to the holy sites in Jerusalem, including the Temple Mount/Haram al-Sharif. The final status of such deeply contested sites cannot be resolved through sweeping legal renunciations, especially not through unilateral legislative acts denying the historical and spiritual connections of either side.

A more viable and constructive approach would involve acknowledging that certain claims persist while mutually agreeing not to act upon them in a manner that disrupts peace or undermines the agreed-upon political framework. Such an arrangement allows for the continuation of negotiations or legal processes over specific issues, without holding the broader peace process hostage to unresolved, and potentially unresolvable, grievances. Ultimately, a sustainable resolution must differentiate between the political necessity of ending the conflict and the practical complexity of addressing all claims. A durable peace will rest not on the erasure of claims, but on the commitment of both parties to resolve them through peaceful and legal means, and in a manner consistent with justice and mutual respect.

Repeated attempts to reach a final status agreement have highlighted challenges on the Palestinian side in consolidating internal consensus. Therefore, Israel must exercise both decisiveness and flexibility, demonstrating a genuine commitment to achieving a permanent status arrangement while remaining sensitive to Palestinian political and societal constraints. A pragmatic and principled approach requires the parties to adopt a *framework agreement* articulating a mutually recognised endgame and a shared vision for peace.

This framework should include a clearly defined roadmap with sequenced steps, interim arrangements and binding deadlines. It must also incorporate mechanisms to mitigate the influence of spoilers, uphold security and provide for international arbitration in cases of disagreement. A phased approach would build confidence and establish cooperative habits. Negotiations should begin with comparatively less contentious issues, such as energy, water, education and agriculture, before progressing to more sensitive topics, including the release of prisoners, the delineation of borders, the status of Israeli settlements, the refugee question and the future of Jerusalem.

In parallel to these discussions, both sides should agree on a structured process for enhancing Palestinian governance in the West Bank, facilitating the orderly withdrawal of Israeli forces and transferring designated areas to Palestinian control. Israel should actively support the creation of territorially and economically viable Palestinian contiguity as a foundational element of statehood. These concrete confidence-building measures will foster trust, enhance legitimacy and generate momentum towards the realisation of a comprehensive peace. The culmination of this structured and incremental process should be the signing of a comprehensive final status agreement addressing all core issues and reflecting the aspirations of both peoples. Such an agreement should be accompanied by a formal declaration marking the end of the Israeli-Palestinian conflict, paving the way for a new era of coexistence, mutual recognition and regional integration.

Four-party permanent team – Egypt, Israel, Jordan and Palestine will maintain a permanent forum that will meet periodically to discuss concerns and resolve problems amicably. It will discuss issues such as the Gaza ports, the West Bank airport, economic development, water, tourism, security controls along the Jordan River, security concerns in Sinai, counter-terrorism and counter-radicalism.

International monitoring and arbitration – experience underscores the necessity of establishing an international monitoring body tasked with ascertaining that Israel refrains from constructing new settlements or expanding existing ones. This entity would also serve as a coordination mechanism for security affairs between Israel and Palestine, ensuring that the PA maintains exclusive control over weapons, and that both Palestinians and Israelis uphold public order and peace. All acts of violence and terrorism would be rigorously suppressed, with extremist actors on both sides prevented from destabilising societal tranquillity.

Complex and intractable issues that elude resolution through direct bilateral negotiations would be referred to a dedicated arbitration committee. The committee would comprise an equal number of Israeli and Palestinian representatives, supplemented by a majority of internationally recognised experts. Membership would be limited to individuals jointly approved by both parties, to guarantee impartiality and legitimacy. The committee would include specialists in law, economics, human rights and Middle Eastern affairs, ensuring comprehensive expertise. Its decisions would be final and binding, with no option for appeal. Both parties would formally commit to abiding by every ruling issued. A precedent for such a mechanism can be found in the arbitration committee established to resolve the Taba dispute between Israel and Egypt.

Four years after the establishment of a Palestinian state in the West Bank, formal negotiations would commence between Palestine and Jordan, aimed at forming a confederation within a twelve-month period. Throughout the process, Palestine and Jordan would maintain transparent communication and consult closely with key stakeholders, including Israel, the United States and Arab states, to ensure regional stability and garner broad support for the confederation initiative.

Stage Two: Palestinian-Jordanian Confederation

In 1920, at the San Remo Conference, it was decided that Great Britain would rule Palestine and Jordan, while France received a mandate over Syria.[136] In July 1922, the League of Nations empowered Britain to administer Transjordan. On 25 May 1923, the British recognised Transjordan's independence under the rule of Emir Abdullah with the proviso that matters of finance, military and foreign affairs would remain in the hands of the British. Jordanian full independence was achieved after the Second World War by a treaty on 22 March 1946 and Abdullah proclaimed himself king. In 1949, the name of the state was changed to the Hashemite Kingdom of Jordan.[137]

In 1947, Emil Sandström, the Swedish chairman of the United Nations Special Committee on Palestine, who was assigned to explore the feasibility of the partition of Palestine, saw no realistic possibility of accommodating two viable states west of the Jordan River. Sandström thought, against the view of the majority in the committee, that the partition of Palestine should have been between a Jewish and a Jordanian-Palestinian state.[138]

In 1948, Jordan declared war on Israel after its proclamation. During that war, Jordan occupied the West Bank and East Jerusalem. Some 70,000 Palestinians were integrated into the Kingdom's population. In December 1948, the Jericho Conference named King Abdullah 'King of Arab Palestine' and called for the union of the West Bank and Transjordan. Jordan was interested in integrating the 'Arabs of Palestine' from Transjordan and the West Bank into one kingdom. An amendment to the Passport Act stipulated that 'every Palestinian Arab with Palestinian nationality may obtain a passport'.[139] With the annexation of the West Bank, Jordan's population tripled. The population of Jordan was around 470,000 people, while the West Bank population was around 740,000 people.

In 1949–1950, the Hashemite Kingdom was home to over 1.2 million inhabitants; two-thirds of the population were of Palestinian origin.[140] Jordan had effective control over the West Bank from the time of the

[136] Efraim Karsh, *The San Remo Conference 100 Years On: How the Jewish National Home Entered International Law*, Mideast Security and Policy Studies No. 172 (Ramat Gan: The Begin–Sadat Center for Strategic Studies, 2020).

[137] Hassan bin Talal, *Palestinian Self-Determination* (New York: Quartet Books, 1981), 41; 'History of Jordan', *Britannica*, www.britannica.com/place/Jordan/Husseins-last-years-and-the-ascent-of-Abdullah-II.

[138] Shlomo Ben-Ami, *Prophets without Honor: The 2000 Camp David Summit and the End of the Two-State Solution* (Oxford: Oxford University Press, 2022), 285.

[139] Al Husseini, 'Jordan and the Palestinians'.

[140] Ibid.

General Armistice of 3 April 1949 until June 1967. During the same period, Egypt occupied the Gaza Strip. In 1950, the Jordanian parliament approved the unification of Jordan and the West Bank. Jordan officially annexed the West Bank and granted Jordanian citizenship to Palestinians who wished to claim it. Egypt made no attempt to annex the Gaza Strip. The same year, 1950, elections were held on the two banks of the Jordan River. The National Assembly, representing the two countries, held an equal session on 24 April 1950 and unanimously approved the unity decision between the two shores on the basis of parliamentary rule.[141] The dinar was proclaimed as the sole currency in both banks.

After Jordan attacked Israel yet again in June 1967, Jordan lost those territories in the Six-Day War, and many Palestinians moved from the West Bank to Jordan. Despite the military defeat, Jordan continued to maintain extensive political and economic ties with the West Bank. West Bankers were still considered full citizens of Jordan. They retained the right to vote in the general and municipal elections of 1972 and 1978. Half the seats in the Jordanian parliament were still held by West Bank representatives.

The idea of a Jordanian-Palestinian confederation was raised again in 1972 and has continued to be mentioned since then, despite King Hussein's decision to sever links between Jordan and the West Bank. In July 1988, under pressure from the Arab League, in a public address to the nation, Hussein renounced all Jordanian claims over the West Bank. He explained that he respected the wish of the PLO, as the sole and legitimate representative of the Palestinian people, 'to secede from us as an independent Palestinian state'.[142] The Intifada in 1987 and the inability to reach an agreement with the Palestinians pushed Hussein to that decision.[143] It was primarily motivated by his interest in securing the Hashemite Kingdom. The decision was never ratified in parliament and is still regarded by many as unconstitutional.[144] The 1950 decision to unify the East and the West Banks was never annulled.

The decision to break all ties with the West Bank is very important. For a decision of this magnitude – and this is a crucial decision – Jordan usually ratifies these decisions in parliament. I asked Marwan Muasher

[141] Hazaimeh, 'Why Jordan Rejects a Confederation with Palestine'.
[142] King Hussein's Address to the Nation, Amman (31 July 1988), www.kinghussein.gov.jo/88_july31.html.
[143] Shlaim, *Lion of Jordan*, 401.
[144] Shlomo Ben-Ami, 'The Return of the Jordanian Option', *Project Syndicate* (6 June 2016), https://tinyurl.com/5n8x2enu.

why the decision was not ratified, and his answer was 'because there was a feeling that the Palestinians need to take their fate into their own hands. There was a general agreement on this, and people went with it.'[145] I asked Muasher whether the non-ratification decision might mean that a window is open for change in the future, and that Jordan might reconsider its position. Muasher conclusively answered in the negative, arguing that 'if anybody suggests today that West Bankers should regain Jordanian citizenship, there would be an uproar in the whole country from East Jordanians and Jordanians of Palestinian origin alike. Because that will be seen today as an effort by Israel to solve the problem at Jordan's expense.'[146]

Prior to 1988, King Hussein hoped that he would bring about a solution on his watch and under his leadership, a solution that would end the occupation of the West Bank and restore East Jerusalem to Arab sovereignty. The First Intifada convinced him that there was a whole new generation in the West Bank that did not know Jordan, and that had not even been born when the West Bank was part of Jordan. Hussein became convinced that he had to let the Palestinians find a solution on their own. There has never been a real movement in Jordan to look at the constitutionality of this move, precisely because the majority of the population agreed with the king's reasoning. Even those who did not think the disengagement was constitutional were not ready to challenge the decision, because, at the political level, a clear majority has supported it.[147]

In 1988, the Jordanian parliament was dissolved and no longer included West Bank representatives. Jordanian involvement in West Bank affairs ceased completely. At the same time, in his address, the king emphasised that he believed in 'one Arab destiny, and committed to joint Arab action'.[148] The citizenship rights of Jordanians of Palestinian origin remained intact. Jordan retained its status as Guardian of Holy Sites in the West Bank, and it has granted special status of free passage to the West Bank for Jordanians of Palestinian origin. As part of the Israeli-Jordanian peace treaty, Israel respects those passes.

But Hussein was still interested in the West Bank. Between the 1980s and early 1990s, King Hussein and Yasser Arafat held strategic discussions on the idea of a confederation between Jordan and a future Palestinian state.

145 Ambassador Forum with Marwan Muasher (8 May 2024), 1.
146 Leadership Seminar with Marwan Muasher (8 May 2024), 2.
147 Leadership Seminar with Marwan Muasher (8 May 2024), 1.
148 King Hussein's Address to the Nation, Amman (31 July 1988).

While Arafat acknowledged the concept in principle, he insisted it could only be pursued after the creation of an independent Palestinian state. In 1989, at its 20th session, the Palestine National Council formally backed the concept of a confederation with Jordan. The confederal model envisioned shared governance structures, especially in practical domains such as water resource management, economic coordination and infrastructure development. These discussions were shaped by diplomatic shifts in the region, US policy interventions and internal Arab world dynamics.[149]

In 2025, Jordan's population was 11.5 million.[150] The Jordanian and the West Bank populations are interlinked. A substantial portion of the Jordanian population is Palestinian. Jordan is the only Arab country that has granted citizenship to Palestinians. The flags of Jordan and Palestine are almost identical (see Figures 12.3 and 12.4). A Jordanian-Palestinian confederation would enable Jordanian-Palestinians to continue living in Jordan while retaining their Palestinian identity if they so choose. Repeated West Bank opinion polls have shown that Palestinians support the confederation idea.[151]

Figure 12.3 Palestine flag.
Source: Orionist, previous versions by Makaristos, Mysid, etc., Public domain, via Wikimedia Commons.

[149] Trudy Rubin, 'Mideast Jigsaw: Arafat and Hussein Try to Puzzle Out Joint Response to Reagan', *Christian Science Monitor* (13 October 1982); Nasseer Aruri, 'The PLO and the Jordan Option', *Middle East Report*, 131 (March/April 1985), https://merip.org/1985/03/the-plo-and-the-jordan-option/; Caryle Murphy, 'Hussein and Arafat Discuss Confederation', *Washington Post* (16 March 1992). See also Rashid Khalidi, *Palestinian Identity: The Construction of Modern National Consciousness* (New York: Columbia University Press, 2009).

[150] Worldometer, Jordan Population, www.worldometers.info/world-population/jordan-population/.

[151] Khaled Abu Toameh, 'Palestinians and Jordan: Will a Confederation Work?', *Gatestone Institute* (25 May 2016), www.gatestoneinstitute.org/8112/palestinians-jordan-confederation; Adnan Abu Amer, 'A Palestine–Jordan Confederation Is Becoming a Very Real Possibility', *Middle East Monitor* (18 February 2019), https://tinyurl.com/yc3j5pk9.

Figure 12.4 Jordan flag.
Source: Construction Sheet, Public domain, via Wikimedia Commons.

Polls conducted by the Palestinian Center for Policy and Survey Research from 13–15 June 2013 showed that 55 per cent of West Bank Palestinians supported the idea, a 10 per cent increase since 2008. On 13 May 2016, a research institute affiliated with An-Najah National University in Nablus published the results of a survey indicating that 42 per cent of Palestinians supported the establishment of a Jordanian-Palestinian confederation and 39 per cent opposed it. Palestinians who welcome the idea of a confederation with Jordan are those who see the end of occupation as a more compelling necessity than separate statehood. President Abbas himself expressed interest in the idea in a meeting with a group of Israelis on 2 September 2018.[152]

The Hashemite Kingdom is an island of stability in a torn and highly complicated region. The idea of a confederation does not aim to threaten the Kingdom or weaken it. The confederation depends on the goodwill of all parties involved. It is not based on coercion. It is not meant to cause an influx of Palestinians from the West Bank to Jordan, destabilising its delicate population balance. It is not intended that Jordan become the representative of the Palestinians against their will. Political and constitutional issues should be resolved by discussions and negotiations.

Jordan has a GDP per capita of around $4,255, reflecting its diversified economy and substantial foreign aid. In contrast, Palestine's GDP per capita hovers around $2,747.[153] In Jordan, the overall unemployment rate is around 15 per cent; in Palestine, the unemployment rate is significantly higher, ranging between 25 and 30 per cent. In Jordan, approximately 15.7 per cent of the population lives below the poverty

[152] Ben-Ami, *Prophets without Honor*, 288.

[153] Jordan vs Palestine – Country Comparison, *World Comparison*, www.worldcomparison.com/jordan-vs-palestine-country-comparison/. Fayyad, however, commented that Jordan is a heavily indebted country with a debt-to-GDP ratio of nearly 100 per cent.

line, reflecting ongoing efforts by the government to address the issue. In Palestine, the situation is more challenging, with around 29.2 per cent of the population living below the poverty line.[154]

At the 1991 Madrid Peace Conference, the head of the Palestinian delegation, Haidar Abd al-Shafi, spoke about a Jordanian-Palestinian confederation in his opening speech. He said:

> We address our Jordanian colleagues in our joint delegation: Our two peoples have a very special historic and geographic relationship. Together, we shall strive to achieve peace. We will continue to strive for our sovereignty while proceeding freely and willingly to prepare the grounds for a confederation between the two states of Palestine and Jordan, which can be a cornerstone for our security and prosperity.[155]

Elyakim Rubinstein confirmed that the Palestinians responded to the confederation proposal by saying that first, they should have a state, and then we shall see.[156] Indeed, Arafat did not rule out the idea of a Jordanian-Palestinian confederation but insisted that it could be actualised only after the establishment of a Palestinian state.[157] In his meeting with King Abdullah II, Abbas said: 'We and Jordan are one … Our interests, concerns, pain and hope are the same.'[158] Abdullah said that the Jordanians are there to 'listen to you and hear from you what is demanded of the Jordanians'. He described Jordan as 'the closest' to the Palestinian cause (see Figure 12.5).[159] Jordanian officials stated time and again that confederation could be an option, provided that the Palestinians agreed to it and that it would be established after Palestine was established.[160]

During the Oslo process, Peres insisted that the term 'Palestinian State' would not be part of the Declaration of Principles. Peres thought the term would be too hard to digest for the Israeli public, and he supported the idea of a Jordanian-Palestinian confederation.[161] He preferred

154 Ibid.

155 Speech of Haydar Abd al-Shafi, Head of the Palestinian Delegation, Madrid Conference, Madrid (31 October 1991), https://tinyurl.com/5bfksjr8.

156 Elyakim Rubinstein's personal communication (9 April 2021).

157 Oded Eran, 'The Idea of a Jordanian-Palestinian Confederation, Revisited', *INSS Insight*, No. 1092 (6 September 2018).

158 Aaron Boxerman, '"We Are One," Abbas Tells Jordanian King during Rare West Bank Visit', *Times of Israel* (28 March 2022), https://tinyurl.com/mrm98ezt.

159 Ibid.

160 Shlomo Brom, 'INSS Insight: Jordanian-Palestinian Confederation: An Idea Whose Time Has Not Come', *Scoop* (17 July 2007), https://tinyurl.com/4mpepcpz.

161 Hirschfeld meeting with Peres, 25 April 1993, Israel Archives (Hebrew), https://tinyurl.com/3hhe6csp.

Figure 12.5 King Abdullah II and Mahmoud Abbas.
Credit: Pool/Pool/Getty Images News.

that Jordan lead the security and foreign affairs of that confederation. As he trusted the Jordanians much more than he trusted the Palestinians, a full-fledged sovereign Palestinian state was not his vision. At certain points, Arafat supported the confederation idea.[162] Ahmed Qurie told Gil: 'I know that your prime demand of us is security. And we failed to provide you with security. So, maybe this is the solution. A confederation, where Jordan will be responsible for security.'[163]

I discussed the possibility of a Palestinian-Jordanian confederation with several Jordanian officials. Before 7 October 2023, they all said the same thing: Palestinian state first, and then we shall see. They did not rule out the possibility. On 24 March 2021, I hosted the Jordanian Ambassador to London, HE Omar al-Nahar, and asked him about the option of confederation between Jordan and the Palestinian West Bank. Al-Nahar did not rule out the option. He said that first there should

[162] Interview with Avi Gil (16 January 2025), 16. Arafat made King Hussein very angry when he told the King: 'And you will be the first, because you are the king, to be the number one. And then I will be the number one.' Ibid. Hussein was not too happy to hear Arafat's rotation idea.

[163] Interview with Avi Gil (16 January 2025), 17.

be a Palestinian state and, once the State of Palestine is established, it would be possible to consider confederation. Al-Nahar echoed what King Abdullah said: 'Only after there is a Palestinian state on Palestinian soil can Jordanians and Palestinians decide on the nature of relations between them.'[164] Olmert told me that he spoke with the Jordanians many times when he was prime minister. From their point of view, they will never interfere with anything that could jeopardise the right of the Palestinians for their own sovereign independent state. After an independent Palestinian state comes into being, *if* the Palestinians are prepared to consider the option of a confederation with Jordan, then Jordan would be prepared to examine it. They would not reject it outright.[165]

In 2022, Muasher said that if there were a Palestinian state, then it would be much easier to consider a confederation. The prelude to discussing the issue from the Jordanian point of view is the establishment of a Palestinian state.[166] In 2024, after the 7 October Hamas terror attack and the ensuing war between Hamas and Israel, Muasher thought that the majority of Jordanians would not accept the confederation idea.[167] He said he supported a one-state solution,[168] which would mean the end of the Zionist enterprise.

During the 1990s, fear of Palestinian instability drove a former royal adviser, Adnan Abu-Odeh, and two former Jordanian prime ministers, Abdel Salam Majali and Taher al-Masri, to advocate a Jordanian-Palestinian confederation. They were on public record for their blunt support of the confederation. Majali even visited Israel to lobby for the idea.[169] Majali's plan was an update of King Hussein's federation plan of March 1972 and the 1985 agreement between Arafat's PLO and Jordan to seek Palestinian self-determination within a Jordanian-Palestinian confederation. Majali also introduced elements of the Lebanese consociation constitution into his plan. Both the legislative and the executive authorities would be based on equal representation for the two states, with a Palestinian and a Jordanian rotating in the positions of

164 Brom, 'INSS Insight: Jordanian-Palestinian Confederation'.
165 Interview with Ehud Olmert (6 January 2025), 10.
166 Raphael Cohen-Almagor, 'The Role of the Arab World in the Palestinian-Israeli Conflict: Interview with Marwan Muasher', *Israel Affairs*, 29(5) (2023): 880.
167 Ambassador Forum with Marwan Muasher, Middle East Study Centre (MESC), University of Hull (8 May 2024), 2.
168 Ibid.
169 Ben-Ami, *Prophets without Honor*, 293; Ian Bremmer, 'A Difficult Plan Whose Time Has Come', *New York Times* (6 June 2007).

speaker and prime minister. The king would be head of state, not in his capacity as Jordan's king, but as a descendant of the Hashemite dynasty and, as such, also of the Prophet. The Palestinians living in Jordan would have to choose between Palestinian and Jordanian nationality. A serious sticking point is what would become of Gaza. Would it be part of the confederation, once it finally merges with the West Bank under a united leadership? Would it remain as an Islamic independent quasi-state? Or would it be absorbed as an Egyptian protectorate? In the grand peace designs of King Abdullah I, Gaza was to be part of the Hashemite Kingdom.[170]

Majali's elaborate 2007 plan, which I assume was shared with King Abdullah and received his consent to be aired, was spurred by the prospect of chaos should an Israeli government decide to secure Israel's survival as a Jewish state through unilateral withdrawal from much of the West Bank. Such chaos, Jordan's government feared, could spread to the East Bank, potentially dealing a fatal blow to the Kingdom.[171] Majali reiterated: 'Jordan cannot live without Palestine and Palestine cannot live without Jordan.'[172]

The important thing is to pursue this option via communication and the ability to secure compromises. During the 1980s, the Reagan administration tried to facilitate Jordanian-Israeli negotiations over the heads of the Palestinians, aiming to return most of the West Bank to Jordan. Then Secretary of State George Shultz thought Jordan would join the negotiations without the Palestinians. He thought that in the aftermath of the war in Lebanon, the PLO was a weakened player and, therefore, he wished to fill the Palestinian lacuna with Jordan as the interlocutor. But Jordan would not simply be shoehorned into the place of the PLO without the latter's involvement. It was only when the Intifada began and King Hussein withdrew all claims to the West Bank that the Americans finally understood that their partner on the Palestinian issue was the PLO.[173] Mapping and understanding the situation are crucial.

A confederation is a political arrangement in which sovereign states retain their independence while voluntarily uniting under a shared constitutional framework to coordinate policies and institutions. In the case

170 Ben-Ami, *Prophets without Honor*, 294.

171 Ben-Ami, 'The Return of the Jordanian Option'.

172 Khaled Abu Toameh, 'Palestinians and Jordan: Will a Confederation Work?', Gatestone Institute (25 May 2016), www.gatestoneinstitute.org/8112/palestinians-jordan-confederation.

173 Interview with William Quandt (11 September 2019), 27.

of Palestine and Jordan, the foundations for such a union are already present. The two populations are linked by deep commonalities – religion, language, culture and values – and maintain long-standing familial, economic and social ties across the Jordan River. Their historical interconnectedness, coupled with geographic proximity and shared interests, makes the prospect of a confederation both practical and potentially transformative.

Palestinians and Jordanians not only share a common identity and social fabric but also face parallel challenges and needs in areas such as infrastructure, education, commerce and public services. A confederation could enhance cooperation across sectors including security, tourism, agriculture, scientific research and transportation, fostering regional stability and development. Given Jordan's demographic composition, with its significant Palestinian population, and its historical and political ties to the West Bank, the Kingdom has a strategic interest in the region's stability. For decades, Jordan has played a key role in West Bank affairs, and it remains highly attuned to the political and social dynamics within Palestinian society. Both Jordan and Israel recognise that the West Bank represents a potential force for either regional progress or destabilisation. Accordingly, Jordan is well positioned to contribute to the future Palestinian state's economic sustainability and security infrastructure. Israel, for its part, acknowledges the importance of closely coordinating with both Jordan and Palestine in any future confederal arrangement. Israeli leaders are acutely aware that destabilising Jordan would not serve their strategic interests. A carefully constructed confederation, supported by regional and international actors, could serve as a viable framework for enhancing cooperation, ensuring mutual security and advancing a durable resolution to the Israeli-Palestinian conflict.

Udi Dekel thought that a Palestinian-Jordanian confederation was a viable option.[174] According to Maj. Gen. (res.) Giora Eiland, a conventional two-state solution is untenable. Israel cannot give up all of the West Bank, support an unviable Arab state and also bear the consequences of the ensuing instability. He suggested the revival of a Jordanian-Palestinian federation or confederation.[175] Benny Morris also suggested renewed Jordanian involvement, in the form of a Jordanian-Palestinian

[174] Interview with Udi Dekel (17 June 2014), 8.

[175] Giora Eiland, *Rethinking the Two–State Solution*, Policy Focus 88, Washington Institute for Near East Policy, Washington, DC (2008).

federation or confederation, to contend with the problems engendered by the potentially limited viability of a small Palestinian state.[176] John Jenkins said:

> I think that the issue of some sort of confederation, which preserves Jordan as a Hashemite state, I think that has to happen. Because otherwise there will be chaos. A collapse of the Hashemites in Jordan would be bad for everybody. It would be bad for Israel. It would be bad for the Palestinians. It would be bad for the Saudis. It would be bad for Egypt as well. I mean, Jordan is one of those states that everybody thinks should not exist, but everybody recognises has to exist.[177]

As an initial step towards deeper integration, Palestine and Jordan would establish a free-trade zone, alongside joint industrial and tourism development areas. These initiatives aim to foster economic synergy by capitalising on the comparative advantages of both populations. Jordan's strategic infrastructure, most notably its international airport and the port of Aqaba, will serve as primary export hubs for goods produced within the confederation.

To enhance the competitiveness of the emerging economic bloc, tax and tariff agreements will be negotiated with key international partners, including Israel, Egypt, the United States and other relevant actors. These agreements will seek to secure preferential trade arrangements for the Jordanian-Palestinian free-trade zone, thereby encouraging foreign investment and export-led growth. Israel may, at a later stage, become a party to such agreements, further regionalising the cooperative economic framework.

The integrated Jordanian-Palestinian economy will leverage the respective strengths of each society, including labour, entrepreneurial capacity and natural resources. Free movement of people between the East and West Banks will be facilitated, allowing Jordanians and Palestinians to work, travel and engage in cross-border economic activities. International assistance will play a crucial role in supporting the confederated economy, particularly in infrastructure development, institutional capacity-building and investment promotion. Such support is essential to ensure the long-term viability of the confederation and to transform it into a model of regional cooperation and sustainable development.

176 Benny Morris, *One State, Two States* (New Haven, CT: Yale University Press, 2009).

177 Interview with John Jenkins (9 December 2022), 32.

The Hashemite king would be the head of the confederation. He would also be the army chief commander. Jordan would be responsible for overall security, in coordination with Palestine. Jordan already has an army. Palestine will have strong police forces in the West Bank and along the west bank of the Jordan River. A joint command centre would be established under the leadership of Jordanian authorities. As security is of utmost importance for Israel, the two countries will coordinate on security matters that may affect Israel.

A united Jordanian-Palestinian judicial system would be established. Local affairs would be decided by the respective governments. The Palestinian government will be responsible for daily life in Palestine. The confederation's foreign affairs would be led by Jordan, with significant Palestinian input. Decisions that may affect Palestine would be made through consultation with Palestine.

The confederation would have a shared parliamentary committee between Jordan and Palestine, and a similar coordination governmental committee. Joint coordination committees would be established in every ministry in Jordan and Palestine, as many interests and concerns are shared by both entities (education, health, economy, agriculture, business, commerce, tourism, environment, water, welfare, technology, culture, sport, etc.). Palestine and Jordan would retain their prime ministers, governments and parliaments. That is, there will be two governments and two legislative parliaments, one in East Jerusalem and the other in Amman. The Palestinian parliament will elect the Palestinian prime minister.

The capital of Palestine would be East Jerusalem. The capital of Jordan would remain Amman. The Al Aqsa Mosque will be administered by Palestine, Jordan, Saudi Arabia and Morocco. As suggested earlier, the Holy Basin would come under a special international regime under the control of a five-nation consortium. The Jordan Valley, separating Jordan from Israel and the West Bank, will be part of the confederation. The valley follows the north–south course of the Jordan River, from the Sea of Galilee to the Dead Sea, and between the Dead Sea and the slopes of the mountains of Hebron and Jerusalem to the west. Its width is up to ten kilometres (six miles). The valley accounts for around one-third of the West Bank (almost 2,400 square kilometres), the majority of its land falling within Area C, as defined by the Oslo Accords. Some 56,000 Palestinians reside in the Jordan Valley, including in the city of Jericho.[178]

[178] 'Israel's Planned Annexation of the Jordan Valley: Why It Matters', *Middle East Eye* (22 May 2020), https://tinyurl.com/3wfsdskp.

Effective security mechanisms must be established in the form of an international peacekeeping force or joint border patrols that include forces from Israel, Palestine and Jordan. Intelligence sharing between Israel and the confederation is also a must.

A Palestinian-Jordanian confederate state, then, has compelling historical logic and political sense. Jordanian-Palestinian confederation would satisfy the Palestinian yearning for statehood and would enhance Jordan's regional standing through the creation of a robust Jordanian-Palestinian entity, whose viability should be boosted by financial assistance and development schemes of great magnitude, which the international community, under American leadership, can put in place. A Jordan–Palestine peace with Israel would realise the dream of King Abdullah II's grandfather, Abdullah I, who was assassinated by a Palestinian in 1951 at the Al Aqsa Mosque for trying to make precisely such a peace with Israel.[179] The confederation would be a more stable state than Palestine, homogeneous in terms of religion, Arab history and socio-economic structures. At the same time, such a confederation will require constant maintenance and reinforcement to withstand the challenges that will surely arise. One can expect it to face immense integration issues. Sustaining such a structure requires a great deal of investment, internally and externally.

To make this work, the Jordanians would need economic and security guarantees for sustainability, as well as an external guarantor of Jordan's security and the survival of the Hashemite Kingdom. The only country that can provide such essential guarantees is the United States, which can lead and mobilise the United Nations and international support. Jordan has considerable economic problems and would accept the idea of a confederation only if it believed that this arrangement would boost its economy and security. It would not opt for the confederation idea if it might possibly worsen its situation.

To be absolutely clear, such a confederation would also entail the abandonment by the Israeli far right of its dream of Jordan as the 'alternative homeland' of the Palestinians, to which they could be transferred. They argue that the Palestinian state already exists – it is called Jordan. The Palestinians must aspire to create a home for themselves in Jordan, not in the West Bank or Gaza. They should immigrate to Jordan and seize power there.[180] This proposal of the Israeli far right is not a just solution.

[179] Ben-Ami, *Prophets without Honor*, 287.

[180] Daniel Tauber, 'Should Jordan Be Palestine?', *Jerusalem Post* (23 April 2013).

Those who promote it do not have Palestinian interests in mind, nor do they care about what Jordan wants. Jordan's former foreign minister, Marwan Muasher, rightly called upon the international community to help forestall any such plan that Israel might harbour.[181] My proposal, in contrast, does not aim to get rid of Palestine and undermine its cause for an independent state. It aims to provide Palestine with a more stable and sustainable backbone.

Gaza

Since Hamas took over the Gaza Strip in 2007, I have doubted proposals that speak of one solution for the West Bank and Gaza. Gaza and the West Bank were never a single unitary territory. The distance between them is too wide geographically, ideologically and politically. The two territories are different in many respects, including curricula and laws. The Gazans have new words that do not exist in the West Bank. I could not imagine Hamas convoys passing above, or below, Israel, delivering people and goods between the two Palestinian entities. The PA and Hamas are rivals that do not hide their disdain for each other. When Hamas took over Gaza, it did so brutally, killing members of Fatah by throwing them from rooftops. Unlike the PA, Hamas has remained committed to the destruction of Israel and has chosen terror and violence over peace and reconciliation. I thought that as long as Hamas remains in control of the Strip and is committed to the ideology of destruction, Israel cannot risk establishing a tunnel, or a bridge, that would connect Gaza and the West Bank – and would create a security nightmare for Israel. This option would entail a Palestinian state in the West Bank and another mini-Palestinian state in the Gaza Strip.

At the same time, I understand that despite substantial differences between Hamas and the PLO, there are psychological and emotional ties between the people of the West Bank and the people of Gaza, including family connections. Gaza and the West Bank belong to one people, the Palestinian people. The people of the West Bank cannot desert Gaza. This would be considered treachery. Therefore, the solution should aim to include Gaza. If and when the people of Gaza join the peace process, the parties will ensure territorial contiguity for Palestine. A corridor would connect the West Bank and the Gaza Strip, to allow safe and free passage. As long as peace is maintained, the road will be permanently open

[181] Interview with Marwan Muasher (25 July 2022).

and solely Palestinian. There will be no Israeli checkpoints. Palestinians will not be able to enter Israel through the corridor, nor will Israelis enter Palestine through it. Palestine will ensure that this safe passage will not be abused for violent purposes.

This option of one Palestine in the West Bank and Gaza became much more problematic on 7 October 2023. The terror attack Hamas launched on Israel was a game-changer for Palestine, for Israel and for other national and international players as well. The ferocity and scale of the attack, the trauma it has inflicted on Israeli society and the dramatic impact it has had on its sense of security, all were unprecedented. The brutal attack confirmed, as if confirmation was necessary, that Israel must take fanatics seriously and not simply say 'there will always be spoilers' and 'we'll have to deal with them at the time'. Zealots like Hamas change the matrix of the conflict. They force Israel to retaliate. After 7 October, Israel opened a wide-ranging war in Gaza that immersed the Palestinian population in its own trauma. According to an independent report, almost 84,000 people died in Gaza between October 2023 and early January 2025.[182] According to Reuters, since the beginning of the retaliation, by March 2025 more than 50,000 people had been killed.[183] More than 17,000 of those killed were children.[184] Over 87,000 received critical care.[185] More than 60 per cent of Gazans report having lost family members in the war.[186] Israel's bombing campaign in this war was one of the most extensive in the history of warfare. Hamas set for Israel what Mervyn Frost calls an 'Ethical Trap'.[187] Its initial attack was ethically obnoxious and was roundly condemned by the international community, yet that attack succeeded in provoking

[182] Rachel Fieldhouse, 'First Independent Survey of Deaths in Gaza Reports More than 80,000 fatalities', *Nature* (27 June 2025).

[183] Nidal Al-Mughrabi and Emma Farge, 'Gaza Death Toll: How Many Palestinians Has Israel's Offensive Killed?', *Reuters* (24 March 2025). See also Emma Farge and Nidal Al-Mughrabi, 'Gaza Death Toll: How Many Palestinians Has Israel's Offensive Killed?', *Reuters* (15 January 2025), https://tinyurl.com/4v3fk5sh; 'Reported Impact Snapshot | Gaza Strip (19 November 2024)', OCHA, www.ochaopt.org/content/reported-impact-snapshot-gaza-strip-19-november-2024; Kiara Alfonesca, Keren Inal and Chris Looft, 'Destruction in Gaza: Side–by-Side Aerial Look at the Israel–Hamas War's Devastating Damage', *ABC* (9 May 2024), https://tinyurl.com/c7zv94yx.

[184] Sheren Falah Saab, 'Israel's War in Gaza Has Killed over 17,000 Children. These Are the Stories of 28 of Them', *Haaretz* (28 June 2025).

[185] United Nations, *Global Humanitarian Overview 2025*, 121, https://tinyurl.com/mraa23a3.

[186] Palestinian Center for Policy and Survey Research, @Press Release: Public Opinion Poll No (92) (12 June 2024), https://pcpsr.org/en/node/980.

[187] Mervyn Frost's comments on a draft of this chapter.

Israel into a counterattack that appears to know no ethical boundaries. It moved Israel from being seen by the international community as the victim of an unethical attack, to being seen as the perpetrator of much worse ethical wrongs. Evidence for this is in the number of people killed by each side. Frost argues that in asymmetrical warfare, this kind of ethical trap has become and will remain the norm.[188]

Other important lessons from Hamas's unprecedented attack are that the concept of divide and rule that guided Israeli leaders in their treatment of the PA and Hamas, aimed at weakening the PA, should end; that Hamas cannot remain a military force;[189] and that the root causes of the conflict must be addressed. Israel has no interest in returning to Gaza, but lacunas must be filled. Since the start of the Israeli onslaught that began in October 2023, Hamas has diminished in power and stature. Still, its leaders strove to maintain control over the Strip.

According to the International Rescue Committee (IRC), more than two million Palestinians in Gaza, half of them children, are living without access to sufficient clean water, food and vital medical services. Over 80 per cent of the current population, or 1.9 million, have been displaced. Every person in the Gaza Strip is in need of humanitarian assistance.[190] The IRC further reported that 75 per cent of the population of Gaza had been displaced, most of them multiple times as they responded to Israel's warnings before it entered certain areas. Israeli bombardment and exchanges of fire have damaged or destroyed over 60 per cent of Gaza's housing. The United Nations estimated that a total of 42 million tons of debris lies across the territory, and that clearing the rubble, which contains human remains and unexploded ordnance, and then rebuilding could take eighty years and cost more than $80 billion.[191] Over half

188 Mervyn Frost's comments on a draft of this chapter.

189 Interview with Maher El-Kurd (30 January 2025), 24. El-Kurd argues: 'Hamas was created especially by Israeli security forces in the First Intifada, and it challenged Fatah and the PLO. And this is documented history.' Asfour said that Hamas was created to replace the PLO. He maintained: 'Hamas was brought in by Israel and the Americans. Why do professional people like you and the academics forget that Israel and the Americans asked us to hold elections with Hamas without any preconditions? Why do not you see that?' Interview with Hasan Asfour (18 February 2025), 15.

190 'Crisis Briefing', International Rescue Committee, www.rescue.org/country/occupied-palestinian-territory-opt.

191 Fadwa Hodali, Fares Akram et al., 'Gaza Reduced to 42 Million Tonnes of Rubble. What Will It Take to Rebuild?', *Bloomberg* (15 August 2024), www.bloomberg.com/graphics/2024-gaza-who-will-pay-to-rebuild/; Lucy Swan et al., 'How a Year of War Laid Waste the Gaza Strip – Visualised', *The Guardian* (10 October 2024), https://tinyurl.com/2m39esxk.

of the water and sanitation facilities in Gaza have been destroyed.[192] In the short term, there is a need to rebuild Gaza from the ashes and rehabilitate the lives of its people. This will require a complete overhaul of its physical infrastructure. The Palestinians are unable to do this on their own. Israel should not ignore its responsibility and it is in its best interest, as well, to see that this is done.

This enormous task requires the involvement of the international community, including the United States, the United Nations, the European Union, Egypt, Saudi Arabia, the Gulf countries and other countries that have the goodwill and interest to re-establish Gaza. The Gulf countries have the know-how and the funds to enable economic growth in Gaza and to expand it into the Mediterranean Sea. Other players can establish a humanitarian relief system to support the welfare of Gazans. The population in Gaza is young and many of them, perhaps the majority, do not have steady employment. It is in Israel's interest to ensure that they do not see terrorism as their profession. Israel must invest in local Palestinian leadership, one that would be willing to see Israel as a partner for securing a better future for Palestinian future generations.

Gaza may benefit from international support and investment in the development of artificial islands as a strategic solution to its acute land scarcity and population density challenges. Artificial islands offer a viable means of territorial expansion, can alleviate overcrowding in Gaza's densely populated urban centres and support long-term socio-economic growth. They can facilitate urban planning by creating new space for housing, office complexes and recreational facilities while also serving as platforms for essential infrastructures. They can function as integrated transportation hubs, hosting airports, seaports or nodes within larger systems of connectivity through bridges and tunnels. They would significantly enhance Gaza's regional mobility and economic integration. Moreover, when designed with environmental considerations, artificial islands can help mitigate ecological degradation by diverting human activity away from sensitive terrestrial habitats.[193] If implemented

192 International Rescue Committee, 'Crisis in Gaza: What Is Happening?', *Emergency Watchlist 2024* (4 July 2024), www.rescue.org/uk/article/crisis-gaza-what-you-need-know.

193 G. Ernst Frankel, 'Prefabricated and Relocatable Artificial Island Technology', *Macro-Engineering, Mit Brunel Lectures on Global Infrastructure*, Woodhead Publishing Series in Civil and Structural Engineering (1997): 155–173, www.sciencedirect.com/science/article/pii/B9781898563334500124; Mehul Hotwani and Priyanka Rastogi, 'Future Possibility of Artificial Islands', *International Journal of Engineering Research & Technology (IJERT)*, 10(1) (January 2021): 583–585.

with sustainable planning and international oversight, artificial islands could serve as a model for innovative and ecologically responsible urban development in resource-constrained environments like Gaza.

The artificial islands project is driven by a vision to encourage progress and cooperation in the region. Gaza leaders can make the Strip a flourishing place, like Singapore and the Gulf states, if they prioritise the economy and the welfare of their citizens over the destruction of Israel. It is in Gaza's interest to model itself after Bahrain's Amwaj Islands, for instance, rather than ISIS. Amwaj Islands is a group of six artificial isles off the coast of Muharraq.[194] Singapore has also cultivated innovation and reclaimed land from the ocean.[195] In 2021, the Danish parliament approved plans for an artificial island to house 35,000 people and protect the port of Copenhagen from rising sea levels.[196] Iconic artificial islands, such as Palm Jumeirah in Dubai (see Figure 12.6) or the World Archipelago, can become urban or national symbols, attracting global attention and becoming tourist destinations in their own right.

As long as the Gazan government remains hostile and terrorist, the border with Israel will remain sealed. If relationships improve and the government is willing to establish relationships with Israel, the three parties – Gaza, Palestine and Israel – can work together to establish a tunnel connecting the West Bank and Gaza.

In February 2025, President Trump announced a bold plan: the Gazan population would be 'resettled in far safer and more beautiful communities, with new and modern homes, in the region' where they would be 'happy, safe, and free'.[197] Egypt and Jordan were mentioned as potential

194 Dianne Apen-Sadler, 'Bahrain Area Guides: Amwaj Islands', *Time Out Bahrain* (3 January 2020), www.timeoutbahrain.com/moving-to-bahrain/428538-bahrain-area-guides-amwaj-islands.

195 Samanth Subramanian, 'How Singapore Is Creating More Land for Itself', *New York Times* (20 April 2017), https://tinyurl.com/4txxuzhx.

196 'Denmark Parliament Approves Giant Artificial Island off Copenhagen', *BBC* (4 June 2021), www.bbc.co.uk/news/world-europe-57348415. See also Oendrila De, 'Top 15 Artificial Islands – Amazing Man-Made Islands', www.wonderslist.com/top-15-artificial-islands-amazing-man-made-islands/.

197 Tharoor and Westfall, 'Trump's Plan for Gaza is a Nonstarter'. See also Raphael Cohen-Almagor, 'Making Sense of President Trump's Plans', *Times of Israel* (11 February 2025), https://blogs.timesofisrael.com/making-sense-of-president-trumps-plans/; Raphael Cohen-Almagor, 'No Threats, No Coercions: The Only Acceptable Way to Relocate Gazans to Egypt, Jordan – Opinion', *Jerusalem Post* (5 February 2025), https://tinyurl.com/ehtrfn88; Raphael Cohen-Almagor, 'President Trump's Policies in the Middle East', *The Cairo Review of Global Affairs* (February 2025), www.thecairoreview.com/essays/president-trumps-policies/.

Figure 12.6 Palm Jumeirah.
Photo: Getty Images.

countries to take the Gazans. The word 'consent' was not mentioned. German Foreign Minister Annalena Baerbock quickly reacted, saying, 'expelling the Palestinian civilian population from Gaza would not only be unacceptable and contrary to international law'.[198] UN Secretary-General António Guterres condemned 'any form of ethnic cleansing'.[199] Trump, as always, was throwing around grand ideas without much elaboration. What is needed is a careful plan carried out in stages and enjoying the consent and approval of relevant countries and the Arab world at large.

In the first stage, the underlying reasons should be family reunification and humanitarian aid. A certain number of Gazans should be agreed upon between the United States, Egypt and Jordan. This number should be based on estimates of the number of families with ties in Egypt and Jordan, and it should be offered first to Gazans with families in Egypt and Jordan, and who voluntarily sign up to immigrate. They would apply to immigrate via the usual immigration channels in Egypt

[198] Tharoor and Westfall, 'Trump's Plan for Gaza is a Nonstarter'.
[199] Ibid.

and Jordan. Both countries should scrutinise applications carefully to ensure that the applicants are not Muslim fundamentalists who might obstruct law and order and who might join the Muslim Brotherhood and other anti-government organisations. The last thing these countries need is a fifth column that would undermine the regimes of Egypt's President Abdel Fattah al-Sisi and Jordan's King Abdullah II. Egypt and Jordan will decide what status these immigrants will enjoy as temporary residents for *x* number of years, with the possibility of becoming citizens in Jordan and possibly in Egypt.

Upon completion of the first stage, lessons should be deduced, after which a further immigration deadline should be offered to new applicants wishing to immigrate on similar grounds, setting another capped quota.

If Trump is serious, then the entire scheme should be sponsored by the United States and executed by Egypt and Jordan. As long as it is based on communication and the consent of all relevant parties, then it is legitimate. Such relocation schemes should not be based on direct threats and coercion.[200] A survey by the Palestinian Center for Policy and Survey Research conducted in May 2025 showed that 49 per cent of Gazans may be willing to apply to Israel to help them leave and immigrate to other countries.[201]

Trump's controversial statements had an immediate effect. They started a conversation about the future of Gaza, a hot potato that most stakeholders have refrained from discussing. And they also moved the Muslim and the Arab world to action. Indonesia proposed to take one thousand refugees from Gaza.[202] In March 2025, the Arab League convened a summit in Cairo. In a rushed attempt to present an alternative to Trump's provocative ideas, Arab leaders quickly endorsed a $53 billion plan to rebuild Gaza by 2030, under the future administration of the PA. The plan includes the opening of an airport, a fishing port and a commercial port. The Gazan population would remain in the Strip. The League called for the Palestinians to unify under the PLO. Hamas would cede power to an interim administration of political independents until a reformed PA can assume control. Egypt declared its willingness

200 Cohen-Almagor, 'President Trump's Policies in the Middle East'; Cohen-Almagor, 'No Threats, No Coercions'.

201 Reuters, 'Almost Half of Gazans Willing to Leave, Survey Finds', *Reuters* (6 May 2025), https://tinyurl.com/mv9wua68.

202 Eka Yudha Saputra, 'Prabowo Clarifies Gaza Refugee Evacuation Plan: "Not Relocation"', *Tempo* (12 April 2025), https://tinyurl.com/3bp7yvjz.

to train Palestinian police to secure Gaza. They would be commanded by former Palestinian officers who served in the Fatah security forces that governed Gaza until the Hamas takeover in 2007. While the plan received the support of Hamas and UN Secretary-General Guterres, Israel rejected it, arguing that the plan ignored facts on the ground. Israel remained adamant that the PA should have no role to play in the reconstruction of Gaza.[203] Trump reiterated his plan, saying that the United States still wished to colonise Gaza and relocate its population to neighbouring countries, mainly Jordan and Egypt, while the Strip would be rebuilt. At the same time, the White House declared: 'While the President stands by his bold vision for a post-war Gaza, he welcomes input from our Arab partners in the region. It's clear his proposals have driven the region to come to the table rather than allow this issue to devolve into further crisis.'[204]

On 13 October 2025, the first phase of President Trump's peace plan was implemented when Hamas released all twenty surviving Israeli hostages who had been held in captivity for over two years, along with the bodies of several deceased hostages. In exchange, Israel freed nearly 2,000 Palestinian prisoners. On the same day, in a festive summit at Sharm El Sheikh, the Trump Declaration for Enduring Peace and Prosperity was issued. Inter alia, the Declaration postulates, 'We are united in our determination to dismantle extremism and radicalization in all its forms. No society can flourish when violence and racism is normalized, or when radical ideologies threaten the fabric of civil life. We commit to addressing the conditions that enable extremism and to promoting education, opportunity, and mutual respect as foundations for lasting peace.'[205] Removing Hamas from its position of power would eliminate a significant impediment to the pursuit of coexistence and lasting peace.

[203] Oliver Holmes and agencies, 'Arab Leaders Endorse $53bn Plan to Rebuild Gaza as Alternative to Trump Idea', *Guardian* (5 March 2025), https://tinyurl.com/5bnf684k; Claire Parker, Susannah George and Heba Farouk Mahfouz, 'Arab States Are Working on a Plan for Gaza's Reconstruction, an Alternative to Trump's Proposal to Take Over the Territory and Displace Its Residents', *Washington Post* (3 March 2025), www.washingtonpost.com/world/2025/03/03/arab-states-propose-gaza-reconstruction/; Wael Hussein, 'Arab Leaders Approve $53bn Alternative to Trump's Gaza Plan', *BBC* (5 March 2025), www.bbc.com/news/articles/cjd32xyjg4eo.

[204] Jerry Fisayo–Bambi and AP, 'Arab Leaders Endorse Egypt's $53bn Plan to Rebuild Gaza Countering Trump's Proposal', *Euro News* (5 March 2025), https://tinyurl.com/2w3hmrze.

[205] 'The Trump Declaration for Enduring Peace and Prosperity', *BBC* (14 October 2025), https://tinyurl.com/mu8zdbd4.

Conclusion

To establish peace, it is essential to have trust, goodwill and security. It would be far-fetched to hope for peace in the short term. Israel and Palestine need new leaders to pave the way forward. We should have no illusions about a fast track leading to a comprehensive peace. In March 2024, 71 per cent of Palestinians in both Gaza and the West Bank thought that the Hamas 7 October attack was correct.[206] Sixty-four per cent of West Bankers and 59 per cent of Gazans preferred to see Hamas in control of the Gaza Strip.[207] Seventy-five per cent of West Bankers and 62 per cent of Gazans were satisfied with the performance of Hamas in the war.[208] The majority of Palestinians perceived violence as the right course of action. As long as this is the case, ripeness for peace is questionable.

The situation is in flux, however; people are reflecting and contemplating, and they remain undecided. This is manifested in a September 2024 poll in the West Bank and Gaza, where, for the first time since October 2023, findings showed a significant drop in the favourability of the 7 October terror attack and expectations that Hamas would win the current war, and a moderate drop in the level of support for Hamas. In the Gaza Strip, findings also showed a drop in preference for continued Hamas control over the area and a rise in preference for PA control. Nonetheless, support for Hamas remains the highest among all Palestinian factions. In May 2025, 48 per cent of Palestinians in Gaza supported the anti-Hamas demonstrations in Gaza, compared with only 14 per cent of Palestinians in the West Bank who supported those demonstrations.[209] Findings also show a significant rise in support for the two-state solution, accompanied by a drop in preference for armed struggle, and an increase in preference for negotiations as the best means of ending the Israeli occupation.[210] Asfour argued that 'it is not easy for Hamas. They will disappear. Maybe Hamas will turn into a new form. The future Hamas I do not think that it will be as Hamas is today.' Asfour maintained: 'Hamas in Gaza is *khalas*.'[211]

[206] Palestinian Center for Policy and Survey Research, Public Opinion Poll, No. 91 (14 April 2024), 5.
[207] Ibid., 13.
[208] Ibid., 16.
[209] Reuters, 'Almost Half of Gazans Willing to Leave'.
[210] Palestinian Center for Policy and Survey Research, Public Opinion Poll, No. 93 (17 September 2024), 1.
[211] Interview with Hasan Asfour (18 February 2025), pp. 13–14.

As for Israel, a poll conducted in March–April 2024 showed that only a quarter (26 per cent) of respondents believed a way can be found for Israel and a Palestinian state 'to coexist peacefully'. Fifty per cent said they did not believe it was possible at all, with 20 per cent saying it depends on future developments.[212] One year after 7 October 2023, two-thirds of Israelis doubted that peace with the Palestinians would ever be achieved, and only 27 per cent supported a two-state solution.[213] In January 2025, over 60 per cent of the Jewish public agreed with the claim that Israel's security needs necessitate both security and civilian control over Palestinians in the West Bank and the Gaza Strip.[214] Two years after 7 October 2023, almost three-quarters of the Jewish public thought that the Palestinian people do not have the right to a state of their own, an increase of 11 percentage points from the previous year (72 per cent in 2025 compared with 61 per cent in 2024).[215] The majority believed that no peace is good for Israel. Israel continues to build the settlements, thus hampering the possibility of striking a deal with the Palestinians in the future. The situation on the ground keeps changing, supposedly in favour of Israel. The Palestinians look on as their future state shrinks in front of their eyes, and there is very little that they can do about it. The occupation is undermining the vital ingredients needed for peace talks, good faith and trust. Under duress, Palestinians lack freedom and control over their lives. Their economic activities, the allocation and management of their natural resources, their freedom of movement, and their health and well-being are all in the hands of Israel.[216]

The road to peace is long, protracted and complicated. What is required is to build trust; consolidate economic conditions for Palestinians; bolster security on both sides; stop enlarging existing

212 David Brennan, 'Most Israelis Can't See Peaceful Coexistence with a Palestinian State – Poll', *Newsweek* (30 May 2024), https://tinyurl.com/yn2n8cmz.

213 Benedict Vigers, 'Dim Outlook for Peace in the Middle East', Gallup (1 October 2024), https://news.gallup.com/poll/650636/dim-outlook-peace-middle-east.aspx; Sara Austin and Jonathan Evans, 'Israelis Have Grown More Skeptical of a Two-State Solution', Pew Research (26 September 2023), https://tinyurl.com/3dmvtu6k.

214 Mora Deitch, Udi Dekel and Noy Shalev, 'Survey Findings: The Intersection of the Israeli-Palestinian Conflict, the End of the War, Normalization, and Regional Coalition – January 2025', INSS (20 January 2025), www.inss.org.il/publication/survey-israel-palestinians-2025/.

215 Tamar Hermann et al, 'Two Years since Oct. 7: Majority of Israelis Say the Time Has Come to End the War', *Israeli Voice Index* (September 2025), https://en.idi.org.il/articles/61845.

216 Omar M. Dajani, 'Surviving Opportunities', in Tamara Cofman Wittes (ed.), *How Israelis and Palestinians Negotiate* (Washington, DC: US Institute of Peace Press, 2005), 46.

settlements; evacuate isolated settlements; dismantle checkpoints to make the lives of Palestinian civilians easier; involve the international community in the trust-building process; and devise ways to address the Iranian challenge. In June 2025, Iran suffered major blows from Israel and the United States, but its leaders remain committed to destroying Israel and to continuing with their nuclear project. The road is long and the challenges are great, but the potential reward is worth the effort.

The Palestinians aspire to have an independent state within the 1967 borders, with Arab Jerusalem as its capital. The Israelis wish to retain the character of Israel as the only Jewish state in the world, and they wish to enjoy life in security, free of violence and terror. Both parties should explicitly accept UN Security Council Resolutions 242, 338 and 1397,[217] and then begin their full implementation. Neither side should define the other; this right is reserved for each party for itself. Erekat told Livni: 'We've never denied Israel's right to define itself. If you want to call yourself the Jewish state of Israel – you can call it what you want.'[218] In turn, Livni accepted the Palestinian right to self-determination.[219]

In Chapters 9 and 10, I highlighted the obstacles that Prime Minister Olmert and President Abbas confronted, obstacles that prevented them from signing a peace accord. To resolve the Israeli-Palestinian conflict, courageous leaders are required on both sides who will seize the opportunities presented to them, who strongly believe that the time is ripe for change, and who will make the most of it for their people. One or more balanced and fair brokers are required to act as intermediaries, considered by *both* sides to be honest, even-handed and reliable.[220] The 1978 Camp David Peace Summit between Israel and Egypt was successful thanks to the tireless efforts of President Jimmy Carter, who was perceived as an impartial moderator by Prime Minister Begin and President Sadat. In contrast, from 1993 to now, the United States has not been perceived as an honest broker by the Palestinians. On numerous occasions,

217 UN Resolution 1397 (2002), www.un.org/unispal/wp-content/uploads/2016/04/SRES1397.pdf.

218 Amira Howeidy, 'PA Relinquished Right of Return', *Al Jazeera* (24 January 2011), www.aljazeera.com/news/2011/1/24/pa-relinquished-right-of-return.

219 Ibid.

220 J. Burton and F. Dukes, *Conflict: Practices, Settlement, and Resolution* (London: Macmillan, 1990); A. Smith and A. Stam, 'Mediation and Peacekeeping in a Random Walk Model of Civil and Interstate War', *International Studies Review*, 5(1) (2003): 115–135. See also Kjell Skjelsbæk, 'The UN Secretary-General and the Mediation of International Disputes', *Journal of Peace Research*, 28(1) (1991): 99–115.

the US has cooperated and coordinated with Israel, drafting documents and initiating proposals in concert with it, without incorporating and consulting the Palestinians in the process.[221]

In the long term, a confederative arrangement between Jordan and Palestine represents the most just, reasonable and pragmatic resolution to the Israeli-Palestinian conflict. This proposal, grounded in regional history and contemporary necessity, would revitalise and formalise the deep historical, familial and economic ties between the West Bank and Jordan. By re-establishing a structured relationship across the River Jordan, such a framework would provide Palestine with a vital institutional and economic backbone – enhancing governance capacity, economic viability and regional integration. A confederation would not erase Palestinian national identity but rather offer a sovereign Palestinian state the structural support to thrive, especially in areas such as infrastructure, trade and international diplomacy. For Jordan, it would deepen its regional relevance and stabilise its western frontier while maintaining its political integrity. Crucially, a Jordan–Palestine confederation could contribute to a broader architecture of peace. It would offer Israel a credible and secure neighbourly arrangement – built not on isolation or perpetual military deterrence, but on regional cooperation. Israelis and Palestinians could coexist not as adversaries or reluctant neighbours, but as distinct communities with interdependent futures – living side by side in dignity, mutual recognition and respect.

This solution will have its challenges – constitutional, territorial and emotional – but it offers a constructive alternative to the perpetual conflict and the moral and logistical crisis of permanent occupation. It builds on existing affinities and shared interests and reflects a commitment to justice and peaceful coexistence in a region long haunted by division.

221 One example is the Sharm El Sheik Summit of October 2000, when the Palestinian delegation was presented with an 'American-Egyptian' working document which was, in fact, an Israeli document. The Israeli delegation had examined and studied it prior to the summit, while the Palestinians saw it for the first time during the summit. Yasser Abed Rabbo, the Palestinian negotiator, complained to the Americans, saying this was not right, 'don't play that game with us'. See Charles Enderlin, *Shattered Dreams: The Failure of the Peace Process in the Middle East, 1995–2002* (New York: Other Press, 2003), 314.

13

Concluding Thoughts

> Peace is the only battle worth waging.
>
> ~ Albert Camus

This book is the culmination of a research journey that started in 2013. It is much more than an academic endeavour. Peace is of existential importance. Israel will be able to survive in the Middle East only if it finds ways to integrate into the region and be accepted as a legitimate international player, where no power would try to eliminate it from the map. For both Israel and Palestine, peace should be a strategy, not a mere tactic.

What is needed at this stage is a series of small trust-building steps that manifest the Israeli and Palestinian commitment to peace; where they show each other that peace is a strategic choice and not mere tactics, that violence is an absolute taboo and that the zeal for peace is unwavering. Only in an atmosphere free of violence is it possible to build peace. Each act of violence throws us back. If the Palestinians think that acts of terrorism will deter Israel from building settlements, they are wrong. Violence does a disservice to Palestinian interests. Palestinian leaders cannot say about their zealots, 'these are rogue flanks that do not accept authority'. If this is the case, then a Palestinian state will remain a dream. The Palestinians who wish for sovereignty must manifest their ability to control their territory; otherwise, why should Israel trust them? Israel, too, should control its own zealots and ensure that they do not derail the peace process.

My extensive research provides historical perspectives and practical suggestions. It explains the three major peace junctions and the reasons for their failure to bring about peace. The book also suggests practical ways to resolve the conflict via negotiations and mediation. I firmly believe in the necessity of resolving the conflict in order for Israel to survive in the Middle East. I also believe that the solution must be just and reasonable, attractive to Israel *and* Palestine. Rawls emphasises that justice in a just society entails settled liberties for equal citizenship, immune to political bargaining or considerations of social interests. The solution cannot be one-sided, ignoring the needs of the other. Furthermore, the Israeli-Palestinian conflict is not only about Israel and Palestine. As recent events have shown, it involves all of Israel's neighbours as well as other countries, including Iran, Yemen, Iraq, Qatar and the United States. In 1936, Haj Amin el-Husseini turned the conflict into a regional one, and it has remained so ever since.[1] In 2023, Yahya Sinwar hoped he could obtain the military and political support of the Arab and Muslim world.[2] For a period of time, his hopes were fulfilled, as Israel was attacked by Hezbollah, Iran, the Houthis in Yemen and Iranian factions in Iraq. Israel found itself fighting on seven fronts – Gaza, the West Bank, Syria, Lebanon, Iran, Yemen and Iraq – but Sinwar's hopes were dashed when the United States stood firm behind Israel. Much of the Hezbollah forces were destroyed and the Assad regime collapsed by the end of 2024.

To resolve the Israeli-Palestinian conflict, both peoples must listen to each other. One of the frustrating things for people who study the conflict is to listen to the same arguments time and again as they are voiced by Israelis and Palestinians. Both sides resort to similar rhetoric to justify their claims. The Israelis say about the Palestinians what the Palestinians say about the Israelis, unaware that the other side thinks about them in similar terms. Both of them have said:

- We are right.
- The other side is wrong.
- We shall prevail because justice is with us.
- Our national movement is strong and just.
- We are resilient.
- Do not underestimate our strength.
- We are here to stay.
- Their national movement is based on wrong ideas.

[1] Muhammad Amin al-Husayni (Haj Amin el-Husseini) was the Mufti (chief Muslim Islamic legal religious authority) of Jerusalem under the political authority of the British Mandate in Palestine from 1921 to 1937. He was an Arab nationalist who played a major role in Arab resistance to the Zionist movement in Palestine. Husseini spent most of the Second World War in Nazi Germany, where he issued broadcasts urging revolt in the Arab world and endeavoured to halt Jewish emigration to Palestine.

[2] Yahya Sinwar was the leader of Hamas from 2017 to 2024. He masterminded the 7 October 2023 terror attack on Israel.

- We are victims.
- We cannot trust them.
- They believe only in violence.
- They want us out of here.

The *lingua franca* should change dramatically, from a language filled with incitement, violence and hatred to a language of peace, mutual recognition, respect and good neighbourliness. Words do matter as they may be levers of action. Intentions, plans and aims should be explained directly. They should be transparent and clear, not open to contrasting interpretations. They should convey a message of peace and coexistence. As part of trust-building, the Palestine Liberation Organization (PLO) should do what is required and publish a new Charter, with a strong commitment to peace, reconciliation and coexistence.

Both Israelis and Palestinians rely on religious and national justifications. Both wish for the same things: the Haram al-Sharif/Temple Mount, Jerusalem and the West Bank. Both fail to acknowledge evil wrongdoing and rely on external powers. Both are unwilling to address core issues and are unwilling to pay the price for peace. Rightly or wrongly, leaders of both societies relate to the conflict in existential terms. Rushed moves are deemed to constitute grave threats to their respective societies. Hence, for many years no significant steps towards peace and reconciliation were taken. Once there were sufficiently brave people to move forward towards peace, the movement was like a waltz: two steps in one direction, one step in the opposite direction; sometimes, one step forward, two steps back. The peace of the brave is still in the making and the process has seen many bumps, challenges, hurdles and obstacles along the way. Spoilers in both Israel and Palestine are willing to pave the way with blood, to see destruction instead of peace. The cost of peace is so high that people ask: why bother? At times of violence and terror, emotions are high and calls for revenge silence moderation.

The conflict is complex, because Israel and Palestine do not share the same religious and ideological values. Israel is a Jewish democracy with links to liberal ideology and socialism. The Palestinians are Muslims. They are more religious, more authoritarian, less democratic, more conservative and less liberal, with a different understanding of human and civic rights. At the time of writing, Israeli democracy is threatened by its own government, exemplifying the democratic catch – the government resorts to democratic rhetoric and, in the name of its democratic majority in parliament, it aims to undermine liberty, equality and tolerance.

To resolve the Israeli-Palestinian conflict, we must learn from history. Both sides should explicitly declare their endgame, be considerate of the other and decide on a shared plan, as outlined in Chapter 12, to achieve it together. Peace should be their mutual strategy. Discussions should be open, transparent and candid. Peace between Israel and the Palestinians must be based on a genuine, mutual desire for tranquil coexistence. Both sides will have to make painful concessions, understand the needs of their partners and acknowledge their fears. Both Israel and Palestine will have to answer difficult questions and devise solutions to the challenges, together.

The conflict is not *only* about territory. It is much deeper than that. To resolve this entrenched and complex conflict, Israel and Palestine will have to converse about history, offer their narratives of history, listen to each other, learn and move forward. This needs to be done if they truly want peace. Both sides should learn about the other's national movement. They should learn what happened in Palestine during the second part of the nineteenth century, when the conflict started to foment. What led to the 1947 UN Partition Resolution, why did the Jews accept it, why did the Arabs reject it, why did the Arabs start the civil war in Palestine, how did the refugee problem emerge and who was responsible for it? Because the conflict is not about 1967, but about the clash between the Zionist movement and the Arabs who were the majority in Palestine, the air must be cleared before the parties sit down to negotiate. Neither side is fully aware of the different interpretations of history and, certainly, they do not empathise with the other's narrative.

Another crucial element missing in the past is the participation of Arab countries in the negotiations between Israel and Palestine. In 2002, the Arab Initiative came about, but the timing was wrong and Israeli leaders overlooked its potential. Yasser Arafat said time and again that he could not decide some of the issues, for example, Jerusalem and the Haram, because these issues relate not only to the Palestinians but to the whole Muslim world. Indeed, Jerusalem and the Haram are the most complicated issues. They cannot be resolved only by Israel and Palestine. Resolving the Palestinian refugee problem also requires wide Arab participation. Constructive input from the relevant stakeholders is vital.

In 1979, Israel signed a peace agreement with Egypt. Israel's strongest and most threatening neighbour was taken out of the Arab-Israeli conflict. Generations of soldiers playing war games in which Egypt featured prominently were greatly relieved. Defeating Israel without Egypt is difficult. The Egyptian-Israeli peace treaty has known many challenges, many ups and downs, but it has remained firm. Both sides are interested in upholding the treaty. The peace also bolstered the relationships of both Egypt and Israel with the mover and shaker of the negotiations, the United States. However, this was the last time the US was successful in mediating peace between Israel and one of its neighbours. Since then, American efforts have come to nought.

In the light of the American failure to bring about peace, we need to study the role that other countries have played in the peace process and examine their likely contribution to future negotiations. This book analyses the roles of Sweden and Norway in the context of their respective Middle East policies and bilateral relations with Israel and the Palestinians. Sweden and Norway uphold strong humanitarian traditions. Both are interested in investing in peacekeeping and peacemaking efforts globally, and in promoting values and norms that enhance their own security and standing among the nations. On the one hand, Norway had a close relationship with Israel.[3] It was reluctant to establish contact with the PLO, and once relations were established, it exhibited cautiousness in its policies regarding the Palestinian organisation.[4] On the other hand, Sweden has traditionally taken a more critical view towards Israeli policies on the Palestinian issue.[5]

Small states such as Norway and Sweden have limited power. They cannot impose a solution or even dictate an agenda. Norway and Sweden lack leverage over the sides, especially Israel. Their ability to offer carrots is limited, although they can assist in the rebuilding of the economy.[6] They achieve no direct gains except enhancing their reputation. Because they do not have a stake in the Israeli-Palestinian conflict, their goodwill is appreciated by both sides. Because they are far away from the

[3] Hilde Henriksen Waage, 'Norwegians? Who needs Norwegians?' Explaining the Oslo Back Channel: Norway's Political Past in the Middle East, A report prepared by PRIO International Peace Research Institute, Oslo Institutt for fredsforskning (2000); Hilde Henriksen Waage, *Peacemaking Is a Risky Business: Norway's Role in the Peace Process in the Middle East, 1993–96* (Oslo: International Peace Research Institute PRIO, 2004), chapter 2.

[4] Hilde Henriksen Waage, 'Champions of Peace? Tools in Whose Hands? Norwegians and Peace Brokering in the Middle East', in Peter Bauck and Mohammed Omer (eds), *The Oslo Accords 1993–2013: A Critical Assessment* (Cairo: American University in Cairo Press, 2013), 31.

[5] Marko Lehti (ed.), *Nordic Approaches to Peace Mediation* (Tampere: Peace Research Institute TAPRI, 2014), 52–53.

[6] John Stephen Moolakkattu, 'Peace Facilitation by Small States: Norway in Sri Lanka', *Cooperation and Conflict*, 40(4) (2005): 400.

Middle East, they can provide privacy and secrecy, using their wealth to facilitate talks away from the public eye, on equal terms, successfully providing the same arrangements for Israelis and Palestinians. Because Norway and Sweden do not have the same global aspirations that major players such as the United States have, they can focus on a given conflict without considering its global implications. For similar reasons, Switzerland can also play the role of a facilitator.

Since the Oslo Accords, the Palestinian Authority (PA) has been unable to establish a monopoly over the use of force, an essential condition for statehood and for securing Israeli cooperation. While former Prime Minister Salam Fayyad spoke of the PA's willingness to confront any military faction, including Hamas, to achieve this control,[7] the enduring reality is that Hamas's violent actions have deeply disrupted Israeli-Palestinian relations. The Palestinians have often sought to gain the maximum from negotiations with Israel, but in practice they have received only the minimum. Entrenched in myths, dreams and rigid aspirations, they have repeatedly missed pivotal opportunities for progress: the 1947 UN Partition Plan, the Oslo Accords (1993–2000), the Camp David Summit (2000), the Clinton Parameters (2000), the Bush administration's Roadmap (2003), the Olmert–Abbas negotiations (2006–2008) and the Kerry Initiative (2013–2014).

Israel, too, has missed significant openings, particularly during the Oslo process, Camp David 2000, the Arab Peace Initiative (2002) and the Kerry Initiative. Both sides, therefore, have valid grounds to reproach the other. This tragic symmetry of missed chances has perpetuated a conflict that continues to cost lives.

Meanwhile, the occupation continues, Israeli settlements grow, more people lose their lives, and Palestinian and Israeli children miss the experience of a normal childhood. Unfortunately, many Palestinians still find solace in violent resistance, viewing it as a means of asserting

[7] Interview with Salam Fayyad (19 January 2024), 26. In his comments on a draft of this book, Fayyad stated (30 June 2025) that during his government career, he did not speak for Fatah or on its behalf. He was, and remains, an independent with no party or faction affiliation. His entire cabinet was made up of political independents. The security doctrine was the PA's policy, and Fayyad 'vigorously worked to uphold it across the board, regardless of the party (faction) affiliation of the men with guns. In fact, early on, my primary focus was on gunmen affiliated with Fatah, not Hamas. Two reasons. First, my assessment was that they were the primary cause of the state of lawlessness that prevailed then. Second, that order of priorities was compelled by the need for our effort to be seen as credible by the public and inspired by the need to strengthen the institutions of the PA, rather than partisan politics. The effort was very successful.'

their presence and expressing their anger. But violence has not improved their living conditions. Instead, it has hardened positions, deepened hatred and delayed peace. Violence is not a solution. It is the perpetuation of suffering.

As long as the occupation persists, violence will remain a grim inevitability. Israel must begin easing the occupation and seriously commit to the path of peace. Speaking of peace while building settlements signals insincerity and erodes Palestinian trust. For their part, Palestinians must engage meaningfully with Israel to define final borders. As long as Israeli leaders resist delineating borders, suspicion will endure that territorial expansion remains a hidden goal.

The 2005 unilateral Israeli withdrawal from Gaza under Prime Minister Ariel Sharon, while significant, did not yield the security dividends Israel had hoped for. Subsequent military campaigns in Gaza and Lebanon failed to neutralise threats or establish long-term peace. Both sides expend tremendous energy preparing for war; they must apply equal dedication to preparing for peace. Without serious, structured preparation, any peace process is doomed to falter and die.

Israel's security remains precarious, largely due to a failure to curtail spoilers like Hamas and Islamic Jihad, who have amassed weaponry and launched repeated attacks on Israeli civilians, especially those living near Gaza. In response, Israel has mounted several major operations: *Cast Lead* (2008–2009), *Pillar of Defense* (2012), *Protective Edge* (2014) and *Guardian of the Walls* (2021). Despite these offensives, Hamas has regrouped and rearmed, culminating in the traumatic events of 7 October 2023, one of the bloodiest days in Israeli and Jewish history outside the Holocaust.

Because the PA has been unwilling or unable to rein in violent factions, and because Israel has struggled to prevent their resurgence, the time has come for greater international involvement. The global community, already affected by the reverberations of this conflict, must take a more active role in addressing spoilers. Goodwill and financial support are insufficient on their own; a coordinated effort to support both Israel and the PA in ensuring security is imperative. However, such support must come after both parties genuinely commit to peace and develop a concrete, time-bound implementation plan.

The international community can help instil urgency in both leaderships. It must work to improve the Palestinian economy, facilitate Israeli-Palestinian cooperation, bolster security on both sides and enforce zero tolerance for violence. It must also press Israel to halt settlement expansion and provide it with the security assurances necessary to ease movement restrictions for Palestinians. Trust-building is essential and achievable.

Peace requires leadership. True leaders understand the context in which they operate, develop clear strategies, adjust to new realities and inspire their people.[8] The Oslo process demonstrated that while vision and planning are critical, implementation is equally vital. Without it, hope fades, and trust dissolves. As Henry Kissinger noted, 'great leadership results from the collision of the intangible and the malleable, from that which is given and that which is exerted'.[9] Leaders must make decisions and lead.

Two Israeli leaders who tried more than others to achieve a long-lasting peace with the Palestinians were Ehud Barak and Ehud Olmert. At Camp David, Prime Minister Barak was willing to confront history and mythology, and to make difficult concessions. However, although his proposal was generous in his own eyes, it was insufficient as far as the Palestinians were concerned; moreover, his tactics were inadequate. He believed that he had no partner similarly willing to confront history and mythology, and to make hard decisions and compromise.

David Ben-Gurion was a visionary leader. He declared that Israel's goal is not to rule others but to be 'masters of our own fate – no more than that and no less'.[10] Ben-Gurion insisted that the justice Israel demands for itself, it must also extend to others:

> What we want others to give us we are prepared to give to others. We do not want to suffer injustice in the diaspora, to have our rights oppressed and to be robbed of justice, and we cannot and do not desire to do that to others in our country; we do not want foreigners to rule over us and our fate ... We who come humbly and sincerely before the entire world to demand total national equality for ourselves are thus committed to put this demand to ourselves as well.[11]

Israeli and Palestinian leaders must take ownership of the peace process. History shows that ownership matters. Leaders such as Anwar Sadat, Menachem Begin, King Hussein and Yitzhak Rabin made peace

[8] Henry Kissinger, *Leadership: Six Studies in World Strategy* (Milton Keynes: Allen Lane, 2022), 415.

[9] Ibid., 416.

[10] David Ben-Gurion, 'National Autonomy and Neighbours' Relations', in David Ben-Gurion, *Us and Our Neighbours* (Tel Aviv: Am Oved, 1931) (Hebrew), 110–130.

[11] Ibid., 122.

because they believed in it and took responsibility for its realisation. Israeli Prime Ministers Rabin, Shimon Peres, Barak and Olmert each risked political capital to advance peace. None, however, could deliver an agreement that the Palestinians could not refuse.

On the Palestinian side, Arafat and Mahmoud Abbas failed to present bold, transformative visions. Arafat, to his final days, remained more a revolutionary leader than a statesman. Abbas, while rejecting violence, has been unable to deliver a better future for his people, despite a promising rapport with Olmert. Meanwhile, the occupation, settlement expansion and violence continue.

The Palestinian people urgently need a leader committed to non-violence and to securing a sovereign, independent and viable state alongside Israel. That leader must focus on security, unifying armed forces, dismantling militias, eliminating corruption, building an economy and channelling human potential towards productivity. This would mark the end of destruction and the beginning of construction.

Arafat feared being remembered as the man who compromised. Abbas, acutely aware of history, fears being labelled a traitor. But fear has never produced great leadership. The Palestinians understand that and are looking forward to a new leadership that could move them forward. In April 2024, after years of delay, Abbas named his close ally, Hussein al-Sheikh, as his deputy and likely successor. Al-Sheikh is widely viewed with scepticism, stained by allegations of corruption and closely tied to the existing regime. While he embodies moderation and supports negotiation, he lacks fresh vision and broad popular support. It is doubtful he can reduce tensions, unite the Palestinian people and inspire the necessary reforms.

Israel, too, must address its internal challenges. As the influence of religious nationalism grows, especially among Orthodox Jewish communities, the likelihood of compromise diminishes. Some religious leaders believe peace can only be achieved through force. Groups such as Chabad,[12] which still reject the 1979 peace deal with Egypt, exert significant political influence, especially on the Likud party and on parties to the right of Likud. This ideological rigidity is a barrier to peace.

'Peace' is a shared word in both Hebrew and Arabic. It is a blessing, a value, a strategy, a hope. For some, peace remains a distant aspiration, something desirable but not essential. I disagree. Peace is both a moral imperative and a strategic necessity. Achieving it in the Middle East will

[12] About Chabad-Lubavitch, https://tinyurl.com/5a9nethv.

require courage, vision and determination. Leaders must seize opportunities and strive for win–win outcomes.

I emphasised that negotiators must listen actively, engage sincerely, show empathy, clarify positions and be willing to learn. They should aim to humanise the process, build trust, establish common ground, take ownership of outcomes and compromise where necessary. Strategic thinking, emotional intelligence and cultural awareness are crucial tools for peacemaking.

The plan outlined in Chapter 12 is doable, if Israeli and Palestinian leaders commit to peace and make genuine, substantive concessions, to be differentiated from tactical concessions. I believe that all conflicts are solvable and that the Israeli-Palestinian conflict is no exception. In 2023, I lived in Lund, Sweden. Lund is situated in Skåne County, a region that previously belonged to Denmark. For hundreds of years, Sweden and Denmark fought each other with gusto. Countless people died in the long, protracted conflict, until they had had enough. Today, one can travel freely between the two countries. The train line between Lund and Copenhagen is very busy. Peace and tranquillity replaced gore and death. The Danish-Swedish wars became part of the countries' distant histories. The two countries share many common interests. If the Danish and the Swedes successfully settled their conflict, so can the Israelis and the Palestinians.

Northern Ireland saw another conflict, much longer than the Israeli-Palestinian conflict. That conflict was resolved once English and Irish leaders were determined to make the necessary concessions. Another example concerns South Africa. Very few people believed that South African apartheid would end peacefully, without bloodshed. But it did. These examples show that prima facie 'unsolvable' conflicts can be resolved once capable, visionary leaders are installed. These leaders were able to redirect their respective societies away from violence to a road of peaceful coexistence. They argued: if there is a will, there is a way. And they led the way. In Israel and Palestine, both sides need to understand that peace is a precious commodity and, therefore, they must be prepared to pay a high price for its achievement, reaching a just solution. The peace deal should be attractive to both equally; it cannot be one-sided, enforced or coerced.

The conversation will continue, as it must. I hope this book contributes positively to that ongoing dialogue. One scratch on a wall may be meaningless, but many scratches can tear a wall down. The insights I offer here are intended to help dismantle the mental and political barriers standing in the way of peace. Even in times of war and terror, we must work to change the prevailing language from one of fear and violence to one of peace.[13] Violence is not the answer. Peace is.

This book begins with the story of a farmer who was unaware of the golden opportunity that was presented to him to improve his life. History has offered Israelis and Palestinians several golden opportunities to make peace. I hope that when the next opportunity arrives, both sides will be ready to grasp it and transform dreams into reality. Together, they can write a new chapter, one in which their children grow up as friends, discover their common humanity and replace the sword with the plough.

13 Prospects for Peace Following the 7th of October Attack, IIAS (December 2024), www .youtube.com/playlist?list=PLTn74Qx5mPsTFGohkQt5E2gju8TB5aWpO.

Appendix A

Interviewees (in person, unless specified otherwise)

Mr Ziad Abu Zayyad, former Palestinian Authority minister; advisor to Yasser Arafat. Jerusalem (14 May 2015)

Dr Hussein Agha, peace negotiator; advisor to Chairman Yasser Arafat and PA President Mahmoud Abbas. London (5 April 2019)

Mr Ghaith al-Omari, former Executive Director, American Task Force on Palestine; peace negotiator and former advisor to PA President Mahmoud Abbas. Washington (2 September 2014)

Mr Shaul Arieli, military expert. (11 November 2024, online)

Mr Hasan Asfour, PLO representative for the Oslo and Camp David talks. (18 February 2025, online)

Admiral Ami Ayalon, former Head of Shabac, Kerem Maharal (28 June 2022) (20 July 2022, online)

Mr Gadi Baltiansky, chairman of the Geneva Peace Initiative; advisor to Israeli Prime Minister Ehud Barak. Tel Aviv (25 January 2016)

President (ret.) Professor Aharon Barak, former legal advisor to Israeli Prime Minister Menachem Begin at Camp David 1978. Herzliya (8 July 2018) and Tel Aviv (30 June 2019)

Mr Ehud Barak, former Israeli Prime Minister (25 May 2022, 21 June 2022, 11 July 2022, online)

Dr Yossi Beilin, former Israeli Deputy Foreign Minister; peace negotiator. Jerusalem (13 May 2015)

Professor Shlomo Ben-Ami, former Israeli Minister of Foreign Affairs. Los Angeles (26 June 2013).

Ambassador Anders Bjurner, former Swedish Deputy State Secretary for Foreign Affairs. Stockholm (20 August 2019)

Brig. Gen. (res.) Shlomo Brom, Senior Research Fellow, Institute for National Security Studies; senior peace implementer. Tel Aviv (17 June 2014)

Rt Hon Alistair Burt, former Minister of State for the Middle East, UK. (22 April 2022, 27 May 2022, online)

Sir Richard Dalton, British Consul in Jerusalem (1993–1997). London (22 July 2015)

Maj. Gen. (res.) Uzi Dayan, former Deputy Chief of Staff, Israel Defense Forces. Tel Aviv (26 July 2017)

Brig. Gen. (res.) Udi Dekel, Deputy Director, Institute for National Security Studies; former advisor to Israeli Prime Minister Ehud Olmert. Tel Aviv (17 June 2014)

Mr Jan Egeland, Secretary General, Norwegian Refugee Council; State Secretary in the Norwegian Ministry of Foreign Affairs (1990–1997). Oslo (2 September 2019)

Mr Stuart Eizenstat, former US Deputy Secretary of the Treasury. Washington (7 July 2022)

Mr Nabil Elaraby, member of the 1978 Egyptian delegation to Camp David. Rhodes (31 October 2019)

Mr Maher El-Kurd, member of the Palestinian delegation to Oslo. (30 January 2025, online)

Professor Salam Fayyad, former Prime Minister of the Palestinian Authority (5 December 2023, discussion at the Prime Minister Forum; 16 January 2024, 19 January 2024, online)

Sir Vincent Fean, British Consul in Jerusalem (2010–2014). London (24 March 2016)

Mr Avi Gil, former senior advisor to Shimon Peres. Tel Aviv (16 January 2025)

Mr Gidi Grinstein, former senior advisor to Prime Minister Ehud Barak. Jerusalem (21 May 2013)

Professor Amos Guiora, former senior peace implementer. Jerusalem (10 July 2018)

Ambassador John Hagard, former Ambassador to Israel and Deputy Director General of Ministry of Foreign Affairs, Sweden. Stockholm (22 August 2019)

Ambassador Professor Manuel Hassassian, PLO Ambassador to the UK. London (17 February 2014); The Ambassador Forum, Hull (20 November 2013)

MK Israel Hasson, former Deputy Head of the Shabac (Israel Internal Security); senior peace negotiator. Tel Aviv (23 May 2013)

Mr Gamal Helal, former American peace negotiator. (11 November 2022, online)

Dr Yair Hirschfeld, main Israeli peace negotiator, Oslo first phase. Jerusalem (discussion on 29 October 2024) (interviews in writing on 15 July 2018 and 20 July 2018)

Ambassador Ulf Hjertonsson, former Deputy Chief of Mission at the Swedish Embassy in Washington, DC. Stockholm (27 August 2019)

Ms Hiba Husseini, former legal advisor to the PLO. Jerusalem (23 December 2024)

Mr Hussein Ibish, former Senior Fellow, American Task Force on Palestine; Senior Resident Scholar, Arab Gulf States Institute. Washington (20 October 2012, 13 September 2019)

Ambassador Dr Martin Indyk, former peace negotiator. (9 August 2022, online).

Sir John Jenkins, former British Consul General. Jerusalem (9 December 2022, online)

Dr Ahmad Khalidi, peace negotiator; advisor to Chairman Yasser Arafat and PA President Mahmoud Abbas. London (5 June 2019)

Ambassador Daniel Kurtzer, former US Ambassador to Egypt and Israel; former US Deputy Assistant Secretary of State for Near Eastern Affairs. Princeton (6 April 2017)

MK Tzipi Livni, former Israeli Foreign Minister. Jerusalem (22 June 2016)

Mr David Makovsky, former peace negotiator, US State Department. Washington (29 July 2022, 29 August 2022, 30 September 2022, online)

Dr Robert Malley, former peace negotiator, the White House. Washington (28 July 2022, 20 August 2022)

Mr Dan Meridor, former Israeli Deputy Prime Minister. Jerusalem (21 May 2013, 20 January 2016, 10 July 2018)

Dr Aaron David Miller, former advisor to both Republican and Democratic US secretaries of state; senior peace negotiator. Washington (October–November 2008, 12 September 2019)

Maj. Gen. (res.) Yitzhak Mordechai, former Israeli Minister of Defense. Jerusalem (19 December 2024); Tel Aviv (7 September 2025)

Ambassador Mathias Mossberg, former Assistant Under-Secretary for Africa and the Middle East, Swedish Ministry of Foreign Affairs. Stockholm (23 August 2019)

Dr Francesco Motta, Chief, Asia Pacific and MENA Branch, Geneva, United Nations. (1 April 2022, online)

Dr Marwan Muasher, former Foreign Minister and Deputy Prime Minister of Jordan. (25 July 2022, online; 8 May 2024, online speech and discussion)

Professor Aryeh Naor, former Israeli Government Secretary. Brandeis (12 June 2017)

Mr Yitzhak Navon, former President of Israel. Jerusalem (21 May 2013)

Brig. Gen. (res.) Azriel Nevo, Military Secretary of Prime Ministers Menachem Begin, Yitzhak Shamir, Shimon Peres and Yitzhak Rabin. Tel Aviv (30 July 2017)

Mr Pär Nuder, Swedish State Secretary and Chief of Staff to Prime Minister Göran Persson, 1997–2002. Stockholm (20 August 2019)

Mr Ehud Olmert, former Prime Minister of Israel. London and Tel Aviv (22 February 2019, 24 April 2019, 17 February 2021 discussion at the Prime Minister Forum, 6 January 2025)

Sir Tom Phillips, former British Ambassador to Israel. London (21 March 2016)

Mr Jonathan Powell, conflict resolution expert. (20 July 2022, online)

Professor William Quandt, member of the American delegation to Camp David 1978 in his capacity as member of the National Security Council. Washington (11 September 2019)

Ambassador Professor Itamar Rabinovich, former Israeli Ambassador to the United States; senior advisor to Prime Minister Yitzhak Rabin. Tel Aviv (21 July 2017)

Ambassador Dennis Ross, special Middle East coordinator under US President Bill Clinton (27 September 2019, 21 October 2019, online)

Mr Yuval Rotem, former Director General, Israeli Ministry of Foreign Affairs. (11 January 2021, online)

Justice Elyakim Rubinstein, Deputy President of the Israel Supreme Court; former senior peace negotiator. Jerusalem (28 May 2013, 10 July 2018) (15 February 2021, online)

Mr Yossi Sarid, former peace negotiator. Tel Aviv (15 May 2015)

Ambassador Pierre Schori, former Secretary General of Sweden's Foreign Ministry; member of cabinet; Deputy Foreign Minister; Ambassador to the United Nations. Stockholm (27 August 2019)

Mr Jonathan Schwartz, former peace legal advisor. Washington (17 August 2022)

Ambassador Svein Sevje, former Norwegian Ambassador to Israel; Head of the Middle East Section, Ministry of Foreign Affairs; Special Envoy to the Middle East; Advisor to the Peace and Reconciliation Division. Oslo (1 September 2019)

Mr Shabtai Shavit, former Head of Mossad. Ramat Hasharon (2 July 2018)

Mr Gilead Sher, senior negotiator; Chairman of the Negotiation Team in Camp David; Chief of Staff and Policy Coordinator to Prime Minister and Minister of Defense Ehud Barak; Coordinator of the Security committee, the Israeli delegation to the Interim Agreement under Prime Minister Yitzhak Rabin. Tel Aviv (26 May 2013) (2 February 2024, 9 February 2024, online)

Mr Joel Singer, chief peace negotiator, Oslo; senior advisor to Israeli Prime Minister Yitzhak Rabin. Washington (29 August 2014) (25 March 2022, 5 April 2022, online)

Ms Annika Söder, State Secretary to Swedish Minister for Foreign Affairs. Stockholm (23 August 2019)

Mr Sven-Eric Söder, Director General of the Folke Bernadotte Academy; former State Secretary at the Ministry for Foreign Affairs; Chief of Staff for the Social Democratic Party of Sweden; Head of the Olof Palme International Centre. Stockholm (20 August 2019)

Mr Tor Wennesland, Special Representative for the Middle East Peace Process, Norwegian Ministry of Foreign Affairs. Oslo (30 August 2019)

Mr Ted Widmer, former speech writer for US President Bill Clinton. Salzburg (27 September 2015)

Mr Gad Yaacobi, former Labour minister and Israeli Ambassador to the United Nations. Tel Aviv (discussions during 2004–2006)

Appendix B

General Questionnaire

What are the keys for successful negotiations?
What are the keys for successful mediation?
What are the keys for successful facilitation?
How important are personal relationships?
Is trust important?
How do you know that the time is 'ripe' for negotiations?
Is US involvement crucial?
Who can mediate?
Which country is best suited to mediate peace?
The role of other mediators: Switzerland? Egypt? Saudi Arabia? Turkey?
UK?
Europe?
Russia?
China?
Other?

Is there a role for small countries to play in mediation?
Is there a role that other countries can play (Russia, China, Europe, others)?

Tell me about your own experience.

Should Arab countries be involved in the process?
Can Israel and the PLO resolve the differences themselves?
What do you think of Trump's peace plan?
What can the PLO do?
What is the PLO's endgame?
What should be the PLO's endgame?
What is Israel's endgame?
What should be Israel's endgame?
What are the possible visions for the future?
How to address spoilers on both sides?
Should we speak to terrorists? How? Directly? Indirectly?

Will Hamas change?
Should Israel negotiate with Hamas?
The differences between the IRA and Hamas.

Oslo

Your opinion of Oslo.
When did you become aware of it?
Were you involved?
Oslo achievements
Oslo pitfalls
Was Oslo a failure?
What do we learn from Oslo?
What could have been done differently?
Was the absence of the US an advantage or disadvantage?

What Do You Think of Stockholm?

Achievements?
Failures?
The Swedish role?
What is the role of small countries in the process?
Are they effective?

Camp David

What could have been done differently?
Were the Americans prepared for the summit?
Was it prudent to convene Camp David at that time?
What were the mistakes in Camp David? How could it be done differently?
American mistakes?
Israel's mistakes?
PLO mistakes?
Was it prudent to demand an end to conflict?
What are the summit's achievements?
Was it correct to put all the blame on Arafat?
Is it prudent to put pressure?
What lessons did we learn?

Future

Are you optimistic? Is there room for optimism?
Is peace in reach, or beyond reach?
What is the solution?
One state
Annexation
Two states
Three states
Jordan
Jerusalem
Refugees
Jewish state
Settlements
Hamas
Separation Barrier

Other issues?

Appendix C

Historical Timeline

1988

31 July. King Hussein announced that Jordan relinquished any claim of sovereignty to the West Bank.
14 December. The Palestine National Council accepted UN Resolutions 242 and 338.

1991

30 October–4 November. The Madrid conference. For the first time, representatives of Israel, Lebanon, Syria, Jordan and the Palestinian territories met face to face.

1992

23 June. Elections were held in Israel. Labour, headed by Yitzhak Rabin, won the elections, receiving forty-four seats in the Knesset.
4 December. Yair Hirschfeld met with Ahmed Qurie privately in his hotel room during multilateral talks in London.

1993

19 January. The Knesset repealed the law that prohibited direct contact between Israel and the Palestine Liberation Organization (PLO).
21–22 January. The first meeting of the Oslo process was held in Sarpsborg, giving the negotiators an opportunity to understand their mutual goals.
11–12 February. The second Oslo meeting took place, producing a basic draft. Sometime after this meeting, the draft was shown to Shimon Peres, who took it to Rabin.
21 and 27 February. Peres met with Faisal Husseini, a senior PLO member, who conveyed Yasser Arafat's desire for the success of the Oslo talks.

20–22 March. The third meeting at Sarpsborg took place.

13 April. Daniel Kurtzer met with Ron Pundak and Hirschfeld and expressed his irritation over Elyakim Rubinstein's tactics in Washington and the Americans' continuing unwillingness to be directly involved with the Oslo channel.

16 April. Hamas member Tamam Nabulsi blew his car up beside an Israeli bus parked near the settlement of Mechola, in the Jordan Valley. Two passengers were killed and five were wounded. This was the first suicide attack in Israel.

30 April–1 May. The fourth meeting in Sarpsborg took place; this meeting produced a preliminary version, the 'Sarpsborg Document'.

8–9 May. The fifth meeting in Oslo took place at the government's official guesthouse not far from the royal palace; it was at this meeting that it became clear that official acknowledgement by the Israeli administration would be needed to strengthen the talks.

21–22 May. The sixth meeting took place at the Holmenkollen Park Hotel, Oslo; Uri Savir made his first appearance at this meeting, legitimising the negotiations and shifting them from an unofficial backchannel to the status of an official secret channel.

11–14 June. At the next meeting at the Holmenkollen Park Hotel, Joel Singer, the lawyer tasked with rewriting the Sarpsborg Document, arrived and presented a series of questions to the Palestinian and Israeli negotiators to clarify his editing of the document.

27–28 June. The eighth Oslo meeting was held at the Fafo Centre in Oslo; Qurie presented his list of counter-questions.

3–5 July. The ninth meeting was held in Gressheim, a hamlet 100 kilometres north of Oslo.

10–12 July. The tenth round of negotiations was held in Gressheim. The Palestinians, concerned that they were being pressured, produced a counter-draft to that written at the previous round. Tensions built between the two sides over unresolved issues, and the talks appeared to be in danger of collapsing.

25–26 July. The eleventh set of talks took place at the remote resort hotel of Halvorsbøle.

13–15 August. The twelfth meeting was held in Halvorsbøle, and it was agreed that talks should soon be brought to a close. A number of issues around border security, terrorism and settlements remained unresolved.

17 August. Peres rendezvoused with Johan Jørgen Holst, the foreign minister of Norway, in Stockholm and, in a seven-hour series of nine phone

calls from his hotel room, communicated directly with Arafat through Holst, finalising the agreement to prevent it from falling through and postponing a solution to many of the areas of tension by pushing them to the final agreement rather than incorporating them into the interim agreement.

27 August. Peres and Holst flew to California to meet with Warren Christopher and Dennis Ross and inform them that an agreement with the Palestinians had been reached.

4 September. Singer, Savir, Qurie and other Palestinian diplomats met in Paris to negotiate a separate mutual recognition agreement for the PLO.

9 September. Arafat presented the agreement for mutual recognition, which took the form of a letter, to the steering committee of the PLO to obtain their approval.

13 September. Declaration of Principles (Oslo A).

1994

25 February. A Jewish settler, Baruch Goldstein, opened fire at a mosque in Hebron, murdering twenty-nine Palestinians and injuring some 125 others.

29 April. Paris Protocol.

4 May. The Gaza–Jericho agreement.

13 May. Israel withdrew from Jericho, followed by Gaza on 18 May.

1 July. Arafat entered Gaza.

29 August. Agreement on the shift of authorities between Israel and the Palestinian Authority (PA).

9 October. Hamas kidnapped and killed Israeli soldier Nachshon Wachsman.

14 October. Israeli Prime Minister Yitzhak Rabin, Israeli Foreign Minister Shimon Peres and PLO Chairman Yasser Arafat were awarded the Nobel Peace Prize for their roles in the Oslo Accords.

26 October. Israeli-Jordanian Peace Treaty.

1 December. West Bank administrative control was transferred to the Palestinians.

1995

27 August. The Protocol on the shift of authorities between Israel and the PA was expanded.

28 September. Second Oslo (B) Agreement.
4 November. Prime Minister Rabin was assassinated.

1996

20 January. Palestinian elections were held for the first time as required by the Oslo Accords. Hamas boycotted the elections. The Palestinian people endorsed the peace process by giving Arafat an overwhelming victory. Arafat was elected president of the PA.
13 March. Egypt and the United States convened world leaders in the Sinai resort of Sharm El Sheik. They called it the Summit of Peacemakers and hoped to influence the Israeli electorate to support Peres in the general elections.
26 April. Israel–Lebanon Ceasefire Understanding ('April Understanding').
29 May. General elections for the 14th Knesset. Benjamin Netanyahu was elected prime minister.
4 September. Netanyahu and Arafat met for the first time.
24 September. Netanyahu approved the opening of the Western Wall tunnel exit. Riots erupted.
5 November. In the American presidential election, Democrat Bill Clinton was elected to a second term, defeating Republican Bob Dole.

1997

15 January. After four months of negotiations, Israel agreed to withdraw from Hebron, leaving behind only a small enclave of Jewish settlers. Arafat's PA controlled all of the major cities in the West Bank and Gaza.

1998

15–23 October. In an attempt to revive the peace process, President Clinton hosted talks between Palestinians and Israelis, who agreed on the Wye River Memorandum. The memorandum drafted at Wye was signed in Washington on 23 October.
10 December. Palestinians voted to change the PLO Charter in the presence of President Clinton.
21 December. The Netanyahu government fell following a no-confidence motion in the Knesset.

1999

17 May. General elections for the 15th Knesset. Ehud Barak was elected prime minister.

3–5 September. Barak and Arafat signed the Sharm El Sheikh Memorandum.

2000

24 May. Israel withdrew its forces from southern Lebanon.

11–25 July. Camp David Peace Summit.

28 September. Ariel Sharon visited the Temple Mount.

29 September. Outbreak of the Second Intifada.

12 October. Two Israeli soldiers were lynched by a Palestinian mob in Ramallah.

28 November. The Knesset passed a no-confidence motion, and general elections were announced.

23 December. Clinton published his Parameters for Peace.

2001

21 January. George W. Bush became president of the United States.

21–27 January. Taba peace negotiations.

6 February. Elections held in Israel. Ariel Sharon was elected prime minister.

7 March. The Sharon government was installed.

6 May. Following the outbreak of the Second Intifada, US Senator George J. Mitchell led an international fact-finding committee; its report recommended confidence-building measures.

11 September. The US suffered its worse terror attack in its history.

2002

4 January. Israel intercepted a massive Palestinian arms shipment on the ship Karine A.

27 March. During Passover, a Hamas suicide bomber murdered thirty Israelis and wounded about 100 others at the Netanya Park Hotel.

28 March. During the 14th Arab League Summit held in Beirut, Lebanon, a landmark proposal known as the Arab Peace Initiative or the Saudi Initiative was endorsed by all twenty-two members of the Arab League.

29 March–21 April. In retaliation for the Passover massacre, Israel launched *Operation Defensive Shield*, during which it occupied much of the West Bank.

23 June. Israel began the construction of the Separation Barrier in the West Bank.

2003

28 January. Sharon led Likud to a resounding victory in the general elections, winning thirty-eight seats in the Knesset. Labour won nineteen seats.

29 April. Mahmoud Abbas was appointed prime minister of the PA.

30 April. President Bush outlined the American Roadmap for Peace.

6 September. Abbas resigned as prime minister of the PA.

8 September. Qurie was appointed prime minister of the PA by Arafat and Fatah/PLO.

14 October. Geneva Accords: Palestinian and Israeli politicians released symbolic peace agreement.

18 December. Sharon announced his plan for a unilateral disengagement from the Gaza Strip.

2004

29 January. Israel swapped prisoners with the terrorist group Hezbollah, releasing 435 Arab prisoners in return for the remains of murdered soldiers and a kidnapped Israeli businessman.

9 July. The International Court of Justice ruled that Israel's security barrier was in violation of international law. Israel was ordered to dismantle the barrier. The UN General Assembly voted and ordered Israel to take it down. Israel officially announced that it would ignore the ruling but did change the route of the barrier.

11 November. Yasser Arafat died. Abbas and Qurie were to share his powers.

23 December. The first phase of PA municipal elections were held; Hamas secured nearly half the seats.

2005

10 January. Abbas was elected president of the PA.

2 February. Prime Minister Sharon and President Abbas met in Sharm El Sheikh, Egypt, and declared an end to hostilities.

15 August. Israel began disengagement and evacuated Gaza settlements and four West Bank settlements.
12 September. Israel finalised its disengagement from the Gaza Strip.
21 November. Israeli Prime Minister Sharon left the Likud party and formed Kadima, a new centrist party.

2006

4 January. Prime Minister Sharon suffered a severe haemorrhagic stroke and fell into a state of prolonged unconsciousness.
5 January. Sharon was replaced by his deputy Ehud Olmert.
9 January. Abbas was elected president of the Palestinian National Authority (PNA).
26 January. Hamas won the Palestinian Parliamentary elections. Abbas remained PNA president.
28 March. Olmert was elected prime minister of Israel.
25 June. Corporal Gilad Shalit was kidnapped by Hamas from an Israel Defense Forces (IDF) army post; Israel responded with a military operation.
12 July. Following a Hezbollah cross-border raid in which three Israeli soldiers were killed and two others were kidnapped, the Hezbollah–Israel war, also as known the Second Lebanon War or the 2006 Lebanon War, started.
14 August. The 2006 Lebanon War ended.

2007

8 February. Hamas and Fatah agreed to share power.
9 June. Hamas seized control of Gaza, routing Fatah forces and killing more than 100 people.
27 November. Annapolis Conference in Maryland.

2008

16 July. Hezbollah released the bodies of captive Israeli soldiers Eldad Regev and Ehud Goldwasser, whose kidnapping sparked the Second Lebanon War.
26 October. Following the resignation of Ehud Olmert, foreign minister Tzipi Livni announced that she could not form a coalition and called for elections.

4 November. Democratic Senator Barack Obama won the American presidential elections. He defeated Republican Senator John McCain.
27 December–18 January. In response to increasing rocket barrages, Israel launched *Operation Cast Lead* against Hamas in Gaza.

2009

31 March. Netanyahu returned to the prime minister's office following unusual parliamentary election results that saw the centrist Kadima party led by Livni win the most seats but not enough to forge a coalition government. Netanyahu succeeded where Livni failed and established a comprehensive coalition.
4 June. President Obama delivered a speech in Cairo.
14 June. Prime Minister Netanyahu delivered the Bar-Ilan speech in which he recognised for the first time the principle of the two-state solution.
26 August. The government of Salam Fayyad, prime minister of the PA, issued a detailed plan to establish a de facto Palestinian state within two years.

2010

31 May. Israel intercepted a flotilla of six ships en route to Gaza.
2 September. President Obama launched direct talks at a White House summit with Abbas and Netanyahu.

2011

4 May. Palestinian rivals Fatah and Hamas signed a reconciliation pact.
18 October. Kidnapped IDF Corporal Gilad Shalit was released in a prisoner exchange deal with Hamas.

2012

25 January. Israeli-Palestinian peace talks in Jordan ended without progress.
6 November. President Obama was re-elected to a second term. He defeated former Republican Governor Mitt Romney of Massachusetts.
14 November. In response to Hamas rocket fire on the western Negev, Israel launched an eight-day military operation called *Pillar of Defence*.

2013

22 January. Prime Minister Netanyahu retained his seat following general elections.

29 July. Israeli-Palestinian peace talks resumed in Washington, DC.

14 August. Israelis and Palestinians officially began peace talks in Jerusalem.

2014

11 January. Former Prime Minister Ariel Sharon died.

23 April. The Palestinian leadership and Hamas forged a new reconciliation agreement. Israel responded by halting the peace talks.

12 June. Israeli teenagers Naftali Fraenkel, Gilad Shaer and Eyal Yifrah were abducted and killed by Palestinian terrorists. Their bodies were discovered on 30 June.

2 July. Jewish extremists kidnapped and killed sixteen-year-old Palestinian Mohammed Abu Khdeir.

7 July–26 August. In response to attacks by armed groups in Gaza, Israel launched *Operation Protective Edge*, a military air and land campaign to knock out rocket-launching sites and destroy the terror tunnels.

2015

May. Prime Minister Netanyahu formed a new coalition government.

2016

14 September. The United States committed $38 billion over the next ten years to military assistance for Israel, the largest such deal in US history.

8 November. Republican Donald Trump was elected US president, defeating Democrat Hillary Clinton.

2017

6 February. The Knesset passed a law which retroactively legalised almost 4,000 Jewish settler homes built on private Palestinian land in the West Bank.

6 December. The United States formally recognised Jerusalem as the Israeli capital and ordered the relocation of the US Embassy to Jerusalem.

2018

14 May. US Embassy opened in Jerusalem, and violence and protests ensued.

March–June: Protests by Palestinian factions in Gaza on the border led to clashes with Israeli troops in which more than 100 Palestinians died and thousands were injured.

2019

21 March. Trump announced American recognition of Israel's sovereignty in the Golan Heights.

9 April. Elections in Israel. No party was able to form a government. The two major parties, Blue and White and Likud, each received thirty-five seats.

30 May. The Knesset voted to dissolve itself and trigger new elections in order to prevent Blue and White party leader Benny Gantz from being appointed prime minister-designate.

17 September. Elections in Israel. Blue and White overcame the Likud by a single seat. Nonetheless, the Likud received the mandate from the president after gaining the support of one Knesset member more than Blue and White. Netanyahu again failed to form a government. Gantz tried to compose a coalition, without success. The president passed the mandate to the Knesset members for twenty-one days. After no other candidate was offered, the Knesset was dissolved.

2020

2 March. Elections in Israel. Likud gained more seats than Blue and White, but Gantz achieved more recommendations from potential allies in the Knesset and received the mandate from the president. Nevertheless, Gantz was unable to unite enough allies to form a coalition.

20 April. Likud and Blue and White agreed on an equal unity government, which included a rotation agreement between Netanyahu and Gantz in the prime minister's office. However, following a failed budgetary vote in December 2020, the government coalition collapsed yet again, and a new election was called for March 2021.

3 November. Former Vice President Joe Biden defeated incumbent President Trump.

2021

23 March. Elections in Israel. Likud received thirty seats. The second-largest party, Yesh Atid, received seventeen seats. However, Netanyahu was unable to garner the needed endorsement of sixty-one Members of the Knesset. The leader of Yesh Atid, Yair Lapid, received the mandate to compose a coalition.

13 June. Naftali Bennet became Israel's prime minister, although his party won a mere seven seats in the Knesset. He signed a rotation agreement with Lapid, who agreed to be second in the prime minister's office. The Bennett–Lapid government collapsed one year later after losing its parliamentary majority, triggering early elections.

2022

29 December. Netanyahu was sworn in for a sixth term.

2023

January. Protests against the government legislation blitz erupted all over Israel, arguing that the government was aiming to annul democracy.

9 May. Israel launched surprise airstrikes across the Gaza Strip, targeting leaders of the Islamic Jihad.

7 October. Hamas launched a coordinated attack on Israeli kibbutzim and settlements outside Gaza, murdering 1,200 civilians and soldiers. Hamas also kidnapped more than 250 people and took them to Gaza.

9 October. Israel ordered a complete siege of Gaza and launched air attacks on Gaza that were followed by an extensive ground operation.

2024

12 June. The United Nations' first inquiry into the 7 October terror attack and resulting conflict found that both Israel and Hamas committed war crimes.

16 October. Yahya Sinwar, the leader of Hamas, was killed by Israeli soldiers.

5 November. Trump was elected president of the United States for the second time.

2025

19 January. Israel and Hamas approved a ceasefire agreement that intended to end the war, exchange Israeli hostages and Palestinian prisoners, and allow international aid. The ceasefire collapsed on 18 March.

18 March. Israel launched aerial bombardments and attacks on the Gaza Strip, killing at least 400 people.

13 June. Israel launched what its leaders described as a pre-emptive attack on Iran, targeting Iran's nuclear infrastructure and military command.

21 June. The United States attacked Iran's major nuclear facilities – Fordow, Natanz and Isfahan.

25 June. The twelve-day war between Israel and Iran ended with a ceasefire brokered by the United States and Qatar.

9 October. President Trump announced that Israel and Hamas had agreed to the first phase of his twenty-point peace plan in which all Israeli hostages are to be released in exchange for Palestinian prisoners, the IDF withdraws from half of the Gaza Strip and a ceasefire comes into effect.

13 October 2025. Israel and Hamas enacted a landmark ceasefire: Hamas released the final twenty living Israeli hostages and returned four bodies, while Israel freed over 1,900 Palestinian detainees. The exchange, part of a US-brokered peace plan, marked a pivotal step towards ending the Gaza war, though tensions remained over the incomplete return of deceased hostages. That same day, President Trump arrived in Israel to declare the war's end, later presiding over a summit in Sharm El Sheikh, Egypt, where global leaders convened to chart Gaza's reconstruction and future governance.

SELECT BIBLIOGRAPHY

Ababsa, Myriam (ed.), *Atlas of Jordan: History, Territories and Society* (Amman: Presses de l'Ifpo, 2014).

Abadi, Jacob, 'Sweden's Policy toward Israel: Constraints and Adjustments', *Middle Eastern Studies*, 37(2) (April 2001): 23–49.

Abbas, Mahmoud, *Through Secret Channels* (London: Garnet Pub Ltd, 1995).

Abrams, Elliott, *Tested by Zion: The Bush Administration and the Israeli-Palestinian Conflict* (New York: Cambridge University Press, 2013).

Abu Nowar, Maan, *The Jordanian-Israeli War, 1948–1951: A History of the Hashemite Kingdom of Jordan* (Reading: Ithaca Press, 2002).

Abu Zaida, Sufian, 'Palestinian Prisoners from Oslo to Annapolis', in Peter Bauck and Mohammed Omer (eds.), *The Oslo Accords 1993–2013: A Critical Assessment* (Cairo: American University in Cairo Press, 2013): 135–146.

Addicott, Jeffrey F., 'Using a Civil Suit to Punish/Deter Sponsors of Terrorism: Connecting Arafat & the PLO to the Terror Attacks in the Second Intifada', *St. John's Journal of International and Comparative Law*, 4(2) (2014): 71–105.

Aggestam, Karin, 'Reframing International Conflicts: "Ripeness" in International Mediation', *Paradigms*, 9(2) (Winter 1995): 86–106.

Aggestam, Karin, *Reframing and Resolving Conflict* (Lund: Lund Political Studies 108, 1999).

Aggestam, Karin, 'Mediating Asymmetrical Conflict', *Mediterranean Politics*, 7(1) (2002): 69–91.

Aggestam, Karin, 'Quasi-Informal Mediation in the Oslo Channel: Larsen and Holst as Individual Mediators', in J. Bercovitch (ed.), *Studies in International Mediation* (Basingstoke: Palgrave Macmillan, 2002): 57–79.

Agha, Hussein, 'Oslo25 | "We Must Liberate Our Thinking from the Oslo Straitjacket": An Interview with Hussein Agha', *Fathom* (August 2018). https://tinyurl.com/cnmr8cyt

Agha, Hussein, Shai Feldman, Ahmad Khalidi, and Zeev Schiff, *Track-II Diplomacy: Lessons from the Middle East* (Boston, MA: The MIT Press, 2004).

Agha, Hussein, and Ahmad Khalidi, *Syria and Iran, Rivalry and Cooperation* (London: Royal Institute of International Affairs, 1995).

Agha, Hussein, and Ahmad Khalidi, *A Framework for a Palestinian National Security Doctrine* (London: Royal Institute of International Affairs, 2006).

Agha, Hussein, and Ahmad Khalidi, 'Yasser Arafat: Why He Still Matters', *The Guardian* (13 November 2014), www.theguardian.com/news/2014/nov/13/-sp-yasser-arafat-why-he-still-matters

Agha, Hussein, and Ahmad Khalidi, 'The End of This Road: The Decline of the Palestinian National Movement', *New Yorker* (6 August 2017), https://tinyurl.com/mn6c8bfj

Agha, Hussein, and Robert Malley, 'Camp David: An Exchange', *New York Review of Books* (20 September 2001).

Agha, Hussein, and Robert Malley, 'A Solution Is Possible Now', *The Guardian* (29 March 2002).

Agha, Hussein, and Robert Malley, *Tomorrow Is Yesterday: Life, Death, and the Pursuit of Peace in Israel/Palestine* (New York: Farrar, Straus and Giroux, 2025).

Akram, Susan M., 'Palestinian Refugees and Their Legal Status: Rights, Politics, and Implications for a Just Solution', *Journal of Palestine Studies*, 31(3) (Spring 2002): 36–51.

al-Arif, Arif, *A Brief Guide to the Dome of the Rock and al-Haram al-Sharif* (Jerusalem: Supreme Awqaf Council, 1965).

Albanese, Francesca P., 'Advancing Palestinian Refugee Rights after a 70-Year Long Impasse', in Pietro Stefanini (ed.), *UNRWA at 70: Palestinian Refugees in Context* (London: Palestinian Return Centre, 2020): 54–69.

Albanese, Francesca P., and Lex Takkenberg, *Palestinian Refugees in International Law* (Oxford: Oxford University Press, 2020).

Al-Hout, Shafiq, *My Life in the PLO* (London: Pluto Press, 2011).

Al Husseini, Jalal, 'Jordan and the Palestinians', in Myriam Ababsa (ed.), *Atlas of Jordan: History, Territories and Society* (Amman: Presses de l'Ifpo, 2014): 230–245.

Al-Khatib, Mahmoud A. 'The Concept of Justice in Islam', *Journal of Ethnic and Cultural Studies*, 10(5) (2023): 45–66.

Alkidwa, Nasser, 'The Oslo Accords: A Closer Look', *The Cairo Review of Global Affairs* (Winter 2019), www.thecairoreview.com/essays/the-oslo-accords-a-closer-look/

Alon, Ilai, and Jeanne M. Brett, 'Perceptions of Time and Their Impact on Negotiations in the Arabic-Speaking Islamic World', *Negotiation Journal*, 23(1) (2007): 55–73.

al-Shafi, Haydar Abd, Speech at the Madrid Conference, Madrid (31 October 1991), https://tinyurl.com/4x73jnn8

al-Shafi, Haydar Abd, 'Moving beyond Oslo: An Interview with Haydar 'Abd Al-Shafi', *Journal of Palestine Studies*, 25(1) (Autumn 1995): 76–85.

Aly, Abdel Monem Said, 'The Road to Oslo and Beyond: Prospects for an Arab-Israeli Peace', *Security Dialogue*, 25(1) (1994): 37–50.

Aly, Abdel Monem Said, Shai Feldman, and Khalil Shikaki, *Arabs and Israelis: Conflict and Peacemaking in the Middle East* (London: Red Globe Press, 2013).

Anziska, Seth, *Preventing Palestine: A Political History from Camp David to Oslo* (Princeton, NJ: Princeton University Press, 2018).

'Arab Peace Initiative: Full Text', *The Guardian* (28 March 2002), www.theguardian.com/world/2002/mar/28/israel7

Arafat, Yasser, 'The Palestinian Vision of Peace', *New York Times* (3 February 2002), p. WK15.

Aran, Amnon, *Israeli Foreign Policy since the End of the Cold War* (Cambridge: Cambridge University Press, 2021).

Arieli, Shaul, *A Border between Us and You* (Tel Aviv: Miskal Publishing – Yedioth Books, 2021).

Aristotle, *Politics*. 350 B.C.E, http://classics.mit.edu/Aristotle/politics.1.one.html

Aronson, Geoffrey, 'Settlement Monitor', *Journal of Palestine Studies*, 29(2) (Winter 2000): 135–142.

Aronson, Geoffrey, 'What Was the 1997 Protocol Concerning the Redeployment in Hebron (a.k.a. Hebron Protocol, Hebron Agreement)?', *ProCon.org* (19 May 2008), https://tinyurl.com/bdf9et5t

Arrow, Kenneth J. et al., *Barriers to Conflict Resolution* (New York: W.W. Norton & Company, 1995).

Aruri, Nasseer, 'The PLO and the Jordan Option', *Middle East Report*, 131 (March/April 1985), https://merip.org/1985/03/the-plo-and-the-jordan-option/

Ashrawi, Hanan, *This Side of Peace: A Personal Account* (New York: Simon & Schuster, 1995).

Atran, Scott, and Robert Axelrod, 'Reframing Sacred Values', *Negotiation Journal*, 24 (July 2008): 221–246.

Avidar, Eli, *The Abyss* (London: Rowman and Littlefield, 2015).

Awad, Mubarak E., 'Non-Violent Resistance: A Strategy for the Occupied Territories', *Journal of Palestine Studies*, 13(4) (Summer 1984): 22–36.

Ayalon, Ami, *Friendly Fire: How Israel Became Its Own Worst Enemy* (Lebanon, NH: Steerforth Press, 2020).

Azoulay, Ariella, and Adi Ophir, *The One-State Condition* (Stanford, CA: Stanford University Press, 2012).

Barak, Ehud, *My Country, My Life: Fighting for Israel, Searching for Peace* (New York: Macmillan, 2018).

Barak, Oren, 'The Failure of the Israeli-Palestinian Peace Process, 1993–2000', *Journal of Peace Research*, 42(6) (2005): 719–736.

Barak's Proposal to Divide Jerusalem, Information Regarding Israel's Security (n/d), https://iris.org.il/divided-jerusalem/

Barari, Hassan (ed.), *The Middle East Peace by Piece: The Quest for a Solution to the Arab-Israeli Conflict* (Amman: Friedrich, 2009), http://library.fes.de/pdf-files/bueros/amman/06836-book.pdf

Barash, David P., and Charles P. Webel, *Peace and Conflict Studies* (Thousand Oaks, CA: Sage Publications, 2018).

Bar'el, Zvi et al., Haaretz e-books – *The Forgotten War: A Year Since Gaza* (2015): 1–37, https://tinyurl.com/2s3m3vna

Barnett, Michael, 'Culture, Strategy and Foreign Policy Change: Israel's Road to Oslo', *European Journal of International Relations*, 5(1) (1999): 5–36.

Barnett, Michael, and Shibley Telhami (eds.), *Identity and Foreign Policy in the Middle East* (Ithaca, NY: Cornell University Press, 2002).

Barry, Brian, *Theories of Justice* (London: Harvester, 1989).

Bar-Tal, Daniel, 'Is A Confederation between Israel and Palestine with Jordan A Viable Arrangement?', *World Affairs* (2022). https://doi.org/10.1177/00438200221128026

Bar-Tal, Daniel, and Amiram Raviv, *Comfort Zone of a Society in Conflict* (Tel Aviv: Stimatzky, 2021) (Hebrew).

Bar-Tal, Daniel, and Izhak Schnell (eds.), *The Impacts of Lasting Occupation: Lessons from Israeli Society* (New York: Oxford University Press, 2013).

Baskin, Gershon, *In Pursuit of Peace in Israel and Palestine* (Nashville, TN: Vanderbilt University Press, 2017).

Bauck, Petter, and Mohammed Omer, *The Oslo Accords 1993–2013: A Critical Assessment* (Cairo: American University in Cairo Press, 2013).

BBC, 'Intifada Toll 2000–2005', *BBC.com* (8 February 2005), http://news.bbc.co.uk/1/hi/world/middle_east/3694350.stm

Beardsley, Kyle C., David M. Quinn, Bidisha Biswas, and Jonathan Wilkenfeld, 'Mediation Style and Crisis Outcomes', *Journal of Conflict Resolution*, 50(1) (February 2006): 58–86.

Behrendt, Sven, *The Secret Israeli-Palestinian Negotiations in Oslo: Their Success and Why the Process Ultimately Failed* (London: Routledge, 2007).

Beilin, Yossi, *Touching Peace* (Tel Aviv: Yedioth Ahronoth, 1997) (Hebrew).

Beilin, Yossi, *Touching Peace* (London: Weidenfeld & Nicolson, 1999).

Beilin, Yossi, *The Path to Geneva* (New York: RDV Books, 2004).

Beilin, Yossi, 'Oslo and Camp David: One and the Same?', *The Cairo Review of Global Affairs* (Winter 2019), www.thecairoreview.com/essays/oslo-and-camp-david-one-and-the-same/

Beilin, Yossi, et al., *The Holy Land Confederation as a Facilitator for the Two-State Solution*, https://ecf.org.il/media_items/1538

Beilin-Abu Mazen Document. Framework for the Conclusion of a Final Status Agreement between Israel and the Palestine Liberation Organization (31 October 1995), www.palquest.org/en/historictext/10467/beilin-–-abu-mazen-document

Bellamy, Richard, *Liberalism and Pluralism* (London and New York: Routledge, 1999).

Ben-Ami, Shlomo, *2000 Camp David Summit: Daily Diary* (July 2000), www.jewishvirtuallibrary.org/jsource/Peace/benamidiary.html

Ben-Ami, Shlomo, *A Front without a Rearguard* (Tel Aviv: Yedioth Ahronoth, 2004) (Hebrew).

Ben-Ami, Shlomo, *Scars of War, Wounds of Peace* (London: Phoenix, 2005).

Ben-Ami, Shlomo, 'So Close and Yet so Far: Lessons from the Israeli-Palestinian Peace Process', *Israel Studies*, 10(2) (Summer 2005): 72–90.

Ben-Ami, Shlomo, 'The Israeli-Palestinian Peace Conundrum', *Currents Briefs on Contemporary Israel* (Los Angeles: UCLA Nazarian Center for Israel Studies, 2019).

Ben-Ami, Shlomo, *Prophets without Honor: The 2000 Camp David Summit and the End of the Two-State Solution* (Oxford: Oxford University Press, 2022).

Ben-Meir, Alon, 'The Case for an Israeli-Palestinian-Jordanian Confederation: Why Now and How?', *World Affairs*, 185(1) (2022): 9–58.

Ben-Porat, Guy, *The Failure of the Middle East Peace Process: A Comparative Analysis of Peace Implementation in Israel/Palestine, Northern Ireland and South Africa* (Houndmills: Palgrave Macmillan, 2008).

Bentsur, Eytan, *Making Peace: A First-Hand Account of the Arab-Israeli Peace Process* (Westport: Praeger, 2001).

Bercovitch, Jacob, 'International Mediation', *Journal of Peace Research*, 28(1) (1991): 3–6.

Bercovitch, Jacob (ed.), *Resolving International Conflicts: The Theory and Practice of Mediation* (Boulder, CO: Lynne Rienner, 1996).

Bercovitch, Jacob (ed.), *Studies in International Mediation* (Basingstoke: Palgrave Macmillan, 2002).

Bercovitch, Jacob, J. Theodore Anagnoson, and Donnette L. Wille, 'Some Conceptual Issues and Empirical Trends in the Study of Successful Mediation in International Relations', *Journal of Peace Research*, 28(1) (1991): 7–17.

Bercovitch, Jacob, and Scott S. Gartner, 'Is There Method in the Madness of Mediation? Some Lessons for Mediators from Quantitative Studies of Mediation', *International Interactions*, 32(4) (2006): 329–354.

Bercovitch, Jacob, and Scott S. Gartner (eds.), *International Conflict Mediation: New Approaches and Findings* (London: Routledge, 2009).

Bercovitch, Jacob, and Allison Houston, 'Why Do They Do It Like This? An Analysis of the Factors Influencing Mediation Behavior in International Conflicts', *Journal of Conflict Resolution*, 44 (2000): 170–202.

Bercovitch, Jacob, Victor Kremenyuk, and I. William Zartman (eds.), *The Sage Handbook of Conflict Resolution* (London: Sage Publications, 2009).

Bercovitch, Jacob, and Jeffrey Z. Rubin (eds.), *Mediation in International Relations: Multiple Approaches to Conflict Management* (London: Macmillan Press, 1994).

Bin-Talal, Hassan, *Palestinian Self-Determination* (New York: Quartet Books, 1981).

Birnbaum, Ben, 'The End of the Two-State Solution: Why the Window Is Closing on Middle-East Peace', *The New Republic* (11 March 2013), www.newrepublic.com/article/112617/israel-palestine-and-end-two-state-solution#

Blair, Tony, *On Leadership: Lessons for the 21st Century* (London: Hutchinson Heinemann, 2024).

Bocco, Riccardo, and Nigel Roberts, *An Israeli/Palestinian Federation: An Alternative Approach to Peace* (Geneva: Geneva Graduate Institute, November 2024).

Boulos, Sonia, and Xavier Abu Eid, 'Recognizing Palestinian Statehood; Some Critical Comments', *Security Context* (25 April 2024), www.securityincontext.org/posts/recognizing-palestinian-statehood-some-critical-comments

Boutros-Gali, Boutros, *Egypt's Road to Jerusalem* (New York: Random House, 1997).

Bowling, Daniel, and David H. Hoffman, 'Bringing Peace into the Room: The Personal Qualities of the Mediator and Their Impact on the Mediation', *Negotiation Journal*, 16(1) (January 2000): 5–28.

Bowling, Daniel, and David H. Hoffman (eds.), *Bringing Peace into the Room* (San Francisco: Jossey-Bass, 2003).

Breger, Marshall J., Yitzhak Reiter, and Leonard Hammer (eds.), *Holy Places in the Israeli-Palestinian Conflict: Confrontation and Co-existence* (London: Routledge, 2010).

Bregman, Ahron, *Elusive Peace* (London: Penguin, 2005).

Brenner, Bjorn, *Gaza Under Hamas* (London: I.B. Tauris, 2022).

Brockopp, Jonathan E., *'Justice and Injustice', Encyclopaedia of the Qur'ān Online* (Leiden: Brill, 2018).

Bronner, Ethan, 'Olmert Memoir Cites Near Deal for Mideast Peace', *The New York Times* (27 January 2011).

Brown, Nathan J., *Palestinian Politics after the Oslo Accords* (Berkeley: University of California Press, 2003).

Brundtland, Gro Harlem, 'Former Premier of Norway Reflects on Oslo Accords 20 Years Later', *Al Monitor* (8 September 2013), www.al-monitor.com/pulse/originals/2013/09/elders-oslo-anniversary-20-peace.html

Buchanan, Andrew S., *Peace with Justice* (Houndmills: Palgrave Macmillan, 2000).

Budd, Eric N., *Conflicted are the Peacemakers* (New York: Bloomsbury, 2013).

Burns, William J., *The Back Channel: A Memoir of American Diplomacy and the Case for Its Renewal* (New York: Random House, 2019).

Burton, J., and F. Dukes, *Conflict: Practices, Settlement, and Resolution* (London: Macmillan, 1990).

Calvo, Michael A. *The Middle East and World War III: Why No Peace?* (CreateSpace Independent Publishing Platform, 2017).

Caplan, Neil, *The Israel-Palestine Conflict: Contested Histories* (Chichester: Wiley-Blackwell, 2010).

Carter, April, *Direct Action and Liberal Democracy* (London: Routledge & Kegan Paul, 1973).

Carter, Jimmy, *Keeping Faith: Memoirs of a President* (London: Collins, 1982).

Caspersen, Nina, *Peace Agreements* (Cambridge: Polity Press, 2017).

Caspit, Ben, *The Netanyahu Years* (New York: Thomas Dunne Books, 2017).

Chaitin, Julia, *Peace-Building in Israel and Palestine* (Houndmills: Palgrave, 2011).

Christopher, Warren, *In the Stream of History: Shaping Foreign Policy for a New Era* (Stanford, CA: Stanford University Press, 1998).

Claudet, Sophie, 'Camp David, One Year Later: Old Myths and New', *Jerusalem Quarterly*, 13 (Summer 2001), www.palestine-studies.org/en/node/78058

Clinton, Bill, 'Proposals for a Final Settlement', *Journal of Palestine Studies*, 30(3) (Spring 2001): 171–173.

Clinton, Bill, *My Life* (New York: Knopf, 2010).

Clinton Parameters, 'Clinton Proposal on Israeli-Palestinian Peace', *White House* (23 December 2000), https://ecf.org.il/media_items/568

Cofman Wittes, Tamara (ed.), *How Israelis and Palestinians Negotiate* (Washington, DC: US Institute of Peace Press, 2005).

Cohen, Roger, 'The Success that Failed', *The New York Times* (14 February 2013).

Cohen-Almagor, Raphael, 'The Intifada: Causes, Consequences, and Future Trends', *Small Wars & Insurgencies*, 2(1) (1991): 12–40.

Cohen-Almagor, Raphael, *The Boundaries of Liberty and Tolerance* (Gainesville, FL: The University Press of Florida, 1994).

Cohen-Almagor, Raphael, 'Disqualification of Lists in Israel (1948–1984): Retrospect and Appraisal', *Law and Philosophy*, 13(1) (1994): 43–95.

Cohen-Almagor, Raphael, 'Administrative Detention in Israel and Its Employment as a Means of Combating Political Extremism', *New York International Law Review*, 9(2) (1996): 1–25.

Cohen-Almagor, Raphael, 'Disqualification of Political Parties in Israel: 1988–1996', *Emory International Law Review*, 11(1) (1997): 67–109.

Cohen-Almagor, Raphael (ed.), *Liberal Democracy and the Limits of Tolerance: Essays in Honor and Memory of Yitzhak Rabin* (Ann Arbor: University of Michigan Press, 2000).

Cohen-Almagor, Raphael, *Speech, Media, and Ethics: The Limits of Free Expression* (Houndmills and New York: Palgrave-Macmillan, 2001, 2005).

Cohen-Almagor, Raphael, *The Scope of Tolerance: Studies on the Costs of Free Expression and Freedom of the Press* (London and New York: Routledge, 2006).

Cohen-Almagor, Raphael, 'Political Extremism and Incitement in Israel 1993–1995, 2003–2005: A Study of Dangerous Expressions', *Democracy and Security*, 3(1) (2007): 21–43.

Cohen-Almagor, Raphael, 'The Failed Peace Process in the Middle East 1993–2011', *Israel Affairs*, 18(4) (October 2012): 563–576.

Cohen-Almagor, Raphael, 'Two-State Solution – The Way Forward', *Annual Review of Law and Ethics*, 20 (2012): 381–395.

Cohen-Almagor, Raphael, *Confronting the Internet's Dark Side: Moral and Social Responsibility on the Free Highway* (New York and Washington, DC: Cambridge University Press and Woodrow Wilson Center Press, 2015).

Cohen-Almagor, Raphael, 'Parameters for Two State Solution', *Palestine-Israel Journal*, 21(2) (2015): 112–119.

Cohen-Almagor, Raphael, 'Fifty Years of Israeli Occupation', *E-International Relations* (14 October 2017), www.e-ir.info/2017/10/14/fifty-years-of-israeli-occupation/

Cohen-Almagor, Raphael, 'President Trump and the Israeli-Palestinian Conflict', *E-International Relations* (10 March 2017), www.e-ir.info/2017/03/10/president-trump-and-the-israeli-palestinian-conflict/

Cohen-Almagor, Raphael, 'In Support of Two-State Solution', *Youth Law Journal* (12 November 2018), www.theylj.co.uk/in-support-of-two-state-solution/

Cohen-Almagor, Raphael, 'The Oslo Peace Process: Interview with Joel Singer', *Israel Affairs*, 24(5) (2018): 733–766.

Cohen-Almagor, Raphael, 'Interview with Former Head of Mossad Shabtai Shavit', *Fathom* (January 2019), https://tinyurl.com/bdhtb6xe

Cohen-Almagor, Raphael, 'Israel-PLO Peace Process: Interview with Ambassador Daniel Kurtzer', *Israel Studies*, 24(3) (2019): 127–156.

Cohen-Almagor, Raphael, 'Keys for Peace in the Middle East: Interview with Ambassador Itamar Rabinovich', *Israel Affairs*, 25(4) (2019): 699–725.

Cohen-Almagor, Raphael, 'Lessons from the Israeli-Egyptian Peace Talks: An Interview with Aharon Barak', *Israel Studies Review*, 34(2) (Autumn 2019): 1–32.

Cohen-Almagor, Raphael, 'Coercion', *Open Journal of Philosophy*, 11(3) (August 2021): 386–409. www.scirp.org/journal/paperinformation.aspx?paperid=111463

Cohen-Almagor, Raphael, 'Genuine, Principled and Tactical Compromise', *Studia Iuridica Lublinensia*, 30(2) (2021): 11–31.

Cohen-Almagor, Raphael, 'History of Track II Peace Negotiations: Interview with Hussein Agha', *Israel Studies*, 26(1) (2021): 47–72.

Cohen-Almagor, Raphael, *Just, Reasonable Multiculturalism: Liberalism, Culture and Coercion* (New York and Cambridge: Cambridge University Press, 2021).

Cohen-Almagor, Raphael, 'Lessons from Peace Negotiations: Interview with Ehud Olmert', *Israel Affairs*, 27(6) (2021): 1160–1189.

Cohen-Almagor, Raphael, 'Stockholm and the Israeli-Palestinian Peace Process – An Interview with State Secretary for Foreign Affairs Annika Söder', *Israel Affairs*, 27(4) (2021): 732–749.

Cohen-Almagor, Raphael, 'Israeli-Palestinian Negotiations through the Eyes of Gamal Helal', *Israel Journal of Foreign Affairs*, 17(2) (2023): 159–174.

Cohen-Almagor, Raphael, 'The Pursuit of Peace with the Palestinians: Interviews with Ehud Barak', *Israel Affairs*, 29(2) (2023): 385–450.

Cohen-Almagor, Raphael, 'The Role of the Arab World in the Palestinian-Israeli Conflict: Interview with Marwan Muasher', *Israel Affairs*, 29(5) (2023): 864–894.

Cohen-Almagor, Raphael, 'Analysis of the PLO and Hamas: Interview with Sir John Jenkins', *International Dialogue*, 14, Article 3 (2024). https://digitalcommons.unomaha.edu/id-journal/vol14/iss1/3/

Cohen-Almagor, Raphael, 'Is Israel a Liberal Democracy?', *The Cairo Review of Global Affairs* (December 2024). www.thecairoreview.com/essays/is-israel-a-liberal-democracy/

Cohen-Almagor, Raphael, 'Thirty Years after the Oslo Peace Accords: Interviews with Joel Singer', *Israel Studies*, 29(2) (2024): 1–29.

Cohen-Almagor, Raphael, 'President Trump's Policies in the Middle East', *The Cairo Review of Global Affairs* (February 2025), www.thecairoreview.com/essays/president-trumps-policies/

Cohen-Almagor, Raphael, 'Resolving the Israeli-Palestinian Conflict', *The Cairo Review of Global Affairs* (Fall 2025), www.thecairoreview.com/essays/resolving-the-israeli-palestinian-conflict/

Cohen-Almagor, Raphael, and Sharon Haleva-Amir, 'The Israel-Hezbollah War and the Winograd Committee', *Journal of Parliamentary and Political Law*, II(1) (2008): 113–130. Reprinted in Athina Karatzogianni (ed.), *Violence and War* (Abingdon: Routledge, 2012): 171–187.

Cohen-Almagor, Raphael, and Mohammed S. Wattad, 'The Legal Status of Israeli-Arabs/Palestinians', *GNLU Law & Society Review*, 1 (March 2019): 1–28.

Corbin, Jane, *The Norway Channel: The Secret Talks that Led to the Middle East Peace Accord* (New York: Atlantic Monthly Press, 1994).

Council Conclusions on the ME Peace Process, 2009, https://tinyurl.com/cy4pt3ya

Crocker, C., F.O. Hampson & P. Aall (eds.), *Turbulent Peace: The Challenges of Managing International Conflict* (Washington, DC: The United States Institute of Peace Press, 2001).

Crocker, C., F.O. Hampson & P. Aall (eds.), *Leashing the Dogs of War: Conflict Management in a Divided World* (Washington, DC: USIP Press, 2007).

Cullen, Bob, 'Two Weeks at Camp David', *The Smithsonian* (September 2003), www.smithsonianmag.com/history/two-weeks-at-camp-david-88891073/

Czarny, Ryszard M., *Sweden: From Neutrality to International Solidarity* (New York: Springer, 2018).

Danin, Robert M., 'A Third Way to Palestine', *Foreign Affairs* (January-February 2011).

Darby, John, and Roger MacGinty (eds.), *The Management of Peace Processes* (New York and Basingstoke: Palgrave, 2000).

Das, Samir Kumar (ed.), *Peace Processes and Peace Accords* (New Delhi: Sage Publications, 2005), South Asian Peace Studies, Vol. 2.

Declaration of Principles on Interim Self-Government Arrangements, 13 September 1993, www.historycentral.com/Israel/documents/Oslo.html

Dixon, W. J., 'Third-Party Techniques for Preventing Conflict Escalation and Promoting Peaceful Settlement', *International Organization*, 50(4) (Autumn 1996): 653–681.

Djeredjian, Edward P., 'War and Peace: The Problems and Prospects of American Diplomacy in the Middle East', *U.S. Department of State Dispatch*, 4(51) (December 1993): 874–878.

Djeredjian, Edward P. et al., *Getting to the Territorial Endgame of an Israeli-Palestinian Peace Agreement*, A Special Report by the Israeli-Palestinian Workshop, the Baker Institute's Conflict Resolution Forum (Houston, TX: Rice University, 2010).

Dowty, Alan, *Israel/Palestine* (Cambridge: Polity Press, 2012).

Dror, Yehezkel, *Israeli Statecraft: National Security Challenges and Responses* (London and New York: Routledge, 2011).

Drori, Israel, and Chaim Weizmann, 'Prime Minister Yitzhak Rabin against the Settlers: A Stakeholder Analysis', *Public Administration Review*, 67(2) (March–April 2007): 302–314.

Drucker, Raviv, 'Olmert, Abu Mazen and Barak Refer to the Political Process', *HaMakor* (17 November 2015) (Hebrew).

Eban, Abba, *The New Diplomacy* (Tel Aviv: Yediot Aharonot, 1985) (Hebrew).

Eban, Abba, 'Prospects for Peace in the Middle East', *Landon Lecture* (29 January 1990), www.k-state.edu/landon/speakers/abba-eban/transcript.html

Echterhoff, Gerald, E. Tory Higgins, and John M. Levine, 'Shared Reality: Experiencing Commonality with Others' Inner States about the World', *Perspectives on Psychological Science*, 4 (2009): 496–521.

Echterhoff, Gerald, and E. Tory Higgins, 'How Communication Shapes Memory: Shared Reality and Implications for Culture', in Gun R. Semin and Gerald Echterhoff (ed.), *Grounding Sociality* (New York: Psychology Press, 2011): 115–146.

Egeland, Jan, *Impotent Superpower – Potent Small State* (Oslo: Norwegian University Press, 1988).

Egeland, Jan, *A Billion Lives* (New York: Simon & Schuster, 2008).

Eiland, Giora, *Rethinking the Two-State Solution, Policy Focus 88* (Washington, DC: The Washington Institute for Near East Policy, 2008).

Eizenstat, Stuart, *President Carter: The White House Years* (New York: Thomas Dunne Books, 2018).

Elchahabi, Samer, 'Shifting the Paradigm: The One-State Solution as a Path to Peace', *Arab Center* (14 December 2023), https://tinyurl.com/5dupx67x

El-Sadat, Anwar, *In Search of Identity* (London: Collins, 1978).

Emerson, Steven, 'Hamas, the PLO, and Terrorist Attacks Against Israel', United States House of Representatives, House International Relations Committee (12 March 1996), www.investigativeproject.org/documents/testimony/5.pdf

Emling, Shelley, *A Forgotten Hero* (Toronto: ECW Press, 2019).

Enderlin, Charles, *Shattered Dreams: The Failure of the Peace Process in the Middle East, 1995–2002* (New York: Other Press, 2003).

Enderlin, Charles, *The Lost Years* (New York: Other Press, 2007).

Erekat, Saeb, 'Bush Took My Job by Siding with Sharon', *Gulf News* (28 April 2004), https://tinyurl.com/2py926nj

Eriksson, Jacob, *Swedish Mediation of the Israeli-Palestinian Conflict: A Study of the Utility of Small-State Mediation and Track II Diplomacy*, Thesis submitted for the degree of Ph.D. (Department of Languages and Cultures of the Near and Middle East, School of Oriental and African Studies, University of London, 2011).

Eriksson, Jacob, *Small-State Mediation in International Conflicts: Diplomacy and Negotiation in Israel-Palestine* (London: I.B. Tauris, 2015).

Eriksson, Jacob, 'Coercion and Third-party Mediation of Identity-based Conflict', *Review of International Studies*, 45(3) (2019): 387–406. doi:10.1017/S0260210518000566

Eshtawi, Mahmud, and Avi Issacharoff, "At Fatah congress, Rajoub – and Abbas – walk away with big wins", *Times of Israel* (4 December 2016), http://www.timesofisrael.com/at-fatah-congress-rajoub-and-abbas-walk-away-with-big-wins/

Evans, Mark (ed.), *Just War Theory* (Edinburgh: Edinburgh University Press, 2005).

Farrell, Witham E., 'An Interview with Israel's Controversial Moshe Dayan', *The New York Times* (5 June 1977), https://tinyurl.com/5ertjta6

Fisher, Roger, and William Ury, *Getting to Yes: Negotiating Agreement without Giving In* (London: Random House, 1991).

Fixdal, Mona, *Just Peace. How Wars Should End* (Houndmills: Palgrave, 2012).

Fixdal, Mona (ed.), *Ways Out of War: Peacemakers in the Middle East and the Balkans* (Houndmills: Palgrave, 2012).

Framework Agreement for Permanent Status, Discussion Draft, 20 May 2000, Harpsund, Sweden, www.brookings.edu/wp-content/uploads/2016/07/Appendix-Z.pdf

Frankel, G. Ernst, 'Prefabricated and Relocatable Artificial Island Technology', in *Macro-Engineering: Mit Brunel Lectures on Global Infrastructure*, Woodhead Publishing Series in Civil and Structural Engineering (Woodhead Publishing Limited, 1997): 155–173. www.sciencedirect.com/science/article/pii/B9781898563334500124

Freilich, Charles D., *Israel National Security* (New York: Oxford University Press, 2018).

Friedman, Thomas L., 'An Intriguing Signal from the Saudi Crown Prince', *The New York Times* (17 February 2002).

From Oslo to Camp David to Taba: Setting the Record Straight, Featuring Dennis Ross, Margaret Warner, and Jim Hoagland, The Washington Institute for Near East Policy Forum (8 August 2001).

Frowe, Helen, *The Ethics of War and Peace* (London: Routledge, 2011).

Gavison, Ruth (ed.), *The Two-State Solution* (New York and London: Bloomsbury, 2013).

Gazit, Mordechai, *Israeli Diplomacy and the Quest for Peace* (Israeli History, Politics and Society) (London: Routledge, 2002).

Gelvin, James, *The Israel-Palestine Conflict: One Hundred Years of War* [Paperback] (New York: Cambridge University Press, 2013).

Geneva Accord: A Model Israeli-Palestinian Peace Agreement (Basel: Geneva Accord, 2004).

Giacaman, George, and Dag Jorund Lonning (eds.), *After Oslo: New Realities, Old Problems* (London and Chicago: Pluto Press, 1998).

Gil, Avi, *The Peres Formula* (Modi'ín: Kinneret, Zmora-Bitan, 2018) (Hebrew).

Gil, Avi, *Shimon Peres* (London: I.B. Tauris, 2021).

Gilman, James E., *How to Resolve Conflict* (Lanham, MD: Rowan and Littlefield, 2017).

Golan, Galia, *Israeli Peacemaking since 1967* (London: Routledge, 2015).

Golan, Galia, 'The Israeli-Palestinian Conflict: Lessons for a Breakthrough', *Middle East Policy*, XXII/3 (2015): 100–108.

Golan, Gaila, and Gilead Sher, *Spoiling and Coping with Spoilers: Israeli-Arab Negotiations* (Indiana: Indiana University Press, 2019).

Goldman, Micah, 'Eight Steps to Shrink the Israeli-Palestinian Conflict', *The Atlantic* (1 April 2019), https://tinyurl.com/3x8pn67z

Grinstein, Gidi, and Ari Afilalo, *(In)Sights: Peacemaking in the Oslo Process Thirty Years and Counting* (Jerusalem: Gefen, 2023).

Guiora, Amos N., 'Negotiating Implementation of a Peace Agreement: Lessons Learned from Five Years at the Negotiating Table', *Cardozo Journal of Conflict Resolution*, 11 (2010): 411–436.

Gunn, Jane, *The Authority Guide to Conflict Resolution*. The Authority Guides; Illustrated edn. (London: SRA Books, 2017).

Guyatt, Nicholas, *The Absence of Peace* (London: Zed Books, 1998).

Haass, Richard, 'Ripeness and the Settlement of International Disputes', *Survival*, 30(3) (1988): 232–251.

Haberman, Clyde, 'Rabin Renews Denunciation of Settlers as "Burden"', *The New York Times* (28 January 1995), https://tinyurl.com/2bupzuu6

Halevi, Jonathan D., 'The Palestinian Authority's Responsibility for the Outbreak of the Second Intifada: Its Own Damning Testimony', *Jerusalem Viewpoints*, (594) (March-April 2013): 1–14.

Halperin-Kaddari, Ruth, Nava Ben-Or, and Sharon Zagagi-Pinhas, *A Quest for Justice* (Jerusalem: The Dinah Project, 2025).

Hammer, Joshua, 'What is Beneath the Temple Mount?', *Smithsonian Magazine* (April 2011), www.smithsonianmag.com/history/what-is-beneath-the-temple-mount-920764/

Handelman, Sapir, *Conflict and Peacemaking in Israel-Palestine: Theory and Application* (London: Routledge, 2014).

Hanieh, Akram, 'The Camp David Papers', *Journal of Palestine Studies*, 30(2) (Winter 2001): 75–97.

'Haram al-Sharif', *Encyclopedia of the Modern Middle East and North Africa, Encyclopedia.com* (25 May 2018), https://tinyurl.com/37uateff

Harel, Amos, and Avi Issacharoff, *34 Days: Israel, Hezbollah, and the War in Lebanon: The Second War in Lebanon* (Houndmills and New York: Palgrave Macmillan, 2008).

Haydar, Bashshar, 'The Ethics of Fighting Terror and the Priority of Citizens', *Journal of Military Ethics* 4(1) (2005): 52–59.

Hermann, Tamar, *The Israeli Peace Movement: A Shattered Dream* (Cambridge: Cambridge University Press, 2009).

Hirsch-Hoefler, Sivan, and Cas Mudde, *The Israeli Settler Movement: Assessing and Explaining Social Movement Success* (Cambridge: Cambridge University Press, 2021).

Hirschfeld, Yair, *Track-Two Diplomacy toward an Israeli-Palestinian Solution 1978–2014* (Washington, DC: Woodrow Wilson Center Press and Johns Hopkins University Press, 2014).

Hirschfeld, Yair, *The Israeli-Palestinian Peace Process* (Cham: Springer, 2024).

Holst, Johan Jorgen, 'Reflections on the Makings of a Tenuous Peace', *Brown Journal of World Affairs*, 1(2) (Spring 1994): 1–16.

Hotwani, Mehul, and Priyanka Rastogi, 'Future Possibility of Artificial Islands', *International Journal of Engineering Research & Technology (IJERT)*, 10(1) (January 2021): 583–585.

Huda, Qamar-ul (ed.), *Crescent and Dove: Peace and Conflict Resolution in Islam* (Washington, DC: United States Institute of Peace Press, 2010).

Human Rights Watch, 'Israel and Palestine', *World Report 2023*, www.hrw.org/world-report/2022/country-chapters/israel-and-palestine-0

Human Rights Watch, 'I Can't Erase All the Blood from My Mind' (17 July 2024), hrw.org/report/2024/07/17/i-cant-erase-all-blood-my-mind/palestinian-armed-groups-october-7-assault-israel

Hussein-Peres Agreement (London Document), 11 April 1987, https://tinyurl.com/26mra67b

Husseini, Hiba, and Yossi Beilin, 'An Israeli-Palestinian Confederation Is the Best Path to Peace', *Foreign Policy* (23 May 2022), https://foreignpolicy.com/2022/05/23/israeli-palestinian-confederation-peace/

Ibish, Hussein, 'Obama's Second Term: Two Views on the Peace Process – View Two', *Fathom*, 3 (Summer 2013).

Ibish, Hussein, Interview with Jeffrey Goldberg in *The Atlantic* (3 November 2009).

Irfan, Anne, 'Whose Agency? UNRWA and the Palestinian Refugees in History', in Pietro Stefanini (ed.), *UNRWA at 70: Palestinian Refugees in Context* (London: Palestinian Return Centre, 2020): 21–29.

Inbari, Motti, 'Religious Zionism and the Temple Mount Dilemma – Key Trends', *Israel Studies*, 12(2) (2007): 29–47.

Inbari, Mordechai (Motti), 'The Role of the Temple Mount Faithful Movement in Changing Messianic Religious Zionists' Attitude toward the Temple Mount', in Leonard J. Greenspoon (ed.), *Next Year in Jerusalem: Exile and Return in Jewish History* (West Lafayette, IN: Purdue University Press, 2019): 247–264.

Indyk, Martin, *Innocent Abroad* (New York: Simon & Schuster, 2009).

Indyk, Martin, *Master of the Game: Henry Kissinger and the Art of Middle East Diplomacy* (New York: Knopf, 2022).

'International Arbitration on Taba Border Dispute Begins in Geneva', *Jewish Telegraphic Agency (JTA)* (11 December 1986), https://tinyurl.com/3czv5s6c

Ish-Shalom, Piki, *Democratic Peace: A Political Biography* (Ann Arbor: University of Michigan Press, 2013).

Israeli Ministry of Foreign Affairs, 'Fatal Terrorist Attacks in Israel (Sept 1993–1999)', *Foreign Policy* (24 September 2000), https://tinyurl.com/4dnp6ez5

Israeli Ministry of Foreign Affairs, '200 Israel Government White Paper regarding Palestinian Non-Compliance with Their Commitments and Agreements', *Israel Government White Paper* (20 November 2000), https://tinyurl.com/mpk8saye

Israeli Ministry of Foreign Affairs, 'Israeli Position on Three Main Points at Taba Talks' (21 January 2001). www.gov.il/en/pages/israeli-position-on-three-main-points-at-taba-talks-21-jan-2001

Issacharoff, Avi, 'EXCLUSIVE: Olmert: "I Am Still Waiting for Abbas to Call"', *The Tower* (24 May 2013), https://tinyurl.com/2r4a67ww

Jackson, Richard, 'Successful Negotiation in International Violent Conflict', *Journal of Peace Research*, 37(3) (2000): 323–343.

Jebsen, Anniken Haugen, *Why Norway? Norway's Involvement in the Middle East Prior to the Secret Oslo Channel 1948–1993* (Ph.D. diss., London School of Economics and Political Science, 1997).

Jerusalem Old City Initiative, *Proposals for the Old City of Jerusalem* (Windsor: University of Windsor, 2010).

Jones, Deiniol Lloyd, *Cosmopolitan Mediation* (Manchester: Manchester University Press, 1999).

Jones, Clive, and Tore T. Petersen (eds.), *Israel's Clandestine Diplomacies* (Oxford: Oxford University Press, 2013).

Jones, Peter, *Track Two Diplomacy in Theory and Practice* (Stanford: Stanford University Press, 2015).

Johnston, Wm. Robert, Chronology of Terrorist Attacks in Israel, Part IV: 1993–2000, last updated 18 May 2013, www.johnstonsarchive.net/terrorism/terrisrael-4.html

Kacowicz, Arie, 'Rashomon in the Middle East: Clashing Narratives, Images, and Frames in the Israeli-Palestinian Conflict', *Cooperation & Conflict*, 40(3) (2005): 343–360.

Kacowicz, Arie, 'Rashomon in Jerusalem: Mapping the Israeli Negotiators' Positions on the Israeli-Palestinian Peace Process, 1993–2001', *International Studies Perspectives*, 6 (2005): 252–273.

Kahneman, Daniel, and Amos Tversky, 'Conflict Resolution: A Cognitive Perspective', in Kenneth Arrow, Robert H. Mnookin, Lee Ross, Amos Tversky, and Robert Wilson (eds.), *Barriers to Conflict Resolution* (New York: W.W. Norton & Company, 1995): 45–60.

Kamel, Mohamed Ibrahim, *The Camp David Accords: A Testimony* (Abingdon: Routledge, 1986).

Kant, Immanuel, *Political Writings* (Cambridge: Cambridge University Press, 1991), 2nd ed., by H. S. Reiss (ed.).

Kant, Immanuel, *Toward Perpetual Peace* (Jonathan Bennett electronic ed., 2017).

Karsh, Efraim, *Arafat's War: The Man and His Battle for Israeli Conquest* (New York: Grove, 2003).

Karsh, Efraim, *The San Remo Conference 100 Years On: How the Jewish National Home Entered International Law*, Mideast Security and Policy Studies No. 172 (Ramat Gan: The Begin-Sadat Center for Strategic Studies, 2020).

Katz, Neil H., Nekeisha G. Bascombe, and Peter Tokar, 'Illuminating Interviews: Insights into the Hearts and Minds of Conflict Resolution Practitioners', *Conflict Resolution Quarterly*, 36 (2019): 345–371.

Kellerman, B. & Rubin, J. Z. (eds.), *Leadership and Negotiation in the Middle East* (London: Praeger, 1988).

Kelman, Herbert C., 'The Political Psychology of the Israeli-Palestinian Conflict: How Can We Overcome the Barriers to a Negotiated Solution?', *Political Psychology*, 8(3) (1987): 347–363.

Kelman, Herbert C., 'Acknowledging the Other's Nationhood: How to Create a Momentum for the Israeli-Palestinian Negotiations', *Journal of Palestine Studies*, 22(1) (Autumn 1992): 18–38.

Kelman, Herbert C., 'Contributions of an Unofficial Conflict Resolution Effort to the Israeli- Palestinian Breakthrough', *Negotiation Journal*, 11(1) (1995): 19–27.

Kelman, Herbert C., 'Some Determinants of the Oslo Breakthrough', *International Negotiation*, 2 (1997): 183–194.

Kelman, Herbert C., 'The Israeli–Palestinian Peace Process and Its Vicissitudes', *American Psychologist*, 62(4) (May–June 2007): 287–303.

Kelman, Herbert C., *Resolving Deep-Rooted Conflicts* (London: Routledge, 2020).

Kelman, Herbert C., Philip Mattar, and Neil Caplan, *Transforming the Israeli-Palestinian Conflict: From Mutual Negation to Reconciliation* (London: Routledge, 2018).

Kerry, John, *Every Day Is Extra* (London: Simon & Schuster, 2018).

Khalidi, Rashid, *The Iron Cage: The Story of the Struggle for Palestinian Statehood* (London: Oneworld Publications, 2007).

Khalidi, Rashid, *Palestinian Identity: The Construction of Modern National Consciousness* (New York: Columbia University Press, 2009).

Khalidi, Walid, *Brokers of Deceit: How the U.S. Has Undermined Peace in the Middle East* (New York: Beacon Press, 2013).

Khouri, Rami G., 'The Arab-Israeli Peace Process: Lessons from the Five Years since Oslo', *Security Dialogue*, 29(3) (1998): 333–344.

Kimhi, Shaul, Shmuel Even, and Jerrold Post, *Yasir Arafat: Psychological Profile and Strategic Analysis* (Herzliya: The Interdisciplinary Center, 2002).

Kimhi, Shaul, and Shmuel Even, 'Yassir Arafat: Behavioral and Strategic Analysis', *Social Behavior and Personality*, 31(4) (2003): 363–374.

Kimmerling, Baruch, and Joel S. Migdal. *The Palestinian People: A History* (Cambridge, MA: Harvard University Press, 2003).

King Hussein's plan for a Federation (15 March 1972). https://content.ecf.org.il/files/M00182_TheUnitedArabRepublicPlan-EnglishText.pdf

King, Mary Elizabeth, *A Quiet Revolution: The First Palestinian Intifada and Nonviolent Resistance* (New York: Nation Books, 2007).

King, Nigel, Christine Horrocks, and Joanna Brooks, *Interviews in Qualitative Research* (London: Sage Publications, 2019).

Kissinger, Henry, *Leadership: Six Studies in World Strategy* (Milton Keynes: Allen Lane, 2022).

Kleiboer, Marieke, 'Understanding Success and Failure of International Mediation', *Journal of Conflict Resolution*, 40(2) (1996): 360–389.

Klein, Menachem, *The Jerusalem Problem: The Struggle for Permanent Status* (Gainesville, FL: University Press of Florida, 2003).

Klein, Menachem, *Arafat and Abbas: Portraits of Leaders* (London: Hurst, 2019).

Klimesova, Martina, *Using Carrots to Bring Peace?: Negotiation and Third Party Involvement* (Singapore: World Scientific, 2016).

Knudsen, Are, and Sari Hanaf (eds.), *Palestinian Refugees: Identity, Space and Place in the Levant* (London: Routledge Studies on the Arab-Israeli Conflict, 2010).

Kresel, Morag M., 'Fractured Oversight: The ABCs of Cultural Heritage in Palestine after the Oslo Accords', *Journal of Social Archeology*, 15(1) (January 2014): 24–44.

Kruglanski, A. W., M. Ellenberg, E. Szumowska et al., 'Frustration-Aggression Hypothesis Reconsidered: The Role of Significance Quest', *Aggressive Behavior*, 49(5) (2023): 445–468.

Kruglanski, Arie W., and Joel Singer, 'The Israeli-Palestinian Deadly Struggle for Significance', *Psychology Today* (17 June 2024), https://tinyurl.com/4whee58j

Kurtzer, Daniel C., *Negotiating Arab-Israeli Peace: American Leadership in the Middle East* (Washington, DC: United States Institute of Peace Press, 2008).

Kurtzer, Daniel C., (ed.), *Pathways to Peace: America and the Arab-Israeli Conflict* (Houndmills and New York: Palgrave Macmillan, 2012).

Kurtzer, Daniel, and Rosemary Hollis, 'An Arab Initiative that Can Work', *International Herald Tribune* (21 March 2007). www.nytimes.com/2007/03/21/opinion/21iht-edhollis.4978404.html?_r=0

Kurtzer, Daniel C., Scott B. Lasensky, William B. Quandt et al., *The Peace Puzzle: America's Quest for Arab-Israeli Peace, 1989–2011* (Ithaca and Washington, DC: Cornell University Press, in Collaboration with the United States Institute of Peace, 2013).

Kushner, Jared, *Breaking History: A White House Memoir* (New York: Broadside Books, 2022).

Lasswell, Harold D., 'The Garrison State', *The American Journal of Sociology*, XLVI (January 1941).

Lavie, Ephraim (ed.), *Israel and the Arab Peace Initiative* (Tel Aviv: Tel Aviv University, 2010) (Hebrew).

Leal, Bento C. III, *Four Essential Keys to Effective Communication* (n.p.: Bento Leal, 2017).
Lehrs, Lior, *Unofficial Peace Diplomacy: Private Peace Entrepreneurs in Conflict Resolution Processes* (Manchester: Manchester University Press, 2022).
Lehti, Marko (ed.), *Nordic Approaches to Peace Mediation* (Tampere: Peace Research Institute TAPRI, 2014). Series No 10, Research Paper No. 101.
Levitan, Nir, *Scandinavian Diplomacy and the Israeli-Palestinian Conflict* (London: Routledge, 2023).
Levitt, Matthew, *Hamas* (New Haven: Yale University Press, 2006).
Luban, David, 'War as Punishment', *Philosophy & Public Affairs*, 39(4) (2012): 299–330.
Makover-Blikov, Sari, 'Architect of the Oslo Accords: "Alone in yearning for peace"'. *NRG* (17 August 2013) (Hebrew), www.makorrishon.co.il/nrg/online/1/ART2/499/557.html
Makovsky, David, *Making Peace with The PLO: The Rabin Government's Road to The Oslo Accord* (Boulder, CO: Westview, 1996).
Malley, Robert, and Hussein Agha, 'Camp David: The Tragedy of Errors', *New York Review of Books* (9 August 2001).
Malley, Robert, and Hussein Agha, 'A Reply to Ehud Barak', *New York Review of Books*, XLIX(10) (13 June 2002).
Mandell, Brian S., and Brian W. Tomlin, 'Mediation in the Development of Norms to Manage Conflict: Kissinger in the Middle East', *Journal of Peace Research*, 28(1) (1991): 43–55.
Mangini, Michele, 'Toward a Theory of Reasonableness', *Ratio Juris*, 31(2) (2018): 208–230.
Markus, Joel, *Camp David: Window for Peace* (Tel Aviv: Schocken, 1979) (Hebrew).
Mason, Simon J. A., and Damiano Angelo Sguaitamatti, *Mapping Mediators: A Comparison of Third Parties and Implications for Switzerland* (Zurich: Swiss Federal Institute of Technology, 2011).
Matthews, Elizabeth G. (ed.), *The Israel-Palestine Conflict* (London: Routledge, 2011).
McMahan, Jeff, 'The Ethics of Killing in War', *Ethics*, 114 (2004): 693–733.
McMahan, Jeff, 'Liability and Collective Identity: A Response to Walzer', *Philosophia*, 34 (2006): 13–17.
McMahan, Jeff, *Killing in War* (New York: Oxford University Press, 2009).
McMahan, Jeff, 'The Just Distribution of Harm between Combatants and Noncombatants', *Philosophy and Public Affairs*, 38(4) (2010): 342–379.
Meridor, Dan, *Camp David 2000* (Hebrew).
Meridor, Dan, 'Camp David Diaries', *Haaretz* (29 July 2011) (Hebrew).
Michael, Kobi, *Arab Peace Initiative – Is It A Historical Opportunity?* (Jerusalem: Jerusalem Institute for Israel Studies, 2007) (Hebrew).
Midgley, Gerald, and Luis A. Pinzón, 'Systemic Mediation: Moral Reasoning and Boundaries of Concern', *Systems Research and Behavioral Science*, 30 (2013): 607–632.

Miller, Aaron David, *The Much Too Promised Land: America's Elusive Search for Arab-Israeli Peace* (New York: Bantam, 2008).

Miller, Aaron David, 'How Not to Host a Summit', *Foreign Policy* (10 July 2012).

Miller, Aaron David, 'Memorandum to the President: Thinking through an Israel-Palestinian Initiative', in Daniel C. Kurtzer (ed.), *Pathways to Peace* (New York: Palgrave-Macmillan, 2012): 135–155.

Miller, Zinaida, 'Perils of Parity: Palestine's Permanent Transition', *Cornell International Law Journal*, 47 (2014): 331–415.

Mitchell, George J., *The Negotiator: A Memoir* (New York: Simon & Schuster, 2015).

Mitchell, George J., *A Path to Peace: A Brief History of Israeli-Palestinian Negotiations and a Way Forward in the Middle East* (New York: Simon & Schuster, 2016).

Mitchell, George J., et al., 'The Mitchell Report Sharm el-Sheikh Fact Finding Committee' (8 May 2001). *Israel Ministry of Foreign Affairs*, Jerusalem.

Mnookin, Robert H., *Bargaining with the Devil* (New York: Simon & Schuster, 2011).

Mnookin, Robert H., Ehud Eiran, and Shula Gilad, 'Is Unilateralism Always Bad? Negotiation Lessons from Israel's "Unilateral" Gaza Withdrawal', *Negotiation Journal*, 30(2) (April 2014): 131–156.

Moolakkattu, John Stephen, 'Peace Facilitation by Small States: Norway in Sri Lanka', *Cooperation and Conflict*, 40(4) (2005): 385–402.

Morag, Nadav, 'Unambiguous Ambiguity: The Opacity of the Oslo Peace Process', *Israel Affairs*, 6(3/4) (2000): 200–220.

Mordechai, Yitzhak, *For My People and for My Country* (Rishon LeZion: Yedioth Ahronoth, 2022) (Hebrew).

Morris, Benny, *The Birth of the Palestinian Refugee Problem, 1947–1949* (Cambridge: Cambridge University Press, 1987).

Morris, Benny, *1948 and After* (Oxford: Clarendon Press, 1994).

Morris, Benny, *Israel's Border Wars, 1949–1956: Arab Infiltration, Israeli Retaliation, and the Countdown to the Suez War* (Oxford: Oxford University Press, 1997).

Morris, Benny, *Righteous Victims: A History of the Zionist-Arab Conflict, 1881–2001* (New York: Vintage, 2001).

Morris, Benny, 'An Interview with Ehud Barak', *New York Review of Books*, XLIX(10) (13 June 2002).

Morris, Benny, *1948: A History of the First Arab-Israeli War* (New Haven: Yale University Press, 2009).

Morris, Benny, *One State, Two States: Resolving the Israel/Palestine Conflict* (New Haven: Yale University Press, 2010).

Muasher, Marwan, *The Arab Center: The Promise of Moderation* (New Haven: Yale University Press, 2008).

Netanyahu, Benjamin (ed.), *Terrorism: How The West Can Win* (New York: Farrar, Straus, Giroux, 1986).

Netanyahu, Benjamin, *A Place among the Nations: Israel and the World* (New York: Bantam Press, 1993).

Netanyahu, Benjamin, *Address at Bar-Ilan University*, https://tinyurl.com/47kxk6c2

Neuman, Tamara, *Settling Hebron: Jewish Fundamentalism in a Palestinian City* (Philadelphia: University of Pennsylvania Press, 2018).

Nitzan-Shiftan, Alona, *Seizing Jerusalem: The Architecture of Unilateral Unification* (Minneapolis: University of Minnesota Press, 2017).

Nusseibeh, Sari, *Once Upon A Country: A Palestinian Life* (London: Halban, 2009).

Obama, Barack, *Remarks at the AIPAC Policy Conference 2011* (22 May 2011), https://tinyurl.com/5n6c9eav

Olmert, Ehud Interview to Stephen Sackur, *BBC HARDtalk* (2009), http://webcache.googleusercontent.com/search?q=cache:RhsmGjUhoY8J:www.bbc.co.uk/iplayer/episode/b00n4fw3/HARDtalk_Ehud_Olmert_Israeli_Prime_Minister_2006_2009/+Ehud+Olmert+talks+to+Stephen+Sackur+about+his+Palestinian+peace+proposals&cd=1&hl=en&ct=clnk&gl=uk

Olmert, Ehud, *In First Person* (Tel Aviv: Yedioth Ahronoth, 2018) (Hebrew).

Olmert, Ehud, *Searching for Peace: A Memoir of Israel* (Washington, DC: Brookings, 2022).

Olmert Peace Map, www.haaretz.co.il/hasite/images/iht_daily/D171209/olmertmap.pdf

O'Malley, Padraig, *The Two-State Delusion – Israel and Palestine – A Tale of Two Narratives* (New York: Viking, 2015).

Palestinian National Charter: Resolutions of the Palestine National Council, 1–17 July 1968, https://avalon.law.yale.edu/20th_century/plocov.asp

Palestinian Declaration of Independence, Palestine National Council, 19th Session, Algiers (15 November 1988), www.palquest.org/en/historictext/9673/palestinian-declaration-independence

Pappe, Ilan, *The Ethnic Cleansing of Palestine* (Oxford: Oneworld Publications, 2007).

Parsons, Nigel, *The Politics of the Palestinian Authority* (New York: Routledge, 2005).

Peraino, Kevin, 'Olmert's Lament', *Newsweek* (12 June 2009), www.newsweek.com/ehud-olmerts-lament-80319

Peres, Shimon, *The New Middle East* (New York: Henry Holt, 1993).

Peres, Shimon, *Battling for Peace: A Memoir* (London: Weidenfeld & Nicolson, 1995).

Peres, Shimon, and Robert Littell, *For the Future of Israel* (Baltimore: Johns Hopkins University Press, 1998).

Perlman, Haim, *On Justice* (Jerusalem: The Hebrew University Law Faculty, 1962).

Podeh, Elie, 'Israel and the Arab Peace Initiative, 2002–2014: A Plausible Missed Opportunity', *Middle East Journal*, 68(4) (Autumn 2014): 584–603.

Podeh, Elie, *Chances for Peace: Missed Opportunities in the Arab-Israeli Conflict* (Austin: University of Texas Press, 2015).

Podeh, Elie, *Villa in the Jungle?* (Jerusalem: Carmel, 2025) (Hebrew).

Podeh, E. & A. Kaufman (eds.), *Arab-Jewish Relations: From Conflict to Resolution?* (Brighton: Sussex Academic Press, 2006).

Podszon, Lucie, *Does Development Aid Affect Conflict Ripeness?: The Theory of Ripeness and Its Applicability in the Context and Development of Aid* (Wiesbaden: VS Verlag für Sozialwissenschaften, 2011).

Political platform for the Norwegian Government, Formed by the Conservative Party, the Progress Party, the Liberal Party and the Christian Democratic Party (Granavolden, 17 January 2019). www.fao.org/faolex/results/details/en/c/LEX-FAOC199092

Powell, Jonathan, *Talking to Terrorists: How to End Armed Conflicts* (London: Vintage, 2014).

Pressman, Jeremy, 'Visions in Collision: What Happened at Camp David and Taba?', *International Security*, 28(2) (2003): 5–43.

Princen, Tom, 'Camp David; Problem-Solving or Power Politics as Usual?', *Journal of Peace Research*, 28(1) (1991): 57–69.

Princen, Tom, *Intermediaries in International Conflict* (Princeton, NJ: Princeton University Press, 1992).

Pruitt, D., 'Ripeness Theory and the Oslo Talks', *International Negotiation*, 2(2) (1997): 237–250.

Prusher, Ilene R., 'Interview: How Salam Fayyad Plans to Save the Palestinian Dream', *The Christian Science Monitor* (3 November 2009).

Pullan, Wendy, and Maximilian Sternberg, 'The Making of Jerusalem's "Holy Basin"', *Planning Perspectives*, 27(2) (April 2012): 225–248.

Pundak, Ron, 'From Oslo to Taba: What Went Wrong?', *Survival*, 43(3) (2001): 31–45.

Pundak, Ron, *Secret Channel* (Tel Aviv: Aliyat Hagag, 2013) (Hebrew).

Pundak, Ron, and Shaul Arieli, *The Territorial Aspect of the Israeli-Palestinian Final Status Negotiation* (Jaffa: Peres Centre for Peace, September 2004) (Hebrew).

Quandt, William B., 'Personal Notes on the Camp David Summit', Peace Research Institute Oslo (PRIO, 1978), www.prio.org/Publications/Publication/?x=11344

Quandt, William B., *Peace Process: American Diplomacy and the Arab-Israeli Conflict since 1967* (Berkeley, CA: University of California Press, 2005).

Quandt, William B., From Comprehensive Arab-Israeli Peace to a Separate Egyptian-Israeli Agreement: 1977–1979, prepared for a conference on Camp David in Oslo, Norway (28 May 2019).

Quinn, D., J. Wilkenfeld, K. Smarick, and V. Asal, 'Power Play: Mediation in Symmetric and Asymmetric International Crises', *International Interactions*, 32(4) (2006): 441–470.

Qurie, Ahmed, *From Oslo to Jerusalem* (London: I.B. Tauris, 2006).

Qurie, Ahmed, *Beyond Oslo* (London: I.B. Tauris, 2008).

Qurie, Ahmed, *Negotiating Palestine: From the Second Intifada to Hamas' Electoral Victory* (London: I.B. Tauris, 2014).

Qurie, Ahmed, *Peace Negotiations in Palestine* (London: I.B. Tauris, 2015).

Rabinovich, Itamar, *The Brink of Peace* (Princeton, NJ: Princeton University Press, 1998).

Rabinovich, Itamar, *Waging Peace: Israel and the Arabs, 1948–2003* (Princeton, NJ: Princeton University Press, 2004).

Rabinovich, Itamar, *Yitzhak Rabin: Soldier, Leader, Statesman* (New Haven: Yale University Press, 2017).

Ramon, Amnon (ed.), *The Historic Basin of Jerusalem – Problems and Possible Solutions*, The JIIS Studies Series, No. 408 (Jerusalem: Jerusalem Institute for Israel Studies, 2010).

Ramsbotham, Oliver, *When Conflict Resolution Fails* (Cambridge: Polity Press, 2017).

Ramsbotham, Oliver and Amira Schiff, 'When Formal Negotiations Fail: Strategic Negotiation, Ripeness Theory, and the Kerry Initiative', *Negotiation Conflict Management Research*, 11 (2018): 321–340.

Raphael, D. D., *Problems of Political Philosophy* (London: Pall Mall Press, 1970).

Ravid, Barak, *Trump's Peace* (Rishon LeZion: Yedioth Ahronoth, 2022) (Hebrew).

Rawls, John, *A Theory of Justice* (Oxford: Clarendon Press, 1972).

Rawls, John, *Political Liberalism* (New York: Columbia University Press, 1993).

Rawls, John, *The Law of Peoples* (Cambridge, MA: Harvard University Press, 2002).

Reidel, Bruce, 'Camp David – The Deal Made between Israel and the USA', *Bitterlemons* 26 (17 July 2002) (Hebrew), www.bitterlemons.org/hebrew/previuos/bl170702ed26extra.html

Renshon, Jonathan, *Why Leaders Choose War* (Westport, CT: Praeger, 2006).

Rice, Condoleezza, *No Higher Honor: A Memoir of My Years in Washington* (New York: Broadway Books, 2011).

Rogan, Eugene (ed.), *The War for Palestine* (Cambridge: Cambridge University Press, 2013).

Ross, Dennis, *The Missing Peace* (New York: Farrar, Straus and Giroux, 2004).

Ross, Dennis, and Gidi Grinstein, With a Reply by Hussein Agha and Robert Malley, 'Camp David: An Exchange', *New York Review of Books* (20 September 2001).

Rothman, Jay, *From Confrontation to Cooperation* (London: Sage Publications, 1992).

Rothstein, Robert L., Moshe Ma'oz, and Khalil Shikaki (eds.), *The Israeli-Palestinian Peace Process: Oslo and the Lessons of Failure: Perspectives, Predicaments and Prospects* (Brighton and Portland: Sussex Academic Press, 2004).

Roy, Sara, 'Why Peace Failed: An Oslo Autopsy', *Current History*, 101(651) (2002): 8–16.

Roy, Sara, *Hamas and Civil Society in Gaza: Engaging the Islamist Social Sector* (Brookings, NJ: Brookings University Press, 2011).

Rubin, Jeffrey Z., and Barbara Kellerman (eds.), *Leadership and Negotiation in the Middle East* (London: Praeger, 1988).

Rynhold, Jonathan, 'Cultural Shift and Foreign Policy Change: Israel and the Making of the Oslo Accords', *Cooperation and Conflict*, 42(4) (2007): 419–440.

Sackur, Stephen, 'Standing by the Olmert plan', *BBC HARDtalk* (24 September 2009), http://news.bbc.co.uk/2/hi/middle_east/8273336.stm

Sagie, Uri, *The Frozen Hand* (Tel Aviv: Miskal, 2011) (Hebrew).

Said, Edward, *The End of the Peace Process* (New York and London: Vintage, 2001).

Sasley, Brent E., 'Affective Attachments and Foreign Policy: Israel and the 1993 Oslo Accords', *European Journal of International Relations*, 16(4) (2010): 687–709.

Savir, Uri, *The Process* (New York: Vintage Books//Random House, 1999).

Savir, Uri, *Peace First: A New Model to End War* (San Francisco: Berrett-Koehler Publishers, 2008).

Savir, Uri, 'Oslo: Twenty Years After', *Negotiation Journal*, 30(1) (2014): 115–123.

Sayigh, Yezid, *Arafat and the Anatomy of Revolt*, www.occupationalhazard.org/article.php?IDD=512

Schiff, Amira, 'The Kerry Peace Initiative in the Israeli-Palestinian Conflict: When Hope and Good Intentions Are Not Enough', *International Negotiations*, 23(1) (2018): 8–41.

Schulz, Michael, *Between Resistance, Sharia Law, and Demo-Islamic Politics* (London: Rowman and Littlefield, 2020).

Schulze, Kirsten E., 'The Hebron agreement', *Mediterranean Politics*, 2(1) (Summer 1997): 201–205.

Sebenius, James K., *Kissinger the Negotiator* (New York: Harper, 2018).

Sela, Avraham, 'Difficult Dialogue: The Oslo Process in Israeli Perspective', *Macalester International*, 23 (2009): 105–138.

Sela-Shayovitz, Revital, 'Suicide Bombers in Israel: Their Motives, Characteristics, and Prior Activity in Terrorist Organizations', *International Journal of Conflict and Violence*, 1(2) (2007): 160–168.

Self-rule for Palestinian Arabs, Residents of Judea, Samaria, and the Gaza District, Jerusalem, 28 December 1977, www.palquest.org/en/historictext/9646/begins-autonomy-plan

Shanks, Hershel, *Jerusalem's Temple Mount: From Solomon to the Golden Dome* (London: Continuum International Publishing, 2007).

Sharon, Gilad, *Sharon – The Life of A Leader* (Tel Aviv: Matar, 2011) (Hebrew).

Sharon, Gilad, *Sharon – The Life of A Leader* (New York: Harper, 2011).

Shavit, Ari, 'The Day Peace Died', *Haaretz* (14 September 2001) (Hebrew).

Shavit, Shabtai, *Head of Mossad* (Rishon LeZion, Miskal-Yedioth Ahronoth, 2018) (Hebrew).

Sheehan, Edward R. F., 'How Kissinger Did It: Step by Step in the Middle East', *Foreign Policy*, 22 (Spring 1976): 3–70.

Shehadeh, Raja, *From Occupation to Interim Accords: Israel and the Palestinian Territories* (The Hague: Kluwer, 1997).

Shenhav, Yehouda A., *Beyond the Two-State Solution: A Jewish Political Essay* (Cambridge: Polity Press, 2012).
Sher, Gilead, *Just beyond Reach* (Tel Aviv: Yedioth Ahronoth, 2001) (Hebrew).
Sher, Gilead, *The Israeli-Palestinian Peace Negotiations, 1999–2001: Within Reach* (London: Routledge, 2006).
Sher, Gilead, *The Battle for Home* (Tel Aviv: Yedioth Ahronoth, 2015) (Hebrew).
Sher, Gilead, and Samih Al-Abed, *A Framework for Middle East Security, Peace, and Normalization* (Houston, TX: Rice University's Baker Institute for Public Policy, 2024).
Sher, Gilead, and Anat Kurz (eds.), *Negotiating in Times of Conflict* (Tel Aviv: INSS, 2015).
Shlaim, Avi, *Lion of Jordan* (Or Yehuda: Kinneret, Zmora-Bitan, 2009) (Hebrew).
Sicherman, Harvey, *Palestinian Autonomy, Self-Government and Peace* (Boulder, CO: Westview, 1993).
Simmel, Georg, *The Sociology of Georg Simmel* (Glencoe, IL: The Free Press, 1950).
Singer, Joel, 'Interview', *Kol Israel Radio* (11 March 1997), https://tinyurl.com/44bfdpar
Singer, Joel, 'Developing the Concept of Palestinian Autonomy', *The Cairo Review of Global Affairs* (Winter 2019), www.thecairoreview.com/essays/developing-the-concept-of-palestinian-autonomy/
Singer, Joel, 'An Oral Agreement Isn't Worth the Paper It's Written On', *Israeli-Arab Negotiations*, 101 (12 June 2019).
Siniver, Asaf, 'Power, Impartiality and Timing: Three Hypotheses on Third Party Mediation in the Middle East', *Political Studies*, 54(4) (2006): 806–826.
Slater, Jerome, 'What Went Wrong? The Collapse of the Israeli-Palestinian Peace Process', *Political Science Quarterly*, 116(2) (Summer 2001): 171–199.
Smith, A., and A. Stam, 'Mediation and Peacekeeping in a Random Walk Model of Civil and Interstate War', *International Studies Review*, 5(1) (2003): 115–135.
Stedman, Stephen John, 'Spoiler Problems in Peace Processes', *International Security*, 22(2) (1997): 5–53.
Steinberg, Matti, *In Search of Modern Palestinian Nationhood* (Tel Aviv: Moshe Dayan Center, 2016).
Stefanini, Pietro (ed.), *UNRWA At 70: Palestinian Refugees in Context* (London: Palestinian Return Centre, 2020).
Susser, Asher, *The Rise of Hamas in Palestine* (Waltham, MA: Brandeis University Press, 2010).
Susser, Asher, *Israel, Jordan and Palestine* (Waltham, MA: Brandeis University Press, 2012).
Swisher, Clayton E., *The Truth About Camp David: The Untold Story About the Collapse of the Middle East Peace Process* (New York: Nation Books, 2004).
Swisher, Clayton E., *The Palestine Papers* (Chatham: Hesperus, 2011).

Tabarani, Gabriel, *Israeli-Palestinian Conflict: From Balfour Promise to Bush Declaration – The Complications and The Road for a Lasting Peace* (Milton Keynes: AuthorHouse, 2008).

Tartir, Alaa, 'International Aid to Palestine: Time to Change Course', *Middle East Eye* (29 December 2017), www.middleeasteye.net/opinion/international-aid-palestine-time-change-course

Tetlock, Philip, and Dan Gardner, *Superforecasting: The Art and Science of Prediction* (London: Random House, 2015).

'Text: Arab Peace Plan of 2002', *BBC* (22 March 2005), http://news.bbc.co.uk/1/hi/world/middle_east/1844214.stm

Tezel, Yönet C., 'International Humility: Rebooting and Age-Old Virtue', *Global Policy* (January 2025). https://tinyurl.com/yzy9c3pt

'The Madrid Peace Conference', *Journal of Palestine Studies*, 21(2) (Winter 1992): 117–149.

'The Taba Negotiations (January 2001)', *Journal of Palestine Studies*, 31(3) (Spring 2002): 79–89.

Thrall, Nathan, 'Israel & the US: The Delusions of Our Diplomacy', *New York Review of Books* (9 October 2014).

Tibon, Amir, and Barak Ravid, 'Obama's Israel Adviser Leaves Trump's White House', *Haaretz* (22 April 2017), www.haaretz.com/us-news/1.784449

Touval, S., *The Peace Brokers: Mediators in the Arab-Israeli Conflict, 1948–1979* (Princeton, NJ: Princeton University Press, 1982).

Toye, P., and Seay, A. (eds.), *Israel: Boundary Disputes with Arab neighbours 1946–1964* (Cambridge: Cambridge University Press, 2013).

Truedson, L., *International Mediation – Case Studies and General Conclusions: Report from a Seminar Co-organized by The Olof Palme International Center and The Stockholm Peace Research Institute, SIPRI* (Stockholm: The Olof Palme International Center, 1999).

Turner, Catherine, and Martin Wählisch (eds.), *Rethinking Peace Mediation* (Bristol: Bristol University Press, 2021).

UN Resolution 242, https://peacemaker.un.org/sites/peacemaker.un.org/files/SCRes242%281967%29.pdf

UN Resolution 338, https://peacemaker.un.org/sites/peacemaker.un.org/files/SCR338%281973%29.pdf

UNHCR, *The 1951 Convention Relating to the Status of Refugees and Its 1967 Protocol* (Geneva: UNHCR, September 2011), https://tinyurl.com/3bbxv33z

United Nations, *Global Humanitarian Overview 2025*, https://tinyurl.com/58utyc9e

UNRWA (n/d), www.unrwa.org/who-we-are

UN Watch, *The Unholy Alliance: UNRWA, Hamas, and Islamic Jihad* (December 2024). https://tinyurl.com/dnrd52jp

US Government and Department of Defense, *Back to Basics: A Study of the Second Lebanon War and Operation CAST LEAD – Israeli IDF Incursions into Lebanon and Gaza 2006 and 2008 against Hezbollah and Hamas, Tactics, Hard Lessons Learned*, https://tinyurl.com/ytcpuf67

Usher, Graham, *Palestine in Crisis* (London: Pluto Press, 1995).

Usher, Graham, *Dispatches from Palestine* (London: Pluto Press, 1999).

Waage, Hilde Henriksen, 'Explaining the Oslo Backchannel: Norway's Political Past in the Middle East', *Middle East Journal*, 56(4) (2000): 597–615.

Waage, Hilde Henriksen, *'Norwegians? Who Needs Norwegians?' Explaining the Oslo Back Channel: Norway's Political Past in the Middle East*, A report prepared by PRIO International Peace Research Institute, Oslo Institutt for fredsforskning (2000).

Waage, Hilde Henriksen, 'How Norway Became One of Israel's Best Friends', *Journal of Peace Research*, 37(2) (2000): 189–211.

Waage, Hilde Henriksen, *Peacemaking is a Risky Business: Norway's Role in the Peace Process in the Middle East, 1993–96* (Oslo: International Peace Research Institute PRIO, 2004).

Waage, Hilde Henriksen, 'Norway's Role in the Middle East Peace Talks: Between A Strong State and A Weak Belligerent', *Journal of Palestine Studies*, 34(4) (2005): 6–24.

Waage, Hilde Henriksen, 'The "Minow" and the "Whale": Norway and the United States in the Peace Process in the Middle East', *British Journal of Middle Eastern Studies*, 34(2) (2007): 157–176.

Waage, Hilde Henriksen, 'Postscript to Oslo: The Mystery of Norway's Missing Files', *Journal of Palestine Studies*, 38(1) (2008): 54–65.

Waage, Hilde Henriksen, 'Proactive Peace Diplomacy: Jan Egeland', in Mona Fixdal (ed.), *Ways Out of War: Peacemakers in the Middle East and Balkans* (London: Palgrave Macmillan, 2012): 91–118.

Waage, Hilde Henriksen, 'Champions of Peace? Tools in Whose Hands? Norwegians and Peace Brokering in the Middle East', in Peter Bauck and Mohammed Omer (eds.), *The Oslo Accords 1993–2013: A Critical Assessment* (Cairo: American University in Cairo Press, 2013): 29–39.

Wallensteen, Peter, *Understanding Conflict Resolution: War, Peace and the Global System* (London: Sage Publications, 2007).

Wallensteen, Peter, *Peter Wallensteen: A Pioneer in Making Peace Researchable* (Cham: Springer, 2021).

Wallensteen, Peter, and Isak Svensson, 'Talking Peace: International Mediation in Armed Conflicts', *Journal of Peace Research*, 51(2) (March 2014): 315–327.

Walzer, Michael, *Spheres of Justice: A Defence of Pluralism and Equality* (New York: Basic Books, 1983).

Walzer, Michael, *Just and Unjust Wars* (New York: Basic Books, 2006).

Walzer, Michael, 'Terrorism and Just War', *Philosophia*, 34 (2006a): 3–12.

Walzer, Michael, 'Response to Jeff McMahan', *Philosophia*, 34 (2006b): 19–21.

Walzer, Michael, 'On Proportionality', *The New Republic* (8 January 2009), www.tnr.com/article/politics/proportionality

Watson, Geoffrey R., *The Oslo Accords* (Oxford: Oxford University Press, 2000).
Waxman, Dov, *The Israeli-Palestinian Conflict* (New York: Oxford University Press, 2019).
Weitz, Gidi, 'Meridor's Diaries: Last Minutes of Dialogue', *Haaretz* (30 July 2011) (Hebrew).
Wendt, Fabian, *Compromise, Peace and Public Justification* (London: Palgrave, 2016).
White House, *Peace to Prosperity: A Vision to Improve the Lives of the Palestinian and Israeli People* (January 2020), https://tinyurl.com/yccdxst6
'White House's Kushner to Finalize Palestinian Economic Plan on Middle East Tour – Official', *Reuters* (21 July 2019), https://tinyurl.com/4zw2eynr
Wright, Lawrence, *Thirteen Days in September* (London: Oneworld Publications, 2014).
Wye River Memorandum (23 October 1998), https://unsco.unmissions.org/sites/default/files/the_wye_river_memorandum.pdf
Yatom, Danny, *The Confidant* (Tel Aviv: Miskal-Yedioth Ahronoth, 2009) (Hebrew).
Yatom, Danny, *The Labyrinth of Power* (Tel Aviv: Contento, 2016).
Yousef, Ahmed, 'Out of the Ashes of Oslo: The Rise of Islamism and the Fall of Favoritism', in Peter Bauck and Mohammed Omer (eds.), *The Oslo Accords 1993–2013: A Critical Assessment* (Cairo: American University in Cairo Press, 2013): 99–108.
Zahar, Marie-Joelle, 'Reframing the Spoiler Debate in Peace Processes', in J. Darby and R. MacGinty (eds.), *Contemporary Peacemaking* (Basingstoke: Palgrave-MacMillan, 2008): 159–177.
Zartman, I. William (ed.), *The Negotiation Process* (Beverley Hills, CA: Sage Publications, 1978).
Zartman, I. William, *Ripe for Resolution* (New York and Oxford: Oxford University Press, 1989).
Zartman, I. William, 'Negotiating with Terrorists', *International Negotiation*, 8(3) (2003): 443–450.
Zartman, I. William, *Negotiation and Conflict Management: Essays on Theory and Practice* (London: Routledge, 2007).
Zartman, I. William, 'Mediation Roles for Large Small Countries', *Canadian Foreign Policy Journal*, 19(1) (2013): 13–25.
Zartman, I. William, and Guy Olivier Faure (eds.), *Escalation and Negotiation in International Conflicts* (Cambridge: Cambridge University Press, 2005).
Zartman, I. William, and Guy Olivier Faure (eds.), *Engaging Extremists* (Washington, DC: US Institute of Peace Press, 2011).
Zilberfarb, Ben-Zion. 'The Israeli Economy in the 1990s – Immigration, the Peace Process and the Medium Term Prospects for Growth', *Israel Affairs*, 3(1) (Autumn 1996): 1–13.

Ziv, Guy, *Why Hawks Become Doves* (Albany: State University of New York Press, 2014).
Zubok, Vladislav, *Collapse: The Fall of the Soviet Union* (New Haven: Yale University Press, 2022).
Zunes, Stephen, 'The United States and the Breakdown of the Israeli-Palestinian Peace Process', *Middle East Policy*, VIII(4) (December 2001): 66–85.

Archives

Israel Ministry of Foreign Affairs, Jerusalem
Israel National Archives, Jerusalem
King's College, London
Library of Congress, Washington, DC
National Archives, Kew, London
Nobel Peace Prize Institute, Oslo
Peace Research Institute Oslo (PRIO)

Interviews

See Appendix A.

INDEX

For EU product safety concerns, contact us at Calle de José Abascal, 56–1°,
28003 Madrid, Spain or eugpsr@cambridge.org.

www.ingramcontent.com/pod-product-compliance
Ingram Content Group UK Ltd.
Pitfield, Milton Keynes, MK11 3LW, UK
UKHW021032041026
15470UKWH00014B/1406
9781108484398